HISTORY AS EXPERIENCE

Aspects of Historical Thought—Universal and Jewish

HISTORY AS EXPERIENCE

Aspects of Historical Thought—Universal and Jewish

Selected Essays and Studies
by
Aaron Steinberg

Published
Under the Auspices of the
World Jewish Congress

KTAV PUBLISHING HOUSE, INC.

NEW YORK

Library of Congress Cataloging in Publication Data

Steinberg, Aaron, 1891-1975.
  History as experience.

  Bibliography: p.
  Includes index.
  1. Jews—History—Addresses, essays, lectures.
  2. History—Philosophy—Addresses, essays, lectures.
  I. Title.
  DS119.S73   1982   909'.04924   82-17273
  ISBN 0-88125-001-5   *84-1099*

        COPYRIGHT © 1983
        World Jewish Congress

Manufactured in the United States of America

CONTENTS

Section C

Varieties and Distortions of Messianism

Section D

Towards the Future

Foreword

On the occasion of Aaron Steinberg's 80th birthday the World Jewish Congress decided to publish, as a personal tribute to the man and his work, the essays and studies which he wrote over a period of nearly 60 years in various languages and which are to a great extent inaccessible. The completion of this project has taken much longer than was first anticipated.

The selection of the essays and studies which are included in this volume was made by Dr. Steinberg personally. His wishes have been respected, with only minor changes. The collection contains both articles in which he shows himself to be an original thinker, and contributions to encyclopaedic works which bear the imprint of his times and personal perceptions.

Originally, the publications appeared in a variety of languages, in Russian, Yiddish, Hebrew, German, French and English. We are most grateful to their publishers for permission to reprint them here in English. We also wish to express our thanks to all those who helped to establish an authoritative English text.

If this volume finally appears, it is due mainly to the erudition and the unceasing efforts of Mrs. Assia Klausner, Dr. Steinberg's assistant and devoted friend over several decades, who saw the project through to its completion. It is with a sentiment of deep gratitude that we acknowledge her loyalty and dedication.

We also wish to express our thanks to Mr. Mark Friedman for reading the proofs and generally supervising the final printing.

November 1981   Gerhart M. Riegner   Uriel Tal

Aaron Steinberg—A Portrait

by Gerhart M. Riegner

To write about Aaron Steinberg is not an easy task. He was a man of immense gifts and a phenomenally rich personality, and had an extraordinary variety of interests.

I had the privilege of seeing him and talking to him in many settings: sometimes we were together for weeks at a time in places as disparate as London, Geneva, New York, Florence, Montevideo, Algiers, Israel—or wherever we spent time or attended conferences together.

I will try to say a few words about Aaron Steinberg, the human being; Aaron Steinberg, the Jew; and Aaron Steinberg, a leader of the World Jewish Congress. But any division I make is artificial, for there has rarely been a personality as integrated as his in whatever he did or undertook or in whatever he said or wrote.

First a few words about the man, the human being. He was descended from a great Russian Jewish family, of whom anyone would be proud. He was an aristocrat in the real sense of the word: he belonged to an aristocracy of the kind developed only by the great Jewish families of the past. At the same time, his was a background deeply rooted in Russian culture. He was a gentleman, in thought and deed. He was a warm person, open to every human being he encountered. He was deeply religious—not ostentatious in his religious manifestations and even ambivalent in his relationship with the official religious establishment, but nevertheless a really committed religious person. At the same time he was tolerant, never trying to force his opinion on others but rather hoping to convince them by his own example. Above all, he had respect and a genuine sense of brotherhood for every human being.

He had a unique gift for communicating with people, for establishing warm human contact with complete strangers in the space of a few minutes. On one of the very numerous occasions on which I saw him make use of this gift, he engaged in conversation a Montevideo taxi driver—with whom he really had nothing in common—and in five minutes the man had told him the whole story of his life and they had found a point of common

1

ground between them. Some people even criticized him for wasting too much time on individuals who, after all, were not all that important. But this commitment to brotherhood impelled him voluntarily to make that sacrifice of his time because he knew what it meant to the other man, particularly when the latter was of a more humble condition. He knew that the other man's sense of dignity was enhanced by the feeling that someone else understood him and cared about his hopes and worries.

He had a uniquely universal outlook in the great humanist tradition—this was perhaps the hallmark of his personality. He was a doctor of law, and very proud of it; he told me many times, "I'm also a lawyer." He wrote an important book on the Russian parliamentary system. He was a genuine philosopher; in his young years he was professor of philosophy at the University of St. Petersburg and secretary of that city's philosophical society; he wrote an outstanding work on the idea of freedom in Dostoievsky; he was at home with German philosophy, Bergson, Sartre, Pascal, etc. He was a historian, not only because he translated Dubnow's *World History of the Jewish People*, but in his own right. He was in reality a philosopher of history; the sense of history—what it meant and what it can mean, what it can teach and where it can lead us—was the great problem with which he struggled all his life. He was also a sociologist, and it was no accident that the idea of *The Jewish Journal of Sociology* came from him and that it was created under his leadership.

He was a man of great artistic gifts. His wife sometimes used to tell me that we did not really know Aaron, that the real Aaron was the artist, the man who had written plays and novels which we had never read. But you could see his artistic ability when he described some event he had witnessed, when he suddenly started imitating people, when he tried to convey a scene in history by assuming the various roles of those involved in it.

His was, in brief, a many-faceted personality; he was a polyhistor. But, though a great scholar, he did not live in an ivory tower; he had both feet on the ground, and followed developments in politics as well as in the spiritual and intellectual world. He not only followed these developments, but at the same time sought a way in which man could help to influence events and thus aid God to complete the Creation which is never finished.

Let me say a few words about Aaron Steinberg the Jew. The most important and decisive element of his Jewishness was the concept of the Jewish people—the Jewish *Weltvolk*, in Dubnow's words—and that idea brought him to the World Jewish Congress. His concept of Judaism was universalist, it was all-embracing. As I have said, he was deeply committed to religious Judaism, to *halakha*, which he considered binding on himself; but he accepted other trends and factors as well. He admitted the validity of all trends of Judaism, of all forms of Jewish self-expression and thought, no matter where they came from—secular, religious, Zionist, Yiddishist,

Sephardi, socialist, or whatever. His concept of Judaism was based on an attitude of positive neutralism vis-à-vis every creative contribution to Jewish life. Just as the trends were important and each of them was to be admitted and recognized, so were what he called the various "tribes" of the Jewish people, meaning the different communities: the Russian Jewish community, the Polish, the French, the German, the Anglo-Saxon, and so on. Each had its special characteristics, its special gifts and shortcomings; each was a current and an offshoot of the one great stream of Jewish tradition that assured the creative survival, the uninterrupted continuity, of the Jewish people.

Judaism for him had a special mission in the world. It was often the catalyst; it was often the test for judging and measuring other ideas and other developments. I should not have been surprised, had he seen what is going on at the United Nations today, if he had pointed his finger at us and said, "You see, it is again on the Jewish question that the world will be judged."

Culture was for him the great spring of man's creativity: all the national cultures of the peoples of the world, including Jewish culture, flowed into and enriched that spring, and together led to the many-faceted universal culture of man. It was no accident that he was particularly at home in Unesco: originally, the great concept of Unesco was that of the friendly competition of all the great cultural contributions of mankind which were to blend into a vast current propelling mankind into progress. It was no accident that Aaron Steinberg devoted many long months to one Unesco undertaking in particular—the publication of *The History of the Scientific and Cultural Development of Mankind*. He was deeply convinced that unless the Jewish people as such, and its special contribution to civilization, were recognized by the world, the Jews would not be acknowledged as a people standing on an equal footing with other nations. I still see him reading the scripts of nine of these enormous tomes written by eminent scholars, volume by volume, and making hundreds of suggestions for a fitting acknowledgment of the many Jewish contributions to civilization, century by century.

This great stream of universal culture (in which the Jewish contribution was merged) also flowed through him himself: his Judaism; his deep roots in Russian culture; the great influence that German philosophy and the German classics had on him; his familiarity with French literature, art, and philosophy; his being at home with the great creative periods of Italy—all that was fused into a unique harmony, which I had the privilege of observing on many occasions. I vividly recall our staying together for several weeks in Florence on the occasion of a Unesco General Conference; his speaking to me of the influence of the great legal men of Bologna in the Middle Ages; his telling me of his philosophic studies in Italy; and our visiting together the great monuments of the Renaissance in

Florence, Siena, and Pisa. There he was at home; every form of human self-expression flowed through him and joined in a unique oneness.

Let me end with a few words on Aaron Steinberg's contribution to the World Jewish Congress. It was a great honor for the WJC that a man of his unique calibre chose to serve it. It was typical of him that he accepted the task, because he was not only a great scholar and a great thinker but also a man of practical dimensions and action. In the WJC London office, during the Second World War, there met the so-called Research Committee of the World Jewish Congress, which was the first body to prepare a postwar program for the Jewish people. In that committee Dr. Steinberg gathered around him a number of outstanding and unique personalities from every walk of life—great scholars and great human beings—to study and discuss the problem. From that group came some of the most revolutionary ideas, such as the concept of crimes against humanity, which became one of the bases of the Nuremberg Trials. It was in that committee that the request for collective compensation, for reparations to the Jewish people after the collapse of the Nazi regime, was carefully considered in very concrete terms. And it was from that group that—to my knowledge, for the first time in Jewish history—a real concept of a cultural foreign policy of the Jewish people emerged. That was well before the State of Israel was created. (The idea that the Jewish people had to be represented in an international cultural organization was later, of course, to lead to his practical work in Unesco and elsewhere.)

He was also involved in all our major political discussions, and participated in the passionate debates that took place during and after the war—discussions on the question of East and West and on relations with the Christian churches and with the cultures of Asia and the Third World. Aaron Steinberg was one of the first to understand these problems; he was deeply involved in all of them, and he left his imprint on many of the policies which were eventually adopted.

He often played the devil's advocate, advancing any negative argument he could think of so that matters might be discussed from every angle and the discussion pushed to its logical conclusion. He made use of his encyclopaedic knowledge and of his sense of history. He knew that if you want to meet the demands of today you have to anticipate what may happen tomorrow, and that planning, foresight, and long-range thinking were the most important elements in every political move.

In conclusion, I would say that perhaps his most outstanding quality, which overshadowed everything else, was his absolute independence. He was a man of independent judgment; he was nobody's tool; he would not swim with the stream; and, as a result, from time to time he was even very unpopular. He was often intentionally provocative, in order to make people see the consequences of their action: his task was to make others think, to guide them in their independent thinking, and to make them see through (and beware of) the slogans of the day.

It was comforting, in times like those in which we live, to see a man who—despite today's secularism, materialism, and conformism—tried to show us that it is still possible to live as an independent thinker and man of action and also as a truly religious person. It is refreshing as well as comforting that he showed us that the choice of freedom is possible in our time. And that is perhaps the greatest message he left us.

He was a man of great labors; he left numerous works and writings, some of which, unfortunately, are forgotten. A number of his essays and studies appear in this volume. They will help to acquaint a wider public with the originality and the dimensions of his thought.

But apart from what he did and wrote and achieved, there was the man himself: a unique example of the universalistic Jewish spirit.

Introduction

On the Thought of Aaron Steinberg

by Uriel Tal

A. *A Sense of Crisis*

The start of the twentieth century, and in particular the years after
World War I and the Russian Revolution, was a period during which a
sense of crisis emerged and took shape in the European *Zeitgeist*.
European society, especially its intelligentsia, showed signs of confusion;
Europeans felt they were at a crossroads, with no idea of where the roads
led, and which one to take; they felt that their world was collapsing, and
that a supreme effort was required to avert a disaster that would turn the
continent into a social ruin or political prison. The traditional foundations
of European civilization, among them the heritage of monotheism and
humanism, were being undermined.[1]

There was a feeling that the "inner struggle in the world of
contemporary culture threatens to turn into its spiritual suicide"[2] and "the
entire universe of European values . . . threatens to collapse . . ."[3]

The feeling that the values of civilization, including its philosophical and
aesthetic aspects, were being devitalized was evident also in the political
map of post-World War I Europe; ". . . we are witnessing the complete
collapse of the old European territorial organization"[4] . . . "fragments
everywhere, splinters, ruin, disintegration . . ."[5]

At the end of the nineteenth century, Steinberg asserts, there still
prevailed the optimistic belief that an integral European civilization and
united European society were being built. It was commonly assumed that
the potential harmony in mankind and human nature would be realized
and produce harmony in practice among nations, religions, classes and
economic sectors, between modern man's chief creative areas such as
philosophy and history, and between those disciplines and science and art.
Moreover, it looked as if the ethical values of the labour movement would
gain universal recognition, and as though "a new nationality had emerged,
a European one, a new European character . . ."[6]

Yet, while the second half of the nineteenth century was conversant with pessimism as well, it was World War I and the subsequent violent totalitarian revolutions which brought home to the Europeans of the 1920s how mistaken that optimism had been. One of the principal aspects of their disappointment was the admission that technology—one of Homo sapiens' greatest achievements—instead of being a blessing, had become "the technology of destruction."[7]

There, in man's failure to control what his head and hands had made, was where Steinberg, as early as the 1920s, discerned one of the most drastic indications of the failure of Western civilization. The consequences, whether blessing or curse, life or death, depend not on technology itself but on man's moral decisions.[8]

Technology in particular, and modern civilization in general, generated a radical change in man's phenomenological and existential situation. Man's uniqueness as a creature formed in the image of God, and the mystery of that uniqueness, and on the other hand man's humanistic uniqueness as a thinking being with a natural ability to shape his life responsibly in freedom and autonomy—those characteristics now seemed to have become dulled and obscured. In modern civilization dominated by science and technology, man was transformed from a creature with the specific status of a subject to one with the specific status of an object. The Kantian heritage—to which Steinberg was faithful mainly through the religious rationalistic philosophy of Hermann Cohen,[9] which maintained that man was not a means but an end in itself—was stripped of all meaning, and man was turned into mere means through processes he himself lost cognizance and control of:

> ". . . the educated European relates to himself in the same way as he does to the external world . . . Am I not a fact among other facts? Is not the soul an object of science . . . Having transformed himself into a laboratory he can no longer observe his own nature in freedom, but rather as if it were in prison. . . . "[10]

This change in man's fundamental status, Steinberg added, is clearly demonstrated on the aesthetic plane, for it is there that technology and art meet as expressions of man's existential quality. The age is reflected on the aesthetic plane as "an age in which organic integrity of means and ends breaks down . . . This technology developing to the level of an end in itself transforms physical and spiritual nature into one expanding *nature morte*, into a stillborn nature, the image and likeness of the self-annihilating spirit."[11]

For decades, this sense of crisis provided the background for Steinberg's rich intellectual activity, his thought, speeches and writings.

Two levels are discernible in this activity. One is mainly Steinberg's reactions to the historical events and processes of his time: the aftermath of the Bolshevist Revolution in the twenties, the rise of Nazism in the thirties, the outbreak of World War II, a time when he was full of dread in anticipation of the Holocaust that was to overtake the Jews and the heritage of Europe. Pertaining to the same level of Steinberg's philosophy are his reactions to the post-World War II years which in his judgment embodied a great potential for the renewed spiritual and moral vitality of the Jewish people in the Diaspora and Israel. The second level of Steinberg's thought consists in the main of historical consciousness and its contribution to an understanding of the uniqueness of the Jewish people and their position among the nations, a uniqueness which in Steinbergs' view was an ethical commitment arising from the law and history of Israel.

B. *The Dynamics of the Russian Revolution*

Aaron Steinberg deeply loved Russia and he cherished Dostoevsky as the symbol and embodiment of the mystique of the Russian unfathomable soul, its burning passion, its dark depth yet also its bright, warm simplicity, its thirst for grandeur and power and its all consuming emotional intenseness. In Dostoevsky Steinberg found the artistic expression of the political and emotional dilemma so characteristic of intellectuals in the days of social and national upheaval. Universalism and particularism, humanism and nationalism, class struggle and national conflict, the authenticity of the simple and harmonious life rooted in the soil and the artificiality of a decadent European bourgeois society, refinement and vulgarity—they all were unresolved contradictions or even irreconcilable oppositions articulated by Dostoevsky in, as Steinberg felt, an unequalled way. Moreover, it was Dostoevsky who exemplified the hostility to the West and the fascination with the West; it was Dostoevsky who taught about the hopes for the realization of a redemptive mission to which the Russian, not any more the Jew, was called by his own national earthbound God, by his destiny and by his intermediary position between Europe and the East.

It was against this background that the disenchantment with the Russian revolution was so painful for Steinberg. On the one hand, still in 1942 Steinberg felt that at first it looked as if ". . . the great revolution in Russia (was) proving that not everything was futile and that there was hope for all who thirsted for justice . . ." (cf. below "Between the Pieces of Abraham's Covenant"). On the other hand, to his mind the Russian revolution turned out to be perhaps the most brutal manifestation of the European crisis prior to the Holocaust. Therefore Steinberg described the aftermath of the revolution as a structure of tension between hope and despair, between great expectations of social redemption and the ensuing profound disappointment as a result of the violence, cruelty and totalitarianism in Russia. At the outset there was hope that Marxism in all its varied political guises, including Bolshevism as well, would bring peace to the world, justice would prevail in relations between state and citizen, employee and employer, man and his fellows; but in fact Bolshevism succeeded only in "echoing the original chaos of universal strife of the bellum omnium contra omines . . ."[12]

Ostensibly, Marxism hoped to overcome the long history of conflicts, disputes and wars in human society. Marxism, as a social movement, before accumulating violent power, held that through material redemption, mankind would be relieved of dependence on narrow sectarian or class or even national interests. The proletariat was to become the redeeming force by freeing the universalist human society from the burden of class wars and power struggles between particularistic social groups.

European socialism hoped that with the elimination of these conflicts a kind of human harmony would be realized. Thus, socialists of diverse varieties imagined that the class war would be the last, for it would lead to man's victory over destructive forces—exploitation, inequality, injustice. The war of the socialists, says Steinberg, was to be different from all others in form and content for it was to lead to "external national and international peace . . ."[13]

In view of this supreme goal of a class war that was to be the last, Steinberg notes, the socialists saw also the more immediate social economic goals as a comprehensive change in the nature of man and society. They therefore wished to understand the workers' control of the means of production, one of the principal goals of Marxism, as a far-reaching change in man's existential status. That control was expected to lead to the liberation of man from dependence on the means of production, that is to "the establishment of an order under which the creative work of mankind will not depend on . . . . the distribution of the material means of production . . ."[14] The original purpose of control of the means of production by the proletariat, adds Steinberg, was conceived as being "to emancipate mankind from the dominance of the means of production . . ."[15] The true aim of the socialist revolution is not the abolition of private property but the eradication in man of the possessive instinct. [16]

In the spirit of the vision held by the Utopians of the early nineteenth century, Marxian socialism too believed that property is not the source of freedom but rather dominates its owners to the point that they lose their self-identity. For this reason, under a capitalist system, the possessive instinct dominates the personality and not vice versa. Following the revolution in the property system, the Marxian socialists believed, man will be emancipated from all external trappings and his personality will no longer be split between his own essential inner nature and his external status in society; consequently, the individual's connection with the community will be based on inner identification and not economic necessity or political domination. Thus, Steinberg concludes, the socialist movement sought to establish universal brotherhood and that was the reason many considered it a movement with a messianic social vision,[17] whose mission it was to "usher in a fundamentally new world."[18] Even the Bolshevik Revolution, although already at the outset showing clear signs of violence leading to despotism and totalitarianism, initially succeeded in awakening public opinion to the ideals of equality and fraternity between social classes and nations.

Years later, in a retrospective survey, Steinberg described the fate of the Revolution as follows:

> "A covenant of peace between the nations, a pact of justice and equity within every people, these were the principal headings in the scroll heralding the future that hovered over the last war's valley of death."[19]

Furthermore, the Revolution enhanced the yearning to create a new human society, shape a new human nature which would not be inclined to war but be based on "everyone's love for everyone else."[20] That socialism, in which Europe still believed in the first quarter of this century, meant "universal collectivity without a priesthood, without ecclesiastical state-hood, without a patriarch-Father Superior, that is, the free community of associated brothers."[21]

These hopes were however dashed, and years before the Revolution set up its regime of terror, it was Dostoevsky, says Steinberg, who best described the fanatic character of the Russians. In contrast to Western man with his rational mentality the Russian zealously seeks a holy cause to which he can sacrifice himself, and with great enthusiasm and strong emotion conducts a "quest for sacrifice and for heroic deeds," for a lofty purpose, or some God, whether spiritual or substantial, or some absolute truth or other; instead of the self-restraint deriving from logical thinking or scientific method or practical considerations as in the case of Western man, the Russian is characterized by enthusiasm to the point of ecstasy, and fanatical faith to the point of violence.[22]

Among the spiritual and political manifestations of these dashed hopes, Steinberg was one of the very first to discern the religious-secular and ecclesiastical-political structure of the Bolshevist regime. The class war, which was supposed to emancipate man from economic or political tyranny, resulted in a different tyranny, that of the Communist Party and the centralistic government. The dream of the international brotherhood of people turned into a reality in which the historical imperialistic aspirations of Moscow and the Byzantine Church persist, now with communist rather than monarchistic slogans, now in the name of the proletariat and the party rather than the Tsar and the clergy. The hopes of a change in human nature emancipating man from the desire for strength, power and domination were dashed, and the "will to power and struggle for power" came back. The aspirations for a new phenomenological status for man as a free individual reaching full emancipation because of the cognitive autonomy inherent in his nature which European socialism and before it liberal humanism sought, were overturned and became a reality in which ". . . human individuals are but the tools used by the great historic forces . . ."[23]

In Bolshevism, all means were considered legitimate by the regime in order to maintain man in the status of a tool. Civilisation, including language and philosophy, education, and modern science including psychology all became instruments facilitating the regime's domination of everything—politics, economics, society—and above all, "the human mind,"[24] and "the human spirit."[25]

Bolshevism thus developed into an ideology and policy depriving man of his special status in the phenomenological world, that of a cognitive creature with a natural ability to evolve cultural and ethical values and historical consciousness. By means of psychological coercion and more brutal violence, Bolshevism robs man of his intellectual capacity and his right to believe in the truth as he sees it, with the result that the Bolshevist regime is characterized by "ethical cynicism,"[26] which is nothing less than ethical relativism. What was termed "the will to proletarian power" became the ultimate goal rather than a means, to the point where "proletarian dictatorship . . . degenerated into a dictatorship over the proletariat . . ."[27] This overall nature of Bolshevism led to a total reversal of values, and to the justification of means which in any other context, religious or secular, are inadmissible, such as prevarication, calumny, torture and murder.[28] Thanks to this reversal of values the political leaders too acquire an aura of sanctity. They now became agents of providence, agents of the proletariat and the party, with a mission so exalted that in contrast ordinary social values and "life itself dwindle into insignificance . . ."[29]

Consequently, the authority of these leaders becomes absolute, and what they say or write in the name of the party becomes sanctified and is credited with "revelatory power."[30] Therefore, Steinberg notes, ". . . before the advent of Bolshevism only the founders of religions were possessed by a similarly all-embracing ambition to improve the world . . . The essential nature of the Bolshevik Party can be grasped by regarding it as a philosophical school with an ecclesiastical constitution comparable to institutions such as the religious orders . . ."[31]

Indeed Steinberg regarded the structure of Bolshevism as one borrowed from ecclesiastical history as a political secular force that adopted a religion-like form and authority. This was the background for his dispute with one of the great Marxist philosophers, Georges Lukacs. In Steinberg's opinion Lukacs exemplified the tragedy of communism as an attempt to provide it with an intellectual foundation by an original and critical study of the Marxist credo, in confrontation with the best modern European thought. But in that confrontation Lukacs went beyond the confines of intellectual discussion and produced a political ideology so that in his conception the proletariat becomes "the absolute bearer of historical freedom (and) thereby in the full sense of the word deifies the proletariat and is thus the first Marxian theologian."[32] However, this approach of Lukacs led to a clash with the communist establishment, for "the communist church cannot tolerate independence and free research even into its own dogmas . . ."[33]

One of Lukacs's achievements, Steinberg notes, is that his neo-Marxist philosophy developed the concept of "alienation" of man in modern society and in the capitalistic system. Except that here too, Steinberg adds, Lukacs went to an extreme and reached a dead end. Lukacs endeavoured to develop the concept of "alienation" in confrontation with the *Lebensphilosophie* of Georg Simmel. Lukacs asserted that Simmel was not consistent in his admission that socio-economic factors have considerable weight in the historical process and in the formation of man's phenomenological image. If Simmel were consistent, in his "philosophy of money" he would have had to admit the correctness of Marx, but instead he remained faithful to German idealism and explained the vast importance of historical materialism as though it was ". . . the result of more profound evaluations and currents of psychological or even metaphysical presuppositions."[34]

Lukacs endeavoured to reinforce the Hegelian structure in Marx's conception of the process of "depersonalization of modern man," by reversing its meaning. While in Hegel's system the process takes place on a metaphysical level, in that of Marx it occurs on the physical level, in society and through the economy.[35] In capitalist civilization man's status is determined according to quantity rather than quality, according to production and not creativity, and so life itself is fashioned in a mechanistic way.[36] The individual is pounded between forces that shape his destiny, but of which he has no knowledge and certainly no understanding or control. Thus, in capitalistic culture, the individual is doomed to remain isolated and powerless. This isolation is a manifestation of the atomization of everything, of the structure of society and of science, and it is also borne out by the fact that in capitalistic scholarship each branch is separate and isolated from the others, so that the practitioner loses all perspective, and is ignorant of the context of his own work:

"Law has degenerated into automatic legal procedure, the state into a bureaucratic apparatus, the family into a business transaction, literature, especially journalism, into a marketable conscience, a marketable emotion, a talent which can be bought and sold. The most inalienable in human

existence, the uniqueness of man, his very spiritual image, his gifts—even
these have been put up for sale, have been put on the market. The logic of
things has transformed man . . . into a thing . . ."[37]

This mechanistic life seems to be organized on a rational basis, for the
aim of capitalism is "rationalizing the whole of life." But the omnipotent
force of reason has been a disappointment, according to Lukacs, and as
long as capitalism must solve problems "of actual social reality" reason fails
and the outcome is that "man is powerless to change that reality . . ."[38]

Just as in the epistemology of what Lukacs called the bourgeois society,
rational cognition cannot arrive at a knowledge of "the thing itself" as
Kantian philosophy teaches, so also the sociology and economics of
bourgeois society cannot solve the real, concrete social problems themselves.

Against the alienation of man in capitalistic society, Lukacs sets a great
vision of redemption, which is, in Steinberg's opinion, and perhaps
despite Lukacs's objections, a guide to a secular political religion with
coercive power. Just as in Hegel, history will reach realization when the
absolute spirit attains self-consciousness, in Lukacs too, following Marx,
history will achieve its goal—that is, social redemption—when man attains
self-awareness. Man now becomes the soul, the inner consciousness of the
thing itself, its self-consciousness, and thus the self-consciousness of the
entire world of things . . ."[39] Following man, now ". . . the class consciousness of the proletariat is the self-consciousness of the historical
process as a whole, is the revelation of history in man, is man's true
knowledge of himself."

Steinberg properly discerned that Lukacs is here proposing a merger
between the rhythm of Hegel's metaphysical redemption and that of
Marx's revolutionary, socio-economic one. Through that merger, Lukacs
hoped to attain a new unity on the metaphysical level between spirit and
substance, and on the epistemological level, between the rational and the
irrational; and on that base, a unity on the level of social reality between
man and the fruit of his labour, and thus, in the Marxian spirit, between
empirical man and man in his anthropological essence.

Lukacs endeavoured to overcome the cognitive antinomies modern
thought inherited from Kant, and develop in their stead total unity which
would eliminate the dichotomy between freedom and necessity, between
consciousness and being. It is here at this point that the totalitarian
character of Lukacs's philosophy becomes evident, says Steinberg. For if
these dichotomies are eliminated, so is man's freedom, and if freedom is
eliminated, so is man's status as endowed with moral responsibility
destroyed. Thus Lukacs arrived at a position opposed to that represented
by Judaism, one Steinberg believed in with all his heart, holding that man
is not located in a mythical unity between consciousness and being, but

because of his nature as God's creature, he is in a constant, permanent duality between himself as a subject and the world as an object, and it is his personal responsibility as a sovereign subject, that is in freedom, to choose an ethical way of life.

Lukacs, on the contrary, elevates the proletariat to the rank of the bearer of the metaphysical unity of subject and object and thus turns the revolutionary world into a kind of unity typical to the intuitive and mythical approach to the world and contrary to the rational, critical, and therefore also ethical approach to the world:

> "and here we have the neo-Marxist Lukacs, taking this very decisive step: proletarian socialism turns out to be not only a doctrine of the super-natural essence of human society and of its historical development, but also a super-rational doctrine."[40]

This total conception transfers the Hegelian notion of freedom as the ultimate unity between spirit and history to society and state. And thus, adds Steinberg, Lukacs arrives at extreme political messianism. For the transformation of the state into a factor which in political reality implements the theoretical principle of unity, that creates the ideological justification for "State power as an instrument of the coercive incarnation of truth . . . the tyranny of the absolute principle over the personal consciousness of its bearer cannot but transform the individual who has 'seen the light' into a tyrant . . ."[41]

In the intellectual confrontation with Bolshevik totalitarianism, Steinberg perceived the fate of the Jews, including anti-Semitism in Russia, Germany and Austria, as a reflection of Europe's inability to solve not only the Jewish question, but also that of freedom, justice, equality, and above all, of man's faith in the modern world. This universalist conception of the Jewish question sharpened Steinberg's discernment of the rise of Nazism.

C. The Nazi Predicament

Steinberg was one of the few first Europeans to understand that Nazi anti-Semitism was an expression of more than hatred of the Jews. It was an expression of the negation of the universal values Judaism and monotheism had bequeathed to the European mind. The rise of Nazism meant a new era in human history, a period of total darkness, of total *Götterdämmerung*. It began a period of destruction of which the world had been warned by some of the greatest writers and thinkers such as Dostoevsky and Vladimir Soloviev.[42] And the Jews, as throughout their history, were chosen to reflect, and symbolize and represent that crisis in practice. The crisis took the form of a number of manifestations, Steinberg explains. Socialism, which basically sought to eliminate social classes and thus also political tyranny paved the way, involuntarily though, ". . . for the theory of absolutism, the total state which brushed aside all ideals of a free society . . ."[43] Consequently, Steinberg adds, Fascism must be viewed as a concomitant of socialism, except that as Fascism and in particular Nazism gained strength, they abandoned the humanistic elements originally contained in socialism. Nazism negated those elements, including the moral-social bases of socialism and its international aspirations.

Important evidence that Nazism is a new, anti-humanistic, anti-religious manifestation was discerned by Steinberg in the opposition of Nazism to Christianity, mainly to Roman Catholicism but also to Protestantism. It is thus possible to show a parallelism between Bolshevik and Nazi opposition to Christianity.[44] In both instances, there is a political struggle of secularism or even paganism against religion. In both regimes, the State seeks to take hold of the youth, of man's mind. In both regimes, ideology adopts a church-like guise, in which, however, politics, the proletariat or race substitutes for God.

Racial anti-Semitism of the Nazi variety, Steinberg adds, included the negation of Christianity in its negation of Judaism. In the thirties, that is even before the Holocaust, Steinberg felt that the Christian world, and thus in effect Europe and the Western civilization in general, were on the eve of a crisis such as it had never known. Until the advent of Nazism, says Steinberg, from the viewpoint of their historical effect, the crises that attacked Christianity contributed to its strengthening in that they indirectly helped it to adapt to changing historical conditions. Thus, for example, the rift between Rome and Byzantium helped to evolve a special type of Christianity more suited to Eastern Europe, and prevented Russia from being lost to Christendom. In the same way the Reformation was able to prepare the ground for the acceptance of rational thought, modern science and humanism and so also of secularism in Christianity, thereby keeping it within the historical development of the modern world. In fact Christianity succeeded in becoming an inseparable part of that world, and was able to absorb the effects of the French Revolution and later the notion of the differentiation between state and society. It managed to keep pace with time and find a path to the national and international labour movements in Europe, so that "all the great crises in the history of Christendom were pains of adaptation . . ."[45] Such was not the case this time, that is under Nazism. Already several years before the publication of Sigmund Freud's analysis on the anti-Christian nature of Nazi anti-Semitism Steinberg arrived at the conclusion that: "It is in fact an anti-Christian revolution among Christian nations . . ."[46]

Steinberg did not believe that this new type of anti-Semitism was likely to alter the theological doctrine of Christianity which held that Jewry was a living witness to the correctness of Christian redemptive history

(*Heilsgeschichte*). But he wished to awaken the Jewish community to a broader political view, to a comprehension of the fact that Nazism's inclusion of Christianity among its foes is indicative of the universal nature of anti-Semitism as such, and that the Jewish people serve as a mirror reflecting the fate of mankind. That, according to Steinberg, was one of the keys to the understanding of the history of Israel among the nations:

> "To look at the Jewish situation with an open mind means to be willing to see it as it is in the light of world history. The historical past trodden by the Jewish people has always been a universal historical path . . ."[47]

Steinberg's intense awareness of the historical reality of Russia in the 1920s and Germany in the 1930s culminated in his conclusion that secularism was evidence of and one of the chief reasons for the European crisis. He discerned this secularism not particularly as an opposition to the institutional or formal character of religion, but primarily in the sense of the loss of true humanism, the loss of spiritual and moral values, the elevation of political interests and of the desire for power to the rank of absolute values replacing God. And as usual for Steinberg, in his conclusion from an examination of the reality of his time, the Jewish question appears like a barometer or a bubble, reflecting symbolically and concisely the fate of the world. The fate of the Jews manifests secularism in the sense of the loss of faith in ethical values in an extreme form, so that now, with the rise of Nazism, Christendom too, and thus all of Europe, faces the danger of destruction.

Internally, within Jewish life, the world situation of the 1920s and 1930s should be viewed as evidence that even though secularism led to the emancipation of the Jews, it is no guarantee that the rights of Jews as a minority will be safeguarded or that the result will be a better, juster and freer world. For an irreligious world is not necessarily a more moral one.[48] On the contrary, a world in which secularism becomes a new religion, a substitute for religion, like the world of the Bolsheviks and Nazis, imperils the existence of Jews, and consequently also of Christians and Western civilization. The universalist view of the particular fate of the Jews was voiced also in Steinberg's impassioned cry to world Jewry on the eve of the Holocaust for *Bitochn*, that is, faith, trust. In 1939 Steinberg asked, "Can the Jewish people, God forbid, cease to exist?" For with the Bolshevik Revolution and the rise of Nazism the Jews were subject to persecution and torture. Their fate is "frightful and bitter . . . , thousands upon thousands curse the day they were born and do away with themselves. We are experiencing the multiple destruction of nearly all our national social and spiritual values . . ."[49]

The hopes the Jews placed in autonomy and minority rights in Central and Eastern Europe, the hopes they placed in the class struggle and ownership of means of production by the proletariat, as well as in emancipation, were all disappointed and dashed upon the rock of reality preceding World War II. In the face of this all-embracing defeat, Steinberg insisted, the Jews had only one way left, "one way for the pious and for the freethinkers. That is the way of wisdom," and by this he meant the traditional Jewish conception of wisdom as "faith based on the foundation of reason . . ." In that fateful hour, the Jews dared not "cut the roots of reason and sow and reap the poisonous harvest of despair . . ."[50]

It was that faith which Steinberg perceived to be the pillar upon which the people of Israel had leaned in the course of its long and unique history.

D. *On History and Jewry*

A central part of Steinberg's historical thought and its main purpose is a confrontation with the problems of the mystery of the Jewish peoples' existence and survival.

Like other outstanding Jewish intellectuals early in the century,[51] for whom the meeting between Eastern Europe and the Western world was a decisive spiritual experience, it was in history that Steinberg sought the answer to the question of Jewish survival. He accepted the analysis of "the enigma of Jewish survival" which Dubnow had published (in 1912 in Hebrew) that "we are confronted with a great and hidden mystery. We try to penetrate the depths of this mystery, the secret of the survival of the Jewish people, and to fathom the forces acting within the soul of the people . . . in order to penetrate the veil of this mystery we have to approach it under the aspect of reason in applying to it rationally conceived general laws of social science. . . "[52]

For empirical, objective, positivistic research is essential, Steinberg agreed, in dealing with a historical question, especially such a theoretical one as that of the forces operating within the Jewish people and enabling them to exist in the course of their particular history. But, he added, this factual, objective study itself is not sufficient for proposing a constructive answer to the question of Jewish existence, for the uniqueness of the Jewish people lies in the fact that besides being an empirical sociological phenomenon, "as it sees itself . . . (it) was created not for itself alone but for the whole world. It was created for God's world and because of that it had to suffer and fight for its existence . . . and to gain the redemption of God's world . . . generation after generation sacrifices itself and offered itself for the Sanctification of the Name (*Kiddush Hashem*) . . . if this idea . . . has no reality from the scientific point of view, then almost our entire history lacks reality . . ."[53]

Steinberg was well aware of the contradiction or even clash between the objective approach to history required of the scholar, and the subjective approach to history as the heritage of living experience and social or national ethical values to which a person of faith ascribes. Each of the methods contains some truth, and Steinberg devoted a considerable part of his historical thinking to the examination of that duality. He found an illuminating example of the problem in N.A. Berdyayev's own testimony:

> "I remember that in my young days, when I was attracted by the materialist interpretation of history and I endeavoured to demonstrate its correctness in the light of the history of the various peoples, the greatest obstacle which I encountered in my enterprise was the history of the Jewish people whose fate seemed utterly inexplicable in terms of the materialistic interpretation. It must be admitted that from any materialistic or positive-historical point of view, that people should have ceased to exist long ago . . ."[54]

The lesson Berdyayev teaches, says Steinberg, is that it is the empirical reality of history, not preconceived views, that compel the student of Jewish history to admit that he is facing a phenomenon in which the spirit or the idea is the real social force. In that spirit, with all its opposition to Simon Dubnow's secularist conception of history, he accepted in principle the latter's definition that "Subjective or spiritual factors are supreme in the development of the national type, while all the material factors are but stages leading to the highest point of this development, namely the crystallization of a well-defined and conscious national individuality . . . spiritual affinity is a more important factor than blood relationship in families."[55]

In his historical thinking, Steinberg aspired to add to the study of world history by Simon Dubnow a "Jewish philosophy of world history" as he himself viewed it.[56] Like other Russian Jewish intellectuals, such as Simon Dubnow, S. Anski, Aaron Liebermann and Chaim Zhitlovsky, Steinberg was also influenced by the historical philosophy of Peter Lavrov,[57] from whom he learned that the interest in history was indicative of the spirit of the times, for "long before Dilthey, before Rickert, before Simmel, he considered the study of history to be the distinguishing feature of our times . . ."[58]

Steinberg further testifies that it was Lavrov's philosophy that reinforced his own belief that the historian as a scholar is confined to the study of the past while, in order to make use of history for an understanding of the present and for a keener vision in regard to processes anticipated in the future, in addition to empirical positive research in history, there is need also for "the philosophical world view"[59] or "the philosophical understanding of history as a whole . . ."[60]

This principle of history as "a whole" is central to Steinberg's thinking, as through it he endeavoured to formulate his own conception that Jewish history is a continuity of a whole embodied in a concrete people. Steinberg was encouraged by the fact that even someone like Lavrov, who described himself as a positivist and socialist, sought to understand history as a continuum from the start of human civilisation to its end, with the notions "end and beginnings"[61] indicating teleological questions "which by their very essence can be solved only by supra-empirical means, by metaphysical means," which is to say, Steinberg adds, that even Lavrov is not a "positivist" in the ordinary sense.[62]

In one clearly defined point of Lavrov's historical thought, Steinberg felt a great kinship with this source of inspiration, but realised too that from that point on their ways parted. This was Lavrov's anthropological interpretation of the Hegelian concept of historical consciousness. Lavrov took from Hegel's historical philosophy the assertion that consciousness is the motive operating in history, whether overtly or covertly, whether potential or actual. Therefore, consciousness involves two sides. One is the metaphysical, which takes the form of the revelation of reason in the world even against the will of historical man, and it is a kind of secular rational guise of the principle of divine revelation in history. The other is the empirical side which takes the form of institutionalization of history in society due to the willful decision of the man and citizen to leave his mark on nature, on life, on society and the state. Under the influence of Ludwig Feuerbach and Karl Marx, Lavrov transferred the metaphysical aspect of history to the empirical and anthropological, i.e. to the realm of sociology, not unlike Auguste Comte. The beginning of human history is not set at the beginning of human consciousness, and now "consciousness" has the meaning of intelligence taking the shape of culture and civilization. In contrast to the Hegelian metaphysical aspect of the spirit, this process does not take place without man's mind, but is his decision. On this point, Lavrov's interpretation is less deterministic than those of Feuerbach and Marx, for he left more room for man's will power and social idealism. Now, since the concept of consciousness was explained as intelligence expressed in deeds, in culture and civilization, Lavrov, and in his wake Dubnow, Steinberg and others could stipulate that the transition from nature to history or from non-historical life to historical life occurred with the voluntary operation of man's practical intelligence, that is, through the realization of material needs to ensure physical survival, in practice:

> "the beginning of history is action in the dawning light of consciousness under the influence of the spirit . . ."[63]

Human life then became historical life when it was consciously directed to satisfy needs and constantly improve the means and tools for satisfying them:

> "as soon as the intelligentsia with its vague thirst for development appears on the scene of social life, a dissatisfaction with the existing forms of culture is

born, and the mental activity of the intelligentsia is directed to changing it . . ."[64]

In this function of developing civilization in order to satisfy the needs of human existence, Lavrov sees the source of the ethical character of history. After having risen to human consciousness, the needs of existence require the creation of tools, the development of technology, and the evolution of a just and reformed society, for without all these man has no existence and there is no history.[65] Consequently, the essence of the socialist ideal which Lavrov preached is likewise to bring history to its culmination, on the one hand through consciousness which will reach its highest stage of development, and on the other through material civilization which will be built with the help of this development of consciousness.[66]

At this point Steinberg diverged from Lavrov. In Steinberg's opinion, neither the actual reality in which socialism turned here into Bolshevik totalitarianism and there into Nazi totalitarianism, nor the method of mathematical analogy[67] used by Lavrov and the Positivists to explain history (a method which grafted the determinism taken from nature on to an understanding of history), nor the secularism and universalism which deprived national particularity of its raison d'être, could help to explain the historical uniqueness of the Jewish people. It is true that Lavrov's teleological principle of history definitely went beyond the limitations of the Positivist definition of the natural sciences, for he defines history among other ways also as a development constructed on "a moral conviction based on a definite belief in the . . . ultimate predestination of mankind as a whole . . ."[68] Yet Steinberg could not be content with that for, according to Lavrov's school, national particularity, including that of the Jewish people, is only a historical phenomenon and consequently ephemeral. The secularized messianic conception of socialism leaves no room for meta-historical matters with peoples or religions, and Lavrov clearly declared that since the world was marching toward a realization of international socialism, "national-religious traditions . . . have long lost their value . . . for a convinced socialist, the national question is eliminated."[69] Thus, redemption will not come through a messianic supernatural process, and not through a chosen people, but through socialism, "from the natural development of the process of nature which enlightens human thought more and more; from the natural evolution of historical events which reveal more clearly the tasks of progress . . . in the form of proletarian masses . . . in the union of all nations and peoples for whom the present universal struggle will be transformed into a universal aspiration to self-development and education . . ."[70]

This conception is inevitable, given the overall world picture of socialist positivism, according to which:

"science and scientific philosophy have long since led all thinking persons out of the dark world of religious illusions and religious traditions (belief in revelation). World industry, world trade and the world market on the one hand, and the union of the world proletariat on the other hand, have brought about a class struggle which has pushed to the side all the false conceptions of national pride . . . critical science . . . has no use for fantastic faith and traditional illusions . . . It is impossible to seek the unity of mankind today in religious and national traditions and it is also useless . . ."[71]

Steinberg's entire spiritual world rebelled against such conceptions for it was in religion and peoplehood that he saw the two foundations upon which Judaism was built both historically and in essence, and without which it could not exist. Moreover, the future of mankind too, especially in the light of the Holocaust on the one hand and the ruin of Europe during World War II on the other—is dependent on the renewal of the ethical values originating in monotheism and the particularist history of nations.

In his attempt to formulate historical thought that would allow for normative values, Steinberg's point of departure was the warnings of Heinrich Rickert and Wilhelm Windelband against the relativism that would ensue from historicism. If all ethical or religious values are the products of historical or material circumstances that are temporary and ephemeral and have no substance of their own, independent of historical conditions, their normative validity is likely to vanish with changing times. If values like the love of man, equality, freedom, social responsibility, or religious faith are conceived of only as the outcome of changing historical circumstances, a change in these circumstances will deprive them of validity, and as Rickert said, "all historicism if consistent, leads to relativism, even nihilism . . ."[72]

One of the ways to avoid relativism in values is to strengthen faith in their super-historical origin whether religious or rational humanist. These two sources of value recognition are exempted from historical relativism, and they show that human reality differs in its ontological quality from the reality of the natural world; the ontological essence of history is such that its manifestations are by nature imbued with values. Historical phenomena are not just facts as in the world of nature, but rather acts and events, or phenomena "which have their origin in the human will and as such point far beyond themselves inasmuch as they derive their value and essence only out of a broad spiritual pattern established in a higher sphere . . ."[73]

However, a methodological conclusion derives from this ontological assumption. The historian may, or even must, select the phenomena for study, and the causal connection between them, in the light of their significance, in the light of their contribution to an understanding of the present and future. Therefore, Steinberg concludes, historical research cannot be conducted without "subjective intellectuality."[74] This is not necessarily detrimental to the objectivity of history as a science and system of thought.[75] Furthermore, objective historic facts become understandable only when the scholar succeeds in discovering the idea that unites all the external aspects of this historical phenomena. In the absence of an idea there is no science, no form making it possible to combine the components of the phenomena.[76] The question which occupied Steinberg in many of his writings was to identify the very idea that binds together all the external manifestations, all the components of Jewish existence throughout the long and varied history of the Jewish people in its many different dispersions. That was one of the questions too at the root of the historiographic work of Simon Dubnow. For Dubnow too endeavoured to discover the historical processes that unify the great mass of facts, and thus the historian's task is "to uncover the organic connection among the individual fragments of time and space distributed over three thousand years . . ."[77]

Against this background, Steinberg turned to Simon Dubnow's historical teachings. Dubnow disagreed with Lavrov's assumption, as expressed in the latter's *Historical Letters*, that the national particularity of every people is a temporary, transient historical phenomenon. Dubnow agreed though with the empiricists and positivists in their critique of the theological explanation of national historical continuity, for a priori assumptions based on faith and not on empirical findings subject to scientific critique are unacceptable and inadmissible. Furthermore, "in the history of Judaism, for example, there is no single definite idea which runs through all periods like a silk thread. There are various ideas with increasing cultural creativity and deep yearning for social progress in every generation . . ."[78]

But in Dubnow's opinion it is precisely the empirical findings that withstand scientific criticism which show that the physical social existence of a national unit, first and foremost the Jewish people within the continuum of changing historical conditions, is possible only thanks to ethical values including values of faith. The Jewish people succeeded in maintaining the continuity of its existence despite its dispersion among various cultures and nations, and despite pressures and persecutions, thanks to spiritual values. Thus Dubnow stated, despite his definitely secular approach:

> "In our time only superficial minds can still believe that religious thought or emotion is in and for itself opposed to morality. On the contrary, it becomes increasingly clear that purified religion, which already at the time of our ancient Prophets advocated lofty ethical ideals, is also destined to fulfil the function of a powerful ethical force in our scientific age . . ."[79]

In attempting to add Jewish traditional aspects to Simon Dubnow's historiography, Steinberg sought to interpret Dubnow's self-definition as a

historian with a secular positivist, sociological approach as an acknowledgment of the significance of tradition in Jewish history. [80] On the one hand,
Dubnow's scientific method seems rooted in the sociological positivism
founded by Auguste Comte, and in the principles of evolution stipulating
in the spirit of Herbert Spencer and the anthropology of social Darwinism.
Accordingly a sovereign factor in history is "the natural instinct of national
self-preservation." [81] Thus, also, "as an opponent of theological and metaphysical theories, he [Dubnow] wants to see his fundamental historical
attitude 'bio-sociologically' buttressed . . . Dubnow's watchword in 'the
rigorously applied principle of evolution'; . . . the subject of scientific
historiography includes besides the origin and growth of national individuality its 'struggle for survival' . . . Dubnow described his approach as 'bio-
sociological' . . ." [82]

But on the other hand, Steinberg stresses, Dubnow was not interested
in the discovery of sociological laws, and did not accept the mythical
aspects of "the organic theory of society." Consequently, despite Dubnow's theoretical declarations that historiography should be built on a "bio-
sociological" foundation, "in his actual exposition the historian never tries
to explain the content and continuity of the Jewish past by deducing it from
accepted general biological principles." [83]

Dubnow's historiography is therefore characterized by most instructive
internal dialectics. The uniqueness of the historiographic material of the
Jewish people, or empirical, concrete sources, is what led to the change:

> ". . . it was contrary to the author's intention to write a story of ideals and
> ordeals, yet that is what his inner sense of truth and his affinity with his
> subject matter compelled him to do . . ." [84]

Dubnow's dialectics culminated in his crucial point that it is in fact
empirical social history that demonstrates that in the history of Jews, "the
spiritual elements outweighed decisively the material and political elements . . ." [85]

But here Steinberg differed from his teacher Dubnow. For in Dubnow
the religious source of these spiritual elements was construed as a source
whose validity had vanished:

> ". . . all the ancient national values of the Jewish nation, the historical
> festivals, customs and usages, laws, social institutions, the whole system of
> self-administration . . . had been incorporated gradually and artificially into
> the sphere of religion . . ." [86]

In Dubnow's opinion, that sphere was only "fossilized tradition" distort-
ing the nation's vital forces. Disagreeing with Dubnow and other leaders of
secular thought in Eastern European Jewry such as Chaim Zhitlovsky, [87]

Steinberg endeavoured to propose the religious tradition of Judaism as a historical force that maintained and will in the future maintain the Jewish people. And within that tradition, the idea that ensured Jewish continuity amid the "diversity of historical life,"[88] is morality, "the faculty of choice between good and evil."[89]

E. *On History and Jewish Ethics*

Steinberg does not mean to draw an ideal picture showing the Jewish people and its history as always ethical. He meant that morality served in the past and does so in the present as an ideal which Judaism aspires to realize in actual social reality. On the ontological plane, that ideal is expressed in ". . . balance . . . between matter and spirit . . ." and on the level of daily life "in the incessant attempt . . . to gain control of the human spirit over the material conditions of life . . . liberation of the human spirit . . ."[90]

The prime and dominant source of this morality, Steinberg explains, is the Torah and its development along the two main directions in the history of Jewish thought and thus also in "the historical development of the typical Jewish outlook on life . . ."[91] The two are Law and Legend, the revealed and the concealed, knowledge and faith. This duality in Jewish history is also reflected in two quite different systems of thought, philosophical speculation rooted in the absolute independence and autonomy of reason, and religious thought rooted in tradition.

These two systems of thought may turn into normative guides for modern man as well, but only on condition that faith and tradition should also become "a source of knowledge . . . which is also in accordance with reason . . ."[92] Steinberg does not ignore the metaphysical level in the history of Jewish thought. He is well aware of the great importance of definitely theological and philosophical questions such as the transcendentality, supramundaneity, and incorporeality of the one God, the negation of any form of concretization of divinity, which were already of concern even earlier than the Middle Ages, in the Bible, expressed as "who is unto Thee" (*Exodus* XV:11; *Psalms* XXXV:10; LXXI:19; LXXXVI:8; LXXXIX:6, 8; CXIII:56; *Lamentations* III:37; *Isaiah* LV:8-9; XLV:5). [93]

On various occasions Steinberg dealt with answers proposed to these questions by medieval neo-Platonic and neo-Aristotelian thinkers, among them Maimonides' answer that God can be known not through attributes but through virtues that are deeds.[94] (*Guide to the Perplexed*, Part 1, Chapter 54.) Steinberg was particularly preoccupied with questions dealt with in Jewish thought from Saadia Gaon through the late Middle Ages, such as the possibility of faith along with speculative thought, how free will is conceivable despite Divine providence and predestination or the antinomy between human freedom and Divine power, and the source of sin and its outcome. Yet with all his devotion to the normative authority of tradition, Steinberg was aware of the dilemma of modern Jewish thought in regard to the need for the precepts in the age of rationalism, since for modern man"whatever is not in accordance with pure reason is false; if its teachings coincide with those of reason, it is superfluous . . ."[95]

Nonetheless, the pivot of Steinberg's Jewish philosophy was not metaphysics but the ethical creed of Judaism, in particular that which was to be reflected in actual human reality. The search for social relevance in Jewish tradition did not derive only from social pragmatism, though that element too was present in Steinberg. The search for relevance was inevitable, given his overall conception of Judaism, according to which "all creation is one entity inasmuch as everything which exists is the creation of God," so that the teachings about man's conduct, about truth and falsehood, about good and evil, about justice and injustice are no less important in Judaism than teachings about metaphysical matters. For that reason a person breaking the rules of social morality also breaks those of universal order. Thus, in contrast to classical philosophy, Judaism, beginning with the Pentateuch and the prophecies, "transformed the natural world into a means of realizing the laws of justice and order. With them metaphysical monism assumed the form of ethical mono-theism . . ."[96] Influenced by Hermann Cohen, Steinberg went on to say that the creation of the world and the creation of the Law are "correlates,"[97] for on the one hand the Torah is of cosmological significance, having, according to the Midrash, preceded the creation of the world. In other words, it was pre-existential and even served as a primordial paradigm for the Creation.[98] But on the other hand, the main historical importance of the Torah is in having served as the source for shaping the day to day life style of the individual and the community, and Jewish history throughout is the annals of the continuous interpretation of these ancient fundamentals. Judaism believes that each successive generation's interpretation according to its understanding and needs is already potentially inherent in the revealed Bible, for "whatsoever a sagacious disciple might one day state . . . even that was declared by Moses on Sinai . . ." (Jer . Tractate *Pea*, Ch. II/4).

Within the Jewish moral law, Steinberg considered the essentials to be a) in principle, man's ability to decide by judging, of his free will, and consequently on his own responsibility and b) in practice, on the basis of this decision of his, love of one's fellow man. This conception is scattered throughout Steinberg's writings in dozens of places, sometimes in systematic historical discussions, sometimes in a wealth of associations cited explicitly and in full, or fragmented and implicitly. Man's ability to make a moral decision was first specifically noted in *Deuteronomy* (XXX: 15, 19):

"See, I set before you this day life and prosperity, death and adversity . . . I have put before you life and death, blessing and curse. Choose life—if you and your offspring would live."

That was one of the sources of inspiration for the Sages' sayings such as Rabbi Akiba—"Everything is foreseen, yet freedom of choice is given," and Rabbi Hanania—"Everything lies in the hands of God except the fear of God" (Tractate *Berachot* 33/b).[99] Under the influence of the Stoics, this was worded in *IV Hasmoneans* as ethical principle that man's virtues can master his lusts and passions. Generations later, notes Steinberg, the principle of moral decision was given a systematic rational formulation by Maimonides. In *Rules of Repentance*, Chapter 5, he warns against deterministic conceptions according to which man is not responsible for his deeds or misdeeds and not endowed with the ability to make moral choices or decisions because everything is predetermined, either by divine providence or heredity. Rebutting this position, Maimonides teaches that "Let it not come into your thought . . . that the Holy One Blessed be He sentences man from the beginning of his creation to be righteous or evil. Such is not the case, but rather every man is capable of being righteous . . . or evil . . . or wise or stupid, or compassionate or cruel, or miserly or noble, and so with other attitudes, and no one can coerce him, but he himself and of his own mind inclined to the path he wishes . . ."[100] According to Maimonides, Judaism teaches that the cosmological structure is such that a special place is reserved for man:

"for in a small way man is himself a Creator, and because he has the choice of creating according to patterns of goodness, he has also the power to improve and make himself more complete in the human community."[101]

This evolution of the principle of man's free will decision as a precondition for morality is clearly reflected, in Steinberg's view, in Hermann Cohen's rationalist-religious philosophy. Steinberg admired the synthesis, in Cohen's thought, of religion with ethics, of the universalism of the prophetic creed with the particularity of the Jewish people, of pure reason with practical reason. This interrelationship with reason retaining an autonomous status and faith remaining in a state of correlation with it, achieved a concrete Jewish-religious framework during Cohen's last years, and Steinberg found in that framework a reflection of his own philosophy:

"As a simple creature of flesh and blood, burdened with the realization of his moral guilt, and a constant prey to the weakness of the flesh and of social ills, man cannot exist without 'love of God,' . . . and hence of his fellow men . . ."[102]

The fellow man—in Hermann Cohen's terms *Mitmensch* (companion) and *Nebenmensch* (associate)—is what the other aspect of morality focuses on, that is, the realization in practice of man's free will decision. In this too Steinberg finds continuity and consistency in Jewish ethical thought from the Bible down to his own time, including the moral teachings different and even opposed to thinkers like Hermann Cohen, Jacob Rosenheim, Isaac Breuer, Leo Baeck, Franz Rosenzweig. The main element in this continuity is in precepts of commission such as "Love your neighbour as yourself" or as the prophet Micah says that indeed, all "the Lord requires of you" is ". . . to do justly and to love mercy and to walk humbly with Thy God" (VI:8), or as Habakuk says on the essence of all the precepts, "And the righteous man will live in his faith" (*Tractate Makoth*, p. 24/a).

Throughout his Jewish thinking, Steinberg stressed the uniqueness of the Jewish people as a chosen people, chosen to carry the burden of universal, moral commitments. The precept to love one's neighbour, says Steinberg, obliges the Jews in regard to all people, not just their fellow Jews. In that interpretation, as in other ideas as well, he was influenced by Samuel David Luzzatto, from whom he took over the notion that the Hebrew views all humans as sons of one father, all in the image of God, and man is judged not for his faith, but for his deeds . . . "The Bible never distinguished between a Hebrew and a Gentile in anything in which judgments of justice and honesty commit every man to his fellow . . ." (*Yessodei Torah* Ch. XVI, paras. 36, 38).

Steinberg's understanding of Jewish ethics is summarized in his conception of the essence of redemption according to Judaism. In many of his writings, he stressed that Judaism considers one of the main reasons for its existence to be working for the realization of redemption, not only with faith, prayer, thought and study, but in one's day-to-day deeds. This redemption is conceived not as a mystic phenomenon,[103] but as a social and even political goal. For the essence of redemption is "rescuing people from its political, social and spiritual misery, and . . . bringing it nearer to the 'End of Days' of universal peace."[104]

Notes

1. "Culture and Revolution—Essay on Lukacs' History and Class Consciousness" (henceforth cited: "Culture"), p. 1.

2. *Ibid*, pp. 1/2.

3. *Ibid*, p. 3.

4. "Development and Disintegration in Contemporary Art" (henceforth cited: "Art"), p. 4.

5. *Ibid*, p. 5.

6. *Ibid*, p. 3.

7. *Ibid*, pp. 4/5

8. One of the major principles of Judaism, Steinberg believed, is that man is a creature endowed with inalienable ethical potential; hence human beings are personally responsible for their decisions and deeds, cf. below, Section B.

9. See below "Hermann Cohen—as Educator (1842-1918)".

10. "Art", p. 8.

11. *Ibid*, pp. 15/16.

12. "Brotherhood", p. 3.

13. *Ibid*, pp. 4, 7.

14. *Ibid*, p. 7.

15. "Bolshevism's 'Weltanschauung' " (henceforth cited: "Bolshevism") p. 6.

16. "Brotherhood", p. 14.

17. *Ibid*, p. 15.

18. "Bolshevism", p. 12.

19. "Between the Pieces of Abraham's Covenant (Ben Habtarim), (henceforth cited: "Covenant"), p. 3.

20. "Brotherhood", p. 11.

21. *Ibid*.

22. *Ibid*. pp. 8/9; Cf. A. S. Steinberg, *Die Idee der Freiheit—Ein Dostojevsky Buch*, translated by Jacob Klein, Vita Nova Verlag, Luzern: 1936, pp. 9ff; pp. 77ff.

23. "Bolshevism", p. 11. Dostoyevsky was one of the major sources of inspiration for Steinberg, cf. below "Dostoyevsky the Thinker". Steinberg's criticism of ". . . the prevailing conception of Dostoyevsky as an advocate of the late nineteenth century antisemitism" as "a superficial one", since "Dostoyevsky's malevolent attitude towards the Jews" had deep roots in his mystical and messianic cravings, has been sustained in recent historiography, see the penetrating analysis by Shmuel Ettinger, *Anti-Semitism in Modern Times*, Moreshet-Siphriat Poalim, Tel Aviv: 1978, pp. 161ff. (Hebrew).

24. "Brotherhood", p. 12.

25. "Bolshevism", pp. 4, 13-15.

26. *Ibid*, p. 11.

27. *Ibid*, p. 7.

28. *Ibid*, p. 12.

29. *Ibid*, p. 6.

30. *Ibid*, p. 12.
31. *Ibid*, pp. 13-14; cf. also "Culture", p. 13.
32. "Culture", p. 12.
33. *Ibid*, p. 14.
34. See also Georg Lukacs, *Von Nietzsche zu Hitler oder der Irrationalismus und die deutsche Politik*, Fischer Bücherei, Frankfurt a/M, 1966: p. 143.
35. "Culture", p. 7.
36. *Ibid*, p. 8.
37. *Ibid*.
38. *Ibid*, p. 9.
39. *Ibid*.
40. *Ibid*, p. 12.
41. *Ibid*, pp. 12/13.
42. "Christianity in Crisis" (henceforth cited: "Christianity") p. 5. Jewish intellectuals in Eastern Europe were quite intrigued by the philosophy of Soloviev, especially in matters of ethics, religion and nationalism, see "The Ethics of Nationalism" in Simon Dubnov, *Nationalism and History—Essays on Old and New Judaism*, ed. with an introductory essay by Koppel S. Pinson, Meridian, Cleveland & JPS, Philadelphia: 1961 (henceforth cited: "Pinson") pp. 116-130.
43. "Christianity", p. 3; p. 17. The term "Total State" was introduced into the official political ideology and jurisprudence of the Nazi regime in 1933 by Carl Schmitt and Ernst Forstoff. One of the first systematic attempts at a critique of political totalitarianism from a Christian point of view, parallel to Steinberg's argument, was made by the "Forschungsab-teilung des Oekumenischen Rates für praktisches Christentum" Vol. VII of the series "Kirche und Welt—Studien und Dokumente" entitled *Totaler Staat und christliche Freiheit*, Geneva: 1937, 177 pp.
44. "Dostoyevsky: the Thinker" (henceforth cited: "Thinker") p. 1.
45. "Christianity", p. 1.
46. "Thinker", pp. 1, 6-11; also see below "Our Controversy with Christianity".
47. "Faith (Bitochn)", (henceforth cited: "Faith"), p. 3.
48. "Christianity", pp. 14-15.
49. "Faith", p. 3.
50. *Ibid*, pp. 1, 2.
51. *He'atid*, ed. by Saul Ish Hurwitz, Berlin: 1911, Vol. IV.
52. "Pinson", p. 83; pp. 325, 335.
53. "Jewish World History" (henceforth cited: "World History") p. 10.
54. "The Philosophical Premises of Jewish Historiography" (henceforth cited: "Histori-ography"), pp. 16/17; cf. "World History", p. 8.
55. "Pinson", p. 87.
56. "Historiography", p. 25.
57. E. Tcherikower, "Peter Lavrov and the Jewish Socialist Emigres". *YIVO Annual of Jewish Social Science*, YIVO, New York: 1952, Vol. VII, (henceforth cited: "YIVO"), pp. 132-145.
58. "Beginning and End of History in the Teaching of P. L. Lavrov" (henceforth cited: "Lavrov") pp. 2, 3.
59. *Ibid*, p. 7.
60. *Ibid*, p. 5.
61. *Ibid*, pp. 12, 13.
62. *Ibid*, p. 13.
63. *Ibid*, pp. 2, 3; pp. 16-18.
64. *Ibid*, pp. 1, 2.
65. *Ibid*, p. 19.
66. *Ibid*, pp. 27-29.

67. *Ibid*, p. 10.

68. *Ibid*, p. 20.

69. "YIVO", pp. 142, 144.

70. *Ibid*, p. 144.

71. *Ibid*, p. 141.

72. "Historiography", pp. 1/2.

73. *Ibid*, p. 8; cf. "Rambam—The Maimonides Anniversary (1135-1935)", (henceforth cited: "Rambam"), p. 13.

74. "Historiography", p. 8.

75. On the roots of the issue of objectivity in modern Jewish historical study and thought, cf. Nathan Rotenstreich, *Tradition and Reality—The Impact of History on Modern Jewish Thought*, Random House, N.Y. 1972, pp. 21-74.

76. "Historiography", p. 15.

77. "Pinson", pp. 336/7.

78. *Ibid*, p. 94.

79. *Ibid*, p. 120.

80. *Ibid*, p. 339; cf. Simon Dubnow "World History" (German Edition), Vol. I, pp. XIII-XX; Vol. IX, 47, p. 429; Vol. X, 37, pp. 345ff; also Idem, *Letters*, No. 1.

81. "Pinson", p. 80; cf. p. 87.

82. "Historiography", pp. 20-21; "World History", p. 4; cf. "The two sources of Simon Dubnow's Thought" (henceforth cited: "Sources") p. 81; "Pinson", pp. 336-353.

83. "Sources", p. 83.

84. "Historiography", p. 21; "Sources", p. 80; also cf. "Historiography" pp. 22, 23; and "Sources", pp. 82, 84.

85. "Pinson", p. 80.

86. *Ibid*, p. 89.

87. "A People and its Ideal", pp. 7, 9.

88. "The Bible in the History of Jewish Tradition", p. 5.

89. "The Scale of Values" (henceforth cited: "Values"), p. 71.

90. "Values", pp. 70ff.; "The History of Jewish Religious Thought" (henceforth cited: "Thought"), pp. 280, 285, 292.

91. "Thought", p. 273.

92. "Faith", p. 2.

93. "Thought", p. 280.

94. Cf. *Exodus* XXXIV: 6, 7; Tractate *Rosh Hashana*, p. 17/b.

95. "Thought", p. 302.

96. *Ibid*, p. 276.

97. "Letter to L. P. Karsavin" (henceforth cited: "Karsavin"), p. 6.

98. *Ibid*, p. 7.

99. "Thought", p. 282.

100. "Rambam", pp. 8, 9.

101. *Ibid*.

102. "Thought", p. 340.

103. Steinberg, in the spirit of the first generations of the "Wissenschaft des Judentums" and under the impact of empiricism and positivism felt that the mystical traditions in Judaism reflected alien influences and rather "naive faith", even though personally Steinberg was deeply attached to the mystique of Jewish existence, survival and destiny. "Karsavin", pp. 9, 10; cf. "Thought", p. 278.

104. "Dostoyevsky and the Jews", pp. 328, 329; also p. 227; cf. "Socialism and Messianism", pp. 4, 5.

SECTION A

The Cultural Factor in Historical Change

1. Development and Disintegration in Contemporary Art

When a living body begins to disintegrate, each one of its particles acquires a life of its own, but it is only the wretched life of maggots.

Hegel

My friends, what do you think? Would you not like along with me to ask death, is this then life? But then I swear upon my love for Zarathustra—once again!

Nietzsche

We are living in a period of transition. Long before the catastrophe of 1914, the premonition of impending doom fell across the European consciousness like a sinister shadow. Eras and epochs were drawing to a close. The old world tried to conceal its age and to live frantically, first charging ahead, then glancing back; it suddenly began to mark time and, as if stumbling in a vain attempt to jump over its own shadow, it collapsed—slain by its own hand. Today we are witnessing the final disintegration of the corpse of defunct European culture.

But there is no real death in nature or in human life, because life itself is a process of constant dying; the very constancy of the process signifies genuine and vital life. Only the rate of the deadly life-process alters, in which death itself is eternally dying. We speak of a blossoming, or of the fullness of vital energy, when in fact the grim reaper still has much work to do; but the end is in sight only when new life though foredoomed begins to stir. Only *sub specie praesentis*, only in the crowded arena of the present are life and death eternally opposed; in the onward rush of time they are inseparable.

It is important to note this distinction in all questions relating to the present age. The old world is no more; in other words, the new world came into being. The disintegration of old culture is the proliferation of possibilities for rebirth, and in our transitional period our contemporaries

This essay was first published in Russian in Volume I of *Alkonost, Iskoustvo Staroye i Novoye,* collected essays edited by Konst. Erberg, St. Petersburg, 1921.

must realize that our own time will soon become the past, and that history continues—and as always, everything is beyond the present. So also are the destinies of art.

Art is inseparably linked with the whole problem of human culture. If a philosophy of culture is possible, then there must be a place within it for the philosophy of art; and if the philosophy of culture must solve the eternal problem of the meaning of human history, then necessarily the philosophy of history must encompass the history of art. In such a way the philosophy of the history of art finds its own justification, at least as a legitimate problem. Firstly, this problem extends to the totality of phenomena defining art as one of the links in our culture, which itself is always developing and which is unified by a single purpose; and secondly, within the bounds of the life of art, it must elucidate those internal laws of its development which autonomously determine its own fate. Both sides of the problem would have to find their application to any period or to any cross-section of the whole historical process.

When applied to our problem, this would mean that from the connection between early twentieth-century art and the general cultural situation of that period here defined as one of disintegration, as well as from the intrinsic aspirations of art itself—it would be possible to extract some general meaning which would illuminate the individual and partial with the light of the general and integral, and so remove the screen which shields the future from our eyes. Thus, irrespective of any one particular aesthetic ideology, we would discover a sound basis for the clarification of the sense and meaning of so many current controversies about old and new art, and, having risen above the present, we would view it with particular clarity.

I. The Elements of European Disintegration

The disintegration of European culture was manifested simultaneously in all its various aspects. Towards the end of the nineteenth century, the concept of a common European culture, as some real entity, became a fact. Philosophy, science, art, and technology came to be seen as one; the labour movement marched forward under the banner of the International; industry and trade were just as rapidly Europeanized in the international sense; dress, manners, and home furnishings became alike. Instead of separate English, French, and German nationalities, it was as if a new nationality had emerged, a European one; a new European character was emerging. Although there was still no common language, knowledge of foreign, i.e. of other European languages became widespread throughout Europe. And Russia, with increasing intensity, was also drawn into this general process.

But at the same time as this integral unity was being formed, there was also revealed with extraordinary force a "centrifugal" nationalistic aspiration; the particular characteristic of this new aspiration was the fact that its goal was openly stated as movement away from the centre. Such a movement away from the centre as an end in itself is the purest ideology of the impending dissolution. In this respect, as in many others, the great war only exposed the development of general history. The exploding structure shattered with its own fragments whatever integrity of the parts still existed, and we witness the complete collapse of the old European territorial organization.

The internal unity of national society also collapsed. The class struggle had never before been recognized as a principle which would, in practice, lead to the total demise of political and social unity. The international character of the workers' movement proved to be an imaginary force. Similarly, the "sacred unity", invented for the integration of classes which had been isolated by the force of events during the war, proved in its turn to be imaginary. Revolutions followed the wars. Political parties were permeated with class consciousness, and the political struggle took on the character of a struggle for economic interests. The author of *Das Kapital* had become a prophet: that is he himself became one of the causes of the succeeding events. But he had not foreseen that within the classes, united in their economic interests, there would appear in turn a new internecine struggle of conflicting interests among groups, factions, circles, and even among individuals, and that the dialectic of disintegration would not stop in the face of projected manifestos. Nor did it stop before such apparently indestructible organizations as the Latin oecumenical church. The unification of people on the basis of religion and dogma stood out in all its unreality. Unified technology achieved its greatest success as the technology of destruction, that is, it revealed its meaning, or rather its meaninglessness, in self-destruction. The struggle with nature degenerated into a struggle with the human kind. Science, which had gradually became the "servant of technology", shares the fate of its master. Philosophy split into a multitude of disputing schools and celebrated the rebirth of Alexandrianism and scholasticism. Even to mention questions of morality is regarded as ill-mannered. The family is the last "atom" which seems as yet not disintegrated completely. Fragments everywhere: splinters, ruin, disintegration.

Yet at the same time, what an extraordinary blossoming of the exact sciences and what an incomparable accumulation of countless treasures! Archeological excavations had unearthed Sumarian remains; philology deciphered and resurrected languages and dialects unknown even to our earliest forebears; microscopes and macroscopes examined the smallest and the farthest objects; even the minutia of some second-rate problem appear too big to the contemporary mind so concerned with precision. Every day brings with it new achievements, new inventions and discoveries. But this accumulation is also a decline: a plurality, which lacks unity; wealth, possessed by no one; infinity, above which no spirit hovers.

Where then is art? Where is its voice in this confusion of tongue? Why is it unable to help with its constructive genius in the European Babel?

Let us then turn to contemporary man, from the creations of his hands to their creator. Then, perhaps, we may come nearer also to the unravelling of the problem of his mediocrity in achieving creative targets.

Contemporary man possesses widespread knowledge. His Bible is the newspaper, a comprehensive daily encyclopaedia. In the cinema he can see what cannot be conveyed in words. He has heard about everything. It is extremely difficult to astonish him. His technologically complex life insistently demands that he should rapidly orientate himself in complicated schedules, byelaws and plans. From this fact derives the particular nature of human relations: people do not converse with each other, they negotiate; they do not ask each other questions, they conduct enquiries. Man has become the reference book for other men: this is the modern adaptation of the ancient law of the jungle. But in order to receive information, other information must be provided in exchange. Hence the desire to be "well-educated", that is, to be a reference book of the latest edition. Furthermore, in order to be really useful to one's neighbours, i.e., to be able to derive real benefit from one's neighbours, it is necessary to specialize in one specific branch of knowledge, since no one person can possess all the required information. The narrow, specialized character of contemporary education is the other side of its superficial omniscience. And what does the average European know about himself? No more than what is known to him within the narrow confines of his speciality. His personality coincides completely with his knowledge of facts. He is conscious of himself as a depository of disparate bits of knowledge, integrated by the unity of a practical, everyday task.

Such is the average European, including not only the residents of Western Europe, but all those associated with Western European culture. Fortunately, in Russia we still have very few of these average Europeans; however, among those who participate in the shaping of culture, we have far too many Europeans. That is why the intention to characterize the creative European applies also to Russia. The correlation, of course, is somewhat different. The dependence of the European creative spirit on the entire European cultural and psychological milieu is a direct and immediate dependence, whereas Russian dependence on this milieu is still determined by the intermediary link of European action and endeavour. Nevertheless, it exists and sometimes even shows up as the unconsciously adopted "measure of things". In this respect the problem of contemporary European culture is also Russia's concern.

The creative man in decaying Europe can be drastically described as follows.

If the average European possesses wide knowledge, then the average representative of the European creative classes is genuinely educated. True specialists in every branch of learning compose the newspapers he reads. It is even more difficult to astound him than even his "younger brother"; but, having more knowledge, he also knows that one should be inured to astonishment, and that astonishment is the beginning of wisdom. That is why he strives in every way to discover something astounding. He prefers exotic countries, ancient epochs, the languages of remote peoples, the most obscure philosophical systems, occult religions, refined speech, and a technology of exceptional value. To be amazed and to amaze: that is the norm of his life. But he also knows the difference between precise and approximate knowledge, and aspiring towards the summit, he demands of himself a methodical and critical attitude towards facts, and the ability to experiment and to observe. Thus he learns to observe himself.

The educated European relates to himself in the same way as he does to the external world—methodically, critically, scientifically. Am I not a fact among other facts? Is not the soul an object of science—of psychology? Is not psychology an exact, experimental science? And there emerges a new type of man who exists for himself only as a scientific fact. The more man learns to see in himself, the less he sees himself; in other words, it is not that he does not see himself, he simply does not exist; he is divided into an observable object and its observer. The complexity of his intellectual life results in his inability to distinguish that which is inherited from his own nature and that which is acquired. He is too much of an experimentalist to be a good observer. Having transformed himself into a laboratory, he can no longer observe his own nature in freedom, but rather as if it were in prison ready for trial, in some laboratory for research exercises—in short, a nature investigated with all the ardour of experimental science. But the scientific ends justify the ordeal of vivisection, if only one fact more, the one millionth psychological "discovery" can be recorded in the results.

It is the Holy Inquisition and—the holy, holy simplicity . . .

II. Development and Disintegration in Art

The history of mankind is meaningful. The meaning consists in the fact that mankind is called upon to embody eternal meaning in its history, and thus to render all history and time itself superfluous. The meaning of temporal events is the future realization of supratemporal being. To understand the history of mankind as a successive series of accomplishments in this direction is tantamount to grasping the philosophical meaning of history.

Thus man is both the instrument and the creator of history, and the diversity of man's works constitutes a necessary multiplicity in the solution of a manifold task. Art embodies the highest degree of possible achievements in every period of human history.

The history of mankind is the history of the development of man's creativity in progress towards overcoming the natural temporal order of events. This development never was, and never can be, an ascent towards a higher stage, higher owing to some non-historical evaluation. From the point of view of the philosophy of history, every later moment is more valuable than any previous one, because it draws history closer to its completion. Nevertheless, development is still realizable.

Time was conceived in timelessness and must return to its eternal primary origin. The history of human consciousness within the limits of time merely continues and completes the primordial breaking away process from the fragmented world of experience, from the integrity and completeness of the ideal cosmos. Time is the principle of disintegration, and the faster its wings revolve, the more productive is the work of its grinding millstones. The whole world of experience must be ground down to the last grain, so that the historically prescribed process can be completed in its entirety. The problem of mankind is to employ time, to speed up its processes, to hasten its end. If history must terminate with the extinction of time itself, and if this can happen only when time has completed its task of atomization, then every disintegration represents progress in the single true historical direction: that is, decay is progress, and disintegration is undoubtedly development. In fact everything which we conceive of as progress and development in human history is primarily the ramification of the simple, solid trunk of the tree of human life into its many branches and direction—each of which in turn ramifies and multiplies, transforming its original state into a network of interlacing and interplaying possibilities. The tree of life is transformed into the tree of knowledge, and in this penetrating consciousness, under its veiled surface, lie hidden the roots of integral unity.

This is not the place to develop these thoughts to their final conclusions and first principles. Rather, let us endeavour to demonstrate in general terms what place art occupies in this creative process of disintegration.

Time and all temporal phenomena are constantly disintegrating; consciousness as a principle of unity is opposed to time. If there were no consciousness in time, there could be no consciousness of the disintegration of unity. Disintegration, which would only be disintegration, would not be what it really is; nor would it consist of the relative unity which enables it to be seen as plurality, engendered by some original common denominator—that is, it would be nothing at all. But consciousness in time is that potential which counterbalances its destructivess and allows it continously to overcome its own discontinuity. That is why by itself pure contemplative inactive consciousness in time is transformed into the creative and unifying principle. Temporal consciousness is creative consciousness.

Creativity is the overcoming of temporality in time and the reason why art is the most intense form of human creativity is due to the fact that it overcomes temporality at its most critical point, i.e., at the boiling point of the present, where, between that which already exists and that which does not yet exist, in the void and isolation of the moment, a bridge is to be thrown across the gulf of complete discontinuance. Art solves the problem in that it preserves the moment, elevating it above time. "The leaf which withered and died, survives as eternally golden in paeans of praise." The temporal non-temporality of the immediate perception of the moment—that is the true element of art.

From this follows the historical nature of art. Genuine art is always art of the contemporary period, and its contemporary nature must remain so for ever. Copernicus erases Ptolemy, but Shakespeare can never annihilate Aeschylus. The Cronus of science is devoured by his own children; the Titans of art live together peacefully in the pantheon of history. Old and new art, future art and contemporary art—if it is genuine art, does not require defense or justification because its worth cannot be subjected to the judgment of history above which it is always elevated. Therefore the argument concerning old and new art, is, as it were, an argument behind the heights of its "hanging gardens" about lowly everyday issues, scarcely vital to it. Still the argument about it does not arise by mere chance.

Art, accompanying humanity on its historical path, in its supra-historicity preserves a constant connection with those underlying layers in which are embedded its lasting monuments. On one hand, it is monumental in each separate authentic manifestation; on the other hand, it is internally differentiated, in conformity with the regularity of the changes of the ground above which it arises. In other words, this means that each work of art by itself stands outside of time, though all taken together make up an integral gallery developing in accordance with its intrinsic evolution. Such is the meaning of the historicity of supra-historical art.

This thought can be expressed in another way: the form of a work of art, or a particular aspect of that unity which constitutes the exclusive world of an artistic whole, is identical in all the multiformity of works of art in all its aspects, and in all the changes of its manifestations; but the elements themselves, organized into a self-contained whole, and its multiformity cannot be conceived outside the swing of the historical pendulum and the dynamism of the life process in its fundamental duality: development—disintegration. Consequently the debate about the formula for progress in the history of art, in this particular sense, is logically involved in the very problem of the philosophy of art.

The elements of an artistic work are the elements of the human culture of the artist's age transformed in the crucible of his creative consciousness. The link with the contemporary age is overshadowed in the creative act, but at the same time it is preserved in the work itself, precisely in its peculiar individual light. In so far as all points of the contemporary age form a single line of historical development, so do all reflections of these points, transformed into an artistic work, deploy a new imaginary line of the particular history of the arts, which urgently demands its individual interpretation from the point of view of rational philosophy.

In application to our age, this view reveals broad perspectives. We attempted to characterize our age as one of disintegration. Disintegration, as we tried to indicate, is the genuine criterion of development. It follows that one or other trend in contemporary art, as a trend, which is the same from the point of view of the philosophy of the history of art, will be that much more topical and progressive, the more clearly it corresponds to this spirit of disintegration and decline which is the spirit of our age. However, such a correspondence by no means determines the purely artistic and autonomous value of separate works of art, because aesthetics and the philosophy of history lead to their own evaluations, each independent of the other. After all that has been said above, this is self-evident.

Wherein is the highest degree of disintegration manifested which could serve as a measure of its relative successes? Now we have all the data to enable us to answer this question. As was said already, consciousness is the principle directly opposed to time, and related to it in the way that pure unity relates to pure plurality. Therefore the pinnacle of disintegration would be the disintegration in time of consciousness itself. Having noted above the elements of European disintegration, we have already touched on the disintegrating unity of consciousness in its form of psychological phenomenon. Now let us see how this stage of development is reflected in art.

Art is always realistic. Yet, the reality which art copies is that reality which is embodied by the ideality of the creative spirit. This spirit, as by now we know, is the spirit of contemporary culture, in that phase of its disintegration to which it was brought by the universal process of development. Therefore, we could, inversely, infer from realized art the spirit of contemporary culture embodied in it. From whichever side we approach it, we meet the wide open but empty gaze of modern art.

What prevails in modern art is consciousness, technical virtuosity, historicism, outspoken subjectivity, and, objectively, insignificant content. Let us assess the progressive character and the justification of these creative aspects of our age.

The consciousness of modern man manifests itself most distinctly in his ability to observe himself, i.e., to relate to himself as an object. But a work which reflects the objective spirit, the spirit of the age in its most involuntary manifestation, thus will remain involuntary only in this limited meaning. The contemporary creative spirit is preserved, as a principle of unity, only in the abstract formal sense. Distance with respect to itself is integrated in this concept, that is, the principle of inner fragmentation. The spirit of the present is a self-disintegrating spirit which, within its own boundaries, breaks down into a variety of objective elements and the empty frame of bare observation. Its efficacity shows itself in its disposition experimentally to juggle with itself, that is, in its skill in putting itself under a diversity of approaches, and to submit passively to the results of these artificially devised experiments. Consequently, the ultimate end of its activity is aimlessness and inactivity. Thus we can understand the enormous role of aesthetic ideologies in contemporary art, in which the justification of meaning mostly precedes the very existence of the object which is being justified. Aesthetics, the theory of creativity, emerges as the aim of creativity, and itself is reduced to a practical means of proving to itself and to others the accuracy of the preconceived theory. Instead of creating in the name of the present, it proclaims the future as the principle of creative work: this work observes itself from the point of view of the future, i.e., looks at itself as it looks at the past, and therefore it is born dead. As art in general, it preserves the spirit of the contemporary age, but alas, of a stillborn age.

In contrast, technology triumphs. Yet again we are faced with centrifugal force. The scaffolding around the building in construction as a part of the architectural whole, creates the style of our age in which organic integrity of means and ends breaks down into elements unified only by an effort of consciousness. To this all its actions are equally important, because they are all equally objective, eliminating any contents of subjectivity. This technology, developing to the level of an end in itself, transforms physical and spiritual nature into one expanding "nature morte", into a stillborn nature, the image and likeness of the self-annihilating spirit. The means are recognized as means and still considered as an end. Thus in the contemporary artistic world-view all subjects and words, being means to an end, like the creative spirit which is conscious of its own disintegration, break down into the smallest component parts, whilst the form of its integration and reunification is preserved only in the bare consciousness of the exposed decay, as a new revelation of the essence of things. Psychopathology has long been aware of the peculiar necrophilic passion, the specific attraction of the odor of decomposition.

Hence the strong inclination for extensive diversification of content. The entire chaotic and aphilosophic mass of factual material extracted from all the secret crannies of history, saturating the contemporary age, is drawn into the whirlpool of art. For the empty form, such as the creative consciousness of the present, any stuffing is aceptable. Lacking immediate criteria and bereft of any substance, this consciousness retained merely the formal standards of difference and similarity. Everything which differs even superficially from the ordinary is preferred by this token alone, whereas anything which formally resembles the ordinary is rejected. Herein lies the source of all kinds of stylization, affectation, imitation, and trends toward the primitive, reached by means of the most sophisticated technological efforts. Incidentally, the entire historicism of the age can be understood as one of the technological devices.

All of this taken together entails an enhanced subjectivism. The personality of the creator has never before been so clearly perceptible in his works. The canvas has become transparent, like a cobweb; granite has become like glass; all music has become vocal: the ego is seen and heard everywhere; it is the beginning of every sentence. But it is by no means a genuine lyricism where the ego is objectified in its own subjectivity. Rather, we are dealing with an ego thrust upon us against its own free will. In its striving towards purest objectivity, the contemporary spirit overlooks only one fact: that genuine objectivity is an entire system of completed, organized worlds of subjectivism. However, when subjectivity is only a shadow of itself, then all of its manifestations are not only far from objectivity but, as far as their objectivity is concerned, it is below the stage of a self-contained subjectivity: these manifestations are simply chaotic and accidental, i.e., individual, yet individual in a specific sense, not unlike the individually troublesome buzzing of a housefly. It is just as impossible to buzz objectively, as it is to create a lyricism of sensations. Scientific objectivity in art is the obverse side of spiritually devastated individuality.

Needless to add that in such an arid individuality there is no place for inspiration by non-aesthetic ideals, which could be transformed into aesthetic values in the very process of artistic creation. This follows directly from that aesthetic self-awareness leading to the hypertrophy of technology, to the absence of material criteria in the choice of content, to bare subjectivism, where even in the creative act, the ego remains buried in the dust of triviality, from which the innocent artist had in days of old been purified before he had the vaguest foreboding that there is no end to the torments of knowledge.

III. Unity to Come

Contemporary art, with its extraordinary virtuosity, all the brilliance of perfected technical skill and the force of creative strength—reveals to us the spirit animating our age in its seemingly hopeless atomization. Is it indeed hopeless?

Hopelessness is the natural condition of old men and historians old and young. To them the present day is both the end of history and the end of the world because, tomorrow, their body will become the abode of maggots whose life they feebly envy and towards whom they have an unconquerable aversion. Valuing most that which they perceive as the remains of their ego, they jealously guard their obsolete past and regard the future, where there is no place for them, as of no concern of theirs. Will they say to death in the words of Nietzsche: "Is this life?" If so, they would then be conscious of themselves as immortal, and would neither grumble and complain about the past, nor would they grow old; they would calmly welcome the triumph of disintegration: historians would become philosophers.

From a philosophical point of view, however, successes in the process of development are the more significant, the nearer historical disintegration approaches its end. In this sense our contemporary age has moved forward considerably in comparison with even the most recent periods. In our cultural consciousness we have arrived at such stages of schizophrenia which in recent times were considered as forms of insanity: today all progressive people to a man suffer from chronic split personality.

Is it possible to go further along this road? It follows from the definition of consciousness, as the last principle of unity in an age of general disintegration, that after the disintegration of consciousness itself, one cannot expect anything substantially new in the process of development; only the degree of intensity can increase. But this critical moment in the history of human consciousness must also become its turning point.

Now we can understand in what sense humanity can participate in the transformation of temporal events into supra-temporal being. The fate of being within the time-frame cannot be decided without man's creative effort. The development of human history from the original synthesis of primordial mystical consciousness towards the gradual blossoming of culture must lead to the gradual dropping of its petals and to the ripening of the fruit with its new seeds. Therefore the seeming discontinuity following in the development is a necessary jump from the height of upswept branches down to the loose, receptive soil which absorbs the seeds for new development and growth. Until the destiny of the particular historical period is completed, one culture will replace another, grow side by side with it, overtake it in its growth or lag behind it, and the human world will resemble a leafy, rustling forest.

Now the withered tree of European culture falls with a crash under the blows of the axe of history; while the helpless shoots of new-born vegetation already appear on the European peninsula. We do not yet know its future fate, but the signs are favourable.

The new culture which replaces the old disintegrating one, cannot but be determined by its predecessor, and if the law of successive development in history is the law of continual disintegration, then the highest degree of disintegration must bring about the creative disintegration of the process of disintegration itself. This would be the turning point in the historical process and would signify man's drawing near to his genuine predestination, to the fulfilment of his philosophical mission.

Intuitively we can imagine a new humanity, one unified in its political existence, organized in all aspects of its practical life, clearly aware of its age-old unity and its high common purpose, living for cosmic creation, and illuminated by one source of light, the central sun of the universe. In this synthetic, conscious humanity each personality will be creative, because no one will lack work in which all will participate together. And in this humanity, co-operating in leading history to its final goal for the perfection of history, every man will have his own place, because everyone's place will be determined by the world-order; everyone will remain himself, because everyone will be in accord with the soul of the universe, which will include everyone within the soul of his own.

Perhaps in this new world art will not exist as a special elevated form of life because the whole would will be a unified work of artistic inspiration and humanity will be, as it was said, "saved by the light of beauty". But then Beauty will be Truth, and its steady light will replace the flicker of the sinister stars of the past.

In any case, the art of the present is not the art of the future. That which is new today will be old tomorrow and by means of its own history will relate in its own language the thousand-year old chronicle of mankind's spiritual disintegration, completed, as we truly hope, by the decaying contemporary age. And if there are still heated arguments about yesterday's truth and about today's truth, then the argument is actually about as to who will be the first in the realm of the future, and who will be the last in the disintegrating present. The difference is clearly negligible.

2. Beginning and End of History in the Teaching of P. L. Lavrov

In the concluding chapter of his last major work on the history of thought Lavrov, contrasting 'pseduo-learning' with true learning, attempts to establish at the same time three different but mutually complementary types of true scholars. There is firstly the methodologist, the creator of new ways of knowing, the 'teacher of those who already know', one who indicates new aims and creates new means of achieving them; secondly there is the systematizer, in whom the interest in a harmonious fusion into one whole of all the diversity of contemporary knowledge outweighs the desire to disclose particular features of that knowledge or to add to their numbers; and there is thirdly the specialist, who "concentrates his thought on one single question, extracting it, as it were, from the body of a particular science, but treating this question in all its details and peculiarities, thus leaving for future generations a model of a special work, on the basis of which they can learn how to work." Archimedes is a classical representative of the first type; Euclid embodies the second; finally Apollonius of Perga, "primarily a geometer", as the Alexandrian scholars called him, is a brilliant example of the third type.[1]

This differentiation, which is so typical for the entire style of Lavrov's thought, reads like some sort of epilogue to all his own work, work which went on for almost half a century, in one special field, on one special problem, namely in the field of history and on the problem of its true meaning. Indeed it is not difficult to guess to which of the three types of scholar, as Lavrov delineates them, he himself is to be assigned, to which he obviously assigns himself. Learning as such, he goes on, would not exist were there no scholars of the first type; though "it would remain forever the property of a very limited number of highly cultured people and would play no part in the history of mankind", were there no scholars of the second type; yet "only scholars of the last type extract from learning the entire wealth of its results and show it forth as the most productive power of the human mind."[2] Did not Lavrov himself, as did once the Alexandrian

---

1. A. Dolengi, *The Most Important Moments in the History of Thought*, Moscow, 1903, pp. 938 *et seq*.

2. *Op. cit.*, p. 943. Cf. also pp. 388 *et seq*.

This essay was first published in Russian in *Kolos*, edited by P. Vityazev, St. Petersburg, 1922.

scholar of old, whom he compares with "the discoverer" Archimedes, did
not he himself strive to extract from history as a science "the entire wealth
of its results", did he not constantly defend it as "the most productive
power of the human mind"? "To understand history in our time is to have a
clear understanding of the moral ideal," he had already written in the
Historical Letters,[3] and it is precisely because of this that still earlier, long
before Dilthey, before Rickert, before Simmel, he considered the scientific study of history to be the distinguishing feature of our time and even
found it necessary and possible to construct a system of education such that
history was its culmination and at the same time its foundation.[4]

Lavrov did indeed, as a specialist scholar in the best sense, in his own
sense of the word, "leave for posterity a model of a special work" on the
basis of which one should learn how to work; but he also indicates in what
further direction such work can and should develop: with the passage of
time, according to his own teaching, the very question of the correlation of
that understanding of history which he developed to the "vital element",
the spirit of the future—embodied not in his own present, but in ours—
must be re-examined afresh. Are the 'tasks of the understanding of history'
the same as they were in the second half of the last century? Does history
itself as a process—not as *historia rerum gestarum*, but as true *res gestae*—
appear to us in the same aspect as it did to Lavrov, who longed to find the
dream city beyond the next turn in the path of history?

The present study attempts to bring together some data towards a
solution of these questions in one specific aspect only, from the point of
view of one particular problem. There can, however, be no doubt that this
problem is central to a whole series of questions connected with the
philosophical understanding of history, nor, moreover, that the problem is
such that it leads immediately to the basic premises of any world-view
which strives towards wholeness, and of P. L. Lavrov's world-view in
particular.

Lavrov himself was fully aware of this. More than once he came back to a
definition of the tasks of philosophy of history and constantly emphasized
that the philosophical understanding of history, as distinct from its
scientific understanding, is a striving to understand history as one "whole".
It is true that in his earlier works Lavrov apparently allotted to philosophy
of history more modest tasks. "In the present state of knowledge", he
wrote in 1863, "the search for unity in the history of the whole of mankind
does not come within the purview of our science", and although philoso-

3. S. S. Arnoldi, *Historical Letters* (in Russian), 2nd ed., St. Petersburg, 1905, p. 261.
4. P. L. Lavrov, *Helge's Practical Philosophy. Biblioteka dlya chteniya*, 1859, Book V,
pp. 49 *et seq;* also 'Some thoughts on the system of general intellectual education of young
people', *Biblioteka dlya chteniya* (*Library for Reading*, in Russian), Vol. CXLVII, No. 2,
1958, Section II, p. 135: "History is the highest result of all human sciences." Or *ibid.*, p.
141: "A pupil finishes off his general education by weaving it into the crown of History."

phy, "being implicated in all branches of human activity as a quest for *unity* [Lavrov's italics], *wholeness* [our italics] and harmony", which is in fact what makes science out of knowledge, whereas the philosophy of history completely satisfied this quest for "unity and wholeness" when it succeeds in understanding what is peculiarly characteristic of "the life of an entire society at a given epoch". "Philosophy of history", he says on another occasion, "indicates in each epoch what constitutes its real *vital wisdom*, i.e. the ability to conjecture what knowledge, what perfect beauty, what realizable ideal of humanity, are attainable."[5] Thus, according to these first definitions, philosophy, whose aim with regard to history is to complete our knowledge, must limit itself to an understanding of some part of history, of a single given epoch as a whole; but this whole cannot in its turn be thought of as a part of a more comprehensive whole, understood as an *object*, and connected with the concept of "the whole of humanity". It is clear that man still overshadows mankind for Lavrov; the "anthropological" point of view in philosophy, when not complemented by the humanistic point of view, turns Philosophy of History into a discontinuous series of generalizing characterizations which are not imbued with the idea of a whole as a total single object.[6]

Lavrov, it is true, could of course not remain content with this result. The deeper he penetrated into the problems of history, making use of his education in mathematics and natural sciences merely as simple "literacy", the more concrete did the philosophical "demand for unity and wholeness" become for him; the "vital wisdom", which had earlier been important to him, principally as a means of defining the mutual relationship of the individual personality and contemporary society, gradually changed into a special critically based method of understanding historical reality as a peculiar "world of aims and means" alongside the world of "causes and effects". The present, however, and this vital wisdom, with its "ability to conjecture" what the possibilities were, was to serve as a means of correct orientation in the present which appeared to Lavrov in a completely Hegelian light: as the currently existing unity of vestiges of the past and germs of the future. From this point of view Lavrov could repeat literally after Hegel the definition of the present which the German idealist had made. For Hegel "philosophy, being concerned with that which is true,

5. For the articles 'Unity' and 'The anthropological point of view in philosophy' see *Entsiklopedichesky Slovar* (*Encyclopedic Dictionary*), Section II, Vol. I and Section I, Vol. V, 1863 and 1862. Reprinted in *Collected Works*, Ser. I, issue II, Petrograd, 1918, pp. 215, 206.

6. This is apparently contradicted by what Lavrov said about the philosophy of history in 1860, in his 'Three conversations on the contemporary meaning of history' (reprinted *ibidem*, p. 149); a closer examination, however, reveals that here, too, the "single harmonious whole" is merely a general definition of the understanding of history as such— of history as knowledge and not as a particular object of knowledge and understanding (Cf. especially pp. 145 *et seq*. and p. 113).

has to do *ipso facto* with the eternal present" and "nothing in the past is lost for philosophy, because the idea is still present, the spirit is immortal, i.e. it has not passed away, and it is not true that it no longer exists—on the contrary it still indeed *is*." For Lavrov, too, in the last count all the past and all the future are always here in the present; and from his point of view the present can only be understood in a historical sense as an essential link connecting all the past of the world with all its future as a single, continuous whole.[7]

Confronted by a more condensed historical reality, parallel with the discovery of the universal character of the historical approach to the Universe at large, which puts the world as a single continuous process of evolution on a level comparable with that of the general sphere of well-construed order, the meaning of philosophy of history was in turn bound to undergo a profound change. The results of this are already evident in works which are separated from the ones just mentioned by no more than a decade. Thus, by 1870, in an article entitled 'The Philosophical Meaning of History', devoted to Edgar Quinet and Laurent, Lavrov gives a definite and quite new indication of where the task of the scientific understanding of history ends and where its "philosophical task" begins. "History is a process which embraces not only the past but also the present and the future." "The scientific historian is limited to the past. But the philosophical world-view is not content with this, and necessarily constructs the future by analogy with the past in accordance with the tasks of the present." The task of understanding history as a single, objectively given whole is clearly brought out and at the same time it becomes clear to us that—using Lavrov's own new terminology—his "Historical Letters", which had just appeared, should in fact be called "Letters on the Philosophy of History."[8]

This shift of Lavrov's to the viewpoint of a concrete philosophy of history definitely reveals that earlier, too, Lavrov had been an adherent of 'left' Hegelianism, simply because that way it was most convenient for him to turn in Hegel's own direction and exactly whence he had come from: i.e. to German classical ethics. Henceforth Lavrov never loses this broad perspective and submits all his scholarly work to the basic purpose thus conceived. In *The Tasks of the Understanding of History*—the systematic

7. Hegel, *Vorlesungen uber die Philosophie der Geschichte*, Brunstad edition, Leipzig, 1907, p. 125. See below for references to parallel texts in Lavrov. Hegel's play on words, achieved by using the archaic "itzt" = *ist*, instead of *jetzt*, cannot, unfortunately, be rendered in Russian.

8. Cf. *Collected Works*, Ser. IV, fasc. I, Petrograd, 1918, pp. 68, 85; also 'Philosophy of the history of the Slavs', *Otechestvennye Zapiski (Notes of the Fatherland)*, 1870, Vol. CXC, Section I, p. 350, and Vol. CXCI, Section I, p. 116. Of particular interest here are the remarks on "the philosophical construction of the future for the *whole of mankind*" [our italics]. The well known article 'N. K. Mikhailovsky's formula of progress', which also appeared in 1870, should be mentioned here. (See *Collected Works*, Ser. III, issue VIII, p. 52.)

index as it were to Lavrov's ensuing major works on the history of thought—though a more detailed definition is given of the tasks of the philosophy of history, yet in essence they remain as they were in the works of the 70s: the philosophy of history is the concrete application to history of a formula which allows the entire sequence of historical stages to be conceived as a single, continuous, developing whole.[9] Hence Lavrov was necessarily confronted with the question of the beginning and end of this historical series.

At first sight it might appear that this is not one question but at least two, moreover such as can be solved independently of each other. But such a point of view is of course quite erroneous. The beginning and end of human history, like the birth and death of the individual, are linked by virtue of the unity of the problem of meaningful life—both that of the individual and that of mankind; and the way we try to solve the question of what awaits us after death depends on how we regard the mystery of birth—depends, that is, on our particular world-view. Conversely, the problem of the origin of mankind cannot but predetermine likewise whether we look upon the future destinies of mankind as something which will be revealed only at the time of their final culmination, or as a potentially endless series such that the idea of its having an actual end is in sharp contradiction with its entire inner structure. "The vessel which I have offered them is full of gall",—thus Vyacheslav Ivanov in his poem *Prometheus*, a creature born of the present, speaks of the form of historical existence. "And they will come to love this gall, and will grow accustomed to existence, from generation unto generation, striving and vying with each other to create playthings, to multiply their pleasures. They will contrive the building of cities, commerce, warfare, art, calculation and enslavement and domination—only, in the tumult of their days, amid their cares and passion, in their dreams, to forget the direct and total freedom of being." It is the very neglect of the primordial "total freedom of being" which prevents any concern with the liberating culmination of the series; and the series without beginning is of necessity transformed into the series without end, the series indeterminate, into formlessness and disorder, held together by one force alone—"the habit of living". As is alpha, so too is omega, without alpha there is no omega, and without them neither is there an alphabet: no alpha, no beta, no gamma; the historical series cannot be constructed; the record of historical existence can never be read to the end, for the first word in this Book of Genesis was and still is: "In the beginning."

But if it is true that alpha determines omega, then it has to be admitted

9. S. S. Arnoldi, *The Tasks of Understanding History*, 2nd edition, St. Petersburg, 1903, pp. 99 *et seq.*, esp. pp. 116 *et seq.*; also *The Most Important Moments . . .*, p. 919 for the formula "real are only those moments of which it is composed". Cf. also P. Lavrov, *Essay on the History of Modern Thought*, Geneva, 1894, Vol. I, Part I, p. 99.

as no less true that history can be read in reverse order: from the end to the beginning, from the final tasks of historical existence to their first origin and understanding. Strictly speaking, the dependence of the end on the beginning is merely the conversion into necessity of the free dependence of the beginning itself on the end of history, on that which we consider a fitting culmination of history and a justification of its entire course, and it is only on the final edge of existence that the mystery of its origin is revealed. Hegel was right in emphasizing that the very separation of the moments of conception and result reveal most vividly the "futility" of an existence without meaning. It is only in their indissoluble fusion, only in the recognition that freedom and necessity are two aspects of one indivisible reasonableness that natural life and historical life are endowed with meaning. "I am alpha and omega, the beginning and the end, the first and the last",—such is the revelation of historical self-consciousness which Hegel expounded and which, after Hegel, Lavrov also taught.

But before going on to a direct exposition of the various aspects of this teaching of Lavrov's on the beginning and end of history, we must take account of that fundamental difficulty which is connected with the very understanding of the historical series as a single whole. It has been shown above that the very idea of such wholeness, speaking in abstract terms, is inseparably bound up with the application to historical existence of the category of continuity, and it may be said that all the achievements of modern historical knowledge amount to the successful concrete application of this particular category to such historical epochs which appeared to be a living refutation of its universal significance. The idea of historical and logical continuity, so convincingly asserted by Hegel, could not but be particularly near to Lavrov's heart, schooled as he was in mathematics, and it is noteworthy that it is a *mathematical* analogy which serves him as a means of elucidating this methodological principle. "For a reader who knows mathematics the business of the philosopher at the present day could be expressed metaphorically," says Lavrov about philosophy of history, "in the following way: he has to find an equation for a curve that passes through all the points denoted by science." "By finding the law for the curve," he goes on, "and expressing it in an equation, the thinker not only satisfies the aesthetic requirement of form but can with greater probability than the empiricist, indicate the position of new, intermediate points which are as yet undiscovered."[10]

In these as yet undiscovered intermediate points, in the very supposition that they must of necessity exist, lies the essence of the matter. Without the hypothesis of continuity the equation for the curve of the course of history cannot even be formulated. But if it is the case that each point on the course of history is to be understood as an unrepeatable

10. *Philosophy of the History of the Slavs*, Article I, p. 350.

combination of that which no longer exists with that which has not yet been, as an always completely unique grouping of "vestiges", "vital elements" and "the characteristic tasks of the given epoch", i.e. of the past, the future and the historical present which is determined by them,[11] — then the question of the beginning and end of this entire course becomes apparently a completely insoluble task.

Indeed, in so far as we restrict ourselves to the consideration of any one particular historical epoch or the history of any one people or institution, the task of understanding this isolated series as a complete whole seems to be soluble merely because the question of the beginning of the given concrete series or of its end is placed outside the special task and is assumed to be solved in terms of the general question of the order of events in time and of the possibility of turning any event into an era. But as soon as one puts the questions of the entire historical series, of—so to speak—the era of all possible eras and of the end of all ends—without losing sight thereby of the inner continuity of this series—then this inner continuity of the series immediately comes into conflict with the very idea of its discreteness—with the idea that it is completed. The philosopher of history is then face to face with the most difficult problem of logic and ontology: the synthesis of that which is outwardly discrete with that which is inwardly continuous. This problem can be formulated in the following way: can—or better how can—a whole, the parts of which begin and end nowhere, or in the given instance begin and end at no point in time, how can such a whole itself have any real beginning or end?

No sooner does one recall that in the history of human thought the apparently insoluble difficulties of this particular problem have led on the one hand to constantly renewed endeavours to create theogonies and cosmogonies, and on the other hand to the creation of particular apocalyptic beliefs—which by the way, Lavrov himself recognized as having great significance as "a special impetus towards intellectual movement"[12]—no sooner does one understand that the very question of "ends and beginnings" is one of those final questions, which by their very essence can be solved only by supra-empirical means, by metaphysical means, then the full sense of that notorious "positivism", in the spirit of which P.L. Lavrov allegedly thought and worked, becomes abundantly clear. No—for the pure Positivists the question of the beginning and end of history simply

11. To indicate all the texts in which Lavrov develops this idea is hardly possible: over 70 relevant references reveal that Lavrov's views on this question hardly changed at all. Suffice it to refer to the *Historical Letters*, p. 232, the *Essay on the History of Modern Thought*, pp. viii, 14 *et seq.*, *The Tasks of Understanding*, pp. 22 *et seq*. Particular note should be made of *Vestiges of the Pre-Historic Period*, which is entirely devoted to this matter. (*Collected Works*, Ser. III, issue V.)

12. *The Most Important Moments*, p. 824. See also his remarks on the historical significance of cosmogonies (*Collected Works*, Ser. III, fasc. I, p. 7).

cannot exist, whereas for Lavrov this very question predetermined decades of searching and effort.

Let us, to begin with, simply enumerate some of the most important completed attempts made by Lavrov in this direction. In 1870, at a time when, as we have seen, Lavrov's views on the tasks of the philosophy of history were more or less finally defined, in his essay *Before Man*, he tries for the first time also to answer the question "where should history be begun".[13] In 1875 he published the first Russian edition of the *Essay on the History of Thought*, the second book of which has the title 'The Preparatory Stage of the Emergence of Man'. In 1883 his articles "on the lower organisms" were finished. These articles begin with "man" and finish with "the establishment of the dominion of man" as the final task of historical existence.[14] In addition, in all the major works of Lavrov, which have been frequently referred to, more and more attention is devoted to the question of the beginning and also of the end of history.

To what results did these numerous and thorough investigations lead him? In a few words the results can be formulated as follows: 1. History begins when the consciousness of freedom arises. 2. The consciousness of freedom arises when the possible becomes the basis of the necessary. 3. The end of history is the coincidence of the realm of possibility with the realm of necessity in the single realm of omniscience. 4. The sense of historical life lies in the conscious acceleration of its process, in bringing the end closer to the beginning.

These results may appear at first sight to be somewhat unexpected. Lavrov himself never expressed them in just such words. On the other hand, his original "anthropological" point of view in epistemology is in sharp contradiction to such philosophico-historical conclusions. Nevertheless the fact remains. We shall try to show step by step that such indeed are the final conclusions of that philosophy of history which does not disdainfully turn away from ultimate questions, even though they lie outside the sphere of exact science. As regards the undoubted contradiction between the basic epistmological conception and Lavrov's philosophy of history, there cannot, it seems, be two opinions as to where to seek the centre of gravity of all his theories and which of them it is quite sufficient to regard as merely auxiliary structures, subject to outside influences: an epistemology of course of course is the first prerequisite of any philosophical thinking, but like any premise it follows from the conclusion, and not vice versa.

So, the first point is the question of the true beginning of history. Lavrov's strictly critical mind, as we see, clearly surveyed the entire

13. Reprinted in *Collected Works, loc.cit.*, p. 5.
14. *Collected Works*, Ser. III, fasc. II, pp. 5 *et seq.*, 142 *et seq.*

complexity of the question in terms of assertion of continuity as the basic category of the historical process, and, naturally enough therefore, he sought solutions on the line of that continuity. History should be begun there where the universal process as a whole continues, as though it never had a beginning.

"The moment of the birth of the earth is the only one which serves as a rational beginning of the process in the midst of which we find ourselves and which has not yet ended. This process embraces the development of the earth, the development of organisms, the development of man as a zoological species, his history as a founder of civilization."[15] The philosopher of history, delving into the question of the beginning of history, should make use of the most reliable and at the same time continuously progressing achievements which are the result of the entire historical process to the present time: he should in fact use the methods of exact science! Herein is the sense of all those introductions to natural science which sometimes outweigh the very works to which they served as introductions, and which Lavrov always prefixed to all his attempts to give a concrete representation to the historical process itself, in the proper sense of the word. The beginning of history must necessarily be at the same time the end of non-history, and it is where this end and this beginning meet that one should conceive, in consequence, of a special transitional, intervening realm between the purely natural and the purely human world. Thus in Lavrov's teaching there are created special categories of "man's emergence" and the "eve of history",[16] and at the same time that medium is defined in which the historical consciousness could actually be first sparked off.

One must not forget however that the only real bearer of historical life for Lavrov always was and always remained a concrete living man, and consequently the actual medium, in the most real sense of the word, in which historical life could arise had of necessity to be for him some living soul in whom for the first time historical consciousness was awakened as a special fact of mental life. In seeking this first "ancient Adam" Lavrov plunged into the labyrinth of the "natural state" of animal man. The beginning of history is thus, according to Lavrov, some indisputable biographical fact in the life of some unknown hero who first rebelled against the entire world of inanimate and animate nature, which he felt to be a "medium" fettering his "individuality". But here, too, always in the name of that same principle of continuity and in accordance with his own general psychological views, Lavrov tries to break down this idea of the

15. *Before Man*, p. 11
16. *The Tasks of Understanding*, pp. 136 and 143; *The Most Important Moments, First Study*, pp. 173, 184, 187; *Essay on the History of Modern Thought*, pp. 123 *et seq.*, 566 *et seq.*

individual consciousness into the sphere of the conscious and the unconscious on the one hand and the semi-unconscious on the other hand. It is in this half conscious-half unconscious awareness made by the true originator of history that one should see the beginning of history. [17] It is only in this way, it seems to Lavrov, that the problem of the beginning of history becomes commensurable with the problem of its end, that end which should, as we shall see, coincide with the task of a knowledge which is perfect both in its scope and its precision.

However, though the point of the beginning of history in time is theoretically found, its discovery has been possible only because we had looked within the past for the ideal of the future, the ideal of freedom. History began, Lavrov teaches, with the appearance on the earth of the first "intellectual"; and this intellectual appeared when the "need for development" was realized or half realized. Let us listen to Lavrov's own words.

"Probably an innumerable multitude of bipeds perished before the fortunate individuals capable of thinking better were evolved", says Lavrov in the fourth of his *Historical Letters*. "This first completely natural aristocracy among the two-legged creatures created humanity. Inherited ability or inclination to imitate transmitted the discoveries of these primeval geniuses to a small minority . . . the existence of mankind was secure." "The individuals of genius in prehistoric humanity hit upon the idea" that it was more advantageous not to kill a conquered enemy but to enslave him. "The defense of the pregnant female while asleep, for the sake of future pleasure or future assistance from her, was probably the first and greatest act in the moral development of mankind." "From personal inclination . . . critical thought worked out the industrial system of division of labour."[18] "The primeval genius", "the intellectually outstanding individual", "the skilful hunter", "the lucky robber"—these are the ones who through some "simple and rational decision" brought about the transition from non-historical life to "the moral development of mankind", to historical life; that historical life begins when "a group of individuals who were capable of enjoying development and who worked out the need for development gained influence on society. We shall give this group," writes Lavrov, "the name of intelligentsia . . . its business is the transformation of culture by means of thought." Thus, "the absorption by the individual of an urge for development is the characteristic feature of this individual's entry into historical life." "Thereby for all societies and for the whole of mankind

17. Cf. works indicated in preceding footnote and also: *The Most Important Moments*, p. 336: "Before history the main task of social progress—a task solved for the most part unconsciously—was to create in society, where solidarity rested on custom, conditions under which the conscious development of the personality and the realization thereby of one's individuality would be possible"; also *The Tasks of Understanding*, pp. 52, 340.

18. *Historical Letters*, pp. 51 *et seq.*, 53 *et seq.*, 152, 156.

the beginning of historical life is connected with the creation of groups capable of enjoying development and feeling the need for it."[19]

Let us summarize and comment on some of the recorded points. The biography of mankind is like the biography of a single individual. Each of us can sooner or later enter into historical life; thus at some time "the whole of mankind" entered historical life. Just as for each of us the beginning of our biography is the memory of the first fission of our world into the opposition of I and Non-I, of the individual and the environment, so the origin of mankind coincides with the moment of recognition of the "enjoyment" of development, i.e. with the unconscious discerning in the inner world of a special kind of "excitation", involved in the opposition of one's own personal fate as against the universe as a whole. In the same way this contrast in each of us is nothing more than the birth within the I of a "second I" ("secondary I"—Lavrov calls it),[20] i.e. an "I" as a still persisting enigma, an "I" as a norm, so for the whole of humanity the "enjoyment of development" is turned into the "need for development", i.e. into some problem which as yet simply demands a solution. For how is this need for development manifested? It is "the need for the development of thought by way of its gradual clarification and the perfection of its methods"; it is "the need for the development of personal life by enhancing its consistency"; it is "the need for the development of life in a community by way of the embodiment of justice in social relations, by way of strengthening the bonds of social solidarity", because in essence the need for development is indissolubly bound up with "moral impulses". "To develop in oneself and others strength of mind and strength of character—this is virtue", thus Lavrov taught already in 1860. "Develop your self"—such was "the moral duty", the "human ideal" which at that time Lavrov put forward against Pisarev and Pisarevism.[21]

From this it follows that Lavrov, with all his intellectualism and rationalism, some striking examples of which have been given above, takes as the final foundation for the definition of the beginning of history not the generalizations of natural science but a moral conviction based on a definite belief in the true meaning of the historical series as a single unit, a belief in the ultimate predestination of mankind as a whole. It is only because the methods of natural science themselves are the result of following the norm of intellectual development, it is only because of this that they are, as we have already noted above, a suitable means for solving

19. *The Tasks of Understanding*, pp. 27 *et seq*. Cf. also pp. 25 *et seq*. 55. 57 *et seq*., and furthermore *Essay on the History of Thought*, pp. 22, 24, 27, etc.; *The Most Important Moments*, pp. 167, 181, 188, 193, etc. Especially p. 204: "Development as a special form of nervous excitation", also *ibid.*, pp. 215, 336 and *passim*.

20. *The Most Important Moments*, pp. 50, 335 *et seq*.

21. See *Essay on the History of Thought*, p. 27; *Collected Works*, Ser. I, fasc. II, pp. 141, 177, and also, on "self development", *The Most Important Moments*, p. 120.

the problem in its own spirit, in the spirit of a continuous whole. From this however it follows that all Lavrov's doctrine of the beginning of history depends in its entirety and in all its details on his doctrine of the end, of the moral ideal. For, Lavrov says, "the moral ideal of the historian is the only light capable of giving a perspective to history as a whole and in its particulars."[22] Alpha is omega. But what is alpha itself?

However, before going on to analyse the second aspect of Lavrov's doctrine of history as a single continuous whole, it will not be superfluous to note, firstly, that the basic character of this teaching, already outlined above, is not in the least at variance with those aspects of it which concern, to put it briefly, civilisations lost. These individual "histories" which apparently ended before the advent of the end of a single history, have not in fact ended, in so far as we know about them, and in so far as our knowledge about them is itself an important historical fact; the hypothetical consideration of them, independently of our knowledge about them, would be an assumption at variance with the formulation itself. Actually, however, the matter is solved not so much by these formal considerations as by the recognition of the fact that the problem of a multitude of historical systems independent of each other, even though on the same planet, does not in the least affect the inner wholeness and completeness of each of them when examined from its own centre, from the focus of its own philosophico-historical view of the world.

Secondly, one must realise that the teaching on the beginning which has been outlined is in fact an assertion of the idea of freedom as a beginning of history and at the same time of the idea of the possible as the basis of the necessary. An attempt to give support to such a summary of Lavrov's doctrine by verbal quotations from his own works would lead us too far. Yet this point is particularly important as to the roots of the doctrine: it is here indeed that Lavrov's teaching on the beginning of history touches on Hegel's well-known formula on "progress in the recognition of freedom". But perhaps an analysis of the results which have already been established, in conjunction with the following survey of Lavrov's views on the end of the historical process, will at least partly serve as a compensation.

History began, as we have seen, with the enjoyment of development and with the need for it. "As soon as the intelligentsia with its vague thirst for development, appears on the scene of social life a dissatisfaction with the existing forms of culture is born, and the mental activity of the intelligentsia is directed to changing it." "In the intelligentsia there prevails a desire to work out all the details of the new culture which is in process of being established, until new manifestations of the need for development provoke a new dissatisfaction." "Until the intelligentsia with its need for development is formed in non-historical society, historical life is impossible. As soon as this has taken place, *possibility* (author's italics) is

22. *Historical Letters*, p. 260.

at hand." "Where historical life has begun, it has an urge to expand and develop."[23]

What do these formulae mean? They mean that the beginning of history is, as it were, a conscious defection from the "eternal rotation", as Lavrov puts it, of natural existence, that the beginning of history is the rebellion of man against nature, is "dissatisfaction" with what is, with what is customary. It is a revolt against the bonds of habit. "Habit," says Hegel, "is something which brings natural death in its train (the clock is wound up and goes of its own accord)." (It is appropriate to quote this passage in full, so that the meaning of Lavrov's teaching should be completely clear.)"Habit," Hegel goes on, "is activity devoid of contradiction, activity in which only formal continuance is preserved and in which the fullness and the depth of the aim may be silent,—it is a kind of outward sensual existence which does not penetrate into the essence of things. Thus individuals and entire peoples die a natural death." "Thus in the beginning Time reigned— a golden age without moral creations, and that which was engendered, the children of Time, were devoured by Time itself. Only Jupiter, who engendered Minerva out of his own head, and who included Apollo and the Muses in his circle, only he conquered Time and set a limit to its destruction."[24]

The beginning of history is action in the dawning light of consciousness under the influence of the spirit of contradiction in the name of that which should be. This is what Hegel taught, and—as we have seen—Lavrov's teaching coincides almost word for word with Hegel's teaching in all three principal points. It is significant that from the very beginning of his own work he rated "Hegelianism" so highly—precisely for its philosophy of history.[25] And though it is about possibility and not freedom that Lavrov is speaking, we shall see in a moment that there too the difference is not so much in the essence as in the outward verbal form. The basic difference between Lavrov and Hegel lies in the fact that for Hegel the bearer of the whole historical process is the collective "national spirit", whereas Lavrov, in his rationalism, knows no other creatures than single real individuals.

What then is "the possible" as a category in the philosophy of history? This is how Lavrov answers the question in one of his final works: "As soon as the intelligentsia has made its appearance, the *possibility* (author's italics everywhere) of historical life for the individual in society is already present. This *possibility* becomes *reality* only under the influence of conditions which allow the emerging intelligentsia to become a historical force, and the character of this historical life is determined henceforth not

23. *The Most Important Moments,* pp. 181 *et seq.*
24. *Hegel, op. cit.,* pp. 120, 121.
25. Cf. article quoted above 'Hegel's Practical Philosophy', pp. 51 and 53 (especially on the idea of "succession", i.e. continuity), also preface to Marx's article on Hegel's philosophy of law, written in 1887 and reprinted in 1906 (St. Petersburg, Vrublyevsky edition, p. 18).

merely by the conquest of technology, by the economic conditions of social life, but also by those ideological currents which are being worked out by the intelligentsia and by the results of the conflict between these newly engendered currents."[26] This means that with the appearance of individuals who act in response to their need for development, in accordance with an accepted norm and with the moral duty "develop your self", the very character of reality is changed in its ontological essence: henceforth the universal process is the resultant of two heterogeneous components—the blind elemental and the ideological current, and consequently it is determined as a whole not merely by causal necessity but in part by ideological resolution as well. Thus Lavrov can affirm that "between the understanding of history as a process which is occurring in communities of individuals who set themselves aims and seek means to achieve these aims, and the philosophical concept of the determinism of everything that occurs there is no contradiction." One may take as the point of departure "the necessity in the objective process",—its culmination will then be "the scientific understanding of history in its subjective elements." If, conversely, we take "as the point of departure the aims set by the individual for himself, as though this individual was autonomous" (this purely Kantian point of view of Lavrov's is worthy of note, especially the "as though"), we shall arrive at "unconditional determinism" as the most mature product of free human development.[27] The antinomy of freedom and necessity is overcome by the adherance of Lavrov to Kantianism which allows him to speak in his philosophy of history of the moment of origin of freedom as a historical force.[28]

We now have all the data to pass from the beginning of history to its end as presented in Lavrov's teaching. The end of history is for him primarily, as has already been noted, its end in the present, i.e. the present's idea of its ultimate tasks. "To understand history in our time"—these words have already been quoted above—"is to have a clear understanding of the moral

26. *The Most Important Moments*, p. 205.
27. *The Tasks of Understanding*, pp. 184 *et seq*.
28. We do not of course pretend with these remarks to exhaust either the problem of possibility in general or even its correct significance in Lavrov's philosophy; it was important for us simply to note that for Lavrov, just as for Hegel, history is the history of freedom—and thus for both of them the search for the beginning of history amounts to a yearning for the revelation of freedom in the realm of necessity; for Hegel however this discovery is attained in historical institutions and thus also in *historia rerum gestarum*, whereas for Lavrov it is in the inmost recesses of subjective experience and therefore in intuitive history. One should also add that B. A. Kistyakovsky, who has devoted a long and in many respects valuable essay to the "Russian Sociological School and the Category of Possibility"—a work which brought him to a purely Lavrovian (Kantian) result—knows Lavrov so poorly that the history of Russian science alone refutes his groundless attack on the Russian sociological school. This essay was printed in 1902 and reprinted in the book *The Social Sciences and Law*, Moscow 1916. Cf., as regards Kistyakovsky, B. D. Kamkov's remarks in *P. L. Lavrov's Historico-Philosophical Views*, Petrograd 1917, p. 18, and in particular *The Tasks of Understanding*, pp. 338 *et seq*.

ideal which has been worked out by the best thinkers of our time." But the "best thinker" in each epoch is he who embodies the "motive forces of the future", who at the level of his own age surpasses it in the same way that every age, by virtue of the principle of continuity, always surpasses itself. "The judge of the present", says Lavrov in another place, "is the as yet unrealised future with its ideals of truth and justice", and only this unrealised but realisable future can be the beginning of the complete culmination of history, because "if the present could be remade in the name of the past, there would be no end to such remaking, since beyond the half-century-old past, there would rise the century-old past, and beyond that the two-centuries-old past, and so on and so on"[29] and we must involuntarily exclaim—would not the future of a century ahead rise up beyond the future of half-a-century ahead, and beyond that the future of two centuries ahead and so on and so on? But this is the very point—that the idea of an infinity of time stretching back into the historical past is distinct from the concept of such infinity stretching forward into the historical future. The whole sense of measuring time in this way by the yardstick of the final moral ideal, by the criterion of the supratemporal, lies in the fact that it makes it possible to reveal not only those supranatural perspectives which are revealed in the historical vision of things past, but also suprahistorical perspectives—in the future. If we find nothing surprising in the "progress which leads from the chimpanzee to Voltaire", then we can imagine—say Lavrov—the advent of such a historical moment "when the Parthenon and the Iliad will seem to a thinking being something in the nature of coral reefs and bird song",[30] i.e. the step from natural life to historical life can be accomplished yet again; then our history will be replaced by a mode of existence in relation to which our history itself will be reduced to the level of natural existence, and from this suprahistorical point of view it will be possible to say of our history that its end has come.

What are the conditions under which one should conceive of this transition from history to suprahistory? For Lavrov these conditions coincide, as could hardly otherwise have been expected, with the tasks of converting the ideal of truth and justice into historical reality. "Have we the right to deny"—thus he concludes one of his last major works—"that a new historical culture imbued with the idea of conviction is possible in the future; that an understanding of and demand for the prevalence of higher interests is possible, a demand conditioned by the scientific hierarchy of convictions; that a mutual understanding of mankind towards a harmoniza-tion of convictions as the most efficient motive of practical activity is within the limits of possibility?"[31] This is that socialist culture which can be "transformed by thought"—only of a suprahistorical character—because

29. *Historical Letters*, p. 232.
30. *Collected Works*, Ser. IV, fasc. I, pp. 88 and 85.
31. *The Most Important Moments*, p. 997.

in this "mature state" of society, the "state of the highest solidarity possible for it, with the highest possible development of consciousness in each of its members", a way will be opened to mankind which will alow it "to proceed freely towards the complete consolidation of the dominion of man over the world."[32] It is true that Lavrov, when speaking of this future society, the culmination of history, admists that "at present it is almost as difficult to obtain a clear idea of the practical and theoretical tasks of a future epoch as it was for the mathematicians of the sixteenth century to imagine the tasks of integral calculus";[33] nevertheless the general direction is clear: "the supremacy of man over the world" is the recognition by man of the full power of the world over him. It seems strange—and yet there is no doubt about it—that Lavrov's Kantianism culminates in his Spinozism. Necessity engendered freedom so that freedom would culminate in a necessity freely recognized and accepted. Hegelianism triumphs both in form and content.

We may say in summing up that history for Lavrov begins with the realization of the antinomy between freedom and necessity and ends with the concrete recognition of freedom as necessity, and of necessity as freedom—because without the triumph of free critical thought in the most remote future, without the complete triumph of knowledge, we shall never reach a concrete understanding of the fact that necessity is "free necessity", as Spinoza taught, and that on the other hand our freedom lies not in the choice between "possibilities" but in knowing precisely which of the apparent possibilities is the only necessity because it is the true necessity. Can history still continue after this? Is is clear that if it can, then it is no longer our history, not that history the only meaning of which is in the speediest solution of the basic philosophical problem, that of the unity of theoretical and practical reason.

It is sufficient here simply to draw attention to this final moment, to the moment of "acceleration" in the historical process. The problem of acceleration in philosophico-historical dynamics is, as it were, the touchstone which shows with the highest degree of accuracy the category to which this or that system of the philosophy of history should be assigned: to the naturalistic or the supranaturalistic type. The fact that Lavrov never lost sight of the possibility of an acceleration of the historical process and constantly returned to this idea[34] bears witness to the bases of his teaching as a whole.

This study has pursued a single aim: to demolish the prejudice that in Lavrov we have to deal with a thinker the basis of whose thought is

32. *Collected Works*, Ser. III, fasc. II, pp. 149, 151.
33. *Collected Works*, Ser. VI, fasc. VII, pp. 101 *et seq*.
34. *Historical Letters*, pp. 60 and 241. S. S. Arnoldi, *Civilisation and Savage Tribes*, St. Petersburg, 1903, p. 243; *Collected Works*, Ser. III, fasc. II, p. 143; Ser. VI, fasc. VII, p. 40; especially *The Most Important Moments*, pp. 117 *et seq*. and 184.

superficial. The philosophico-historical problem which we chose with this object in mind was to reveal the wealth and variety of the motives which determined the structure and progress of his ideas. It may be that a more careful study of everything which Lavrov did in the sphere of philosophy and in the general theory of history would reveal that, if contemporary criticism can hardly be completely satisfied with the solutions which he reached, then it is not because his mind constantly sought the answers to supra-empirical questions but because in Lavrov's "utopianism" there still remained too many vestiges of timidity—a timidity which was so characteristic of the entire development of philosophical thought in the second half of the last century. On the other hand how many undoubted "germs of the future" are revealed even at the first attempt to trace in detail the development of but one particular problem in the general structure of his world-view! What could more clearly elucidate the "productive power" of a man's world-view and at the same time the great strength and the true significance of the thought of this, the greatest of the Russian rationalists?

3. On P. L. Lavrov's Philosophy of History

"The unforeseen is expanded into Newton's binomial"
V. F. Odoyevsky, *Russian Nights*

The significance of Lavrov for the history of philosophical thought in Russia has not yet been sufficiently evaluated. Moreover, the place of a correct and adequate assessment, based on a thorough study of all the many influences which Lavrov's thought underwent in the lengthy course of its development, has been occupied by trivial definitions and superficial characterizations, without critical verification. The very fact that Lavrov's philosophical views developed has remained almost unnoticed, as if the thinker's scientific horizon, which broadened continuously for forty years, could have failed to displace the centre of his world-view, as though the *Tasks of the Understanding of History* was merely a repetition of the *Historical Letters*. The apologist of critical thought still awaits a criticism worthy of him.

We have become accustomed to uttering the name of Lavrov in one and the same breath with that of Mikhailovsky. It is perhaps in this association, dictated by the history of social thought, that there is to be found the clue to that negligence with which the characterization of Lavrov's philosophical views is usually approached. Lavrov the political pioneer, Lavrov the founder and ideologist of populism, Lavrov the socialist and the "Lavrovian" still overshadow the image of a thinker who went his own way, of one who battled not only in the arena of history but also in the supra-empirical realm of ideas. Meanwhile, the pre-revolutionary period of Russian history is already at an end, and in face of the vast perspectives which have opened it is time to sum up, to survey the past, to preserve for the future the continuity of the link with times and epochs already brought to an end. It may well be that many of Lavrov's solutions have been revised and even actually rejected in the formulation usual for him and his time, but his problems are still alive today and these problems are far wider and deeper than is usually supposed, because Lavrov was not only a sociologist and the inventor of "the subjective method" but also a philosopher of history.

This essay (jubilee address given at St. Petersburg in 1920) was first published in Russian in *Vpered* (*Kolos*, edited by P. Vityazev, 1920).

One of the most eminent disciples and successors of Mikhailovsky and Lavrov speaks of the "poverty of the philosophical equipment" of the former and considers that "the entire enormous and elegant edifice of his world-view stands on the shallow foundation of positivism", i.e. "is built on sand". Of Lavrov he says that "his world-view lacked elegance and wholeness, since he always endeavoured to unite that which could not be united and to reconcile the irreconcilable". Thus the assertion that Lavrov is guilty of "eclecticism" leads to a sentence far more severe in the philosophical sense than that which falls to the lot of Mikhailovsky's edifice "built on sand", under which one could "insert the foundation of critical philosophy" and thus easily strengthen the entire edifice while merely eliminating its insignificant flaws (cf. Ivanov-Razumnik, *History of Russian Social Thought*, 5th ed.,vol. V, pp. 35, 48, 118). Is this indeed the case? Is not an assessment guilty of prejudice which attempts to measure by the same yardstick groundless assumptions and philosophical investigation in depth? It appears to be overlooked that in the sphere of systematic philosophy all non-philosophical scales turn into variables and that therefore here, in the sphere of philosophical construction, the preference of the vertical as against the horizontal is a striking change of direction in the argumentation.

The object of Lavrov's philosophy was history—and with that one has said everything. It may be that as a sociologist he betrayed internal contradictions and was not a very independent thinker, but his very problem is far closer to the ultimate foundations of a systematically thinking philosophy than the entire complex of questions assembled in the confused Greco-Roman concept engendered and baptized by Gallic positivism. And not only can the fact that he was saturated in the tradition of German classical philosophy be detected in the very name of Lavrov's problem but also his very close relations with the independent philosophical tradition of Russia itself. True, the very existence of such a special philosophical tradition in Russia is questioned but this very argument is at all conceivable only because the problem of the philosophy of history alone could be firmly claimed to be the true basis of the particular history of Russian philosophy in the nineteenth century.

And indeed, on the plane of *this* problem the movement of Russian philosophical thought intersects with the development of artistic thought. In the beginning there was the fact, the deed of Peter, the fact of Russia's East-West position in historical life and all that ensues therefrom for the destinies of Russian culture. When Herzen wrote that in answer to the great reformer's call for enlightenment Russia responded one hundred years later with the formidable phenomenon of Pushkin, he could not yet see as clearly as we can that in the person of Pushkin Russia answered in a language which was not only poetic but also deeply philosophical, for Pushkin responded not merely like an "Echo", the title of his famous poem, but spoke of Peter and his work as an equal of an equal. Since that time Russian thought has worked tirelessly on the questions of the fate of its native Rome and of the universe. Pushkin and Chaadayev, the "two-headed eagle" of Westernism and Slavophilism, Odoyevsky and Herzen, Dostoyevsky and Soloviev, the two-in-one socialism of Russian scope—all this is linked by the unity of the problem, the name of which is *urbs et orbis*, Rome and the world—the philosophy of history.

Neglect of the role of the philosophy of history in Lavrov's "anthropologism"—this is the ultimate reason for the fact that we begin Lavrov's spiritual genealogy with Comte and not with Kant and his successors; the roots of this many-branched genealogical tree lead far away from the "positivism", the "subjectivism" and the "relativism" with which Lavrov is characterized first in the "general opinion" of our "doctors" and, following them, in foreign philosophical compilations and dictionaries (cf. for example R. Eisler, *Philosophen—Lexikon*, p. 389).

But there is yet another reason for such an erroneous confusion of ideas, and here Lavrov himself is at fault. "Positivism" has a two-fold meaning in philosophy: it is either the tendency to make philosophical conceptions conform with the "data" of a positive science, or—independently of these data and the conclusions to be drawn from them—it is the borrowing of the method of philosophical thinking itself from some particular but idealised positive science. In neither sense is positivism a gnoseological term and is certainly not identical with empiricism and much less with psychologism, but is simply a definition of the limits of philosophical freedom in the one case, and a choice of the shortest route towards that freedom in the other case. One can well maintain, however paradoxical this may seem at first sight, that in the best sense of the word all the great systematisers of philosophy were positivists, not excluding of course Hegel himself, to whom Lavrov was so close as regards his basic task, since Hegel too did not, as is customarily thought, have a disdainful attitude towards "facts", but simply demanded that they should be strictly and systematically deduced. (Cf. for example Ch. Rappoport, *The Main Currents of the Philosophy of History*, 1899, p. 30 and his later work, *The Social Philosophy of Peter Lavrov*, 1906, pp. 62 ff.) This is why, for example, it is incorrect to maintain on the basis of Lavrov's article "The Philosophical Meaning of History" (cf. *Collected Works. Historico-Philosophical Articles*, fasc. 1, pp. 67 ff.) that in it he breaks with the traditions of the classical philosophy of history merely because he bases the solution of philosophico-historical problems on the entire complex of historical facts; one might similarly assign to the category of works of a positivistic character Hegel's *Lectures in the Philosophy of History*. Or the question might be transferred to the sphere of the psychological analysis of the conscientiousness of the handling of facts peculiar to a particular thinker—this however is not a question of principle, of course, and the arguments adduced in this connection are typical in their lack of logic. Any philosophy of history is a philosophy of historical and not of falsified facts. What facts are worthy of the name historical is another question, but it was in this very question that Lavrov, as is well known, was least naive and thought through to the end what the very task of the philosophy of the concrete requires.

Lavrov moreover is a positivist in the second of the senses delineated and, what is most striking, an unconscious and unintentional positivist at that. Here too, however, it is necessary to distinguish the positivism of Bacon and Condillac from the positivism of Plato or Spinoza. For Lavrov, as for many other subtle thinkers among those who did not realise that philosophy has not only its own task but also its own way, the prototype of true scientific thinking was the clear and distinct constructionism attained in mathematics. Without apparently being aware of his own methodological sympathies inspired by the mathematics so close to him, Lavrov feels that even in his philosophico-historical vision he is a "sober" scholar only because his utopias are defined by quasi-geographical degrees and minutes; he speaks of the future as of an as yet not finally formed link of an algebraic series; "truth and justice" he opposes to "savagery and dead-weight inertia" as a maximum to a minimum. Here is the source of those delusions about himself which prevented even Lavrov from seeing his own subject in its truly metaphysical, truly philosophical light. Hence the natural deviation from Kant, Fichte and Hegel, the three undoubtedly most influential figures in Lavrov's spiritual communion—to the Feuerbachian simplification and to a psychologico-evolutionistic lowering of the level in the formulation of the epistemological targets. On the latter point Lavrov is indeed an empiricist, psychologist and a positivist in the generally accepted meaning of the term. But what follows from this? Only the fact that Lavrov, aspiring "to understand history" as the "history of thought" and as a personal creation in the name of a "future which belonged to nobody" (cf. 'To Whom Does the Future Belong?', 1917, p. 123), that he indeed always remained a "positivist" with regard to this future. For it was precisely in it that he laid the foundation of his system—in that future, which is not as yet, in this "u-topian" something which is nowhere, unexisting, because it is ideal. In consequence, Lavrov, utopianist, idealist and criticist, simply by virtue of the fact that he was, as regards his gnoseology, constrained by his mathematical past, developed his system not from its positive to its superlative degree but on the contrary degraded it to a level which was quite unsuited to it. But it must be repeated again and again: to understand means to distinguish, and "one can understand a philosopher better than he understood himself". What Kant said about Plato must be said to himself at the very outset by any commentator on any thinker the tissue of whose philosophical body, burdened by heredity, has not yet dissected into its ultimate fibres. As a typical Russian philosopher, as a philosopher of history, Lavrov is not a positivist in the crude sense of the word but he is a positivist in the gnoseological foundation of the philosophical system which he was in process of constructing but did not finish. Can we have any doubt where the centre and kernel and where the shell and periphery of his life's work and achievement lie! The contradiction is easily resolved by an insight into Lavrov's personality.

It is worth dwelling on this. It is well known that in his political activity too Lavrov "quantified" social relations, made calculations and computations. He thought of the contingent of the Revolutionary Army as a function of the number of propagandists; of the moment of revolution as a function of the duration of propaganda; and whereas for Herzen the Hegelian dialectic became the "algebra of revolution", for Lavrov on the contrary the revolutionary algebra was the most serious obstacle in the way of evaluating the entire significance for his own thought of the Hegelian dialectic, of Fichte's ethic, of the transcendental theory of knowledge. Odoyevsky would hardly have recognized in Lavrov the double of his Segeliel, and yet it *was* Lavrov who in the full sense of the word expanded "the unforeseen into the Newtonian binomial".

In this respect Lavrov's polemical article "N. K. Mikhailovsky's Formula for Progress" (*Collected Works, Scientific Articles*, vol. VIII, pp. 52 ff.) is a striking example, although in a less generalised form; the same mathematical analysis figures in a number of his major works. "One who knows what a formula means for a mathematician," says Kant in his *Critique of Practical Reason*, "will not look upon a formula as something insignificant, which one could manage without." Lavrov himself was a mathematician and, as if against his own will, he thought of the formula for progress as in fact a mathematical formula—more than that—as a binomial to the nth degree—$(a + b)^n$.

Civilisation and culture, already distinguished by Herzen, became for Lavrov the $a + b$ of the universal history of mankind. Conceiving historical time as a series which begins with culture (in the contemporary meaning of the word) at the degree of zero and finishes with civilisation at the same degree, Lavrov defined the historical present, the contemporary, in a general manner, as a constantly varying combination of two principles: of the inert, the factual, the traditional principle of history inherited and accepted uncritically, with its other, second principle, the creative one, which ought to be expanded, developed in a critical spirit, subordinated to a free, autonomous, individual will guided by an ideal of truth and justice. In a certain sense one can say that the entire life work of Lavrov was limited to the development of this general formula, to expanding it into the fullness of its algebraic content. It goes without saying that a mind hypnotised by the means of solving his entirely non-mathematical problem, unwittingly applied to certain aspects of this problem the elements of that "bad" positivism which was fundamentally at variance with the very essence of the problem.

Such an evaluation can easily be tested against an analysis of

Mikhailovsky's "formula"—an analysis which is so interesting in the psychological aspect. What is the philosophical content of the debate between Lavrov and Mikhailovsky? Lavrov invokes against Mikhailovsky the principle of the "unconditional" and maintains that this principle remains unchanged throughout the whole of human history. We deliberately leave aside here the question of the ethical significance of this principle: the basic ideas and even the terminology of *Fundamentals of a Metaphysic of Morals* and *The Critique of Practical Reason* shine clearly through every line of these pages. But as applied to history the term "unconditional" *(das Unbedingte)* has no other meaning than that which is concentrated in the term. The Absolute, from Hegel through Fichte to Kant, this is indeed the clue for deciphering Lavrov's own philosophico-historical formulations.

This is not a hypothesis, or rather it is the only hypothesis which makes it possible to comprehend as a single whole all the "facts" of the philosophical and even the scientific work of Lavrov. It is well known that one of the most significant results of such an early work as the *Historical Letters* was the identification of the historical with the individual and the unique. In the literature on Lavrov, as yet very sparse, it has already been pointed out in what detail he developed this very fruitful idea—an idea which had occurred more than once to Herzen thus anticipating contemporary research in this sphere (cf. B. D. Kamkov, *P. L. Lavrov's Historico-Philosophical Views*, 1917). This fact itself demands the further explanation of the delay in its discovery. "Happy" ideas occur only to second-rate thinkers. For the first-rate thinker they are merely the natural fruit of that philosophical ground from which they spring. It has been shown how the entire road from Kant to Hegel can easily be measured by this very problem of the individual and unique. This is why it is only in such a historico-philosophical perspective that this most important detail of Lavrov's philosophy of history also appears to us not as a happy discovery but as the indispensable exposition of a single problem, ensuing from his philosophy as a whole.

The philosophy of history has its own logic—even more so than history itself. Precisely this *pure* logic, which animated Lavrov as the deepest inner motivating force of his entire work, impelled him on the one hand towards that organic world-view which was to draw into its orbit the whole of classical metaphysics and on the other hand, given the psychological make-up of Lavrov's mathematically positive mind, made him constantly shun the very purity of that logic in favour of "applications". Lavrov's psychology overcame the logic of his problem; his life was spent in attempts to create an "applied" philosophy of history. Faced with his enormous unfinished edifice we can only divine its true structure on the basis of its incomplete outlines, which always remained the single plan of a systematic philosophy, without which there can be no philosophy of history worthy of the name nor any genuine historical creative initiative.

4. The Philosophical Premises of Jewish Historiography

The discovery that history as a discipline stands in a much closer, yet at the same time far more complex relationship to philosophy than the natural sciences may well be counted among the least controversial findings of epistemological study of the last century. As a result of this insight—which stems ultimately from German idealism with its historical orientation—the old dichotomy of matter and mind, nature and spirit, which used to dominate the realm of learning and to govern the classification of sciences, has given way to the new polarity of nature and history, or nature and culture. And so it came about that many problems of the questing mind and spirit—religious problems no less than philosophical ones—found themselves expelled from their home ground in the now dethroned *Geisteswissenschaften*, the sciences of the spirit, and took sanctuary under the wings of cultural history. The resulting situation has not been a happy one either for the protecting power or for the new denizens of its domain: for while philosophy and philosophical interpretation of the world see themselves threatened by the danger of historicism,[1] historiography is tempted to opt for a subjectivist approach of "endowing the meaningless with meaning."[2] Yet the fate of modern philosophy as such may remain in this context outside our analysis; on the other hand, seeing that the relationship between the study of history and philosophy has become reciprocal, it is all the more pertinent to ask how far the former is bound to be influenced by the latter, whether in fact historiography is still in a

1. This is aptly pointed out by Rickert in *Die Grenzen der naturwissenschaftlichen Begriffsbildung*: "All historicism, if consistent, leads straight to relativism, even nihilism, or else it covers its entire lack of substance and emptiness by focusing attention on some arbitrarily selected historical figure and constructing in its image a world view bounded as a rule by a horizon that is even more narrow than in the naturalistic approach." (Third and Fourth Editions, 1921, p. 6.) Cf. also pp. 531 and 546 ff. Rickert's attack on historicism must not make us lose sight of the fact that this particular brand of relativism has received one of its most potent impulses precisely through the endeavours of the so-called "South West German School" which included Rickert himself.

2. See the symptomatic book of Theodor Lessing, *Geschichte als Sinngebung des Sinnlosen*, Fourth Edition, 1927.

This essay was first published in German in the *Dubnow-Festschrift*, Berlin, 1931.

70

position to claim any objective validity, and if so, under what suppositions such a claim can be recognised as legitimate. It will be readily understood that this tripartite problem must first be clarified in its most general form (Chapter I) before it is possible to draw conclusions that can be applied to historiography, and Jewish historiography in particular. An attempt to draw such conclusions is made in Chapter II. Finally, the character of Simon Dubnow's *World History of the Jewish People* is to be adduced as evidence to prove that the results flowing from general considerations have been anticipated, as it were, in the practice of Jewish historical research (Chapter III)—a statement that could never have been placed on record, were it not that Dubnow's "historia rerum gestarum" forms itself part of the Jewish "res gestae".

I

That beside the past the present also, with its specific hopes and worries, is bound to be mirrored in historiography; that, in other words, every historical work constitutes a document of contemporary history, a document of the time in which it was conceived, is an insight of comparatively recent date, but one which nevertheless has retroactive force.[3] In contrast to the natural sciences where the results of research are in principle independent of the scientist's individual mind, the historian was always a focal point within his sphere of action. From the earliest beginnings of historiography the personality of the historian and therefore his personal world view informed his entire work even when, like Julius Caesar, he chose to refer to himself in the third person. How far, then, it may be asked, has the problematic aspect of history as a science been rendered more acute by the change, outlined above, in the relationship between the study of history and that of the philosophical approach? Should not this change, from the point of view of history, be appraised as a step forward on the way to methodological self-awareness? Or can such progress in methodological self-awareness entail disadvantageous consequences? To show that this is indeed the case shall be our first task.

Setting out from the well-known Hegelian distinction between three approaches to history—primitive, reflected and philosophical[4]—it may seem, at a first glance, as if modern historiography, in its growing awareness of its philosophical premises, had reached the third and highest stage of development; as if, that is to say, the goal set up by Hegel were about to be attained at last. But this is utterly deceptive. To Hegel, the "reason" which he wanted historiographers to perceive in the occurrence

3. Cf. Benedetto Croce, *Zur Theorie und Geschichte der Historiographie*, German edition 1915, pp. 144 ff.
4. Hegel, *Vorlesungen über die Philosophie der Geschichte*, Einleitung, ed. Brunstäd, pp. 33 ff.

and interplay of historical events, represented the logical consistency of a "plan" independent of all human subjectivity, whereas to the modern historiographer the "point of view" from which he approaches the historical matters he is dealing with has in the first place a purely personal aspect. As for the "values" which he relates to his subject matter, he disregards the philosophical emphasis on their universal validity, since in the "age of history" the study of philosophy itself is held to be no more than a transient product of its time. This situation is in no way altered even if the historian looks upon his own personality as the instrument of some kind of supra-individually determined collective consciousness. The class consciousness of an historian thinking in Marxist terms, for instance, is no less subjectively conditioned than the consciousness of the historiographer who openly avows his own, purely personal world view. In either case the standpoint adopted actually presupposes a personal decision. What we are faced with today, then, is not the "philosophical" approach to history in the spirit of classical German idealism but a derivative of the "reflected" treatment of history, a mode of treatment that in some degree must be considered a regression even by comparison with the "primitive", naive, form of historical narrative: for reality as portrayed, say, in Herodotus or the Books of Kings speaks for itself, as it were, whereas the modern historian, conscious of the plenitude of his authority regarding all problems of the objective "spirit", has very little use for "facts". It makes no difference that, contrary to the usual manner of the reporting and pragmatic historiography of antiquity he has become a partisan of the modern genetic method:[5] abandoned to subjective discretion, the method itself aiming at the establishment of an evolutionary nexus is bound to become a tool for the crippling of facts. It almost looks as though the "spirit", subjected to the sway of cultural history, wanted to take revenge by unleashing anarchy in its own domain. Religion, now secularised, and philosophy involving subjectivism in the interpretation of history now turned scientific thus represents the reaction to the relativistic degradation of philosophical thinking through modern historicism.

But is it true that modern scientific history distorts the facts? Does it not pride itself, and with good reason, on having rediscovered and brought to light countless facts that had been left unrecorded? Has it not uncovered

---

5. The division of history into the categories respectively of narrative or reporting, didactic or pragmatic, and developing or genetic history is due to Bernheim, *Lehrbuch der historischen Methode*, Third and Fourth Editions, 1903, pp. 17 ff. The belief in progress, so characteristic of Bernheim, induced him to identify those three approaches to history with the "three principal stages in the development of historical knowledge" (cf. notably pp. 26 ff. and 184). That in this field as elsewhere development cannot simply be equated with "progress" is demonstrated by the situation outlined above. Moreover the conspicuous growth of biography as a separate branch of literature which has been observed of late indicates a wide-spread interest in purely narrative history.

sources that had been untraceable for ages, has it not gathered materials now brought together in vast and monumental works of learning? Who would deny it! And yet, for all that, it must not be overlooked that what matters in the science of history, precisely because it constitutes the opposite pole to the natural sciences, is not facts but acts—events, that is, which have their origin in the human will and as such point far beyond themselves inasmuch as they derive their value and essence only out of a broad spiritual pattern established in a higher sphere. One is reminded here of Hegel's warning not to crush the "objects worthy of history" by "superfluous rubbish".[6] Hegel goes on: "To embroider the representation of the general interests for the sake of so-called truth with the detailed trivialities of the time and of any individuals runs counter not only to judgement and good taste but to the very concept of objective truth, by whose canon the only things acceptable as true by the Spirit are matters of substance but not the vacuity of outward existences and adventitious phenomena. Indeed, it makes no difference at all whether such irrelevancies are formally documented or, as in a novel, freely invented and related to some specific name or circumstances." In this passage the principle of the selection of material, which is fundamental for all historiography, is formulated in utter sharpness and raised to the level of historical con-sciousness,[7] but, in addition, this passage contains something yet more significant: the insight that such a selection can and must be determined solely by the criterion of what to the "Spirit" are "matters of substance". And the matters which in that sense are of substance to the "Spirit", or at any rate to the individual historian's mind, are again matters spiritual, matters human, the purposive human act and in conjunction with it the entire organism of humanity, but never mere factualness.

Similia similibus evocantur. The unreflecting historian rooted in a supra-individual spiritual context carried out the selection incumbent on him with a corresponding matter-of-fact and unreflecting sureness of touch. What has been called "historical congeniality" was in the literal sense an inborn quality with him. How different the modern individualist with his brittle tablets of values![8] Everything is affected by his subjective interpretation of the world: the selection of historical material, the choice and delimitation of the subject of his narrative, as well as the arrangement of the subject matter, the tracing of internal and external historical

6. Hegel, Enzyklopädie der philosophischen Wissenschaften, §549, ed. Lasson, 1920, p. 460.

7. On this point see Rickert, *Grenzen*, e.g., p. 225: "History has everywhere the task of separating the essential from the inessential" and pp. 254 ff; Bernheim, loc. cit., pp. 94, 148 ff. and especially 704 ff. Cf. also Franz Eulenberg, 'Are historical laws possible?' in the collection *Hauptprobleme der Soziologie*, 1923, vol. I, p. 24, footnote.

8. Cf. Ernst Troeltsch, Uber den Begriff einer historischen Dialektik, *Historische Zeitschrift*, Third Series, vol. XXIII, 1919, p. 376.

interconnections, the sequence of epochs, even the method of investigation he chooses to employ, not to speak of the basic tendency of the historical process under scrutiny. Built on "facts", on meticulously accurate data concerning time and place, the completed historical work nevertheless is in danger of being no more than the fruit of subjective intellectuality. Those of its elements which are objective in the common sense of the word are in themselves unhistorical because they belong to the context of nature, whereas the elements that are historical in the ordinary sense are not objective. In such circumstances, can we still speak of science? Or must we conclude that those are right after all who, following Schopenhauer, have relegated history to the arts?

That would be the inevitable consequence of the existing relationship between the study of history and that of philosophy if the latter-day logic of history were right in its basic premise that the difference between natural and historical science lies not in their subject matter but solely in the difference of methodological approach.[9] As against this, we propose here to set out a view which deviates from the currently dominant one in some essential points but, simultaneously, opens up the prospect of a positive solution of the problem facing us. This view can be presented here only in a brief outline and leaves aside an elucidation of its epistemological foundations. The application of this conception to the problem of Jewish historiography will on the other hand provide indirect support for our general analysis and offer an opportunity of developing it in more concrete terms.

History, it is said, transforms the past into the present. The past is the unalterable. How, then, can the past be altered even in the sense of making it once more present or actual? Thus the difficult problem of memory arises in history in a new and more complex form. To deal with it adequately it is necessary to keep two modes of Being strictly apart: on the one hand the everlasting form of Being that exists from eternity to eternity and is revealed in the law of nature,[10] on the other the ever nascent form of happening that is never completed, always in flux. It is that mode of happening that constitutes the proper subject of history. Wherever we encounter traces of human action we perceive the changing world as an immediate experience. That which is seemingly past emerges as something impending, tending towards a goal, facing the future. It is only from the future ahead that the historical can be understood, interpreted, grasped. Thus the "facts" of history can be seen as a sequence of flowing waters, and the historical process as a whole as the totality of various criss-

9. It will suffice here to refer to the memorable inaugural address of Wilhelm Windelband, *Geschichte und Naturwissenschaft*, 1894, which exercised a dominant influence on the subsequent interpretation of history. See also A. D. Xénopol, *Les principes fondamentaux de l'histoire*, Paris, 1899.

10. Here we advisedly leave out of account the so-called "evolution of natural laws".

crossing currents. In short, the difference between history and natural science rests not on methodological but on ontological foundations.

This entails extremely important consequences for historiography. If the material of history as such, by its own inherent goal, is independent of the treatment applied to it, then any interpretation that may be imposed on it by the historian's subjective intellectuality must become readily discernible. In other words, the flow of historic events carries its own objective truth with it. No matter how sharply the historian's world view may be defined, the greater the discrepancy between it and the subject matter to which it is applied, the easier will it be for the student of the narrative to decipher the sense of the original language of the events themselves. For it is the peculiar quality of historical science that it speaks not "of" facts but "to" men, and in doing so never appeals to the senses but always to the mind. But why "science"? Because the interest of history is directed chiefly to the identification of what is objective. The problem of historical objectivity, however, requires further clarification.

Just as there are two different modes of Being, so there are two modes of objectivity: one concerning stable states of things, and another objectivity which is a projection from a mobile on a mobile. Such, indeed, is the objectivity of history. As yet, mankind as one entity is but an idea. Accordingly, from the angle of the future as seen from the present, the flow of history is composed of a multitude of currents, so that the truth which it carries with it is in turn broken up into a host of partial, relative truths. Yet to make them accord at some point in the future, each one must first be worked out in isolation. There are as many separate historic currents as there are historically effective forms of world interpretation. As the historical process as a whole so the concept of historical objectivity is gradually being defined, by no means finally determined.

II

The notion of the philosophical premises of historiography has undergone a transformation in the course of the foregoing examination. Seemingly an indivisible conception, it revealed itself under closer examination as an alloy of two elements that must be assessed separately: the historian's subjective world view on the one hand and the world of ideas inherent in the historical subject matter on the other. Yet, as has been pointed out, the two elements are fused and can be separated only in the realm of abstraction. The scientific character of history and its claim to objectivity rests to a certain measure on the interpenetration of the two elements. That means that the historian in his scientific approach, irrespective of the specific character of his individual world view, cannot help identifying himself more or less with the basic elements of the subject matter concerned. The "congeniality with the subject treated" postulated by historical methodology[11] must embrace above all the ideas alive within the compass of the subject. Where the premises of such a philosophical affinity are missing, the attempt to produce an objective presentation of genuine historic reality is foredoomed to failure. The history of the Jewish people can serve as a paradigm to illustrate that point.

The very act of recognising the historical significance of the Jewish people's destiny presupposes that the historian must have steeped himself in the separate Jewish stream of world history. If, on the other hand, he had completely identified himself with some other separate stream, say the "Christian-Germanic" one, then the main line of Jewish history (that is to say, the ever-present hope of redemption) will either not exist for him at all, or it will appear to him to be discontinuous and repeatedly abruptly broken. Indeed, from the point of view of an observer carried along with the motion of an unfolding internally coherent sequence of events other sequences of similar character are bound to appear either incoherent or, foreshortened in perspective, continually shrinking. A strictly objective distinction between historical motion and historical immobility could only be made on the basis of a system of coordinates pertaining to universal history and absolutely at rest, which, however, would be tantamount to the anticipation of the absolute end of history.[12] But the historian, as we know, is no more than a "backward-looking prophet". And so, swept along with the particular current that carries him, he must, in his attitude to all other separate historic currents, act of necessity as an exponent of the relative truth embodied in his own specific current. A few examples may bring out that relationship in full relief.

One has to be a Christian in order to break off Jewish history with the advent of Christianity, as does Wellhausen. Methodologically even more instructive is the manner in which Hegel, polyhistor and philosopher of history at the same time, contrives to settle the historic status of Judaism: without acknowledging here any coherent and continuous context whatever, he deals with the lot of the Jewish people at one point in the context of the "oriental world", and at another in conjunction with the origin of the Christian message of salvation.[13] The subject as a whole is thus torn apart into two loosely connected fragments and, having duly discharged what is supposed to be its sole function, vanishes from the stage of world history. It must appear nothing short of uncanny, then, when "secret Jews" emerge all of a sudden in the "modern age".[14] Another example of the way in which historical judgment can be clouded by objective circumstances is provided

11. Bernheim, loc. cit., p. 577 (cf. also pp. 534 and 548).
12. This point is discussed at greater length in my Russian paper, *Beginning and end of history in the work of P. L. Lavrov*, Petersburg, 1922.
13. *Vorlesungen über die Philosophie der Geschichte*, pp. 262 ff. and 410 ff.
14. loc. cit. p. 533.

by Oswald Spengler's contention that "history had ceased to exist" for the Jews "approximately since the time of Judah ben Halevi".[15] Whereas as far as Hegel is concerned, Jewry forfeited its role in world history because of its supposed incapacity to form a state, Spengler considers himself constrained to deny the Jews the right to historical existence for the diametrically opposite reason, to wit because Jewry had continued even in the Diaspora to conduct itself as a state within the state.[16] So we see that neither Hegel's Christian-Germanic State embodying the "absolute spirit" nor Spengler's "Faustian idea" is compatible with the Jewish people's collective consciousness acting, as it did, as an effective force in world history. One has to be a Jew, i.e. to be capable of identifying with that consciousness in order to grasp and delimit the subject matter of Jewish history with at least a modicum of accuracy. But to those who have absorbed, though perhaps unconsciously, the world view inherent in Jewish history, the issue of the State loses its overriding importance irrespective of the particular value attached to statehood.

A further, yet more cogent demonstration of our fundamental thesis that each historical continuum is held together by its own specific idea will be obtained by focusing attention on the methodological form immanent in the factual matter of Jewish history. In general, there is as yet little inclination today to treat problems of methodological form on the ontological plane. Again, the question as to whether the historian ought to adopt the nomothetic (generalising) or ideographic (particularising) method and the related question as to whether history can hold its own as a separate branch of learning, independent of sociology, are usually decided not on the strength of considerations of substance but in the light of the logical concept of science. Yet it is scientific insight which depends on its specific subject and not the other way round. Incongruous as the notion of allowing for the application of different methodological attitudes to the different currents of world history may seem, it is plain that even the most cursory contact with Jewish history must convince the staunchest supporter of the sociological school that here he is outside the sphere in which the "historical laws" are applicable. For it is chance, the direct opposite of law, which—to put it in the language of logic—is decisive for the structure of Jewish history. We know that in the language of religion the concept of chance as a happy coincidence of favourable circumstances is called providence. That is the reason why to those with religious leanings the

15. *Der Untergang des Abendlandes*, II, 1922, pp. 388 and 396.
16. Hegel, loc. cit., p. 265: "The state is the element inconsistent with the Jewish principle and alien to the legislation of Moses." Spengler, loc. cit. p. 391, speaks of the Jewish "*state* which had a law and a public law of its own—though the Christians did not even notice it—and which looked down upon the surrounding world of the host peoples as upon foreign parts", and notes that Spinoza and Uriel da Costa "as the result of a formal trial on charges of high treason were expelled" from that state.

continued existence of the Jewish people has always appeared as a miracle. But even the most sober-minded adherent of the doctrine of the validity of historical laws will be compelled in the face of the dominant part played by chance in Jewish history either to regard the Jewish people as "unhistoric" or to be shaken in his conviction.[17]

In particular, it would be wrong to search for a corroboration in Jewish history of any general theory of progress. No doubt, the Jewish world view, whose pivot is the unshakable belief in world redemption, is thoroughly optimistic in its essence; nevertheless the optimism of Judaism is by no means as "false, shallow and pernicious" as Schopenhauer would have it,[18] although it has certainly nothing in common with the exuberant belief in progress characteristic of the modern Enlightenment.[19] In the modern view, which equates development with progress, the state in the historical process reached at any particular time is deemed to be higher and more valuable than the preceding stages of development, whereas Judaism always keeps its distance from the present as an historical epoch, accepting and rejecting it at the same time: accepting it, in so far as Judaism tenaciously clings to life as such for the sake of life's most exalted purpose, yet also rejecting it, for Judaism must judge the present by the ultimate and highest standards, by the standards of the time of fulfilment. That restraint towards the surrounding world, which is peculiar to the Jewish consciousness, imposes a thoroughly uniform pattern on the whole subject matter of Jewish history and it must be vicariously experienced and relived by the historiographer, if he is to swim with, rather than against, the stream of the events he is dealing with. And here emerges the decisive criterion for an appropriate division into periods applicable to the treatment of Jewish history.

The Hebrew language has two terms for "history": *Toledoth* and *Divre*

17. This is the case with the former orthodox Marxist N. A. Berdyayev, who testifies: "I remember that in my young days, when I was attracted by the materialistic interpretation of history and I endeavoured to demonstrate its correctness in the light of the history of the various peoples, the greatest obstacle which I encountered in my enterprise was the history of the Jewish people whose fate seemed utterly inexplicable in terms of the materialistic interpretation. It must be admitted that from any materialistic or positive-historical point of view that people should have ceased to exist long ago" (*Der Sinn der Geschichte*, German edition, 1925, pp. 128 ff). In connection with the foregoing cf. also L. P. Karsavin, *Philosophy of history*, §§ 58 and 59, Russian edition, 1923.

18. *Die Welt als Wille und Vorstellung*, ed. Griesebach, vol. II, p. 734. Incidentally it is worth noting that Schopenhauer believed that under certain positive and negative conditions "there will be only a very few Jews left in a hundred years" and that "soon after, the ghost will be finally laid, Ahasverus will lie in his grave and the chosen people will no longer know what has become of itself" (*Parerga*, § 132, ed. Griesebach, p. 272), and shows how readily the philosopher committed to pessimism fell into a baseless "optimism" in respect of the Jews.

19. A different view has lately been expressed by S. B. Rabinkow, 'Individual and community in Judaism', in *Soziologie der Person*, vol. IV of *Biologie der Person*, 1928, p. 818.

Hayomim, which only seem to be synonymous. In contrast to the latter term which, literally, means "matters of time" and thus relates directly to chronology, the former term points to the chain of "births" and so to the procession of the generations that stands out clearly from the natural division of time in the universe. This again is a methodological form impregnated in the material itself; it reflects the dual attitude of the Jewish spirit to the surrounding world—which has just been outlined—and it must be taken into account when choosing the most suitable subdivision into periods. Seen from within, the historical process is an unbroken continuum which, so to speak, knows nothing, and does not wish to know anything, about the entire outside world of nature and of history. But the sub-division into periods, the division of the flow of time, is concerned with caesurae, with pauses, and seeks to break up the continuous web of the inner history, as there is indeed no other way to represent a continuum. Hence the time pattern can only be introduced from the outside, from the aspect of the "matters of time". Taken together, then, the two Hebrew terms for the single concept of history signify that the Jewish destinies merge into a separate current, but only within the compass of the broad channels of world history.

The last philosophical premise which can be considered here in our context concerns the question as to the significance of outstanding individuals in Jewish history. The answer to that question, too, is already to be found in the material itself. As for devotees of the cult of heroes, men of the mentality of a Carlyle or Cousin, Jewish history—to put it bluntly—is none of their business, there is nothing in it for them. Not that the Jewish people was ever short of outstanding men, only they were never "declared demigods or elevated above the compass of earthly life".[20] It is easy to realise that the history of a people that from its earliest beginnings has been collectively conscious of its role as the carrier, witness and guarantor of a supra-historic promise, is bound to be a people's history rather than a chronicle of individual feats of genius. The immediate awareness of the absolutely unique destiny of the Jewish people is in fact the first and last philosophical premise of Jewish historiography.

III

The results of the foregoing general considerations are brilliantly confirmed by S. M. Dubnow's *World History of the Jewish People*. There is undoubtedly a certain tension between the personal world view of the author, set out most succinctly in the introduction to the whole work,[21] and

20. S. B. Rabinkow, loc. cit., p. 812.
21. World History, German edition, vol. I, pp. XIII ff; cf. also vol. X, § 37, pp. 345 ff. as well as *Letters on old and new Judaism,* especially letter 1. (The page numbers given in brackets in the text refer to the "Introduction", German edition.)

the intrinsic general premises of Jewish history. In emphatic contradiction of the "one-sided spiritual interpretation" of earlier Jewish historiography, he openly declares his support for an "achievement of the recent past", to wit the "purely scientific sociological view" (XIV f.), which he also characterises as the "realistic" one (XVII). As an opponent of "theological and metaphysical theories", he wants to see his fundamental historical attitude "bio-sociologically" buttressed (XX), and takes even a sociologist of Max Weber's standing to task for having interpreted the history of Judaic antiquity "in a theological or metaphysical spirit" (XXX).[22] Dubnow's watchword is the "rigorously applied principle of evolution" (XX). In common with all forms of sociological approach, Dubnow's variety has a touch of naturalism, and so in his eyes the "subject of scientific historiography" includes beside the origin a growth of national individuality its "struggle for survival" (XVI). "The secularisation of the Jewish national idea", he holds, "had to be followed by the secularisation of historiography, its liberation, to begin with from the shackles of theology, and subsequently from those of philosophical spiritualism and scholasticism" (ibid.). The non-Jewish sources of that general approach to history can readily be identified: they are French positivism and English biologically founded evolutionism.

On the strength of his personal world view Dubnow thus ranks as an advocate of the latest secular phase of Jewish intellectual development, which was dominated by foreign influences.[23] Nevertheless, he could not be the born historian that he was if his basic personal views had not fused into a unified whole with the ideas animating his entire subject matter from within. How thoroughly that fusion has in fact been accomplished can be seen from the use which the Jewish universal historian makes of the basic West European methodological concepts. Thus he terms his approach sociological not, perhaps, because he is striving to single out laws and regularities governing history, but solely on the strength of his view that the Jewish people ought to be recognised and acknowledged as the "actual subject, the creator of its history . . . in the field of social life as well", in short as a "living national organism" (XV and XXX). The same relationship is revealed even more sharply in the meaning attached by Dubnow to the concept of life. So far from equating the biological element in a rough and ready manner with the animal element, he invokes the principle of life in his attempt to circumscribe the unified spiritual substratum beneath the unbroken course of Jewish history over thousands of years (XVI f.). To him also only "matters of substance" are true, in accordance with the Hegelian

22. We cannot here enter into the merits of his argument, but it must be stressed that the concepts of "sect" and "caste" have a completely different meaning for Dubnow on the one hand and Weber on the other (see the latter's *Gesammelte Aufsätze zur Religionssoziologie*, 1921, vol. I, pp. 217 ff. and vol. III, pp. 392, 403).

23. World History, vol. IX, § 47, p. 429.

maxim.[24] In keeping with this approach even the concept of evolution in Dubnow's thought forfeits its primary naturalistic connotation and acquires instead a tendency to maintain the peculiar continuity in the process of cultural change. In his usage, then, the term "bio-sociological" has the meaning both of supra-individual continuity and the uninterrupted chain of works produced by the creative genius.

One might be tempted to look upon Dubnow's reinterpretation of concepts such as sociology, life and evolution as an indication of a concession to the "organic theory of society",[25] ill-reputed as metaphysical; yet the entire content and structure of his life's work make it clear beyond any doubt that it is not some modern sociological theory or other but the very subject matter of Jewish history by which the Jewish historian has been swayed. A brief review will bear this out.

By what principles is Dubnow guided in the selection of his material, in the separation of the essential from the inessential? Above all, surely, by the principle of the continuous evolution of the people's collective consciousness. That is why, and indeed the only reason why, he records with meticulous accuracy the progressive expansion of the Diaspora, the migration, even the fluctuation of the Jewish population in the various countries and continents. The road of Jewish history as a whole in his eyes runs from an infinitely remote past into an infinitely remote future. The Jewish people is an "eternal" people, it has its own "world history".[26] And the dominant force in that history, especially at its critical turning points, is a happy coincidence, a lucky change.[27] Dispersed over the whole globe, the Jewish people, gradually developing from a union of kinship groups into a "spiritual nation", is held together by the consciousness of a common destiny, by cultural bonds, by the "spiritual hegemony" radiating from national centres. And so Dubnow is consistent in arranging the structure of the individual chapters of his work by starting from the outward happenings affecting the people as from a periphery, then working his way inwards, first to the social-economic relations and finally to the true centre: the people's intellectual and spiritual life and creativity. As in the architectural arrangement, so in respect of the basic principle of his time pattern, his procedure is in complete harmony with the old Jewish view that any breaks in the continuous flow of events can only come from outside, from the "matters of time" (see above, Chapter II). The chronological frame of Jewish history thus delineates the area where the people of

24. See (Hegel quotation) above.

25. Cf. Paul Barth, Wrong and right of the organic theory of society, *Vierteljahresschrift für wissenschaftliche Philosophie*, vol. XXIV, 1900, pp. 69 ff.

26. It was precisely the title of Dubnow's main work that was most frequently subjected to criticism by reviewers who utterly misunderstood the author's intentions. It is significant that most of those objections came from non-Jewish quarters.

27. See World History, e.g. vols. V, p. 452; VI, 18, 425, 443 and X, 276.

Israel meets the non-Jewish surrounding world. With all that the distance towards the outside world in Dubnow's ten-volume work is in consonance with ancient Jewish tradition which, however, is rather overemphasised. Seen from the angle of the Jewish separate stream of world history, the movement of world history in its totality appears as a progression but not as progress. An austere air pervades the whole work throughout its ten volumes. It was contrary to the author's intention to write a "story of ideas and ordeals", yet that is what his inner sense of truth and his affinity with his subject matter compelled him to do.[28] And that is why his work ends on a note of messianic yearnings and why "autonomism" and "spiritual nationalism" are interchangeable ideologies for him.

Such is the logic, not of science but of the flow of history itself, not of facts but of that unique perpetually unfolding action of which the Jewish People is the originator and protagonist. Dubnow's work compels us to identify that unity of action as a reality, irrespective of the endless diversity of places and epochs, to grasp it as living purposefulness, to see it as a meaningful whole. Dubnow, however, in a spirit of epic severity refrains from unveiling the meaning immanent in that whole. He has thus with his *World History of the Jewish People* accomplished a deed in the domain of intellectual creativity which demands to be continued directly through a Jewish philosophy of world history.

28. The difference of principle that separates him from Graetz remains none the less unmistakable: indeed, Dubnow's great predecessor was so wrapped up in the inner history of Judaism that he overlooked the continuity of the outward history almost completely (cf. Hermann Cohen, *Jüdische Schriften*, 1924, 'Graetz's philosophy of Jewish history', vol. III, pp. 203 ff, and also vol. III, p. 452).

5. Jewish World History (on the Occasion of Simon Dubnow's 70th Birthday)

I

The seventieth birthday of Simon Dubnow is a threefold occasion for jubilation. It is the day on which our famous historian and publicist, still fully engaged in scholarly projects and with the creative power of a 30-year-old, has happily passed the limit of the biblical span. Secondly, it is fifty years, a jubilee in fact, since he began his writing career; and thirdly, it happens that this is the year of Dubnow's "Rejoicing of the Law" marking the completion of his ten-volume work, "World History of the Jewish People" to which he has devoted nearly half of his life.[1]

The Jewish world has already expressed its gratitude to him, first of all for his magnificent history in the innumerable congratulatory messages which have been showered upon him from all parts of the world for this threefold celebration. (Only in Russia is there an imposed silence.) He himself, in the preface to his just published "History of Hasidism", has referred to his main work as 'my own Talmud'. And indeed, like the Talmud, Dubnow's "World History" is in itself an encyclopaedia. No one has tried his hand to construct such an edifice since Heinrich Graetz. And it is worth remarking, as has already been done by the Jewish-German scholar Elbogen in the inaugural article of the "Festschrift zu Simon Dubnow's siebzigsten Geburtstag" published in Germany in Dubnow's honour, that from the last volume of Graetz (1876) to the first volume of Dubnow's "World History" (1925), there has elapsed a period not less than half a century. Dubnow's festive day is, in short, a festive day in Jewish historiography, and itself a jubilee, the sort that occurs only once in a half-century.

The Jewish world of to-day owes only to Dubnow a debt of gratitude for being enabled to witness this Rejoicing of the Law. The modern Jew who is still imbued with national feelings, but has turned his back on the old festivals, has only his history to be proud of. Now all that remains of the

---

1. The work has so far been published only in German in my translation. The further quotations are taken from the full edition.

This essay was first published in Yiddish in *Fraye Shriftn*, Warsaw, May 1931, No. 11.

commandment 'Observe and Remember', which used to be one word, is merely 'Remember!' which moves him to recollect. "Torah", tradition, faith, have all been carried away into a river of historical memories. During the festival of the Rejoicing of the Law, when the whole congregation, men, women and children, assemble for a few moments to form a round choral dance, so on Dubnow's festive day, the festival of Jewish history, all the divisions in our present-day community have fallen away and Zionists and Hebraists, anti-Zionists and Yiddishists, socialists and anti-socialists, even agnostics and rabbis, all join hands in one jubilant circle.

Certainly, without the focal figure, without the presence of the guest of honour himself, these general festivities, this circle, would not have been possible. The personality of Dubnow, his all embracing understanding, which permits him to judge with sympathy nearly all Jewish parties, is so deeply anchored in Jewish history that often it becomes difficult to distinguish if we are listening to his own voice or to the echo of the Jewish past. He and his work have become welded together even more closely than that of a poet and his poem. Nevertheless, Dubnow's work is not art, but scholarship, to use his own expression, Talmud, which offers not only enjoyment, but calls for continuous study. The holiday is over—the studies go on. And what does 'study' mean to a Jew? Asking questions! It is related of Rabbi Jochanan that his favourite pupil was Resh Lakish, because he used to bombard his master with the most impossible questions. Just so, the ten volumes of Dubnow's "World History" must not be devoured as though they were epic poetry, but examined like difficult complex problems. They call for commentary. They call for discussion and even for research into their implications and perhaps also their secrets.

II

I wish to start with a comment on Dubnow's scientific approach; then to explain what is to be understood by the idea of 'Jewish world history', and finally to try to divine the great secret of our 3,000-year existence, a secret of which I can find but a hint in Dubnow's ten volumes. [2]

When Dubnow had once again successfully traversed the prodigious distance from the earliest generations, the times of Abraham, Isaac and Jacob, to the present day and was able to report to us so lucidly and engrossingly on his historic journey it can only be explained by the fact that he had from the start decided on a detailed itinerary. He made discoveries because he knew what he was looking for. He was seeking, first and foremost, for confirmation of his own method in Jewish history. The

2. Part of the remarks that follow have been included somewhat differently in my German article "Die weltanschaulichen Voraussetzungen der juedischen Geschichts- schreibung" published in the "Festschrift zu Simon Dubnows siebzigstem Geburtstag"

thought will immediately arise that for the historian, method is only a means to an end, the safest way of reaching the objective results of research. As a matter of fact, such an assumption, as it is known today is erroneous in respect of history, and especially so in the case of Dubnow. *Method*—from the Greek meaning *way*—is a word which in reference to history is closely equivalent to the Hebrew expression *derekh*. Dubnow approached the material of the Jewish past with his *derekh*, that is to say, with his system, his own world-view and completed pattern. His intention was to demonstrate that this pattern was as though made-to-measure for the entire three thousand year process. At the same time he had to show that the *derekh* itself was the right one and that the systematic approach was valid. I cannot tell how far the young Dubnow was influenced by Lavrov's "Historical Letters". In his own "History" he himself mentions the currents of thought which influenced his generation, namely positivism and evolutionism (Vol. 9, p. 429), that is to say those trends with which the founders of the so-called "subjective sociological school", Lavrov and Mikhailovsky, were permanently preoccupied. Thus it may be accepted that he absorbed the ideas of Russian historical "subjectivism" with the air he breathed in his youth—the theory that the doors of history must be for ever closed for him who is without a *derekh* in its study. For this reason, indeed, Dubnow began at an early stage to lay stress not on special historical research but on the need of a suitable key to the main gates of Jewish history; and as soon as he sensed that he held the key firmly within his grip, he felt as secure in the historic past, as he did in the living present. He began to build with materials which became, so to speak, his own property. If we do not wish to remain outside his edifice and consider him only with aesthetic eye, we must turn back to Dubnow's original ideas, look into his building plans, and examine the approach which led him to his wide building site.

Dubnow described his approach as 'bio-sociological' (Introduction to *World History*, 2, I. 8, XV and XX). What does he mean by this and how did he arrive at it? The father of sociology and of the word 'sociology' itself, was the positivist Auguste Comte. Sociology, the science of the laws which govern social life, was for Comte the summit of human knowledge. If we recognize the laws according to which our lives run their course—so he believed—then we shall become the masters of our future; mankind will become divine. To know these laws, however, one must not confine oneself to only a portion of the social world, only to the present that is; but it is necessary to take into account everything within the bounds of human experience, and that means the whole story of civilization. But while the present in relation to the historical past is like a drop in the ocean, it is history which has necessarily to provide almost all the material for sociological study. To put it differently, the sociological method is for Comte the means to learn that which must be from that which has always been. With its rigid iron laws, Marxism is, as may be seen, a spiritual offspring of Comte-ism. Herbert Spencer went even further along a branch road of Comte's theory. Comte laid down the general rule that life as far as history has revealed it, is governed by laws. Spencer tried to prove that the social laws are the same as those which control all living nature, that they are in a word, biological laws. Thus the 'bio-sociological' approach to Jewish history should have signified an effort to discover the general biological laws which governed our past, which govern our present, and will govern our future.

Comte's formula was: "Know in order to foresee, so as to have power." Is that the intention of Dubnow? To think so would be a grave mistake! Dubnow calls this approach 'sociological' because his basic assumption is 'that the Jewish people, in all countries, always and everywhere, in both its spiritual and social life, was the subject and the creator of its own history'. Another reason he has for using the word 'sociological' is the recognition that 'the subject of Jewish history' must be regarded as 'a living national organism' (I.7,XV and XXX). The science of Jewish history is concerned, according to Dubnow, not merely with a religious association, but with a living people, a 'nation'; it is a phenomenon falling within the province of sociology, therefore sociological, and by the same argument also basically 'bio-sociological': biology is the science of life and the Jewish people is 'a living organism'. Thus as 'subject' and as 'national individuality', it has always 'grown' and 'struggled for its existence', for its 'singularity' (7, XVI and II). On the one hand its history is a sociological process, and on the other a biological one, or more briefly a 'bio-sociological' process. It is necessary to attain a clear grasp of the meaning that Dubnow attached to his terminology in order to avoid being misled into serious error. The question remains, why did Dubnow choose words which are ordinarily used in quite a different sense? To understand this, it is necessary to consider 'genetically' how Dubnow arrived at his own approach. Even the historian has to be explained historically.

Dubnow's first important independent work was the history of Hasidism. The more deeply he became immersed in the struggle that the Hasidic popular movement waged against the old forces in Jewry, the more obvious it became to him that the organic unity of the Jewish people was by nature not just an idea, but, at least in earlier times, a real socio-historical fact. In the atmosphere strongly prevailing in russified intelligentsia among whom the young Dubnow lived, such perception amounted to a discovery. The impression grew stronger when Dubnow undertook wider research into Jewish history in eastern Europe. Almost until the end of the XVIIIth century Poland was the classic land of Jewish self-government, of communal regime. In this area, while gathering material for the history of the Jews in Poland, Lithuania and Russia, Dubnow realized quite clearly that even in exile the Jewish people had not ceased to be an organic whole and that even after losing its land and statehood it had remained a social reality, a 'nation'. He knew from that moment that what he had to seek in Jewish history was the proof of this 'national point of view'. If the ordinary rank and file Jew had been told of Dubnow's discovery, he would surely have shrugged his shoulders and inquired in amazement—'What does it mean? What is new in what this scholar brings us? Don't we know that we are a people, and even a chosen people as of old, today in exile as in olden times and until the days of the Messiah Himself?' Dubnow was, however, far removed from the ordinary 'rank and file' Jew. Moreover, the old faith had in his estimation fully completed its purpose. In his general view of the world he was a positivist, an evolutionist, just as the entire young Jewish russified generation. His discovery was a novelty not for the old but for the young Jews, for those who were half-assimilated and at best preached, as they did in the west, that Jews were linked to one another no more than by a common place of prayer. When he realized that there were two radical sections, Dubnow had to emphasize that his 'approach' was a middle course between the way of burning faith, and that of cold-hearted assimilation. On one side his approach was not religious but scientific, positivist and evolutionist; on the other side it was not assimilationist, but national. The sociological perception was for him the characteristic of a scientific attitude, in contradistinction to the old world of religious piety. The 'biological' perception was a proclamation to the outer world that the Jewish people was 'alive' and that it was a 'living organism'. The 'biological' method teaches that also the non-religious Jew can grasp Jewish history from the beginning to the end, as long as it is clear to him that he has before him an organized 'national' unity.

At the cradle of Dubnow's "World History" there stood a worldly or secularized Jewish nationalism. Dubnow sought in Jewish history not general laws, whether sociological or biological, but the hallmarks of a national organized existence. He collected any evidence in every land of manifestations of Jewish autonomy, of a way of life pursued in accordance with their own law. And for every epoch he determined the centre which forged the whole of Jewry into one people and which, according to his terminology, wielded the spiritual leadership, the 'hegemony'. This is directed against those who deny the national character of Jewry. His anti-religious and positivist tendency is reflected in his search for a natural explanation for every phenomenon, and reason for everything that was. If there is no reason to be found in the historical material, then Dubnow follows the rule, 'The end of a deed is in the initial intention', or 'When men have done something, they intended to do it from the beginning'. The objectivity of Dubnow's explanation, its scientific basis, often rests on the extent to which his psychological conjectures appear reasonable. I offer one example from among hundreds:

The Twelve Tribes entered the Land of Canaan as one people because in the desert they had already acquired national consciousness, instilled in them by Moses. 'For this purpose Moses had chosen just those instruments which were in his possession' . . . . 'With the help of Moses at Mount Sinai the Covenant was sealed between the people of Israel and its God, an act by which the link between the individual tribes had to be strengthened' (I. p. 22 and fol.). Plainly, this is a conjecture which will appear reasonable only to rationalists, to those who believe that in the history of human life everything permits of a simple explanation. True, there are events in Jewish history which perplex even Dubnow. 'One is almost moved to talk of Providence', he observes, for example in one passage, 'when considering that Holland, which at the beginning of the XVIth century became subject to Spanish rule, had by the end of the century freed itself of Spain in order to become a 'city of refuge' for the Marranos suffering in the lands of Inquisition (Vol. VI, p. 425; see also p. 18 and 443, or Vol. V., p. 425, etc.). 'Almost Providence', however, it goes without saying, is a long way from 'God's verdict': it is a matter of chance. We may observe here from another angle how great is the difference between Dubnow's sociological approach and ordinary sociológical theories. In sociology there are only laws which seek to reduce everything that seems accidental to general rules. Dubnow knows that such a method will not take one far in Jewish history.

There are times, though not often, when Dubnow shows astonishment at remarkable encounters with historical forces that came, as though deliberately to the aid of the Jewish people. He is not astonished at the exceptional phenomenon within the realm of individual human life and creation. In this case he takes the point of view that all the elements of psychic life are known and where individuals are concerned it depends to a greater or lesser degree on their spiritual force. I have already given the example of Moses. The Prophets, Christ, Mohammed, the false messiahs, the holy mystics, the thinkers and poets appear in Dubnow's works in a similar way. He brings them all closer to ordinary understanding. In this respect he is a true man of his time. Later psychological research takes quite a different course; its followers having lost their fear of belief in God, they are no longer afraid of looking more closely into the divine and demonic forces in man. Dubnow is a freethinker. Wherever in Jewish history he comes upon such free spirits as 'Acher' (Elisha ben Abuya) or Uriel Acosta, he is in deep sympathy with them. He sees them as men who were in advance of their time, and because of the conflict between their individual needs and the practical requirements of society in general, found themselves in a tragic dilemma. Dubnow himself was spared such tragedy. The road which he as historian chose unhesitatingly for himself was the *Derekh Ha-Melech*, the Royal High Way of his entire generation.

III

Historical material is never entirely without shape or form. The connection between separate facts which the historian seeks is mostly contained in the facts themselves. These facts are really waves of a single continuous stream in which earlier and later waves become inseparably mingled. That is the principal feature of spiritual life in general and the degree in which historical life is really spiritual is characterized by "continuity", by flowing unity. Naturally, there is room for argument here. Can the history of a people be compared with the fate of an individual? Is it possible, in a word, to write 'biographies' of whole nations as of individual persons? Such controversy turns into empty words at the very moment we step into the field of Jewish history. The Russian philosopher Nikolai Berdyaev who was a Marxist in his youth, relates that the moment he began to take an interest in Jewish history, he found himself compelled to become a heretic in respect of historical materialism. He suddenly perceived that here at the very least was a considerable historical process that came within the realm not of material motives, but of the spirit. He had no choice, either to deny a long series of facts, or to renounce Marxism. Accordingly, in the Marxist sense he became a heretic. The non-Jewish Marxist did at least have a choice, but the Jewish historian has no choice but to recognize the spiritual character of Jewish history. This teaches us that concrete historical material can be approached only with a formula to fit; in other words, the subjective approach of the historian must often adapt itself against his will, and even unconsciously, to the historical material on which he is working. This process of adaptation, I think, explains the long scholarly career of Simon Dubnow and was fully realized in his most mature work, the ten volumes of his "World History".

Even the title "World History" is evidence of this. The title has its own story. The German philosopher Ernst Troeltsch in his work "Der Historismus und seine Probleme" shows how the very idea of a world history developed from Jewish prophetic monotheism and passed into Christianity in the form of universalism, originating from the thought that the whole of mankind having one God, also had one fate. Naturally, 'world history' is to be understood as the history of mankind, or at least of civilized mankind. The question, therefore, confronts us: is not the concept of "world history" of one people a contradiction in terms? When the first volumes of Dubnow's work appeared in German, the learned critics at once drew attention to the title page. They said that the work should really have been called 'History of the Jewish People within World History'. They had not noticed the most important point which the author himself had made in explanation of his title, namely that 'Jewry is actually a historical microcosm', i.e. a historic world on its own (Vol. I, p. XIII). Little by little, Dubnow had become so deeply absorbed in the material of Jewish History that at the end of his task he was himself talking in terms of the facts he examined. Only one kind of phenomena can be considered a 'world on its own' in terms of history of civilization, a fully rounded welt anschauung (world-system). When Dubnow tells us that the subject of Jewish history is the people, it must be a people complete with a welt anschauung and its own idea of the world. If one reads Dubnow's history, volume after volume, without prejudice, forgetting his subjective approach, then it becomes obvious that the title "World History" for a historical work of such scope is thoroughly justified. What concerns us is that Dubnow keeps firmly to his elected approach according to which the Jewish faith was created for the people and not the people for the faith. Also it would be erroneous to think that the facts presented by the historian were in contradiction to his own theoretical approach: they do not deny it; they supplement it. Assuredly, the faith was created for the people; yet the people as it sees itself was created not for itself alone, but for the whole world. It was created for God's world and because of that it had to suffer and fight for its existence; and to gain the redemption of God's world, as Dubnow himself tells us, generation after generation sacrificed itself and offered itself for the Sanctification of the Name (*Kiddush Ha-Shem*). Holiness!—that in a word is the content of Jewish 'world history'. If *Kiddush Ha-Shem*, I stress the word *Ha-Shem*, i.e. the Sanctification of the Name, the Idea, has no reality from the scientific point of view, then almost our entire history lacks reality and all that is left of it are meagre crumbs.

Meagre or not meagre—whatever the representatives of today, who are already of yesterday, wish to call them—the crumbs are still a reality. Should we then exclude from Jewish history everything that lacks the stamp of religion? In that case, what should we do with the whole of the XIXth century, and with the period in which we ourselves are living? The answer to this question I find in Dubnow's book which is a kind of scholarly 'Ingathering of the Exiles'. Is not secularized Jewry, so long as it considers itself Jewish, still under the influence of Jewish world history, and is it not illuminated by its reflected light? As I have already said, it may be 'non-observant', but it 'remembers'. The less it observes, the more it lives with the historical memory. Moreover, the Jewish historical memory is a reliable guardian. When the right time comes, it reminds us to do what is necessary and what we must do, the things indeed that older generations had done with all their hearts and souls and strength. For tens of thousands of Jews Dubnow's "World History" will renew and refresh the memory and this way will serve as an iron bridge from our own time into the future . . . What sort of future? Whither?—This brings us to the great secret of Jewish world history.

Dubnow's principle, in dealing with any particular period of history, is to let it speak in its own language. As far as possible he quotes the contemporary documents verbatim together with the comments with which each generation followed its own fortunes. In his first volume he talks to us through the Bible; in the second through the mouth of Josephus Flavius; in the third, his voice is that of the Talmud, and so on, until the end. Every Jewish generation has its own fortune, and the thoughts which it evokes have their own particular colouring. Nevertheless, the reader feels, as he closes the last volume, that he has been listening throughout to one voice, and that the Jewish people, in all languages, at all times, and in all countries, have continually spoken of one subject and lived with one thought. What is this subject? What kind of thought? The last lines of Dubnow, while they offer some pointers leave the question essentially unanswered. World peace and justice which Dubnow mentions here, referring to the Prophets, are ideas (Vol. X and end of Epilogue) too abstract for the explanation of so concrete a phenomenon in the world as the struggle of the Jewish people for its historical existence. Reluctantly, I recall "Historical Miniatures" by the profound Swedish poet, August Strindberg. In the series of images he tries to convey some idea of general human development, and in each image, whether of the Socrates' Circle of Athens, or of St. Petersburg of Peter I, he introduces a figure of a Jew constantly repeating throughout thousands of years, 'Not this I mean! We still wait! Our Redeemer has not yet come'. Is the reason why the Jew does not wish to cling to the richest and grandest culture of the world because he still believes that the future will confer peace and justice on us? The loud echo which international socialism evoked among the Jewish people may possibly be treated as evidence that this is indeed so. The Jew finds it easiest to desert his Judaism for the sake of universalism. Before, however, socialism could absorb the core of the Jewish people, it became split into two camps, each of which, after its own fashion, as soon as it passed from precept to action, betrayed its universal mission. If Strindberg could today complete his historical picture gallery, he would have to add a small picture of "the Kremlin" and another of 'the Labour Government' and neither of these would be without the figure of the Jew who argues: 'Once more, this is not what I mean. The time is not yet for which I wait! . . . .' And if he is interrupted with the question, 'Then tell us, what do you mean? When will your time be?', the Jew would reply, for every Jew is a prophet 'I do not know when it will be, but I know it will come'. The prophetic spirit, the conviction that everything around us and within us can and will change completely—that is the basis of our whole world history.

How do we know what we know? What is the source of the super-natural, super-historical force of our faith?—This is the secret for which we must keep listening.

6. Simon Dubnow (1860-1960)

In memory of a master-builder

It is impossible for me to mention the name of Simon Dubnow without adding the age-old and uplifting words, "Blessed be his memory!"

The entire Jewish world knows that Simon Dubnow's life, which began a hundred years ago on the second day of the Jewish New Year 5621 (1860 c.e.) in the town of Mstislavl, Belorussia, came to a tragic end in the ghetto of Riga where the octogenarian was destined to find a martyr's crown. It is also known that he and his name are firmly engraved in the roll of honour of Jewish modern secular historiography. Simon Dubnow and Jewish "world history" have become for us inseparably linked like one of those pairs of sentinels who, in olden times, stood guard on the road to our people's spiritual progress. But is it enough to know more or less closely the building a man has constructed without having a clear conception of the builder? The builder and his work are often bound to each other much like body and soul. As one who was privileged to spend a considerable time in Simon Dubnow's closest company, I believe that this centenary year of his birth is the right time to devote ourselves primarily to a study of his personality and to try and assess how far his spirit lives in the body of his achievement. Perhaps this may even result in a better understanding of the work itself.

To digress for a moment, I should like in these prefatory remarks to make plain that Simon Dubnow did not only die a martyr, but that he also lived his life like a saint, as it is written of Noah: "He was a righteous man and perfect in his generations" (Gen. 6:9). Amid the worldly-minded surroundings of his long life, he was a "wholly righteous man". If there are orders of piety among the nations of the world, why should it not be possible for a Jew, a "free-thinking" man of the world, to reach the level of saintliness? I firmly believe that without this quality Simon Dubnow would never have been able to produce the remarkable work that goes by the name of "The World History of the Jewish People".

I

It is difficult to describe the significance which Father Noah and the whole Story of the Flood had in Dubnow's attitude to the destiny of his

This essay was first published in Yiddish in *Di Goldene Keyt*, Tel-Aviv, 1961, No. 39.

own "generation of the flood". There is no doubt, however, that the line quoted from Genesis with its use of the plural form "generations", had an influence on his outlook. In a letter which I received from him in London in the autumn of 1935 when he was living in Riga, his city of refuge (after Berlin), shortly after his 75th birthday, I read: "My life may be measured in quarter-centuries . . . For a historian it is a great achievement to have lived in three "dimensions", three generations, because in this way he can more deeply penetrate the secret of epochal change. It is also a source of great sorrow if the change is from bad to worse, because then the thought crosses one's mind that the thread of life will be broken in a time of darkness. We live in dreadful times and only my two-fold faith in life as a Jew and a chronicler gives me the strength to endure." (Original in Russian.)

On the threshold of the fourth "dimension" of his life, Simon Dubnow sensed palpably the approaching storm that would swallow him, the rising waters that would engulf the world and already scarcely left any dry land. Yet he has the courage to endure and lives on only by reason of his faith as a Jewish historian—as it is explicitly written: "A righteous man lives in his faith" (Habakuk 2:4).

I met Dubnow in Riga twice, the first time at the beginning of 1934 and then in the autumn of 1937. To this day, his handsome dwelling outside the town in the quiet Kaiserwald is clearly before my eyes, bright and tidy, with elegant stacks of bookshelves against the walls, pine branches showing through the window-panes, and in the middle of it all the figure of the dear master of the house himself. I see it all as clearly as on the day I enjoyed his warm-hearted hospitality. Truly, "the beauty of Japhet in one of the tents of Shem!" I painfully picture to myself the scene when our dear Simon Dubnow was taken away from this his home to be thrown into the ghetto and destroyed there. But however much I try, I see always the same image of the man—unperturbed, with a calm, serious face and tight lips, his eyes turned away from the assassins around him, a bundle of books and manuscripts under his arm. And this is how he is led away, stepping softly but firmly on his last journey. The picture I have before me of a true Jewish Stoic, who is always prepared to take upon himself the yoke of martyrdom, mirrors for me the chief impression I retain of Simon Dubnow's character since those years when I had the privilege to know him, the years 1918 to 1922, when we lodged, so to speak, in the "same inn" in Bolshevik Petrograd.

There I met Dubnow for the first time in the house of my uncle, Dr. Eliashov ("Baal Machshoves"). That was at the end of 1918. The terror was at the height of its ferocity. Old liberals and radicals like Dubnow or Israel Zinberg were far from sure of survival. Nevertheless, a group of Jewish scholars with Dubnow at their head decided that this was just the time to do something to raise the state and prestige of Jewish education among

Russian Jews. A glass of tea at the doctor's house, far from any contact with Russian politics, was intended as a precautionary prescription against interference by the Cheka, in case the suspicion arose later that the deliberations for the founding of a Jewish Research Institute in Petrograd was in fact a political conspiracy.

So we sat around the table confiding in each other, to start with, our serious doubts whether anything like that was possible in the prevailing darkness. Perhaps it was better to wait until the passing of the fury, was the suggestion at this point by Saul Ginsburg. But more persuasive was the view of Simon Markovitch, i.e. Simon Ben Meir, Dubnow's unshakable pride. "What do you mean by darkness?" he demanded, directing for a moment his piercing eyes on everyone around that table. "Of course it is dark, dark in fact with the darkness of Egypt! So when do we have to light a candle? In broad daylight? We must learn from our past . . ." And in a few ardent words he drew up for this handful of Russian-Jewish intellectuals, sitting in the dim light of this dining-room, a list of all the periods in Jewish history when the nation owed its deliverance to a few individuals. He ended with a quotation from Jeremiah (30:7): "It is a time of trouble for Jacob, but out of it he shall be saved." Whether it was the word of the prophet that did it, or Simon Dubnow's brief historical survey, the end of it was a unanimous decision to join forces and establish in Bolshevik Petersburg a "Jewish People's University". Out of this there grew not long after the "Institute of Higher Jewish Studies".

That same evening I recorded Dubnow's words in my diary, as I did frequently in the ensuing years, and added the following notes: "In the words of Simon Markovitch one heard the heroic voice of our past. How modest is his appearance! But should not a true hero be modest or unassuming?" I dare say it would have been more appropriate on that Petersburg night not to use the word "hero", but the much more heroic name of "saint" (Tzaddik). But that became clear to me only later, particularly in the Berlin years (1923-1933), the years of my closer association with Simon Dubnow.

The sure sign of a saint is, I believe, that he lives by virtue of his faith in a spiritual impregnable stronghold, invulnerable to any warlike tactics or satanic cunning. The translation of the "beth" in Habakuk's phrase "b'emunato" ("by his faith", Hab. 2:4) is not "by" or "through" but "in", thus making the line "The righteous shall live in his faith". Indeed thus, "in" his faith, was Simon Dubnow able to survive his Bolshevik years in Petersburg. Faith is primarily a steadfast trust. Not for a single moment during those dreadful years was there any weakening in Dubnow's trust that ultimately liberty and not servitude would prevail. And his belief in the Jewish prophetic vision of humanity's redemption, in an everlasting bond of fraternal peace, was a belief without any reservations. When he moved through the streets of half-empty, half-deserted Petrograd, in the armour of his faith, he proclaimed in a truly tragic moment of our contemporary history, "With Satan there can be no compromise!" And it will repay us to dwell a while on that point of time when Dubnow's innermost character was revealed to us all in its exemplary clarity.

We had gathered in the Troitzkaya Road, in the administrative room of our Institute. There was only one subject on the agenda. Face to face with the danger that at any moment the Whites might force their way into Russia's imperial capital, what should we do? That was in October 1919, when General Yudenitsh was already encamped no more than ten miles from the city centre. No one among us entertained any shadow of doubt but that if it came to it, the Jews would be the first victims. Knowing that Trotzky had arrived from Moscow and had taken command of the defences of "Red Petrograd", one of our members, though a dyed-in-the-wool enemy of Bolshevism, proposed that we should contrive to see "Lev Davidovich" (Trotzky) and ask him to make separate arrangements for the security of the Jews apart from a mass evacuation of the Jewish population. (Such a meeting would have been quite possible, Trotzky's personal adjutant being a son of our colleague, Julius Hessen, historian of Russian Jewry.) No sooner, however, was the proposal made than Dubnow rose from his chair shaking with indignation in a manner I never saw him either before or after, and raising his voice called, "Heaven forbid! You don't ask mercy of the Devil and you don't make any pacts with him! If that is our destiny, we shall be destroyed, but the Jewish name will remain unsullied. To bow to the embodiment of terrorism is worse than idol-worship! This is a case of 'be killed rather than transgress'. We certainly need an organised defence, but it must be Jewish self-defence, and that's what we should talk about."

The other details are not important here. It is enough to recall that Dubnow, now approaching sixty, put to shame with his Hasmonean zeal the other, mostly younger, members, and after a short argument they decided to follow him. Meanwhile the wheel once more took a turn to the left. Petrograd remained "Red" and "the permanent pogrom against Jews and non-Jews", in Dubnow's phrase, became more drastic. It would be quite wrong to think that Dubnow's anti-Bolshevism in general and his revulsion—there is no other word for it—for Trotsky in particular, had any other reason than his "faith", his ethical conviction that the Jewish people could and would maintain its position in the world only in the ways of freedom and peace. "Terror is unclean," he would often exclaim in those years, with an air of disgust not unlike that of pious Jews faced by a gross breach of the Law. Before Passover in 1921 he provided himself with half-a-dozen *matzos*, explaining that a time when freedom, "the most sacred of all human values", was being suppressed, it behoved every Jew, whether observant or not, "to make at least a historical-symbolical protest by a conspicuous allusion to our ancient way of life, the ritual supper glorifying liberty."

In later years I happened to hear the accusation made more than once that Dubnow was too accommodating or broad-minded and was prepared to accept into the Jewish fold any sort of "heretic" as long as he was "national"; to put it briefly and colloquially, he was ready to "dance at anybody's wedding". Such accusers did not understand and did not want to understand, that Dubnow's tolerance was not weakness, but rather one of his strong moral principles. And when it came to tolerance, he was really a zealot. He believed with complete faith that at a time of world crisis Jews must make an effort to understand each other, even if they were spiritually as far from one another as East and West.

An illustration of this can be found in his Petersburg period. There were differences of opinion in our Institute concerning the language of study. Dubnow's way was to insist at all times on equal standing for all three languages, i.e. Hebrew, "our ancient national tongue"; Yiddish, "our vernacular"; and Russian, "the language of the country". (Most of the lectures were given in Russian.) In 1920 it was important to extract from the authorities a formal sanction of the Institute's statutes. Accordingly, some voices among us were heard suggesting that it was advisable not to mention the question of language, or at all events, to maintain silence about Hebrew so as not to provoke the Red "turkey-cocks". On the other hand, others believed that to specify Yiddish could be interpreted as a concession to the Jewish Communists. But Dubnow put an end to all argument with the statement that on the question of language we had no option but "to fight fanatically for the principle of tolerance", and as was his habit, he gently made clear that "any betrayal of such a sacred principle" would prevent him from taking part in the Institute. And once again the ruling remained "according to Simon Dubnow".

The months and years meanwhile rolled on and on, and always downhill. Dubnow became impatient. At the meeting in celebration of his sixtieth birthday, after the Tabernacles festival (*Simchat Torah*) 1920, he light-heartedly interpreted the letter-numbers of the Hebrew calendar year (hatirpa = 5681) as meaning, "Will you be healed this year? What are you doing to escape from the dreadful epidemic, the plague of the country?" He then confided to us his secret, that he himself was preparing to emigrate, to use the "remedy" that had already helped millions of Russian Jews to rid themselves of the terrible plague of persecution. Sadness fell upon us all to hear this. We all felt that without Dubnow our small Petersburg *kibbutz* would lack its moral pillar. But at the time we all knew that Dubnow's decision was in accordance with his personal mission. He had for decades been assembling, brick by brick, the building material of his comprehensive work, which in his view was to add the last word to modern research in the wide field of Jewish history. By 1920, however, it became clear to him that he would never live to see his multi-volume work published in Russia; and if not in the Russian original, in Russia, thought Dubnow, it had better appear in a German metamorphosis "in the classic land of Jewish learning".

When we bade farewell to each other in Petersburg in 1922, it occurred to neither of us that quite soon we should meet again under the same roof, this time in the free city that was the capital of the Weimar Republic; and it would then fall to me to lend both my hands to Dubnow's work.

II

If I have previously allowed myself to associate Simon Dubnow's name with the exalted idea of a saint, it is not merely because he was for me so bright a figure against the dark background of Bolshevik Petersburg, but mainly thanks to my experiences in Berlin. It was there where for years I shared his cares during the cradle stages of his gradually developing works then emerging in their German version. These were the ten volumes of "The World History of the Jewish People" (1925-1929) and two volumes of his "History of Hassidism" (1931), not counting the three volumes of the abridged "World History" (1937-1938). During this period of his life it was possible for me to assess him not merely over the span of a century, as it is done the world over today, but according to the fine scale of minutes that add up to a man's every-day life. One way or another, the counts agree: in the final reckoning he remains the same Simon Dubnow, the "upright man" of his and our generations.

He himself would certainly not have minded to be portrayed in the natural setting of his daily surroundings, in the first place not as a modern European scholar which in fact he was, but as a Jewish sage of ancient times. At most he would have smiled thereat and observed that it was no more than a new-fangled symbolist stylisation. His irony would not, however, have been justified. It would merely have reflected his deep unconscious humility, since he had not noticed or perhaps had not wanted to notice that his real life had bit by bit become transformed into the symbolism of "Torah and service", and that the order of his days and years had accordingly assumed the style of the ancient sages, with the difference only that his Torah was Jewish history and that he served the spirit of eternal truth as he conceived it through his own common sense. Actually, if he firmly held also to practical rules of behaviour, they were prescriptive of his own personal ritual. The most important of these rules was not to waste time. They were strictly adjusted to his way of study and to his ardent desire to make discoveries in the six-times-six "orders" of our people's past. Half in earnest, half in jest, he would often cite the adage, "In doing a good deed, one is absolved of another good deed."

As the sages of old, Simon Dubnow was both of the world and unattached to the world. He was closely interested in all that was happening in the world of so-called higher politics, especially in so far as it might affect the Jews. He would begin his day scrutinising the newspapers. Facts which appeared to have historical significance were at once recorded in his "journal", his private diary. On the other hand he would ignore completely any recent achievements in the natural sciences or technology if they disclosed no positive bearing on moral progress. When the whole world, for example, marvelled at Charles Lindbergh's success in flying across the Atlantic (in 1927), Dubnow only laughed. "Where do they have to hurry like that? Where do they fly? People have not learned yet how to behave properly towards their next-door neighbour or a neighbouring nation. Material progress that comes too soon can become the greatest danger to the spirit!" I regularly made notes in my diary of such extempore comments so characteristic of Dubnow's individuality, made as it were on the margin of contemporary history. I had occasion to tell him of this once. He was quite pleased and asked me to make no secret of any critical notes I might add to his comments. "When one is entirely absorbed in scientific research," he was at pains to explain, "one becomes almost detached from the world and it is then easy to fall into error respecting one's own period and one's own attitude. A diary is a safeguard against this, enabling one continually to maintain control. There is a specific saying on this: two heads are better than one. It may be useful one day to hear what both have to say." I set this down, too, in my notebook, having thus Dubnow's explicit encouragement to my further study of his personality.

Be he a historian, true to the modern type, or a Talmudical scholar of the old pattern, the habits of life and research displayed by Dubnow are in every way similar to those described in "The Sayings of the Fathers". There we learn (Chapter 6:4), "This is the way of study of the Torah: Your food will be bread and salt . . . You will live a life of poverty while you toil in the Torah. But if you do this, it will go well with you!" How often did I recall this description of a Talmudist's way of life when I saw unrolled before my eyes, day in day out, the scroll of Dubnow's "Chronicles".

His industry had no limits. There were weeks and months when he used to sit at his desk from early morning till late at night, often devoting hour after hour to establishing the exact spelling of a name or a date in a historical document. In such a case he would quote the Talmudic saying, "It is presumed that a colleague (i.e. another Talmudist) will not let anything pass from his hand without correcting it." At the time of his acute attacks of research fever, his life's partner, the pious Ida Yefimovna, would not infrequently have to force him to take some food. Almost always short of money, he never wanted to accept a loan from well-to-do admirers and would always quote the verse from Proverbs, "The borrower is serf to the lender" (Pr. 22:7). "You insult me!" an old friend of his from the Odessa days once ventured to protest. "On the contrary, you insult me," was the calmly insistent response of Simon Meyerovitch. "Am I not able freely to decide when I am a freeman and when a slave?" And Dubnow closed the argument with a laugh. Indeed he felt free and in good heart. Generally speaking, all the seven features which, according to the "Sayings of the

Fathers", characterise a wise man were as though designed for Simon Dubnow, more particularly the last of the seven, which is perhaps the most important in the life of a research worker—the ability to face the truth, to admit one's own mistakes and seek to correct them.

Dubnow's last work, his autobiography entitled *Sefer Ha-Hayim* (Book of Life; in Russian, *Kniga zhizni*), in three volumes, affords singular evidence that he was constantly trying to get the better of his own faults and reprove his own greater or lesser transgressions. Towards the end of his life, he divided it in retrospect into three stages—Thesis, Anti-thesis and Synthesis. Some were inclined to see in this the influence of Hegel, but far be it from that! Dubnow was a convinced opponent of dialectic logic which, as he liked to put it, "removed it from reason". He used the Hegelian "triad" only for the purpose of clarifying to himself and others that until the concluding period of his spiritual "Synthesis" he had strayed down blind alleys. He had been constantly seeking, however, the connecting and unifying element, the "synthetical" in himself, around himself and principally in the historical world.

Simon Dubnow was clearly far from the simple man that the world wanted to make of him, in his own "three generations". In the third of these, I can myself testify, he was by no means uniform or simple but almost the opposite, being, from whatever angle one observed him, a harmonious synthesis of dissonances and contradictions. Let us take, for example, his attitude to people. Superficially one might suppose that, wholly absorbed as he was in his work and little interested in the world, he did not see individuals at all, and that his polite friendliness to a visitor who happened to call at his study with the window wide open to the past, was no more than a tepid indifference. But, in fact, this seeming courteous indifference of his was, on the contrary, often a disguise for a warm affection for people. One example may suffice. An occasional visitor at Dubnow's was a Jewish writer whose philosophy should have created an abyss between the two men. But this young "anarchist" was very hard up and too proud to mention it. As soon as Dubnow became aware of this he at once made an appeal for the establishment of a special fund for the man's needy family. Time, as we have noted, was the most precious commodity to him, but nonetheless Dubnow spent two whole days, together with a friend, knocking at the doors of rich emigrants until the target was attained. On the third day he said to me with a shining face, "I told them I was celebrating my own "Holy Day in Exile" and, you know, it worked!" Apparently our worldly-minded historian was also somewhat caught up in Hassidic custom and it was no accident that from youth onwards he was captivated by Hassidic history.

Bearing always in mind that he represented the honour and glory of Jewish history, Simon Dubnow became in old age its symbolic embodiment. Its splendour shone in his face. People with an aesthetic sense were at once struck by it. Chaim Nachman Bialik was such a one. Saul Tchernichowsky was another. I once spent an evening with Dubnow and Chaim Zhitlovsky. On our way out Zhitlovsky repeated, as though to himself, "What a beautiful old man!" Next morning I asked Dubnow what impression Zhitlovsky had made on him. "I believe that in respect of Yiddish, Zhitlovsky is too one-sided," he answered. "But what a beautiful old man!" I was truly delighted and made a note: "The echo of beautiful is beautiful."

I have already mentioned in passing Dubnow's extraordinary modesty. This persisted so that even on his seventieth birthday he absolutely refused to appear at a festive gathering arranged in his honour in Berlin by German, Russian and Jewish friends and admirers. Shaking his fine grey head he said, "Rather something different . . . at home, at the close of Rosh Hashanah, a glass of tea among our dear friends." He was thinking of course of the Lestschinskys, the Tcherikovers, the Rawidowiczes, the Krupniks—not forgetting the Steinbergs. So Ida Yefimovna's tea party was joined also by a guest from Eretz Israel, Zalman Rubashov (Zalman Shazar, President of Israel) who had been a student of Dubnow's in St. Petersburg in the years "before the Flood". Although a cup of tea is not usually accompanied by speeches, nevertheless each one there felt called upon to say something. Zalman held forth with almost volcanic ardour, claiming that it was high time for the historian of the people of Israel to come to the Land of Israel, where even the stones talk the language of history. The host (who was also our guest of honour) observed quietly, with some embarrassment, that he had probably not been worthy of that as long as his labour of research remained incomplete. But now, having put his signature to it, he hoped soon to find it possible to fulfil his heart's desire, and that he would then be forgiven his sin in accordance with the Gemara saying, "He who is busy fulfilling a commandment is dispensed from another commandment."

By the month of Tishrei, September 1930, all ten volumes of Dubnow's "World History" had been distributed in thousands of copies among Jews and non-Jews throughout Germany, and eulogies were coming from all quarters. Professor Adalbert Merks of Heidelberg wrote that "Dubnow's magnificent work is a singular monument to Jewish diligence." Congratulations came in personal letters and published reviews. A former cabinet minister, a member of the Catholic "Centre Party", who was laid up in a hospital, wrote to the author of the "World History" that he was reading the work volume by volume "like a novel" and he believed it was the best remedy he'd had. But the author himself paid more attention to criticism than to songs of praise. In the very days of his apotheosis he remarked to me suddenly that if there was to be a reprint of the ten volumes he would have to take into account many of the critical observations that the past five years had produced. "We know after all," he added with some concern, "at least some of them are not undeserved." Bearing with a sense of pride the imposing title of a Jewish historian, he was often at the time prone to ask himself whether he really merited such dignity. On the occasion of his seventieth birthday, the Berlin community honoured him with a commemorative volume, which included among other writings a critical objective evaluation of Dubnow's philosophy of history. The contributor, with whom I am well acquainted, had some doubt as to how Dubnow would receive this sharply flavoured contribution. But it transpired that precisely this peppery flavour afforded Dubnow the greatest satisfaction. "This is criticism in its own right!" he exclaimed when the "sinner" appeared before him at his house, "and most important, it is *en connaissance de cause*. What more can one wish!" Simon Dubnow liked to make use not only of a verse from the Bible or a saying of one of our sages, but also of a French or English *bon mot*.

Also in the ordinary sense of Jewish piety, Simon Dubnow was far from simple minded. Not only did he live in the stronghold of his theoretical, or more precisely abstract-ethical *credo*, he had during his period of synthesis, as he called it, a warm if concealed attitude to the Jewish traditional ritual observance for which time and again he would find a kind of secular excuse. I have already mentioned the *matzoth* in Bolshevik Petrograd. But also in democratic Berlin it became his custom to spend the first Seder night of the Passover at the Lestschinskys and the second at my brother's. On the Ninth of Ab my brother took him to the Synagogue to the "Lamentations" reading. Dubnow explained, "The Ninth of Ab is not a religious but a national day of mourning." On Shavuoth (Pentecost), he used to stop work and go walking in the woods around Grunewald, because as I heard him say, "Nature, when regarded face to face, can reveal to us the deepest secrets of Creation." During the year of mourning for my father, he occasionally joined us at prayers, and one evening going home with me after the service, he remarked suddenly: "The commemoration prayer (*Kaddish*) is a very important cultural institution. A pity that in our younger years we became too formalistic and lost the habit even of observing mourning anniversaries (*Yahrzeit*). The death of one's parents is an important chronological date in a man's life."

Much to my surprise, however, I discovered in the recesses of Dubnow's heart even a chord of true mysticism.

One of Dubnow's old friends, by training a naturalist, had, for a variety of reasons, come to the conclusion that he had been chosen to redeem the people of Israel and through them the world. This illumination descended on him nowhere else than in the middle of the Bois de Boulogne in Paris. The vision by which he was graced was a pair of scales suspended in the air whilst a voice commanded: "Take the scales in your hand." He obeyed and the scales in his outstretched right hand went up and down, up and down. And again the voice called out to him in sing-song, "Think a while!

Meditate, meditate!" The moment he heard this, his glance fell upon a tumble-down kiosk at the side of the driveway. Now his eyes were opened: the hut was "David's ruined *succah* (tabernacle)" and he grasped that he was called to "meditate" how the Temple could be rebuilt. A moment later all had vanished and what remained was the thought that he, the man of the vision, had the mission of redeeming the world.

He wrote of it at once to his old friend in Berlin. Who else but the great Jewish historian could be his adviser in his "world-historical" assignment? How great then was my astonishment when early one fine morning Dubnow telephoned me to say that he wanted to consult me on a matter which had nothing to do with our normal work, but was connected with my "sympathies with Messianism!" When subsequently he gave me the letter from Paris to read, he observed me closely to see what sort of impression it made on me. Then he inquired: "Do you think this is quite mad, or is there something in it?" In complete amazement I thought—Who is speaking? Is this the confirmed positivist, evolutionist and rationalist? The straight thinking father of Autonomism and Dubnowism?

Thus began for me, in partnership with Dubnow, a long and entangled chapter of practical "Messianism". The basic text was provided by the man of the vision, who had temporarily settled in Berlin, whilst the comments were formulated by me to the best of my abilities. Let me be brief. The whole world knows that to this very day it remains unredeemed. Both Dubnow and his friend have by now for many years passed on to the better world. Nevertheless, after thirty years the question still remains a question. What did it all mean? Was the source of Dubnow's very real and warm interest in the bizarre experience of his visitor from Paris merely an old affection for an old friend? Or was it perhaps no more than compassion for a man who had taken leave of his senses? (In other respects the visionary was entirely clear-headed and down to earth.) Or was there in the last resort something in the ultimate essence of Dubnow's personality that was even deeper than all his professed convictions and theories made explicit?

This supposition I believe to be the most realistic.

III

Seen from outside, Dubnow's main creation, his ten-storeyed "World History of the Jewish People", gives the impression of an architectural structure built according to strict and well-tried principles of modern design, with a frontage in symmetrical transparent style without any superfluous embellishment. In length, breadth and height, the whole edifice is evenly balanced. Behind this facade there are at once apparent the workings of an acute mind of strict planning. And that was indeed the chief impression made by Dubnow's sky-scraper on the general public in

Germany. When the structure was complete to its uppermost peak, the "Epilogue", people marvelled how it was possible for one man to achieve so much in so short a time—ten volumes in five years. "This is indeed cyclopean work" was the remark made to me by Professor Elbogen, the eminent German-Jewish historian, when the work was only half-finished (Dubnow himself used to call it "my own encyclopaedia"). And Elbogen said furthermore, "I have no doubt that we shall never again have a Jewish historian with courage equal to anything like this."

The professor's prognosis, as we know today, was not justified. All depends on courage, on the belief of the Jewish historian that his research work can go on throughout his life, without pause or break, which is the case of our people's whole story. The plea that quality, the true scientific spirit, does not go well with quantity, i.e. with a field of research too widely spread, is also not convincing. Once again, all depends on the intensity of "the courage", the determination that the historian brings to his research programme from the outset. Simon Dubnow proves it! Is he not indeed the living proof that where there's a will, there's a way? His confidence in his aims is the key to a comprehension of the "cyclopean" or "encyclopaedic" character of his achievement. It is especially important to appreciate the steadfastness of his will when one begins to read and study his major work. It is necessary, firstly to peruse it from beginning to end, more or less like a flowing many-volumed novel. Dubnow's "World History" is really no more, but also no less, than the biographical account of a hero—the People of Israel. The moment one becomes caught up in Dubnow's creative impulse, which is the inner spirit of Dubnow's creation, one is carried away by a torrent which bears the reader without pause from millennium to millennium, until they restore him to his own day and age.

Dubnow's courageous purpose, as I have already attempted to describe, lay in the security of his faith. But both, courage and confidence, drew their nourishment from a deeper source, from his overflowing love for his people. Can love be scientific? The answer to this is already anticipated. Master Simon embodies it! Just as his love for a person, an individual, would often arouse his warm interest in the man's individual history, in his relatives and dear ones, and even in his material needs and problems, so Dubnow's scientific method in Jewish history was inspired by his deep love for the Jewish people, both in respect of its spiritual development and the economic basis of that growth. In his own terminology he called it the "bio-sociological method". But only when one has a closer knowledge of Dubnow's inner character can one understand precisely what he meant by this. "Bios" means "life". To seek and to find in the great past of the Jewish people its spiritual and vital strength, to range retrospectively and look backwards to the origins of the "Jewish nation" and its profession of faith— "The People of Israel is alive!"—this was the historian's main endeavour and perpetually stimulated and renewed his own joy in life. Is it not natural for one who loves to take joy in every living characteristic of the beloved? In order to enjoy a full spiritual delight in Dubnow's magnificent edifice, it is necessary to share not only the creative urge and confidence of the builder, but even more so his illuminating love for the perennial tradition of "Israel the Old" wherever and whenever it existed.

Here one may ask: Is it not too metaphorical to talk of love for the historical life of a people as if it had anything to do without feelings for an individual? For the third time, therefore, let me say that Simon Dubnow and his sociological method is rather in tune with such imagery. His own interpretation of "sociological", should one seek a deeper understanding of it in the light of his personality, arose from his conviction that it is scientifically justifiable to regard a collective unit, such as the people of Israel, as an organic whole, as a single body with an everlasting collective soul which unifies in time and space all its widespread components. The date, 15 October 1931, when he had just completed his "Short Jewish History for Children", is marked by Dubnow with an entry in his diary: "The story of four thousand years in a little book—that was not easy," but "the hero of the story was throughout the people as a whole", that is to say, precisely as in his major work. It is therefore no figure of speech or exaggeration to say that, seen from within Dubnow's own character, his bio-sociological method was only a means of translating his subjective feelings, his love of his people, into an objectively conceived story in the form of a people's biography. Love works wonders. It has the power to make the abstract concrete, and to transform the general into the tangible particular.

It thus becomes clear that for Dubnow the principle "The People of Israel is alive!" was no more than another version of the formula, "The People of Israel is one", in both meanings of the word—one and unique. In a sense, a living creature is always both one as well as unique, in particular when it is the object of love. Then how could Dubnow, no matter what historical period he was dealing with, avoid stressing the objective and subjective conditions of Jewish unity? When he turned seventy and tried to draw up for his own benefit the sum of his labours, he set it down in his diary (25 September 1930) in these terms: "My only achievement. Not in vain have I toiled these fifty years. I have united East and West in one feeling."

In this context I wish to recall that in 1924 in Berlin, soon after his arrival in Germany, Dubnow became one of the founders of the "Jewish Scientific Association", the principal aim of which was to create a permanent link between East and West European Jewish scholars. As formerly in St. Petersburg, Dubnow held firmly to the principle that all three languages, Hebrew, Yiddish and the language of the country must have equal status, and he himself in Germany used Yiddish so that the Germans should know that Yiddish was also one of the languages of scientific research. At this time he was, by the way, also taking part in the founding of YIVO, the Institute for Jewish Research, and in 1930 the Dubnow Fund was established in his honour and with his blessing for the publication of a "General Encyclopaedia" in Yiddish.

The title page of Dubnow's principal work at once proclaims that the Jewish people—the hero of his ten-volume massive novel as well as of the love story of his own life—was for Dubnow unique "in its generations", unique among all nations of the world in all periods of Jewish existence. He called it, as we know a "World History". The term is, in its application to the story of one people, Dubnow's own coinage, a neologism, as he notes in the third volume of his autobiography. He tells there that originally he had his doubts as to such usage of the term and therefore consulted Professor David Koigen and me. "After some hesitation," he writes, "we came to the conclusion that the term was justified in the context of the history of Jews throughout the world, especially in the sense, so important to me, attaching it to the history of a "world-wide people not confined to a particular territory" (Russian original, pp. 41-42). Assuredly so! The crucial word in Dubnow's conception is "world-people", the people concerned being a world on its own. Thus, the history of this people is by definition a world-history. And this indeed was the true intention of the historian—to present his beloved hero, the people of Israel, in its own "centres of spiritual hegemony" and its "autonomous existence—an existence in its own right, as a separate entity both spiritually and materially.

Here we may inquire again: Is not such an approach to Jewish history entirely metaphysical, if not even mystical? How can it be reconciled with Dubnow's modern rationalism and with his own tendency to bring common sense to the treatment of even such extraordinary "historical manifestations" as, for example, the Patriarchs, the Exodus, the figure of Moses and the giving of the Law on Mount Sinai, up to the rise of a united people of Israel? In the light of Simon Dubnow's personality, it is possible, I believe, to dispose of the apparent contradiction by remembering that our own conception of the rationalism of the secular intelligentsia is far from exact. Not unlike the word "world", the word "worldly" has more than one meaning, and so has the philosophical idea of "rationalism". We learn from Dubnow's work that while presenting the plain meaning of Jewish history to his secularised "generations", Dubnow nevertheless in no sense disowned his inner faith, his enthusiastic appreciation of the great miracle of a world-people with its own world history. Again and again this pious enthusiasm of his wells up in the text of his narrative, especially when recording that in a time of trouble the remedy appeared to be at hand even before the disease. This happened, for instance, in the fourteenth century when the persecuted Jews of Germany found a land of refuge in Poland, which just at about that time was developing urban life. By the next century, the Ottoman Empire was powerful enough to accept the

Jews expelled from Spain. And almost in our own times, America was able
to rescue millions of Jews from Russia (see "World History", vol. V, p. 62;
vol. IV, p. 47 and p. 49; vol. X, p. 29). Although Dubnow describes such
events mostly as happy coincidences, his real intent is to show the hand of
Providence, since in respect of the historical destiny of the Jewish people
he was essentially not an agnostic but a believer. He not only lived and
died "in" his faith, but he also thought, worked and wrote in its spirit.

Shortly before the outbreak of World War II, I received in London from
Dubnow his last "Epilogue" to the "World History" (A Review of the
Historical Events of the Years, 1914-1938), with the following lines on the
title-page: "My wish is that in time you will be able to write a happier
epilogue." Let us hope that such a blessing will be fulfilled, and that in the
footsteps of Dubnow the Jewish people will produce a whole series of new
world-histories which will together ring out a rousing final chord. But even
that which is recorded here is in a certain sense correlated with it. It is
"epilogue" material, a testimony for the memorial which the Jewish world
is now erecting on the unknown grave of the biographer of all of us, whose
centenary we now celebrate.

7. The Two Sources of Simon Dubnow's Thought
On the 100th Anniversary of His Birth

In the homage paid throughout the Jewish world to the memory of Simon Dubnow on the occasion of the centenary of his birth, much emphasis is laid on the fact that he is claimed by our modern secularized historiography as its true progenitor. That this claim is fully justified is a view expressed by such a thinker as the late Simon Rawidowicz. Professor Koppel S. Pinson points in the same direction in his most valuable introduction to the volume of Dubnow's writings edited under the title *Nationalism and History* (Philadelphia, 1958). The underlying assumption in all statements of this nature is the tacit identification of Dubnow the historian with Dubnow the thinker. In other words, it is being taken for granted that since Dubnow's thinking was informed by the general secular trends of his time, his writing of history and, in particular, his *opus magnum*, the ten-volume *World History of the Jewish People*, must needs bear the same imprint and testify to the spirit of nineteenth-century secularism.

Is there no alternative to such an approach? Is it true that the ideas imbibed by Simon Dubnow in the early period of his worldy self-education were the only source of his general conception of Jewish history? Could it not be that even then, when he came under the spell of Auguste Comte's Positivism and Herbert Spencer's Evolutionism, the fountain-head of his inspiration remained, though hardly noticed by himself, the spiritual storehouse of his ancestry, the eternal truths of Judaism?

Bold as this question may sound, a thorough examination of Dubnow's crowning work, of its inner structure and the central idea which permeates the whole narrative, poses the amazing puzzle: How was it possible for a worldy-minded skeptic and agnostic, steeped in the methodological principles of modern science, to present the Jewish people as a unique phenomenon in universal history, with a "World History" all its own, with a staying power outweighing any accumulation of physical strength in the

This essay was first published in English in *Jewish Book Annual*, New York, 1961-62, Volume 19.

whole of humanity's past? It appears that the image of Dubnow the "free thinker" is strikingly inconsistent with his historical and historic master-piece; that the creation belies its creator; that his thought as reflected in the immense mirror of his main work is different from that revealed in his theories related to the contemporary currents of Jewish opinion and practical problems, for example, Zionism and Diaspora Nationalism.

The Complexity of Dubnow's Thought

In view of the complexity and apparent inconsistency of Dubnow's thought, any adequate presentation of its proper character has to be based on a clear distinction between its two main layers, the one nearer the surface and the other pointing in the direction of depth, each drawing its nourishment from a separate source. The confluence of both sources in the integrated personality and life of Simon Dubnow is the most impressive aspect of his biography as narrated by his daughter, Mrs. Sofia Dubnow-Erlich, and especially as expounded by himself in his three-volume autobiography with its sub-title, "Recollections and Meditations."

In the light of his self-awareness, Simon Dubnow remained faithful to the philosophical convictions he had hammered out for himself towards the end of his 20's. Since then he never ceased to believe that the principle of gradual evolution was the real clue to an all-comprehensive understanding of human destiny on earth. At the same time he firmly believed, in accordance with the first principles of sociology, that human life stood under the unrestricted rule of general laws which made it possible to provide a rational explanation for any sequence of historical events. Such were the fundamental ideas which Dubnow held in common with the avant-garde of contemporary Russian intelligentsia (see *World History*, vol. IX, para. 47, "The Cultural Revolution") and which determined the substance of the upper layer of his thought. And yet, beneath its surface other forces and factors were unceasingly at work, which in the end proved no less decisive in delineating the thinker's profile and in giving a coherent meaning to his whole life.

When in his early 30's Dubnow finally made up his mind to dedicate his life to Jewish historiography ("History has revealed herself to me," he recorded in his diary, quoting from Victor Hugo), his decision was far from being in line with Jewish secularism then current in Russia. The Jewish intellectuals around Dubnow did not care for the past of their people and would under no circumstances choose it as a subject of their study. No doubt Dubnow's original preference for his people's past derived from no other source than from this past itself.

With his first step, in essence an act of faith, the Jewish historian and his thought unavoidably became hostages to fortune, to the fate and fortunes of the Jewish people since the days of its creation. Every student of the philosophy of history knows of the inextricable interdependence of the historian and his chosen subject which, with the progress of study, increasingly gains momentum. The historian himself may or may not be aware of the "evolution" in the identification of his thought with its object, but the final result of his research will implicitly bear witness to the "law" which compels him to gravitate towards his material. This is exactly what happened to Simon Dubnow's thought. A parallel phenomenon can be found in the natural interplay between creation and creator in the domain of artistic activity, and we should not overlook the fact that the architect of the monumental Jewish "World History" was not only a historian and thinker but also an artist.

True, the terminology Dubnow adopted in his "pre-historical" phase was not discarded even in the final formulation of his "General Conception of Jewish History" dating from 1925 (see the mentioned volume edited by Prof. Pinson, pp. 336-353). A careful analysis, however, of the true meaning of the terms "sociological" and "biological" in the historian's own usage will disclose that Dubnow superimposed on them an entirely new connotation. In his autobiography he emphasizes that the term "World History," in its application to the history of the Jewish people, is in fact a "neologism" (see the Russian original, vol. III, pp. 41-42). In the same way the scientific reputation of sociology and biology served his purpose of presenting for the benefit of a secularized world the spiritual content of the story of Israel in modern guise.

Indeed, Dubnow describes his "general conception" as "sociological" not, as one should have expected, because his over-all purpose was to discover the general sociological laws governing the flow of events in the Jewish people's past. It was solely for the reason that, according to the "idea" he "derived from the totality of our history, the Jewish people has at all times and in all countries, always and everywhere, been the subject, the creator of his own history, not only in the intellectual sphere but also in the general sphere of social life" (English version in Pinson, l.c., p. 338 and particularly p. 351). Thus we find once more that in Dubnow's usage "sociology" and "sociological" are "neologisms" and that above all the new connotation is based on an "idea" inspired by the material of Jewish history.

A similar transformaton took place in Dubnow's attitude to the natural sciences and in particular to biology, the basis of his constant affirmation of the principle of evolution. Though his *credo* in the Introduction to his "World History" includes the article demanding that Jewish historiography should be placed "upon a firm bio-sociological foundation" (1.c, p. 342), in his actual exposition the historian never tries to explain the content and continuity of the Jewish past by deducing it from accepted general biological principles. Life, "bios," is to him first and foremost the conspicuous characteristic of the historical existence of the Jewish people as an "organic collective individuality," ever growing in stature in its endless struggle for autonomy and independence, always impelled by its innate will to survive as a separate "nation." This singular notion of a collective will may partly be traced back to the "volonté générale" of the romantic Jean Jacques Rousseau, but never to the sober teachings of modern biology. The real source of this whole idea, so relevant to Dubnow's thinking, lies obviously elsewhere; it is hidden and revealed once again in the very facts of Jewish history and in the spirit which holds them all together.

The Enigma of Jewish Survival

In consonance with the "secularization of the Jewish national idea" Simon Dubnow endeavored to revise Jewish history in the light of modern rationalistic secularism; instead, Jewish history brought about a revision of his original endeavor. Despite the fact that he meticulously avoided in his ten-volume narrative reference to any factor of a supernatural character, the sum total of all the related events, of their natural causes and effects, i.e. the survival of the Jewish people, remained to the narrator an enigma, and for this we have his own authority.

In 1912, when Simon Dubnow was well beyond the midway of his life and was making final preparations for his crowning feat, he published an essay in Hebrew entitled, "The Mystery of Survival and the Law of Survival" (the English version now available in Pinson, pp. 325-335). While Russian was the language of Dubnow's brain and Yiddish that of his heart, Hebrew came to him *M'maamakim,* "out of the depths" of his soul. How significant then are the opening sentences of his authentic testimony: "We are confronted with a great and hidden mystery. We try to penetrate the depths of this mystery, the secret of the survival of the Jewish people, and to fathom the forces acting within the soul of the people, forces whose results lie often before us but whose inner workings are shrouded in darkness, like all basic forces operating in the souls of both individual and community." He goes on to say that "miraculous and unique" as the historical destinies of old Israel may be, in order to penetrate the veil of this mystery we have to approach it under the aspect of reason in applying to it the rationally conceived general laws of social science. This essay is a confession and a manifesto. Until the very end Dubnow's thought was incessantly active on both planes, on that of "sweet reasonableness" and of a mysticism only rarely avowed. How else could he have erected his magnificent edifice with its clearly and symmetrically articulated facade, but entirely dedicated to his mystical, passionate love for his chosen people?

The deeper source of Simon Dubnow's thought, mostly indiscernible from the outside, was always at the threshold of his mind. His reflections on the subdued conflict between the rational and irrational elements of his soul fill many pages of his diaries, and it is most telling that the first of his "Meditations" appended to his autobiography bears the title, "The Integration of the Soul" (vol. III, pp. 125-131). Can such an integration be achieved at all?—asks the thinker; and the historian replies—only by conceiving one's life as a meaningful whole.

No doubt Simon Dubnow's end is the ineffaceable seal on the integration of his blessed personality.

8. The Impact of History as a Discipline on Contemporary Historical Experience

Some fifty years ago, Wilhelm Windelband, the eminent historian of philosophy, ventured to predict that as much as the 19th century deserved the title "the scientific century", the 20th was likely to be distinguished by posterity as the "historical" one ("das historische Jahrhundert"). Rapid progress in all fields of historical research, the growing interest which the generations to come would take in this progress, and the deep influence the unprecedented concentration of the human mind on historical problems might exercise on the destiny of humanity as a whole, would—Windelband thought—in the end produce a new phase in universal history, as different from the preceding past as the age of triumphant science differs from its own merely preparatory stages. Having gained certainty about the possibility of extending its domination over Nature indefinitely, the human mind would at last turn to the conquest of History, once more relying on the irresistible power of rational delimitation and penetration of the object to be brought under control. As Scientific Man in the sphere of Nature, so Historical Man in his specific sphere would be enabled to advance by methodological elucidation both of the goal ahead and the best means to its attainment.

Such expectations were obviously based on a philosophy of history which implied, inter alia, the possibility of turning the results of historical research to practical account in the same way as mathematical knowledge and exact or descriptive natural sciences find their technological application in the service of every-day human needs. Kant's Idealism is, of course, the epistemological background against which this kind of reasoning must appear most plausible. Indeed, if it be true, as the Neo-Kantian School of Marburg (Cohen, Natorp, Cassirer) taught, that there is no nature apart from the "nature of natural science", i.e. from that constructed on foundations a priori in a steady process of scientific exploration; and if, on the other hand, Windelband, Rickert, Lask, and their followers of the German "South-West School" were right in opposing

This essay was first published in English in the Proceedings of the XIth International Congress of Philosophy, Volume XIV (Additional Volume and Contributions to the Symposium on Logic), Brussels, 20-26 August 1953 (North-Holland Publishing Company, Amsterdam; Editions E. Nauwelaerts, Louvain).

History to Nature as a methodologically autonomous province of knowledge with a priori foundations of its own—then the anticipation of an age characterised by prevalence of the historical interest acquires clear philosophical meaning. It would be an age in which "history" as res gestae, as an empirical process, would present itself, in the idealistic perspective, as a gradual projection on to the screen of reality of a coherent system of the universal historia rerum gestarum; an age—in which "applied history" would become, in analogy to applied science, a singularly practical proposition.

The idealistic approach in its radical form which asserts the logical precedence of conceiving, interpreting and preserving history in relation to any flow of occurrences in time lays bare, quite independently of the general philosophical conception at its base, a problem of vital importance not only for the understanding of our time, but also for one's free choice between the various available blueprints designed to quicken our pace on the road to the future. In full accord with earlier predictions, our century has indeed revealed itself as a time of formidable experiments in shaping universal history; moreover, all the initiated attempts in this direction have been undertaken on the strength of some pre-conceived philosophy of history derived from a more or less unbiased study of the recorded past. In other words, the general trend of our time, the contemporaneous "Zeitgeist", appears to be tinged by the originally idealistic belief that history as an empirical process may become essentially dependent on the skilful application of historical knowledge integrated in all embracing generalisations. The problem thus facing us can aptly be traced back to Nietzsche's enquiry as to the "Use and Abuse of History" ("Vom Nutzen und Nachteil der Historie für das Leben" in "Urzeitgemässe Betrachtungen", 1874). A closer re-examination of this problem might indicate that the very idea of man's limitless mastery over history is studded with pitfalls both in the theoretical and practical spheres.

However, before proceeding any further let us recall the relevant facts.

For a period extending over more than three and a half decades, a school of historical thought, priding itself on the exclusive possession of adequate knowledge of the past attained allegedly by virtue of an infallible method of approach and based on a philosophy of history embracing the future not less than the past, is persistently carrying out a gigantic experiment in "applied history". True, the general philosophy of this school is not "idealism" but "materialism", and its historiosophy is specifically labelled as the "materialistic conception of history". The student of the history of philosophy can, nevertheless, hardly fail to recognise in the teachings of Marx, the progenitor of the Russian school of "dialectical materialism", their hereditary components deriving from Hegel and thus, once removed, from Kant. Were it not for the "Copernican Revolution" in metaphysics proclaimed by Kant in 1787, many a subsequent revolution would perhaps have taken a different course. Be that as it may, there is a well discernible thread connecting the modern conception of Man as the maker of history with the main idea of the *"Critique of Pure Reason"* that "objects have to conform with our apprehension". Yet another fundamental idea inherent in the Marxian conception of universal history clearly derives from the rationalistic idealism of the 18th century. It is the dogmatic conviction that with the discovery of the economic factor as the "true" substance of the historical process the latter was bound to be transformed, thanks to the newly discovered truth, once and for all into a process of man-made history, ever more thoroughly planned and ever more forcefully directed.

Other instances of man's self-reliance in the field of "applied history" witnessed in our time possess the same symptomatic significance as the Marxian experiment. Racialism, too, presented itself to the world as a philosophy of history intended to be applied in the practice of historical life. Within this conception, "superior" race was assigned the same revolutionary role in the drama of world history, which the proletariat, "the chosen class" in Boulgakov's phrase, had assumed in the historical conception of Marxism. Once more history was singled out as a target for a mass experiment in the course of which the natural condition of human life, the very physique of man, was to have undergone a violent change. Thus, in the perspective of modern historical conceptions, the distance from pure reason to absurdity appears not much greater than the step from the sublime to the ridiculous in the days of Napoleon.

Many other instances, even if on a smaller scale, could be cited to illustrate the modern belief in man's boundless power to alter the very course of historical life on the basis of historical study. A case in point is the recent ill-starred attempt to resuscitate the ancient Roman Empire on the shores of the Mediterranean. Even such an event as the revival of a Jewish State in Palestine could hardly have materialized in an age less possessed than ours by the idea of history as a planned effort.

Considered from the philosophical point of view, modern totalitarianism with its concentration of oligarchic power appears not as an end in itself but rather as a technical invention in the service of the guiding idea of the century. The "volonté générale" of our democratic age induces, as it were, the individual to forgo his personal freedom ad maiorem gloriam Hominis, with a capital H. The most modest share in the "greater freedom" of man-made history has become the price of subservience and self-abnegation.

Simultaneously, Historical Man has learned how to harness written history to the paramount task of history-making. He writes and re-writes it as he goes, to adjust even the remotest past to the particular needs of the present, for the sake of an anticipated future. In a truly paradoxical way, the higher criticism of the sacred books, which flourished in the last century, has in our time brought about a marked propensity not to rejct but to overdo the "unmasked" historiography of antiquity by deliberate distortion and falsification of facts. New "Bibles" have been produced, the heroes in charge of experimental history have been invested with superhuman abilities, and prophecy has become the natural charisma of those who were supposed to hasten the advent of the Millennium.

If Nietzsche were to renew today his enquiry as to the "use and abuse of history" he might have recoiled from his own qualified appraisal of history's "usefulness" advanced at a time when the specific impulse given by "monumental history" to forceful personalities was still a thing of the future. A special effort to eliminate the sting from the challenge of the Historical Man has recently been made in England. However, the impressive attempt of the new English School of philosophy of history (initiated by Oakshott and Collingwood from the idealistic point of view, by Toynbee on a positivistic basis, and by Butterfield on the basis of faith) to restrict historical thought to the past and to divert it from the temptation to divine the future seems to be of no avail on the philosophical plane, since the deeper roots of our time's aberration are left untouched.

Indeed, how could modern historical thinking be converted to see things historical exclusively sub specie praeteritorum, as postulated by Oakshott or Collingwood, while the epistemological presuppositions of the modern experiments in historical prognostication, and of all it practically implies, remain undiscerned and the limitations inherent in those premises are not recognised?

To modern man, the historical process, both as reflected in written history and projected into the future, seems to present a phenomenon differentiated within the realm of knowable nature by the singularity that throughout this process human nature appears constantly as the natura naturata which is simultaneously a natura naturans. Mainly by reason of this coincidence, the historical process is appraised as the most workable material for rational penetration as far as the past is concerned, and for rational prefabrication in respect of the future. In strict contradiction to Kant's critical idealism, according to which creativeness regarding nature can be attributed to the human mind only under the supposition of the hypothetical existence of the "thing in itself", the Historical Man of our time, though inadvertently acting under the spell of the idealistic conception, has entirely failed to grasp the essential meaning of the "thing in itself" as a "regulative idea". This fundamental notion has been discarded both in relation to nature and to history.

This misconception of the true spirit of the idealistic tradition may well be at the root of many perversions typical of our "historical century". For with the abandonment of the "regulative idea" embodied in the "thing in itself", man has become soulless, a phenomenon pure and simple, uncorrelated to any noumenon—an apparition to others not less than to himself, essenceless in his existence, and consequently a Proteus-like object of experimental history. A post mortem analysis of the contemporary history-makers strikingly confirms that they believed to be merely the tools of an impersonal fate, of the all-embracing historical process they appeared to drive forward.

It is obvious that in such a world of unsubstantial history, with phantoms as its protagonists, encompassed by a nature which is itself of a purely spectral character, there is no room for values other than of a relative, transient significance. The metaphysics, ethics and also the aesthetics of our time are intertwined with its predominant philosophy of history. They all bear the mark of the devastation produced in the human mind by its loss of contact with the absolute, be it even in the guise of a necessary presupposition of a coherent system of philosophy. The unprecendented rise of history as a discipline and the annexation by modern historiosophy of practically the whole sphere of influence previously reserved to a hierarchy of philosophical disciplines are the characteristic symptoms of this situation.

Can it be reversed? It appears that to this end it would first be necessary to re-establish the principle that man's mind is commensurable with the idea of the absolute. With the reaffirmation of the relationship between the individual human being and the absolute, a limit would be set both to the dependence of man on the everchanging conditions of historical life and to the senseless ambition of fellow-men arbitrarily to determine the meaning of personal existence. In consequence, philosophy of history would lose its disproportionate influence, and the unhealthy excess of the general interest in historical findings (which, incidently, can never be final) would disappear. A regenerated idealistic tradition would help to restore to Historical Man that humbleness of mind without which there can be no genuine step forward along the road to freedom.

9. The Man of Tomorrow

In projecting the image of the Man of Today onto the screen of Tomorrow, our mind's eye is turned not towards today's sunset, but towards tomorrow's new sunrise, towards a new morning in the calendar of universal history. We aspire to a new age, prompted and compelled to do so under the impact of what was fittingly described as "cultural uneasiness". Since the middle of the last century, the oncoming twilight has been foreshadowed in many a noble heart by anxiety and anguish. Today we are bracing ourselves by a concentrated effort to pierce the veil of the future, to look beyond the threatening darkness, and to meet the ancient challenge, "Watchman, what of the night?" (Isaiah 21,11-12) with the hopeful response: What of the Day, what of the Morrow?

By these exertions, contemporary thought is indulging neither in prophecy nor in crystal-gazing. Its firm ground is historical knowledge, a sober analysis of the human condition at the present time, and philosophical conviction extending on a broad front—from traditional faith to Positivism—according to which Man is free—free in anticipation of the future, freely to participate in its final forming.

Past and Present

History teaches us that, like nature which abhors a vacuum, the process of universal history is a *continuum* in which there is no room for unbridgeable gaps. Whatever the ideal Man of Tomorrow will be, whether, in the terms of our theme, essentially a "Scientist" or a "Humanist", or both in personal union—as the substratum of a new phase in mankind's destiny—he will certainly incorporate, willingly or unwillingly, the Man of Today, and the Man of Yesterday, and even the Day-Before-Yesterday. If that be true, any speculation in respect of the ideal Man to Come must be based on an adequate idea of the human mind and its intrinsic tendencies in our own day. Only on such a basis will it be possible to form a view as to whether the so widely-spread forebodings of the contemporary prophets of doom are grounded in fact and, further,

The text of this address delivered at the Seventh General Conference of International Non-Governmental Organizations attached to Unesco, held in Paris in June 1960, was first published in English in *World Jewry*, London, September 1960, Volume III, No. 9, and in *Jewish Affairs*, Johannesburg, 1960, Volume 19, No. 12.

whether it is justifiable to expect that the Man of Tomorrow will be vigorous enough to shake off the deficiencies of the mentality of modern Man, which are coming to the fore throughout the habitat of the human race. And who knows, perhaps the revival of the Man of Yesterday in the Man of Today will in the end reveal itself as the best answer to all our anxieties regarding the future of the *Homo Sapiens?*

The sub-title of our theme, "The Scientist and the Humanist", which points to the growing tension between the two main streams of modern intellectual endeavour, implicitly suggests that, for the sake of the Man of Tomorrow, it is our task to examine the possibilities of a reconciliation between the exponents of the two seemingly incompatible attitudes of mind and to explore the ground for a mutual understanding. Here, indeed, we are putting our finger on the sorest point of our modern civilisation, including its educational system, the safeguard of its continuity. The rift between the Scientist and the Humanist, which widens steadily and makes both inaudible to one another, concerns us all, and not the world of learning alone: *De nobis fabula narratur!*

Splitmindedness

C. P. Snow has strikingly brought into relief the fact that we all begin to breathe the air of "two cultures", thus exposing ourselves to the dangers of splitmindedness. This is, of course, the effect of the "Scientific Revolution" which has forced the Man of Today to succumb to its spell. At the same time, the human values inherited from the past, Religion, moral principles, the autonomy of the beautiful, and, more than that, the autonomy and independence of the individual, appear to be on the down-grade, condemned to disintegrate with the further progress of Science. Is the Humanist still able to stand up against this devastating onslaught?

One thing must be clear from the outset. The magnetic attraction of Science working on the mind of the Man of Today is due not to the highly developed logic of scientific research, nor to the whole apparatus of checks and balances by which scientific progress is kept constantly on the move—science is worshipped mainly and chiefly for its palpable results, for the marvels of its application in everyday life, or more precisely, for the amenities derived from modern technology. In humanistic terms, the ascendancy of the scientific disposition in our time is rooted in the hedonistic propensities of modern Man wherever he may dwell on earth. Would the Scientist, be he an exponent of pure or applied Science, agree to take the responsibility for this by-product of the scientific-cum-technological progress? If he did, he would divest himself of his specific privileges *qua* scientist and express no more than a "subjective" opinion. In his own strictly scientific confines, the Scientist is logically bound to profess and to exercise disinterestedness in all questions affecting Man's moral dignity.

This was not always so. In the age of the Renaissance of Science and Art, which preceded and prepared the age of Humanism, men of the stature of a Giovanni Pico de la Mirandola based their discourses *De hominis dignitate* on science not less than on a vast spiritual tradition comprising even the Jewish Kabbalah. Descartes lives in our memory as the author of the *Discours de la Méthode* and as the founder of Analytical Geometry as well; the name of Blaise Pascal is inscribed both in the annals of philosophy and of science, and so is the name of Leibniz. It is this intellectual universalism which already in the Middle Ages inspired the Jewish humanist and scientist, Moses Ben Maimon (Maimonides).

Philosophy "Undesirable"

However, after the bifurcation of the one highway of human culture became historical fact, the ensuing mutual alienation between the Scientist and the Humanist imposed on the latter a new task, that of accounting not only for his won creed, but also for the creed of incredulity, of sceptical aloofness, of agnosticism propounded by the Scientist in regard to all things which, in the phrase of the Book of Daniel, cannot be "numbered, weighed and measured" (Dan. 5, 25). For, whilst the Scientist is supposed, in conformity with his methodical principles, to discard any trace of subjectivity, looking away as far as possible even from his own self, the Humanist accepts no science outside the History of Science, which is to him indissolubly intertwined with the history of Man's creative activity in all its aspects, with all its attainments and aberrations.

Whereas the Scientist is inclined to disregard the strivings and findings of the Humanist as though at best they were the efforts and achievements of an artistic character, to the Humanist science is science, whatever the philosophical superstructure may be which is often put on top. And this for the simple reason that "scientific philosophy" is by the very definition of the notion "Science" a contradiction in terms. One can safely say that the Scientist's motto is *Humani omne a me alienum puto* which, in his empire, automatically reduces philosophy to the status of an undesirable "alien". In other words, whereas to the Humanist the Scientist is one of his own kith and kin, his scientific "relations" reject him as an undisciplined and illegitimate intruder in their enlightened midst.

Crucial Poser

And yet, in his unflagging effort to restore the ancient unity to integrity, the Humanist keeps a crucial poser in reserve for the unsympathetic

Scientist: How can it be explained scientifically that within the endless cosmological process its whole majestic magnitude should become revealed in such a cosmologically negligible space of time as the six to seven thousand years of mankind's recorded history? If the unknown and unimagined universe is to be represented by the idea of pure indefinable Being shrouded in utter darkness, is it not the marvel of marvels that this all-comprehending object of science stands at this moment of astronomical time suddenly revealed in its fantastic dimensions, all thanks to a chink—narrow as narrow can be—torn in the curtain—thick as thick can be—which divided darkness from light, the Universe from the Knowledge of the Universe? Is it possible to deny that, in the light of this heroic feat, Man who brought it about occupies by the very standards of modern science a unique place in Nature? And if so, is he not worthy of special study on the same scale as the objects of the natural sciences, though in a different way, in accordance with the human condition which is partly sub-human, yet partly super-human?

In this context, let us remember the immortal words of Pascal: *"Qu'est ce que l'homme dans la nature? Un néant à l'égard de l'infini, un tout à l'egard du néant, un milieu entre rien et tout"*. ("What is man in Nature? A cypher compared with the Infinite, an All compared with Nothing, a mean between zero and all.") (*Pascal's Penseés*, trans. by H. F. Stewart)—*"Un tout"*—a whole world!

Modern science predisposes the Man of Today to overlook this aspect of his essence; the humanities are trying to keep this notion alive by building up the universal history of Mankind. Under the impact of applied science the *homo technologicus* of our time is tempted to worship the work of his own hands, like the idolator of the days of old, expecting to be awarded by his idol with the benefits of material prosperity; the humanities remind him that in the past his self-respect was based on the idea of his Godlikeness. The Scientist says: I don't know whether God exists; the Humanist is justified in replying: Well then, let us see what the idea of God-likeness stands for!

According to the Jewish tradition, the first chapters of the Book of Genesis relating to the creation of Adam in the likeness of God imply that any single human being is as unique—irreplaceable by any other human being—as the Universe and its Creator are unique. In contrast to all other creatures created "after their kind"—emphasises the Talmud—Adam appears alone, to teach us that to sustain one single man is equal to the sustenance of the whole creation (Sanhedrin iv, 5). Whatever the Scientist may think about the existence of a transmundane Creator, he will hardly oppose the self-assertion of Man as the crown of creation and his claim to be chosen to rise above his own level and to direct his own evolution.

If that much could be agreed upon by the two parties, the Scientist and the Humanist, then there is hope for the Man of Tomorrow. Many a danger could thereby be warded off. It would become possible to conceive a universal cultural policy aiming at a balance of power as far as the scientific and the humanistic elements of education are concerned. Philosophy might once more get afloat and resuscitate the ideal of Man's perfection both in the intellectual and emotional spheres, in theory and in practice. The overgrowth of specialisation, which—to use "Zarathrustra's" simile—sometimes prompts the research worker to inquire into the workings of the non-existent brain of the leech, would disappear. But first and foremost, the freedom of the individual persistently assaulted in our time from so many directions would become as sacred as it was yesterday and the day-before-yesterday. If for no other reason, this prospect alone may give to both the Scientist and the Humanist a new impulse to delineate their respective spheres of interest and to join forces in the service of their common cause—the freedom of the Man of Tomorrow.

10. Hermann Cohen as Educator

> The grave threat which lies hidden in modern, supposedly crystal-clear enlightenment is the belief that it destroys only religion, whereas, in fact, it simultaneously jeopardizes ethics and all philosophy.
>
> Cohen—"Ethics of Pure Will"

Almost four years have passed since the death of Hermann Cohen. The complicated circumstances of our own age have not yet permitted the "Society for the Dissemination of Enlightenment among Jews in Russia" to respond to the passing of this outstanding European thinker and Honorary Member of the Society. The first available opportunity must be used. The four years which separate us from Cohen's death, years of great upheaval and great change both in Russia and in Cohen's native Germany, not only fail to blur the imposing image of the late thinker; but make him all the more significant, and present his life work even more clearly in its true historical light. The laws of perspective in time are different from those in space: as they fade into the past, great historical occurrences do not diminish, but rather increase in their dimensions; great men of the contemporary age grow into heroes; defenders of ideas are gradually transformed into creators of historical life, thinkers—into rulers of destiny. The furious tempo of recent years makes these last four, which were so completely saturated with events, seem like a long historical period; an entire epoch divides us from that day on which the wise, aged Cohen passed away—and we come to his grave not merely to "question the deceased about the living"; we preserve a memory not of a monument; rather we continue that living dialogue into which Cohen drew not only his contemporaries, but even more so—his teachers, his successors, and all those for whom his books are not merely valuable relics—but a source of life and living instruction. Cohen is alive. That is the message which we already have the right to utter at his graveside.

But, if Cohen is alive, then it is for us to speak. We do not question him—rather he poses questions for us and forces us to answer; he continues to teach us, and consequently, to educate us—because, as

This essay was first published in Russian in *Yevreyskaya Mysl*, St. Petersburg, 1922, and later in Yiddish in *Davke*, Buenos Aires, 1958, No. 33/34.

122

Cohen stated, "the problem of education is the problem of instruction"; this according to him is the most valuable kernel of the precepts of Socrates and of Hellenic wisdom in general. "Without logic, there can be no ethics. Outside this foundation there can be no truthfulness because there is no truth." Thus Cohen, as a living teacher of the present generation and of the following ones, must be one of the integral elements of their education for conscious activity whilst our urgent problem is to realize his lasting educational significance.

What does Cohen teach us? What would he want to instill in us? How did he rise to the rank of our spiritual guide, to one of our "eternal companions"? It is possible here to answer these questions only in the most general terms and only from the Jewish point of view. But more than ever, in the given instance, the Jewish point of view coincides with the general human one, because Cohen, as one of the acknowledged educators and teachers of the Jews, teaches us first and foremost the spirit of systematic philosophy, which knows neither Greek nor Jew; and secondly, he teaches us to recognize clearly the place of philosophy in the system of a unified culture of unified humanity. So, the third foundation of his world-view, his conception of Judaism, confronts us as one of the chapters of the philosophical interpretation of universal history. If it was still possible to doubt the vitality of his teaching during his lifetime, then in the current storm we realise even more clearly than before that the question of the existence or non-existence of the Jews is a problem of philosophy of history, that there is no culture outside philosophy, and that philosophy is effective only within a system. We shall examine each of the three precepts of Cohen and Cohenianism separately. In our interpretation by means of this three-sided approach, both the personality of the philosopher, and his life's work will emerge in all their natural simplicity with all its multi-coloured variations.

I

"Philosophy is systematic philosophy"—Cohen never tired of repeating this in all his systematic works as though these words were his battle cry. In order to evaluate the significance of this seemingly pleonastic utterance—one which, like a glittering drop of water, reflects the entire inspiration of Cohen's work and the ardent passion of his oratorical style—one must clarify the role which fell to Cohen in the philosophical life of the second half of the last century. Herein lies the key to the understanding of Cohen's place not only in the history of German philosophy, but of European philosophy in that period in general; and hence light can be shed on the internal philosophical development of Cohen himself: the originality of an individual thinker is most clearly outlined in its natural and inescapable limits.

At the time when Cohen definitely recognised his philosophical vocation and turned from the humble rabbinical path to that of a teacher of philosophy, philosophy lingered in Europe almost in a state of inertia; even "the country of thinkers" designated its philosophy and philosophers, in Nietzche's accurate phrase, as its *Gedankenwirtschaft* and *Gedankenwirte*—a complete parallel with other practising experts. The fields which had been plowed up by preceding generations of giants were merely covered with manure and artifically fertilized; no one had the courage to deal with virgin land. Philosophy was transformed into the history of philosophy, and the history of philosophy—into the history of human delusions and fallacies. Owing to Fredrich Albert Lange, though due to no fault of his own, the condescending attitude towards philosophy as the "poetry of concepts" became current. Kant and critical philosophy fell to "philological criticism". The vainglorious Schopenhauer attained at long last his posthumous fame: pessimism became the fashion and the collapse of the grandiose systems of the past met with almost general applause. Like all of Germany, intoxicated with its physical might, so, too, German Jewry had withdrawn into itself in all its helplessness, continuing to live on the crumbs of its poor Mendelssohnian heritage and feebly defending itself against the anti-Semitic demagogy.

It was at this time that a little known Marburg professor published his first work: "Kant's Theory of Experience" (1871). It would be difficult in this modest, conscientious, thoughtful (in the German sense), refined (in the Talmudic sense) commentary to the "Critique of Pure Reason" to divine something more than the book claimed to do: to think out and verify anew the critical formulation of the problem of knowledge. And this is how it was accepted. Cohen's book attracted attention as one of the events in the Neo-Kantian movement. Since then the fame of a subtle and difficult commentator on Kant has remained with Cohen and, like a ghost, persistently followed him even when Kant was left way behind and Cohen had begun to reinterpret and then to criticize—and finally, feeling certain of himself, he progressed to his own independent "System of Philosophy". But in fact, from the very first steps, Cohen proceeded along a path which was completely new for his own generation. Kant served merely as a device for self-testing, a voluntarily imposed act of obedience, because Cohen was not attracted by the historically correctly recorded works of Kant, but venerated the spirit of Kantianism. And the spirit of Kantianism was to him from the very beginning the spirit of systematic philosophy.

Indeed, already in "Kant's Theory of Experience" the general plan of the commentary to the most fundamental of Kant's three "Critiques" did not tempt Cohen to follow slavishly Kant's own path of literary development simply out of admiration for his teacher. The commentator's first work was devoted not to an interpretation of the fundamental component of the canon of Kantianism, but to the very problem of theoretical philosophy, in other words, to the philosophy of being. Thus, even in his first work, Cohen included the fundamentals of the teleological approach developed by Kant in conjunction with his philosophy of art in his "Critique on the Force of Judgement", along with the theory of scientific knoweldge. Forging anew the weapon of criticism, the Kantian Cohen ventures to treat the heritage of his master as though it was raw material: working on it, Cohen reshapes it in the furnace of his own genius. Under the pressure of Cohen's thought, Kant's texts are ground to a fine dust and reintegrated into new components. Cohen's books of this so-called first period represent in this respect what may be a singular phenomenon in all philosophical literature. Here, between the crushing millstones of two systematic minds, the reader witnesses the consistent process of creation of a philosophical system. The boulders of Kant's cyclopean structures were the hard granite upon which Cohen learned his art of fine craftsmanship in chiselling the "Philosopher's Stone". The disciple struggles with the master, and in this singular duel he hardens himself for battle with all the anti-philosophical tendencies of his contemporary culture.

Of course this is only one facet—perhaps the most external facet at that—of Cohen's first major work. Far more important than his unconstrained treatment of the Kantian literary heritage, is his perspective on the entire philosophical system which is clearly revealed in his very approach to Kant. In connection with his exposition of the full significance of the Kantian antinomies, there emerges the problem of freedom, i.e., the problem of philosophical, systematic ethics, rooted in logic. Thus his "Kantian Foundation of Ethics" (1877) and "Kantian Foundation of Aesthetics" (1889) were the natural sequence of his first work. Even this order of Cohen's works, repeating that of Kant's three "Critiques", appeared to be no more than the faithfulness of a disciple. But such an evaluation reflects the general lack of understanding for genuine originality in the philosophical literature of that time. The choice itself of developing a system already foreshadowed "deep waters". In this style Cohen was preceded only by the great German idealists, while in his own generation only the historians of philosophy—with their necessarily limited philosophical horizons—took an interest in Kant as a whole. That is why Cohen's interest in "all of Kant's works" in itself bore witness to the fact that he revived that spirit of post-Kantian systematic philosophy, which had seemingly gone out forever. Could neo-Kantianism without Cohen have preserved the Kantian theory of knowledge at the cost of conceding all remaining philosophical problems to positivism? And did not Cohen object to this "bad peace", demanding philosophy's natural and ancient boundaries? The future demonstrated that this was so.

However, even that answer is not completely accurate. In fact, this first period of Cohen's literary activity, in spite of its subordination to the problem of Kantianism, far surpasses in importance those purely historical results of "Kant's rehabilitation" which are usually connected with it. In other words, it would have been impossible to rehabilitate Kant in all his historical authenticity if, in order to defend him, it had been impossible to defend him against himself. The deeper Cohen went into the problem of the Kantian system, the more decisively he began not only to transpose and to modify, but also to sweep aside, and to combine more and more new elements from outside and from himself. The thirty years which separate "Kant's Theory of Experience" from "The Logic of Pure Knowledge" (1902), the first volume of Cohen's "System of Philosophy", present us with the uninterrupted growth of a single organically expanding world-view. Even if it may be true, as it is sometimes thought that Cohen's originality consists merely in his original synthesis of Kantianism and Hegelianism—even then, one must search for the first stages of this complex process of synthesis in the very first works of one of the greatest European thinkers of recent generations. We will be convinced of this as soon as we take into account that fundamental concept with which we began—Cohen's concept of systematic philosophy.

What is Cohen's idea of systematic philosophy? To answer this question, it is best to turn to the clearest point of divergence between Cohen and Kant at its earlier stages. This is the problem of "the thing in itself". Just as immediately following Kant this problem aroused Maimon to doubt the correctness of Kant's path, and then through Maimon, it again determined the future development of philosophy towards a philosophy of the Absolute, so too did this problem expose once again the impossibility of returning to Kant and stopping just where he did. If in Kant's "Copernican deed", by virtue of which it was not reason which had to revolve around objects, but the objects around reason, some sort of meaning could still be preserved only if a single centre was admitted in the ratiocentric system. But the Kantian world is dominated by a central dualism; on the one hand, there is the nature of mathematical science, i.e., the result of methodical intelligence, and its being is existence in scientific thinking; on the other hand, reason itself moves methodically only in the direction of a goal given to it from without, towards that objectivity rooted in chaotic sensory material, which, self-contained like a thing in itself, constantly entices it to a tireless, but equally fruitless chase after it. We are not transcending our own boundaries, rather they are constantly broadening because there is some centripetal force lying outside which drives us to rise above ourselves in our knowledge. Thus in the realm of conscience the thing in itself paves the way for a duality which leads unavoidably to a multiplicity of dominating principles with its final dissolution of any principles at all. Kant's conception takes us to crossroads: if one proceeds straight on after him—then one must sacrifice the principle of consistent unity; to relinquish the autocracy of reason in the world is tantamount to opening one's heart to romantic mysticism for there is no break-through from closed human consciousness to the other-worldly realm in itself but that of mysterious insight and vague forebodings. Thus there remains the third possibility of rejecting the world which would not be a world of reason and logic from beginning to end. This is Cohen's choice. Cohen is a panlogist.

But this transition from Kant to Hegel, perhaps through the intermediacy of the concept of space held by the mathematician G. Grassman, a transition entirely predetermined in Cohen's first work, is in no way a break with Kant or a betrayal of him. Cohen seeks and finds in Kant himself all those allusions which, making Kantian relativism absolute, allows him to revere and to read Kant according to Hegel. Kant's "thing in itself" stands before us as an idea, i.e. as an eternal problem of knowledge itself. That which is understood within consciousness itself as its provisional external limit, is the external for knowledge, singled out as such in order that the progress of knowledge should lead to infinity making the endless progress of science rational. Thus the alogical emerges as a factor in the very organism of Logos as a necessary logical prerequisite.

It would be a misunderstanding to assume that Cohen himself ever realized that his work constituted a return of Hegel into the fold of Kant. For Cohen Hegel always was and remained a Spinozist and, hence, a romantic. Spinozism, according to Cohen, is pantheism which is not able to distinguish the existing from that which ought to be, and consequently, does not even recognize the problem of ethics. The genuine theme which forced Cohen to reform Kant according to Hegel is the decisive theme for his whole pursuit of philosophy: the theme of unity coincidental with the need for a systematic approach. The original sin against the principle of unity is revealed in Kant's problem of "the thing in itself". How would a systematic philosophy be possible, i.e. a philosophy which conceives of the entire cosmos of philosophical problems as a unified, continuous whole, if, already in dealing with the basic methodical problem, it were necessary to accept a breach from within the closed system? For the sake of a supreme first principle as a fundamental premise of all philosophy in general, Cohen rejected a second world contemplated alongside with the world of "experience", the world of knowledge and science. And if here he turns to Hegelianism, then it is not because he rejected that ultimate element of the unity of all philosophy which he found in Kant, but solely because on this point absolute idealism is closer to the ultimate foundations of systematic philosophy than Kant himself. The essence of Kantianism is in its transcendental method; the value of this method is in its universal significance for the totality of the philosophical problems, in other words, in that it is the single principle for all components of a philosophical system. The fate of philosophy, therefore, depends on the unity of its method; without this unity, no unity in general is possible; however, without unity, philosophy is not what it should be, i.e., it is not systematic philosophy.

The example of Cohen's reinterpretation of Kant's "thing in itself" should have clarified to what extent the principle of systemization is fruitful in the most critical problems of knowledge and understanding and, on the other hand, how this same principle was decisive for Cohen from the first flights of his thought into the realm of infinity. Yet, in a more abstract, though also more precise, form, the spirit of systemization can be grasped only in the application which Cohen discovered for Kant's concept of transcendentalism. At this turn of Cohen's creative life, it should be realized that the clue to the correct understanding of Cohen's new position was not his work on Kant, but the three volumes of his own unfinished system.

According to Cohen, Kantianism is transcendentalism; whilst transcendentalism is only a method, a way—but one which leads from a single centre directly to a goal in any direction. If philosophy had to proceed from something given in advance, then the nature of this datum would certainly be reflected in all its diversity in all its subsequent radiation. A philosophy, whose starting point were some external entity, could not by virtue of this alone be a unity and of a systematic character. Therefore the opposite is true: a systematic philosophy can proceed from nothing other than itself, i.e. from its own method. That which is true for the problem of theoretical understanding of the world, is true in general. Reason is given only to itself in its own rational methodology. But this reason is not that of man as a singular, natural phenomenon, but that of mankind, the reason of human culture. As much as critics have objected to the rationality of human culture, Schiller was nevertheless right when he wrote that "even in opposing reason, men were still taking it into consideration in one way or another, and in general were acting in agreement with it." Thus we have in human culture that homogenous material (in relation to consciousness) on which the continuous progress of rationality can be demonstrated. But human culture in itself, outside of its philosophical evaluation, is not a fact, but rather a problem; not a datum, rather an aim. Transcendental philosophy evaluates, purifies it in as much as it clarifies its original founding in consciousness itself. The transcendental method, consequently, is a way of "purity", of "purification"—in Cohen's own Platonic terminology. This way consists in the fact that, from the problems of continuous development of culture, philosophy turns to the question of the possibility of this development; in the objective directions of cultural life, it tries to find the elements of consciousness which constitute this continuousness. In other words, as mathematicians have always done, philosophy starts with an analysis of the conditions of the solution of its problems. This means that the transcendental method is one of delving into premises as assumptions. And if the indivisibility of the philosophical target is bound up with the unity of its method, then it is clear that ultimately this unity of method is based obversely on the unity of the goal. Cohen's pan-methodism, like Hegel's pan-logism, has as its ultimate foundation the unity and rationality of universal culture. Of course, this is not the place to try to describe, even in the most general terms, that complicated path which led Cohen from "The Logic of Pure Knowledge" through "The Ethics of Pure Will" and "The Aesthetics of Pure Emotion" to the unsolved problem of completing a system endeavouring to encompass the entire reality of human culture—that of a "Philosophical Psychology". In this limited space it would be even less appropriate to try to characterize Cohen's originality in his approach to the interpretation of the history of human culture. But several of his results from the point of view of the history of most recent philosophy must be related.

Kant and Hegel are the alpha and the omega of German classical philosophy. If it is true that in Cohen's work, the end leads to the beginning, and the chain of the idealistic tradition, which seems broken and suspended in mid-air, is re-fastened by the link of Cohen's philosophy, then a great deal is implied by it. The entire path from Kant to Hegel appears in turn as one large closed link in the history of recent thought, which has only now been revealed in all its entirety. This means that the history of philosophy of the second half of the 19th century can no longer appear as aimless wandering around and near central problems, as it had seemed before Cohen; on the contrary, a definitive direction in development clearly emerges amidst the endless multitude of literary phenomena. In the person of Cohen there stands before us a man worthy of his teachers, a consummation of this great period of Western philosophical thought. At the same time a way is paved for a continuous development of philosophy—in as much as in the person of Cohen, classical German idealism demands an answer not on any one specific point; rather we must be with it or against it in the entirety of its problems and ways. This means that the history of philosophy in all its complicated side issues is alive to this very day because there is no system more saturated with philosophical traditions than the Kantian-Hegelian system, conceived as one. But most essential in a system so grandiose in its tendencies is that Plato, the origin of idealism and systemization, arises anew. Thus while Cohen was advocating systematization in philosophy, he first and foremost reinforces anew the ancient belief in the possibility of a methodically verifiable, strict and integral world-view, not recognizing ultimate unanswerable questions.

In one of the last pages of his "Aesthetics" Cohen for the first time uses the word "metaphysics" not in his usual sense. He calls his future "Psychology" "not that imaginary metaphysics which so calls itself, but which does the work of materialism and sensualism"—not that, but then which? Obviously—genuine metaphysics. Cohen was not fated to realize this genuine, non-materialist, non-sensualist metaphysics. But did he not bequeath it to successive generations? Does not Cohen demand that in better times than his own, when belief in the infinite power of human reason and in the unlimited possibilities of philosophical architecture would be renewed, simultaneously would be revived that great style of systemization, for which he was only the herald and precursor in our own intoxicatingly sober age? Because after all the style of Cohen's own system is a product of old age, a specimen of the baroque style, that of Faust, Part II. In his system Cohen no longer initiates, but only finalizes. Yet as the author of a majestic epilogue which challenged and cut across the spirit of his age, Cohen teaches us to begin again and again, because there is no bold beginning in philosophy which would not be fruitful if only it were inspired by the spirit of systemization and rational methodology. Methodical systemization—that is the first commandment which is left to us by Cohen's legacy.

II

However, is not all of this taken together the exclusive concern of the philosophical guild? Anyone who is not dedicated to special philosophical interests should certainly ask this question. Cohen answers clearly and intelligibly: the fate of philosophy is the fate of our whole human culture; without it "belief in a new world is merely an ideological illusion". If in his commandment to think methodically and systematically Cohen seems to be addressing a narrow circle of philosophers and only those engaged in philosophy, then in his own teaching on the place of philosophy in the system of culture, he is addressing the world of culture at large, all those who are not indifferent to its fate. But in order to understand correctly this second of Cohen's commandments, we must turn again to the definition of philosophy given by Cohen.

"Philosophy is systematic philosophy"—this means that the unity of a system presupposes the unity of cultural creation. But this unity, like every unity, is not a given phenomenon but set as a goal; it does not exist, but is being realized, or more correctly, it exists only in its realization. But how and in which way does this develop? The entire history of philosophy answers this question.

It should be noted that Cohen's contribution to the history of philosophy as a special branch of historical study is in no way less significant and, in its immediate tangible impact, may even be more influential than his immense contribution to the systematic elaboration of philosophical problems. "I do not hesitate to say," wrote Natorp, "that Hermann Cohen opened our eyes not only on Kant, but also on Plato." From Plato to Kant, and to Cohen himself, the whole history of philosophy, thanks to Cohen, appeared in a completely new light. One can argue endlessly about those entirely new valuations and confrontations concerning the history of philosophy which are scattered in such great abundance in all of Cohen's works and which sometimes appear as independent themes of his separate monographs. Here Cohen, like anyone who really knows what he wants and what he is searching for, is extremely biassed. Cohen does the same thing to all the old and new thinkers as he did to Kant: he often sees in them what perhaps he alone could see. But his subjectivism is the fruit of his most genuine intuition. A completely independent school in the interpretation of the "Platonic question" grew out of his academic address on Plato and mathematics; Descartes and Leibnitz were resuscitated and revived; Kepler, Galileo, Robert Meyer and Johann Müller were included in the history of philosophy for the first time. Nonetheless Cohen could hardly be described as an historian of philosophy. Whence then originated his extraordinary fruitfulness precisely in the historical field? The answer is simple: it is rooted in the systematic valuation which Cohen gave to the interrelationship between philosophy and culture. That the history of philosophy as a discipline, properly speaking, still does not exist, that there are merely mounds of raw or semi-raw material available—this realization has only recently begun to penetrate into philosophical circles. The history of philosophy simply shares the common fate of all separate historical disciplines: their mutual estrangement, and consequently, their internal incoherence. The arbitrary delineation of any one field of historical life as an object of isolated historical research is methodically inadmissible, for the sole reason that culture is one and indivisibly integrated in all its diverse directions. But, as we have seen, this is the fundamental premise of Cohen's entire systematic thinking. And it is quite natural that he to whom the thesis of the unity of human culture was the system's corner stone should, in the historical manifestations of philosophical thought, have seen what actually they are: carriers of the integral world—views of their time reflecting their contemporary culture. Thus, on the one hand, in the philosophers themselves, there was revealed to Cohen their designated place within the surrounding culture which enabled him to see in them much more than they often saw in themselves; on the other hand, this culture itself was illuminated in a new way and gave new meaning to its philosophical exponents. Be that as it may, the definition of philosophy had to appear in the same new light as that of the philosopher.

And in fact if philosophy is both consciousness and the foundation of human culture in the continuity of its development, then necessarily he who is conscious of and furthers any advancement of culture--is a philosopher. But advancement is possible only in the presence of clear consciousness of the way. The "way" is the "method", the methodologist the guide. Hence, anyone is a philosopher who builds and founds new ways of thought and action, of feeling and consciousness in general. So in the gallery of philosophers there is created a place for ordinary scholars and statesmen, revolutionaries and artists, prophets as well as thinkers in the accepted meaning. Hegel called these great men beacons on the paths of human wandering. If we accept this definition, then we can say that according to Cohen, all great men are philosophers, or, that he who is not a philosopher has no claim to historical greatness.

According to Plato, philosophers were supposed to govern; according to Cohen, they are the only genuine rulers, i.e. the mentors and educators of mankind. Thus a whole series of familiar names disappears from Cohen's history of philosophy; on the other hand, its former continuity is restored by previously unnoticed newcomers.

If such is the nature of philosophers and philosophy, then its place in the system of culture is indeed paramount. "I am culture"—philosophy could say about itself paraphrasing the well-known royal saying—if, like culture itself, philosophy were not in the process of eternal coming into being, not in the eternal, everlasting aspiration towards its infinite goals. Moreover, in this eternal striving, philosophy is precisely that principle which upholds the will to expand. Knowing the ways pointing beyond the limits of the given, philosophy, in deepening the foundations, enriches culture in all its manifestations—in science, in politics, in art—by giving it the possibility of elevating itself higher and higher, infinitely expanding the horizons of mankind.

But at the same time philosophy is also the centre of this horizon, or more correctly, there is no horizon without it, no integrated culture, but only fragmentary facts with their contingent and arbitrary valuation. Without the future which is anticipated by the method, there is not only no present, but also the past dissipates into ruin. And with the disintegration of culture, there is no concrete unity of human consciousness, for human personality is non-existent without the unity of its goal which, in turn, is tantamount to the totality of cultural consciousness. The human person is personalized culture, culture carried by man and vouchsafed in its integrity only and exclusively by systematic philosophy.

Hence it necessarily follows, firstly, that philosophy carries its own special indebtedness to the culture which brought it forth and would be furthered by it, and secondly, that culture as such will finally become free and conscious, which is tautological, when both culture and philosophy will tend towards growing approximation. And just as from the perspectives opening before a self-conscious culture it follows that the only rational religion, i.e. that the only rational bond of culture, is its internal duty to become free, so too, on the other hand, from the fundamental duty of philosophy to culture, there emerges a whole chain of necessary consequences for philosophy itself.

In this context Cohen faces us as the true teacher and prophet of his generation.

Firstly notice should be taken here of Cohen's closeness to the spirit of the age. It goes without saying that philosophy must stand on the level of contemporary science. This seems obvious. Nonetheless, even the greatest of the great are not without blame on this point. But the problem of systematic philosophy is not only scientific knowledge. Ethics and aesthetics are no less important than logic. As much as aesthetics relates philosophy to "the art of genius", so ethics is based on Law, and, consequently on politics. But just as the spirit of science and art is incessant yearning for unexplored horizons, so too the spirit of politics, inspired by philosophy, is the spirit of universal brotherhood and world justice, the spirit of socialism. The Kantian formulations of the categorical imperative, writes Cohen, "proclaim the idea of humanity and the political idea of socialism". Understanding and vivid concern for these two ideas remained alive solely in Fichte. "The idea that man is in essence purposefully chosen, a goal in itself, is transformed into the idea of socialism." And in another place in his "Ethics", "the current objection that socialism is a matter of the stomach exposes the callous prejudice in all its shameless nudity." But he goes even further. In his "Aesthetics", considering "France's mission" in the development of contemporary art, he defines France as a carrier of the revolutionary spirit, preordained to initiate the "social revolution" (vol. II, p. 413ff.). Thus Cohen converted his abstract concept of systematic philosophy into concrete actuality.

But is philosophy capable of realizing such immense tasks? For philosophy is only a concept. Only philosophers are concrete. Whereas the more the sphere of culture expands, the more difficult it is to include its boundless worlds in a frame of a single horizon. Cohen's answer to this question was the creation of the Marburg school.

The term "school of philosophy" has gradually acquired a metaphorical character in philosophical literature, having been connected only with the conception of a purely literary succession of scholarly opinions and a community of views. That a school could become an organization with the most essential characteristic of any organization, the principle of the division of labour consciously carried out—this, in the 19th century, could seem one of the most abstract illusions; yet in the very energy of Cohen's teaching, there was that creative principle which, after an interval lasting for centuries, again led to the realization of a philosophical school in the classical Platonic-academic sense. The Marburg school was just that. Everything was kept together by the unity of the problem, by the unity of the method, indefatigably propagated by the founder and head of the school—a unity creative in character in which the subject of study was not a ready-made philosophy, but the very skill of philosophical thinking. The internal life of the Marburg school which represents one of the most interesting and instructive chapters in the history of modern philosophy, was determined by that concept of systematic unity which lay at the basis of all of Cohen's works. He wrote as early as 1877: "A method which one could only copy is bad." "Science, although it must be dogmatic, nevertheless is not dogma." Accordingly the whole Marburg school, faithful to the adopted principles of systematic methodology, never inhibited the personal independent development of its adherents and produced already in the first generation a whole series of brilliant and original thinkers. Cohen's educational significance in the metaphoric sense in which the term is used in the title is, so to speak, the logical foundation of Cohen's entire academic and educational activity in the direct and immediate sense. Only a philosophy which again sees itself as the ideal focus of the entire cultural life of an epoch was capable of, and had to give birth to a special reform of philosophical education carried out by "direct action". This reform represents, as it were, the first step on the way towards an active intervention of systematic philosophy in cultural life lacking self-awareness.

In consonance with the best traditions of Platonism, Cohen reaffirmed anew philosophy's "claim to law-giving", because according to Cohen, to legislate means to realize in concrete historical life the highest ethical principles, the pinnacle of which is the "virtue of humaneness". Only in the close connection between "the goal of self-realization" and "the mission of legislation" does there appear what in ethics can be called the self-determination of man. That is why without a close relation to concrete politics, which is a struggle for the power to legislate, there can be neither individual morality in general, nor practical philosophy in particular. Practical philosophy is, in this sense, the law of lawmaking itself, the basis of rationality in all objective human actions always and everywhere. Therefore, "The Ethics of Pure Will" uncompromisingly rejects Kantian doubts regarding the possibility of strict "material" ethics. In place of Kantian formalism we have before us the Platonic doctrine on philosophical virtues elaborated anew. The true "landmarks" on man's path towards his own self are the ancient virtues: truthfulness and modesty, bravery and faithfulness, justice and loving-kindness. And just as in his anti-formalism Cohen harshly opposes Kantian ethics, so too in his teaching on affects, he breaks with all the prejudices of formal stoicism: without the affects of honour and love, a doctrine on virtue would be impossible; whilst without it ethics would be only logic—true, not of natural sciences but of humanities, still, a doctrine about the existing, concerning being, and not a doctrine about what ought to be and its being, which, as to its degree of reality, is even superior to anything simply "existing".

The last point, Cohen's doctrine on the primacy of practical reason and his own social school structure (prompted by this doctrine) may surprise only those who did not grasp that in the "Logic of Pure Knowledge", though the first, it is still only one of the components of the system, while the problem of a system again places logic before the necessity of its deepest reform—not only outlined but realized by Cohen, namely the transformation of "formal" logic into an aspect of the transcendental. This is the profoundest connection between Cohen and Hegel, but it is conditioned by the fact that systematic ethics must follow logic; that, so to speak, in spite of chronological order, Hegel had to be followed by Fichte.

Rooted in ethics as it is, the fact that logic must be a logic of pure knowledge is a reflection of Cohen's primordial interpretation of transcendentalism. If the unity of the system is merely another expression for the unity of culture; if in this unity of cultural consciousness, the centre is the philosophical realization of the methods and aims of the progressive development of cultural activity—then the central philosophical principle is, of course, the idea of Good, and the philosopher whose life is determined by systematization must be a creator of new forms of community, albeit in the dimensions of exemplary models.

Therefore, it was precisely this idea of the Good, which Plato already had compared with God, with Helios, that Cohen had to transform into "the idea of God". All of Cohen's optimism in his evaluation of the place and meaning of systematic philosophy in the history of human culture would rest on unverified prejudice, if Cohen had not decided to include a fundamental concept of religion in his systematic ethics. But having taken this step also, he only revealed more profoundly the last of these premises which he himself sometimes calls his "creed", the "ethical monotheism". In the last foundations of his system Hermann Cohen appears before us "like his own name" with his own purely German first name—but in a truly Jewish spiritual rank—the Priest Hermann! Prophetic monotheism, i.e., a continuation and development of those ideas propagated by the great Jewish prophets and priests of antiquity—that is what in the last analysis inspired Cohen, and that is what constitutes the ultimate transcendental premise of his whole system. "My predecessor Micah"—with such, one may say, arrogant words Cohen established his spiritual genealogy towards the end of his life. Perhaps Cohen's greatest merit lies in this presumption—but it also contains his most valuable legacy intended, as it were, only and solely for his own Jewish people. —Solely?

III

What is prophetic or messianic monotheism in the sense of a transcendental proposition sponsored by systematic philosophy? The answer to this question should finally clarify the ultimate meaning of Cohen's life-work; simultaneously, Cohen himself, in all his vitality, should arise before us as that teacher and educator of Jewry without whom a Jewish House of Learning and even Jewish self-awareness itself would remain precarious.

If it is true that philosophy is systematic philosophy; and if, on the other hand, philosophy can be systematic only because it merely reflects that continuity in the development towards rationality which is continuously realized in universal culture striving towards unity and integrity, then the ideal of universal rational unity and its continuous realization in historical life are the methodological precursors of all philosophical systematization. But the reality of the moral ideal is only conceivable in line with the reality of nature in whose formation there emerges initially the power of rationality in general. However, this reality of nature would not be true to itself, if it were a reality determined exclusively by the methods of mathematical and descriptive natural science. Thus ethics expose a deficiency in Being itself, qua natural Being: as natural Being it is ethically neutral, but bearing in mind that the reality of this Being is founded in systematic philosophy, it implies the assumption of its correspondence with the ultimate foundations of the general principles of philosophy, including those concerning the realization of the Ideal. It follows that the ethical neutrality of nature seemingly contradicts its philosophical foundation. This contradiction is only solved in that the *inde*pendence of the concept of Being in logic from the concept of Being dictated by ethics is turned into its opposite, namely, into the *inter*dependence of the Being of nature and the ideal Being of what should be: the reality of nature is of such a character that it is potentially both the arena for the embodiment of the ethical Ideal and also augurs well for the progress of the service to this end. All this is warranted by the Idea of God.

But if God is a God of the embodiment of good in the sphere of its kinetic state and if God is a God of the world-process, a God of the universal history of humankind, then He is the God of the prophets, and faith in the Messiah is belief in the salvation of the world through good, truth, and justice. The fundamental methodological "law of truth" requiring the unison of logic and ethics is realized in the "idea of God", as in its rational, methodically based "offspring". "Prophetic Messianism", as a methodological premise, finds its justification in its fruitfulness for philosophical systematization: serving as a foundation, it acquires its own character as a fundamental proposition. This is precisely the logical meaning of transcendental teleologism in general. Thus in his rejection of metaphysics, Cohen transcendentally re-affirms a "religion of reason", or simply the inherited Judaism.

Had Cohen, from the very beginning, set himself such a task, he never would have become that "inspired herald of the prophets' tenets and a learned champion of the eternal truths of Judaism", which he became towards the end of his life, a title rightly bestowed on him by the best representatives of Jewish learning in Germany in their dedication to his 70th birthday in 1912. He is one of the most brilliant examples of that unconscious searching for personal truth which is the true basis of a scientist's conscience. Abandoning his own self and his internal tension, Cohen found his peace of mind as well as himself in their objective rationality: the foundations of Judaism are not inconsistent with methodical philosophy because Judaism is methodical philosophy which includes the foundations of Judaism as its own presupposition. This is the result which Cohen reached towards the end of his life-work. But if this is so, then the philosophy of his own life, so to speak, and of the life of his people, must have been understood by Cohen in all their compelling deeper meaning.

The history of the Jewish people is a struggle for the *Logos* of history, for the rationality of the historical process. It can be nothing other than struggle because the meaning of history is "coming-into being", i.e. elucidation of its meaning. The children of Israel as personified by the prophets, who were first conscious of man's vocation on the high road of history, naturally had to oppose everything in human culture which contradicted rationality and misplaced the proper emphasis of the various aspects of cultural life. So Christianity, for example, which rests on pantheism and on the stoical, i.e. pagan image of the sage, is like any pantheism an overemphasis of the aesthetic principle in human life, and therefore it is a principle philosophically irreconcilable with genuine systematic rationality. The Jews were as unable to be reconciled with it as with paganism which is in essence merely a grounding for systematization, but not the thing itself. Genuine philosophy is a unification of Plato and Isaiah; without Isaiah it would be impossible to appreciate the true greatness of Plato. And if the goal of history is the reign of reason, and if the content of Judaism is the meaning of history, then, of course, the significance of the existence of the Jews is in the purity with which they preserve their ethical monotheism, their ancient Covenant on the coming of the Messiah. Cohen wrote in his "Ethics": "The preservation of Jewry rests upon the fact that in the messianic idea of a united humanity the Jews are preparing a universal union of nations." He continues: "Neither tribal attachment nor the millenia of historical isolation is that which might solve the historical enigma of the Jewish survival; it finds its explanation only in the forceful conviction that this historical idea is a specific manifestation of the category All-in-one." *(Allheit)*

Cohen tried to prove his conception of Jewish existence in a series of special expositions illuminating various sources of Jewish culture. To these series belong his essays: "About neighbourly love in the Talmud" (1888), "Love and Justice in the Concepts of God and Man" (1900), the address "On the significance of Judaism in the Religious Progress of Humanity", "German and Jewish Spirituality" (1916), and a considerable amount of research devoted to the history of Jewish philosophy. Through Hasdai Crescas and Maimonides, Bahia-ibn Pakuda and Saadia he goes back to the prophets and even to the Ten Commandments. It goes without saying that Cohen's history of Jewish philosophy is acceptable only to adherents of Cohenianism. Yet here, too, the problem of an integral history of Jewish philosophy completely depends on an integral philosophical understanding of the content and meaning of Jewish history in general. Also in his special historical writings Cohen first and foremost teaches how to interpret philosophically, and then to analyse and to reassemble.

Furthermore, all this determined Cohen's image as a political thinker, in the philosophical sense of the word. In turning to the outside world he addressed it not so much as an apologist for Judaism, but rather as a preacher *in partibus infidelium*. From his interpretation of the Jewish message it immediately followed that every single Jew had to be a missionary of the prophetic spirit; even in Marx Cohen saw a "messenger of the God of history" ("Ethics", 296). Within Judaism he stressed faithfulness to the Jewish predestination through its realization, through its philosophical reaffirmation. Herein lies his deepest significance as an educator of the Jewish people.

This is not the place to go into the question whether Cohen was right or not in his interpretation of Judaism. One thing is certain: as an example of how a philosophical mind, at the pinnacle of contemporary scientific, artistic, and political aspirations, can in our time find in Judaism an inexhaustible reserve of strength and inspiration for preaching its "eternal truths" not only to the Jews themselves, but to the whole world, so alien and uncomprehending of the Jews—Cohen proclaimed to all those who doubted or wavered: seek and you will find. He also told them where, in what direction, to seek—in that of philosophical penetration of the essence of Judaism, in a methodical and systematic way.

Jewish enlightenment, which in a trivial and superficial form considers that under the cover of populist phrases or a purely philological guise, it is possible to build a system of Jewish education outside a continuous connection with the whole spiritual heritage of past millennia in all its wealth of content, cuts the thread which links the past with the present, and consequently cuts off any possibility of an ethical justification of the very fact of Jewish existence. But to justify ethically means to found national education on supranational, universal principles; just as, on the other hand, the philosophical re-interpretation of Judaism must inevitably lead to a new verification and to a re-enforcement of the ages-old principles of the internal history of the Jews. But if Cohen is right in his general doctrine about philosophy, and if he is right in his doctrine on the significance of philosophy for human culture in general, then only by virtue of the formal application of these general principles to Jewish enlightenment, there inevitably appears the necessity of finding a place for systematic philosophy in the system of Jewish education, together with a place for the philosophy of history, and consequently, for the philosophy of Jewish history, and therefore for the history of Jewish philosophy, i.e. for the history of those ideas which, by and large, coincide with what Cohen called prophetic messianism.

Thus in Jewish education itself the adoption of Cohen's guiding principles would lead from an expansion of the spiritual horizon to the strengthening of the Jewish will to exist and fight. And once again the personality and life of this inspired thinker in this respect also would be a living example of the educational significance of his seemingly abstract ideas.

It is well known how long the "Kantian" Cohen had to struggle in Kant's own native land for a prize even much lower than simple recognition, when hardly any one took notice of his existence. In the initial misfortune of his own philosophy Cohen was inclined to see merely another example of that inertia and irrationality against which scientific philosophy on the one hand, and the Jewish people on the other, were called upon to put up a fight. However, in the sinister silence of his Kantian contemporaries, Cohen saw and could see only one thing: that "universal-historical affect of hatred for the Jews" which one could oppose only in a struggle for culture in general, i.e., for the "idea of God" in all its purity. His whole life in this sense represented an example of exclusive determination and uncompromising consistency in matters of philosophical convictions and dedication to them. Cohen was dedicated to philosophy, as a devout Jew is to the faith of his fathers; and he was dedicated to Jewry, as a devout philosopher is to the truth he had discovered—the Jewish attitude to philosophy, the philosophical relationship to its Jewish fate—these were indivisibly interconnected. Is there a formula which would ever be more to the point, and in particular at our time, when the question of the education of the Jewish will to exist and fight faces us in all its severity? And is there not contained herein an indication of those ultimate problems of education which are connected with the idea of aesthetic education? If the singular character of Jewish aesthetic education is the aim to create an aesthetically valuable Jewish personality, then here too Cohen is the mentor who affirms that: "The hard but reliable touchstone of genuine art is that in it nationality and humanity do not present contradictions." If that be so, then truly Cohen, as a future educator of Jewry, will be an educator of a generation of beautiful people, i.e., of human beings in whom nationality and humanity will not oppose one another; and of whom, therefore, each one may and will be the authentic product of the great educational art of Hermann Cohen.

11. Around the Departure Point of Existentialism

I

What is "Existentialism"?

The question is not a simple one. Ordinarily one understands the term to indicate a particular direction taken by the contemporary philosophical thinking and to be connected at root with the idea of "existence". This leads to the further questions: Wherein lies the particularity of this new thinking? How did it force its way through the labyrinth of modern thought? Who are its most acknowledged representatives and what is the common element in their world concept? As soon as one poses these and similar questions, one is confronted with quite extraordinary difficulties which cannot be considered without a thorough acquaintance with the history of philosophy since the first half of the last century.

As it is known, the earlier decades saw the greatest triumph of systematic philosophical thought, and very soon after, its complete overthrow. The great universally inclusive systems constructed after Kant, particularly that of Hegel, had turned into a heap of fragments almost before one had a chance of considering them. So it was in Germany, while in France there arose at the time the positivism of Auguste Comte. European thought reached the stage in which Marx was able to carry out his dialectic operation on Hegel and "put him on his feet", that is to say, on the base of positivist science. Instead of merely trying to understand the world, Marx demanded that philosophy should assume the power of changing it. This revolt against Hegel ultimately led, as we know now, to a revolution with which the whole world has to reckon to this very day. Almost at the same time, in an isolated corner of Europe (Denmark), there appeared another rebel against Hegel who called almost as urgently for an end to speculative idealism and to Hegel's claim that he was qualified to understand the world. Søren Kierkegaard, only five years older than the leftist Hegelian, Marx, also declared that instead of trying to understand the world, the time has come to change it. The difference between these two was "merely" that Marx strove to change the objective world, while his contemporary thinker of North Europe, absorbed in quiet meditation, was

This essay was first published in Yiddish in *Davke*, Buenos Aires, 1959, No. 37/38.

solely concerned with the inside of the subjective world. In accordance with its basic aims, Marxism very soon became a force in world politics, while the melodious mutterings of Kierkegaard's deeply muted ideas had to wait for recognition, and then only in Christian religious and philosophical circles, till after World War I, when the non-Marxist and anti-Marxist world realized that philosophically speaking Marxism became almost naked. It was then that people first began to lay stress on "existence", because according to Kierkegaard it was considerably more important that man should really "be", or should be a real "entity", or that he should concretely "exist", than that he should have an abstract conception of himself, of another, and of the world's "meaning". Could it be mere chance that one generation produced two philosophical revolutionaries whose achievements are as far apart from each other as East and West, so that one is a sort of polar opposite of the other? That is a question for quite another historico-philosophical inquiry.

Explain it how you will, the fact remains that it was in Germany, soon after the first World War and the Marxist revolution in Russia, that the first voices of Kierkegaard's discoverers and admirers became audible. The most important of them was the Heidelberg professor, Karl Jaspers, who in his Psychologie der Weltanchauung (1922) devoted a place of honour to Kierkegaard's philosophical, or more accurately anti-philosophical heresy. Ten years later his friend and disciple, Professor Martin Heidegger of Freiburg, joined forces with him with the result that in the inter-war years a movement arose in France, in philosophy and literature, which aimed at turning Kirkegaard's "Existenz" idea into the so-called system of "existentialism". Its leading representatives in France were Jean-Paul Sartre, Albert Camus and Gabriel Marcel, but the German thinkers already mentioned do not deny that they also represent the same point of view. What is this point of view? Can it be defined with any precision?

The answer lies in the expression itself "point of view" or "standpoint". A point of view is not a system; it is not something that can be enclosed in a series of logical, inter-related arguments and conclusions; in order to grasp it properly, one must stand exactly in the place of the person whose standpoint is being considered. The old rule, "Do not judge another until you stand in his place" applies literally to all known existentialists of our times. Each of them honours Søren Kierkegaard's achievement, each from his own standpoint. This unites them all. But the achievement itself consisted precisely in this, that the lone thinker of Copenhagen clearly contrasted—to use Sartre's terminology—"existence" with "essence"; he set the concrete in opposition to any sort of abstraction, of general ideas which in his view merely float in the air. He set the single and singular individual "here and now" against the idea of man in general or some sort of humanity in being. If this is so, how can all this possibly be turned into a system of abstract ideas, a theory which allows of acceptance by a group of thinkers in common and be transmitted in generally understandable language? Kierkegaard's first principle, his point of departure, contradicts the very thought that "existence" in its true unfalsified sense should suddenly give birth to a new "ism", even if it is no more than "existentialism". In so far as that which bears this label has a "basic assumption", it is an assumption or hypothesis without words, indeed the hypothesis that one can really and concretely exist merely by deciding that one can get along without any intelligible, logically defined hypothesis. As Kierkegaard himself once observed in reference to the Christian religion, "To understand it means primarily to understand that one cannot understand it." (German edition of Kierkegaard's works, vol. 6, p. 258.)

Does it mean that all this existentialism, which has been the cause of so much agitation in modern philosophical literature, turns out to be a plain and simple paradox? And if so, is the so-called "existentialist standpoint" no more than the expression of complete skepticism about the real possibility of systematic philosophical thought? Clearly, such a supposition would itself be more than paradoxical.

II

The matter is far from being simple. Even supposing that the "ism" in "existentialism" is in fact only a dialectical play with a syllable, there still remains in the term the weighty content of "existence". So let us analyse this Latin word and consider each of its three aspects separately, each of which has its own meaning: "ex" indicates "exclusion". In the term existentialist "ist" stands for something that "is", and "ens" ("ence") in existence is Latin for "being". Together all three syllables indicate some sort of state of "being" which is "without", in the sense of outside, as to everything else. In other words, only that has an existence which is and remains identifiable apart from all other things, and therefore has independence in respect of the world around it and is established within itself as a world in itself and of itself. Have we therefore to admit that, strictly speaking, we know only one way of "being" which is in this sense fit to possess existence, and it is nothing other than man and only man, as a concrete unit, man in himself, by himself and with his own will? This is precisely what Søren Kierkegaard meant when, instead of a basic hypothesis, he made use of the term "existence" as the "concrete-real" against all sorts of abstractions. And just by reason of this in our epoch of hesitant individualism he lives as the "father of existentialism".

It seems indeed right that a philosophical system, as for example, the Kantian or Marxist, cannot be erected on such a foundation. But this was exactly what Kierkegaard was at pains to emphasise: the man who truly has "existence", or better, whose life is not aimless or haphazard, but real, concrete, independent reality, such a man has nothing to do with theories woven out of abstractions. Every moment presents him to a unique situation, which he and he alone is able to assess in order to decide freely what he ought to do in this situation. A man who sees himself only through the mist of abstract ideas, as other "non-existent" creatures see and judge him, as for example according to his descent, his age, his occupation, his merits and faults, or according to his material condition, such a man lives, breathes, works and perhaps writes wonderful books, but essentially has not begun to exist. And this also holds true between man and his fellows: true human relationships between man and man are possible only when they are "existential" and not based on a foundation of formal or informal "arrangements" according to the customs of the world. With his "existence" idea Kierkegaard aimed at nothing more or less than setting up man in his temporary span face to face with eternity, with the absolute creator of man and his world. His follower in France, Jean-Paul Sartre, expresses the same thought in his agnostic fashion: "Man makes himself man, in order to become God", because he is that which he is not, and he is not that which he is (*L'Etre et le Néant,* 1943, esp. p. 720).

Now it becomes clear what sort of standpoint existentialism envisages in our time, and how it is connected with the "first point" of the Copenhagen rebel of a hundred years ago. Modern existentialism is not a system; nor is it an abstract definitive approach to "existence" in the sense of Kierkegaard's revelation; but the most prominent, the main aim is a constant tendency of the human spirit, its intention and desire to make "existence" real, primarily in oneself but also in one's environment, and in whatever manner it may be. It may be by means of philosophic expression, or by action, or by an artistic miracle, just as happened with Kierkegaard when he changed himself and remade the broken fragments of his life in a flood of exuberant existentialist worship. The existentialist of today, whoever and whatever he may be, wants exactly the same, not simply to be, but truly to exist in existential association with other existences. The world must and will change, he believes, if only existentialist theory remains unshaken at heart, for according to this theory "existence" is possible and can be realized, for man is endowed with the additional grace which made him in the image of the Creator and accordingly free and able to bear full responsibility for his own existence.

It is thus entirely natural that all three of the leading representatives of this trend in France (Sartre, Camus and Marcel, a son, by the way, of a Jewish mother) should have synthesised in themselves philosophic and artistic elements. He who wishes, for example, to adopt Sartre's "existentialist standpoint" should not confine himself to a study of his *L'Etre et le Néant,* already quoted, and similar works, but he should also take well into account his novels and dramas. Together they may constitute unique evidence that each of us is "composite", being made up, so to speak, of the lowest degree of "something in being" and a higher state of "being" which is hidden under the cover of "nothing". It does not matter that existential-ists express themselves differently. What matters principally is that one should be able to feel, sense, touch, conceive and grasp that there exists, above all within the limits of reality, some level of human existence that is beyond comparison more human than the ordinary, average life of man in our world. It is possible for us to achieve all this; it is within our grasp—that is the "point of departure", and, if we wish so to label it, the "basic hypothesis" of existentialism in all its modifications.

Take a closer look at just this "basic hypothesis", and at once it becomes clear that what is really new in this modern philosophical trend or direction is only the name. Kierkegaard who, according to certain accounts, was a converted Jew, revolted against the Christian Church and against Hegel's Christian philosophical idealism, and did it without doubt following the footsteps of a tradition much older by thousands of years, the tradition of the uniqueness of the human race and every one of its members. Without him and his modern mainly unbelieving followers, the idea that man can and should always stand face to face with the Absolute would not have become so vital in the thought of our times. Truly remarkable are the secret and impenetrable ways of the spirit. Even today, in the face of the systematic philosophers, existentialism is active as a kind of yeast in the almost empty kneading troughs of Western thought. "If there is the dough, the spirit will flourish; and if it will flourish, there will be dough." It will be thanks to the first principle of existentialism which has initiated a truly fresh philosophical way of thought. This is something of which our western world stands much in need. It requires a moral awakening of the individual, a deep ethical urge, which is the first spur both in Kierkegaard's work and its offspring in the existentialist movement of our generation.

III

Our own Jewish world stands in a similar if quite separate need. It is of no consequence, whether it is true or not that the father of existentialism was "the son of a Jewish merchant" and "that he was baptised in 1848", that is at the age of 35, as I find noted in Hutchinson's *Encyclopaedia of the Twentieth Century* (London, 1951, p. 597). Even if Kierkegaard had been and remained formally a Jew until the end of his days, this would not have altered the fact that the modern existentialist movement to which he gave the impulse, quite apart from the consideration that its principle expo-nents are un-believing Christians, is in its essentials a Christian move-ment. In order to recognise this, it is necessary to dwell on the method by which such existentialists as Heidegger in Germany and Sartre in France try to overcome the cardinal difficulties of every anti-rationalist philoso-phy.

Exactly in the manner of Kierkegaard, they reject the thought that philosophical thinking has to determine as a point of departure, some first principle or axiom (as, for example, Spinoza's substance), or an axiomatic basic hypothesis (like Descartes' "I think, therefore I am"). The starting point must be a fact, something that is picked up immediately without examination or any prompting from outside, and in all simplicity. It must be entirely free of any logical "deduction", of any sort of "wherefore" or "therefore", and that is the fact itself "of my being". Only when one is completely identified precisely with this fact does it permit of close analysis with the help of the "phenomenological" method and of description or expression in words also intelligible to others. And this is so for the simple reason that anyone has the power to identify himself with the same "phenomenon", the same "manifestation" of his own being. A more astute critic of this phenomenological "leap" from the world of chaos into himself, could, I believe, misjudge that there is here a concealed compromise with rationalism far from Kierkegaard's radical anti-rationalism. And indeed, why should we begin by accepting as the "first fact", so to speak, that the "first fact" is one and the same for all creatures that are endowed with consciousness? "Existentially" speaking, that is an unproven rationalist supposition.

Let us not argue, however, and let us consider further what can be discovered in the first or "prime" fact by phenomenological analysis. Both Heidegger and Sartre find there a dualism of "I and the world", more exactly, "I in the world", and Heidegger describes it even more distinctly: "I have been cast into a world", flung into the midst of some sort of world "on the way from nowhere to nowhere". That is my "existence", a tragic existence, and yet this is man's way in the world.

Here, I think, is the point where the Jew who immerses himself in the world of Kierkegaard's modern followers, must reluctantly exclaim: "Thus far! But no further can I go with you!" And thereafter, the Jewish protest will go something like this: According to your account of your first and original intuition of your "being", you find yourself in an "existence" (in a border-situation, according to the terminology of Karl Jaspers), at the bottom of an abyss; you have been flung there as though out of the blue, but, to put it crudely in the Yiddish vernacular, you burst in like a "Hellene into a Tabernacle". This arises from the fact that your intuition, whether you are believers or not, is a Christian intuition, and therefore also hellenistic by the classical Greek concept of the world, and Greek wisdom. Your "I" is a creature that is naturally isolated and yearns for personal redemption, and your world is by its nature an un-created world. And as for your intuitions in the terms of your credo, the son and his tragic emergence in a sinful world is much nearer to you than the "Father in Heaven". Just suppose for a moment that a Jew had travelled along your phenomenological road and had described, as precisely as you do, the reality that he found there. He would surely have become conscious of and discovered the fact of "I and a world", but the "I" would not have been your "I", the "world" not your "world", and he would certainly have discovered the "and", the relevance between man and world.

A Jew whose mental make-up is naturally Jewish would be able to argue with modern existentialism that "I" and "Jew" were for him one and the same thing. A generation or two ago there were many people among us whose first principle was the "Jewish Iota". It is possible, as Descartes taught, to have doubts on everything; but it would be a contradiction in terms to have any doubt about the sentence "I think". Exactly in this way, the first and absolute truth for Jews was their being Jewish, and Jews were even in the habit of swearing with the words "As I am a Jew!" Those among us for whom the words "I am a Jew" still have the logical importance of "I am I", will certainly recall that Moses was summoned to his mission with these words "I am that I am" or more exactly, with a glance towards the future, "I shall be that I shall be", which can be treated as a mystic symbol of intelligible indentification. But can it be taken for granted that a phenomenological analysis of a Jewish consciousness that is not merely abstractly human, but on the contrary, concretely Jewish, would reveal not only an isolated detail, but man in the history of humanity; "homo historicus"? Not just a world, any world, but the concrete world to which man is bound through the eternity of "I am that I am"? In other words, is it really true that the Divine is not immanent in man's very centre?

That at any rate was not the opinion of the father of modern existentialism. In his self-analysis he discovered "existence", but only by reason of the revelation to him of the ultimate meaning of faith, which is to stand face to face constantly with eternity in the sense of the Psalmist's words, "I have set the Lord always before me" (Ps. 16, 8). In his famous work, *Fear and Trembling*, he set forth the story of Abraham and Isaac at its central point as the prime example of true faith (our own Leivick did it for us in his own way). People have tried to ascertain among us if "Midrash Kierkegaard", Kierkegaard's exposition, agrees with our own tradition. It is not so much a matter of detail, however, as of principle: The existentialist intent and the leap into real existence, are according to Kierkegaard himself, at least as old as the faith of Abraham. The question thus arises: Do we live only as Abraham's seed, or are we able even in our own times to receive the command "Get thee and go . . ." which he had the grace to hear on two occasions? Will we station ourselves on our old inheritance of hardened tradition, or do we still possess the power to leap up and become "go-ers" and marchers once more?

That is the old question with which existentialism confronts us once more in a new style.

SECTION B

Jewish Morals and Messianic Hopes

1. The Bible in the History of Jewish Tradition

The significance of the Bible in the shaping of Jewish history

The Bible—that is the totality of the 39 books of the so-called old "covenant" (Testament)—constitutes the pivot and focal point of the entire spiritual and cultural history of the Jewish people and thus provides the most solid foundation for the continuity of Jewish history in general. Though in itself no more than the slowly unfolding epiphenomenon of a complex spiritual development spanning a thousand years, the corpus of writings gathered in the biblical canon so as to form a unified whole, the Book of Books, has acted throughout the subsequent millennia as an immutable point of origin—anchored, as it were, in supra-temporal spheres—for the spiritual life of the Jews, for all their creative endeavours.

From the time of its completion, the canon was not only the terminus a quo, the constant guide for Jewish thought and action, but it became the people's cherished treasure whose preservation was henceforth understood to be the nearest and self-evident goal of collective as well as individual life, of theory as well as practice. It can be said that the intellectual, notably the literary achievements of that people—scattered as it was in all directions and exposed to overwhelming pressures from the outside world—present a paradigmatic picture of continuity: stage follows stage in a sequence reflecting an accurate image of the process of organic growth, and the successive strata of post-biblical literature seem to form concentric layers around the Bible, comparable to the rings of a growing tree. That is the most striking feature of Jewish cultural history, and it stems primarily from Holy Scripture itself, where we find the idea of historical continuity ever present as an explicit or tacit assumption, documented in one majestic scroll and thus by implication proclaimed as the highest normative principle governing human conduct. The character of the Bible as a guide to progress of a kind that takes its bearings from the past is manifested most tellingly in the relationship which it establishes between its own main components, between the Torah on the one hand and the Prophets and Hagiographa on the other: inseparably united by the predicate of holiness, the Pentateuch nevertheless assumes within the canon a position of pre-eminence as the holiest of holies, an inexhaustible

This essay was first published in German in *Encyclopaedia Judaica*, Berlin, 1929, Volume IV.

fount of knowledge and thus reveals itself immediately as a beginning, the
initial term, as it were, in a series pointing in essence beyond itself. The
Jewish conception, it is true, was guided from the outset by a religious
view of history, a view which mirrored the most decisive facts of the
opening period of the nation's spiritual history in inverse sequence. The
prophets who, as originators of the idea of an organic development of
spiritual life, according to its own immanent laws, had been foremost in
demanding that the teachings of the faith, as laid down in the written word,
should be handed over to the people themselves, and came to the fore not
in their true character of heralds and precursors of the canonized law, but
disguised as mere devotees and servants of older traditions. In any case the
collection of the most important portions of Hebrew literature in the form
of coherent and generally accessible documents, which was the work of the
prophets (notably in 621 B.C.E. when Deuteronomy was published at the
inspiration of Jeremiah, and above all in 444 B.C.E. when the complete
Torah was first published in its final form), assumed exemplary significance
for the whole post-exilic Jewry. Loyal disciples of the prophets and their
successor, Ezra, the so-called "scribes" progressed in the literary domain
continually from one editorial conclusion to the next, for in their eyes each
section, once traversed, was finally completed and resting in the lap of
eternity, yet far from being the terminal section. So far from wishing to
deprive literary activity of the opportunity of further development by the
delimitation of writings singled out as classical, the men who increased the
treasure in the people's store acted on the assumption that the time was
ripe for the "making of books" (Eccl. 12,12) only if provision had been
made for the future productivity of the mind and if the core of the
intellectual products handed down by tradition and now due to be
perpetuated in documentary form was adequately safeguarded by a
protective cover of "oral", that is to say unfinished doctrine, developing
dynamically in the living interplay of utterance and response. That at each
stage the conclusion of the canon should have entailed at the same time the
exclusion, irrevocably as a rule, of certain parts of the national literature,
that the canonization of some books should have gone hand in hand with
the demotion or even the proscription of others (such as the Apocrypha) is
merely the obverse of a basically creative effort of construction. Thus, on
the count of its sharply accentuated internal structure alone, the complete
Bible was to act as a guide to a creative process governed by the same
structural pattern tending towards infinity. When the first "Saying of the
Fathers" (Avot 1,1) clearly proclaiming the principle of tradition, demands
the erection of a "fence round the Torah", it does no more than restate the
fundamental law of continuity that was previously manifested in the
organic formation of Holy Scripture and in the relationship established
therein between the Torah and the Prophets. This structural principle is
already clearly visible in the arrangement of the five books of the

Pentateuch subdivided in two parts—the four first books and the fifth, singled out as the "Second Torah", the Deuteronomy.

The historical background of the conclusion of the Bible

The definite completion of the canon, however, coincided in time with the rapid expansion of the Diaspora and the decay of the Jewish State. Representing the fruits of spiritual life in the preceding historical era of political and territorial independence, the Bible came to appear, by accident rather than design, both as an eloquent memorial to a past now surrounded with an aureole and as the guarantee of a yet more glorious future, and thus won the status of a document belonging to a sphere outside and above the realm of historical experience. It was only then, on the strength of that new status, that the biblical canon was finally sealed, an event that made a deep incision in the hitherto continuous line of literary tradition. As early as in the first century B.C.E. the Greek translation of the Bible, just completed at the time, showed clearly that the primary concern of that people, journeying into an uncertain future, was not with the empirically determined linguistic form but with the supra-empirical content of the revelations manifested in the sacred texts. The same attitude was reflected in all the subsequent Bible translations undertaken by Jews faithful to tradition, up to and including that of Mendelssohn. In effect, because they were now consigned to the safe keeping of each Jewish individual, the books of the Bible lent themselves readily to unlimited reproduction as the insignia of the Messianic realm awaited with fervent longing. Yet, with all that, the biblical injunction to foster the organic development of national literature continued to be heeded without a break, though the people's spiritual leaders were no longer leaning on Holy Scripture but rather looking up to it. Having become the fixed point amid the growing diversity of historical life, the Bible in fact exercised forthwith great influence within as well as outside the narrower domain of literary activity, and in both fields the effects can be traced in detail.

The Bible as reflected in post-biblical literature

The creative activity which adopted the Bible as its point of departure was confronted with a work which in its overall structure was a Book of History. Even such books as Psalms or Proverbs, which do not fit into the historical frame, were only included in the canon as products of the heroes of the history of the people as narrated in the Bible itself. Doctrinally, however, the biblical account of history makes a claim to absolute truth only in so far as it has been included in the core of the canon, the Pentateuch. "The Prophets and Hagiographa"—Rabbi Yohanan taught—"will one day be dispensed with, but the five books of the Torah nevermore" (Jerusalem Megillah 1, 70d). In contrast to the books following after the Torah, a series that can be described as an historical work in the broadest sense of the word, the five books of Moses together form an unmistakable entity as an history of legislation and the creation of law, a history of law in short. The historical account given in the Pentateuch, beginning with the creation of the world and of man and ending with the death of Moses, the law-giver illumined by the divine spirit, impresses on world history as such the stamp of an history of law. According to the Torah, the people of Israel holds the centre of the stage of world history as a whole only because it is linked with the Creator by a covenant that is a source of law, because the creation of the world and the creation of law are correlates. The most momentous event of the time encompassed in the narrative of the Torah is the revelation of the Torah itself, and the entire subsequent development—which is the subject of the remaining books of the Bible—appears to be no more than a consequence flowing from the Sinai revelation. The primacy of law and moral custom over unbridled, teeming life, attested by the very structure of the Bible and reflected in the different ranking accorded to the various ages, was to be of crucial importance for post-biblical Jewish literature, both as regards its inner structure and the mutual relationship between the several structural components involved.

The dual character of post-biblical literature

It is owing to the dual character of the Pentateuch both as a law and a history book that the single mainstream of Jewish literature was transformed into the twin streams of Halakhah and Aggada. Accordingly the historical aspect of the Torah, after it had gained a measure of self-sufficiency in line with the scale of values underlying the central testimony of revelation, could only materialize in the Bible as narrative and devotional books of lesser rank, as compared with those parts of the post-Biblical literature which continued the setting up of legal rules. In consequence, the Aggada, building on the canon as a whole, and the Halakhah, continuing the development of Mosaic law, were closely at one in accepting the Pentateuch, whose subject in unique paradoxy, as indicated above, is the story of its own origin—a design for the creation of the world as the prototype of the universe which was in being before the beginning of time. "God," it says in the Midrash, "looked into the Torah and created the world" (Yalkut Shimoni 1,2); and also in Genesis Rabbah 1, the Torah is explicitly described as "pre-existential". Regarded as the paradigm of the universe, a unified entity abolishing all time differences within the story of revelation ("In the Torah there is neither earlier nor later", Pesahim 6b); conceived further as a likeness of the people according to esoteric tradition, as the sum total of all the treasures yet to be unearthed by those learned in the law ("Whatsoever a sagacious disciple might one day state before his master, even that was declared to Moses on Sinai", J. Péa II 17a). The Torah came to be taken as composed not of words and written letters but of living cells each one of which must needs have its special function. Thus, according to the Talmud, the 248 commandments of the Torah constitute a counterpart to the same number of members of the human organism, while the 365 prohibitions form a parallel to the days of the solar year (Makkot 23a). It was that basic attitude, shared by Halakhah and Aggada alike, which inspired a man like Rabbi Akiba to introduce the method of interpreting the law by attaching special meaning to individual syllables and letters of the Torah text (Menahot 29b). All the same, the margin for free creative work was much narrower in the domain of the Halakhah than in that of the Aggada. The component parts of which the laws and rules of the Torah are made up are concepts appealing to reason and fashioned to meet the requirements of harsh reality, whereas the tales surrounding the Torah commandments are born of living sense-perception spreading out amid the inexhaustible richness and variety of the world, and are addressed in turn to the human imagination capable of bursting all the fetters of reason. But the wider the margin offered to the Aggada to encircle the Bible, the greater was its endeavour to follow the Bible at least to the extent of arranging its subject matter in the order indicated by the sections of the Torah and by other self-contained parts of the Bible. The Halakhah, by contrast, inextricably bound up as it was with the conceptual components of the law, was bent—a few exceptions apart ("halakhic midrashim")—on extending the development of the conceptual framework inherent in the system of Mosaic law as such and therefore independent of the outward arrangement of its treasure trove of formulae. That development is most clearly attested by the composition of the Aggadic midrashim on the one hand and the Mishnah on the other. The completion of the Mishnah in the second century C.E. furnished the first tangible evidence that the injunction of the Bible to continue the organic development of the national literature was faithfully observed, and that, accordingly, the norm of historical continuity was effective without a break in the Jewish people's life. This completed summary, then, was bound to be followed by further similar summaries and so the Mishnah was, indeed, followed in the fourth century by the Palestinian and at the turn of the sixth century by the Babylonian Talmud, the relationship of both of which to the Mishnah, their core, was the same as that of the Mishnah itself to the Torah. More even than their completion, the history of the gradual formation of those ultimately anonymous works, fruits of centuries of collective industry, bears witness to the fact that the unique literary structure of the Bible stamped its impress on all the creative spiritual activities of the following ages.

The Bible in the spiritual under-currents and parallel developments

Although Halakhah and Aggada appear to be as inextricably intertwined in the Talmud as are history and law in the Bible, creative spiritual activities linked with the Bible followed a course of their own, a course off the beaten track throughout the Talmudic era. The very beginning of the Bible, the story of the creation, a subject for thought fired by imagination, represented an irresistible temptation to venture into the fields of metaphysics and mysticism with all their manifold dangers to naive faith. Long before the completion of the Talmud, the first chapters of Genesis together with Chapters 1 and 10 of Ezekiel dedicated to the splendour of God's glory, had given rise to clandestine theosophic speculation (Hagigah 2, 1). Out of that "hidden midrash" there gradually developed an independent metaphysical "tradition", the Kabbalah, a phenomenon paralleled by the rise of a philosophy of religion which, for all its closeness to the Bible, had ever since the times of Philo of Alexandria taken its bearings partly from non-Jewish systems of thought. The underlying connection of both with the basic tendencies of the midrash, itself a by-product of the Aggada rooted in the Bible, is hardly questionable. Thus the "Zohar", the canon of the Kabbalah completed in the 13th century, asserted itself as a commentary on the Pentateuch aiming to bring the "mysteries of the Torah" to light. Similarly, the most important work of Jewish philosophy of religion, the "Guide of the Perplexed", produced by Maimonides in the second half of the 12th century, treated the theology and the very terminology of the Bible among its chief subjects. As much as a century earlier Rashi, following in the footsteps of the geonim, had evolved a commentary which encompassed nearly the whole of the Bible together with its close companion, the Talmud, thus completing another turn on the ascending spiral which characterizes the motion of Jewish spiritual life. In such a manner the vivifying influence radiating from the Bible as the core spread out in widening circles to the consecutive layers, the periodical growth rings, as it were, of the national literature, with poetry forming the outermost boundary. The flowering of Hebrew poetry in the 11th and 12th centuries coincided with the rebirth of the biblical style in whose mold all the great Jewish lyrical poets, from Samuel ha-Nagid to Yehudah Charisi, voiced their experience of which the "Zionides" cycle of Yehudah Halevi is the most outstanding example. In their turn, the monumental codes of Maimonides and his successors (the Poskim of the 12th—16th centuries), for all the originality of their structural form, had been intended as a "second", condensed Halakhah, once more erected as a "fence" round the Torah. Commentary, supercommentary and super-supercommentary was and remained the almost magic watchword of traditional Judaism. At the same time the continuous and hence almost imperceptible development of Jewish spiritual life was inevitably accompanied by some drawbacks, crises of growth which in the literary sphere—at times even in poetry—were manifested in a more or less marked loss of feeling for the language of the Bible, for Hebrew. It is true, the original language of Holy Scripture was held to be holy itself, so that the cultivation of the original text of the Bible counted among the self-evident obligations of the class of learned men ever since, and to some extent even before, the Massoretic era, reaching back into the fourth century. Nevertheless, in the eyes of the scholar, linguistic expression appeared understandably as of secondary importance rather than something to be cultivated for its own sake. Accordingly, it was left to modern Jewish journalistic and literary writing, as it developed under the impact of the Enlightenment, to rediscover the vitality immanent in the biblical language as such and to harness its creative potentialities promptly and effectively in the service of everyday life. The very secularisation of Jewish literature and national self-awareness, then, proceeded ultimately under the aegis of the Bible.

The Bible in Jewish daily life

The supremacy of the Law and its written record over life, proclaimed in the Torah and perpetuated by its authority, turned the Jewish people—as the outside world correctly realised—into a "people of the book", a repository of an organically unfolding erudition. In consequence, the essential trend of the spiritual movement set in motion by the Bible acquired formative significance for Jewish history as a whole. Until very recent times even those who took no direct part either in the further development of the religious teachings or in creative literary activities were still serving the cause of national literature, helping to preserve it and to hand it down to the following generations within the family. It is the duty of the individual, according to Deuteronomy 6, 6-9, to keep the words of the Torah ever before his own eyes and of those of his family and that duty was faithfully discharged. The family became the germinating cell of the school, of the Beth-ha-Sefer, i.e. the "House of the Book", the Bible, followed on a higher level by the house of "the midrash", i.e. exegetics, and higher still by a court of law engaged in formulating responsa and making decisions on points of law. Eventually, the Rabbi came to unite in his person the functions of teaching and instructing on the one hand and of spiritual care on the other, under the roof of the most fitting place for exercising these functions, in the house of prayer linked to the house of learning. The Bible continues to this day to hold the pre-eminent position where it stands for the holiest of holies. The Ark sheltering the Torah Scrolls represents the ancient Temple, and the reading of the Torah is the climax of the Sabbath and Festival services. In line with the Biblical hierarchy, congregants are called to these readings in the old order of

priorities: first, the priest (a Cohen or an Aaronide), then a Levite and last a
"plain Israelite" (cf. Gittin 59a). And so, countless believers staked their
lives for the preservation of the Torah Scrolls in times of persecution.
Judaism as a whole, firmly founded as it was on the Bible, its teachings, its
histories and its prophecies—so that the commonly applied label of
"Talmud Judaism" is clearly a misnomer—retained as its supreme
principle the norm of the continuity of cultural history and the closely
related assumption that the course of world history which began with the
creation of the world must be meaningful in each of its stages. Indeed, the
belief that history, Jewish history in the first place, is meaningful has
become an essential feature of the Jewish outlook, a postulate of the Jewish
natural view of the world. It is the educational force of biblical optimism
which is the key to an understanding of the Jewish people's character. If
there were times (such as in Poland in the 16th-18th centuries) when the
rank growth of Talmud study threatened to stifle the study of the Bible
within the set-up of Jewish education and instruction, the Bible still
proved strong enough as a vital force to provide the impulse for great
movements of regeneration which seized hold of a large mass of the
people, as did the Hasidic movement a breakthrough of the Kabbalah into
Jewish daily life—thus leading the people back to the Bible, the
fountain-head of Jewish spirituality.

The Bible in the inner Jewish splinter movements

By elevating the basic law of the continuity of cultural history to the
status of a norm, the Bible marked out the major line of Jewish history, but
at the same time it created also one of the basic conditions for the sectarian
and alienation processes which recurred over and over again in the course
of the millennia. In fact, all inner Jewish sectarian movements, however
different otherwise in their attitudes to the world and to their people,
shared one essential characteristic. Setting out from the Bible as their
starting point, they rebelled each and all against the Bible's assumption
and postulate of a continuing organic development of the substance
contained in the biblical canon. Whether it was the case of Christianity or
the later Karaism spiritually akin to the ancient Sadducees, or of the
various Messianic movements or, for that matter, modern secularism, the
issue separating all those spiritual trends from traditionalist Judaism
invariably concerned the attitude to the tradition which thrived on biblical
soil and derived its solemnization from the Bible. In fact, time after time it
was confirmed that, once adopted as the point of departure for spiritual
creativity, the Bible unfailingly led towards paths running more or less
parallel to the dominant line of Jewish spiritual development. Pre-Pauline
Christianity challenged the injunctions of the scribes who sought to adjust
Holy Scripture to the demands of practical life, and the Apostle Paul, by

invoking the Prophets, wanted Charity not only to fulfil but to supplant the Law. But the Bible, taken over by the Church in its infancy, compelled the Christian believers to tread the road of the scribes and to add to the original Jewish canon a "new" canon which was instrumental in the transition first to the patristics, and subsequently to the era of scholasticism. Similarly, the Karaites who, in the name of the Bible, were up in arms against its legitimate heir, post-biblical literature, ended up by creating a new "Talmud". Again, it was characteristic of the Messianic sectarianism in its diverse forms that it turned always to the Bible, especially the Prophets, so as to prove the legitimacy of a sudden interruption of the organic development of Judaism. Adopting the same procedure, the Jewish Enlightenment which culminated in the Reform movement of the 19th century (having been represented a full two centuries earlier by men such as Uriel da Costa or Spinoza) somehow felt that its reverence for the Bible gave it a right to attack the Talmud and the Rabbinical system.

The pre-eminent position maintained by the Bible in Judaism as a Code without a break over two millennia may be one of the reasons why modern Bible criticism which dissolves the "Old Testament" into several single components has had little appeal even for many Jewish scholars not committed to religious tradition. Indeed, over by far the longest stretch of Jewish history, leading directly up to the present, the Bible has made its influence felt—as the Torah, its core, had done in the more remote past—not as perceived by the analytical mind, but as a living, organic, indivisible entity.

2. Jewish Morals

1. Introduction

The survival of the Jews as a coherent community is generally attributed to their religion and their peculiar morality. Opinions may differ widely as to the intrinsic value of this morality; no one, however, will question the fact that Jewish society, since time immemorial, has been based on certain moral principles typical of this group and of this group alone. To those who regard true morality as a standard of general human conduct fundamentally independent of historical antecedents, the distinctive character of Jewish morals may appear deficient by definition. However, this is a matter to be examined only after the essence of Jewish morality has been clearly defined. Jewish believers, those who abided by the law of their fathers, for their part, deprecated any attempt to reduce the mass of commandments, precepts and regulations to general moral principles. To them, every distinction between morality and legality within the flow of religious tradition meant lowering the status of obligatory law as against the dictates of the heart. Inspirations of this kind, as reflected in Musar, Aggada, Midrash, were at best regarded as substitutes for or accessories to the law. It was only in times of crisis and spiritual confusion that Jewish moralists raised their voices, and even then their guiding maxims were:

This essay was first published in English in *The Jewish People: Past and Present*, Volume II, Jewish Encyclopedic Handbooks, Inc., New York, 1948.

"The fear of the Lord is the beginning of knowledge," and "My son, forget not my law" (Proverbs I, 7 and III, 1). Any investigation into the essence and development of Jewish morals must thus first establish the place actually occupied by morality within the compact reality of Jewish history, and its true relation to the accepted sacred law.

This historical approach, far from conflicting with the traditional Jewish attitude, may make the latter comprehensible even to those who are indifferent to the validity of the Law. In the written history of ancient Israel all crucial moments are presented as landmarks in legislation (cf. Jewish Law, Introduction). The lawgiver and supreme judge is God, and His will is revealed to the people through His faithful servants. No other authority exists to draw a line between right and wrong, between good and evil. As far as the people itself is concerned, its own moral attitude and ability to tell good from evil are generally presented as vitiated by blind impulses and an innate want of constancy. The people is "stiffnecked," readily deceived by false prophets and seduced by "other gods." In their natural morality the Children of Israel are thus merely descendants of Adam, of man in general, of whom it is said that "the imagination of his heart is evil from his youth" (Genesis VIII, 21). Left to itself and to its own instincts, without the guidance of divine law, the people would succumb to the forces of evil and cease to exist. This basic conception of the natural weakness, if not wickedness, of the human heart, and of its constant need for a legal harness, underlies the Hebrew Bible from beginning to end. It may be assumed that the Scriptural exposition of Israel's ancient history was in itself influenced by an unyielding mistrust of morality as an independent factor in human progress. This mistrust of natural morals inevitably determined the moral and ethical reasoning of the post-Biblical generations. Encloistered in its legal armor, Judaism became suspicious of its own moral vigor and preferred to by-pass it in silence. Not until the age of Emancipation, the time of its self-imposed disarmament, did the Jewish people feel an urge to speak to itself, as well as to the world at large, of the moral foundations of its real existence.

Seen in historical perspective, these foundations stand revealed in their true light. They cannot be of a later origin than the original community built upon them. The order of social creation cannot be reversed: the community always precedes the legal principles which it is challenged to implement. Even as a divine revelation the Law is assigned to a "chosen people," a people predisposed to accept it. This, as is well known, is the established doctrine of the Bible. Powerful as may have been the opposition of the moral élite, which speaks through the Bible, against the immorality of the people, to the historian this moral aristocracy is still bone of the people's bones and flesh of its flesh. Good laws could not have been assigned to an altogether bad people, and must consequently be credited, at least in part, to the moral atmosphere in which they were engendered.

And what is true of the Biblical period of Jewish history is no less true of the later periods. Side by side with the evolution of Jewish law, and interwoven with it, went another process by which the moral principles, whether already embodied in legal statutes or still tending toward such embodiment, found an ever higher degree of clarification. It seems obvious, then, that a reconstruction of the Jewish past from a strictly historical point of view has to concentrate no less on this moral evolution than on the more easily traceable advancement of the Jewish law.

A comprehensive exploration of the inner moral fabric of Jewish life in its development through the centuries will have to take cognizance of every force which determined that life, be it from within or without. Charity, for instance, becomes a different proposition in a community deprived of solid economic foundations, as compared with the practice of the same virtue under more normal economic conditions. Thus, the evolution of Jewish charitable institutions and the prominence they have gained within the general framework of Jewish morality remain a historical enigma, unless viewed against the background of the external factors which have shaped the political destiny of the Jewish people. And the same is true of almost every other characteristic feature of Jewish morality.

As to the sources to be consulted, clearly the history of Jewish law, or more precisely, the sources of that history, must take precedence over every other kind of historical testimony. One illustration may suffice: at a very early period of Israel's history a measure of legal protection against the "avenger of blood" was accorded to the "manslayer that killeth unwittingly and unawares" (Numbers XXXV, 11-34; Joshua XX, 2-9). Whatever else this legal innovation may have signified, the curtailment of the private right to avenge blood with blood indicates that the primitive moral notions of human responsibility, guilt and duty were at that time undergoing a process of reformation in Israel. And when we learn that centuries later even the judicial imposition of capital punishment was circumscribed in such a manner as to make it almost impossible (e.g., see Mishnah Sanhedrin, IV-V), we have every reason to assume that in the period between the canonization of the Torah and the codification of the Mishnah, the value placed on individual human life was steadily increasing. Is there a more reliable yardstick for measuring moral progress than the actual price, fixed in terms of law, which society is prepared to pay for each individual's right to live?

The continuous and well-documented history of the development of Jewish law provides the explorer of Jewish morals with a never-failing guiding thread. True, he may sometimes question whether or not the promulgation of a certain law can be taken as an adequate reflection of the moral climate of the time. For just as laws are often merely forerunners and stimuli of moral progress, so may they sometimes lag behind or retard it. However, such difficulties are more likely to confront the historian who probes the morals of its evolution. The explorer of Jewish morals, on the other hand, confronted with an uninterrupted process of three thousand years, is justified in dealing with periods of such length as enable him to draw general conclusions. No law can stand the test of time if it is not congruous with the general trend of morals within the community which gave it birth, and no community will, in the long run, suffer an ancient law to persist unless it be adaptable, by way of interpretation, to higher levels of moral achievement. This, incidentally, is the story of the Ten Commandments with their enduring moral significance both within and beyond the Jewish world.

The clue to the problem of what moral teachings, as distinct from the accepted law, contributed to the actual reformation of Jewish moral life may often be found in liturgical literature. The composition of the Jewish prayerbook reflects a concurrence of factors of which the most important, apart from Law, are the moral and ethical tenets approved and gradually absorbed by the mass of the people. Though formed by law and comparable in some respects to a legal code, the Jewish prayerbook testifies to the permeation of the whole community by the loftiest moral ideals of its spiritual guides. Generation after generation could not have prayed for the transfiguration of "all creatures" into "one unit," as is done annually on New Year's Day and the Day of Atonement, had not the idea of universal brotherhood become an integral part of Jewish morality.

Like the morality of every other community, that of the Jews had to pass through a succession of stages. Their conceptions of the ideal man, of the good life, of the moral tasks of the community as such, of its obligations toward other communities, of the duty to translate solemn exhortations into deeds, and the coordination of all these concepts within the framework of one morality—all this was the product of a long and extremely painful process. At its end, marked by the first codification of the "oral law," the Mishnah (about 200 A.C.E.), we find that the people's heart had undergone a tremendous change. The lawless, quarrelsome, rebellious nation of the Bible had disappeared. "Since the destruction of the Temple, prophecy has been suspended" (Babyl. Talmud, Baba Batra, 12b)—there were no prophets left to castigate the people, and no people to stone its prophets. Scribes and Pharisees—the successors of those who in the days of old had poured out their wrath upon a sinful people—and the people itself had merged into one. Nothing short of a miracle—not recorded in our sources—could have brought forth this unity, had not the body politic itself been singularly receptive to the Prophetic ideals. At least from the time of the Babylonian Exile, the discrepancy between Jewish law and Jewish life, however great it may have been before, diminished steadily, and the morality of the people began to take shape. Henceforth the community knew what it was living for; and its members realized that their mutual relations, as well as their relations with non-Jews, ought to be built upon this knowledge. They gained an ever clearer idea of who and what should be qualified as "good," what should be aspired to and emulated. At the conclusion of the Mishnah, the Jewish moral ideal had fully emerged and the essence of Jewish morality had grown into a force decisive for the entire future of the people. The end reveals the beginnings. From the viewpoint of the history of morals, all that preceded was but a succession of preparatory stages tending towards this final realization; and all that followed, but a sequence of attempts to bring the adopted moral ideal to an ever higher degree of materialization, to implant, as it were, the rediscovered "tree of knowledge of good and evil" in the firm ground of ordinary human life.

2. The Godlikeness of Man

The quintessence of Jewish morals is the belief that man is created "in the image of God" (Genesis I, 26) and that his human dignity derives therefrom. This belief underlies the Biblical idea of the universal fellowship of men and of their mutual obligations. Their common likeness to the Creator is their indissoluble bond. Though "formed of dust" and destined to "return unto dust," all sons and daughters of Adam breathe the same spirit, that "breath of life" which is their "portion from above" (Genesis II, 7 and III, 19; Job XXXI, 2, XXXII, 8 and XXXIII, 4; Zechariah XII, 1; Isaiah XLII, 5). In the order of creation man is thus both the last and the first; condensed "earth" (the name "Adam" derives from "adamah"—earth) and part of heaven; animal and angel. He is nearest to God in his faculty "to know good and evil" (Genesis III, 22), because this knowledge makes him free to choose one or the other, and by the assertion of his freedom he, a creature, becomes himself creative—like his Maker.

It is difficult to say precisely when this Biblical doctrine of man's twofold nature first captured the people's mind, so as to affect its everyday life. But in retrospect, looking back from the moral heights reached by the fathers of the Mishnah, universal history, both in its political and spiritual aspects, appears determined by the revelation that man is half beast, half God, and that it is his own fault if the earthly part of his nature outweighs the celestial; if he gives ear to the voice of his subhuman rather than his superhuman component. In accordance with this moral conception, the misfortune of individuals as well as of entire peoples was explained by their inability to strike the balance between the two extremes. It was this failure, too, which condemned Israel to undergo successive catastrophes. Its past had already been presented in this light by the Prophetic school, whose exponents painted the people in darkest colors, now so arrogant as to challenge the Almighty Himself, now so depraved as to descend to the level of beasts. This exposition of history had sunk deep into the people's consciousness, and after the restoration of its autonomous life in the 5th century B.C.E., the Jewish community was resolved to side with the forces of good. Conformity with the divine law became the criterion for the right choice between good and evil. Thenceforth this first principle was implied in the people's morality.

How acute the consciousness of the god-like character of man became by then can be judged by the general tendency governing the evolution of the "oral law." The rigid formulae of the inherited written law were interpreted and re-interpreted in such a way as to make them adaptable to specific circumstances of individual life. The severe sanctions of the ancient criminal law gradually fell into disuse. "A Sanhedrin (the Supreme Court) which pronounces one death sentence in seven years," says the Mishnah, "deserves to be called murderous. Rabbi Eleazar ben Azariah says: 'One in seventy years.' Rabbi Tarfon and Rabbi Akiba say: 'Had we been in the Sanhedrin, no man would ever have been put to death' " (Makkot I, 10). Thus high had the price of every human life risen, even the life of one against whom there was strong evidence of guilt deserving the death penalty. A formula never before heard was coined: Man equals World; a formula deduced from the very story of the Creation: "Man was created as a singular (i.e., in contrast to the animals which were created 'after their kinds') in order to teach thee that whosoever annihilates one of the sons of Adam is deemed by Writ as though he had annihilated a whole world, and whosoever sustains one of the sons of Adam is deemed as though he had sustained a whole world" (Mishnah Sanhedrin IV, 5). These words firmly established the foundations for the essential moral idea that every human being is a microcosm in himself.

At the same time another great discovery was made: the absolute uniqueness of every human individuality. The same Mishnah continues: "(Man was created as a singular) in order to reveal the greatness of God. Unlike man whose coins, if stamped with the same seal, are all alike, the King of Kings has stamped every man with the seal of the first man, and yet, not one of them is like unto the other. Therefore, it behoves each man to say: 'The world was created for my sake' " (ibidem, in fine). In other words, every single human being is as unique as the Father of the Universe.

The universalism of this moral idea, presented—anonymously—in conjunction with its correlated and strongly emphasized individualism, must be conceived as the final result of the people's education in the spirit of its sacred literature. From the Patriarchs' Saga down to the Psalms, the Bible abounds in vivid presentations of individual human characters, shown with all their virtues and vices, their hopes and fears, their holy aspirations and diabolical depravities. The Bible thus opened the eyes of the people to the phenomenon of human personality. Only against this literary background does the discovery of man's uniqueness cease to appear as a miracle in itself.

3. The Impact on the Law

The written law of Israel did not evaluate the relative worth of its integral parts. One could, therefore, assess the greater or lesser importance of the various commandments only indirectly and approximately, for instance, by comparing the respective sanctions threatening the transgressor. The oral law, however, introduced an essential distinction between them—one of the most striking examples of the impact of general moral ideas upon legislation: against the commandments governing relations "between man and his fellow." And what is more, the latter appear to rank higher than the former. The classical passage which refers to this distinction as to a well-digested general idea, reads: "From transgression between man and God Yom Kippur cleanses; from transgression between man and his fellow-man Yom Kippur does not cleanse, unless the transgressor has reconciled his fellow-man. Thus did Rabbi Eleazar ben Azariah interpret the verse (Leviticus XVI, 30), 'From all your sins before the Lord shall ye be clean' " (Mishnah Yoma VIII, 9). With this restrictive interpretation of the Torah's phrase "sins before the Lord" a new category of "sins before man" was established, and man achieved godlikeness in a new respect, being invested with the power to forgive or not to forgive offenses committed against him by his fellow-man. Without presupposing a steady moral development towards such a deeper apprehension of the idea of man's godlikeness, the quoted Mishnah would have to be classified as an anti-religious manifesto. In reality, it signifies but another step in the moral progress of the Jewish people.

The new disjunction implied one of the most far-reaching consequences in interhuman relations. Murder, for instance, became literally unpardonable, at least in this world. For to pardon his murderer, the murdered man would have to be resurrected, since under divine law even the Lord Himself appears divested of the right to act for the victim. No wonder that in the community in which this conception prevailed, murder became worse than a crime—a life-long curse brought down by man upon himself. The very idea of shedding blood became horrifying. No sane man could envisage the commission of a crime which would automatically rebound upon himself.

It was probably by this time that the ancient Jewish idea took root that "the Sabbath is for man, not man for the Sabbath." The Talmudic parallel to this Evangelical dictum is: "Preservation of life pushes Sabbath aside," that is to say, the very sanctity of the holiest day must retreat before the sanctity of a single human life (Babyl. Talmud, Shabbat 132 and Tosefta Shabbat XVI, 12).

The scale of legal values, through the medium of the oral law, was gradually adjusting itself to the broader requirements of the people's morals.

4. Israel and Humanity

Within the family of mankind, every member of which was presumed to be born with Adam's stamp of godlikeness upon his face, the Jewish community regarded itself as a family within a family. Through the fatherhood of the first man all human beings were, according to common belief, interrelated, but only the descendants of Abraham were brothers one to another. How far this distinction between the degrees of relationship affected the moral obligations towards individual fellow-men will be considered later (see 9. Relations with Non-Jews). The immediate point here is whether the adoption of the genealogical conception of the Bible (Genesis X) had a direct effect on the attitude of the Jewish people as a whole towards alien peoples, its partners in history.

There is no doubt that one of the most difficult tasks facing the spiritual leaders of Israel was to infuse into their people's mind the notion that it had been raised, by God's grace, to the rank of a "chosen people." This apparently privileged position carried with it the arduous obligation to bear the burden of the Law, and all available evidence of history shows that, up to the breakdown of Jewish political independence, the nation as a whole was rather disinclined to play the ordained role. The responsibilities involved in the privilege of being God's "firstborn son" (Exodus IV, 22; Jeremiah XXXI, 9) did not appeal to the main body of the people. It preferred to maintain its relations to other peoples on an equal footing, to mix with them, to imitate their ways of life, to share their tastes, even to worship their "no-gods" (Deuteronomy XXXII, 21; Jeremiah II, 11; Hosea I, 9). The strong reluctance evinced by the Houses of Israel and Judah against constituting themselves as a spiritual aristocracy among the dwellers of the earth, as "a kingdom of priests and a holy nation" (Exodus XIX, 6), led the Prophets to emphasize over and over again the everlasting validity of the Covenant between the Lord and "His people," according to which Israel ought to be, in things spiritual, the legitimate representative of all mankind. Within the framework of God's Covenant with all the sons of Noah, this eternal treaty with Abraham's seed contained, as the Bible has it, the special obligation to collaborate with the Creator in reaching the moral goal of universal history (Genesis IX, 8-17; Isaiah XI, 9). It took nearly ten centuries to instil into the Jewish mind the consciousness of Israel's duty towards the world at large, but in the end it became as integral a part of the people's morality as the idea of human godlikeness itself. The result was the remolding of the Jewish community in conformity with its moral ideals.

5. Peculiar Features of Jewish Society

Constituted as a family within a family, on the basis of a Covenant within a Covenant, the Jewish community developed features which seem to be unique in the history of social life. United in their common obligation to bring nearer "the end of the days" (Isaiah II, 2-4; Micah IV, 1-5), the age of universal peace and universal wisdom (Jeremiah XXXI, 31-34), each son of the Covenant was called upon to make his personal contribution to an effort pointing toward a distant future. To participate in this assignment with which the House of Israel had been charged was the only thing which really mattered in the individual's life, giving it meaning and direction. Each generation was but a link between ancestry and posterity, and the individual but a means for maintaining the continuity of the national effort. Hence the inclusion into the living community of those who were no more, as well as of those who were not yet, as if all of them were its permanent members. Thus veneration of the forefathers and anxiety for the weal of the unborn generations were merged into one. The people was addressed as though it were one being, and the individual was regarded, and regarded himself, as the embodiment of the whole people. The promise "that thy days may be long" and the reminder "that thou wast a servant in the land of Egypt" (Deuteronomy V, 15-16) deliberately effaced the distinction between the people and its individual members. Accordingly, death meant to the individual being finally incorporated into the national body or, in the Biblical phrase, "to be gathered to his people" (Genesis XXV, 8 and XLIX, 29). In relation to the very distant ancestors at one end of the lineage, and to the no less distant offspring at the other, it was quite natural to recognize all contemporaries within the community as "brothers."

But the great fraternity of Israel was not fatherless. Their ever-present, ever-watchful head was the Creator of the Universe Himself. Without His perpetual presence Israel would cease to be a society of brothers; by His grace, whenever two of the Children of Israel met, the Lord was the third in their company. And even face to face with his own soul, the Jew knew that he was not alone. Rabbi Akiba expressed it thus: "How distinguished is man, since created in the image of God, and still more distinguished in the consciousness of having been created in the image of God . . . and how distinguished are Israel, since called His children, and still more distinguished in the consciousness of having been called His children, as it is said, 'Ye are the children of the Lord your God' " (Sayings of the Fathers III, 14). The Torah passage quoted by Rabbi Akiba proceeds: "For thou art an holy people unto the Lord . . . out of all peoples that are upon the face of the earth" (Deuteronomy XIV, 1-2; cf. also VII, 6-9).

A society which included past and future generations, as well as God Himself, as its integral parts, and which conceived its own perpetuation as a means to the fulfillment of a moral obligation, i.e., the realization of the Prophetic ideal of universal harmony in this world, was bound to evolve its own peculiar structure. As a fraternity it could not but be a democracy. But its aristocratic notion of being the spiritual élite of the human race—humanity itself being the aristocracy of the created world—led to ever more pronounced distinctions of spiritual rank within this primarily democratic society. Like the entire people, so a certain tribe or group within this people could gain distinction by its greater nearness to the source and final end of Creation. Genealogy thus acquired importance second only to Cosmogony, while the idea of spiritual primogeniture did not clash with that of general brotherhood. Having accepted the burden of representing God's will in this world, the Jewish community acquiesced also in its own division into the two classes of spiritual leaders and followers, with the understanding, however, that everyone was eligible in principle to pass from the latter group to the first. Taken as a whole, the community presented the rare phenomenon of a democratically organized aristocracy, its coat of arms emblazoned with the words of Moses: "Would God that all the Lord's people were prophets" (Numbers XI, 29).

6. Personal Relations Within the Community

In the popular conception, the emotional relationship between God and man was based on bonds of mutual love. So was the relationship between man and man. The commandment, "Thou shalt love thy neighbor (the other) as thyself" (Leviticus XIX, 18), was proclaimed by Rabbi Akiba to be the "all-embracing principle of the Law" (Sifra on the quoted verse). This applied to human beings in general (Sayings of the Fathers I, 12). However, the members of the Jewish community were expected to be bound together by a more specific kind of benevolence, by the closer ties of brotherly love. The word of the Torah, "That thy brother may live with thee" (Leviticus XXV, 36), became the guiding rule in both legal and extra-legal relations between Jew and Jew.

Within the pattern of this general brotherhood, all types of personal relationships were subordinated to the ideal cause which the community as a whole was destined to serve.

The family was transformed into a unit best fitted to cultivate the national tradition and to maintain the cohesion between past and future. The primary duty of the father toward his children was to "teach diligently" all that he himself had absorbed of the knowledge accumulated by the older generations, and always to be prepared to satisfy the child's curiosity concerning Israel's history (Deuteronomy VI, 7, 20). That this paternal duty was, on the the whole, conscientiously discharged is proved by the early history of Jewish educational institutions. Only in a society where the family itself functioned as a preparatory school could the idea of universal obligatory instruction be conceived and implemented. The enhanced authority of the father in his twofold capacity as head of the family and headmaster of the domestic school by no means infringed upon the authority of the mother, the second in command. In our sources, father and mother go together, with the latter sometimes taking precedence (Exodus XX, 12; Leviticus XIX, 3). For a son not to "obey the voice of the mother" was an offense no less grave than disobedience toward the father (Deuteronomy XXI, 18-21). No one, however, thought it possible that a daughter might turn "rebellious" like a son. (Mishnah Sanhedrin VIII, 1; Josephus was of a different view.)

The relative equality of husband and wife in the domestic sphere was, no doubt, rooted in generally accepted principles of sexual morals. Legitimate sexual intercouse was invested with a halo of holiness (Leviticus XIX, 2; XX, 7-26). Notwithstanding the legal recognition of polygamy, the union between man and wife for procreation was considered a relationship of a unique character, as if "the first man", Adam, were to know Eve in order to continue the divine work of Creation. Accordingly, any deviation from sexual normalcy was regarded as an "abomination" (Leviticus XVIII, 22-30). Though considered less firm than the man, not only in body but also in spirit, the woman was still his blessed helpmate without whom he would be incomplete; and, because of her very feminine weakness, it was thought she needed special protection. Her womanly reputation was untouchable, her honor sacrosanct (Deuteronomy XXII, 13-19). The purity of Jewish family life, which in later centuries was to be so much admired even by opponents of Judaism, was in essence the result of two interrelated factors: the elevation of the mother to equality with the father and the sanctification of the conjugal relationship.

The inclusion of sex behavior in the code of ideal Jewish morality curbed the development of ascetic tendencies which had made their appearance as early as the Biblical age. All precepts of the Law were interpreted with reference to the Torah phrase, "He shall live by them" (Leviticus XVIII, 5), repeated also by Ezekiel (XX, 11) and in Nehemiah IX, 29, in such a sense as to exclude behavior detrimental to life. Self-imposed deprivation, according to Rabbi Joshua, is tantamount to an attempt to destroy the world (Mishnah Sota III, 4 *in fine*). At the end of the Mishnaic period the saying "He shall live, and not die, by them" (i.e., by the commandments) had become almost proverbial, providing each member of the Jewish community with a moral criterion for his relations with himself.

In sanctifying legal sexual relations and the biological existence of man in general, Jewish morality created a basis for a humane attitude also towards animal life. Protection of a bird's maternal feelings, the extension to cattle of the privilege to rest on Sabbath, and a number of similar legal institutions (Deuteronomy XXII, 6-7; Exodus XXIII, 12; Deuteronomy XXV, 4) were all based on the fact that the righteous in Israel, as the popular saying went, "regardeth the life of his beast" (Proverbs XII, 10; cf. Bab. Talmud, Nedarim 50a, the jest ascribed to Rabbi Akiba's wife). To this aspect of Jewish morality belongs also the methodical cultivation of feelings of abhorrence for whatever is hideous, unclean and repulsive in nature. The commandment, "Ye shall not make yourselves abominable with any creeping thing that creepeth, neither shall ye make yourselves unclean with them, that ye should be defiled thereby" (Leviticus XI, 43 and XX, 25), had been taken to heart by the people and prompted a reaction against evil and evildoers as if, like creeping snakes, they were by nature disgusting and repulsive.

Practical and realistic in its appreciation of the hard facts of man's individual life, Jewish morality brought the same attitude to the harsh realities of social co-existence. The most striking of these was the uneven distribution of wealth within the great fraternity of Israel. Though poverty was regarded as a natural phenomenon, like physical deformity ("For the poor shall never cease out of the land"—Deuteronomy XV, 11), the destitute "brother," he who had "waxen poor" (Leviticus XXV, 25, 35, 39), remained a source of constant worry both to the community and to each of its more fortunate members. It seemed a matter of fairness that the misfortune of the indigent brothers be corrected by allowing them to share in the affluence of their wealthier brethren. Consequently, the material assistance extended to them was not "charity" in the modern sense: it was their due, as testified by the derivation of the Hebrew term for this kind of voluntary aid, *Tsedakah*, from *Tsedek*, Justice. In a sense, all private property was part and parcel of the people's heritage and its possessors were charged with maintaining the poor in the common interest. Under the impact of these ideas, the ancient institution of "Hebrew bondmen" (Exodus XX, 2-11) was bound to disappear. Neither could distinctions of wealth develop into class distinctions of a permanent character. Luxury was deprecated even when displayed by kings, and in the end poverty itself rose to the distinction of being the mark of righteousness.

This was the moral atmosphere in which, towards the conclusion of the epoch under review, the idea of rebuilding Jewish society in accordance with the highest requirements of social justice began to gain ground, and in which sectarian movements, like that of the Hasidim Rishonim or the Essenes, could grow and flourish. One such movement was Christianity.

It may be assumed that by this time an expanding market economy with its unavoidable temptations had done considerable damage to the brotherly relations among Jews, especially in the sphere of trade. The morally alert felt called upon to cast about for emergency measures. Stengthening the law was one of them; forming closer fraternities within the greater fraternity of Israel was another, the latter being probably inspired by the traditional Jewish conception which saw humanity in an essentially concentric pattern.

7. The Ideal Man

Jewish morality found its most condensed expression in the image of the ideal man, an image set up to guide the individual through the straits and travails of earthly life. No moral ideal is ever complete without its incarnation in a life story, whether it be a true story or merely legend. When the moral ideal of the Jewish people had finally emerged, it was linked closely to the personality of Moses, in whose face no trait had been more fascinating than the look of modesty.

In emphasizing the modesty of its greatest hero, Jewish tradition implicitly reaffirmed the meaning of man's godlikeness as a moral principle: the nearer man comes to God, the clearer is his realization of the distance separating him from perfection, the closer is he united with the rest of humanity in the common duty of self-perfection. Thus Moses was extolled as the "Father of the Prophets," men who never spoke in their own name and who, in their turn, were followed by the Soferim (Scribes), the modest interpreters of the law. Down to the fathers of the Mishnah, modesty remained the traditional virtue of the Jewish spiritual élite and, more precisely, the virtue of tradition itself. In the Jewish view, the ideal man must not try to begin a new beginning, but rather carry on the work of his predecessors. "Moses," states the Mishnah, "received the Torah from Sinai and passed it to Joshua, Joshua to the elders, these to the prophets, the prophets to the men of the Great Synagogue . . ." and so from generation to generation (Sayings of the Fathers I, 1-12; II, 8). Therefore the ideal man must be a learned man, versed in the sacred law which he is called upon to implement and to enrich. The greater his scholarly achievements, the more pronounced his modesty. Again in the words of the Mishnah: "If thou hast studied much Torah, do not take pride in it, for to this end thou wast created" (*ibid.* II, 8). These words are attributed to Rabbi Johanan ben Zakkai who, after the destruction of the Second Temple, restored Jewish communal independence on the basis of study.

Modesty may be regarded as the key to all the virtues which were supposed to be engraved on the souls of the best among men. With modesty went self-restraint, contentment with one's lot, consideration for the humble, a mild, serene and open mind, and a pure heart full of mercy and forgiveness. A "clean heart" and "right spirit" were the bounties prayed for by the pious Psalmist (Psalms XXIV, 4; LI, 12). In consonance with the endeavors of more ancient piety, Rabbi Johanan ben Zakkai declared that a good life is unthinkable without a "good heart" (Sayings of the Fathers II, 9). And still another trait typical of older piety was integrated in the image of the ideal man: his "right spirit," like that of the "righteous" (*Zaddik*) and the "gracious one" or "saint" (*Hasid*) of the Psalms, was winged with cheerfulness. At peace with himself, with his fellow-men and with God's world, he was able to enjoy life, even when it demanded, as from Rabbi Akiba, the supreme sacrifice in the service of his Maker. All he did was done "for the sake of heaven," unselfishly, without expectation of reward. It was at this time that the House of Prayer, where the people learned the Psalms by heart, and the House of Learning, where the virtues of the ideal scholar were evolved and cultivated, united in one, so as to produce the composite image of the righteous *Talmid Hakam* (Pupil of the Wise), the ideal of manhood for a long chain of later generations.

8. Guilt and Self-redemption

Realistic, in a higher sense, as it was, Jewish morality could not conceive even the ideal man as being entirely free from sin. "Surely there is not a righteous man upon earth, that doeth good, and sinneth not"—this generalization of Ecclesiastes (VII, 20), which we also find in Solomon's prayer (First Kings VIII, 46), may well be a reference to the life of Moses and its tragic end (Deuteronomy XXXII, 51-52). At the same time this conception provided the Jewish conscience with an answer to Job's question: Why is it that the wicked often prosper whilst the righteous often come to grief? Not unaccountable fate, but personal guilt, attributable even to the most perfect among the sons of Adam, was thought to be the real cause of human suffering. This doctrine, proclaimed by the Prophet of the Exile (Ezekiel III, 20-21; XVIII, 1-32), was progressively assimilated by the mass of the people and helped to sustain its belief in the existence of a moral world order. The core of this doctrine was the recognition of the individual as the real center in any pattern of social morality. No one could henceforth shift moral responsibility to someone else's shoulders; no one could ascribe to himself a definite moral character, be it good or bad, so long as his individual life was not accomplished to the very end. "The righteousness of the righteous shall not deliver him in the day of his transgression; and as for the wickedness of the wicked, he shall not fall thereby in the day that he turneth from his wickedness" (*ibid*. XXXIII, 12). Instead of being taken as a static fact, moral personality, in this fundamental conception, becomes a dynamic factor which, at any moment, can propel the individual either in the right or the wrong direction.

The prophet's term "one's way" *(darko)* became as classical as his trust in man's faculty to "turn away" from lifelong habits and pursuits. In this fundamental Jewish conception, neither sacrifice nor material reparation could efface moral guilt, unless prompted by a genuine sense of culpability and an innermost desire to "turn away" from evil and "come back" to the path of righteousness. Man's power to accomplish his own moral "return" *(Teshuvah)*, to convert himself, as it were, was discovered to be the most adequate expression of his godlikeness as well as of his freedom. For the Jew, there could be no other redeemer from his sense of guilt than his own free will, and no redemption from sin but self-redemption—through prayer and change of heart. These are the moral implications of Rabbi Akiba's laconic dictum: "The power is given" (Sayings of the Fathers III, 15).

However, the stress laid upon the moral responsibility of the individual

did not restrict its scope to one's own acts or omissions. Responsibility for
the moral well-being of one's neighbor (Leviticus XIX, 17; Ezekiel III,
17-18) involved an extension of the sphere of actual or potential guilt far
beyond the limits of individual life, culminating in the image of God's
servant laden with "the iniquity of us all" (Isaiah LIII, 6).

9. Relations With Non-Jews

In their personal relations with non-Jews, the members of the Jewish
community were expected to comply with two apparently contradictory
guiding principles. The first obliged the Jew to respect the human dignity
of the non-Jew and to accord him all the privileges due to a son of Adam;
the second required him to keep the non-Jew at arm's length, never
admitting him to the intimacy of Jewish private life. However, this attitude
of aloofness, which became a more and more conspicuous feature of the
Jewish mind, indicated not a retraction of the universalistic tendency in
Jewish morality but, on the contrary, its very triumph. It resulted from the
fact that this universalistic tendency had so impressed itself upon the mind
of the individual that it determined the patterns of his personal behavior.
At the time of the conclusion of the Mishnah the Jews, with rare
exceptions, knew that every one of them had to live up to the Jewish moral
ideal which embraced all humanity and that, in consequence, it was the
individual's task to keep the House of Israel intact, for humanity's sake.
Hence the reluctance to make proselytes and the aversion to
intermarriage: "They prohibited the drinking of the wine of non-Jews,"
states the Talmud, "because of their daughters" (Abodah Zara, 36b). Far
from regarding non-Jews individually as inferior to themselves, and
attracted to them by natural instinct, the Jews threw the full weight of their
moral discipline into the fight against this ever-present temptation.

Anxious to preserve the integrity and homogeneity of their closed
society, the Jews tended to show all the more consideration to the alien
who, for whatever reason, had to live amongst them. Even the kings of
ancient Israel were famed as "merciful" (First Kings XX, 31). In the Bible
the "stranger" *(Ger)* and the "sojourner" *(Toshav)* come nearest to the
"brother" (Leviticus XXV, 35). Special protection had to be extended to
them, as to the widow and the orphan (Exodus XXII, 20-23 and
Deuteronomy XXVII, 19), "for ye know the heart of a stranger, seeing ye
were strangers in the land of Egypt" (Exodus XXIII, 9). The same reason is
given for the commandment: "Thou shalt love the stranger as thyself"
(Leviticus XIX, 34 and Deuteronomy X, 19). The oral law enhanced and
further developed these same precepts. It was one of the fathers of the
Mishnah, the disciple of Rabbi Akiba, Simeon ben Azzai, who declared
that the scope of the verse, "This is the book of the generations of Adam; in
the day that God created man, He made him in the likeness of God"

(Genesis V, 1), was even more significant than the commandment to love others as one loves oneself (Sifra on Leviticus XIX). The idea of the unity of the human race, with all that this implied in the relations between man and man, irrespective of origin, was thus established as the essence of the Jewish moral tradition. The spirit of the Law, of the Prophets and of the Mishnah merged together to justify the self-imposed segregation of the Jewish community in its humble service to a universal cause.

The self-preservation of Israel through the subsequent centuries is sufficient proof that the moral ideas of its teachers had become habitual motives in its reaction to the contingencies of historical life.

Bibliography

Baron, Salo W., *The Jewish Community*, Vols. I-III. Philadelphia, 1942.

Baron, Salo W., *A Social and Religious History of the Jews*, Vols. I-III. New York, 1937.

Benamozegh, Elia, *Morale juive et morale chrétienne*, 2nd ed. Paris, 1922.

Cohen, Hermann, *Die Religion der Vernunft aus den Quellen des Judentums*. Leipzig, 1919.

Cohen, Hermann, *Juedische Schriften*, Vol. I-III. Berlin, 1924.

Finkelstein, Louis, *The Pharisees: The Sociological Background of their Faith*, Vols. I-II. Philadelphia, 1938.

Guedemann, Moritz, "Moralische Rechtseinschraenkung im mosaisch-rabbinischen Rechtssystem", in *Monatsschrift fuer Geschichte und Wissenschaft des Judentums*, Vol. LXI. Breslau, 1918.

Herford, Robert Travers, *The Pharisees*. London, 1924.

Herford, Robert Travers, *Pirke Aboth: The Tractate "Fathers" from the Mishnah, commonly called "Sayings of the Fathers."* New York, 1925.

Lazarus, Moritz, *Die Ethik des Judentums*, Vols. I-II. Frankfort-on-the-Main, 1904-1911.

Moore, George Foot, *Judaism in the First Centuries of the Christian Era*, Vols. I-III. Cambridge, Mass., 1927-1930.

Rabinkow, S. B., *Individuum und Gemeinschaft im Judentum*. Leipzig, 1929.

Rosenzweig, Franz, *Der Stern der Erloesung*, 2nd ed. Berlin, 1930.

Schechter, Solomon, *Studies in Judaism*, Vols. I-III. New York, 1896-1924.

Steinberg, A., "The Jewish Scale of Values," in *Freedom of Expression*. Ed. H. Ould. London, 1945.

3. Messianic Movements up to the End of the Middle Ages

Introduction

Among the characteristic phenomena of Jewish history, perhaps the most remarkable is the succession of great popular movements—recurring periodically from the pre-Christian era to the 18th century—whose sole aim is the hastening of the time when the supra-historic Messianic ideal would, in accordance with the words of the ancient prophets, be realized. The general conditions which call forth these Messianic movements change from century to century; changes occur in the scope, the content and the driving force of the ideal. At times the entire people is caught up in it; at other times only a single community is affected; at times the movement spreads through all strata of the people; at other times the poorest elements alone make it their cause, so that it acquires a revolutionary character. But beyond these variations, all popular Jewish Messianic movements are marked by one unifying aim: they invariably seek to hasten the fulfillment of Jewish history in general. Parallel with this, the yearning for the "End of Days" always projects the post-historic dream in the form of the ideal personality. Although the aim of every Messianic movement has always been the redemption of the people of Israel and of the world in a universalist sense, the specific problems of every given period were invariably reflected in the picture of the redeemer. Hence, even he whose personality incarnated the ultimate redemption, changed in consonance with the spirit of the age which brought him forth. Nevertheless, he, too—whether he existed only in the imagination of the people or was a demonstrable historic reality—never ceased to be the messenger of God, elected and anointed by Him, and, therefore, a "Messiah."

This essay was first published in English in *The Jewish People: Past and Present*, Volume I, Jewish Encyclopedic Handbooks, Inc., New York, 1946.

The king of the Jews had from of old been a "Messiah of the Lord," God's anointed, worthy of bearing the crown of the people, in particular if he had also been of the House of David. The High Priest, too, naturally laid claim to the distinction. Under the Hasmonaean dynasty the anointed King and the Messiah Priest were united in a single person. But it was the Hasmonaean period which witnessed the deepest disappointments both in the socio-political and the spiritual fields; that same period, therefore, gave birth to the concept that those who stood at the head of the people and ruled it in the name of God, could merit their claim only if they added to the ideal qualities of King and Priest, those of the prophet or, at least, of the kind of man who was the ideal of the prophets. Only such a chosen man, "anointed of the Lord," would—in accordance with this view—be capable of rescuing the people from its political, social, and spiritual misery, and of bringing it nearer to the "End of Days," of universal peace, absolute justice and perfect piety which an Isaiah, a Micah, and a Jeremiah had prophesied. Of the three personalities who were thus merged into one, the first two, because of the burden of historic sin weighing upon them, had been relegated to the background, while the ideal man of the prophets became primary in importance; although a prince of the Davidic dynasty, the Messiah of the future was to be "a poor man, riding upon an ass"; and, although elected to fill the whole world with holiness, he nevertheless was to remain God's simple "servant."

Such was the will and demand of the masses who yearned for redemption, not in behalf of this or that group, but for the benefit of all the people. The destiny of the redeemer, and the destiny of the entire world—such was the view of the believers who prepared the soil for the first Messianic movement in Jewish history—depended on whether he would find in himself the power to fulfill here and now that which had centuries before been foreseen and foretold in Divine prophecy. Should the fulfillment prove to be impossible in a natural manner, it would come about miraculously—only a strong enough faith was needed. A vast Apocalyptic literature spread and elaborated these thoughts and dreams; ancient saints were resurrected—at least in the writings of these dreamers—and they testified that the "true redeemer," the righteous one, chosen by God, would soon appear and renew the whole world with a "new covenant" (according to Jeremiah XXXI, 30). Already in the Book of Daniel (VII, 13-14), there is talk of a "Son of Man" (*Bar Enosh*), who would unite all the kingdoms of the world under the sovereign rule of God. The Book of Enoch of the 1st century B.C.E. was inspired by the same Messianic-theocratic ideal; the same influence is apparent in a series of other works which are spiritually related to the Essenes. For this widespread longing to blossom into a genuine folk movement, there was wanting only the tangible "Son of Man," who would take upon himself the supra-historic mission in consonance with the Messianic ideal. That which the times demanded came to pass; such a "Son of Man" soon appeared. Indeed, he appeared again and again; and since none of these "Sons of Men" had more than a temporary success with the Jewish people, they all fall, in the Jewish tradition, under the concept of "False Messiah"—a parallel to the "False Prophet."

I. Messianic Movements under Roman and Byzantine Rule

In the last century B.C.E., the Messianic element in Judaism assumed the status of an independent spiritual factor in Palestine. A century later it began to develop as an independent belief which severed itself gradually from its Jewish soil in order to dominate the world. But with that the history of Jewish Messianism was by no means concluded; it continued to develop out of its ancient prophetic roots, in conscious contrast to non-Jewish Messianism which functioned in the outside world under the Greek name of Christianity (the Greek "Christos" is a translation of the Hebrew "Mashiah"). This world-historic movement was at the outset a typically Jewish popular movement; it rose shortly before the collapse of the Jerusalem aristocracy, against whose nearsighted politics and moral depravity it was directed; and it parted company with other similar movements in Jewish life only in one respect: while other Zealots believed that the first step toward the redemption was the liberation from Roman domination, the Messianists held that the hour had struck for the realization of the highest Jewish ideal, i.e., for the initiation of God's rule, the Kingdom of Heaven, throughout the world. They therefore pinned their hopes upon the great miracle of spiritual world revolution, and not upon a physical triumph over a few Roman legions. Their "King," Jesus, was neither a hero of the battlefield nor a diplomat of the courts; he was a popular preacher, a "rabbi" (see this Jewish word in the Greek text: the Gospel according to St. John I, 38; XX, 16 etc.), a wonderworker and a healer, as were the oldest prophets. But the general movement also produced, in the first half of the 1st century C.E., claimants to the crown of the Messiah who were closer to the other type of popular liberator. There had appeared in Palestine, for example, a Jew by the name of Theudas who gathered round him several hundred people, intending to lead them in a struggle against the Romans. He had boasted that he would repeat in the middle of the Jordan the miracle of the Red Sea. His ideal was apparently neither a hero of the post-biblical period nor even of the prophetic age; it was Moses, the "Father of the Prophets." The same sources also tell of a Palestinian "redeemer" of about the same period who was to have come from Egypt and who was to have gathered a multitude of Jews "in the wilderness." Even if the second story is merely an episode detached from the previous narrative, it has an importance of its own: we learn from it that the Messianic movement had already drawn into its sphere the Jews of the Diaspora. These attempts to hasten the redemption were drowned in blood by the Roman authorities. The Messianists whose attitude toward the world of reality, to *Olam ha-Zeh* (this world), was one of great disdain, certainly regarded redeemers of Theudas' caliber as "false Messiahs" and "false prophets." And to Jews, who even after the catastrophe in Palestine continued to believe in the coming redemption, all these Messianists whose "righteous redeemer" belonged only to the past, were for that very reason *Minim*, that is, heretics and schismatics. Into the *Amidah* prayer (the eighteen benedictions), which is the most eloquent monument in the Jewish liturgy to the Messianic movement of that day (see, for example, the first benediction: "And bringeth a Redeemer"; the eighth benediction: "Redeem us Speedily"; the eleventh: "Blow a great Trumpet"; the twelfth: "Do Thou Reign over us Alone," etc.), there was inserted a special imprecation against the *Minim* (in later prayerbooks: *Malshinim*, denouncers).

The depth of the chasm between the Jewish Messianists, who lived in the hope of the future, and the Christ-Messianists, who deified the "Son of Man," Jesus, and the story of his suffering, became particularly clear in the 2nd century C.E., when a new Jewish redemptive movement arose in Palestine. At its center stood Bar Kochba and Rabbi Akiba, the latter being the purest incarnation of the Jewish idea of *Kiddush ha-Shem* (Sanctification of the Name). The most noteworthy element in this movement, which soon assumed the character of a military uprising against the power of the Emperor Hadrian, was the fact that its leader became not the representative of the spirit, but of physical might, and that Rabbi Akiba himself, in spite of the opposition of some of the sages, proclaimed Bar Kochba as a Messiah. The very essence of Jewish Messianism, it appears, militated against any kind of aristocracy, even against that of the spirit. Whether the aim of the Bar Kochba rebellion (132-135) included, beyond the liberation of Palestine and the people of Israel, the redemption of the world, remains unclear. But Rabbi Akiba's life and martyrdom testify definitely to his Messianic concepts which were faithful in the last detail to the prophetic program of "the End of Days." In his person the Oral Law (interpretation of the Torah) merged with the ancient prophetic spirit and, far from representing the close of a supposedly antiquated legal tradition, as the followers of Paul thought, it became—thanks to Akiba's Messianic impulse—the natural heir of the true eschatological hope, namely that of the "End of Days." The Messianists, whose orientation was based mainly on the past, *i.e.*, the Christians, would not acknowledge this fact. Thenceforth, Judaism and Christianity part company for ever.

Three hundred years later, when Christianity had itself become a worldly power, and began to translate its hostility toward the Jewish tradition into action, it called forth a new attempt on the part of Jewish Messianism to realize its program. Thus we hear that in the time of Theodosius II, there appeared on the island of Crete a Messiah by the name of Moses (ca. 440); he also attempted to repeat the miracle of the earlier Moses, promising he would lead the Jews back to Palestine across the Mediterranean Sea as if it were dry land. A multitude of the faithful was drowned, and in the history of the Church the incident is cited as a new evidence of Jewish tenacity. Less than three centuries passed and Jewish Messianisn was again embodied in a living personality: this time it was a refugee from Byzantium, Serenus, who aroused the entire Jewish world from Syria and Babylonia as far as Spain. In a number of details this popular movement was reminiscent of the beginnings of Christianity. The devotees of the new "Messiah" wanted to ease the yoke of the law for the masses (mainly those laws which had been instituted by the Talmud); the movement was grounded in the belief that the world-political crisis of that time, *i.e.*, the conflict between Christian "Edom" (Rome, Byzantium) and "Ishmael" (Islam), would be the transition to Messianic days. As had happened eight hundred years earlier, an Apocalyptic literature appeared. In the apocryphal work of that period, *Nistarot de-Rabbi Simeon ben Yohai*, the dramatic denouement of world history is envisaged as occurring in three separate acts: first a pre-Messiah *(Mashiah ben Joseph)* would restore the Jews to Palestine and rebuild the Temple; this however, would end in a new catastrophe, because a mighty king, Armilus, would drive the Jewish people into a wilderness; not until its sins shall have been entirely washed away by these last calamities would the true and righteous redeemer *(Mashiah ben David)* appear. In this wise Jewish Messianism anticipated possible failure for which it prepared comfort. Thereby it also confirmed anew, in the spirit of ancient prophecy, the belief that the restoration of a free Jewish state in Palestine was not of itself the last guarantee of complete redemption. Already near the end of the 4th century, when the Byzantine Emperor, Julian the Apostate, had manifested the desire to effect a restoration of Jewish Palestine (362), the Jewish people showed that the spirit in which such a "redemption" was carried out was by far more important than the redemption itself, and Julian's offer touched no Messianic chord within the people.

II. Messianic Movements under Islamic Rule

Christianity had from the outset held, and always retained, the belief in the first and only "Messiah"; Islam had originally been the religion of the last "Prophet." While Jewish Messianism, therefore, found itself in permanent conflict with the Church, and always strove to convince it that the true Messiah was yet to come, no such difference divided it from Islam, toward which it could remain neutral. One trend in Islam, the Shiites, had already, toward the end of the 7th century—and that under the influence of a Jew who had embraced the new faith—entered the stream of Messianism by its anticipation of a second coming of Mohammed at the "End of Days." Thus, in the Islamic world, too, occasion was given to the Jews to testify to their own Messianic tradition.

We encounter the first Jewish Messianic movement in the Moslem world approximately at the beginning of the 8th century. Its central figure is the Persian Jew, Abu Isa, or Isaac Obadiah, an illiterate man of the masses who nevertheless felt called upon to proclaim the coming of the Messiah. He preached an ascetic morality, bade his followers devote themselves to prayer as much as possible, and was also prepared to take up arms for the redemption. The universalistic element in his Jewish Messianism found expression in his assertion that not alone Mohammed, but Jesus, too, was for him a true prophet, sent by God to the heathen peoples. After he had fallen in battle against a Moslem army, his devotees announced that he lived on, and one of his disciples, Yudghan, the Paul of Abu Isa, evolved an entire system whose main principles were man's freedom of will and the rejection of all anthropomorphisms with reference to God. This Messianic sect, having crystallized into a system, was to branch out in later times, and we find traces of it in the region of Damascus as late as the 10th century. The travels of Eldad ha-Dani toward the close of the 9th century are evidently bound up with this flowering of Jewish Messianism in the Orient. His mission was to establish contact with the "lost ten tribes": it was clear that without them perfect redemption was impossible.

The close of the 10th century was a time of world unrest. The year 1000 was, in the belief of many Christians, to open the Millennium; Jesus was to descend anew from Heaven. Although divided between Christian and Moslem, the religious world of that day was, nevertheless, united in its ancient Jewish and, *ergo*, Messianic roots. From the depth of Central Europe the "men of Rhenus" (Jews of the Rhine Valley) inquire of the scholars of the Holy Land whether they should get themselves ready for the "End of Days." According to the computations of Saadia Gaon (in the first half of the 10th century), the time was at hand. The caliph of the Fatimite dynasty, al-Hakim (996-1021), began to look upon himself as a sort of Messiah. Three faiths simultaneously anticipated the same miracle. Jewish Messianism, however, proved to be the most patient: if the miracle did not occur when it was awaited, it would come a century later—that, at least, was the mood of the Jews among the Moslem peoples; and so in the 12th century Messianic movements blazed forth anew among them. The most powerful was kindled (ca. 1155) in Persia, the country which had witnessed a similar phenomenon three and a half centuries earlier. Its effects were felt as far as Baghdad, perhaps because this "Messiah" was a former pupil of the Yeshivah of that city. To his name, David Alroy, was added the epithet Menahem, *i.e.*, the Comforter. Primarily he wanted to comfort the "Mourners of Zion," little groups of pious ascetics, who, in the period of the Crusades, had brooded on the question: When will the people of Israel, the party chiefly concerned, intervene in the conflict for Palestine between Christians and Moslems? When this "Messiah" had, like his predecessors, been sacrificed on the altar of his idea, remnants of the "Menahemist" movement continued to endure. About twenty years after the death of the "Comforter," David Alroy, there appeared in Yemen an illiterate Jew who regarded himself as the herald of the coming redeemer. No less a personality than Maimonides warned his contemporaries (in his *Epistle to Yemen*) against the temptation to follow all kinds of illiterate dreamers who promised to perform miracles with the power of the Holy Spirit. Nevertheless, it was precisely Maimonides who included the constant expectation of the Messiah among the Thirteen Articles of the Jewish faith; and another Jewish thinker of that day, Abraham bar Hiya, attempted in his *Megillat ha-Megalleh* (The Scroll of the Revealer), to compute the time of the apocalypse of human history. A typical representative of this Messianic 12th century was also Judah ha-Levi. Jewish Messianism, more clearly than heretofore, recognized itself in the subjective form of "patient impatience," according to the twelfth of the Thirteen Articles of Faith: "Even if the Messiah shall tarry, I shall wait for him every day."

III. Messianic Movements During the Christian Middle Ages

While Jewish Messianic movements in the Orient, and particularly under Mohammedanism, frequently assumed an aggressive and even a military-revolutionary character, they were, in consonance with the general living conditions of the Jews, much more passive in Christian medieval Europe. They find expression partly in a yearning to return to the Orient and partly in polemics against the pseudo-Messianism of the non-Jewish environment. Even these polemics were evoked by an assault of the stronger party. Thus, at the close of the 9th century, the Bishop of Lyons, Amulo, charged the Jews not only with the denial of the true Messiah, *i.e.*, Jesus, but also with the erroneous conception of the two Messiahs (ben Joseph and ben David). It is evident therefrom that the Messianic conception as set forth, for example, in the apocryphal *Nistarot* of Simeon ben Yohai, had spread as far as France. In general there must have existed Jewish circles where the yearning for the Messiah was especially cultivated. This is indicated by a contemporary document, the Midrash, *Tanna debe Eliyahu*, dating from the 10th century, which speaks repeatedly of the coming of Elijah, who would announce the approach of the righteous redeemer. During the persecutions in connection with the first Crusade (end of 11th century), Jews of Central Europe took to the road. Many refugees arrived in Constantinople, and soon the rumor spread among them that the Ten Tribes and the Jews of the Khazar countries were marching from the fabled "Hills of Darkness" and would precede the Christians in the conquest of the Holy Land. Already some ten years earlier a "Messiah" had appeared in Southern France, only to encounter the same bitter fate as many earlier Messianic pretenders. During the course of the 12th century, while Jewish Messianism flourished mostly in Moslem lands, it provided in the Christian Occident the main theme for the oral and written disputes between Jews and Christians. From the same period dates Joseph Kimhi's *Sefer ha-Berit*, in which the internal contradictions of the Jesus story are presented. Joseph's son, David Kimhi (d. ca. 1235), puts this query to the Christians: How can they view Jesus as the true Messiah, when they know from the prophets of Israel that his main mission was to be the creation of permanent peace on earth, whereof no sign was evident? The same arguments are presented by the Jewish group during the celebrated disputations which took place in Barcelona (1263) and again in the Tortosa debates (1413).

This strongly polemical attitude toward non-Jewish Messianism, *i.e.*, toward Christianity, was a symptom of the readiness on the part of the Jewish masses in the Christian Middle Ages to receive with enthusiasm every announcement concerning the "End." Indeed, less than twenty-five years before Nahmanides' dispute with the Christians in Barcelona, the "righteous redeemer" had been impatiently awaited in all Jewish communities, simply because the year 1240, according to Jewish chronology, opened the sixth millennium, with which, a Talmudic dictum states, the period of the redemption was to begin. When the invasion of Mongolian tribes a year later crossed the German frontiers, a rumor spread among Christians that this was a result of a Jewish Messianic plot. There followed a wave of anti-Jewish persecutions; one of its motifs, then as always, was the tenacious "heresy" of the Jews, *i.e.*, their belief in a Messiah who was yet to come, rather than in one who had already lived on earth more than a thousand years before.

If the unrest which marked the middle of the 13th century was a Messianic movement with a "Messiah" (at any rate we have no knowledge of "leaders"), there appeared, toward the end of the same century, several "redeemers" who, per contra, attracted very few followers. The most significant personality among the new claimants to the Messianic crown was Abraham Abulafia, who in 1284 had proclaimed himself in Italy as the redeemer. Some time earlier he had proposed merging the Jewish faith with the Christian; the "arrogance" of this proposal, which he presented to Pope Nicholas III, nearly cost him his life. His end is unknown, but after his disappearance, disciples of his continued to prophesy about the "End." Almost simultaneously with Abulafia a Messiah appeared in Avila (Spain), an illiterate, who denounced the "non-believers" as Abulafia had earlier denounced the men of learning. The leading rabbis of the day, headed by Solomon ben Adret, were bitter opponents of the new Messianic tendencies; there are reasons to believe that these tendencies, too, had a definitely anti-aristocratic character. Nonetheless, a century later, according to the report of a Christian divine who participated in the Tortosa debate, the Spanish community brought forth another false Messiah. From the 13th century on the Kabbala introduced a new element into Jewish Messianism. It was the main source from which Abraham Abulafia drew his inspiration for the belief in his universal mission of the redemption.

Bibliography

The history of the Jewish Messianic movements is treated in the general literature on Jewish history, the history of Christianity, and religion in general. The most important special works are:

JULIUS H. GREENSTONE, *The Messiah Idea in Jewish History*. 1906.
HUGO GRESSMANN, *Der Messias*. 1929.
JOSEPH KLAUSNER, *Yeshu ha-Notzri*. 1922.
JOSEPH KLAUSNER, *Ha-Raayon ha-Mashihi be-Yisrael*. 1927.
EDUARD MEYER, *Ursprung und Anfaenge des Christentums*. 1920-1923.
EMIL SCHUERER, *Geschichte des juedischen Volkes im Zeitalter Jesu Christi*. 4th ed., 1901-1911.
ABBA HILLEL SILVER, *A History of Messianic Speculation in Israel*. 1927.

4. The History of Jewish Religious Thought

Introduction

Many of the questions about which religious thought revolves have also been, from the earliest times, the essential questions to which philosophy has sought the answers. However, the basic approaches of religion and philosophy toward these questions are entirely different. Whereas the primary postulate of philosophic speculation is the absolute independence and autonomy of reason, the basis of religious thought is *the word of God*. The convergence of interest of these two schools of metaphysical thinking far from closing the breach between them, has usually resulted in estrangement and antagonism. This will explain why the treasures of Jewish culture, in accordance with their strictly religious character, contain so little of the type of reasoning to which the Greek word "philosophy" has been applied. Instead, Jewish thought has concentrated on religious speculation.

It is true that at various times and in various lands, especially in Western Europe in modern times, we find a great number of individual Jews prominent in the field of philosophy. But these men, however deep their own roots in the Jewish spiritual past, devoted themselves to a line of thinking which had very little in common with the intrinsic development of Jewish thought. Very often, in order to turn to philosophy, the Jew had to step out of his background. This was true in the case of Spinoza. Regardless of the fact that he was greatly influenced by such Jewish thinkers as Maimonides (Rambam), Gersonides (Levi ben Gershon) and Hasdai Crescas, he was nevertheless a link in the chain which continued

This essay was first published in English in *The Jewish People: Past and Present*, Volume I, Jewish Encyclopedic Handbooks, Inc., New York, 1946.

the Cartesianism of modern times rather than the philosophical trends of the Middle Ages. It is significant that whereas Descartes prepared the field for an independent French philosophy, and Leibniz (who took up the thread of modern philosophical tradition where Spinoza had left it off) became the father of a specific German philosophical school of thought, Spinoza exerted but slight influence on the Jewish way of thinking.

However, without continuity there can be no history, and especially no history of human speculation. No isolated episodes, however important, can take its place. The history of Jewish religious thought is therefore the only basis for understanding the historical development of the typical Jewish outlook on life.

At first glance, it may seem that even the development of the rationalistic aspect of Jewish religious thought lacked continuity. There is a series of distinct flourishing periods, separated one from another by centuries: the Prophetic era, the Hellenistic phase, the Jewish-Arabic renaissance, the period of modern Jewish-religious thought, each period having not only a specific geographic center but to some extent its own language (Hebrew, Greek, Arabic and German). This very fact would seem to indicate that these stages in Jewish rationalistic religious thought did not result from any immanent process of development but were due to outside influences. Closer study, however, shows that despite these historical pauses, that is, despite the intervals of decline in Jewish theological speculation and the influence exerted on Jewish thought by the outside world, its development runs parallel with the development of Jewish spiritual life as a whole. The earmark of the development of Jewish religious thought is the influence which its basic ideas exert on later stages, and in this regard the evolution of Jewish thought is the best example of an immanent development. The teachings of the Prophets, and the Bible which is the testimony of these teachings, were and are the classic norm for all Jewish thinkers—from Philo of Alexandria down to our own contemporaries.

Incidentally, no matter in what tongue they wrote and spoke, almost all these men knew the Bible in the original. Influences from without always had the effect of stirring Jewish religious thought to profounder introspection. When universalistic Jewish monotheism was confronted with Hellenistic universalism, it reacted with an interpretation of the "Ionian wisdom"—Greek philosophy—in a Mosaic spirit. This need for a sharp demarcation line between Jewish monotheism and its cultural environment grew even more acute with the rise of rigid Moslemic monotheism. Even the so-called deism, the philosophical monotheism of the 18th century, could not but have a similar effect on Jewish religious thinking. In other words, we find that whenever Jewish religious thought meets another worldview displaying certain common fundamentals, it makes a new effort to strengthen its traditional foundation. Herein lies the roots of the intrinsic antagonism between the positive-religious and the philosophical way of thinking. A negative substantiation of this is the fact that there is no specific "anti-Christian" phase in the history of Jewish religious thinking, unless we choose to view certain currents of Jewish mysticism in that light. It is very likely that Christian metaphysics was viewed as mere heresy by medieval Jewish thinkers. We can say that the magnificent creative epochs in Jewish rationalistic thought were not periods of spiritual dependence but periods of determined struggle against the dangers of such dependence; and the periods of decline simply represented intervals of spiritual tranquility and consolidation when the outside world did not threaten Jewish religious thought—interludes of serenity which prepared the rising generation for a resumption of the struggle against external onslaughts.

It would still be an error to assume that Jewish religious thought has been either apologetic or has repeated persistently—in all languages and under all historic conditions—the traditional and eternally-graven *word of God*. Had this been the case, its history would not have been one of living development but merely one of mechanical reproduction. Though bound by the sanctity of tradition, Jewish religious thinkers very early felt free to seek in the holy text meanings to satisfy their own spiritual needs, and to interpret them in accordance with reason. It was this attitude which enabled the orthodox seeker after knowledge to accept, in principle, the influence of foreign metaphysical fundamentals—whether formulated by the Greek Plato, the Arabian ibn Roshd or the German Kant—and so to assimilate them that they eventually became an organic part of the Jewish outlook on life. Thus, very often Jewish religious thinking was strong enough to exert an influence in *its* turn on the world about it: on Hellenistic philosophy, on Islam and even on certain forms of Christianity. The immense spiritual wealth garnered through the long centuries of its existence, not only from within but from the world surrounding it, explains why to this very day it holds much more than a mere historic interest for metaphysical research.

I. The Classical Era

The basic principles of Jewish religious thought were clearly formulated between the 9th and 5th centuries B.C.E. During this period, the Hebrew literature of Palestine first began to formulate an original Jewish philosophy of life; and, simultaneously, there emerged a number of eminent personalities who were the heralds and bearers of the new outlook—the so-called Book Prophets (Amos, Hosea, Isaiah, and others, up to the time of Ezra). The early prophets who have left us the heritage of their own words unquestionably did not plough virgin soil; they leaned upon an older tradition. However, they did not accept this religious tradition unquestioningly; they submitted it to sharp critical scrutiny, thus extracting the valuable kernel from the ancient popular beliefs and discarding the empty shell. Despite the fact that they were not formal "thinkers" in the accepted sense of the word, and regarded the conclusions at which they arrived as divine revelations and not as their own spiritual accomplishments, "the word of God" as expressed through their lips is nevertheless so logical and so realistic in its congruence with the political, social and cultural conditions of their time, that, especially from a non-religious standpoint, these men emerge as metaphysicians, moralists and philosophers in the classical, non-Jewish sense.

Even today after the considerable achievements in the field of biblical criticism it is still difficult to point out with certainty the new ideas introduced by the prophets into the Jewish outlook on life. We are also unable to circumscribe with accuracy those portions of the Bible (especially in its first part, the Pentateuch) which bear the undeniable stamp of the prophetic and, particularly, "Deuteronomic" influence. It is equally difficult to isolate the individual contributions of any prophet. Despite these limitations of our knowledge, the spiritual world of the prophets rises as a firm structure with an individual style, a system both clear and transparent with regard both to itself and later developments.

The three cornerstones of this structure are: God, His Commandments, and Man. This is clearly brought out in the older parts of the Pentateuch in which a strong prophetic influence is discernible. The first word of God to man is a commandment, and because the first man transgressed this commandment he was expelled from the Garden of Eden. God's commandments, however, are not the product of the arbitrary will of an autocrat; indeed, the reverse is true. They are an expression of the eternal laws of the divine order of things, and as such they apply even to the Creator Himself. Thus Abraham could ask of God: "Shall not the Judge of all the earth do right?"

The entire history of the world beginning with Adam, through the catastrophes of the Flood, the dispersion of mankind, etc., are explained and made clear in terms of these relations between God and man. These principles are especially applicable to the history of Israel. It was to the children of Abraham, Isaac and Jacob that God's teachings and commandments were revealed. God, the Torah (God's teachings) and the people of Israel are therefore the three fundamentals of the prophetic doctrine as preached to Israel by the Prophets.

"Hear the word of the Lord, ye children of Israel," exclaims Hosea, the prophet of the 8th century B.C.E., "for the Lord hath a controversy with the inhabitants of the land, because there is no truth, nor mercy, nor knowledge of God in the land." And further:

"Seeing thou hast forgotten the law of thy God, I will also forget thy children" (Hosea IV, 1 and 6).

Here we have not only the three cornerstones—God, Torah, Israel—but also a very clear idea of the inter-relationship ascribed to them in the prophetic teachings. The people of Israel is bound to God through the Torah. As long as Israel does not *forget* its teachings but pursues its way in truth and righteousness, God concerns himself with the welfare of His people and its land. But the moment Israel disturbs this harmony, God sits in judgment upon Israel (see Isaiah III, 13-15 and Jeremiah XXV, 31). Even here, God is bound by His own code of laws and wishes to remain ever just; even though His verdict is harsh, His final words—as can be seen from the entire book of Hosea—are love, mercy and kindness. This highly complicated metaphysical-ethical formula for the explanation (the diagnosis as well as the prognosis) of the events taking place in and around Palestine bears witness to the heights attained in the "knowledge of God" at the beginning of the Prophetic era. It also casts a light upon the array of basic problems which preoccupied contemporary Jewish spiritual thinkers. There was one question of general concern: how is one to conceive the nature of the world if its primary function is to serve as a home of justice for the nations and men? This was the question from which all Jewish spiritual contemplation developed in an ever-widening spiral.

Several centuries later, when Greek philosophy was grappling with the problem of the nature of the world—that is, how to encompass this problem in one single idea—Jewish monotheism evolved this answer in its search for the one common element inherent in all phenomena of the universe: all creation is one entity inasmuch as everything which exists is the creation of one God. Therefore, since the world and all that is in it, including man, is the creation of God, Who is the creator of heaven and earth and at the same time the Giver of the Torah—the teachings about man's conduct, about truth and falsehood, about good and justice and evil and injustice—it follows that conduct conflicting with the Holy Commandments is equivalent to transgression against universal order and defiance of the Lord of creation. Whereas Greek philosophy traced the principles of right and justice to the laws of nature, the prophets of Israel took the contrary stand, and transformed the natural world into a means of realizing the laws of justice and order. With them metaphysical monism assumed the form of ethical monotheism. This prophetic doctrine is most perfectly expressed in the words of Isaiah (Isaiah XLII, 5-6):

"Thus saith God the Lord, he that created the heavens, and stretched them out; he that spread forth the earth, and that which cometh out of it; he that giveth breath unto the people upon it, and spirit to them that walk therein:

"I the Lord have called thee in righteousness, and will hold thine hand, and will keep thee, and give thee for a covenant of the people, for a light of the Gentiles" (see also Isaiah XLV, 18 and XLIX, 8).

The word "thee" toward the end of the passage refers both to the prophet and the people. This double address is due to the fact that the advancement of ethical monotheism did not merely deepen the concept of God and the teleological world-view, according to which the world was created for man to live in and man was created to live in probity and justice; parallel with this the role of the people of Israel and the prophet's conception of himself and his own mission had assumed a new aspect in prophetic doctrine. The more clearly there emerged the idea that all living beings were *God's creatures*, the more difficult it became to understand why only the children of Israel were bound to God through His commandments. The answer is implied in the above-quoted passage of Isaiah: the people of Israel are to the other peoples of the world what the prophet is to his own people; just as he is the corporeal manifestation of God's *covenant* with the children of Israel, so is it Israel's mission in turn to be a *light* for the rest of the world (see Isaiah XLIII, 1; XLIV, 1).

The earliest, primitive Jewish concept of the relationship between God and man undoubtedly bore a strong resemblance to the prevalent religious beliefs of the neighboring Oriental peoples. The fact that from these primitive and particularist ideas there could eventually develop the ethically-cast universalism of the prophets—with their idea of a God who is one universal God and of a people whose mission it is to disseminate this *awareness of God*, together with social justice and harmony among peoples—can undoubtedly be ascribed to a peculiar appreciation of historical values by the people of Israel, even as far back as the pre-Prophetic era, presumably in consonance with its own individual historical experiences. At any rate, from the very first the prophets held strictly to historical tradition, and their empirical proofs are, more often than not, based on history. Thus, for instance, the Exodus from Egypt furnished them with one of their chief arguments for the justification of God's charges against His wayward people:

"Hear this word that the Lord hath spoken against you, O children of Israel, against the whole family which I brought up from the land of Egypt, saying,

"You only have I known of all the families of the earth; therefore I will punish you for all your iniquities" (Amos III, 1-2; see also Amos II, 9-10, and Hosea II, 17; XII, 13-14; XIII, 4-5).

Although the "Torah" of the prophets is not quite identical with our Pentateuch, they are both based on *Hukkim* and *Mishpatim* (statutes and laws), as well as on facts at the time generally accepted as based on history. We are given the *mathematics of history*, specific time chronology, as for instance the *forty years* of the sojourn in the desert (Amos V, 25). On such a basis, the *knowledge of God* assumed a historical character and, since God is the God of the world, as a consequence it also assumed a universal-historical character. *To know God* now became the equivalent of knowing the history of the world, from the *six days of Creation* till the current period with its outlook on a future along the lines of God's world-historical plan. In this framework the people of Israel is a *family* among all other *families*, created by the same Creator and all descending from Adam, the first man, who was the only creature to be made in the image of God. If God's will manifested itself most clearly in the annals of Israel, it Israel was rendered worthy of recognizing the true God, His intentions and His commandments, this, too, was but an expression of God's will. Just as the Lord designates His prophets without consulting the wishes of those He chooses (Jeremiah I, 4-10) so did He *recognize* the fitness of Abraham and his family to seal a historical *bond* with the Creator of the Universe (Genesis XVIII, 19). Therefore this bond or *covenant* is a privilege, and it also imposes a burden—a burden of strict responsibility toward the Divine partner who had shown man *what is good* (Micah VI, 8) and toward all the rest of God's creatures. For the Lord made a covenant with Israel, as well as with all the rest of creation, an *everlasting covenant* (Isaiah XXIV, 5; LV, 4; Ezekiel XXXVII, 26 and Genesis IX, 16; XVII, 7) and at the end of time all the earth "shall be full of the knowledge of the Lord, as the waters cover the sea," and equally blessed shall be "Egypt my people, and Assyria the work of my hands, and Israel mine inheritance" (Isaiah XI, 9; XIX, 24-25).

Simultaneously with the development of the idea that made Israel God's collective messenger to the world (Deuteronomy XXVI, 18-19 and Isaiah XLIX, 1-7) the prophets deepened the idea of personal mission and responsibility of the individual as such. According to prophetic theism, the ultimate in absolute perfection is possessed only by God, the holy, just and mighty Judge of the world; the nearest approximation to this perfection is vested in the prophet through whose lips God speaks (Isaiah VI, 6-7; Jeremiah V, 14, 23, 29; Deuteronomy XVIII, 16-18). But all God-fearing men, whoever they may be, have it within their power to come close to God just as have the prophets: "But the word is very nigh unto thee, in thy mouth, and in thy heart, that thou mayest do it" (Deuteronomy XXX, 14). Whether due to universal cultural-historical causes or the independent development of the prophetic spirit, the fact remains that as we follow the prophets further in their growth, we find them ever more insistent on the personal self-awareness, and together with this the emphasis on individual ethical responsibility in general. It is, therefore, not by mere chance that Jeremiah, the most subjective of all the prophets, formulated the theory which is the basis of all ethical teachings, including the a-religious: *i.e.*, the individual must bear the responsibility for his own destiny, and must not rely either on the *merits of his forebears* or on the chance that his own deeds, either meritorious or blame-worthy, are only trivial episodes in the life of the community, of his people, of mankind, or of the world as a whole. "In those days they shall say no more," Jeremiah tells us, "The fathers have eaten a sour grape, and the children's teeth are set on edge. But every one shall die for his own iniquity: every man that eateth the sour grape, his teeth shall be set on edge" (Jeremiah XXXI, 29-30 and Lamentations V, 7).

It was this idea that formed the basis of Ezekiel's entire philosophy. By his time, the period of the Babylonian Exile, Jewish thought had delved so deeply into these main problems that the previous thesis—that the bearer of moral responsibility is the community as a whole, and the new antithesis, that the real bearer of moral responsibility is the individual—resulted in a synthesis: the true religious-ethical ideal, the perfect human or *Messiah* who will redeem mankind "at the end of time," is an individual who bears moral responsibility for all men, as described in the Book of Isaiah (LIII, 11): "He shall see of the travail of his soul, *and* shall be satisfied: by his knowledge shall my righteous servant justify many; for he shall bear their iniquities." Several centuries later Christianity sought to use this as a support for the extreme-individualistic doctrine of redemption.

In the 5th century B.C.E., after Ezra's reform, when the Torah began to govern Jewish individual and public life, Jewish religious thought was able to bring about a deepening of personal morality alongside of personal piety. The Book of Psalms is the finest monument of this form of piety, characteristic of the period of transition when Jewish thought was just emerging from its classical stage toward its first encounters with Hellenism. Even Jeremiah was already not merely a passive instrument of God; he frequently engaged in dialogues with the Almighty (XIV, 11-14; compare this with the primitive dialogue-form of Amos VII, 4-6 and VIII, 1-2). In Psalms we return again to the monologue—this time not addressed by God to a human audience but on the contrary addressed by His devotees to Him (see Psalms X). And the pious man had many things to discuss, questions to ask, doubts which pursued him, and even objections to the ways of the Lord; all of which he poured forth in the form of personal prayers. If God is just "and God has authority," he demands an explanation for the injustice implicit in the fact that often "the wicked are at ease," whereas men of virtue who "are pure of heart" are plagued (LXXIII, 1-12). Jewish thought was now confronted with problems regarding the theodicean philosophy, which underlies the entire Book of Job. The absorption in individual creative thinking and in personal piety with its belief that God watched over each of his creatures, led by natural stages to a freer and more conscious consideration of God's world (see the celebrated Chapter CIV of Psalms and Job XXXVIII) and to a deeper human understanding. Such books as Proverbs and Ben Sira indicate clearly that concurrently with the intensification of theological speculation, the Jews were developing psychological generalizations and their practical application, particularly in the field of pedagogy. There is no question that, from ancient times to the Hellenistic period, Jewish sages drew on many non-Jewish sources but never deviating from their elementary thesis that "fear of God" is the beginning of all wisdom and that the ultimate aim of wisdom is the "nearness of God" (Proverbs I, 7; IX, 10; Ben-Sira I, 1; Psalms LXXIII, 28). External influences, even as far back as the era of the Prophets, can probably account for the introduction of the mystical element in Jewish religious thinking (see Isaiah VI; Ezekiel I, X, etc.; Zechariah V, etc.) and its later blossoming forth more extensively in the Apocrypha. The story of Jewish mysticism, however, is the concern of another part of this volume. Characteristic of Jewish thought and of the true prophetic spirit is, on the contrary, the doctrine of eschatology—concerned with the "end of time," the final stage, or the consummation of the pre-Messianic phases of universal history. This is most strikingly illustrated in the Book of Daniel and in Ezekiel's vision of the "dry bones" and Gog and Magog.

II. From Hellenism to the Middle Ages

By the end of the 4th century B.C.E. the foundations of Jewish monotheism had been so firmly established that, without fear for its future independence, it could welcome contact with Greek ideas and the achievements of the Greek philosophers. (Traces of this can even be found in the Bible—in its final books, *The Writings*.) However divergent the opinions may be concerning the time of composition, the internal structure and meaning of the book Ecclesiastes, it must be conceded that it reflects a phase of Jewish thought distinguished by the assimilation of ideas which had their birth in the Hellenic world and not in Western Asia or Northern Africa. The gist of this book is nevertheless not the skepticism and pessimism of the "vanity of vanities" outlook on life, set against a background of Greek cosmology—according to which laws of nature impose an eternal repetitive cycle on events. Its intention is to show that acceptance of a materialistic (Democritic or Epicurean) outlook as the final and definitive basis of a world-view inevitably connotes the acceptance of blind chance as dominating the world, that man's life (both individual and historical) is purposeless and meaningless and that there is essentially no difference between knowledge and ignorance, good and evil, and consequently, between "man and animal." The moral implied here is that too much philosophizing is not good: ". . . God is in heaven, and thou upon earth; therefore let thy words be few" (Ecclesiastes, V, 2).

Thus the initial Jewish reaction to Greek philosophy expressed itself in profound polemics, a sort of *reductio ad absurdum*. But Greek philosophy was multi-faceted and, in addition to those abstractions which were offensive to the Jewish concept of life, it possessed many features with which Jewish thought could accord, as, for instance, the Stoic interpretation. Because of this, Jewish thinkers began to translate and thereby transfer Greek concepts and terms into Hebrew. The hypostatization of *wisdom* in Proverbs VIII, 22-31 (see also I, 20-33; IX, 1) is probably a translation of the Greek *sophia*. Even the Pharisaic theories of immortality and their attempts to link up the idea of personal moral responsibility with that of freedom of will probably did not develop entirely without Greek influence. The rapprochement between Jewish and Greek reasoning increased with the introduction of Greek concepts as well as the Greek language into the literature of the Jews.

On the eve of the rise of Christianity, the countries bordering on the Mediterranean had so far succumbed to Hellenistic influence that it could almost be said of them: "And the whole earth was of one language, and of one speech" (Genesis XI, 1). The restoration of the unity of mankind—one of the basic conceptions of Israel's prophets—was, according to the Holy Scripture, a continuation of the state of man in the Garden of Eden. However, the delusory reversion of mankind to its pristine youth during the Hellenistic period seemed to Jewish thinkers a mockery rather than the realization of the visions of the prophets. Although united superficially, the world—both in its cosmic attitude as well as in its individual and social morality—was now in a state of greater chaos and confusion than ever before. Despite this, Hellenized Jews joined non-Jews in attaching more importance to form than to content. Jewish thinkers were now confronted with the task of so interpreting the inherited Jewish tradition, that the contemporary cultural world could immediately grasp the essential difference between pure universalism and the superficial pseudo-universalism or cosmopolitanism of the Hellenized world. The most effective weapons they had for attacking this syncretism were those furnished by their opponents, the Greek philosophers' methods of reasoning. Thus even then philosophy became the handmaiden of theology, if not for its own benefit, then undoubtedly for the benefit of religious thought not only among the Jews but also among Christians and Moslems at a later period.

The foremost Jewish thinker of the Hellenistic period was Philo of Alexandria. The way had been prepared for him gradually since the 3rd century B.C.E. Already in the Septuagint (the first Greek translation of the Bible), the biblical anthropomorphisms had often been interpreted in an abstract sense, in accordance with the requirements of consistent, logical reasoning (see, for instance, the Septuagint translation of Exodus XXIV, 10). In the apocryphal *Wisdom of Solomon*, which probably antedates Philo's writings by a hundred years, the dualism of body and soul, of matter and spirit, is brought out in clear-cut Platonic fashion (as for instance, I, 4; VII, 1-6), At the same time, *wisdom* is endowed with the significance of a spiritual substance which unites the human soul with God and thus renders it immortal (chapters II-III). A closer examination of this *wisdom* reveals that this is merely a Greek (more accurately, a Stoic) metamorphosis of the old Jewish divine Torah, or "God's word."

A similar work is the so-called IV Maccabees (believed to have been written by an older contemporary of Philo) wherein the deeds of the Jewish heroes merely serve as a historic illustration of the ethical principle that man's virtues can master his lusts and passions ("affects"). Though one of the fundamentals of Stoicism, this reasoning accorded in principle with that of traditional Jewish morals; but whereas the Stoic wanted to destroy man's "affects," ascetic tendencies are alien to the Jewish author of this fourth Maccabean book and he contents himself with the moderate control of mind over animal instincts within the limits of Jewish law. The derivation of ethical precepts and metaphysical principles from the wealth of Jewish law and historical records, and their interpretation in an allegorical form—as parables and symbols of profound ideas and purposes—began to manifest itself in the Judaeo-Hellenistic literature as early as the middle of the 2nd century B.C.E. (Letter of Aristeas; Aristobulus). Here, too, the Jewish thinkers of Alexandria had much to learn from the Stoics who often sought philosophical truths in the naive tales of old Greek mythology. Simultaneously, there flourished in Palestine a school of Bible-commentators, the fathers of the "Oral Torah" who, by means of rational interpretations, did as much for the further development of the Jewish religious outlook as the prophets had done in their time through prophetic inspiration. Accordingly, it may be assumed that this method of allegorical biblical interpretation which is the most striking characteristic of Philo's approach had its inception in the Jewish as well as in the Greek "Midrash." From the concrete results of his work, it is apparent that the Jewish thinker of the 1st century C.E. was a deeply conscious Jew who, like many Jews of that generation, wished to disseminate the Torah among the peoples of the world, and was not an epigone of Greek philosophy among the barely Hellenized Oriental *barbarians*.

For this very reason, Philo's work in the field of Jewish thought was doomed to remain an isolated phase. His primary purpose was to emphasize the transcendentality or supramundaneity of the one God who is, therefore, not only immaterial, but beyond any quality of the spirit as possessed by man. This concept, which was perhaps too abstract for the average Jew, was no novelty to the leading representatives of the idea of ethical monotheism who, from the very first, had adopted the formula: "Who *is* like unto thee" (Exodus XV, 11; Psalms XXXV, 10; LXXI, 19; LXXXVI, 8; LXXXIX, 6, 8; CXIII, 5-6, Lamentations III, 37 or Isaiah LV, 8-9 and particularly XLVI, 5). The more profound interpretation of these words perforce remained far beyond the grasp of the plain people with their naive, anthropomorphic conceptions about the Creator, while to the thinkers of the people they constituted self-evident truths.

The very doctrine of ecstatic union with God which made Philo a predecessor of neo-Platonism and, as some will have it, a typical representative of mysticism, is really only an exemplification of prophetic inspiration. Even the passage in Genesis (XII, 1): "Get thee out of thy country, and from thy kindred, and from thy father's house" Philo considered a hint, in line with a pattern of metaphysical exegesis of the meaning of true prophecy: when God orders Abraham to leave his country, He means Abraham to become a prophet, to *discard* his body, which is earth and dust, his senses, which are his property, his father's home, which is the human brain, and even his own ego, since man cannot be at one with his Creator unless he divests himself of his own conscious "I" (*Legum Allegoria III, 40;* and *Quis Rerum Divinarum Heres, 69-70*). This metaphysical theory of prophecy is not entirely at variance with the deductions that can be made from various Bible stories concerning the ecstasy of the prophets. The same can be said of Philo's greatest cultural-historical contribution, his doctrine of Logos. "The word" or Logos, which becomes an independent entity for Philo—a mediator between God and the world or, more accurately, between the Creator and the created—is again only a generalization based on the Bible, in which God's will is realized mainly by the word, as for instance, in Psalms (XXXIII, 9): "He spake, and it was *done;* he commanded, and it stood fast." "He spoke, and it came to pass" was, from the very first chapters of Genesis, an established formula. On the basis of such premises of religious thought, Philo advanced a step further in logical thinking and found in the biblical images and tales hints of various metaphysical, ethical and psychological theories which had long since been evolved in Greece. In methods and principles this was about as much as tradition-bound Jewish speculation could gain from contact with alien philosophical sources. Though Philo did not lay the foundation for a new Jewish philosophy, he did succeed in fructifying the Hellenistic-Roman world with the spirit of Jewish universalism, and thus helped to crystallize the Christian belief—the most widespread and universal faith up to the present time.

Whereas the superficial Hellenization of Jewish religious thought was a fleeting episode in its history, the main line of its development was along the broad highway of the Oral Torah—a natural sequence to the more ancient Written Torah. The Mishnah, Gemara, and Midrash are the literary monuments of this development. True, not one of the hundreds of great men whose names have been immortalized in this literature can be compared to a Philo as far as systematic speculation in the metaphysical field is concerned. If, among the great teachers of the Halakah and the Agada there were such great thinkers—and many of the aphorisms and parables of Rabbi Gamaliel the Second, Rabbi Akiba, Rabbi Simeon ben Johai, Resh Lakish, etc. quoted in the Talmud would justify such a conclusion—it nevertheless is obvious that they must have kept their systematic speculations secret. It was their principle never to speak openly about metaphysical problems, such as the nature of God (*Maase Merkabah*—literally, Divine Chariot), the Creation of the world (*Maase Bereshit*) and its infinity in space and time (see: "*Ein Dorshin*"—*Mishnah Hagigah II, 1*). The Jewish great men felt a mistrust of every attempt at logical rationalization of faith; this mistrust was given additional impetus by the fact that at about this time Christianity began to put forth religious dogmas patterned after the structure of philosophical thought. Philo Judaeus thus became an authority in the Church and was for many centuries forgotten by his own people. Whenever a Tanna (one of the authors of the Mishnah) felt a need to offer logical proof of the existence of God, he did so for the sake of a controversy with an idol-worshipper or atheist, according to the precept set down by Rabbi Eliezer: "Know whatever answer to give to the unbeliever" (Sayings of the Fathers II, 19).

Still, it cannot be said that the centuries between the conclusion of the Bible and the completion of the Mishnah were sterile. Though they produced less original Jewish thought than had the Classical Period, they were distinguished by a far greater maturity and precision of expression; by a superior versatility in the art of conveying abstract principles and especially ethical concepts in sharply defined formulas; by greater adeptness in the application of logical lines of thinking, as, for instance, arriving at clear classifications, consistent divisions, correct argumentation, etc. The keen minds of the sages of Halakah (Law) enabled them to deal with all problems which came before them. It was only after long and careful reflection that Hillel was able to produce his famous summarization of Jewish ethics: "Do not unto another that which is repugnant to you" (Talmud Babli, Shabbath 31 A). That this was not an isolated conclusion can be seen from other aphorisms which are ascribed both to Hillel and to his followers: "Love thy fellow creatures and bring them nigh to the *Torah*," says Hillel (Sayings of the Fathers, I, 12). The very use of the new term "creatures" for the concept of man, and the conviction that love for one's fellow-men is primarily a concern for man's spiritual elevation, *i.e.*, to bring him nearer the source of truth, justice and righteousness, indicates how far the teachings of the prophets had advanced in the preceding centuries in their view of life's meaning and the ultimate aim of history—from an ideal it had become a practical norm of daily life. This went hand in hand with the widespread recognition that man must possess freedom of choice in order to participate actively in the realization of the universal-historical ideal. Rabbi Akiba's laconic formulation of the basic principle of the Jewish outlook: "Everything is foreseen, yet freedom of choice is given"—for man to do good or evil (Sayings of the Fathers III, 19) which was based on two passages in Deuteronomy (XXX, 15 and 19); and Rabbi Hananiah's like precept: "Everything lies in the hands of God except the fear of God" (Berakot 33 B)—since fear of God is up to man himself—both testify to the thorough consideration given by Talmudical sages to the problem of man's freedom of will, and to the antinomy between human freedom and Divine power which later challenged so many Jewish and non-Jewish minds.

For Jewish thought, from then on, the freedom of man to follow his good or his evil impulses became a sort of dogma; and, though "reward and punishment" in this life as well as after death play an important role in determining man's *free will*, the Talmud evolved a clearly defined religious-ethical concept of "virtue for virtue's sake" and strongly emphasized the idea that the "recompense of virtue is virtue" (Ben Azzai, Sayings of the Fathers, IV, 2; Antigonus, ibid. 1, 3; Rabbi Zadok, ibid. IV, 5).

The belief in another world where the soul is to reap the reward for its deeds on earth, lay at the very foundation of the theodicean motive, from ancient times on. In the Talmudic era, this belief assumed almost the form of a dogma. However, the voluntarism and activism in Jewish thought, characteristic of it from its very inception, prevented this theory from ever becoming petrified. The idea of an *after world* and the *future which is to come* are sometimes intended to mean "that world where the virtuous will bask in Divine glory" and the evil ones will burn in the fires of Hell. Sometimes, again, they simply imply "the days of the Messiah," *i.e.*, the eschatological finale of the world, in the prophetic sense. This double meaning would seem a further proof that Jewish thought never ceased to concern itself with the universal-historical role of the Jewish people. According to the Talmudic concept *Shekinah* (a new term for "God's *nearness*") itself is in need of "redemption"—how much more, therefore, must it be a concern of all mankind. On the basis of the Torah and perhaps remotely influenced by the ideas of Graeco-Roman Stoicism in accordance with this viewpoint, the Talmud evolved theories of universal human right founded on natural law. Many of the prayers which were composed during the Talmudic era breathe forth this universalist spirit. We find, for instance, the following passage in one of the Rosh Hashanah and Yom Kippur prayers: "And all creatures shall bow unto Thee and they shall all make an alliance in order to fulfill Thy will wholeheartedly." The prayer "Aleinu," ascribed to that great figure of the Babylonian Amoraim, Rab, deals with the perfection of the world and expresses the hope that soon "every creature will call on Thy name" and "all inhabitants of the world will recognize and know that every knee must bend before Thee and every tongue swear to Thee" (see also Isaiah XLV, 23).

If, since the close of its Classical Period, Jewish religious thought has not developed much in depth, it can be said to have so expanded its range that, just before the Middle Ages, there was no other course for a Jewish thinker to take than either to desert "the house of his fathers" or to concentrate entirely on the solution of those problems which are the essential basis of Jewish religious culture itself. This became the foremost task of the so-called "Jewish religious philosophers" of the Middle Ages.

III. The Jewish-Arabic Renaissance

The most important event in history and, therefore, also in the spiritual development of the Jews, at the beginning of the Middle Ages, was the advent of Islam. It almost seemed as though there were a repetition of what had happened some thousand years earlier when Hellenistic culture began to spread. Precisely as in that time, the neighboring non-Jewish world began to embrace universalism, with this difference, that now the monotheistic idea was the focal point in world culture. Jewish thought was compelled to recognize in it a spiritual kinship, and inevitably there sprang up the crucial question: does the traditional Jewish world-view possess intrinsic justification for its special existence, or is not the fact that the one and only God had manifested Himself to other peoples of the world outside of Jewish history, a downright contradiction of its essential meaning and spirit? In other words, is not the entire "Sinaitic revelation" threatened with extinction once it can be shown that man's own reason will naturally lead him to conclusions approximating those set forth in the Holy Scripture?

This question became particularly acute for Jewish religious thought in the 9th century, after Islam had assimilated the old Hellenistic heritage with its philosophical elements and produced the Kalam, an independent school dealing with the metaphysical fundamentals of the new faith. A number of the adherents of the new school exalted the rationality of the Islamic fundamentals and commandments. Whereas in the Hellenistic period Jewish religious thought had had to contend with any number of philosophical trends, it now found itself defied by a single school of thought—in itself profoundly religious—which demanded an accounting in the name of reason. Under such a stimulus, it now became the all-absorbing task of traditional Jewish thought to achieve clarity as to the nature of Judaism and reason within the framework of Jewish tradition itself. What was done in this respect by the most original Jewish thinker of the Oriental-Islamic period (Saadia Gaon, born 892 in Egypt) set the tone for the entire period of Jewish-Arabic renaissance. If not for him, it is questionable whether the Jewish element, in this period of joint cultural development, could have had the strength to preserve its independence.

Saadia is frequently referred to as the "father of the Jewish philosophy of religion." But, taken in the modern sense, this term presupposes a free, philosophical approach to the phenomenon of religion itself. It was, however, the intention of Saadia, who was the head of the Yeshibah in Babylonian Sura, to prove in his book *Emunot ve-Deot* (Doctrines and Religious Beliefs), written in Arabic (ca. 933), that actually there is only one faith revealed by the Lord—the Jewish faith, and this faith demands that its followers apprehend its truths also by means of reason. Even in the other faiths man has produced for himself, Saadia contended, there are vital metaphysical and ethical elements identical with those found in God's

Torah and in the words of His prophets. In his polemics against Parseeism, Jewish agnosticism and the Christian dogma of the Holy Trinity, Saadia's weapons were those of pure logic; he went a step further and declared that the rationality of the Torah was proof of its divine character. Nevertheless, in the introduction to his main work, he states that no speculation by man can lay the basis for the discovery of pure truth as firmly as, by the grace of God, it is found in the Torah. And, moreover, not every man is a born thinker. Saadia then comes back to the ancient maxim that "the beginning of all wisdom is the fear of God." This establishment of the reciprocal relationship between faith and knowledge, between revealed truth and man-discovered truth, was transmitted about two hundred and fifty years later by Maimonides to Christian Scholasticism and was even current during the period of 18th-century enlightenment.

Saadia also exerted a considerable influence on subsequent thought by his doctrine that tradition, flowing uninterruptedly through generations, is the chief source of knowledge that is also in accordance with reason. On this he posed his argument that if not for the constantly nurtured Jewish traditional concept of the divine source of the Torah, the truth about the one and only Creator would be left hanging in the air, not to speak of the belief in the redemption of the world "at the end of time." As for the precepts set down in the Torah, the real basis of Jewish faith, the moral commandments, are rational, while the other commandments are to be observed simply because they are God's commandments and their *raison d'être* is hidden from us. In other words, reason itself teaches us that not everything about us is or can be open to full comprehension. In later theological speculation, this difference between comprehensible and incomprehensible precepts became classic.

Saadia's conclusions concerning the rational basis of the Jewish religion were influenced by Islamic philosophy and by religious currents in Judaism itself.

The traditional Jewish world was greatly shaken by the rise of the Karaites who had produced, half a century before Saadia, a thinker of the stature of Benjamin Nahavendi. About the same time there appeared a Jewish heretic, Hivi al Balkhi by name, whose book criticizing the Torah was based on the internal contradictions he believed he had discovered in the Pentateuch. Saadia devoted an entire volume to polemicizing against him. An older contemporary of Saadia, Isaac Israeli (born ca. 850 C.E.) made a deliberate effort to strengthen Jewish faith by applying the principles of Greek philosophy, and attempted to harmonize the Jewish doctrine of the Creation of the world with the neo-Platonic theories of emanation. Israeli's chief aim is clearly reflected in his definition of philosophy as an attempt to have man approximate God as far as possible. Like his medical treatises, his philosophical works were intended for all readers, regardless of creed. However, they exercised a greater influence on the Christian scholastic world than on Jewish theology. At about the same time there appeared on the scene the Jewish thinker David al-Mukammas who also displayed a leaning toward neo-Platonism and argued that God's attributes, such as life, power, wisdom, do not really reveal another divine facet—He is one in perfect unity—but, in ever new details, they exclude any imperfection from His nature. Even Saadia came close to the conclusion that God's attributes can have only a negative signifi-cance—a thought which runs through Philo's works and which later became a pivotal idea in the theology of Maimonides.

For several generations after Saadia, a number of Geonim grappled with the solution of certain perplexing problems springing from the strictly monotheistic outlook. There is, for instance, the Gaon of Pumbedita, Hai ben Sherira, whose reply to the question—How can man be said to have free will if God knows in advance how his creatures will act?—was as follows: God's vision of the future covers not only actual occurrences but even what might happen were man's will to go in another direction; divine prescience is therefore no hindrance to man's choice. In devious ways this doctrine reached the Jesuits in Spain, and Leibniz still gave it serious consideration.

Eighteen years before the death of Hai Gaon in 1038, Solomon ibn Gabirol was born (1020) in Spain, the western outpost of Moslem culture. He was both poet and thinker, and heralded a resurgence in Jewish-religious thought. At that time the nature of the problems confronting Jewish thought became clear and definite. The central question was this: how is it possible, on the basis of reason, to include in one concept the absoluteness of God with the relativity of the temporal spatial world? The more firmly the monotheists stood by their theories of the absolute, transcendental character of the infinite Creator, the more difficult they found it to explain the finite and limited nature of His world; the more supramundane God appeared, the less the world seemed to be the work of His hands. In order to surmount this intellectual obstacle, ibn Gabirol built up a firm bridge resting on the theory of *Emanation*. However, his approach was altogether independent of those of his predecessors whether Jewish, Arab or Greek. In his greatest work, *Fons Vitae* (Source of Life), a title based on a phrase in Jeremiah II, 13; XVII, 13, and in Psalms XXXVI, 10, he developed an original doctrine about *matter* and *form* and, eight hundred years before Hegel and six hundred years before Spinoza, substituted for the theory of real being and of the chain of real causes and effects, a logical "world-process" wherein *form* in all its manifestations, phases and changes is the final result of varying degrees of *matter*. With him matter itself became a logically necessary premise, and with the spiritualization of all life, the creative and driving forces in nature were transformed into the multi-ramified streams of a single dynamic force, the force of Divine Will. Ibn Gabirol's voluntaristic panlogism, which displays a close affinity with various forms of pantheism, greatly influenced the development of European metaphysics. But among Jewish thinkers it was never accepted *in toto* and did not become a model for other thinkers, principally, perhaps, for the reason that it would make it difficult to find a way to the actual history of the Jewish people and therefore likewise to the concrete forms of Jewish religious life. However, one point of Gabirol's system was eventually incorporated as a vital component of the living Jewish tradition, *i.e.*, the thought that God is more than eternal, not only because He always was and always will be, but because, generally speaking, He is outside of time, a concept, incidentally, which figures prominently in Spinoza's system. Ibn Gabirol expressed this thought in many variations in a separate religious hymn of praise, the *Keter Malkut* (Royal Crown) which to this day is read on the eve of the Day of Atonement. Similar liturgical poetic echoes are found in the *Shir ha-Yihud* of Judah Hasid (12-13th century in Regensburg, Germany) where we read for instance the following verse: "Chance and Time exist not in Thee; Thou holdest in Thy hand the order of the ages." The same formulas are to be found in the hymns of the Middle Ages, *Adon Olam* and *Yigdal*, both distinguished by abstract and dialectical verses, as for instance: "He is the first, and yet there is no beginning to His firstness," or "He is and yet there is no 'when' for His being."

Such highly abstract concepts could become rooted in daily religious life only after a number of thinkers had accepted them and then disseminated them among the educated elements of the people. Even then, the essence of neo-Platonism and its direct product, Islamic mysticism (especially of the *Brothers of Purity*) would undoubtedly never have become an organic component of Jewish religious thought, had not a school which undertook to discover the most profound concept of God in the Holy Scriptures arisen simultaneously in Spain. The foremost figures of this movement were Abraham bar Hiyya, the Prince (ca. 1136), who revived the use of Hebrew in Jewish religious philosophical literature; Joseph ben Jacob ibn Zaddik of Cordova (d. 1149) who, in his famous work *Olam Katon* (Microcosmos), resuscitated the theory that man, as the "image of God," incorporates in his own *ens* the Almighty's world in its entirety, a theory which had been fully developed 150 years earlier in southern Italy by Sabbatai Donnolo in his commentary on the *Sefer Yetsirah:* and finally, by Bahya ibn Pakuda of Saragossa, surnamed the Judge (a contemporary of ibn Gabirol) whose book *Hobot ha-Lebabot* (Duties of the Heart), written originally in Arabic, rapidly became popular in Judah ibn Tibbon's Hebrew translation. In this galaxy of great men may also be included Abraham ibn Ezra (d. 1167) who was inclined to interpret the relationship between God and the world in a pantheistic spirit (see, on the one hand, his exegesis on the concept of "man in God's image," Genesis I, 26-27, and, on the other, the formula which is repeated throughout *Shir ha-Yihud:* "Thou art in everything").

The fact that a work like *Hobot ha-Lebabot* could become widely popular indicates what great strides Jewish religious thought had made from the times of Saadia, especially among the Jews of Spain. Abstract thinking became a sort of religious-ethical duty, a divine command and, as a natural consequence of this, logical reflection gained impetus. For instance, we may note the way Bahya undertakes to prove the impossibility of the existence of more than one Creator of the world: "If we are to believe that there is more than one Creator, we must assume that the substance of each is different. It then follows that, owing to this difference or disparity, they are independent of one another. But that which is independent is finite and that which is finite must have an end; that which comes to an end is a composite entity which must have been created; and everything which is created must have a creator. It thus follows that the proponent of the theory that the world may have had more than one Creator must of necessity arrive at the conclusion that the Creator Himself was created—but we have commenced with the presumption that He is eternal, the Cause of all causes and the Beginning of all beginnings. Thus, He is One, as we are told in Nehemiah IX, 6: "Thou, *even* thou, *art* Lord alone." This argument is the fourth in a series of seven proving the unity of God which appear in the seventh section of *Shaar ha-Yihud,* at the beginning of *The Duties of the Heart*.

But the development of metaphysical thought, even in religious tradition, brings with it a threat of spiritual division and is usually a symptom of a sort of internal crisis. Although the Jewish thinkers in the Islamic world of the 12th century were still following the course set by Saadia and were considering Judaism as the only revealed religion, the concept of faith was nevertheless no more than an abstract idea to them, bringing them ever closer to the non-Jewish adherents of monotheism. If at first their aim had been to establish a rational foundation for their inherited positive faith—in opposition to other positive religions and especially Islam—gradually, as time went on, this became an end-in-itself, all else became subordinated and revolved about this foundation to the exclusion of interest in the positive features of Judaism and especially its social-historic elements. Once more as in the days of early Christianity, there is a resurgence of a strong individualistic tendency, the inevitable result of the fact that the ultimate problems of Jewish life and thought were as a matter of fact posited by outstanding individuals, each treating them in his own peculiar way and colored by his individual development and training. As early as the 11th century, Solomon ibn Gabirol had erected a system of thought which was almost entirely divorced from the Jewish classical historico-philosophical system. And even in his ethics of the knowledge of God, Bahya projects the figure of an isolated individual, face to face with the Creator, as though the Jew could dispense with his real social environment—the Jewish nation. The perils of this a-social and hence anti-social tendency in Jewish religious speculation were felt more strongly by the poet in Judah ha-Levi (ca. 1080-1140) and, spurred by an intense spirit of disapproval, he undertook to lead Jewish religious thought back to its original prophetic roots, aiming thereby not only to rekindle its religious intensity but to render it completely Jewish in spirit.

The historical phenomenon of "prophecy" had long been the concern of both Arabic and Jewish thought. However, up to the time of Judah ha-Levi it had been propounded as a special sort of metaphysical-psychological question: attempts were made to explain in various ways how a man of flesh and blood could share God's knowledge, since only God can prevision the future of the world to the end of time. It was the Jewish thinker of Toledo who was the first and the only one to accord this problem—the phenomenon of prophecy—the greatest importance in his world-view and who pictured the supernatural in life in such a fashion as to make prophecy seem a most natural and fitting manifestation. The basis upon which he built his theory was the doctrine of the prophets themselves, their fundamental formula: the prophet is to the Jews what the Jews are to the peoples around them. Thus the question of the possibility of prophecy automatically took on the character of the historico-philosophical query: what must be the state of the world if the Jewish people is to fulfill its mission in accordance with that which its prophets have themselves experienced, known and foretold? Whereas the prophets had been content simply to proclaim the fundamental principles of their philosophy in the categoric form of God's word, Judah ha-Levi, as a son of his philosophically-schooled generation, felt the need to justify the prophetic doctrine that is, to differentiate it from other forms of monotheism, especially that form which was a direct outgrowth of Greek philosophy. A similar polemical attitude toward philosophy now became recognizable among the orthodox elements of Islam (Al-Gazali). In disputing with the "philosophers" and their "faith," it was not Judah ha-Levi's aim to minimize rational reflection in favor of blind belief; on the contrary, he sought to clear the field systematically for profounder and more concrete knowledge which could absorb the prophetic conception of universal history, a conception whose heirs and guardians, until the coming of the Messiah are, according to Jewish tradition, the people of the Torah (see, for example, Judah ibn Tibbon's Hebrew text of the *Kuzari* I, 4 and IV, 13). Judah ha-Levi thus arrives at the conclusion that besides having the essential attributes of man (character, soul and reason), the Jew, the "keeper of the Torah," is, in addition, endowed with the special ability to "apprehend the divine": this was another way of saying that only from such material could "prophets" be molded (see *Kuzari* II, 14 ff). Side by side with this Jewish-metaphysical anthropology, Judah ha-Levi outlined a geographical and philological theory whereby he showed that Palestine and Hebrew were the land and language of the true knowledge of God and prophecy, just as the people of Israel are "the people of God" (ibid II, 8-10; IV, 26 referring to *Sefer Yetsirah*). It is clear that God, referred to here, is not an abstract concept and that, for this reason, there is a sharp demarcation between the "God of Abraham and the God of Aristotle" (ibid, IV, 15).

Since this abstract-philosophical monotheism constituted the common ground upon which Jewish religious thinkers met those of Islam, the whole purpose of Judah ha-Levi's thought was directed toward undermining this common basis and setting up a chasm between them.

Judah ha-Levi marks the most critical point in the development of the complicated relations between Jewish tradition and philosophic thought. It seemed that a complete break between them was unavoidable. That it did not occur was primarily due to the rise of a *Jewish Aristotelianism* and especially to its most important representative, the Rambam (Moses ben Maimon, Maimonides, 1135-1204). In speaking of the history of Jewish religious thought, the use of such concepts as Stoicism, neo-Platonism or Aristotelianism is not to be taken to signify systematic schools of philosophy based on clearly self-centralized systems of thought, as was the case in the general history of philosophy. Jewish religious thought was less independent of tradition than was even that of the Moslems. Not one of the Jewish religious thinkers ventured to oppose the authority of the Torah; and if some of them undertook to interpret the nature of the universe in the spirit of neo-Platonic *emanation,* while others chose to cling to Aristotle's cosmological dynamism and teleology, both schools were convinced that their respective interpretations were in accord with the spirit of the Holy Scriptures. However, this period of close cultural contact with the surrounding world demanded a conclusive rational accounting of the Jewish concept of monotheism. Even the romantic Judah ha-Levi built up a "fence" around metaphysical speculation with the methods of rational speculation. It was thus that Judah ha-Levi's younger contemporary, Maimonides, the great systematizer of the Halakah, realized that the only way to arrive at a decision in the matter of the merits of Judaism and reason was to confront Jewish tradition with the foremost philosophical system of the time—Aristotelianism—in order to establish once and for all that unless reason goes hand in hand with the tenets of the Torah, it contradicts itself. Maimonides did not seek the approval of Greek philosophy for the Torah, but emulated Philo in seeking to hitch Greek speculation to the *Merkabah,* the heavenly chariot of Divine Grace *(Shekinah).*

Chronologically as well as from the standpoint of contents, the work which formed a link between the *Kuzari* of Judah ha-Levi and the *More Nebukim* (Guide for the Perplexed) of Maimonides was the *Emunah Ramah* (Sublime Faith) of Abraham ibn Daud, Rabad I, whose work was originally written, as were the aforementioned two, in Arabic. Like Judah ha-Levi, Rabad came from Toledo. He died in 1180, a martyr for his faith, about ten years before the completion of Maimonides' metaphysical life-work. Whether or not Maimonides was familiar with the work of his predecessor, who is often referred to as the "first Jewish Aristotelian," is still a moot question; but there can be no doubt that both were motivated by the same desire—to allow of no compromises with Aristotelianism but to assimilate it and Greek philosophy in general to such an extent as to put an end to the independent influence they exerted on Jewish thought, and the consequent threat it held for prophetic monotheism. In this respect, both resemble Judah ha-Levi, although their attitudes toward "Greek learning" are basically different. Whereas Judah ha-Levi completely rejected philosophy, Maimonides and ibn Daud wanted to see it absorbed by Judaism. Ibn Daud summed this up most cogently: "The ultimate end of philosophy is the deed," *i.e.*, traditional Jewish conduct. For this reason he was at odds with ibn Gabirol, about whom he wrote that "his book displays a tendency to use philosophy in such a way that all peoples should partake of it, while the Jewish people is not set apart therein as a separate matter." Nevertheless, contrary to Judah ha-Levi, the author of these words hoped to see Jews restored to "the strength to bear two torches—in the right hand the light of Jewish tradition and in the left, the light of reason." As a supporting illustration, he points to the confusion that prevailed among educated Jews in his own circle. By means of his system of thought, Maimonides hoped to end this confusion and chaos in the Arabicized Jewish religious thought of the second half of the 12th century.

The world of Maimonides can be viewed from two aspects, the outer and the inner. Observed from the outer aspect of general philosophy, it presents the typical general picture of medieval Aristotelianism, with its partial absorption of neo-Platonist elements, the only difference being that the controlling power is not Aristotle's "First Mover" in His majestic eternal immutability, but a divine, all-powerful Will, simultaneously King and Ruler, Who is concerned with the conduct of the world, Whose providence reaches even unto the individual and Who sanctions excep-tions in the eternal order of natural events, since all that exists is His doing. In brief, this is Aristotle's world, where generous room has been found for the God of the Jewish Torah. An altogether different picture emerges from an internal examination of Maimonides' system. It is at once apparent that here we find ourselves within the borders of the ancient, purely-Jewish religious tradition which stretches without interruption from biblical times and the days of the Talmud to the period of Saadia and his followers, even to Judah ha-Levi. But again there is a difference; the ancient Jewish heritage and outlook are now dominated by a systematic order and an atmosphere of speculative, or better still, terminological clarity, which are all indicative of the Greek classical spirit. It is no longer Judaized Aristotelianism but rather, Hellenized Judaism. The very fact that all the elements of Maimonides' system summed up into a harmonious whole is evidence that the basic aim of the Jewish thought of the Middle Ages—in its striving to preserve its historical independence with regard to non-Jewish monotheism—was to achieve a synthesis which should embrace the scientific elements of the surrounding culture wherever they did not contradict the Jewish religious tradition.

The point at which Maimonides dissented from the philosopher (Aristotle) was the question whether God's world is eternal or the result of creation. Aristotle contended that the world is just as eternal in time as is its "First Mover," while according to the Torah, life commences with "*Bereshit Bara*" (In the beginning God created). However, since there is no logical argument for either the thesis or the antithesis and the human mind is here confronted with what is now termed an "antinomy," Maimonides concludes that logical reasoning itself compels us, in this metaphysical basic problem, to rely upon the truth revealed in the Torah, and not upon logic and argumentation.

"Is then our whole, Torah," he wrote, "less worthy than their empty phrases? If Aristotle may invoke the opinions of the Sabians, why may we not base ours on the words of Moses and Abraham and all that follows therefrom?" His advice therefore was that in dealing with this difficult question, man must ever "suspect his own reason" and follow the tradition of the "two prophets" who are the pillars on which humankind with its beliefs and peoples rest (*More*, II, 23). In the terminology of modern philosophy, this may be described as "critical irrationalism." It is the method of acknowledging super-rational sources of wisdom only when the object lies outside the realm of rational apprehension. Maimonides never questioned the existence of such "objects" and certainly not of the most exalted of them—God. In a most radical manner, Maimonides sets out to prove the ancient Jewish idea of "God's oneness" by showing that He is the perfection of unity and uniqueness and that His attributes must therefore all be negative; when we speak, for instance, of God's infinite wisdom or goodness, we can mean only that any form of finiteness or ignorance or evil is not applicable in His case.

"The more emphasis man lays on the negative in connection with God, the nearer he approaches to the concept of God and to Him, praised be His name," declares Maimonides (ibid. I, 59). It is best not to speak about His essence at all, as we are told in Psalms: "Fitting priase for Thee is silence" (I, 59 and 50). If we are to speak of divine attributes, they must be found exclusively in the "character and quality of His acts"; attributes and acts which we humans must seek to emulate and which may be indicated as God's "ways" (ibid. I, 54). Thus the theosophy of Maimonides leads to the fundamental principle of his ethical system. If, despite its closeness to neo-Platonic mysticism, his theosophy is thoroughly impregnated with the Torah, so his system of ethics, regardless of the echo of Aristotle to be found therein, is essentially Jewish, especially in the so-called *Eight Chapters*.

Like Aristotle, Maimonides regarded it as man's supreme aim to strive for the cognition of God and the approach to Him. This God, however, is not Aristotle's God, but the "God of Abraham." Moreover, to Maimonides, the greatest nearness to God is attained not by abstract metaphysical reflection, but by prophecy, a concept which in this form is essentially alien to Greek philosophy. In his teachings about prophecy, Maimonides comes closest to a number of Arabian thinkers (Al Farabi, et al.) and, more particularly, to his Jewish predecessors—ibn Daud and Judah ha-Levi. It was Maimonides' conviction that to be a philosopher one must be virtuous himself, and in order to be a prophet, one must be something even more than a philosopher: side by side with logic, there must be the highest form of intuition and only when all these elements are at hand, can the miracle of Divine Revelation come to pass (ibid, II, 36). The "Master of all wise men" and the "father of the prophets," Moses, is, however, unique in history, since his Torah is one, and God, from whom Moses received the Torah, is the One and Only God (ibid. II, 39). It therefore follows that unique in its kind and hallowed is also the people of Israel; unique in its kind and hallowed, even its tongue, Hebrew, a "holy tongue" (ibid. III, 8).

This was the metaphysical background against which Maimonides codified his Jewish religious dogma (in his commentaries on the Mishnah, from which is taken the "Ani Maamin"—credo—of the prayer-books and in the first book of his Halakah codex "Mishneh Torah"). Maimonides' greatest contribution to the history of Jewish and even non-Jewish religious thought was especially the systematic and logical order he introduced into these studies. The great Christian scholars of the 13th century—an Albertus Magnus, a Thomas Aquinas or a Duns Scotus— discovered in Maimonides' *Doctor Perplexorum* (the Latin title of *More Nebukim*) a classic example of positive faith which fits in harmoniously with universal knowledge and learning. At the same time Maimonides' system represents the point where the paths of Christian Church and traditional Judaism meet for the last time and then part again—a logical inevitability once it has been granted that regarding its fundamental truth positive faith can permit no compromise on the basis of merely human knowledge. His insistence on the "oneness" of God, the Creator's absolute unity, supra-mundaneity, incorporeality, etc. was applied by Catholic teachers to the church dogma of the Trinity and the Man-God. It was only in comparatively recent times that even the non-Jewish world began to appreciate how much more stress Maimonides had laid on wisdom and logic than on the irrational element.

Maimonides' religious-philosophical system represented a milestone between two eras of Jewish thought. It marked a departure from which there set in a period of critical analysis of naive traditionalism. With his older contemporary, the Arabian Aristotelian ibn Roshd (Averroes), Maimonides shared the theory that metaphysical speculation is beyond the grasp of the masses and can only serve to deflect the man of no or little education from the path of piety. Nevertheless Maimonides' entire system evinces an impulse to a differentiation in the traditional attitude of the Jewish masses toward their spiritual heritage. His very vindication of the sources of truth—knowledge and faith—in matters regarding the national outlook on life was in itself enough to rouse discussion as to their respective prerogatives. For instance, to what extent is an abstract, metaphysical interpretation of the Torah justified? Or, may one, as a pietist, discover in the accounts of the sacrifices, etc., merely a concession on the part of the Torah to more primitive habits, upon their flight from Egypt? (see *"More"* III, 35 and 46). In general, is not such "heresy" the result of absorption in "secular" studies? These, and similar questions, stirred the Jewish world and for several centuries were the shibboleths of sharp controversies. The great number of commentaries on the *"More Nebukim"* (from Shem-Tob ibn Falaquera, Joseph Caspi and Moses ben Joshua of Narbonne in the 13th and 14th centuries down to the *Gibeat ha-More* of Solomon ben Joshua Maimon at the close of the 18th century) testifies how deep and multifarious Maimonides' influence on Jewish religious thought has been. Ever since, every Jewish thinker has first had to determine for himself whether he is with Maimonides or against him. In the latter case, he has had to decide whether to follow the path back to ancient tradition or to go forward along the road of critical reason. The conflicts which arose as to the borderline between faith and knowledge awakened in the Jewish world such an awareness of metaphysical and scientific problems in general that, alongside with Hebrew translations of Jewish philosophical studies originally written in Arabic, Jewish scholars at the end of the 12th and during the 13th centuries translated more and more works of non-Jewish thinkers and scholars, from Aristotle to Averroes. For the first time in Jewish history, the "holy tongue" became a language of philosophy and science and endowed them thereby with a measure of "holiness."

IV. Between the Middle Ages and Modern Times

In the history of Jewish religious thought, the Middle Ages are, in the first place, the period in which a clear contrast is drawn between prophetic-biblical monotheism and all the other forms of belief in One God which did not directly cling to the Jewish historical tradition. At that period, this second category was primarily represented by Arabic philosophy. The 12th century, when Maimonides lived, is also the period when the center of Jewish national life began to shift more and more from Islamic lands to those of Christendom. However great the dangers that thus threatened the very survival of the Jewish people, as far as Jewish monotheism was concerned, it escaped therewith the peril that might have faced it. Only in the purely emotional spheres, Christian mysticism may have exerted a certain measure of influence on Jews. Thus it probably was not a matter of chance that in the 13th century, when Latin, the language of philosophy and science was also mastered by a considerable number of Jewish scholars, a new form of Jewish mysticism came to light, the Kabbala. Just as the Rambam (Maimonides) was the symbol and representative of the previous century, so Ramban (Moses ben Nahman, 1195-1270), one of the Fathers of Kabbala in Spain, became one of the outstanding figures of the next period. Nevertheless, the development of philosophical thought, from Saadia to Maimonides, continued to hold sway for several centuries, even under these changed conditions. The history of thought has its own immanent logic. Incompletely answered questions demand solutions, even though the circumstances giving rise to the problem have long since disappeared. Even at the very threshold of modern times, we thus find Jewish sages and scholars who prefer to follow old traditional paths and still try to build up metaphysical bases for the Jewish world-view along the lines of the old Hellenic-Arabic ways of reasoning. Regardless of the rich quality of their minds and their spiritual scope, these men are essentially still futilely engaged in settling old accounts for people who are long gone.

Among the tendencies of Jewish thought in the post-Maimonides era, the one most violently opposed by the zealots of tradition was allegorism, that form of metaphysical commentary familiar to us from Hellenistic times and now allegedly sanctioned by Maimonides himself. The interpretation of the Pentateuch tales in the allegorical-metaphysical sense was carried so far that Abraham, for instance, was translated into the concept of "form" and Sarah became "matter." The foremost figure of this movement was Levi ben Abraham ben Hayim or Ralbah of Southern France (d. ca. 1315). His contemporaries in Italy were Zerahiah ben Shealtiel Hen of Rome and Hillel ben Samuel of Verona, the author of *Tagmule ha-Nefesh,* a book in which the doctrine of reward and punishment in the after-life is treated in a strictly rationalistic manner, in the spirit of Maimonides. It is of historic significance that, in his polemics with Averroes, Hillel has recourse to a Christian source (a Latin tract of Thomas Aquinas). The new Catholic speculation now becomes an object of spiritual assimilation on the part of Jewish thinkers, as had once been Greek and, later, Arabic philosophy; with this difference, however, that Christian speculation was itself now in a great measure the result of the assimilation-process which had been greatly stimulated by essentially Jewish methods and thought.

Isaac Albalag's doctrine of the "twofold" truth—paralleling that of the Christian Averroists of the 13th century—now becomes historically comprehensible. This Jewish thinker, who lived either in Southern France or Northern Spain, developed the thesis that the spirit of philosophy and prophecy are diametrically opposed; in philosophy even concrete reality is apprehended conceptually, while in prophecy even concepts are apprehended concretely. From this, he infers that the truth of rational reflection and the truth of prophetic Torah have nothing in common—a thing may be true from the philosophical standpoint and yet may seem entirely false from the standpoint of faith and belief. Thus, Maimonides who wished to make concessions to both knowledge and faith, actually did injustice to both of them. This dual radicalism, which sacrificed the highest principle of the spirit—the one and only truth—in order to defend knowledge against faith and faith against knowledge, was symptomatic of the confusion then existing in Jewish religious thinking. The systems of Levi ben Gershon, Ralbag (1288-1344) and of Hasdai Crescas (ca. 1340-1410) attempted to overcome this confusion by a resorting to ancient metaphysics in the spirit of a changing world.

The system developed by Ralbag and especially evident in his work *Milhamot Adonai* (Wars of the Lord) is partly patterned after Maimonides, but whereas Maimonides regarded the orthodox Aristotelianism of Averroes as offensive from the Jewish standpoint, Ralbag attempted to improve on Maimonides in the rationalistic spirit of classical Arabic Aristotelianism. At almost every point where Maimonides diverged from ibn Roshd's Aristotelianism, we find Ralbag in the opposite camp, commencing with his discussion of divine attributes. The essence of God is not such as to preclude any positive predicate; first, He is pure thought, as asserted by Aristotle; unity and being in their turn are inseparable from the essence of substance, hence it is a contradiction only for the analyzing reason to comprehend the One God's essence, in an aggregate of attributes such as thought, unity, existence, etc. (*Milhamot*, III, 3). Furthermore, Ralbag could not agree with Maimonides that the world was created *ex nihilo*, and held that on this point the Torah was on his side. He claimed that there existed a primordial substance without which even the Supreme Form, Divine Thought, could not have shaped anything. This primordial substance, he declared, was only the pure *potentiality* of being. It would be false to assume from this that the world is eternal and not the work of God. Here we hear in Ralbag's work again the echo of Jewish tradition; not only was the world *created* but "with every instant God renews His *Maase Bereshit* (creation)." The antinomy between creation and the eternity of the world leads to the concept of "eternal creation." With this is linked an entirely new concept of time: God is outside of time; time applies only to the world; viewed from within, the world renews itself every instant; viewed from the divine aspect, its very temporality, eternal in nature, is the conceptual substratum of all divine creation. It would thus seem that creative thought and time are correlative, and Ralbag substitutes them for the Aristotelian-scholastic formula of primordial form and primordial matter (*Milhamot*, VI, 1). Thus a cornerstone for the classical idealism of modern times was laid by a Jewish religious philosopher of the 14th century.

Typical of Ralbag's system are the indications of a new phase in the history of human thought. God is the Supreme Thought and hence the basic laws of thought apply to Him, too. His providence dwells in the wisdom, harmony and purposefulness which govern the universe. Hence it cannot affect the accidental nature of concrete individual existence. In this, too, Ralbag clashed with Maimonides (ibid. III, 2 and 4). For Ralbag, this did away with what constituted a mystery for Maimonides, how to reconcile man's free will with God's foreknowledge of everything that every man of flesh and blood would ever do.

As a student of astrology, categorically rejected by Maimonides, Ralbag so interpreted it that nature emerged as an organic entity ruled by its own immutable laws. Ralbag even attempted to explain miracles and prophecy according to natural laws. Most significant are his conclusions about immortality, since they are based on the premise that acquired or cognitive reason (according to Aristotle, the "immortal" in man) is a continuous ever-developing thought-process which constantly transcends itself (see *Milhamot* I, 13)—approximately the same axiom as that evolved by modern apperceptive psychology.

The advent in the Jewish world of the sage of Avignon (the Christian world knew him as Gersonides), whose scientific works were translated into Latin at papal behest and were said to have exerted great influence on Kepler, was tardy rather than premature. Aside from his influence on the youthful Spinoza of the 17th century, we may regard Ralbag as the final link of a broken chain. Even the philosopher Hasdai Crescas, the second great Jewish systematizer of the 14th century, who was born some four years before the death of Ralbag, followed a system entirely opposed to that of his older contemporary. The Chief Rabbi of Aragon, who lost his only son during the persecutions of 1391, hearkened back to the period preceding that of Maimondes and adopted approximately the attitude of Judah ha-Levi in his approach toward philosophy. His cry was: Torah, not philosophy! Following the method established by his 12th-century predecessor, Crescas, at the beginning of the 15th, fought philosophy with its own weapons; and, since at that time philosophy and Aristotelianism were almost identical, Crescas turned his weapons against the antiquated Aristotelian metaphysics and thus unwittingly furthered the development of European thought.

Crescas' anti-Aristotelian system was carefully grounded. First, he attacked the scholastic theory of *matter,* asserting that even without form primordial matter is an *ens.* In other words, it is *matter* in the physical sense; where material substances do not exist there is vacuity, emptiness of space characterized merely by extension. Space is thus unbounded, infinite, just as are time and number. Thus, Crescas erected his framework in which the modern view of nature was to be set. Galileo, Bruno and especially Newton, meet, in very important details, with the arguments advanced by Crescas at the beginning of the 15th century, in his work *Light of God (Or Adonai* I, 2). Just as for the rabbi of the 15th century, so for Newton infinity of space was the natural symbol of God's omnipresence. Actually, this thought is an ancient Jewish heritage: *Hu mekomo shel olam* (He is the world's space. Cf. Maimonides' *More* I, 70). In the light of these arguments, the question of the Creation assumed a new aspect: if space, time and number are infinite, it must be assumed in principle that the chain of causes is also infinite, and it does not therefore necessarily follow that there must be a First Mover, Aristotle's God. If there is a logically necessary correlation between the world and God, it is because everything that exists can also be conceived as non-existent; consequently the world cannot have any real validity, unless there is some source whose existence is not only possible but absolutely essential, and that source is God, the only stable basis of being and existence. Thus, God is the only cause of the world's existence, its only guarantee of continuity from eternity to eternity (*Or Adonai* III, 1), a point of spiritual agreement between Crescas and the older Kalam on the one hand and all the later proponents of the so-called "ontological argument" on the other.

Crescas' theories here have points of contact with those of his opponent, Ralbag, since with the latter the world's dependence upon God takes also an almost transcendental character. However, Crescas feels that, according to the Torah, we must assume that the world was created in time. Thereby he did not succumb to the philosophical heresy of advocating "double truth" (one for the philosophers and another for theologians) since the *time* he had in mind was not strictly that which man's ordinary language conveys.

A consistent opponent of Aristotelian rationalism, Crescas, together with Judah ha-Levi, is the foremost exponent of Jewish anti-intellectualism. In all his teachings about God, man's essence, immortality and "punishment and reward," he stresses the point that will and emotion, not intellect, are predominant and all-important. Supreme among God's attributes is His benevolence, His desire to create and do good; the joy engendered by His goodness becomes God's love for His creatures. The greatest height to which man can aspire is the love of God: "Thou shalt love the Lord thy God" is consequently a greater deed of merit than cognition of Him. And, since this is taught us by the Torah, and its commandments aim at evoking and fostering this emotion in man, the Torah towers far above all philosophical speculation. If man is immortal, his heart—"the love of God"—must be preserved even more than his intelligence. True paradise is to feel eternally this love of God (ibid. II, 6). Reward and punishment presented a particularly complex problem for Crescas since he was a stern determinist in his attitude toward natural philosophy. He had this to say about man's freedom of will: despite the fact that man's deeds are the natural consequence of a series of all kinds of causes, his own volitions are a vital link in that chain; should he incline toward evil ways, there will be an immediate and direct consequence, as though he had touched glowing iron (ibid. II, 5).

It is characteristic of this period which produced the Marranos, that the author of *Or Adonai* also wrote polemics in Spanish against Christian dogma. There is even a somewhat polemic undertone in Crescas' emphasis on the "love" element in classical Judaism; the same applies to his complicated doctrine of divine attributes which, according to him, stand in their multiplicity in the same close relation with God's indefinable essence, as light with a lighting substance (ibid. I, 3). His chief purpose was to strengthen Judaism in a positive fashion, even though it might occasionally be with a thought or argument from the works of a Thomas Aquinas (as, for instance, in his doctrine of *Creatio ex Nihilo*).

In general, now there began to manifest itself in the sphere of Jewish thought a conservative tendency and a trend toward mysticism. As early as 1360, Meir ibn Aldabi declared war on philosophy in his *Shebile Emunah, The Paths of Faith*. Whatever merit there might be in the systems of Plato and Aristotle he ascribed to the fact that they were disciples of Jewish sages. Aldabi and his younger contemporaries, Rashbaz (Simon ben Zemah Duran, 1361-1444) and Shem-Tob ben Joseph ibn Shem-Tob (d. ca. 1440), often resorted to Kabbala, especially in their doctrine of the soul. In his work *Magen Abot*, Rashbaz aimed his polemics especially at Paul the Apostle. Even Efodi (Profiat Duran), the famous commentator of Maimonides' *More*, published two tracts against the Christian dogmas of the Trinity and the Man-God. In order to rescue the vestiges of philosophical tradition among the Sephardim, ibn Shem-Tob's son, Joseph ben Shem-Tob (d. 1460), the author of *Kebod Elohim*, set out to prove that it was possible to be an Aristotelian and, at the same time, even more pious than Maimonides. Nevertheless, his own son, Shem-Tob ben Joseph (d. 1489) had the courage to write a comprehensive commentary on Maimonides' *More*. This was approximately four years prior to the expulsion from Spain. The two Sephardic thinkers who were fated to end their days in exile—Isaac Abravanel (1437-1508) whose name is so closely linked with the catastrophe of Spain, and Isaac ben Moses Arama (1420-1493), the Baal Akedah (thus called because of his popular Bible commentary)—are the symbolic figures of the conservative-mystic leanings of the period. Although thoroughly versed in philosophical literature Arama wrote *Hazut Kashah* in which he excoriated all ventures into the field of philosophical speculation, and the insolence of philosophy toward true faith, he compared to the temerity of the servant Hagar in setting herself up against her mistress Sarah, the wife of Abraham the Patriarch. Isaac Abravanel was just as harsh in his condemnation, and laid the blame for the Expulsion at the door of philosophy, just as the Kabbalist ibn Shem-Tob had previously held it responsible for mass conversion to

Catholicism. In his commentary on *More Nebukim*, as well as in his own writings *Mifalot Elohim* (The Works of God) and *Rosh Amanah* (Foundation of Faith), Abravanel not only challenged Maimonides' theories about prophecy and miracles but also strove to refute Crescas' views of the Creation.

It is highly characteristic that to this last Jewish thinker of Spain, the very idea of Jewish dogmaticism was offensive. Following Maimonides, Albalag, Crescas and Rashbaz attempted to establish their own systems of Jewish dogma. Somewhat later, their disciple Joseph Albo (d. 1444) published his work *Ikkarim* (Principles). Just as with Rashbaz, his three fundamental principles are the three fundamental premises which the essential concept of a divinely revealed faith demands as a logical necessity: there is a God in the world; He reveals His wishes or Torah to man; He rewards him according to his deeds, since therein the actual importance of His Torah manifests itself (*Ikkarim* I, 10 and 13). In the tree of dogma, these three principles form the main "roots" from which spring any number of other "stems," each a different "shoot," displaying individual "strains" or dominating principles. With these are linked the "branches" of religion, that is, the specific commandments. Although every religion which regards itself as "divine" must incorporate these three basic "general dogmas," this is not necessarily proof that every faith which accepts them is revealed of God. Thus, neither Islam nor Christianity can qualify as pure, divine religion, since the only revelation made by God to man after Adam, Noah and Abraham, was through the Torah at Sinai. Although, in his philosophy of history, Albo closely approaches the materialistic naturalism of ibn Khaldun (see *Ikkarim* I, 25), he has no doubt whatever as to the special spiritual destiny of Israel in the world's history. Everywhere in his book, which is patterned after Latin scholastic works, one feels the anti-Catholic spirit (see III, 25) which filled him during the famous disputation at Tortosa (1413); and still, by the end of that century the whole problem of fundamental dogmas lost all *raison d'être* for Sephardic Jews. Abravanel contended that faith once granted demanded absolute faith in every letter of the Torah, without distinguishing between "roots" and "branches," between principles and corollaries (see especially *Rosh Amanah*). The Sephardic thinker and leader had now concentrated most of his attention on the consideration of a problem completely outside the sphere of philosophy—he was preoccupied with mystical calculations of the year of the Messiah's arrival. Later, at the beginning of the 17th century, distant Poland produced two commentators on Albo's *Ikkarim*, Jacob Koppelman of Brisk and Gedaliah ben Solomon of Lublin (author of *Sharashim ve-Anafim*, Roots and Branches).

By the end of the Middle Ages, Spain shared with Southern France the distinction of being practically the last outpost where the tradition of

Jewish-Arabic philosophy was still influential in the midst of the new Christian world. Just on the eve of modern times, these traditions found a new refuge in Italy, where Christian-humanism was then flourishing. The direct Jewish thinkers to spring up in Italy beginning with Hillel of Verona, had been pupils of the Sephardic sages. It was not until the 15th century that the field of Jewish research in Italy produced figures of more or less original stature. First among these were: that savant in Christian, Greek, Arabic and Jewish philosophical literature, Judah ben Jehiel of Mantua, better known by his Italian cognomen of Messer Leon (ca. 1440-1490), and the friend of the Florentine Platonist Pico della Mirandola, Elijah Delmedigo (ca. 1460-1497) who translated Hebrew and Arabic philosophical works into Latin and, leaning on Averroes, attempted to find a golden midway between pious rationalism and Kabbalistic mysticism in his book *Behinat ha-Dat*, Scrutiny of Religion. But the most eminent among the Jewish thinkers of Italy was a pure Sephardi, the son of Isaac Abravanel, Judah Abravanel or Leo Hebraeus (ca. 1460-1530) in whose *Dialoghi di Amore*, Dialogues of Love, written in Italian, or possibly originally in Spanish, the spiritual influence of his old and his new home are evident to an equal degree. Though Leo Hebraeus still employed Aristotelian scholastic concepts, he nevertheless managed to introduce into his work a Platonic spirit, then experiencing a revival in Italy. Like his father before him, he espoused the theory that the *cosmos* was created by the One and only God and *in time (bizman);* but with him it is, in the best Platonic manner, a single organism, held together by the love of God toward His creation, a love which permeated the world from end to end, binding all its parts and drawing man and all creation back to God. He, the all-Powerful One, is the God not only of truth and justice, but also of beauty. Attempts have been made to trace the influence of Crescas, Solomon ibn Gabirol and the Kabbala in this work of Judah Abravanel. At any rate, it is clear that its author was the product of a generation which was on the road to a new era. Significant in this respect is the fact that his "discourses" rapidly gained favor in the Christian world, whereas they met with no response among the traditionally religious Jews.

The philosophic-scientific works of Joseph Solomon Delmedigo (1591-1655), the great-grandson of Elijah Delmedigo, have but a symptomatic significance in the history of Jewish religious thought. In his youth a pupil of Galileo, Yashar of Candia, as Joseph Solomon Delmedigo was called among Jews, oscillated between Kabbala and rationalism, between tradition and modern science. Born in Crete, fate cast him as far as Lithuania, and a number of his works first saw the light of day in Holland where, a few decades later, there was to burgeon forth Spinoza's *Amor Dei Intellectualis*, Intellectual Love of God.

In Spinoza's system, traditional Jewish speculation left its confines which had remained steadfast during the Middle Ages. The tide of the times broke down one barrier after another, even in the neighboring Christian world. For the first time in its history, Jewish religious thought was compelled to ask what purpose it had to fulfill in a world which sees its holiest possession neither in tradition nor in this or that positive faith nor even in disbelief, but in transhistorical reason.

V. The Period of Pure Reason

The periods of Humanism, of the Renaissance, and of the Reformation gradually widened the spiritual horizon of Western Europe. In place of the Catholic outlook which had previously united all of educated Christendom, there arose now a new world-view. This world-view gradually liberated itself from any bonds with a definite theological tradition and sought its roots in the universal spirit of man, on the basis of experimental natural science and under the strict control of impartial reason. Arguments stressing the inviolability of tradition or prescribed opinions were no longer regarded as valid. The "chain of tradition" had, however, always been the prevailing factor in Jewish religious thought. Now, in the new era when reason took precedence over all else, Jewish religious speculation had only three possible roads open: to point out and emphasize the purely rational elements in Jewish tradition and threby forever renounce its right to an individual historical existence apart, or, on the contrary, to delve more deeply than ever before into the treasures and hidden mysteries of the Jewish spiritual past; the third choice was to seek some middle course between Judaism and pure human reason. The first course was followed by a few isolated individuals who divorced themselves completely from the Jewish community (the classic example here being Spinoza). The second course had been followed as early as the 16th century by the large majority of the more educated among the Jewish masses who, contrary to the tendency of the individualistically-minded thinkers, cut themselves away ever more sharply from the surrounding non-Jewish world. The third course open to Jewish religious thought, to follow with the spirit of the time, was taken by the Haskalah.

From the time immediately after the expulsion from Spain almost to the end of the 18th century, Jewish religious speculation was dominated by the advocates of theoretical and practical Kabbala (together with the Messianism which had now become an integral part of Kabbala) and by the adherents of the strict rabbinic tradition. At that time, the reign of the Kabbala spread wherever Sephardic influence prevailed—from the Near East as far west as Holland. Parallel with it was the ascetic *Musar* (moralist) literature. The 16th and 17th century Messianism was the spiritual offspring of the Kabbala, but in the 18th century it degenerated into the Frankist movement, simultaneously encouraging the revival of mysticism in the form of the Hassidic movement. Rabbinical learning regarded these

new spiritual currents with reserve, but on the whole accepted the
Kabbala tradition and especially the newly-risen Zohar tradition.

To such great Halakah scholars in Poland (which now had become the
center of rabbinical learning) as Solomon Luria, "Rashal" (1510-1573) and
Joel Sirkes, "Bach" (d. ca. 1640), Kabbala represented *true wisdom*. It was
far more significant for the further development of Jewish speculation that
among leading Ashkenazic rabbis of Poland there were many for whom the
attitude of reserve toward the Kabbala was not merely a matter of choice
but a result of their adherence to the pre-Kabbalist school of Spain,
primarily that of Maimonides. Moses Isserles, "Rama" (1520-1572), who
first introduced the *Shulhan Aruk* (code book for ritual and legislative
questions) in Poland, was also the author of a work purporting to interpret
the commandments of the Torah in the light of Maimonides' teachings.
Thus, in the 18th century, Maimonides' *More Nebukim* was still an
important factor in the life of the Ashkenazic orthodoxy. Whereas in the
case of the Lithuanian Solomon Maimon (1754-1800) the *More* served only
to arouse his interest in general problems of philosophy which ultimately
led him away from the Jewish world, for the German Moses Mendelssohn
(1729-1786) it opened a completely new horizon and he saw therein a new
path for Judaism to tread, leading directly to the Haskalah period in the
history of Jewish religious thought.

When the time came to make an about-face toward the surrounding
non-Jewish world, German Jewry became the vanguard and, for that
reason, the qualified heirs of the Sephardic culture. Enthusiasts of the
Haskalah compared the Ashkenazic thinker Moses Dessau or Rambaman,
as they called Moses Mendelssohn, to Moses ben Maimon of Cordova.
Both dreamed of terminating the conflict between Torah and Reason. But,
whereas the Torah remained the old one, the prestige of Reason,
commencing with the 12th century, had greatly risen. As it gained in
importance, it grew less and less tolerant of rivalry in the field of
metaphysics.

The method of the rationalist era was to argue that if the Torah teaches us
about metaphysical matters—God, freedom, immortality, etc.—whatever
is not in accordance with pure reason, is false; if, on the other hand, its
teachings coincide with those of Reason, it is superfluous. Mendelssohn
favored this approach. His first metaphysical works, *Ueber die Evidenz in
metaphysischen Wissenschaften* (1764), *Phaedon* (1767), and others,
appeal to human reason as such and do not seek their support in Jewish
sources, although their themes were the positive attributes of God,
especially His absolute moral perfection, the question of an after-life and
other such topics which had heretofore been regarded by orthodox Jewish
thinkers as the basic principles of the Jewish religion.

In seeking a reply to the question: Why is the Torah necessary at all if
reason need have no recourse to it? Mendelssohn finally came to the

conclusion (particularly in *Jerusalem oder ueber religioese Macht und Judentum*, 1783) that, in contrast to the mystical Christian faith, Judaism is a system of practical commandments and "Ceremonial" laws imposing no obligation to "believe" in a metaphysical premise. The purpose here is to educate an entire people to a point where it will be capable of comprehending "the eternal truths of Reason" (*Jerusalem*, II). In his *Tractatus Theologico-Politicus*, Spinoza had already pointed out that Moses' Torah was not a system of dogmas but a code of laws. Judah ha-Levi, long before and from a different standpoint, had been very insistent on the *Mitsvot Maasiot*. A sharp opponent of Spinoza's pantheism and a warm admirer of the great poet Judah ha-Levi, Mendelssohn employed modern *heresies* in order to strengthen the structure of the Jewish tradition of the Middle Ages. It is interesting to note that already at the beginning of the 18th century, David Nieto (d. 1728), the Sephardic rabbi of London, who was wrongly suspected of leaning toward Spinoza's pantheism wrote *Kuzari Helek Sheni* (Second Kuzari) in his own defense, patterning his work after the model of Judah ha-Levi.

Mendelssohn's effort to divorce ethical monotheism from the Torah and make the former the common property of all mankind while at the same time declaring the Jews to be the sole owners of God's Torah, was in sharp conflict with his own metaphysical conviction that God's absolute goodness belongs to all men, Jews and non-Jews alike. If it is true that all Jewish *mitsvot* "remind and stimulate to reflect on the eternal truths of Reason" (*Jerusalem*, II), why were only the Jewish people worthy to receive the Sinai revelation? The answer to this was Mendelssohn's philosophy of history which, in sharp contrast to the current optimism of the times, testified that in the field of historic reality Jewish rationalistic universalism had its own experience after all. Man, declared Mendelssohn, is a naturally reasoning creature and yet permits himself to be led astray; it was therefore necessary that there should spring up a group of people whose particular task it was "through the fact of its very existence, so to speak, to disseminate among the rest of mankind healthy and unadulterated ideas" (ibid.). This group is the Jewish people, "a kingdom of priests." This was the seed from which there later sprang the *mission*-theory of the Reform movement.

Not ten years had passed after Mendelssohn's death, when his followers began to interpret his *mission* theory in complete opposition to his original intentions. The Kantian scholar, Lazarus Bendavid (1762-1832), held that if Jews had any contribution to offer to modern times it was through the tidings that they were prepared to follow the path of "pure reason" (Immanuel Kant's *Pure Reason*) and convert their "church beliefs," *i.e.*, their synagogue faith, into a pure philosophic "religious faith." In Mendelssohn's terminology, this meant capitulation to the "unification system," or to a would-be universalist and, actually, a Jewish-Protestant syncretism. Whereas individual Jewish thinkers of the 17th century had striven to separate themselves from Judaism, now it was quite the contrary: isolated thinkers were making efforts to wrest it from the spiritual perils besetting it on all sides through the rising flood of rationalism. Since post-Kantian German idealism left room in its system for transcendental reason certain Jewish philosophers found that this offered them new opportunity to ground their ancestral faith in the spirit of the times. In this connection, two names in particular must be mentioned: Salomo Ludwig Steinheim (ca. 1789-1866) and the Hegelian scholar, Samuel Hirsch (1815-1889).

In his four-volume work *Die Offenbarung nach dem Lehrbegriff der Synagoge,* 1835-65 (Revelation According to the Teachings of the Synagogue), Steinheim postulated that critical reason must avow its inability to find a bridge between itself and empirical reality, whether in the matter of daily experience or in the actual revelation of religious truth. The reaction against Kant's "critical idealism," which was evident at the end of the 18th century and led Solomon Maimon to his "critical skepticism," was used by Steinheim for the purpose of reinforcing anew traditional anti-rationalism. Our knowledge of the existence of God, freedom of the will and immortality of the soul, is much more accurate than our knowledge of natural laws and, therefore, "the faith of the synagogue" is "an exact science." However, we owe this science not to reason but to God's revelation. The philosophical foundations on which Samuel Hirsch, Steinheim's younger contemporary, sought to strengthen Jewish faith were much deeper. He published his *Religious Philosophy of the Jews* in 1842 when only 27 years old. However his application of Hegel's dialectic method ran so counter to German Jewry's general trend to retain only the smallest possible vestige of Judaism, that they declared his system sheer impudent "heresy." In contrast to Hegel, Hirsch maintained that religion is not merely an element in the development of Absolute Spirit but that precisely within religion and, more concretely, within the Jewish religion, this spirit reveals itself in its genuine essence. Thanks to his original synthesis of Hegel's theories of human self-consciousness and Fichte's doctrine of the creative force of human freedom, Hirsch outlines a scheme of universal history with the people of Israel at its center, as in Judah ha-Levi's *Kuzari*. Idolatrous cultures were characterized by a passive piety which granted nature's sway over man's free will; on the contrary Judaism, the religion of active will, placed man above nature. As soon as this active religious devotion became rooted in the Jewish people, miracles and prophets became superfluous; the time had now arrived to draw all of mankind into the Jewish-religious cultural sphere. This originally was, and continued to remain, the purpose of Christianity—to lead man from idolatry to God. As long as this task has not been fulfilled, Israel remains the living embodiment of the idea that man has been created to be his

Creator's refulgence in nature, to be a "free man" and to be the Creator's free "first-born son." Since the beginning of the Christian era, the only miracle in the natural world has been the survival of Israel who is the suffering but, nevertheless—or more precisely, therefore,—the chosen "servant of God" (according to Isaiah, XLI et seq., especially LIII). Modern philosophy, from Descartes to Hegel, is not just "universalist" at all but specifically and definitely Christian. For this reason, it is still half-way to its goal and has still far to go to attain its real mission—to lead the Christian peoples to the threshold of the Messianic era.

With Hirsch, Mendelssohn's *mission* theory thus became a sharp weapon of self-defense for Judaism. In general, however, the *mission* theory of the Jewish Reform movement of the 19th century was inclined to drift along with the tide of compromise. *Religion des Geistes* by Solomon Formstecher (1808-1889), which appeared one year before Hirsch's book and was based on Schelling's philosophy, stressed the ethical side of Judaism in contrast to the aesthetic tendency of every sort of natural religion and set out to prove that in the Reformation, Christianity had moved in the direction of the Jewish spirit. Whereas Hirsch maintained that even when the Messiah arrived, the world would need the Jewish people and for this reason it must return to Palestine, Formstecher contended that the disappearance of Jewish political independence was a step forward in universal history and, therefore, on philosophical grounds, he became the apologist of the Diaspora as well as all manner of reforms which may eventually bring about a closer contact between Jewry and the rest of the world. Another disciple of Schelling, Meir Heinrich Landauer (1808-1841) sought ideological contact with Catholicism through the medium of Kabbalist doctrine and through the interpretation of the Torah in the light of the triadic theory. In so doing he based his arguments on the variations of God's name in the Torah (Adonai, Elohim, etc.). Although friendly toward Schelling's romantic philosophy, Landauer's older contemporary, the Rabbi of Hamburg, Isaac Bernays (1792-1849), leaned toward a strict traditionalism. At the same time, in Italy, Samuel David Luzzatto or Shadal (1800-1865) had formulated much more sharply than Formstecher and without any thought of compromise, the contrast between the intellectual-aesthetic (and therefore non-Jewish) and the emotional-ethical (the Jewish) factor in human history. The former factor, that is the Hellenic, he designated as *Atticism* which he considered the eternal opposite of *Abrahamism* which was the essential basis and meaning of Israel's eternal existence.

Together with a galaxy of more or less traditionally-minded German-speaking Jewish savants (Nachman Krochmal, Solomon Judah Rapoport, known as "Shir," Zunz, Geiger, Graetz, etc.), Shadal belongs among the founders of the new *Wissenschaft des Judentums* which also included the history of Jewish religious thought. All of them fervent adherents of objective scholarship and of unalloyed historical truth, these modern Jewish scholars differ sharply in their subjective basic outlooks, and this, in turn, determined the special place of each of them in the evolution of modern Judaism. At a time when Abraham Geiger (1810-1874), who inspired the Jewish Reform movement, regarded the scientific approach to the historical evolution of Judaism as a means by which he could demonstrate its need and justification for adapting itself to the changed times; at a time when even Nachman Krochmal (1785-1840) in his *Emunah Zerufah* (Pure Faith), which was published posthumously (1851) and accorded by Zunz the honorary title of *More Nebuke ha-Zeman*, "The Guide for the Perplexed of Our Times," had placed greatest emphasis on the vicissitudes in the history of the Jewish religious spirit, Shadal and his peers were resolved to elaborate most clearly whatever, in their opinion, was absolute and eternal in Judaism.

In his *Nineteen Letters on Judaism* (1836) and shortly thereafter, in *Horeb* (1837), Samson Raphael Hirsch (1808-1888), the father of modern orthodoxy in Western Europe, came out with the following maxim: "The Torah is as undeniable a fact as heaven and earth, *i.e.*, its decrees and commandments are as immutable as the laws of nature since the object of both is to *hallow* human life and impart true joy ('the joy of life') without which life can have no meaning."

If it was the hope of this pious rabbi of Germany to revive the traditional Jewish way of life in Jewish hearts, two other Jewish thinkers of the 19th century, Joseph Salvador (1796-1873) in France and Elijah Benamozegh (1822-1900) in Italy, were also engaged in defining the universal-historical worth of Israel's perpetuity. In Salvador's work, *Paris, Rome, Jerusalem* (1860), the link connecting Moses Mendelssohn's *Jerusalem* with Moses Hess' *Rome and Jerusalem* (1862), the old mission theory is concretely formulated: Judaism is the universal faith of the future which will effect complete harmony between Catholic orthodoxy and the ideas of the French Revolution. Benamozegh was less optimistic and therefore closer in spirit to his countryman Shadal. In his works, written partially in French (*Morale juive et morale chrétienne*, 1867, and *Israel et l'Humanité*, 1885), the rabbi and Kabbalist of Leghorn sharply contrasted the non-Jewish world outlook which recognizes moral behavior essentially between individuals only, and "Hebraism" with its original feeling for brotherhood between peoples: only because of this, is Israel the "priest" among the peoples of the earth and must so remain until the redemption of all mankind. The emphasis placed on the ethical aspect of Jewish monotheism evoked a revival of interest in the prophets. In a treatise, *Les Prophètes d'Israel*, one of Salvador's admirers in France, James Darmesteter (1850-1894), declared that "a bond between prophetic ethics and science" is the only possible conclusion to the course of religious development (1891). In England at the same time Israel Abrahams (1858-1925), found that the genuine substance of Jewish spiritual history "no matter how many changes the abstract conceptions of Judaism may have undergone" was always the "Jewish moral code which was evolved from the noblest of ideals" (1891). On the basis of emphasis laid on the ethical-universalist element in the Jewish religion, Claude G. Montefiore (1858-1938), together with Abrahams, the founder of liberal Judaism in England, preached a "theism" which was to become a Jewish-Christian faith, although its theoretician himself realized that the new "truth" would prove "too Christain for its Jewish critics and too Jewish for the Christian critics (Introduction to *The Synoptic Gospels*, 1909). For this reason it was truly astounding that another Jewish thinker of almost the same generation, Moritz Lazarus of Germany (1824-1903), at the end of his life published a work *Die Ethik des Judentums* (Vol. I, 1898, Vol. II, 1911) in which he clearly pointed out the progress made by Jewish religious morals in the post-prophetic and, especially, in the Talmudic era. He reaches the same conclusions as the author of *Horeb*, that the meaning of all Jewish *mitsvot* is "the hallowing of life."

Hermann (Ezekiel) Cohen's (1842-1918) *Die Religion der Vernunft aus den Quellen des Judentums*, 1919, represents a magnificent synthesis of all the main tendencies and motives in Jewish religious thought in Western Europe since Mendelssohn. The rationality of Judaism, the bond between religion and ethics, the universal role of the prophets and their Messianism, the significance of the continuous development of Jewish spiritual tradition from oldest times to the present era, the question of the Jewish mission, the opposition to all forms of pantheism and naturalism, all of these elements which we find scattered or assembled in various combinations and expressed more or less clearly by various Jewish religious thinkers, were utilized by Cohen as essential cornerstones in the structure of his philosophic system. What Maimonides was in regard to his predecessors, Cohen was in regard to the Jewish thinkers of the early 19th century; Kant together with Plato represented for him what Aristotle had been for Maimonides. At first Cohen, as was the case with many Jewish religious thinkers before him, turned toward philosophy in general. For him, God was that concept, that idea which combined within a single realm of creative reason "the nature of natural science" and the moral order of the universe; or, expressed differently, that concept which postulated the possibility of realizing the highest ethical ideal, the ideal of social justice among united mankind. Cohen's system was in the tradition of Kant; his logic was that of "pure" cognition; his ethics, that of "pure" will; his aesthetics, a doctrine of "pure" feeling. This idea of "purity" bears the stamp of Kant and expresses the "autonomy" of reason, its independence from any other factor, whether empirical or super-empirical. In the course of these several decades, however, the purity of Kant's transcendental idealism became fused, in Cohen's thought, with the Jewish "holy

Scriptures," as well as with the entire structure of commentaries and philosophical speculation reared upon them during some two thousand years. It now became "purity," "holiness." The motto of Cohen's final work was Akiba's famous exclamation (Talmud Babli, Yoma, 85): "Praise be to you, Israel! Who purifies you and for whom do you purify yourself? It is your Father in Heaven."

If under transcendentalism the basic sense of "purity" is the idea that the tasks of theoretical as well as practical reason are endless, exactly so genuinely-Jewish holiness, man's striving to be worthy of "the image of God" which he bears in his individual lineaments, has essentially the same purpose. This Cohen came to see toward the end of his life. As a simple creature of flesh and blood, burdened with the realization of his moral guilt, and a constant prey to the weakness of the flesh and of social ills, man cannot exist without "love of God," without the religious feeling which binds God to him and him to God, and hence, to his fellow men, the "other one" (see *Religion der Vernunft*, especially chapters VII-X). This knowledge we acquire through "reason"; and whatever reason dictates in this connection has been taught from the very beginning by the "Jewish source"—the Bible and its qualified commentaries in the entire history of Jewish religious thought.

Cohen's spiritual development is typical of the entire era. It would seem that the Age of Reason gained its highest triumph at the beginning of the 20th century. And yet there began to manifest itself a yearning for those "sources" belonging to a former period and to other lands, sources which the scientific mind of the 19th century had heretofore accorded merely an objective, historical interest.

VI. Recent Trends

The spiritual crisis which, at the end of the 19th century, became apparent in the intensification of social and political contrasts all over the world, also brought in its wake a regrouping of the creative forces in all spheres of Jewish cultural life, even in the closely circumscribed field still left for Jewish religious thought. The spirit of religious rationalism which had at first inspired the Haskalah began to disappear gradually, and to assume, especially in Eastern Europe, a purely secular character—whether a-religious or even anti-religious—in a well-nigh sheer national-Jewish form. Jewish thought now became nationalistic, humanitarian, socialistic; insofar as it remained religious it seemed to be dormant and lifeless. Only the decadence of rationalism and intellectualism in Europe called forth a "revaluation of values" also among the Jews. While a number of Jewish thinkers opposed Jewish "spirituality" in general (Micah Joseph Berdyczewski, and others) or still sought to interpret it in the spirit of evolutionism as a means to biological ends—the preservation of Jewish national life (Ahad ha-Am, Simon Dubnow)—there were indications that the apparently dried up spring of traditional speculation was capable of again gushing forth as it had in previous periods.

It was highly characteristic of the mood of the times that this revival was stimulated by an aesthetic interest in the Jewish believer, the Hasid, the man of faith who remained unaffected by the course of historical events, who got along without philosphical deliberations and was content with aphoristic gems of Hasidic "Torah." At first the object of a romantically nostalgic literature (J. L. Peretz, and others), the religiously devout soon drew the attention of the Jewish thinker to that world of speculation in which personal piety had long found refuge. It was principally Hillel Zeitlin who undertook in Eastern Europe to make the world of Hasidism better comprehensible to the Jew of modern times. However the development of religious thought, insofar as it has found expression in recent Yiddish and Hebrew literature, will be treated in another place. In Western Europe it was Martin Buber (b. 1878) who set out to familiarize the outside world with the ideas of Hasidism. In the course of his labors Buber emerged as an original thinker who considered Hasidism as a necessary element in the religious world-view in general, and all the more so, in Judaism. If at first he regarded himself a mystic, he later came to the conclusion that mysticism which seeks, through "nearness to God", to submerge and efface man's individual character, is essentially anti-religious and, therefore, non-Jewish. In his book *Ich und Du* (1923), written under the influence of German idealism and even more under the influence of Henri Bergson, he says that at the core of the world unfolded to us by natural science there lies a profounder world of genuinely *real* being. He describes it by means of the concept *relationship*: only through the completely personal relationship between "I" and "Thou" is this revealed, and it depends upon "me" always and everywhere to find and hear "thy" voice. The beast and the plant emit this voice (an echo of Hasidic panpsychism); but above all, it is God, who speaks eternally to the people of Israel. His voice and speech are the Holy Scriptures and also the entire created world. Only occasionally was the individual deemed worthy to hear this voice from the depths: "One does not find God by remaining in the world; one does not find God by going outside the world; whoever, heart and soul, goes out to his 'thee' finds Him who cannot be sought . . ." "The eternal voice sweeps on—when that is all." And yet the meaning of all history is that the world becomes God's realm "Malkut Shaddai," as one of Buber's last works is entitled.

Whether this semi-rational, semi-mystical conception of the world is Hasidism's legitimate heir is a question per se; at all events Buber became the center of a circle of his own Hasidim. Such circles and little groups were in general symptomatic of the post-war revival of Jewish religious thought in Western Europe.

Parallel with these partly supra-scientific, partly anti-scientific trends which became particularly strong during the great upheavals of the period after World War I, there once more rose to the surface of Jewish religious thought the older major West-European trends: neo-orthodoxy and Liberal or Reformed Judaism. Among the exponents of these trends may be mentioned Jacob Rosenheim who, in his *Orientierung im juedischen Geistesleben der Gegenwart* (1920), seeks to shield Judaism from the rationalism of Hermann Cohen's variety and the irrationalists of Buber's school; likewise Isaac Breuer (b. 1883) whose object it was to entrench the ancient Jewish ideal of "God's governance over the united people of Israel" with the aid of modern theology. Breuer, incidentally, was the author of a *New Kuzari*.

The more liberal-minded Judaism of the period is most clearly expounded by the German rabbi, Leo Baeck (b. 1873), in his book *Das Wesen des Judentums* (new edition, 1926). According to him, Judaism is first of all, a "religion of deeds," ethical in essence and therefore "classical" in form in contrast to Christianity which is thoroughly "romantic"; and at that—one must distinguish between the eternal essence of Judaism and the chaff, which cannot withstand the test of time.

This is 19th century relativism which on the one hand inspired the Jewish Reform movement and, on the other, promoted the scientific investigation of the history of Jewish culture, a study which now, in the period of recent spiritual confusion, once more has focussed on an investigation of the history of Jewish religious thought and especially on the epoch of its Jewish-Arabic Renaissance. Among the liberal religious thinkers belongs David Koigen (1879-1933), the author of *The Moral God* (1922) which summons Judaism to bring the universal development of religion to its last and highest level.

The most eminent figure among the religious thinkers of this period, Franz Rosenzweig (1886-1929), cannot be classified as either an orthodox or as a religious liberal; he also cannot be bracketed as either a rationalist or its contrary, an anti-rationalist, since his *Star of Redemption* (1921) is an organic synthesis of the most diverse shades of thought which one-sidedly dominated the majority of his contemporaries. In his Jewish-religious world-view, Rosenzweig is closely connected with both Cohen and Buber: with the former, in his striving not to overlook the "two thousand year old history of philosphy" but to transcend it; and with his friend Buber, because he, too, sought to find something more in Judaism than merely the "knowledge" of God. To Rosenzweig this "something more" represents neither more nor less than the true "redemption" of the people of Israel, of all mankind and of God's entire world. To him the "star of redemption" is symbolized by the star of David—two triangles intercrossing, each representing only half of the truth, from below to the top—toward God, from above downward—toward the world. Only when intertwined in one "pattern" do these triangles radiate as a star, which is God's "visage," that is, his "eternal truth" (*Star of Redemption* III, "the Gate"). "He is the One Who plants eternal life among us," among us Jews, and among us human beings, in whose midst we, the children of the "eternal people" live. Is this a knowledge? Is this a Faith? "We make Faith"—replies Rosenzweig, the exponent of a would-be new school of rationalism—"entirely as the content of knowledge, but of knoweldge of a sort that has at its base a fundamental concept of faith" (ib. II, Introduction: "The Probabilities of Living to Witness a Miracle"). These words clearly echo the magnificent Jewish philosophical speculations of the Middle Ages. Rosenzweig's "sources" however, are even more ancient: the Bible, Talmud, Midrash, the Prayer-Book and even the "Passover Haggadah." His book rings with the "words of God":

"He hath shewed thee, O man, what is good; and what doth the Lord require of thee, but to do justly, and to love mercy, and to walk humbly with thy God."

This is just the passage which Hermann Cohen declared to be the *leitmotif* of every religious thought (cf. *Religion der Vernunft*, Introduction III, 15 and chapter XVII at the end).

A sign of this disturbed epoch is the fact that even the Russian language, which had formerly been with Jews as a rule a language of religious indifference—now became a means of expressing pious thoughts. On the eve of World War I, Baruch Stolpner (d. 1937), the "Jewish Socrates" among Russia's thinkers, barely mustered sufficient courage to become like them a "God-seeker" but quickly repented his effort to unite Marxism with faith. After the Russian Revolution, the former "Slavophile," M. Gershenzon (1869-1923) suddenly discovered that the Bible is an inexhaustible source of profoundest wisdom. A year before his death, in a treatise entitled *The Destiny of the Jewish People*, he unfolded the religious significance of the biblical "Thou-hast-chosen-us" idea. Even Leo Shestov-Schwartzman (1866-1938) the "Nietzsche of Russia," former exponent of metaphysical "rootlessness," at the end of his life put the Bible and the God of Abraham over against philosophy. Another Russian émigré, M. Hirschkopf, in his book *What is the Meaning of Life?* (1926) attempted to establish a connection between Jewish faith and modern natural science.

From the end of the 18th century German became the language of Jewish learning and, of course, of Jewish religious-philosophical literature. This spiritual hegemony of German-Jewry lasted through almost the entire 19th century. The cultural rise of Eastern European Jewry, with the consequent development of a many-sided and valuable Yiddish and Hebrew literature, together with the growth of large Jewish communities in the English-speaking countries, led to the creation of a rich Jewish literature in Hebrew, Yiddish and English. At present Jewish life and Jewish thought are reflected mainly in these three languages.

The newest tendencies in Jewish religious thought, insofar as they are expressed in Hebrew, Yiddish and English, are discussed elsewhere in this work.

Bibliography

I. ABRAHAMS, *Some Permanent Values in Judaism*. 1924.

I. ABRAHAMS, E. R. BEVAN and CH. SINGER, *The Legacy of Israel*. 1927.

S. W. BARON, edit., *Essays on Maimonides*. 1941.

J. BLUVSTEIN, Hebrew translation of Gabirol's *Fons Vitae*. 1926.

A. CAUSSE, *Les "pauvres" d'Israel*. 1922.

JAKOB GUTTMANN, *Die Scholastik des dreizehnten Jahrhunderts in ihren Beziehungen zum Judentum*. 1902.

JULIUS GUTTMANN, *Die Philosophie des Judentums*. 1933.

P. HEINISCH, *Griechische Philosophie im Alten Testament*. 1913-1914.

G. HOELSCHER, *Geschichte der israelitischen und juedischen Religion*. 1922.

I. HUSIK, *A History of Jewish Mediaeval Philosophy*. 2nd ed. 1930.

M. JOEL, *Zur Genesis der Lehre Spinozas*. 1871.

D. KAUFMANN, *Geschichte der Attributenlehre in der juedischen Religionsphilosophie des Mittelalters von Saadia bis Maimuni*. 1877.

A. LEWKOWITZ, *Das Judentum und die geistigen Stroemungen des XIX. Jahrhunderts*. 1935.

A. LODS, *Des prophètes à Jésus*. 1935.

M. LOEHR, *Sozialismus und Individualismus im Alten Testament*. 1906.

A. MARMORSTEIN, *The Old-Rabbinic Doctrine of God*. 1927.

G. F. MOORE, *Judaism in the First Centuries of the Christian Era*. 1927-1930.

S. MUNK, *Mélanges de philosophie juive et arabe*. 1859.

D. NEUMARK, *Essays in Jewish Philosophy*. 1929.

D. NEUMARK, *Geschichte der juedischen Philosophie des Mittelalters, nach Problemen dargestellt*. 1907-1928.

E. PACE, *Ideas of God in Israel*. 1924.

H. W. ROBINSON, *Religious Ideas of the Old Testament*. 1913.

C. ROTH, *The Jewish Contribution to Civilization*, ch. VII, by Leon Roth. 1938.

L. ROTH, *Spinoza, Descartes, Maimonides*. 1924.

S. SCHECHTER, *Some Aspects of Rabbinic Theology*. 1909.

W. R. SMITH-CHEYNE, *Prophets of Israel*, 1895.

L. STRAUSS, *Philosophie und Gesetz, Beitraege zum Verstaendnis Maimunis und seiner Vorlaeufer*. 1935.

M. WAXMAN, *A History of Jewish Literature*, Vols. I-IV. New York, 1938-1941.

M. WIENER, *Juedische Religion im Zeitalter der Emanzipation*. 1934.

H. A. WOLFSON, *Cresca's Critique of Maimonides*. Cambridge, 1929.

D. NEUMARK, *Toldot ha-Filosofyah be-Yisrael*, Vol. I. New York-Warsaw, 1921.

S. BERNFELD, *Daat Elohim, Toldot ha-Filosofyah ha-Datit be-Yisrael*, Warsaw, 1897.

5. Jewish Law

Introduction

In Jewish history law occupies an even more prominent place than it did in ancient Rome, the principal source of jurisprudence in Western civilization. This is to be explained by the fact that the existence of the people of Israel as such was conceived at a very early period as an essential factor in its religion. The interdependence was clear: just as Israel cannot exist without its faith, so its religion in turn presupposes the existence of the people of Israel. Consequently, Israel's religion lays great stress on the concrete forms of social life, in particular on the legal system which must regulate the most divergent and conflicting private interests and constantly reconcile them, in accordance with the principles of equity, with the welfare of the nation as a whole. The basis of the Holy Scriptures accordingly consists of "statutes and judgments," "justice and righteousness." The most important part of the Scriptures, the Pentateuch, is the earliest history both of the nation and of its most sacred law, a record of the origins of its legal institutions. How deeply the idea of law and of a harmonious legal system penetrated into the minds of the people is evident from the dictum of Rabbi Simeon ben Gamaliel: "By three things the world is preserved: by truth, by judgment, and by peace." (Sayings of the Fathers I, 18.) Commenting, as it were, on this, the Talmud observes that "the three are one," for where the law is enforced, truth prevails and peace is maintained (Perek ha-Shalom). In other words, the ultimate foundation of social peace is the rule of the true and just law.

All of the characteristics of Jewish law derive from the fact that it has its roots in the Jewish faith. Inasmuch as the supreme lawgiver is God Himself, the legal norms, the positive and negative precepts, receive a corresponding significance; the law ranks above the highest authorities in national life, including the anointed King. Indeed, not only the mighty of the earth but even "the Judge of all the earth," the Lord Himself, is bound by the fundamental principle of law (Genesis XVIII, 25). Thus, Jewish law acquired, in theory, a force independent of the state's boundaries, and

This essay was first published in English in *The Jewish People: Past and Present*, Volume I, Jewish Encyclopedic Handbooks, Inc., New York, 1948.

extended its authority over all the members of the nation wherever they might dwell. Moreover, in the course of time certain norms were defined which applied not only to the Jews, but to the civilized world at large (the seven Noahian Laws), and which may be described as natural law (Sanhedrin 56); among these laws is the commandment to establish courts of law. The unlimited validity of Jewish law was an important factor in the consolidation of the Diaspora, enabling the scattered communities to retain their connections with the homeland and with each other by virtue of their common system of law.

The uninterrupted evolution of Jewish law over a period of almost 3,000 years—a cultural process without parallel in world history—is in itself a result of the close connection between the people's attitude to law and its religious tradition. For since, according to that tradition, the original norms are of divine authorship, they cannot be abolished by human beings; at the most they may be reinterpreted in accordance with the new requirements of the times. Consequently, the method of commentary, a new interpretation of an ancient text or of its accepted explanation, became the principal instrument in the enactment of new laws and the progressive development of juridical thought. The whole body of Jewish juridical literature, almost up to the present day, constitutes a great monument to this process. Each new layer encircles its predecessor like a ring and is in turn surrounded by a wider ring. In a sense even such legal codes as Maimonides' *Mishneh Torah* (12th century) or Joseph Karo's *Shulhan Aruk* (16th century) are essentially a systematized interpretation of the older sources.

As a result of the central place occupied by law in the Jewish outlook, those forms of creative thought and effort, which in other civilizations remain strictly within the domain of law, achieved almost complete sway over the entire range of Jewish life. The spiritual possessions of the Jewish people consisted for a long time chiefly of a vast stock of norms: of a purely religious, ritual, ethical or hygienic, as well as of a legal character in the modern sense. Already in Talmudic times a distinction was made between the precepts governing the relationship between God and man, and those concerned with the relations between man and man. A system of law in the modern sense must deal chiefly with the latter sphere, and to a large degree it was law in the narrower sense that determined the development of Jewish social and economic life, whether in an independent state or in an autonomous group under foreign rule. Autonomy for Jews within the framework of non-Jewish states always meant, above all, the privilege, recognized by the dominant power, to live according to Jewish law and to seek justice, in matters not involving non-Jews, in a Jewish court of law (*bet din*).

Jewish law which was always regarded as a means to a higher end—the preservation of the people—succeeded in avoiding the extreme formalism characteristic, for instance, of the older Roman law *(ius civile)*. While the Romans taught that the formal requirements of justice must be enforced at all costs, Jewish law characteristically held that man was not created for the legal norms but that they were created for him, to enable him to lead a worthy life (Leviticus XVIII, 4-5; Deuteronomy XXX, 19-20). This notion harmonized with the principle of "the perfection of the world," or social progress. While Roman law is, as a rule, individualistic and therefore extremely cautious about restricting the rights of private property, Jewish law limits such rights by prescribing a variety of restrictions designed to benefit society, and above all to protect those who are socially the weaker. Thus, it gives concrete effect to its principal purpose, which is to safeguard the people as a whole down to its humblest member—the pauper, the stranger, the widow and the orphan. In accordance with this purpose, there developed in the Talmudic period a ramified social legislation, including a very detailed labor code, which enabled many communities to survive the most severe oppression in the course of their historic journey, and which even in the post-emancipation period remained, among the lower classes, one of the factors responsible for the preservation of tradition in its most intense form. By virtue of their distinctive system of law, Jews for centuries formed a kind of state within a state, and their scattered communities were consequently able, insofar as they possessed the means, to establish trade relations transcending far and wide the boundaries of single states. With the rise of the modern system of world trade and finance, the wealthier Jews began to lose interest in retaining their inherited legal system, and thus the emancipation became the means of their liberation not only from the anti-Jewish but from the Jewish laws as well.

Although built on a completely independent foundation, and pursuing a distinctive course of evolution, Jewish law was naturally often influenced by other systems, and in turn contributed in no small measure to their development. Biblical law was influenced by the systems of the ancient Orient from the time of the Hammurabi Code (17th century B.C.E.), Talmudic law developed under the dual influence of the East (chiefly contemporary Babylonia) and of the Graeco-Roman world. In the Gaonic period, Islamic jurisprudence and, at a later age, the Christian systems exercised their influence on the Jewish courts and legal literature.

The extent of this foreign influence has not yet been thoroughly investigated. Even less attention has been given to the contribution of Jewish law to the development of other legal systems. Through the channels of the *ius gentium* (the law of nations), Hebrew laws undoubtedly found their way into Roman legal practice, especially after the translation of the Bible into Greek. Once the Bible became a part of the sacred scriptures of the Christians, its precepts acquired the status of "natural law" in the eyes of the Fathers of the Church. Thus, the prohibition of usury, for example, is merely a new formulation of the law found in Leviticus XXV, 36-37. The legal authority of the Bible continued to be recognized right into the modern era, as shown by the work of the outstanding 17th-century jurist, Hugo Grotius. Talmudic and the later Rabbinic law, moreover, also found their way into Christian jurisprudence, chiefly because Jewish and Christian merchants in the Middle Ages often engaged in business transactions on the basis of Jewish legal principles, with both parties agreeing to submit disputes to the *bet din*. There is good reason to believe that in this way certain legal institutions, destined to be of the utmost significance in the economic development of Europe, were introduced by Jews in accordance with their own civil law.

6. The Jewish Scale of Values

I. Principles

The Institute of Jewish Learning represented at this Commemoration Conference by Dr. Kobler and myself is very grateful for the opportunity given to us by the London Centre of the P.E.N. to put before you a Jewish view on the crucial question:

> What is the true perspective in which we, at this fateful juncture, are called upon to visualise the relation between Matter and Spirit?

For this, I believe, is the kernel of the problem before us.

In taking the liberty of stating the theme of our conference somewhat differently than the official formula, I am putting, I am fully aware, a certain construction on the point in question which anticipates the answer. But in so doing, I feel I have on my side both the high authority of the immortal patron of this assembly, John Milton, as well as that of the unbroken tradition of Jewish thought and learning. To Milton, not less than to the Jewish creed, things economic could qualify as human values only after Paradise had been lost; only after Adam—lifted in the act of Creation by the force of the Spirit above the "Adamah" (the ground)—has first come under the full sway of gravitation, bound "to return unto the ground."

It is indeed this verse 19 of Chapter 3 of Genesis which impresses upon Adam's mind, in the same breath, Man's earthly origin, the material aspect of his existence, and his dependence on the daily bread and the many exertions indispensable to gain or earn it. To keep body and soul together is, accordingly, not merely the minimum of economic achievement, but at the same time the fulfilment of a divine command which certainly appears to be a curse, a curse, however, apt to be turned into a blessing, if only the balance between Matter and Spirit, between the sub-human and superhuman in Man, could be restored in conformity with the original design.

History is, in this view, the incessant attempt of the *B'ne Adam*, the

This essay was first published in English in *Freedom of Expression*, London, PEN Club, 1944.

children of Adam, to regain—by their own effort, and in the clear light of consciousness—the control of the human spirit, of Man's "portion from above," to say it in Job's phrase, over the material conditions of life and living which are, within human society, based on its economic structure.

To participate in this great work of liberation, the liberation of the human spirit from the fetters of *economic gravitation*, i.e., from the purely earthly and physical conditions of human life; to contribute to the elevation of the human being to that dignity which is conferred upon Adam since his creation, the dignity of a free citizen of God's Universe; to keep this goal of universal history in untarnished clarity before the eyes of humanity; to remind it again and again, by word and by exemplary deed, that the sons and daughters of Adam are born into this world to be always and everywhere on the move—this is what Israel is for among the peoples of the world.

Looking around and ahead at this critical, but not less inspiring, moment in human and Jewish history, one cannot help feeling that despite all the contentions of the devil's advocates, the sowing was not in vain. As ever before, Israel is still a living exhortation—a stumbling-block to some, a stepping-stone to others, an enigma to all, including itself. And yet, in the endeavour to assign to the values of the spirit their proper place alongside the economic, those values which are capable of being adequately expressed in quantities of ponderable matter—in this bold undertaking of readjusting the primary correlation of Spirit and Matter for the generations to come—where can we turn for a guiding light? Surely not to the twilight of some present-day myth. Shall it be the searchlight of modern science which can well do without the hypothesis contained in the word "spirit," and would not know what to do with it? Obviously there is no other light to guide us, if not the unextinguishable light of our civilisation's sunrise, *ex oriente,* or in Hebrew, *me' Misrach.*

Whether the present Jewish generation is worthy to take an active part in the universal work of the rehabilitation of man's prime dignity is beyond the scope of our judgment. The future will show. The past (which Dr. Kobler is going to survey) leaves us in this respect, to say the least, not without hope. That much seems, however, certain that no exploration of mankind's promised land would be complete, should the explorers not avail themselves of that instrument which Israel applied throughout the ages as an unalterable scale of values.

May I therefore, Mr. Chairman, give now a brief description of this ancient but by no means obsolete instrument? The fundamental principle underlying all the markings on this Jewish scale of values, its whole gradation, has by implication already been touched upon in the introductory remarks. It is the spirit, man's "portion from above," which, or shall I say, who prevails. What makes man man is the bond of likeness linking him with his Creator, who is the Maker of all things perceptible, thus Himself beyond sensual perceptibility, beyond space and time, pure spirit. Man is man in so far as he incarnates spirit, by definition supernatural. Consequently, human values in the proper sense are all without exception spiritual values; real objects of free human will governed by reason, because, to put it in the Miltonian way, "reason is but choosing," the faculty to choose between good and evil.

That is why we are entitled to say that economic values are either related to the human will and subject to valuation under the moral aspect of good and its opposite, thus representing only a particular variety of spiritual values; or, they are not human values at all, something which in point of value is quite neutral and indifferent. On the Jewish scale of values this reasoning is symbolised by zero point.

Real things, life itself and even existence in general, are to the traditional Jewish view in themselves quite irrelevant. Let me explain this truly essential point, "by what is contrary" to put it again in a phrase out of the *Areopagitica*. There is a widespread belief that to the Jews endless continuation of life, stubborn persistence, unconditional survival is an end in itself, a belief embodied in the well-known medieval legend of the "eternal" *Wandering Jew*. Nothing is farther from the truth. The paradox of Jewish survival is actually the test case in human history destined as it were to prove that life attains its highest intensity only when it is stripped of all its tempting qualities, when it becomes a means to an end, which has nothing in common with life in the purely biological meaning of the word; when it is entirely subordinated to that value which is supreme on the Jewish scale—to holiness. "Ye shall be Holy; for I the Lord your God am Holy," thus is introduced the Chapter of Leviticus, wherein we find the command, "Thou shalt love thy neighbour as thyself" (19, 18).

From the Holy One, the Pure Spirit, the Value of Values, all their gradation must needs derive. The criterion is holiness, and only owing to the faculty of sanctifying life conferred upon man does life derive its value and dignity. But then—in all its length and breadth. Holy may become a land, its inhabitants, their laws and customs, their language, even their daily bread not to speak of their writings. It is perhaps fitting at this *Areopagitica* Conference to say a few words more on the last point.

How strangely familiar sounds to the Jewish ear the famous passage on the "Potency of Life" contained in books! Is the *Sefer Torah*, the "Book of the Law," not a living entity to the Jews? The copying is a holy craft. The accomplishment of every copy is marked by a feast as if a child were born. Later it is provided with a luxurious girdle, clad in satin and velvet, and adorned with a crown. Before and after reading it is kissed, and when, after a long and useful life, it begins to disintegrate, it is carried in solemn procession to the graveyard to be buried to the sound of Psalms. So deep is the love of holiness, and so holy and innocent is the face of love.

Here is the point from which it can be clearly seen where, according to the Jewish table of values, the economic activities find their proper place. If they are put into the service of sanctification of life, if they are subordinated to the sacred principles of social justice, human solidarity and brotherly love, they reflect immediately the dignity of the spiritual values guiding them; if not, if these activities are a law unto themselves, they go down on the scale of human values, at the best, to zero. But they may fall even below the moral freezing point.

For there is yet another alternative, apart from holiness, to the point of moral indifference, namely—unholiness, and it is, I believe, essential for the Jewish scale of values, that it points not only upwards to the highest possible degree of human achievement in the service and emulation of the divine Spirit, but also the bottomless abyss of human depravity and wickedness. Evil is as bad as good is good. Hence the "choosing" of good must imply the active and forceful rejection of evil. This is what probably accounts for the remarkable fact that at all critical turns in human history the Jewish table of values was a bone of contention not only to evil-doers but also to the lukewarm, those who try to disguise lack of purpose as love of peace.

They failed to notice the place peace occupies in Judaism and in Jewish history. When Israel, scattered all over the world, lives in peace, the whole world enjoys it. World-peace and "Schalom al Israel," "Peace over Israel" are identical. So all our prayers culminate in the word "Schalom." But craving for universal peace with passionate impatience we know full well that the way to God's Kingdom of Freedom is as long as the way back to the Garden of Eden. To deserve it, we have yet to conquer ourselves, our own selves.

"We" means, of course, all dwellers of this earth. The Value of Values, the Holy One, is not the God of Jacob only. His image is impressed on all children of Adam, from "sunrise to sunset," wherever they may be. Potentially all life is holy. However, *the potential of holiness* is not evenly distributed, and it is perhaps still a blessing to humanity that in a continuous succession of a hundred generations a human community *preserved* the original meaning and *sound* of the word: *"Kedoshim t'hiyou,"* "Ye shall be holy." If all of us unite in the common endeavour to *observe* it, the Divine Tragedy of human history will come to a universal *Kátharsis*.

7. The Maimonides Anniversary (1135-1935)

In the year of this jubilee ye shall return every man unto his possession. Lev. 25:13

I

Last year we mourned the death of Bialik. And this is the year of the eight-hundredth anniversary of the birth of Maimonides. There is no need for us to turn prophets to foresee that in 1935 there will be no more spiritually exciting event than the Maimonides anniversary. Here are two occurences separated from each other by a stretch of not less than eight centuries; and yet as one listened to the overtones of last year's funeral orations and this year's eulogies, they became as two verses, one following the other, or as two rhymes in the same penitential prayer. Yes, there is in each the tone of penitence, the echo of longing, heart-ache, and the yearning for a lost spiritual grandeur. That, as it seems, is the secret behind the clamour which keeps on growing around our great names.

It makes no difference if the name is that of a poet who was lately among us, flesh of our flesh, a contemporary of ours, burdened with all our troubles, doubts and sins, or the good name of an ancient genius whose religious-philosophical principles are to most of his modern devotees no less a load than the 613 commandments (mitzvoth) of the many-stories structure of his "Second Torah". Let it be but a name, and it is one more resounding name in the summing up of our cultural balance sheet. Maimonides' credo (Ani Ma'amin) becomes just as much a secondary matter as that in which a Bialik believed or did not believe. People want to know only that the statement of the current account of our history shows one more credit, and they feel assured that the longer the deposit remains, the greater will be the accumulated cultural-historical interest. A wrong sort of accounting, of course, but where does this sort of appalling error arise? Appalling, because nowhere has this self-deception such devastating results as in the spiritual sphere.

True, we live in times of dread. We are being expelled from a world

This essay was first published in Yiddish in *Fraye Shriftn*, Warsaw, 1935, and in Hebrew in *Davar*, Tel Aviv, 1935.

which we thought was ours. A sense of loathing is awakened in us for the sanctities of a world which has suddenly shown us a hideous face. If we were proud, we would shake the dust of that world off our feet and withdraw into our own "four ells". We are not wanted as spiritual partners? Very well, we shall live in a spiritual ghetto. But we shall also show that we can only win that way. Look how rich we are! Every year another great name, whether of the present or the past, and now a name of eight hundred years ago! And we do not notice that we do not merely return to the ghetto—we escape thither, and all our pride is but a tortured pretence. The ghetto itself is the subject of our delusion which emerged under the impact of the alien treacherous world and, worst of all, shaking the dust from our feet, we did not lift a finger to wipe away the stains which spotted our souls after we left the ghetto. Among the darkest stains on our modern culture acquired outside the ghetto which brought us to our present plight, we must consider, in the first place, its purely aesthetic attitude to the profoundest manifestations of the religious spirit. A pure aesthetic attitude rules out the question whether anything is right or wrong, good or bad, and seeks to know only whether a particular creative work "appeals to us", whether it is "magnificent" or "beautiful", the creation of a great and rare talent which mirrors a strong creative individuality. If such an attitude is adopted, however, towards the creations of religious spirit, it must eventually lead to the most severe crippling of the entire cultural life. Anything which has any relationship to the religious spirit demands an appreciation not merely according to its degree of beauty or lack of it, or according to whether we like it or not, but according to the rules of right or wrong, good or bad; and if anyone has taken to exchanging these judgments with those of aesthetics—is there any room left for the sense of truth or right? In short, as soon as in any culture the category of sanctity, of holy truth and holy goodness is eliminated, then honesty is at once impaired in questions both of theory or morality. In the old-time ghetto this was impossible; in the new ghetto—would that this were untrue!—the damage has already been done.

And in truth, how would our world of to-day have been able to receive the whole of Maimonides, its confines, its "four ells", but for its aesthetic rapture over the "magnificence" of his spiritual structures, and but for the decadent confusion of the greatest systematic thinker in the history of Jewish religious thought with something great in the realm of thought-architecture in general, as one of any other epoch or other style? It is this aestheticism which is historically so thoroughly alien to us, this strange and evil contagion from outside, that makes possible our new-fangled cultural evaluations in general, and in particular the degrading of Maimonides to a sort of statue in a national museum.

If we are indeed to take with us something from outside, then let us bring to our anniversary celebration Goethe's strict rule: "What you have inherited from your Fathers, deserve it in order to possess it." Best of all, let us remember, on just this occasion, the principle contained in our own ancient laws of the jubilee: "In the jubilee year let every man return to his land and to his inheritance." Maimonides belongs to the entire people; his spiritual kingdom is world-wide. Each one of us can, and each trend within our people can and will seek there what belongs to them and to them alone, their own particular portion of Maimonides' world. Then those who are able to confess that they have dug there and found nothing will have the right to retain their enthusiasm for the "magnificent" individuality and "beauty" of its creation.

II

Maimonides' world, and especially his view of nature, is an edifice which Maimonides himself, by his almost superhuman intellect, regarded to be exactly as it had emerged from the divine will, measured with a pair of compasses, the earth as its foundation "below" and the *galgalim*, the heavenly spheres "above". There is a system like the mechanism of a gigantic clock: A heavenly sphere within a sphere, the lowest that of the moon, and every planet moving in its own circle, each successively higher, each encompassing more and more, and in their midst the sphere of the sun and the sphere of the fixed stars. The spheres do not move at the same speed—some faster than others—but the sphere of the fixed stars describes a full circle exactly in a day and a night. The world of matter is composed of four elements: earth and water, whose natural rectilinear motion is downwards; air and fire, whose constant tendency, also rectilinear, is upwards. This four-element matter can take many forms, any of which is not less stable than its four material components. Everything that exists in the "lower world", that is to say in the world under the lowest lunar circle, is also divided into four classes: stones, plants, animals and men. They are all composed of matter and form. The form of the human body is its soul, and when this departs from him, his body disintegrates. Man, however, is "the highest to be found anywhere in our lower world." (Guide to the Perplexed, III, 12).

Even in Maimonides' time, this picture of the world centered on man and the earth (geo-and anthropocentric) must have evoked many questions and doubts. Anyone interested in the history of the natural sciences knows that the principal lines of Maimonides' world-picture is identical with the general portrayal of nature that prevailed in the Middle Ages, and which had come to him as a legacy from ancient Greece, particularly from the work of Aristotle. So why mention it at all? Maimonides' astronomy, physics and chemistry are indeed little popular among us even in this anniversary year. And yet it is important to know that Maimonides lived with a conception of a world of which almost nothing has survived. When we first grasp it in full clarity, our impression is—what a difficult relationship it is: we and Maimonides, especially when we learn how highly he himself valued the knowledge of his time. For instance, he argues polemically against certain points in the astronomical hypothesis of his teacher, Aristotle. "He undoubtedly knew the weakness of his theory. It is obvious when we take into consideration that mathematics was not fully developed in his time, and the motions of the spheres were not as well known as they are to-day" (Perplexed, II, 19). Later in the same chapter he adds, "But as I have said once before, in his time the science of the world's structure (astronomy) was not what it is to-day". Does that not sound rather patronizing? Not unlike the words of an enlightened modern man well educated in the natural sciences. But what if Maimonides' metaphysics and even theology, what if his own approach to *Ma'seh Bereshith* or *Ma'seh Merkavah* should be only a super-structure on his own medieval physics, which is now in ruins? We scarcely stop to consider this, but it calls for a closer examination.

A feature of the ancient and medieval image of the world and thus also of that of Maimonides is that the world is finite and is limited in space. To-day, even if we stood on our heads, we could not understand what it means that the world is not unlimited (if it may be so according to Einstein's theory of relativity, it is not in the Euclidean space that all of us have in mind). The problem becomes more difficult when we learn that according to Maimonides the world is also finite in time. Here, as is known, he parts company with the Greek science of Aristotle, and holds that even Aristotle, "the Master of the Philosophers", believed in the world everlasting, agreeing with the "suppositions of the Sabeans" (ancient idol-worshippers). we may, therefore, go along with "the two prophets Moses and Abraham who are the two pillars of humanity in all its religious and social groups", and believe that the world was created not only in time, but also together with time (Perplexed II, 23 and II, 13: "Time itself is among the things created"). But if time was created, if it is a creation, then that raises another question: Will time ever come to an end? (Perplexed II, 28). These are all questions which Maimonides himself could not answer by pure reason and which six hundred years later became for Kant proof that the mind must become involved in innermost contradictions when it undertakes to solve them independently of experience (the first of the antinomies in *The Critique of Pure Reason*). But this is not the place to demonstrate the right or wrong of Maimonides' arguments, except to say that his metaphysics, his theory of space and time, is dependent on his physics; that he is, in other words, in respect of his metaphysics also a child of his generation, and man of his time, of the 12th Century of which he considered that he had a right to boast.

One can hold that time is finite, as the Greeks and Arabs did, and yet see no beginning or end for time. Conversely, it was impossible for

Maimonides to accept that space is without end and time nevertheless finite. In other words, the finite space was for him the logical premiss that time is finite and therefore finite time the logical result of finite space. But the belief that time is a creation, that it had a beginning and can therefore be reasonably expected to come to an end, is for Maimonides not merely a hypothesis but a basic principle in his belief. It follows that he derives from it all his religio-philosophical system in the centre of which rests the Throne of Glory of God, the Creator of the World, and this system is founded on historically conditioned allegedly scientific foundations. Just as Kant's theoretical philosophy is an offspring of Newtonian mathematical natural science, so also are Maimonides' basic metaphysical beliefs deeply rooted in the natural science of his time. When in the realm of astronomy he adopts such a highly patronizing attitude even towards Aristotle, it is not out of vain scholarly pride but from dignified awareness that thanks to the progress of science profound religious thought has also acquired incomparably firmer foundations. This, however, has a lesson for us, namely, that true respect for Maimonides in this anniversary year imposes on us as a first duty the redemption of the "possession", the inheritance, which belongs to him, to his time and to his own logical "prolegomena".

There is yet another lesson to be learned from all this: it is useless to drag Maimonides into the ghetto. The spiritual territory of "four ells" which is supposed to suffice for us to-day, is too narrow to provide a resting place for Maimonides, not to speak of room to live and work with any freedom. His world is the world of his time, the whole of it. True, it was a world deeply influenced by Jewish ideas, a world comprehended in the spirit of Jewish prophecy, the Torah of Abraham and Moses, created, sustained and led by the one and only Absolute, and moreover the Absolute Spiritual Creator of the World. All this, notwithstanding, it was not a "Jewish" world, because according to the Jewish outlook of Maimonides "the world was created only for the sake of his beloved Name", and "He" is not a Jewish God, Heaven forbid, but "the God of the World" (*Mishneh Torah Vol. I, Yesodey HaTorah* Chap. I, 5).

III

The mechanics of the world as seen by Maimonides, his astronomy, is the foundation not only of his metaphysics and his theology, but also to a certain degree, of his ethical concept of the world. It points to a characteristic streak, his great optimism, his conviction that all is well with the world, and regardless of all its turmoil, the world is about human criticism. Maimonides expresses it in the word "perfection". The world was created "fully perfect", "perfect in the highest degree". It is enough to remember that "Shlemuth" ("perfection") implies at the same time both "wholeness" and "perfection" in order to grasp why the conviction that the

world is finite in space and time, i.e. that it was given to us in its
"wholeness", a belief, inherited from the Greeks inevitably led to the
further optimistic belief that the world is "perfect". It is "perfect" for the
sole reason that it is "whole", that means not infinite. Even the ancient
Greeks held that things without an end were only fragments, and the
rounder they were, the more complete. Yet the student of Arabic "Greek
science" had to be a Greek and not a son of Israel to be satisfied with this
sort of "perfection". For he was born not only in the twelfth century of the
present era, but also in the eleventh century since the Destruction of the
Temple. In the astronomic space, a citizen of the bright cosmos, he was in
historical time a child of the Dark Exile. The reality of the human history
compelled Maimonides to draw a line through his optimistic evaluation of
the world and divide the wholeness of the world into two parts: one part of
the actual, realized perfection, and the other which is only "potentially"
complete, no more complete than within the limits of the possible.

Touching on history in the concept of Maimonides (a matter of which it
may still be possible to deal in detail), we approach closely to a "possession"
which in this anniversary year should have become the personal riches of
all those for whom ideals and life are the things that matter. And this
because Maimonides' interpretation of history, not only of Jewish history
but history in general, both human world history and the history of the
divine world in its entirety, is idealistic throughout, supranational and
uniting in a singular manner the social, one may safely say the socialist,
element with an extreme individualism, mystical in essence. Without
doubt the interpretation is traditionally Jewish; and this is where Jewish
tradition is revealed not as a chain that shackles us to a dead past, but a
living link which binds innumerable generations to the most idealistic
mission of the future.

God's world is only in part really perfect. The reason for this is man. He
enjoys free will, freedom to choose between good and evil, and mostly he
chooses what is evil. The entire human history from Adam to the twelfth
century after the Fall of Jerusalem, is for Maimonides the sole evidence of
this. That is how it is "in fact", in plain reality, not so "potentially" as a
possibility open to mankind. Apart from a body and a soul which is only the
"form" of the body, man possesses a soul (nefesh) and a spirit (ruach).
Because of this he resembles God, the Creator of the world. For in a small
way, man is himself a creator, and because he has the choice of creating
according to patterns of goodness, he also has the power to improve and
make himself more complete in the human "community". He has to keep
constantly and clearly before his eyes the aim towards which he must
strive. In the social sense the aim is the Time of the Messiah.

In what wonderful language does Maimonides describe Messiah's
Kingdom! And it is certainly not by chance that this description closes his
most complete and happiest work, the many-storeyed edifice of his

Mishneh Torah: "The sages and the prophets longed for the coming of Messiah not in order to take dominion of the whole world, not in order to oppress other peoples, not that the other nations should respect them, or that they themselves should be able to eat, drink and be merry. [they longed for the Messiah] but that they should be able to devote themselves to the Torah and its wisdom without an oppressor standing over them to steal their time, and that they should become worthy of the life to come. Then there would be neither famine nor war, no envy or strife, while good things would be in great abundance, the best foods would be as plentiful as sand, and the whole world would apply itself to know God . . . (Maimonides, Mishneh Torah, Vol. VIII, Hilkhot Melakhim, Chap. 12, 4-5).

"Neither famine nor war"—the material needs would be fully satisfied, and at the same time envy and hate would vanish, and the spiritual urge to know the Highest and the Profoundest would unite all men and nations in one union. Has human history ever brought forth a richer or more manifold ideal? Whoever thinks so, has the duty to prove it. For the benefit of our positivists it should further be added that according to Maimonides the great ideal can be realized in the most natural way: "Let it not be supposed", he declares at the beginning of the same chapter, "that when Messiah comes anything will be annulled in the world order, or that there will be any new addition to the Creation. On the contrary, the world will continue as it is. . . ." (See also Mishneh Torah, Vol. I, *Hilkhoth Teshuva* Chap. 9, 2.) The end of famine and the end of war would come about not in any way contrary to nature, but actually in a way that was from the beginning comprised in the natural order of the world, which was, so to say, completed during the six days of Creation; therefore, it depends on us whether or not we shall realize its potential. The term "the world to come" (*olam haba*), possibly betrays a deviation in the direction of another sphere; but precisely here in his teaching on the "world to come", the socialism of Maimonides achieves a synthesis with his individualism, and one which is so fully harmonized that it can only be described as no other than classic.

Olam Haba, the world to come, in Maimonides' view, is the integration of the highest in man with the highest in the world—with God. The road from man to God is infinite, because it leads out of this world, limited in space and time, to the world's Creator, who is—must one repeat?— beyond both space and time. It is in a sense and geometrically speaking, perpendicular to all other roads of the world, i.e. the world that is, the *olam haze*, together with its provisional historic conclusion in the coming of universal Messianic rule. Precisely for this reason the coming of the Messiah is only the beginning of the new era in which every man will be entitled to take part in the *olam haba*. Does this therefore mean that there are two ideals: the individual attainment of *olam haba* which a man can

gain only for himself, and the collective ideal of Messianic times, each
being the contradiction of the other? At first glance, so it seems, for even
to-day, as in the days of Maimonides, the individual who immerses himself
in the knowledge of God, can find his way to the Highest. What then can it
matter to the seeker of God, the individual, whether humanity at some
historical time will win freedom from the tribulations of famine and war,
envy and hate, as long as his own soul is saved, perhaps even now? To this
question Maimonides gives a clear answer, to be found by the seeker, in his
Hilkhoth Teshuva (Mishneh Torah Vol. I): "*Olam haba* is the reward
prepared for the righteous" (Chap. 8, 1). And who are the righteous? Says
Maimonides: "Every man has merits and sins" (Chap. 3, 1). The righteous
one is the one who has more merits than sins. To win merit, however,
means doing God's commandments, and the commandments have no
other purpose than to "better the world", on *Tikun ha-nefesh* (betterment
of the soul) and *Tikun ha-guf* (betterment of the body) (see *Perplexed* III,
27) and to make the world fit for the Messiah. It is therefore not possible to
strive for an *olam haba* for oneself alone, especially if one does not dedicate
oneself, life and soul, to the common good. In order to raise himself from
earth to God, a man must travel God's way here on earth without cease. It
will be otherwise only when Messiah comes. Only then, when the
individual becomes entirely free of concern for the community, will it be
possible for him to immerse himself, head and all, in knowledge and love of
God. Thus the social ideal and its realization become an organic part of a
true personal moral mission, and the liberation of the individual is not
possible otherwise than by the liberation of all humanity. Maimonides'
ethics can be seen either as individualist-socialist or socialist-individualist.

How closely Maimonides unites the two impulses is made clear in a
remarkable way in the third chapter of *Hilkhoth Teshuva* already quoted.
Just as the individual can be righteous, wicked or a mixture of both, so can a
whole state or the whole of mankind. If its merits predominate, or they
outweigh their sins, they are righteous; if it is the other way round, the
state is in peril of destruction like any wicked individual. A man must
therefore regard himself and the whole world as in an intermediate
condition, "half innocent, half guilty". "Should he commit one more sin, he
will drag himself and the whole world into guilt and be the cause of its
downfall. With one righteous deed, however, he puts the whole world
right and brings help and salvation to himself and the world. "With this
remarkable thesis, which is without doubt an extension of the principle
that free will can choose between two absolutely equal motives (the
celebrated *liberum arbitrium indifferentiae*), Maimonides makes the fate
of the whole world ultimately dependent on every step of every man. No
one had placed a greater responsibility on the individual, and if to follow
this rule is to be an individualist, then just imagine how different the world
would have been, if all of us had been such individualists.

This opens a wider approach to an understanding of Maimonides' own personality. He has been described as a confirmed "aristocrat"; he has been called the "Jewish Aristotle"; he has been likened to Moses and has been praised as the master of Spinoza, of the great men of Catholicism, Albertus Magnus, St. Thomas Aquinas, and latterly of the German mystic, Meister Eckhart. It is possible even to draw a parallel between Maimonides and the Ba'al Shem Tov—but it is enough to know that each of us can find what he seeks in Maimonides' work, and everyone has the right to seek. Then let this be the rule and meaning of this anniversary: "Go ye and proclaim freedom in the land for all its inhabitants!" And what is "freedom" at the celebration of a jubilee of the spirit? As Kant said concerning Plato and the most important of his concepts, the "idea": "By comparing his thoughts it may be possible to understand him even better than he understood himself".

SECTION C

Varieties and Distortions of Messianism

1. Dostoevsky and the Jews

For the majority of Dostoevsky's readers and admirers the question of the author's attitude towards the Jews and towards the historical fate of the Jewish people is extremely simple. Is it not clear from the start that in the person of Dostoevsky we are dealing with one of the typical representatives of that hostility towards the Jews which first took root in Europe, and then in Russia, and was known by the pseudo-scientific, though by no means ambiguous, name, "anti-Semitism"? To put it bluntly, is it really possible to doubt that during his entire life Dostoevsky remained a steadfast "Jew-hater"? This is certainly the generally held opinion, both in Russia and abroad, among Jews and non-Jews, a view reflected also in Russian literary criticism. A. G. Gornfeld, a thoughtful critic and an expert on Dostoevsky, begins his essay in the "Yevreyskaya (Jewish) Encyclopedia" with the phrase: "Dostoevsky, Fedor Mikhailovich, is one of the most important advocates of Russian anti-Semitism". A few lines below, he continues: "Neither serious arguments nor original ideas can be found in his accusations; it is a banal anti-semitism." It goes without saying that Dostoevsky's banal anti-Semitism, if Gornfeld's definition were even remotely plausible, would necessarily present a curious enigma, deserving of extensive investigation. Could it be that the presence of the "ordinary" amidst the "extraordinary" is less original and mysterious than anything admitted out of the customary? Or was Dostoevsky not such a thoroughly "distinctive" genius, as he sometimes referred to himself, whose imprint must lie on all aspects of his life without exception? Does not the very banality of Dostoevsky's attitude towards the Jews indicate some insurmountable feature in the fate of the Jewish people, something portentous in its most significant historical encounters and confrontations?

It is sufficient to pose these questions in order that the juxtaposition "Dostoevsky and the Jews" should emerge in all its philosophical, even metaphysical, significance. In any case, the matter is not settled simply by including Dostoevsky in the crowd of adherents of a modern bastardised political terminology. Whatever Dostoevsky thought about the Jews, his attitude must necessarily reveal those features which are characteristic of his own unique spiritual outlook. This must be understood first of all. Only

This essay was first published in Russian in *Versti*, Paris, 1928, and later in English in *Problems*, New York, 1949, Volume II, No. 1.

then, for this essay is but the first step in this direction, will it be possible to approach the question of "Dostoevsky and the Jews" objectively, with either a positive or a negative appraisal. However, we must emphasize that such an appraisal would also constitute a solution to the broader question concerning the ultimte meaning of the historical coexistence of the Russian people and the Jewish people—a question which in turn is relevant to Dostoevsky's attitude towards the Jews.

I

The prevailing conception of Dostoevsky as an advocate of late nine-teenth-century anti-Semitism is a superficial one. We shall endeavour to make this clear. However, a superficial impression is, nevertheless, an impression formed by the "surface" of something, consequently there must be something in the external characteristics of Dostoevsky's work which provokes or prompts this impression. Let us consider those passages which provide a basis for including Dostoevsky in the ranks of the Jew-haters with such ease: the error of the majority is almost always a one-sided projection of the truth; only after we have clarified its limited probability can we completely overcome it.

The first, and perhaps decisive, basis for assigning Dostoevsky to the sworn haters of the Jews is his vocabulary. A writer's vocabulary, his verbal material, delineates his scope no less distinctly than the more noticeable and indelible traces of his activity. For the "word" is not only the means of revealing the author's thought and will, but also the herald of his most secretly kept self-awareness, his unspoken and unexpressed feelings. Whatever Dostoevsky may have stated about his attitude towards the Jews (see below, section V), one can never expunge from his vocabulary the particularly expressive monosyllable, "Yid". Even before Dostoevsky arrived on the literary scene, the words "Yid" and "Jew" were competing for supremacy in Russian literature and in the Russian language in general. These words were no longer synonyms; even in the works of Pushkin and Lermontov one can recognize the profound abyss which separates the "accursed Yid" from "Jew" and his melodies. Dostoevsky knew well that as a Russian author, responsible for the fate of his native language and people, he had to make a choice; but instead of choosing, he vacillated between the two words throughout his life, even when speaking in the first person singular (see *Diary of a Writer*, 1877, III, chapter II, p. 1). To see the subtlety with which he evaluated all the decent and indecent variants, it will suffice to recall only a few lines about Fedor Karamazov's arrival in Odessa: "At first he made the acquaintance, in his own words, of a lot of Yids, little Yids, and dirty little Yids; but he ended up by being invited not only by the 'Yids', but even by the 'Jews' " (Book I, chapter IV; cf. Book VII, chapter III). "In his own words . . ." One cannot keep from smiling when one recognizes that this same verbal range is repeated many times over in many other works and in Dostoevsky's letters to his wife (e. g., the letters written on 30 June and 4 August 1879, while he was working on *The Brothers Karamazov*). No, in this passage Dostoevsky is not merely reporting Karamazov's words; on the contrary, Karamazov is echoing Dostoevsky, using Dostoevsky's vocabulary which he always held in readiness to designate representatives of the "eternal tribe" by a whole set of effective verbal instruments: from the simple, untainted "Jew", to the hideously indecent "filthy little Yids". How can one avoid exclaiming, "Jew-baiter"?

The second, no less compelling, reason for including Dostoevsky among the sworn Jew-haters is easily discovered in those traits with which he endows his Jewish characters, unforgettable in their genuine, full-bodied reality. Of course the Jew is an infrequent guest amidst the ranks of Dostoevsky's fictional characters, but we need only look at one: we are confronted with a human being almost bereft of human characteristics; he is some sort of chimera in the flesh, alien in both body and soul to the world of real people. Isaiah Fomich, for example, in *Notes from the House of the Dead*, is described as a "mixture of naivete, stupidity, cunning, insolence, open-heartedness, timidity, boastfulness, and impudence; "laughable and ridiculous"; "full of unparalleled conceit"; "It goes without saying that he was also a usurer" (chapters IX and IV). Therefore it seems to the author of the *Notes* "very strange that the convicts never ridiculed Isaiah Fomich": this is explained inasmuch as "our little Yid", a faithful copy of Gogol's "Yid Yankel", "obviously served as an object of general amusement and fun". After all, Isaiah was "gentle as a mother hen", and one could play with him, "as with a parrot or a puppy".

That was Dostoevsky's first Jew; it shows the gradual development of the general concept "Yid" to the more concrete "filthy Yid". We are facing here the "explication of a certain principle a priori, a preconceived formula, the outcome of a literary tradition (Gogol's), inadvertently emphasized by Dostoevsky himself, particularly in his introductory phrase, "it goes without saying". It also results from one small, but very characteristic feature, which, for readers unacquainted with Jewish ritual, would pass completely unnoticed. Dostoevsky describes in great detail how Isaiah Fomich greets the arrival of the Sabbath on Friday evenings; he depicts his "hero" in his ritual prayers with philacteries on his forehead and arm— which is totally impossible and in complete contradiction to all the customs of Jewish ritual. A mistake of this sort, almost unbelievable in Dostoevsky's work, can only be explained by assuming that although he was looking at a real live Jew, Dostoevsky could not see him at all, or rather, he saw him through a preconceived image. Therefore we also meet the phrase "of course", in the description of the "filthy Yid's" effusive prayers: "Of course, all this was prescribed in the prayer rituals, by the Law".

"The Law"! Even before he wrote *Notes from the House of the Dead*, Dostoevsky had some sort of preconceived ideas about the person of the contemporary Jew; his image and likeness were determined in advance for every individual case. Therefore it is only natural that another of Dostoevsky's Jews, the convert Lyamshin in *The Devils*, in spite of all his idiosyncracies, is, generally speaking, "our little Yid", with the typical mixture of perfidy and stupidity, timidity and insolence, vanity and conceit. And he too, "it goes without saying", was a usurer. There are traits in both Isaiah Fomich and in Lyamshin which make one think that Dostoevsky himself saw something more significant than only this canine capacity to bristle and snarl, or than the warmth of the mother hen. This is only one of the contradictions in his attitude towards the Jews, and will be discussed below (see section V). Undoubtedly the Jew, as a type in Dostoevsky's work, possesses invariable characteristics; he is presented as the most appropriate receptacle of a well-known type of human nature which is at the same time both revolting and engaging, dangerous and extremely ridiculous, be he devoted to the faith of his fathers, or converted.

That is why even the most radiant of Dostoevsky's heroes are not completely free from fear and hatred of the Jews. Significantly, the God-fearing Alesha, for example, when asked, "Is it true that the Yids steal and cut up children at Passover?" cannot find a better answer than that of the Pharisees: "I don't know." (*The Brothers Karamazov*, Book II, chapter III.)

Methodological pedantry could raise an objection here: should we not draw a distinction between the personality of the author and that of the narrator, as well as that of the characters created by the author's fantasy? How is it possible to identify the narrator in the *Notes* or in *The Devils* with Fyodor Mikhailovich Dostoevsky? In order to remove even these last, not unfounded, doubts, let us turn to those writings in which Dostoevsky talks about the Jews directly, not through the mouth of fictional characters, but in his own words and in his own name.

II

Dostoevsky wrote about the Jews and Judaism in his own words and from his own person at every convenient opportunity—principally in his *Diary of a Writer*. It is well-known that one of the articles in this publication is entirely devoted to the "Jewish question" (March 1877), and is an answer to a letter written by the ill-fated A. Kovner, about whom L. P. Grossman has collected and published all available material. It is precisely this article which has generally been considered as Dostoevsky's "main anti-Semitic pronouncement". Later we shall consider the nature of Dostoevsky's outlook as expressed in his various discourses on the Jewish question; here it will suffice to emphasize only those passages which most convincingly bear out the view of Dostoevsky's "banal anti-Semitism". At first glance, this seems a relatively simple task. Dostoevsky makes an accusation against the Jews which cannot be called anything except "banal": "The Jews, of whom there are so very many on the earth", are, in his words, born exploiters, lying in wait to pounce on some "fresh victim"; in America, according to the evidence provided in the last volume of the monthly *Vestnik Evropy*, the Negroes fulfil the role of victims; in Russia, this is the fate which awaits the emancipated peasantry. How could it be otherwise: "Although other nations do exist, the Jews still act as if no other nations existed at all." Thus, according to Dostoevsky, the Jews are full of disgust and scorn for all their fellow-travellers on earth, now settled in Western Europe and, sitting on top of their money-bags, are planning to direct their destructive policy against the last bastion of Christianity on earth—against Russia. The policy of Beaconsfield-Disraeli, the *piccola bestia*, as Dostoevsky calls him elsewhere, would be incomprehensible if we could not assume that it was pursued "partly from the point of view of a Yid". If the whole world has unanimously hated and persecuted the Jews for forty centuries on end, "this hatred must have some reason, and this general loathing must have some ground. The phrase 'the whole world' must mean something." And Dostoevsky hastens to provide a sufficient foundation and justification for this eternal hatred: namely, "the immutable idea of the Jewish nation", the "idea of the Jews overpowering the whole world and replacing unsuccessful Christianity with the "materialism" which is inherent in Jews, with the "blind, carnivorous hunger for personal material security", in direct contrast to the "Christian idea of salvation through the closest possible moral and fraternal unity of all men". The practical conclusion which Dostoevsky reaches on the basis of all these "considerations" is that the Jews in Russia must be granted "everything that humanity and Christian law demand", i.e., the "fullest equality of rights with the native population", however, only after "the Jewish people demonstrate an ability to accept and apply these rights without harming the native population". Even this stipulation, however, is not the last one. The argument concludes with a question mark: will the Jews ever succeed in showing that "they are capable of fraternal unity with people who are alien to them in faith and in blood?" Granted this approach to the "Jewish question", is it surprising that Dostoevsky finally reached the position of excluding the Jews entirely from the fraternal union of humanity? While he never expressed this openly, the conclusion suggests itself when one looks at the speech he made about Pushkin towards the end of his life. In it Dostoevsky movingly extols the universal and genuine Christian spirit of the Russian people; unexpectedly there arises a new concept—that of the "Aryan strain". This universality, comprehended by the Russian nation in all its profundity, and perceived "with love", is unexpectedly identified only with "the peoples of the great Aryan species", i.e., those excluded from the definition are not the Mongols or even the "Semites"—but the Jews. Thus, towards the end of his life, Dostoevsky, probably under the influence of Pobedonostev, began to employ the unambiguous terminology of banal Western European racial anti-Semitism. Does this mean that even more research will eventually produce similar results, which might have been obvious even without any investigation; in other words, is the initial impression the only sound one?

Yes and no. Yes, if we suppose that the human spirit is like a geometrical figure with all its sides and angles, and can be reduced to a single plane; no, inasmuch as we realize that the human heart is a limitless concept, a mysterious and secret world, full of undeciphered implications and insuperable contradictions. But first of all, we are heavily indebted by this ultimate knowledge, by this more profound penetration into the true essence of man, to the creative spirit of the seer Dostoevsky, who derived his wisdom almost exclusively from his own mind. After this, how can one permit Dostoevsky, in whatever manifestation, and consequently, in his relation to Judaism, to be subjected to measurement by a common yardstick, which is definitely lacking direction into depth?

III

Dostoevsky's malevolent attitude towards the Jews is an indisputable fact. The style in which he expresses his "considerations" about the Jews bears witness to this even more than the evidence presented so far. Dostoevsky's style is twisting and elusive, evasive and inconsistent, sprinkled with reservations and stipulations, innumerable counter-arguments (see, for example, even the heading: "But(!) long live brotherhood" in the *Diary*, 77, III). It is precisely his style, whose graphic representation would require a sketch of the Volga together with an abundance of tributaries, which imparts the particular enigmatic nature to Dostoevsky's anti-Jewish outlook and prompts further search for its deeply buried roots.

It has been noted in passing that Dostoevsky's life-long conception of the Jews was in no way a generalization based on his own fortuitous life-experience, as is often the case among the most stalwart anti-Semites; on the contrary, his conception was based on an adaptation of some idea *a priori*, which also determined the features of those individual Jews which he depicted. In order to support this argument from another point of view, one need only recall the aphorism of Dostoevsky's "Isaiah": "If the Lord God existed and I had a few kopeks, then everything would be all right." We noted that Dostoevsky's idea of Jews as depicted in the *Diary of a Writer*, derives albeit with numerous reservations, from this utterance. It is difficult to grant that in this insight into the supposedly Jewish correlation between God and kopeks, Dostoevsky was indebted to Isaiah

Fomich Bumshtein. Even the literary tradition mentioned above by no means solves the problem of the sources of Dostoevsky's anti-Jewish bias. Its actual roots are located deep within the history of Dostoevsky's spiritual development.

In earliest childhood, well before he embarked upon his life's career, the Jews made a powerful, profound impression on Dostoevsky, an impression which he could never discard during the rest of his life. This impression did not derive from any particular Jewish individuals (and where indeed could the young Dostoevsky have encountered any Jews in the capitals of Russia at that time?); nor is it due to any more or less fortuitous image current in literature; rather it can be traced back to the very source of the life and works of the Jewish people, to the sacred monument of Jewish as well as Christian faith—the Bible.

Instead of any biographical evidence, we shall refer to the testimony of Dostoevsky himself, as enshrined in *The Brothers Karamazov:* "In addition to my family reminiscences, I will add my reminiscences about the Holy Scriptures . . . I had a book with beautiful illustrations called 'One Hundred and Four Sacred Stories from the Old and New Testaments', and I learned to read from this book. It is still lying here on my shelf; I keep it as a precious keepsake of my childhood." We know from the testimony by Andrei Mikhailovich Dostoevsky that these words spoken by Father Zosima are an accurate account of Fedor Mikhailovich's own biography. But the confession which follows is particularly meaningful and valuable for the clarification of the process of Dostoevsky's spiritual development; it tells how "at the age of eight, he was granted some spiritual insight". We shall soon see that this story, related by Alesha using Father Zosima's words, is a record of Dostoevsky's own spiritual fate.

Zosima tells how "for the first time he consciously received the seed of the Words of God into his soul". "My mother led me to the church of the Lord . . . A boy stepped forward into the middle of the church carrying a large book, so large that it seemed to me then that he could hardly hold it; he placed it on the lecturn, opened it and began to read; suddenly, for the first time in my life, I understood what was being read in the Church of God." This book was the Bible; the reading from it concerned "a certain man in the land of Uz who was upright and devout"; God's servant Job and his combat with Satan—"And God handed over the righteous man, whom He loved so well, to the Devil . . . And Job rent his garments and fell upon the earth and lamented: 'Naked came I from my mother's womb, and naked shall I return to the earth; the Lord gave, and the Lord hath taken away; Blessed be the name of the Lord now and forever!' Fathers and teachers", the elder interrupts his narration, "forgive the tears which I shed now; it is as if my whole childhood rises again before me; as if I breathe now as I did then at the age of eight; as if I experience the wonder, amazement and gladness which I felt then."

"Lord, what a book this is and what lessons it contains!" exclaims Zosima (the elder), and in moving words he persuades the "priests of the Lord", most of all the village-priests, to make the Holy Scriptures available to all. "Open up this Book," he appeals to the priests, "and begin to read, without any learned words or self-conceit; love these holy words yourselves. Have no fear: everyone will understand; the orthodox heart will understand it all! Read them about Abraham and Sarah, about Isaac and Rebecca, about how Jacob went to Laban and how he wrestled with the Lord in his dream and said: 'How fearful is this place'—and you will amaze the devout minds of the common folk." Thus in the sermons of the elder, endless ranks of Old Testament fighters against Heaven and righteous men, martyrs and sinners, even the "beautiful Esther and the arrogant Vashti", pass before our eyes illuminated by unearthly light. Only near the end, as if suddenly recollecting, the elder adds: "Do not forget the parables of the Lord, especially those from the Gospel of St. Luke (as I did), and the conversion of Saul from the Acts of the Apostles (this is absolutely indispensible!), and finally the Calendar of the Saints". What a striking preference for the Old Testament over the New. "For I love this Book!"—exclaims the elder, referring to the Holy Scriptures of the Jews: "With what wonder and strength does it imbue mankind! It is like a carved image of the world and mankind; in it everything is called by its right name and stated once and for all time."

If until recently it was possible to doubt that this is Dostoevsky's own confession, then now, after the publication of Dostoevsky's letters to Anna Grigor'enva, even the last doubts must have been removed. On 10 June 1875 Dostoevsky wrote from Ems: "I am reading the Book of Job, and it transports me to painful ecstasy: I stop reading, pace my room for hours, practically weeping . . . Anya—this Book—strange as it seems—is one of the first which affected my life, when I was but a child." Just like the most saintly of his fictional characters, Dostoevsky himself was indebted for the words of God, which were reborn in him with new strength, to the Law, the Prophets, and the Scriptures.

And in this heart could there arise and grow a hostility for the people who brought the sacred book into the world, who accepted for its sake the torments of their historical existence? Now we see it: the "banal" anti-Semitism of Dostoevsky ceases to be ordinary and simple-minded, it is enveloped in some sort of enigmatic, almost un-natural form. In any case, the initial impression was deceptive; only now the question of Dostoevsky's attitude towards the Jews begins to emerge in all its complexity.

IV

In order to expose this contradiction even more sharply, it is useful to pose the co-related question: and what was Dostoevsky's attitude towards other nations, apart from the Jews? His artistic and publicistic works provide a wealth of data which will enable us to answer this question, not only concerning his attitude towards the Russians' closest neighbours, the Poles and the Tatars, but also concerning all the leading nationalities of the West, such as German, French and English. It is difficult to say who received more abuse from Dostoevsky: the kinsmen of the humble "Isaiah", or the countrymen and contemporaries of the Polish insurgents of 1863, or for instance Bismarck and MacMahon. The Pole, according to Dostoevsky, is a vain, presumptious, and cowardly busybody; the German, although good-natured and respectable, is slow-witted, like a country-bumpkin; in contrast to him, the Frenchman is clever and sly, but empty, like a sack full of holes; unlike the Frenchman, the Englishman can be relied upon like a stone mountain, but God help you if you look for any clarity of mind in him; the Swiss are simply little "asses"; the Turks and Tatars—what could possibly be worse than the Tatars' despicable deceit? But what is the most depressing is that all these nations whether taken together or each separately are condemned by Dostoevsky to inevitable doom; the ultimate sentence is pronounced for all of them. There is only one nation on earth to whom the future belongs; one nation, which is destined to rule the earth and to save it: Russia, the nation of God-bearers.

It is well-known that Dostoevsky most clearly expressed his cherished Messianic thoughts and dreams through the words of Shatov in *The Devils* : "If a great people does not believe that it alone possesses the sole truth, if it does not believe that it alone is destined to, and is capable of, resurrecting and saving all by means of that truth, then it immediately ceases to be a great people and becomes merely an ethnographical designation. A truly great people is never able to reconcile itself to playing a secondary role in the development of mankind, nor even a primary role; it must by necessity be a first and exclusive one."

How strange these words sound! It is as if they come to us out of the depths of antiquity, of Old Testament times; it is as if they are being spoken not by a Russian about the Russians, but by a Biblical seer about his own people, Israel. In fact for Shatov-Dostoevsky, it is the Russian people which has been chosen by God and which is called upon to become a resurrected Israel. One need only recall the words spoken a few lines above: "A people is a people only as long as it has its particular god, and excludes all other gods as irreconcilable, and only as long as it believes that with the help of its god it will conquer and expel all other gods from the earth. All great peoples have believed this from the beginning of time, at least all those who have left their mark as peoples and have led mankind. It is impossible to dismiss this fact. The Jews lived only in anticipation of the coming of the true God, and they bequeathed the true God to the world" (*The Devils*, part II, chapter I, vii). "A Jew without God is somehow unimaginable; one cannot even conceive of a Jew without God", wrote Dostoevsky in his *"Diary"*.

This is indeed the source of Dostoevsky's extraordinary contradiction.

From the Jewish people, from their ancient, majestic monument, the Bible, Dostoevsky inherited his guiding ideas: his Messianism, his belief that the Russian people was chosen by God, and his religion of the "Russian God" (a phrase used by Dostoevsky in a letter to Maikov). Suddenly, in the middle of his path, as if it had sprung up from beneath the earth, there appeared the puny, ridiculously amusing figure of the convict Isaiah, who bellows out strenuously: How inherited? By what right? What about me? Do I not exist at all? . . . "But there is only one truth," Dostoevsky interrupts him, beside himself with rage, "and therefore only one people can possess the true God." And therefore (we can continue the argument for him) it is either we Russians or you Jews: more precisely, the true Israel today is the Russian people. Russia need only reject the belief that it alone has a claim on the Jewish Messianic idea enshrined in the Holy Scriptures, it need only waver in its faith, and will disintegrate at once, disperse, and become merely an "ethnographical designation". And the converse is also true: if historical truth, the future, and the salvation of humanity are entrusted by Providence to Russia and to the Russian people, then all Jews who are still wandering over the face of the earth are but historical dust . . . "Yids, little Yids, and dirty little Yids." In a relatively insignificant episode in *Crime and Punishment* (part VI, chapter 6), the attentive reader will arrive at once at this same conclusion, a conclusion which was thrust upon Dostoevsky with all the force of logical cogency.

When Svidrigailov reaches his ultimate decision and walks out on to the muddy Petersburg pavement to take his own life "in the presence of official witnesses", his attention is attracted to a "smallish man in an Achilles helmet" on duty at the fire-tower: "With a somnolent gaze he looked askance at the passing Svidrigailov. On his face one could see that age-old querulous grief, which is so sourly imprinted without any exception on the face of every member of the Jewish tribe. Both of them, Svidrigailov and Achilles, silently eyed each other for a few moments . . . " Svidrigailov reaches for his revolver, while the mythical hero who has emerged from the thick milky fog, lisps continuously: "Eh, it's forbidden here, this isn't the place." But what does Svidrigailov care for the vile warning of the puny Achilles: he cocks the trigger and the shot rings out. If we recall that in Dostoevsky's most perfect work there is not one scene, not one image, not one word which has some more profound allegorical meaning, then Svidrigailov's death seems at first like an insoluble enigma; however, it is easily explained as soon as Svidrigailov's "idea" is compared with Dostoevsky's own conception of the Jews. Svidrigailov is profoundly indignant at the ideas of eternity and immortality, like Hegel's bad infinity; he rebels against the endless tautological stamping in one spot against eternal recurrence. What sort of encounter could more graphically portray the meaninglessness of existence simply for the sake of existence, than an encounter with a Jew who has always existed as a spectre—the Eternal

Jew! Like a pet parrot, he repeats always and everywhere his pitiable: "this isn't the place!"—not the place to die, not the place to rebel against the unassailable laws of existence. Let spectres mournfully content themselves with such a negative affirmation of life—a genuinely living human being prefers complete self-annihilation to the curse of self-preservation. Only he who is not led by his God like a mute victim, but who himself blazes the path for God and for His anointed Saviour, only he has the right and duty to live.

Thus Dostoevsky's anti-Semitism is revealed as the opposite side and true basis of his own "Judaism". The apparent contradiction is really straightforward iron logic.

V

But our problem is not yet completely exhausted.

If Dostoevsky were merely a dry theoretician, obsessed with a desire for consistency, then perhaps his mind would have been content with his cunning conceptions, and his peculiar, purely theoretical fear of the Jews would have been no more than a shadow cast by his "Russian God". But in his attitude towards the Jews Dostoevsky remains invariably faithful to the depths of his being; his heart, a battleground of good and evil, plagued with tormenting doubts and contradictions, reserves even here the final word for itself. That same chapter on the Jewish question mentioned earlier as a document of unquestionable anti-Jewish hatred, contains a number of passages which do not fit into any concept of anti-Semitism but rather contradict it.

First of all, we must note the reverence with which Dostoevsky approaches the so-called "Jewish question" (the inverted commas are his)—a reverence so extreme that it is rarely encountered even in statements by passionate Jewish nationalists. "Do not think," exclaims Dostoevsky at the beginning of the summary, "that I will really attempt to raise the 'Jewish question' . . . I am not able to raise a question of such magnitude as the position of the Jews in Russia, or the position of Russia, which numbers among its sons some three million Jews. This question does not lie within my capability." And further: "The time has not yet come, in spite of the forty centuries which have gone by, and mankind's last word about this great people has not yet been spoken." "Even the most powerful civilizations in the world have not endured half of forty centuries, and yet have lost their political significance and their exterior appearance. The main ground is not self-preservation alone, but some inborn and centripetal idea, something so universal and profound, that mankind may yet not have been able to pronounce its final word." "The Jews," exclaims Dostoevsky, almost in a frenzy, "are in another context a people completely without parallel."

Has "an anti-Semite" ever been heard to speak like this? In this essay which abounds with every possible "pro and contra", Dostoevsky strongly protests against the "grave accusation" that he hates "the Jews as a people or as a nation." This is the second most original characteristic of his personal attitude towards the Jews. We see a "Judeophobe", ashamed as it were by his own "phobia", struggling within himself, contradicting and disgracing himself. "When and how have I ever exposed my hatred for the Jews as a people?" exclaims Dostoevsky. "This hatred has never existed in my heart, and those Jews who are acquainted with me or who have had dealings with me, know that this is so; right from the very beginning, I reject this accusation once and for all, and trust that it will never again be mentioned." This is more than a categorical declaration; but apparently it did not sound convincing enough for Dostoevsky; he obviously felt that it was very difficult for him in his own words, to "justify himself"; again and again he almost swears that he is not "an enemy of the Jews". "No, I rebel against this assumption, I deny the very fact." Dostoevsky rejects his own hostility towards the Jews with such stubborn insistence on those very same pages which marshal the most popular and nonsensical slanders against the Jews "just as a people". Moreover, immediately following an allusion to the inner justification of this "universal" hatred, Dostoevsky advances the assertion that among Russians there is "no preconceived a priori, stupid, religious, or any other kind of hatred for the Jews . . . Our whole people views the Jews, I repeat, without any preconceived hatred." So much for the "universal" hatred! Does the phrase the "whole" people still have any meaning? One exclaims involuntarily against Dostoevsky using his own words (see above, section II).

The outlook reflected in all these, almost chaotic, declarations contains not merely a theoretical contradiction, which could perhaps be surmounted by some abstruse logic; rather, it throws light on that terrible struggle which rent Dostoevsky's heart, and on that acute internal conflict which burdened his conscience. As we have seen, the Jewish question for Dostoevsky was not a subject of abstract philosophizing, but one of the most pressing problems of his personal creed, sustaining his faith in the ultimate meaning and the significance of his own life's work. In such a frame, Dostoevsky, Russia's seer, appears in his conflict with Israel, like some "double" or reverse-image of the ancient soothsayer Balaam. Balaam was ready to curse Israel, and yet was unable to refrain from blessing it; Dostoevsky, full of ecstatic admiration, would like to glorify the Jewish people, and yet is unable to keep from damning it. He is ready to exalt the Jews, as the son exalts his spiritual father, yet he is unable to refrain from renouncing the parental relationship because he was so wholly obsessed by that falsely understood Messianism, on account of which historical bliss in every age is thought to rest on one nation alone. In spite of his obsession, Dostoevsky is continually plagued by doubt: he is never convinced, right up to the very end that the Jews are merely a spectral shadow of their former greatness. "Clearly its own beneficent God, with His own ideal and convenant, continues to lead His people towards their constant goal. It is impossible, I repeat, impossible even to conceive of a Jew without God . . ." Doesn't this mean, in other words, that it is impossible to conceive of God without the Jews? Dostoevsky could well have asked himself whether his immeasurable love for the Russian people had not led him astray. Who guarantees that the Russian land and the Russian nation are truly destined to give birth to the Saviour to come? The most insignificant Jew "on duty" seemed to be a decisive witness for the opposite side, the side which refuted Dostoevsky's greatest hopes.

What was there left to do? Convulsively clenching his fists and gnashing his teeth, Dostoevsky, in spite of himself, returns again and again to his initial thought: that the Jewish people do not exist; that all of its force and energy are mere appearance, only vain attempts at being; that all the religious emotion of the Jews, all their prayers and aspirations, their sorrows and joys, are but a pitiful masquerade, only mechanical movements of the body. Towards the end of his life, Dostoevsky wrote to his wife: "Jews even talk differently—whole pages at a time, as if they are reading a book . . ." "Whole volumes of conversations . . ." (Letters from Ems written on 28 and 30 June 1879).

In order to sense even remotely the full bitterness of the doubts which tormented Dostoevsky, one should not forget, even for a moment, that his boldest practical conclusions followed from the postulates of his faith. The passionate enthusiasm with which for decades he asserted the rights of Russia over Constantinople, was, in the last analysis, nourished on the invincible conviction that the keys for the Holy Land, for Palestine, would come to Russia, together with Tsar'grad (Constantinople); this is easily verified by more attentive reading of Dostoevsky's writings on the Eastern question. According to Dostoevsky, Palestine had to be, whatever else came to pass, an inseparable part of Russia; there, where the First Coming took place, the Second would also occur; and if it were true that this was to occur in Russia, then Palestine not only would be, but already was, Russian land. While the people of Israel existed, while it was not yet expunged from the lists of the living, the Holy Land would remain as before, the promised land of the seed of Israel, and the rights of Russia, together with its universal-historical mission, were once again called into question.

Thus, in every possible area Dostoevsky came into conflict with the Jews: in the world of dialectical thought, within his soul torn between faith and doubt, and in the sphere of current political conflicts. However, all these dimensions of his spiritual horizon always intersected at one single point: in that ultimate source of his inexhaustible creative energy, for which he knew only one sacred name—Russia.

Truly a Biblical image in its greatness! An image which unintentionally recalls the ancient Jewish prophets, still unworthy to ascend to that elevated height of prophecy which was soon to be revealed to their heirs and successors in all its infinite, all-embracing, and all-reconciling universality.

2. Dostoevsky the Thinker

There is no need to be ashamed of one's idealism.
A Writer's Diary, 1876, October

The recognition of Dostoevsky as an original thinker came even later than that of his outstanding importance as an artist. In each case one of the main obstacles to recognition was the predominance of accepted standards of expression. While the artistic writings of Dostoevsky appeared to disregard the minimum requirements of the conventional novel, his philosophical thought found expression in a manner which, in the view of the professional thinkers of the time, most of them professors of philosophy, bore the mark of diffuse and irresponsible thinking. At that time, the second half of the 19th century, Kierkegaard had not yet been discovered, Nietzsche was at best counted among the poets and, in Russia herself, Tolstoy was regarded as a preacher rather than a thinker.

At the turn of the century, however, with the gradual consolidation of Dostoevsky's artistic frame, it is already possible to record the first, though still half-hearted, attempts to do him justice also as a thinker in his own right. Yet, those who, like V. V. Rozanov, realized the importance of 'bringing the intellectual treasures left by Dostoevsky into a system' were discouraged by the fact that the thinker himself never tried to give a coherent exposition of his general philosophical ideas. The articles of his philosophical creed, in so far as he expressed them in his own name, are widely scattered in his journalistic writings (the essays and notes published by him since 1860 in a number of periodicals, including his personal monthly *A Writer's Diary*) as well as in letters and in records of private conversation. The recasting of all the relevant fragments into one systematic whole was in itself a hard task. But the greatest impediment appeared to be the indissoluble personal union between the thinker and the artist in Dostoevsky, which made the one indistinguishable from the other.

Indeed, we already know to what an extent the artistic work of Dostoevsky is saturated with philosophical speculation, so that many of the

This text was first published in English as Chapter III in *Dostoyevsky* by A. Steinberg, Bowes and Bowes, London 1966.

central characters created by him represent philosophies endowed with life, breathing, moving and acting. Does this not imply that at least some of these characters, single or taken together, were the author's mouthpieces and that his thought coincided with theirs? That was actually the common assumption of the Russian and non-Russian critics engaged since the beginning of this century on the assessment of Dostoevsky's merits as a thinker. Nearly all of them adopted the device of presenting a distillation of the essence of the world views embodied in certain artistic images of Dostoevsky (be it 'the Idiot' Prince Myshkin, the saint Zosima, or the semi-'Possessed' Shatov) as an adequate substitute for the reconstruction of his own 'system' on the basis of his lifework in its entirety. In all these cases it was presumed that the characters were nearest to the author's heart and consequently also of one mind with him. It is obvious that such an approach oversimplified the problem.

There can certainly be no doubt that Dostoevsky the thinker is reflected in the convictions, thoughts and utterances of his personages; but who would be able to discover in the world created by him Dostoevsky's own singular silhouette, let alone his fullsize self-portrait? Though auto-biographical components are discernible in many of his characters, none of their biographies is a replica of his. Complex and seemingly inscrutable as many of them are, Dostoevsky himself was of still greater complexity and still more of an enigma even in his own perception. This applies in particular to the various stages in the evolution of his thought. Did he not declare a decade before his death that try as one may to convey to others a 'new thought', the very essence of the new 'idea' will remain undisclosed 'even if one were to fill volumes with its explanation and keep interpreting it 35 years on end'. (Cf. *The Idiot*, Part III, end of Chap. V; Dostoevsky's literary activity lasted exactly thirty-five years, and long before the end he anticipated that he would die at sixty.) To make proper use of his artistic work in the reconstruction of his philosophy one must, therefore, first of all take care to avoid the pitfall of simplification.

If the notion that Dostoevsky occupied a niche of his own in the history of human thought is well-founded, then it must be presumed that there exists a close correlation between his original way of thinking and his artistic inspiration. Therefore, the first question to be asked in any effort to define the true significance of this correlation is whether the world created by Dostoevsky's imagination corresponds essentially, and in its whole extension, to the author's fundamental attitudes of mind, and it seems that a full appreciation of the originality of Dostoevsky's art must implicitly suggest the sought-for answer.

We may remember that already, at the beginning of his creative life, Dostoevsky expressed his heart's desire to become 'an artist in science', and that the 'science' which he hoped to advance by artistic means was no other than a consistent moral philosophy based on a comprehensive philosophy of history. Inspired by this aim he succeeded in enriching literary art with a new synthesis of concrete imagery and abstract thought. Would it then not be right to see in this characteristic feature of his art the most promising starting point for an objective reconstruction of his theoretical world view, and to presume that its evolution was running parallel to the intensification of the productivity of his imagination? There is good reason to suppose that in the process of his evolution as a thinker Dostoevsky, instead of imparting his innermost thoughts only to a selected group of characters, brought them all into an intimate and meaningful relationship with certain aspects of his 'system' as a whole. It would at all events be rash to brush aside such a conjecture merely because Dostoevsky's characters seem to represent quite frequently irreconcilable points of view in strictly logical contradiction one to another. The answer to the question how could one and the same thinker be represented, for instance, by all the brothers Karamazov, including even Smerdyakov, might possibly be found in the assumption that it was far from Dostoevsky's mind to entrust the essence of his 'new thought' to any one of them in particular, not even to Ivan or Alyosha, but that nevertheless he needed them all to make explicit the various turns and twists of his own dialectical thinking.

In this context it may be useful once more to cite the analogy with Plato. How does one know who among the persons appearing in his Dialogues spoke for their author and to whom he assigned the part of the devil's advocate? Is Socrates, his spiritual father, and Socrates, the issue of his own mind and imagination, always one and the same person? And is Plato himself always one with Socrates or perhaps sometimes with the others— with Gorgias, Protagoras, or Parmenides? Still all these difficulties and doubts notwithstanding, no one questions the identity of Plato's philosophy in the whole process of its evolution. Could it not be that the relation of Dostoevsky's thinking to his artistic work is similar to that of Plato to his Dialogues? Surely, a symphonic dialectic reigns supreme in the world of his imagination. Is it then not appropriate to compare him with the conductor of an orchestra, who, not playing any particular instrument himself, turns his back to the audience and, swinging his magic baton, extracts from each instrument its singular individual contribution? But even such a comparison is not exact enough. For in relation to the 'orchestra' conjured up by his imaginative thought Dostoevsky is simultaneously conductor and composer of the work performed. His personal thought and way of thinking could, therefore, be discovered only in the composition as a whole projected through the composer's individual style of orchestration. This indeed is the general methodological conception underlying the following analysis.

The preliminary question as to whether Dostoevsky was sufficiently qualified to build his artistic work on philosophical foundations does not present any difficulty. We know that already at a very early age he was fascinated by the intimate relationship connecting poetry with philosophy and religion. Later he assiduously studied the philosophical classics and became particularly impressed by the exponents of German Idealism, above all by Hegel's system; when still an exile in Siberia, he even planned to translate some of Hegel's works into Russian. As to Plato, his complete works were in the last period of Dostoevsky's life constantly by his side in his private library. Parallel with his philosophical studies which as a matter of course included philosophy of history Dostoevsky pursued the study of history proper in all languages at his command. His first biographer, N. N. Strakhov, himself a philosophical scholar of repute, records that Dostoevsky was always attracted by 'questions concerning the essence of things and the limits of knowledge', and that it caused him 'amusement' whenever it was pointed out to him how much his general ideas resembled 'various philosophical views known from the history of philosophy'; 'it transpired'—relates the biographer in conclusion—'that it was difficult to invent something new, and Dostoevsky jokingly reassured himself by the fact other that in his thoughts he coincided with one or the other great thinker.'

The salient point in this account, of course, is not the insinuation as a thinker Dostoevsky was prompted by a naïve ambition to 'invent' something entirely novel, but, on the contrary, that he was rather anxious to ascertain to what an extent his intellectual intuition was in consonance with the recorded history of human thought. In view of his intimate acquaintance with this aspect of universal history, there can be no doubt that his vast learning was a potent factor in the gradual crystallization of his personal philosophical creed. But is it possible to single out the foundation-head of a specific philosophical tradition which might decisively have informed Dostoevsky's thought enabling it also to assume control over his art?

The prominent place accorded in his art to 'ideas' as real entities is a clear indication that Dostoevsky was under the spell of Plato's metaphysic and used his theory of ideas as a safe springboard for his own speculation. This is borne out by a close examination of the use Dostoevsky made in all his writings, artistic as well as non-artistic, of the very term 'idea' (in Russian *eedeya*). True, here and there he deviates from his personal usage and implies the more common connotations in the sense of ideal, design, principle or abstract thought in general; but whenever his aim is to focus attention on the real essence, be it of an individual human being or of a whole nation or of a spiritual tradition, he invariably denotes it by the term 'idea' in its metaphysical, its Platonic meaning. It was, therefore, quite natural that referring to his own specific view of life he defined it as 'idealism', and it was this 'idealism' which in the domain of art provided the philosophical basis for his 'realism in a higher sense'.

Faced with the positivistic and materialistic trends which were then holding sway in Russia, and not there only, over the minds of the younger generation, Dostoevsky never tired to stress that 'in essence Idealism is exactly as realistic as Realism and can in no circumstances disappear from the world'; 'the idealist and the realist'—he explained—'have one and the same object: Man, and they only differ as to the forms of perception of this object' (*A Writer's Diary*, 1876, July–August, Chap. 2, II). Similar statements abound in Dostoevsky's non-artistic writings of the 1870s and culminate in the address on Pushkin of 1880. However, the rehabilitation of the idealistic philosophy, including its ancient metaphysical antecedents, was initiated by Dostoevsky much earlier; in fact—since the world created by his art began to emerge as a new autonomous reality existing, as it were, in accordance with laws as yet undiscovered by natural science. Not questioning the validity of the general principles constituting the natural order of things, such, for instance, as the nexus between cause and effect, Dostoevsky succeeded through the medium of fiction to convey an awareness of most real links between man and man, between man and his 'idea' as well as between the 'ideas' themselves which were beyond the grasp and outside the jurisdiction of common science. Thus the artist undermined the despotic rule of the accepted 'ironcast notions', to use his phrase, and opened up a vista to a philosophy which was so much in contrast with the predominant 'scientifism' in all its varieties and so much nearer to the classical tradition of Idealism, on the one hand, and to the Christian tradition, on the other.

To Dostoevsky the point of intersection of both traditions was the concept of the 'immortality of the human soul', an 'idea' which in the end he came to identify with his own self. 'The idea of immortality'—he wrote in 1876—'is life itself, living life, its final formula and the source of truth and of wholesome consciousness for mankind.' Whatever else this affirmation may signify, it is clearly a profession of faith which contains the 'final formula' of Dostoevsky's personal existence, the sum total of his singular experience as artist and thinker. A close scrutiny of the context in which the quoted sentence appears and of other correlated statements dating from the same period makes it clear that in his relentless quest for a pivotal point in his own thinking he at long last discovered it in his 'unshakeable conviction' that 'immortality is beyond doubt real'. (Cf. *Diary*, 1876, October, Chap. I, IV: December, Chap. I, III, and letter to N. A. Ozmidov of February 1878.)

Having discovered his personal 'idea', the soul of his soul, as it were, in the awareness of the indestructible nature of his individual 'psyche', Dostoevsky thus vindicated the seemingly supernatural character of the world brought forth by his imagination; though different from the physical world comprising nothing but ephemeral phenomena in space and time, it could nevertheless claim to represent reality not less real than the human soul. In his enthusiastic self-identification with the 'idea of immortality' he contemplated the reaffirmation of his innermost 'conviction' in a logically cogent exposition, apparently intending to make use of some of Kant's arguments and to apply the 'transcendental method' of deduction. In contradistinction to Kant, however, to whom the 'transcendental ideas' God, Freedom, and Immortality were of equal significance, Dostoevsky singled out the last one as the real foundation of the other two; for—he argued—without the intuitive perception of the real existence of the immortal soul, of an entity which by definition and immediate experience was not material, no one could believe in the existence of God and no one would ever care for man's real freedom. In this respect Dostoevsky was in line with Plato and metaphysical realism in general rather than with Kant and his critical idealism.

To Dostoevsky, not less than to Plato, the 'idea' was the real thing in the midst of shadows; accordingly, he drew a sharp line between 'ideas' and general concepts, the products of generalization. (Cf. *Diary*, 1876, October, Chap. I, II.) To him the 'idea' was as real as the concrete individual soul, since the essential uniqueness and indivisible singleness of every soul in its endless manifestations could, in his view, find no expression more adequate and concentrated than that which is attainable through the medium of the consciously or unconsciously active idea. 'There are ideas'—he explained in the essay on 'Philosophy of the Mileue'— 'which remain unexpressed, unconscious, and are only strongly felt; there are many such ideas fused together, as it were, with the soul of man. They also exist in a whole people as well as in mankind taken as a whole. So long as these ideas are unconsciously embedded in the life of the people and are merely strongly and properly felt, only so long can the people live a powerful living life. All the energy of its life is but a reflex of its strivings to make those hidden ideas clear to itself' (*Diary*, 1873, No 2). In these few lines we have before us a concise outline of Dostoevsky's general theory of ideas, and they also indicate that he saw in his idealism a reliable instrument to unravel the mysteries of individual and historical life, and above all a clue to the true meaning of universal history.

To forestall inevitable assaults on his idealistic view of life, incompatible in its very essence with the philosophical climate of the age, Dostoevsky tried to buttress his general position by a variety of pointed aphorisms, such as: 'It is possible to know a great deal unconsciously'; 'Ideas are infectious'; 'Ideas live and spread in accordance with laws which it is too difficult for us to grasp', or, to cite yet another example, 'It can hardly be assumed that science already possesses enough knowledge of human nature that it should be able infallibly to set forth new laws of the body social' (*Diary*, 1876, December, Chap. I, III and March, Chap I, IV; 1873, No. 2). These aphoristic utterances reveal that, in line with the Platonic tradition, Dostoevsky unhesitatingly accepted the existence of a realm of ideas with its own 'laws', independent of the world of common experience and yet firmly implanted in it, coexisting with it like soul and body. Any variety of idealism which divided the world into two halves, an ideal and a real one, placing the first somewhere 'beyond the stars', was rejected by Dostoevsky as 'transmundane romanticism' doomed to degenerate in our earthly life into an irresponsible 'cynicism' (*Diary*, 1876, July-August, Chap. 2).

But could an account be given also of the inner structure of Dostoevsky's realm of ideas and the direction in which he visualized its co-ordination with the physical Cosmos?

It seems that the answer to both questions may be found in Dostoevsky's instinctive Panpsychism which, intertwined with his not less spontaneous Panpersonalism, permeated his whole lifework. According to his primordial intuition, everything existing and capable of manifesting an individual character was, by this token alone, an animated entity. The paradigm was to him the human body as the dwelling place of an imperishable soul whose uniqueness was symbolized by the individual character of every human face and whose link with the world of eternity was determined by the idea engraved in it. Yet, a 'psyche' of their own could also be imputed, according to Dostoevsky, to collective entities: to peoples, to cities, and institutions, if only they revealed in the course of historical time a distinct individual character finding expression in a specific clear-cut 'idea'. In this respect Dostoevsky's thinking was undoubtedly influenced by the exponents of German Idealism of the post-Kantian period. Not only by Hegel but also by Fichte and Schelling, though they themselves would hardly ever have accepted the hyper-realistic interpretation of their metaphysics propounded by their bold follower in Russia.

Not afraid of being denounced by scientifically minded contemporaries for his indulgence in 'mystical' speculation, Dostoevsky extended to the whole sphere of historical life the application of the same pattern which, in conformity with his general theory of ideas, typified the relationship between body, soul, and idea in the life of a single human being. Precisely—he thought—as an original idea of an individual was the expression of the uniqueness of his soul, while this, in turn, was the principle of the organic unity of the living body animated by it, so every people with an historical mission, asserting its own 'idea', was endowed with an undying soul as well as with a body—i.e. its preordained homeland. Thus, speaking about the different characters of Moscow and St. Petersburg, he emphasized that nonetheless 'the soul was the same in both cities as also in all the rest of Russia, for everywhere, at every place in the whole of Russia was present Russia as a whole'. The analogy with soul and body of an individual is complete (*Diary*, 1876, May, Chap. I, II). But it is more than an analogy, let alone a patriotic metaphor. In the same vein Dostoevsky referred to 'Italy' as the physical substratum of the 'idea' of a united human race kept alive on Italian soil since antiquity; to 'Germany' with her own 'idea' of non-conformism; to 'Europe' as a Continent faithful to the vision of a universal Christian civilization, of that 'idea' to which he himself laid claim in the name of Russia's immortal soul; and finally—to the whole Earth, the habitat of mankind whose common ideas were still immersed in the slumbering psyche of our unique planet (Cf. *Diary*, 1877, January, Chap. I, I and Chap. 3, I: 1876, June, Chap. 2, IV; 1877, April, Chap. 2, III). In short, Dostoevsky based his philosophy of history on the assumption that the ideas whose evolution, interplay, and collision made human history meaningful were linked by the souls of the historical nations with the respective physical conditions of their earthly life. This was, incidentally, the source of Dostoevsky's vivid interest in current international affairs in which, in his view, the nations were always involved with body, soul, and idea.

Dostoevsky's historical Panpsychism implied that his ideal world was not divorced from the real world in space and time, but on the contrary fitted into the same universe which is the object of natural science. The inner structure of his world of ideas largely coincided therefore with the network of mutual relations which are, in the traditional and popular view, constitutive for any community of human souls. In essence, we can say, the fabric is the same, if only we do not overlook that, according to Dostoevsky's Panpersonalism, every human soul is, at least potentially, a person distinguished by its own idea which is the soul of its soul.

It was this metaphysical background of his art which prompted Dostoevsky to describe himself as a 'realist in a higher sense'. Not claiming inside knowledge of a purely spiritual world, he tried to demonstrate that a truly realistic treatment of human nature could not ignore and should not neglect its ideal dimension. In the last resort, he felt, all relations between human beings were determined by the direct contact of their souls experienced either consciously, through the medium of their respective 'ideas', or unconsciously, as in the case of love relations between man and woman. Accordingly, Dostoevsky had no inhibitions to re-examine biological phenomena, including heredity, in the light of his realistic idealism.

A detailed analysis of Dostoevsky's allusive accounts concerning the succession of generations within any one of his 'accidental families' proves beyond doubt that procreation and physical descent were to him tantamount to a process of filiation of ideas. It remains uncertain, for instance, whether Verkhovensky junior, the cynical ringleader of the 'Possessed', was his father's son or his 'nephew'; this may appear awkward indeed, if one does not remember that the 'father' himself, Verkhovensky senior, stands revealed as the personification of twin-ideas: of that abstract pseudo-idealism which carries unmitigated cynicism with it as its reverse. The offspring of this dual personality, the personification of unqualified cynicism can, therefore, be regarded as a descendant not only of his father but also—and rather more correctly—of his father's twin brother, as it were, that is of his 'uncle' (Cf. *The Possessed,* Part One, Chap. 2, VI and Part Two, Chap. 4, II). Such subtly concealed hints served Dostoevsky's purpose to infiltrate the texture of his narratives with the essence of his speculative thought.

Another more comprehensive illustration of Dostoevsky's metaphysical interpretation of heredity is contained in the matrimonial chronicle of the Karamazov family. The four sons of old Karamazov are the children of three different mothers. They are all in various degrees tinged by their father's peculiar idea which is, in essence, a passionate affirmation of life liable to explode in fits of frenzied voluptuousness almost indistinguishable from animal lust. However, every one of the four sons lives up to his own original idea in which the father's consuming thirst for life is but a component. Mitya, the eldest, is the fruit of his father's union with a 'hot-tempered, courageous, swarthy, impatient lady of remarkable physical strength'. In this union the naked idea of life for life's sake collided with another living soul, and it is on record that Fyodor Karamazov's first wife used to 'thrash' him. In consequence, the idea of his firstborn son is to force upon himself a ruthless mastery over his wild propensities; it is the idea of man's innate faculty to assert his privileged position in the physical world by taming his chaotic subhuman instincts. A Karamazov like his father, Mitya personifies the rebellion of human nature against itself in the name of a humanism which must unavoidably be chaotic at its first awakening.

Thus, the thesis represented by an older generation fatefully collides with its antithesis in the succeeding generation and expands farther towards the germination of a synthesis, i.e. towards the idea of human perfection. The two aspects of this idea, the secular and the traditional Christian, are embodied in the two younger brothers, Ivan and Alyosha. Sons of the same mother, 'the humble and meek Sophia', they are meant to supplement one another, while their mother's name stands for Russia's still subconscious unuttered 'Wisdom' slowly maturing through suffering.

There still remains the fourth brother, the horrible Smerdyakov. Almost an outsider, he nevertheless also personifies an 'original idea' rooted in the Karamazov breeding ground—that of extreme rationalism culminating in the exultation of formal logic. His existence is a by-product of his father's measureless lust for life and power. Impelled by his extravagant life-affirmation the father had found gratification in taking possession of a vagrant imbecile, with the result that the offspring of the unholy union evinces the idea that the unredeemed fortuity of individual existence must be counter-balanced by generalizing reason mercilessly nullifying the specific differences of being. In this genealogical frame Smerdyakov's moral insanity stands out as a concomitant of his perverted intellectualism which is thus exposed as a fatal fallacy threatening to bring to nought even the noblest aspirations of his half-brother Ivan.

The complex set-up of the Karamazov family enabled Dostoevsky to interlace the tangled web of his narrative with a multitude of very thin, almost imperceptible lines of thought pointing from various directions to that general genealogy of ideas which was conceived by him as the real substratum of an adequate philosophy of history and, consequently, as the basis for a realistic moral philosophy. Since the early 1860s, his goal in both these coalescing fields was the assessment of the stage reached by the human race in the gradual evolution of ideas from generation to generation, and the evaluation, on the strength of this appraisal, of the prospects for a moral regeneration of humanity. For, since his first journey abroad, in 1862, he was firmly convinced that the moral crisis in the West was not less devastating than the vacillations of mind and philosophical aberrations endemic among the Russian intelligentsia.

It may well be that the conception of a genealogical tree of ideas had developed in Dostoevsky's mind in deliberate opposition to Charles Darwin's *Origin of Species* published just three years before the Russian adept of philosophical spiritualism set foot on English soil. A full record of the indelible impact made on Dostoevsky by the technological civilization and, in particular, by its gigantic shop window, the London World Exhibition of 1862, can be found in his incisive *Notes from the Underground*. In this semi-philosophical, semi-artistic inquiry Dostoevsky's intention of advancing his method of investigation into the genealogy of ideas, as a kind of antidote against the scientific approach to the delineation of man's place in nature, becomes clearly discernible. Here, moreover, we find the reason which prompted him to restrict the field of his investigation to Russia. His 'anti-hero', as the fictitious author of the *Notes* describes himself, is a 'Russian European', which means that he represents the Russian 'educated class' in its eagerness to assimilate the ripest fruits of Europe's civilization in order to judge their intrinsic value from the inside, as it were. In other words, the life story of Dostoevsky's 'anti-hero' is synchronized with that critical stage in the evolution of ideas at which Russia's partnership in the European legacy markedly gained momentum and which brought the Russian intelligentsia to the dilemma whether to join the general trends of European thought or to blaze its path into the future independently. As to Dostoevsky himself, in the light of his experience abroad, his choice was obvious. Although it would be wrong to identify the actual author of the *Notes* with his anti-hero, it remains true that both were reasoning on parallel lines. In fact, the same philosophical problems which tormented the mind of the First Person Singular of the *Notes* did not cease to harass Dostoevsky himself till the end of his life. Was human freedom still an attainable goal under the reign of natural science? If not, how can human consciousness avoid disintegration in the setting of our time? These were the essentially moral problems which occupied Dostoevsky.

Indeed—asked Dostoevsky—what would freedom mean if the scientific approach to human nature were the only one possible? Natural science recognises only phenomena in space and time interconnected by innumerable chains of causes and effects by which the individual is so tightly hemmed in that, being aware of what science stands for, he does not even dare to claim for himself the dignity of a free agent. However, continuing the line of thought pursued by Dostoevsky since his fascinating experience in the Western temples of triumphant science, the voice 'from underground' exclaims: 'Wherefrom shall I take primordial causes to lean on? Where—the grounds? I practise thinking and, therefore, any primordial cause drags another still more primordial one immediately in its wake and so *ad infinitum*. This is the very essence of all consciousness and thinking' (*Notes*, etc. Part I, V). Like his imaginary thinker Dostoevsky was fully aware that, apart from the endless external physical world, there existed yet another infinity, that which man might discover within his own consciousness, and that it was precisely this inner human endlessness where a solution of the crucial problem of human freedom in a world of necessity ought to be sought and could perhaps be found. If the Western world which first brought to light the significance of man's awareness of his own self (Descartes' *Cogito ergo sum*) was about to surrender its great philosophical tradition to the powers that be, to exact science and the laws of nature, then, Dostoevsky thought, it was incumbent on the 'Russian Europeans', including himself, to pick up the broken thread and to think for themselves. With his general theory of ideas as a basis and forearmed by his intuitive knowledge of the immortality of the human soul, Dostoevsky carried out in his artistic laboratory a series of thought experiments designed with the dual purpose of disproving pseudo-philosophical approaches to the freedom problem, and of pointing to its proper place in the consciousness of the individual. Just as Dostoevsky reveals himself as an original thinker through the medium of his art, his art will appear in a clearer perspective when perceived through the medium of his spontaneous thinking.

The first great experiment in the series devised by Dostoevsky for the exploration of the ways and means at the disposal of modern man in his struggle for the survival of human freedom is recorded in the story of Raskolnikov (*Crime and Punishment*). Raskolnikov is conceived as a true son of the new age, free from the so-called religious superstitions and entirely in line with modern positivism equating reality with what empirical science knows about it. But he is also a 'Russian European' who cannot look away from his own blurred consciousness and disregard his intense longing for absolute independence. Thus an 'original idea' imposes itself on his whole being: if there is nothing in the world but pure and simple factuality—he reasons—whence could then be derived a criterion for the distinction of good and evil? This implies that a consistent follower of the positivistic philosophy is *a priori* justified in transgressing at will any norm of conduct, that he is absolutely free to deal with other human beings at his own discretion, and generally to behave as though he was the sovereign of the universe.

On the face of it, it may appear that this Individualism incarnate solves the problem of human freedom at least for one person. But even this, as Dostoevsky tries to demonstrate *ad oculos,* is not true. The price of such absolute freedom is absolute loneliness, absolute isolation, and where there is no Second Person, either in the plural or in the singular, even a godlike First Person hovering above good and evil is bound to discover in the end that it is no person at all, but a phantom among phantoms. Instead of solving the problem of freedom, positivistic individualism deprives it of meaning and precipitates the disintegration of individual consciousness. Raskolnikov's apocalyptic dream in his Siberian prison puts the seal on his philosophy: it exposes his original idea and the crime engendered by it as a symptom of the general mental disarray of the age, and is a stern warning against worse things to come. If no heed were to be taken of this and similar warnings—this is the message conveyed by Raskolnikov's nightmarish vision—the whole of mankind would be engulfed by universal infectious madness resulting in a war of all against all and of everyone against everyone else; but even then, on the very verge of total extinction, the infected ones will as never before rely on their reasoning and cling 'to their scientific deductions'. Salvation may hinge on the survival of a few pure souls 'predestined to incept a new human race and new life on a rejuvenated and purified earth' (*Crime and Punishment,* Epilogue II). As in a number of analogous thought experiments Dostoevsky applied in his argumentation the method of reducing the contested proposition *ad absurdum,* contrasting it by significant allusions to the highest goal of his own thinking.

On the last page of *Crime and Punishment* devoted to the prospects of the 'criminal's' spiritual regeneration our eye meets the reassuring words: 'Replacing dialectics there entered life, and something entirely different was bound to take shape in his consciousness'. The notion implied in this sentence that dialectial thinking divorced from real life must of necessity lead astray is one of the principles which guided Dostoevsky in all his philosophical experiments. And there was no truer and loftier manifestation of life for Dostoevsky than that which revealed itself in love. For love in which one immortal soul found immediate access to the core of another unique and immortal being, this alone was the real safeguard against the threat of absolute isolation inherent in any 'original idea' rebelling against the spiritual 'commonwealth of ideas' and groping on its own for an outlet from the maze of dialects. It is remarkable that Dostoevsky pronounced his word of warning already in the laconic summing-up of the *Notes from Underground.* Entrusting his 'anti-hero' with the representation of all exponents of modern speculative separatism and isolationism, he wrote in

VARIETIES AND DISTORTIONS OF MESSIANISM 273

their name: 'We are stillborn, and what is more, for quite a while we are being born not by living fathers, and we like it more and more. We have got the taste of it. Soon we shall contrive somehow to be born by an idea.' In fact, already then Dostoevsky saw clearly that his genealogical tree of ideas enshrined in the succession of living generations was in danger of being torn out by the roots.

His anguish as to 'the possibility of a continuation of world history' is most tellingly reflected in the image of the 'possessed' Kirillov, the would-be deicide. Like Ivan Karamazov later on, Kirillov personifies the idea of man's rivalry with the Creator of the universe. To both, God is a reality, but while Ivan rises in dialectical armour to expose the moral deficiency of God's creation, Kirillov sets out to discard God altogether as a fictitious hypostasis of man's 'fear of the pain of death', in order to clear the way for the transfiguration of humanity into a divine entity: Man should become God. As a typical 'Russian European' who, moreover, had some experience even of America, he strongly believes in the experimental method; if, he thinks, he would commit suicide for no other reason than for the sake of proving that man was capable to free himself from the deadly fear of death, the 'main freedom' would be conquered and man's power would become limitless. With his bold hyper-dialectical idea in mind, Kirillov sees himself in the mirror of his consciousness as though he already possessed the power to destroy and recreate the world, as if he were in fact identical with God on the threshold of creation, making the choice between the divine 'Let there be' and self elimination. (Cf. *The Possessed*, I, Chap. 3, VIII.) This whole monstrosity of God contemplating suicide might have been invented by Dostoevsky as a counterblast against Auguste Comte's Positivism culminating in his 'Religion of Humanity'. Once more a popular philosophical position was probed by the method of *reductio ad absurdum*.

However, in its general form Kirillov's idea that suicide was a shortcut to the solution of the freedom problem was taken by Dostoevsky most seriously. In three consecutive issues of his *Diary* he discussed at length the temptation haunting the enlightened atheist of the scientific age to assert the freedom of his will by cutting the line of his own life (*A Writer's Diary*, 1876, October-December). Every single case of suicide which comes to Dostoevsky's knowledge struck his imagination, tormented his mind and spurred his sense of guilt. For, perhaps even more than laxity towards another creature's life, the allurements of suicide appeared to him as a 'logical' consequence of the ascendancy of the world view which rejected the validity of the spiritual and condemned man to solitary confinement within his own self; yet, knowing what he knew—whispered to Dostoevsky his guilty conscience—was he not personally responsible for the fact that close to him, in his own Russia terrible things did not cease to happen, whereas he merely registered and analysed them?

In any appraisal of Dostoevsky's thought it is not irrelevant to bear in mind that he himself was the most exacting judge of his metaphysical hypotheses. Applying all his artistic skill in testing them by confrontation with real life, he singled out in his imagination murder and suicide as the most revealing projections of self-centered 'pride'. But—he thought—the fatal self-adoration may overreach itself to such an extent that, to overcome his absolute isolation, the 'proud man' of the new age might even contemplate the creation by sheer willpower of another human being whose relationship to the self-appointed creator would be similar to that of man to God. Quite appropriately the account of such an experiment, recorded in the short story *The Meek One*, was inserted by Dostoevsky among his reflections on suicide, because in the case in point the meek creature, 'born', as it were, by the embodiment of an 'original idea', was foredoomed to throw away her artificial existence. (Cf. *Diary*, 1876, November.)

It may be pertinent to ask in conclusion whether Dostoevsky's metaphysical resources were sufficient to balance his sinister diagnosis of the time's diseases by a reasonable hope for recovery in the future. For that much is certain: his thinking, as his art, were inspired by the same painful anxiety not to miss the point at which the decline of Christian civilization might be brought to a halt and its downward movement reversed towards a new uplift. It seems, however, that the only remedial asset at his disposal was his reliance on the efficacy of the 'Russian idea'. This, as expounded with ardent enthusiasm by Dostoevsky in his Pushkin speech, was the genuinely Christian endeavour of the Russian people to bring about a 'universal reconciliation of ideas', i.e. the harmonization of all the great ideas which left their mark in world history, combined with the people's unconditional trust, that the Russian idea, as the very essence of the Christian faith was predestined to conquer the whole of humanity. (Cf. *Diary*, 1880, August, Chap. 1–2 II.)

Has Russia given the lie to the prophetic message of Dostoevsky's philosophy? Has the subsequent course of Russian and universal history exposed his thinking as illusory and deceptive? Dostoevsky himself might have countered these and similar sardonic questions by reiterating what he wrote in his own name nearly a hundred years ago: 'In the end the triumph belongs not to material forces, frightful and unshakeable as they may seem, not to wealth, not to the sword, not to power, but to some at first unnoticeable thought often deriving from the apparently humblest of men' (*A Writer's Diary*, 1876, December, Chap. I, III).

These are proud words, indeed, but they derive from one whose humbleness was as genuine as his faith.

3. A Reply to L. P. Karsavin

Dear Lev Platonovich,

I gratefully accept your suggestion to reply to those views which you expressed in your article "Russia and the Jews"; please convey to the editors of *Versty* my deepest appreciation for their kindness. Reading the manuscript of your article, I automatically recalled our conversations on the same subject, and my doubts and objections naturally assumed the form of a personal reply addressed to you. I should like to maintain this form in my answer even though it is to be published. You know that I can approach the question which you raise only from the opposite side; in such cases a meeting is possible only when people look at one another eye to eye.

It seems to me that the greatest merit of your article lies in the fact that you pose the question of Russia's relationship to the Jews as a religious question, I would say as a question of religious toleration. For me, as a Jew, this formulation of the question seems not only the most fruitful, but also the most natural. The so-called "national intolerance" towards the Jews is, in my deepest conviction, in the last analysis only a degenerate, deteriorated, decayed form of religious intolerance; thus it can be overcome only on the basis of intensely active toleration of other alien faiths, with full cognizance of their essential difference and their ineradicable originality. The faith of the Jewish people appears to you to be just such an alien faith; therefore, as a Russian and a Christian, you try to discover, along the path of loving understanding, the best religiously-justified means of establishing the Jews in Russia. All possible assistance to Jewish independence for the aspired union with the people of Israel in the bosom of the orthodox and oecumenical churches—that is the final, ultimate solution which prompts all your partial and provisional solutions.

Allow me to reply to these partial and transitory solutions afterwards. Here I shall only note that I observe in them your fundamental aspiration to follow exclusively the priniciple of toleration. How else could one explain the logically consistent differentiation between the kernel and the husk—*sit venia verbo*—of Israel? The dividing sword, or as one used to say

This text was first published in Russia in *Versti*, Paris, 1928, No. 3.

not long ago, the surgical knife of analysis, is, in your hands, merely a means of saving or securing the kernel, even at the price of casting off the "peel". (Thus in private relationships we sometimes condemn isolated acts in order to affirm the indissoluble essence of a man with even greater force.) However, it seems to me that the fact that you operate with the logical tool of differentiation indicates a certain defect in the very definition of the ultimate goal of Russian-Jewish relations, a certain schematism in your primary synthesis. Therefore I shall start where you end.

Did the priest who baptized the old Jew in Leskov's story act correctly? I think not. It seems to me that the old man who attempted to preserve his son's freedom by buying the freedom of another man was even less "deserving" of baptism than the fraud who played such a spiteful trick on his paternal feelings. And was it to Christ that he was converted? More likely it was only to the Christians. However, you are against such particular solutions of the Jewish question, and in any case, you are against those Jews who, after they have been converted to Christ, are then filled with loathing for Judaism. And how could it be otherwise? According to the apostle Paul you set great hopes on the inevitable salvation of "all" Israel; these hopes are the dynamic force of your active, practical religious toleration: it is at this point that the whole circle of historical and eschatological questions related to the Jews closes. But, as you know, it is precisely here that the fundamental point of our disagreement lies. How can I speak about the parts, without saying anything about the whole?

I shall state the main point directly: not only do I not believe in the conversion of Israel, but I also consider that a Christian who believes in such a conversion thereby displays a certain imperfection in his own belief in God. Forgive me, Lev Platonovich, for having expressed my idea so harshly. But I really cannot conceive of Israel's conversion to Christ in any other way except as a defection from God the Father, or as a betrayal of Him; how can a Christian desire such a betrayal, such treachery? Have you ever heard of a Jew who had never doubted, and whose faith was impregnable, and was nonetheless converted to Christianity? (I am referring to "our" own age, i.e., that age which, from the Christian point of view, lies "between" the two Comings.) Consequently, in order to be converted to Christ, a Jew would first of all have to lose his faith in God; in order that all Israel be saved, all Israel would first have to perish. There remains, as it were, only one last possibility: "Christ", to whom Israel will convert, would be recognized by the Jews as their longed-for "Anointed One", whose Jewish name is the Messiah. But at the time of what you call the Second Coming, and what we call the First Coming, will there really be any place for different faiths, for several churches, for the "Jewish question"? Verily: "They shall no longer instruct each other, 'Acknowledge the Lord', for everyone will know Me, from the small to the great," saith the Lord; "For I will forgive their iniquity and will remember their sin no more." (Jeremiah, 31:34)

What should a Christian do once he has realized that for Jews the path to the font inevitably leads through mortal sin; or if animated by a "compassionate" love towards Israel and by a desire to get along with Israel here and now and in all circumstances on a religious basis. Such a Christian would necessarily reach the conclusion that the Jewish religion is guilty of a paradox in its own position, that the vice of contradiction is contained within it: a most intense quest for the true God of the living, together with absolute negation. This is the view of the essence of Judaism which you, Lev Platonovich, are defending—a view which I consider completely false.

You transform the Christian dialectic and your own toleration of the Jews into an internal dialectic of the Jewish revelation of God. I understand the difficulty of your position; must I repeat that I deeply respect each of the grounds which you cite in support? But the fact remains: it is easier for the Jew to relate lovingly to the Christian, than for the Christian so to relate to the Jew. (It does not follow that this is always the case.) The Jews only have knowledge of the Christians' empirical sins and transgressions. Christians are compelled to blame the Jews, the people "wedded" to God and obsessed by Him, for deicide and for apostasy. You consider that the rejection of "Godmanhood" alone inevitably involves "dualism", i.e., the expulsion of God from the world, a breach between man and his Creator; you say that the "abundant, but terrible proximity between man and God which Orthodoxy professes to be the foundation of knowledge, life and being"—is inadmissable for the Jews; along with an endless chain of Roman Catholic missionaries you add that "the Psalms and Prophets became unintelligible for the Jewish soul". No. Lev Platonovich, forgive me, but here you are mistaken. Your "love for your enemy" has gone too far; you are attempting to rob the Jews simultaneously of their God and their Scriptures. Your second point is as impossible as your first. Jeremiah, in his chapter on the false prophets of Israel, writes: "The Lord saith, 'Am I really only God when I am nearby, and not when I am far off? Can a man really conceal himself so that I cannot see him,' saith the Lord; 'for heaven and earth are filled with Me,' saith the Lord." (Jeremiah, 23:23-4). Lev Platonovich, if our prophets really are no longer intelligible to us, please explain the "nearness" and the "fullness" which are mentioned in this passage. We Jews have always thought about the "abundant" and the "terrible", about the "foundation of knowledge, life and being." No, Lev Platonovich, we are neither atheists nor agnostics; many of our school-children know the Bible by heart and cherish it. If Christianity can be reconciled with Judaism only on the basis of such expropriations, then let us settle it the old-fashioned way . . .

I have become agitated. This is both bad and good. It is bad because it hinders the coherent development of my argument, and I still have a great deal on my mind which I want to state intelligibly. But it is good because my reaction to your words is completely natural; it would be very sad if we all became completely indifferent to our sacred things. In addition, although I am writing directly to you, our words will be read by many Russian Christians and Jews, and it is necessary that we finally learn to take seriously all conversations not only those about "anti-Semitism" and "equal rights", but also those about the essence of Judaism and Orthodoxy. Although I have passionately objected to your views, I have not forgotten even for a moment that your attitude towards the Jews is by no means exhausted by the statements quoted from your article. I should like only to emphasize that the Jewish question, as a religious question, is fraught with great difficulties and dangers, and that we must expend considerably greater efforts in order to find a common language.

Only by pointing out these internal difficulties inherent in the very problem of Christian tolerance for the Jews can I explain the fact that, with your undoubtedly prejudiced and unfounded view of Judaism as a religion, you are able to appreciate Judaism as a culture so highly. For Jewish culture is entirely religious and, consequently, it is completely permeated with that "passionate enthusiasm of its faith", that "dualism", which in your own words, makes it the "most powerful and most terrible enemy of Christianity". Nevertheless, you wish to preserve the Jewish people, and therefore, its culture, as a special "Orthodox Jewish church"? I do not understand this at all. On the other hand, if all Russian Jews became Orthodox Christians, how would the Jewish church in Russia differ from the Russian Orthodox church? Would the language of the divine service be the crucial point? Obviously, the Orthodox Russian Jew would still remain invariably Jewish in his age-old culture; he would remain a "theomachist", as the ancient God made him when He chose the Jews and set them apart. Thus it seems to me that your faith leads you to two mutually exclusive alternatives. Or will you dispute the fact that Jewish culture and the Jewish religion are identical? This would be all the more difficult, since in those Jews who have fallen away from the "kernel" you see an aspect of the same religious element of Judaism, albeit distorted. But I should like to consider this point in greater detail.

I have already mentioned in passing that the opposite side of your synthesis can be seen in your analysis. Now I can explain what I mean by this. It seems to me that true religious toleration, like toleration in general, rests on an absolute affirmation and acceptance of the existence of a "substance" essentially different from one's own, and therefore, of its "accidents", in as much as the substantial kernel is active in them. In your acceptance of the kernel of Jewish culture and the heart of the Jewish people, you provide an excellent example of such a comprehensive, purely Russian freedom of attitude; but your rejection of the Jewish religion forces you later to wipe out all the positive results of the preceding analysis: the kernel itself turns out to be harmful, and it suddenly becomes clear why for you the shell of the Jewish people is all the more worthless, the more one sees its former attachment to the kernel. Thus the kernel must inevitably be discarded along with the husk. In other words, in your attitude to the Jews there is a certain unavoidable duality which results, as far as I can deduce, from your belief in the inevitability of an anti-Judaist attitude in Christianity. Otherwise, even in the "periphery" of Judaism, you would not have been able to see only a negative aspect of contemporary culture. It is true that you are willing to grant concessions to individual "assimilated" Jews, but you ruthlessly reject the idea of assimilation in general. If you were a believing Jew with a sense of national identity, instead of an Orthodox Christian, then this would be more understandable. It seems that each of us could compose a very detailed indictment of our apostates, all the more so since the accusers themselves, in all probability, would find themselves on the bench of the accused. But I for one could not refrain from noting in passing a whole series of circumstances which partially counterbalance the guilt. Wherever I could acknowledge the action of the true religious spirit of the Jews, I would consider it necessary to defend those who verbally reject this spirit, but whose actions bear witness to it. You are doing just the opposite. To pause on one detail: Europeanized Jewry is clearly involved in the development of the contemporary workers' movement; does this speak against it? Quite the contrary: it speaks not against it, but for it; the dream of a just organization of man's social life is the age-old ideal of Jewish culture; if a Jew who has fallen away from the Jewish kernel, really is entirely inspired by the idea of serving the workers, then he is really not so bad; sometimes he is even very good. In general, Jewish assimilation and its relationship to the hard, indissoluble kernel of Judaism is not adequately covered by the analogy of kernel and shell. I would prefer, in this connection, to speak of the radioactive substance of Jewry, of its radiating energy, of its constant disintegration— all as integral parts of its indissoluble essence. Jewish assimilation is as old as the organized existence of Jews as a nation. May I remind you that for those of us who consider ourselves somehow connected to this kernel, the apostle Paul is a typical representative of assimilated Jewry. We are used to thinking that all of the major occurrences in Jewish history cannot be totally devoid of meaning; consequently, assimilation must also have some purpose. In this plane of universal Fate, we can see the reflection of that bend in our historical path which led us to Russia.

I have spoken at some length of my inevitable disagreements with you, allow me now to express myself, though briefly, on those points which I am in complete agreement with you.

Yes, Russian Jewry represents a certain organic unity, although it belongs simultaneously to two different comprehensive "wholes": to the universal Jewish community and to Russia. Russian Jews have problems with respect to world Jewry, and problems with respect to Russia. Moreover, in as much as we can judge, historical fates take shape so auspiciously that the duality of our problems does not give rise to any internal conflicts for the Russian Jews, because in serving Russia, we are at the same time able to serve our Jewish calling. Our mission is revealed to us by our Prophets; the path which has been indicated to Russia by her prophets and pioneers, is leading in the same direction. Russia holds a course towards the unfading light from the Orient: we are going in the same direction.

Let us not argue about whether Russian Jews are Russians or Jews. I think, Lev Platonovich, that your Jewish friend who objected to being called a Russian was not objecting out of "tactfulness" or out of "national pride", but solely because he wished to be truthful. In Russia and among Russians, of course, we are not Russian; but outside of Russia, even among foreign Jews, we feel how Russian we are, how free we are from any social prejudices, from any attachment to the material things of this world—how much closer we are to the true sources of religious life and to the ultimate depths of the human heart: and for all of this we are grateful to destiny for having led us to Russia, and for having given us the chance to know and to love the Russian people. Are we not really the only Asians in Europe? But our European Brothers are afraid to acknowledge this to their arrogant fellow-Europeans, whilst how easy it is for us to be ourselves in Russia.

It does not follow that life in Russia is always easy for us. I am not referring to the difficulties of the present or even those of the past; I am referring to the future. It is necessary for Russians, (those Russians about whom there is not doubt as to whether they are Russians or not), to understand once and for all that the Jews are not their "enemies", but their "allies". This is extremely difficult for many Russians to accept. Lev Platonovich, you know this as well as I do. Not by chance do you turn, with what seems to be a half-turn, to those people in Russia who consider us a "thorn". That is why I take the liberty of considering your article as a first step on a long and tortuous path.

4. Brotherhood

(Heresies aloud!)

"Alle Menschen werden Brüder"
Ninth Symphony

Schiller's simple words which were embodied in Beethoven's harmonies resound once again in the rhythm of revolutionary events: "All men are brothers." Anyone who has a sensitive ear and a heart attuned to contemporary events cannot keep from hearing these words, from feeling their significance. But deafening "external noises" do not fade away even for a moment. "Be silent, hide yourself, and conceal your feelings and your dreams!" (Tutchef). Thus do we tell ourselves, and thus do frantic decrees, laws, and constitutions enjoin us. Men are not brothers at all: they are not children of one father, not conceived of one flesh. There is black and white, wolves and lambs, friends and enemies. The sons of man are the sons of Adam, Cain and Abel, victim and executioner; only fratricide brings them together. Nearly everyone agrees with this—those engaged in social activities and those in theoretical historical creativity, for whom only the thought that is spoken (in cause and effect) is not a falsehood. And our age is, as always, an epoch of class struggle.

Marxism is right. It seems to be incontestable, like a strict generalization based on the experience of contemporary European life. Indeed, who will not see that everything which lives and fights, both in the traditional sphere and in that of the revolutionary history of the last half-century, is almost a continuous struggle of economic interests. As to those who take no interest in economics or in material organization as such, and for whom there is not, and cannot ever be, any truth in "facts" or events, in so far as they are in the field of historical experience (because truth and justice are to them not facts or given phenomena, but rather lofty ideas and unconditional criteria)—all of them in our age are taken to be "romantic dreamers—far away from life", "degenerates of scholastic philosophizing", and sometimes "superstitious renegades", harmless individuals when in their own isolated chambers, studies or cells, but dangerous promoters of

This essay was first published in Russian in *Znamya*, Moscow, March 1922, No. 11/13.

disintegrating infections, when they try to emerge from their involuntary solitude and enter the broad social and historical scene. Intellectual theoreticians have no place where economic ideas are seething.

So we are told and so we tell ourselves; the straining chorus of our own voices and those of others, all singing in unison, tries to stifle the as yet hardly perceptible music of the conscience of affairs, of the meaning of events. And in the meanwhile events irresistably move forward at their own steady pace; the waves spread wider and wider; people with their long lists of tasks, programmes, and forecasts mercilessly vanish from the customary shores; already new words, previously so concealed and inexpressible, are born in the foaming surf, in the obedient rhythm of the tides: "All men are brothers".

Really?—Is this only a dream? Only one's personal feelings? Is history in fact only "we", "us", our plans and our predictions?

"We" are merely the fragments of past shipwrecks cast ashore; the most valuable pearls of our words and our ideas are but the fossilized life of oceanic primordial elements; and when we put our sensitive ear to the twisting labyrinths of the scattered shells of culture, is it not the boom of earlier storms which echoes in their mournful monotony?

"War is the mother of everything; sovereign of all"; thus taught the ancient Heraclitus, called the Dark One. The darkness of Heraclitus is the light of our eyes: we acquired the revelations of the first half of human history as a gift. In the logic of Heraclitus' inextinguishably burning formulation, Hegel was merely a follower and Marx only a pupil. The truth regarding the class struggle is tarnished, fossilized knowledge, mutely and inarticulately echoing the original chaos of universal strife, of the *bellum omnium contra omnes*. In this truth there is only the experience of formal generalization, based on observation of European man during half of the last century. During this period, in a more profound sense, men were no longer struggling; instead they acted out the comedy of struggle which was called variously the struggle for national unification, for national independence, for economic expansion, for economic class interest. It would be worth making the following question a subject of particular consideration: Was the so-called class struggle in its internal essence, its modes of manifestation, decisively different from the struggle between nations and state-governments? Perhaps this would demonstrate that the ultimate originality of Marx is merely this: that Marx thought to draw the psychological distinctions within humanity, which had previously been drawn according to racial and national characteristics, in a direction perpendicular to that historically adopted according to occupation and profession and the related material condition. In other words, the Communist Manifesto was a manifesto about the "constitution" of the classes as nations; human interaction on the basis of economic relations was proclaimed as historically more relevant than international relations; a transverse section of the integral organism of humanity made according to the difference of class psychology was supposed to erase all the distinct traces of the longitudinal section, made according to the generalizations of national-racial psychology.

But the events of the last years have clearly rejected this crude defection from the Hegelian dialectic: classes did not replace nations, but added an additional complication to the development. The internal division of nations into classes merely created a new manifestation of that phenomenon which in sociology is called the "intersection" of social groups. Together with this, however, a new content was also created for the new form of social interrelationships: the opposition of classes within a nation which sharply divides them distributed their components among new universal subdivisions. Marx was the creator not only of the international solidarity of workers, but also of the international bourgeoisie. Hence, the international class struggle in a new, though already tarnished aspect, resurrected the age-old struggle of races and peoples: war, with all its scheming, tactics, and strategy, with all its morality and amorality, with everything which results from the concept of war for the combatants and for the neutrals,—all of this found its full application in the newly perceived class struggle, invented, allegedly, to replace the struggle of races and governments.

Moreover, for the socialists who declared that this war was the last war, a war for eternal national and international peace, this simple use of the age-old forms of war, not even imposed by the hostile side, should in itself have presented a complicated problem. Class war, as the antithesis of all preceding wars, was supposed to differ both in form and content from its predecessors. However, its form remained identical; nor did it change in its content. This is the "heresy" which it is now time to formulate, because history itself is loudly proclaiming it already.

One must distinguish sharply between genuine war as our "maternal" overlord, "the mother and sovereign of all", and war as a farce, a spurious war or pseudo-war.

During the post-revolutionary period European man has not known any "true wars" (in Fichte's phrase). "True war" is spiritual and a conflict of ideas. Not that this type of war was not also waged in the materialist plane of iron and fire. Rather, the fire was at the same time that fiery Logos, about which Heraclitus taught some 2500 years ago; and the iron was the malleable armour of new moral and cultural achievements; in the confrontation of arms, conflicting ideas also confronted one another, and new life for a revived humanity was conceived in this "fateful duel". That is why true wars were not fought over the ownership of the object of the struggle, but total wars for the annihilation of the hostile idea.

Yet class struggle in Europe during the nineteenth century was a struggle for ownership of the means of production. The means of production, as the object of the argument, remain outside that contention; both sides are agreed that the essence of their aims lies in this supreme good. But when the supreme value for the two opposing sides is not in question, and the whole conflict concerns merely possession, then the struggle itself must necessarily be mute and beneath logic; strictly speaking, it is not a struggle of ideas, thoughts, or human values, but a conflict of elements— blind natural forces.

Now, with what category of historical phenomena do we associate the Russian revolution?—At this point we have reached the very centre of the philosophy of history of the last decades.

If capitalist development in Russia at the end of the nineteenth century forced Russian populism to resign itself spiritually to foreign Marxism, then the revolutionary dawn of the twentieth century, principally the history of the last years, must arouse Russian socialism with new vigour to clear self-consciousness.

It is not true that "scientific" socialism was invented to replace "utopian" socialism; nor is it true that the history of socialism is identical with the history of the class struggle of the proletariat; nor is it true that the events of the Russian revolution are merely one chapter in the "European workers' movement of the first half of the twentieth century".

On the contrary, the scope of Russian Marxism is merely one offshoot of that particular socialism which is rooted in genuine Russian black earth; the table of sociological "Latin" terms attached to it should not deceive us as to its nature. This Russian socialist movement only partially coincides with what can be called the class struggle; finally, this socialism, if it is not so evident in its theory, is, in its practice, undoubtedly thoroughly "utopian"—i.e., everything depends on the meaning of the words "science" and "utopia".

Earlier, when the "heresy" concerning the equivalence of the class struggle and intergovernmental wars was touched upon, the doubt was bound to arise: is not the entire socialist "heresy" merely another device of the purely bourgeois polemic against socialism? The very identification of the class struggle of the proletariat with the struggle of leviathan-governments for material spoils,—does this not suggest primarily the outright negation of the very basis of socialism, of the socialist belief that socialist society must necessarily be collectivized humanity, no longer subdivided into classes? And, therefore, whatever the apparent form and content of this war of the proletariat against its class enemies, in essence its true form is its unique place in the series of human wars; its mission to be the last war against the very principle of human internecine strife. Its content, consequently, is not the conquest of the means of production, but the establishment of an order under which the creative work of mankind will not depend on the fact of the distribution of the material means of production. The proletariat struggles with the bourgeoisie not in order to gain ownership of the means of production, but rather to emancipate mankind from the dominance of the "means of production", the "means of life", in general, any "means" over purely human ends, embodied in class society, in particular in capitalist society, with its customary way to trade in things and people.

How can one object to such a "utopian" objection? One cannot—nor is it necessary to contest it. What is necessary is to provoke the objection in every way possible, to emphasize it, and to draw out all of the conclusions it implies. Socialist theory of the class struggle has more profound, idealistic "utopian" premises which are manifested not in the superficial, pseudo-scientific foundations of the theory itself, but in its actual practice; and this practice, not only be means of its theoretical concepts, carries the erroneously conceived doctrine ad absurdum; and in as far as it is based on the experience of its concrete application, it also exposes its original roots and its spurious arguments which do not stand up to the critical pressures of life.

Here, in the realm of practical action, is the watershed between spiritually strained currents of European socialism and the boundless floods of the overflowing Russian waters. The practice of European Marxism revealed the "practicality", in the European sense, of its "scientific" theories: this is the science which makes plausible only the pseudo-confrontation of two camps and not the real opposition of fundamental principles. Between the contestants there is full agreement as to the aims and means of the struggle and the substance of its real object: the contested object is economic power; above all, economic prosperity appears to be an absolute goal in itself. How can socialists encroach on the integrity of the economic whole, if this "whole" is the sole foundation of both doctrine and life? Western socialists are not only sponsors of compromise, but are in total agreement with the other side, and their struggle is merely a game in which the preservation of the stake itself, even though it is in the hands of their opponents, is more important than the resulting gain, so long as the game called European life keeps on going. Western socialists are not utopian, but realistic scientific politicians whose science does not divide them from the bourgeoisie, but rather unites them closely together in the unity of one "scientific", relativistic, utilitarian, materialistic world-view.

Not so in Russia. Here we plunge at once into the realm of "utopia". Dostoevsky was right a thousand times over when he pointed out that "in Russia words mean nothing". Let "our young people frequently worship the most simple-sounding paradox and let them sacrifice everything on earth to it—their fate, their life—but this is only because to them the paradox is the truth." The "quest for sacrifice and for heroic deeds"—"this is the best" (*Diary of a Writer*, February 1876). This indeed is the best and highest in Russian socialism. As opposed to Western socialism, Russian socialism was always inspired not by a craving for vengeance or for glory, not by the will for power or for possession, but by the quest for sacrifice for the good of the people, and by the will to perform heroic deeds in the name of absolute truth and eternal justice. "Paradoxical" or "scientific", as words, "mean nothing", or more precisely, meant nothing. While words remained words, deeds were, in spite of the words, sacrificial deeds, and practice was self-sacrifice.

But even in most recent years, when paradoxical works revealed such a yawning abyss, to put it mildly, of "paradoxical" gestures and actions, scientific "paradoxes", as before, exposed beneath their mask the same age-old Russian socialist utopia. There was not a half-ounce of European "science", European reckoning or calculation, European balance of ends and means. It is true that very little was disguised as European "electrified" and "galvanized" concepts, but this masquerade during the revolution deserves special, more detailed consideration. For the most part Soviet rule was the rule of dictatorial Counsels (in Russian, Soviets) and of their philosophical precepts. Plato, the greatest utopian, said that either philosophers must become kings, or that kings must become philosophers. In the Russian Utopia, under the red banner, the latter alternative has been almost completely fulfilled. They have philosophized with words and, in the phrase of Nietzsche, with the hammer as well as with the deadly scythe.

What should all this signify? Customary "class struggle"? A chapter out of the story of the European proletariat, urban and rural taken together? A struggle for the ownership of the means of production? Will Russia echo the tongues and dialects of the German and Roman worlds, or will she proclaim loudly, in her own voice, her New Word, conceived in torment and blood?

If until now Russia, steeped in blood and only just alive, was not able to give a full answer, nevertheless this answer is clearly sounded in the thunderous chorus of the global uproar: "All men are brothers."

The Russian revolution resulted in the hitherto unknown upheaval in the whole established system of equilibria: of intercontinental, interracial, international, intercommunal, interprofessional, interoccupational, even within the family—and that all over the globe. From the equator to the poles, from the first meridian to the last; but the harmonious hymn of the joy of brotherhood, of Man's longing for emancipation, already resounds on earth. The hitherto unprecedented universal catastrophe engulfed the sober concepts of the necessary and the possible. Side by side with evil, good has become a ponderable reality, and the consensus as to their most dangerous divide can already be sensed. "There is no power, if not the devil's"—this is the fruit which has once again ripened for mankind on the tree of knowledge of good and evil in the infernal "paradise" of history.

Are all men indeed brothers? The twilight of fathers and of all patriarchal hierarchy in social and cultural life is approaching. The equivalence of human personalities is no longer conceived of as merely formal, along Kantian lines. Everything hitherto existing in the universal history of culture is being rearranged into one advancing front line of humanity. There is no poor or rich, no Mongol or Aryan, no man or woman—not because all distinctions have been erased, and all faces, all personalities have not fused into one impersonal mass—for the "Hellenes" and the "Barbarians" must learn from and teach each other. The whiteness of light contains seven different colours.

The ancient teaching about war as everyone's struggle against everyone else is under attack by the new teaching of everyone's love for everyone else which is new not in its logical meaning, but in its real historical significance. Socialism means collectivity. Universal collectivity without a priesthood, without ecclesiastical statehood, without a patriarch-father-superior—that is the free community of associated brothers.

Even those socialists for whom "utopia" is an ideological "reserve", secreted well in the rear—cannot completely forget this freedom, and be it in the heat of battle. But this "reserve" must be brought into action at the very start of the decisive battle, and the long history of the Russian revolution clearly demonstrates the superhuman force contained in the words: "Man! My brother!"

When, in one of his letters, Innokentii Sibiryakov, a contemporary heroic fighter, urges victorious socialism not to "take revenge", he concludes with the exclamation: "Love! Equality! Brotherhood!" "The power of the working people" in his vision is a self-denying power, overpowering the very principle of suppression by violence. The hammer, beating the sword into a ploughshare, is the hammer which is fraternally linked not to the scythe of death, but to the sickle of the sower and the reaper.

Is it to say then that socialism cannot be revolutionary? Does this mean that its only choice is between reformism or total passivity? Not at all! Even from the point of view of the materialist concept of history no one ever denied that there were wars and revolutions before the rise of the theory of class struggle. Marxism pursues merely the exposure of earlier allegedly ideological battles as purely economic confrontations, and it accuses history of the incessant falsification of its own evidence. But are these distortions of events nothing else than self-distortion and not simply their automatic reflection projected on to a disfiguring surface?

The concept of revolution is not identical with the concept of class struggle, and consequently, the concept of a socialist revolution does not necessarily coincide with the concept of the struggle between the industrial proletariat and the class of capitalists. Thus, the revolutionary-socialist party is not necessarily the party which represents the interests of the working class. This is the "heresy" which results from the very rejection of the Marxist philosophy of history and the proclamation of Brotherhood as the guiding idea of the new age.

But if this is the case, what then is the socialist revolution and what the social-revolutionary party? It would be more correct to formulate the second question with greater precision: not what is, but what should the social-revolutionary party be and should it be a "party" at all, i.e., a part, a fraction and a fragment? Should the social-revolutionary organization conceive of its own integrity as a derivative part of that social-psychological whole to which it subordinates itself, and which is defined as contemporary political life? Is this not too great a submission by the prophets of the future before the present which is doomed to destruction?

However, it would be possible to answer all of these questions only if the problem of the socialist revolution were not so paradoxically and inextricably tangled—as occurred at the very moment of its completely unexpected manifestation in Russia.

The socialist revolution differs from all other upheavals and revolutions in human history primarily for the fact that it is a universal revolution; for the first time it involves the participation of all humanity in a single burst of enthusiasm for construction. That is why even within the boundaries of one state or one nation it is necessarily a mass movement, a supernational event. The socialist revolution is the baptism with fire for everyone without exception, and through it for all those deeper levels of the population which, even though living in a civilized environment, have remained by the will of fate outside the realm of higher culture, "cultural savages" (to use Lavrov's term in a wider sense); these strata, too, are bound to partake of the sacraments of historical life. Physical labour is by no means less worthy than intellectual work. Russian populism has for generations fought against such a reversed proletarian aristocratism. But for the first time the manual labourer and the intellectual worker recognize each other as brothers; they no longer harbour jealousy for each other's historical fate which equally accepts the sacrificial bonfires of vital economic efforts and the not less vital, though non-material thought. The true aim of the socialist revolution is not the abolition of private property, but the eradication in man of the possessive instinct, which is often stronger among the "have-nots" than among the "haves", and which is much stronger in the production of non-material goods than in the production of physical goods. Property is a crime ("vol" according to Prudhon) because in expanding one's property by violating its borders, man robs his inviolable domain; he transforms his internal self into an external possessive "mine". The first principle of the socialist code is: Know how to be oneself. The true self is freed from the burdens of its manifestations, from everything which could be conceived as property. The true self is therefore not divided by any partitions from other selves; free from the rights of property, it creates on the basis of its "I" the collective "we"; it gives birth to that equality of the incomparable, where each is the first and the last among equals. The socialist revolution is a "plot of equals" where all men are each other's brothers because every man is son and father to all.

Does this mean that the socialist revolution has no enemies to fight against, that it is meant to mobilize the Salvation Army of humanity with military orchestras, but without any armaments? Can the walls of capitalist Babylon crumble, as did the walls of Jericho at the sound of trumpets which encourage the Biblical Argonauts to penetrate the heart of the promised land?

Yes and no. Of course, in the last analysis only music, according to the ancient myth, could both erect and destroy walls. Yet, when weapons resound, the muses do not fall silent; they merely evoke sounds from new instruments. Still, the socialist revolution can really have no other enemies besides the very principles of enmity and hatred. With these enemies the struggle is one of life and death. The Russian revolution knows a considerable number of tried and tested teachers and founders of such a struggle with its real enemies: suffice to recall the name of Ivan Kalyaev, the hero of 1905. But the enemies, wherever they face us, are the same: be it in front of the bulwarks of the Bastille, or in the class ideology of the bourgeoisie, or in the caste isolation of the intelligentsia, and even among the champions of the socialist revolution. The most dangerous enemy, of course, is the internal enemy, the worm in the maturing fruit of the new revelation.

That is why the idea of universal brotherhood must first find its purest incarnation in a certain concrete brotherhood, as a bearer of this idea in all its clarity and tangible consciousness. The social-revolutionary "party" should have been precisely that sort of brotherhood. Is a party a union or a brotherhood? That is the question which urgently demands an answer.

5. Bolshevism's "Weltanschauung"

1. The Problem

Bolshevism is perhaps best described as an intellectual movement of our age set apart from all others by the mode and intensity of its response to its environment, i.e. to the existing historical world. To a degree unique among contemporary movements, the response of Bolshevism is intrinsically and fundamentally practical, determined to shape reality, both in the negative destructive, and in the positive constructive senses. This interpretation tallies with the picture of Bolshevism seen in the mirror of its self-interpretation: it presents itself primarily as a programme, a challenge, an action profoundly recasting world history. It likes to call itself "revolutionary" Marxism, so as to draw a clear dividing line between itself and all the other movements and tendencies which derive their inspiration from Marx's philosophy of history and society without, however, trying to apply insight as a lever of revolutionary action and use theory as the springboard of practice. What matters to Bolshevism above all is, therefore, not to "have" a theory but to "handle" it as a tool. The idea is not to draw conclusions from premises, but to consummate knowledge through conclusive action.

This entails very important consequences for any valid exposition of the "Weltanschauung" of Bolshevism, its way of viewing and interpreting the world. For if we are to lay bare the spiritual kernel of Bolshevism by a process of dispassionate analysis, if we are to perceive its intellectual dynamic, its root idea, we must clearly understand from the start that what is needed here is not so much an attempt to rehash the more or less compelling thoughts of this or that party "theoretician", as an effort to grasp the inner structure of a world in which thoughts have become facts of history, and concrete historical facts, in turn, vital germs of constructive thinking. Indeed, the interaction between being and thinking is so integral an aspect of Bolshevism, viewed as a phenomenon of cultural history, that strictly speaking we ought to avoid altogether referring to Bolshevism's "world view", except metaphorically. The Bolshevik world leaves no room

This essay was first published in German in *Symposium: Der Staat, das Recht und die Wirtschaft des Bolschewismus*, Berlin, 1925.

for a pure perception of that world by "viewing" or visualizing it, anymore than for a pure, objective cognition supposed to depict reality faithfully without falsifying it. According to Bolshevism, the world cannot possibly be "cognized", but it can be "grasped", and here the term "to grasp" implies to grip, to hold, to master. If, then, we are to do full justice to the Bolshevik conception of a "Weltanschauung", we have to tap sources that will rise far beyond the limits of purely literary works and creations. What we have to examine in the first place, therefore, is not the output of Bolshevik authors and orators, but the handiwork of Bolshevism as a whole: Soviet Russia itself. And seen against the background of Soviet Russia, the purely intellectual product of Bolshevism must be recognized as no more than a part—albeit a vital part—of the whole. "By their fruits ye shall know them"—that is the principle which must be applied as the primary criterion in judging the world view of Bolshevism.

This point leads on to a further point of major significance for determining the concept of Bolshevism: Bolshevism as an intellectual entity must be ranked among those great categories of cultural history which have stamped their unifying seal on entire ages, microcosms of history. What distinguishes Bolshevism from entities such as the Middle Ages, the Reformation, the Enlightenment is its short span of life; yet that deficiency is amply made up for by the conscious urge to be "epoch"-making, by a clear awareness of measuring up to the task of opening a new chapter in the history of human culture. It is on these grounds that we may legitimately discuss Bolshevism in terms of a great religious movement. Before the advent of Bolshevism only the founders of religions were possessed by a similarly all-embracing ambition to improve "the world".

Here the question arises: does all this not apply to modern socialism in general? Have we not singled out Bolshevism as the sole exponent of what is in fact a far wider movement of which it represents but a section? This question is all the more crucial in our context as it gives rise at once to another question: is it possible in principle to expound the ideology of Bolshevism independently of its historical development?

Here the following points have to be considered: as an organic fact of history "proletarian" Bolshevism was neither born "sine matre" nor is its father unknown: it was begotten by Western socialism and the native Russian revolution with its own century-old history, so that the family tree could readily be traced farther back. Nonetheless, in its basic features, the baneful offspring does not bear too close a resemblance to either of its parents. The event that transformed Bolshevism overnight into a novel and independent phenomenon was the conquest of power in October 1917. Only by creating the basis on which it could take broad and effective action designed to mould reality was Bolshevism able to become true to its very concept. For it was only then that Bolshevism began to be what it had meant to be from the outset. Whereas in the past it had merely been capable of making converts, it had now reached the point of becoming truly epoch-making. At the same time the formerly latent ideological world view became manifest, beginning to grasp the world, and the programme sprang into life. Since then it had become a meaningful task to study specifically the world view of Bolshevism, to follow and interpret it step by step.

In pursuing this investigation we may disregard all the internal transformations and regroupings as well as the manifold tensions and cross-currents within the Bolshevik movement. Not that such antagonistic tendencies and cross-currents were unimportant in themselves. But what matters here in the first place is to expose the innermost homogeneous core which generated the whole development and made it possible, with all its complications and internal conflicts. And that hard core, that root idea of Bolshevism has so far come intact and unchanged through all vicissitudes. Had it been otherwise, there would be no more sense in speaking of the world view of Bolshevism than in exploring the world view of any other social entity that appears fleetingly like a speck of foam on the beach which, washed ashore by one wave, is sucked back by the next without leaving a trace.

2. The Subject

Our very first attempt to approach our problem has led us to the conclusion that Bolshevism as an ideological world view is manifested in a peculiar, indeed in some respects unique, marriage of concept and reality, of theory and practice. This aspect has perhaps been expressed most succinctly by Trotsky who in an essay on the occasion of Lenin's fiftieth birthday called attention to the antithesis between the figure of his fellow-fighter and rival and that of Marx. Trotsky wrote: "The whole of Marx is present in the 'Communist Manifesto', in the Preface of his 'Critique', in 'Das Kapital'. Even if fate had not allowed him to become the founder of the First International, he would still have been, and remained for all times, the same man, precisely as we see him standing before us today. Lenin, by contrast, lives entirely in the revolutionary deed. His scientific publications are but preparation for action. Even if he had not published a single book up to now, he would yet live on in history as he has entered it: as the leader of the proletarian revolution, the creator of the Third International" ('Pravda', 23rd April 1920). In this sense Lenin can indeed be considered the outstanding representative, the living incarnation of the Bolshevik world view.

Such generalities, of course, however revealing, can do no more than provide an abstract frame for a starkly concrete content. It is that content which we have to uncover here in all its details, as far as space will permit.

The "active attitude" so characteristic of the Bolshevik world view—we are using here a term applied by the modern psychology of world views (K. Jaspers, "Psychologie der Weltanschauungen", 2nd edition 1922, p. 52 ff.)—can be fully illuminated and comprehended from two angles: 1. from the angle of the subject and 2. from the angle of the object; for in the world view of Bolshevism subject and object are as closely related as two co-ordinates in a frame of reference where any attempt to follow either of the directional axes to its origin leads automatically to the point of intersection which the two intercrossing directions have in common. If for the purpose of our investigation we prefer to make our approach from the subjective angle it is only because it seems the one most apt to reveal the full depth of the gulf that separates Bolshevik "Marxism" from the world view that is commonly, and most manifestly in Germany, decried as Marxism.

Who, then, is the exponent, the subject, the originator of the Bolshevik ideological world view? The apparently trivial and at first sight orthodox-Marxist answer says: the proletariat! So far all is in order and plausible, but at the same time utterly unoriginal. Here, however, the methodological maxims must be applied which we adumbrated at the outset when we formulated our problem: never take Bolshevism at its "word". Additional support for this rule, incidentally, is provided by a consideration of the problem from the angle of a critical study of sources: as we shall see later (Section 3), Bolshevism treats the very language of the philosophy of history and social relations merely as an instrument of leadership which, moreover, is used often enough for the purpose of misleadership.

According to the word, the proletariat, and the proletariat alone, is to be the true originator, exponent and subject of the world-transforming world concept of Bolshevism. But the word is written in ineffaceable letters in the book of history, and it must be interpreted within the context of the whole.

The proletariat which is supposed to carry on its shoulders the world view of Bolshevism and at the same time, like the classical Atlas, to uphold the pillars of the whole world of Bolshevism is all too confused and many-faceted a concept. Clarification is needed in two respects. Above all Bolshevism uses the term in the widest possible meaning, as the entire Bolshevik literature makes emphatically clear: the proletariat, whose ideological world view is Bolshevism, is by no means confined to the sum total, still comparatively modest for the time being, of Bolshevik-inclined individuals working in industry. The proletariat, indeed, is the proletarian "class", the world proletariat, a collective entity that cannot be defined except from the higher point of view of the process of world history as a whole. Thus it may be said that the concept of the proletariat represents the correlate on the subjective plane of the world-transforming objective task confronting mankind in the age of capitalism. Seen in this light, the concept of the proletarian which may be used with advantage, say, in economic statistics is clearly not coextensive with the same concept as it must be interpreted in terms of the philosophy of history from the Bolshevik point of view, although the two circles intersect and have some elements in common. The latter concept, in fact, is on the one hand much wider, yet on the other hand, as we shall see presently, also much narrower in extent than the former. Bolshevism, however, tends to mix up the two concepts, and it is doing so quite deliberately for the following reasons:

Elevating the entire actual as well as potential "world proletariat" to the rank of the initiating subject of an ideological world view, Bolshevism seeks to use this very procedure as a device to win the primary object of its ambitions over to its side. Whatever else may form part of the Bolshevik objective—which will be treated at greater length in Section 3 below—it goes without saying that the overwhelming majority of the human race is comprised in it. The notion that the Bolshevik world interpretation is supposedly the "natural" world view of "productive labour" is to be dinned into the minds of the working people qua working people till the individual is brought to the point of drawing what must seem to him the inescapable conclusion: "As sure as I am a proletarian, I am a Bolshevik as well; but if I am a Bolshevik I must think the Bolshevik way, i.e. act accordingly."

How striking a contrast presents itself here between Bolshevism and all other, Marxist as well as non-Marxist, modes of politics and policies designed to promote human "interests"! What Bolshevism strives to uphold is not the immediate, empirically perceived economic (and intellectual) interests of any human group that derives its cohesion from those very interests but the unique, great and indivisible interest of contemporary humanity as a whole, which the world proletariat has been called upon and chosen to serve. Measured by the yardstick of that unique, indivisible interest—which could more aptly be termed mission or destiny—all the other concerns and desires usually covered by that term, such as higher living standards, the eight-hour working day, but also health and life itself, dwindle into insignificance. The proletariat, indeed, is something which—to use Nietzsche's well known expression—must be overcome, for the sake of the supra-proletariat, of the classless communist society, of the historical age of socialism. Thus the customary and generally most prominent phraseology of Bolshevism, referring to the proletariat as the true exponent of the Bolshevik world view, is used as a device to disguise the deeper esoteric meaning of the doctrine in which, it should be noted, the actually existing proletariat is fully recognised as a nucleus, the appointed power base, for the imminent Bolshevik world revolution. In a nutshell the contrast between the common variety of Marxism and Bolshevism can be summed up by saying that Marxism serves the interests of the proletariat, whereas Bolshevism makes the interests of the proletariat subservient to its own cause.

Bolshevism itself in these circumstances was faced with the necessity of supplementing the wide, and from the non-Bolshevik point of view grossly misleading, concept of the proletariat as the initiating subject of the Bolshevik world view by a second, narrower concept in an attempt to bridge somehow the striking contradiction between word and deed so conspicuously manifested above all in Russia, where the "proletarian dictatorship" degenerated into a "dictatorship over the proletariat". This need was met by distinguishing within the proletariat a multitude of strata shading off into each other rather than separated by clear dividing lines, and presenting a whole spectrum of degrees of intellectual maturity. Whereas the bulk of the proletariat could not be counted on except as a potential exponent of the Bolshevik idea, this process of differentiation singled out from among that bulk above all the "class-conscious" proletariat, i.e. that section which, in contrast to the "bona fide unattached", had in some form or other taken the side of Bolshevism. In that way the Party organisation itself became the "elite" of the class-conscious proletarians, or their "vanguard", and the organisation was to be headed, ex definitione, by those who had most fully mastered the practical theory of Bolshevism, i.e. the pioneers and trail-blazers, the actual originators of the Bolshevik world view. Thus Bolshevism came to be transformed into "Leninism" (although this term only gained currency after the master's death). This does not mean, of course, that Ulyanov-Lenin as a man was credited with being a living incarnation of the world-historic spirit of the proletariat, but it does mean that only those can be accepted as true exponents of Bolshevism who keep faith with the spirit of Bolshevism, whose whole being is absorbed by the doctrine and the cause, and whose individuality is no more than the empty subjective form of the supra-individual, objective task dictated by impersonal circumstance.

The true initiating subject of the Bolshevik world view is the objective sense—a sense outside and independent of human consciousness—to be attached to the historical process in its essence as manifested in the teachings of Bolshevism. The empirical human subject embracing the Bolshevik world view thereby becomes an organ of the world-historic process; he only seems to be an initiating subject of the world view: not Lenin is the originator of Leninism, but on the contrary it was Leninism that picked Vladimir Ilyich Ulyanov for the task of letting the historical facts speak for themselves. It is this objective historical constellation which matters above all.

3. The Historical Process

It may seem that such a view of the subject of the Bolshevik world view is in direct contradiction to the fundamental tendency of Bolshevism characterised in the foregoing (Section 1): How, indeed, is it possible for a world view which on principle denies the existence of cognition as a mental process orientated towards values of objective truth, to enunciate statements of the type of which we have just given some examples, in which reference is clearly made to objective sets of circumstances, such as the world, historical processes, culture, historic mission and so on? Bolshevism is by no means at a loss for an answer to this question: in its view the objectivity of the sets of circumstances on which its schemes are based is safeguarded from arbitrary subjective influence only inasmuch as it stands entirely unaffected and unimpaired by any personal, individual mind; on the other hand, that very objectivity must be seen as the reverse side of a supra-individual subjectivity once the concept of the subject as a human individual is replaced in our picture by the true exponent of the Bolshevik world view, the world proletariat.

Such a picture fully reflects the correlativity between subject and object within the Bolshevik world view, which has been stressed in particular by G. Lukács ("Geschichte und Klassenbewusstsein", Berlin 1923). This correlativity at the same time casts a revealing light on the Bolshevik interpretation of history as a whole.

The historical process as such cannot become an object of conscious contemplation except from a clearly determined, in fact from a subjectively determined point of view, for the process itself is determined by the historic force which is mirrored and manifested in it. Every age, or rather the age in which we actually live, i.e. the present, appears as a system of contending historical forces each of which considers, indeed must consider, its entire environment to be its proper field of action. Thus each of those forces, taken by itself, is a world-spanning monad, as it were, which experiences the other, coexisting monads only as barriers to be overcome because they oppose the infinite urge for expansion immanent in each. Yet this system of forces should not be regarded simply as a set of objective facts absolutely independent of all subjectivity: for it is only to the contemporary "class-conscious proletariat" that the world presents itself in that way, the proletariat whose sole raison d'être is the mission of bringing the class "struggle" to a victorious conclusion and ushering in a new age in which this "materialist" interpretation of history—which might have been more aptly named "dynamist"—will most probably cease to be valid.

Thus the objective aspect of the Bolshevik world view resolves entirely into the concept of a subjective purposiveness that can be perceived only from within, into the concept of the historic task. Put differently, the objective task is only the terminus ad quem of the "subjective" proletarian striving, in the same way as that striving itself is nothing but the force directed to the objective realisation of the end envisaged by that striving. A dialectic interrelation which immediately calls to mind Hegel and Fichte is clearly present here.

Now, we do not, of course, adopt the Bolshevik standpoint and we firmly believe that objective states of affairs can and should be viewed objectively, that they can and should be examined as to their objective logical premises. We are also well aware, it may be added, that, seen from the angle of the Bolshevik world view, such an attitude appears to be merely strikingly illustrating the mentality of a modern "section of the intelligentsia aimlessly straying between the classes". This point seems worth making because it brings the basic standpoint of Bolshevism, its collective solipsism, yet more sharply into focus. Let us now turn to the detailed implications of Bolshevism's dynamist view of history.

The concept of the historic force as an all-embracing monad has so pronounced a metaphysical, not to say mystic flavour that its use in an exposition of the Bolshevik world view is bound to arouse a suspicion that we may be guilty of an arbitrary re-interpretation or even a falsification of the facts. Is not Bolshevism by its very nature committed to an implacable struggle against any brand of "metaphysics", let alone "mysticism"? Is it not totally dedicated to its "materialism", is it not wholehearted in its predilection for the natural sciences and science-based modern technology?

Most certainly. Yet, here as elsewhere words want to be confronted with deeds and facts, basic principles with basic trends.

As for the term "materialist" we took the liberty, in a preceding passage, of translating it as "dynamist". Let us now consider how far this interpretation is justified.

The concept of "materialism" is indispensable for Bolshevism's "colloquial language" because "material", economic interests are of decisive importance in its missionary activity from two different aspects, one positive, the other negative. In the positive sense, the material interests of labouring humanity constitute for Bolshevism, as we have seen before (Section 2), the primary pivot and power base for the historic upheaval that is to be initiated; in the negative sense, the concept serves as a polemical device to unmask, in the eyes of its supporters all the arguments advanced against Bolshevism as so many cloaks for the purely "material" interests of the opposing party, which is thereby to be relegated to a level lower than that of the proletariat, for, through the mouths of its legitimate representatives, the proletariat, at any rate, can and may and does speak the naked, unvarnished "truth". All things considered, then, "materialism" is for Bolshevism nothing but an instrument for the unfolding of its power, and the solid core behind that conceptual guise is not inert "matter", not the substance, the "stuff" of things, but the ever mobile and moving "force". Just as the true and ultimate "interest" of the proletariat lies in the fulfilment of its world-historic mission rather than in the immediate improvement of its economic situation, so on the opposing side the decisive interest is not so much the retention of material goods and privileges as the preservation of the crucial and controlling power position which, again, depends in every way on the possession of the means of production. The "bourgeoisie" may not even be clearly conscious of that fact, but this merely supplies an additional, negative proof confirming that the "proletariat" alone has the capacity to see the contemporary historical situation as a whole, thus also to see through appearances and penetrate to the true background of the opposing world view, whereas the other historic forces in their purblindness for the future have lost even their ability to form a coherent picture of the present.

This signifies in other words that, seen through Bolshevik eyes, historical reality appears as a system of active forces whose direction is determined by the tendency of each to establish its exclusive predominance within the social totality, that is to say within contemporary history. Will to power and struggle for power—that is the true stuff of history from the modern proletarian point of view, the stuff, too, of the entire historical past. He who holds power in his hands at the same time controls reality as a whole; he also grasps reality in fashioning and mastering it.

Human individuals are but the tools used by the great historic forces to achieve their immanent goals. The individual as such is blind, but even the "classes", i.e. the historic forces, lack vigour and direction so long as they have not taken hold of the tool of the human mind. Their path leads through men, to conquer them must be the first of all aims: blessed is he who has become a tool wielded by the arm of historic providence.

Seen in this light, the Bolshevik brand of "materialism", too, may be said to acquire a proper relevance, not in terms of physical "matter", of substance amenable to the processes of weighing, counting and measurement, but in terms of the immediately given and experienced naked fact of the actual historical power struggles. Indeed, if we look upon psychological coercion backed by the instruments of naked physical force as the antithesis of intellectual superiority and the power of intrinsic objective values, then Bolshevism surely appears as a form of "materialism" which, however, is derived not from physical substance, as perceived by the senses, but from what may be called ethical "matter", as opposed not so much to the soul but to the mind. In that sense the Bolshevik world view can certainly be characterised as an ethical "materialism" or, better still, "cynicism".

4. The Problem of Culture

It would none the less be misleading and utterly wrong to regard Bolshevism for that reason as a doctrine of "amoralism". Bolshevism's connection with the problem of culture, its enchantment with the overwhelming consciousness of its world-historic mission alone ought to warn against hasty conclusions. In actual fact Bolshevism is proud of its "cynicism", because it hopes to have found in it the shortest route by which to attain its overriding goal which, of course, is at the same time the objective task confronting mankind in the field of cultural history. Moral "scruples" and "inhibitions" are to be abhorred for the simple reason, among others, that they cause the acting individual to hesitate in the course of action, that in fine they inhibit him in every way. The highest commandment is the good of the cause itself rather than the clear conscience of the individual, let alone his spiritual salvation. The good and pure will is the will to "proletarian" power; good is everything that meets and serves that will and evil everything that obstructs it, or indeed is merely indifferent towards it. Yet, as stated before, the power position is not an end in itself. The historical process has not come to an end, nor is its end within the range of our foresight. The proletariat has been able to perceive the essence of all human history as an unceasing struggle for power because, and only because, it is called upon to usher in a fundamentally new world epoch in which, above all, the historic struggles will come to a final halt. And it is this sublime end that sanctifies, and thus morally justifies, all the means of frightfulness. Evil is to be vanquished with its own weapons and on its home ground. It is not an immoral doctrine, then, which Bolshevism preaches nor a moral indifferentism, but a "new" higher and more practical morality which, however, it must be admitted, is all too strongly reminiscent of many a moral system well known to the human race from time immemorial. However that may be, it remains an immutable article of faith with Bolshevism that the devil can be exorcised only through Beelzebub.

Lies and calumny, torture and murder, fraud and blackmail—all is fair, is justified, indeed is sanctified provided only it serves and promotes the cause of seizing power, of holding and extending it, for there is no other way out of that lowest circle of Dante's inferno that is called the history of the human race up to the present time except the road of the "proletarian dictatorship". But is that really a way out? Whither is it to lead?—Thus the problem of culture acquires a central significance for Bolshevism, and it is only in its light that the world view of Bolshevism emerges coherently in its entirety.

It is often believed that Bolshevism can be characterised by stressing its alleged hostility to culture, by linking it with the Rousseauesque moods of a Tolstoy and thus contrasting it as a "barbaric", "Asian socialism" with the Western European denomination of socialism. Nothing could be more superficial or onesided than such a view. If some parallel with non-Russian cultural phenomena must be found, it would perhaps be more appropriate to compare Bolshevism with what has been called "Americanism". But, as we shall see in a moment, this comparison, too, though nearer the mark, is completely onesided and misleading.

Like all the problems presenting themselves to Bolshevism, the problem of culture is distinctly two-faced: looking upon itself as the element of transition between the old and the new historic order, Bolshevism, on the one hand, is bound to reject the culture that has been handed down, while eager to erect in its place the new, more habitable cultural edifice as quickly as possible. On the other hand, Bolshevism sees itself as an element of transition in the specific "dialectical" sense, which implies that its role is a dual one of separating and simultaneously linking the two antithetical cultural systems. This means that Bolshevism must, inevitably, seek not only to destroy the old system but to utilise its components for the projected new construction and make sure they can bear the load. Thus the problem of culture is clearly one of the most difficult and controversial within the Bolshevik ideological world view as a whole.

It is unfortunately not possible here to enter more closely into these highly interesting complexities. We will confine ourselves to some of the most important points so as to spotlight this most intricate web of facts.

In its practice, Bolshevism, true to its basic attitude, has on the one hand established an internal "intellectual front", as the phrase goes, promising a relentless fight against the "intellectual enemy", and it has in fact carried out that threat, while on the other hand it has turned with the greatest vigour to the cultivation of intellectual values. In the course of these endeavours it has actually launched a novel institution, the so-called "Proletkult" ("proletarian culture") charged mainly with the task of fostering the culture of the "upward striving class". Tempting as it may be to place in relief the unity of the Bolshevik world view amidst so multifarious a variety of activities and manipulatory devices, we are obliged here by lack of space, if for no other reason, to follow a different path and confine ourselves to an examination of the Bolshevik attitude to the great spheres of culture severally.

Religion and philosophy (non-"Marxian", of course)—"c'est l'ennemi", there is the arch-foe. And how could it be otherwise: Bolshevism, after all, was conceived from its earliest beginnings as an ideological world view, as a philosophy—a philosophia militans, to be precise—as a system, that is to say, which for a start, following the example of other systems with a claim to "universal validity", contests the adversary's very right to live while asserting in theory its own right to exclusive domination. But the Bolshevik system does not stop there, for it believes that in the actual enforcement of its claim, in the elimination and even the physical destruction of the opponent, in the conversion of mankind as a whole to the new world view lies the most essential aspect of its own "truth" and consistency. Tolerance is known to the ethical system of Bolshevism only as a vice, though it becomes readily transformed into a virtue whenever a display of tolerant behaviour seems indicated by "tactical considerations", meaning opportunism. But, as a matter of principle, dissidents are heretics deserving to be burnt at the stake. The only distinction made in that respect between philosophy and religion is that the former is held to direct its attention more to the tight organisation of the enemy's world of thought, whereas religion is more concerned with rallying the masses, that is to say with the tight organisation of the human material itself; both, however, are equally compromised as representatives of a hostile principle of organisation that must be mercilessly consigned to destruction. In the light of these facts the Bolshevik world view stands transparently revealed as a world view bent on assimilating the social motives both of religion and philosophy. Indeed, the essential nature of the Bolshevik "Party" can be grasped by regarding it as a philosophical school with an ecclesiastical constitution, comparable to institutions such as the religious orders. One cannot help being reminded of the Middle Ages: a comparison, it may be pointed out in passing, noted very often in Russia itself.

Once the corner-stones of faith and a comprehensive world view have been wrenched off the cultural edifice of the old world, the whole structure is shaken to its foundations and is inevitably doomed to collapse. What remains after that is merely building material, matter in the raw that needs to be formed and fashioned anew.

Accordingly, Bolshevism seeks to harness to its use above all the full range of the achievements of modern experimental pedagogies and of psycho-technological science in general so as to be in a position to place all human energies that can in any way be mobilised in the service of the Bolshevik cause. An excessively harsh organisation of work, even American Taylorism—which in America itself is being decisively rejected by the more humane economists in view of the psychological damage which it causes—are practices which Bolshevism not merely sanctions but elevates to the position of the guiding principles of economic life as a whole. A closely related feature is the high appreciation accorded by Bolshevism to the natural sciences. This attitude, however, is prompted neither by an untainted interest in our objective knowledge of the world nor by the intrinsic value of the mathematical-scientific theorems but solely by the selfish motive of the quest for more and more power. After all, the representatives of Bolshevik educational theory did not even shrink from proclaiming the existence of a specific "red mathematics", i.e. a brand of mathematics that serves the Bolshevik regime. So it is always the concrete task, the exact nature of which has been sufficiently outlined here, that remains in the foreground.

For the sake of completing the picture it may be mentioned here that the great power which art can exercise over the human spirit is not neglected by Bolshevism: art, too, in all its manifestations is to be integrated with the uniform power system, as an instrument for influencing the human will, as a device to make it pliable and tame.

It will not come as a surprise that all the technical devices of social organisation, so richly and subtly developed by the "Old World" in the State and the legal system, are highly appreciated as well as handled in masterly fashion by Bolshevism. A single name will suffice here to characterise the substance of the case: Machiavelli!

Having portrayed, however sketchily, that Russian Americanism, that communist capitalism in all its soulless, barren desolation, one cannot help asking: where, then, are we to find the new culture? Where the ultimate justification of all atrocities and sufferings? Where is the ultimate goal of all Bolshevik aspirations? Self-assured, confident of victory, Bolshevism answers: ex ungue leonem! What today still seems imperfect and fragmented at a time when the task has only just been taken in hand is bound to ripen by and by till it yields a full harvest. Yet even the first step already indicates where our road leads. Above all it is the great highway of world history, and thus the new culture cannot attain to its full efflorescence till the Russian experiment has become the decisive world event. The national element acts as a brake on culture. By freeing culture finally from the shackles of national peculiarity, by placing humanity in relation to the supra-individual element of mass production, Bolshevism achieves a unifying effect which is actually capable of embracing all mankind over the whole of the globe.

How mankind will develop within that all-embracing cultural system cannot, of course, be foreseen in all its details, although—in the Bolshevik view—there can be no doubt that we have an inkling of the shape of that future even today. It will be a realm of labour (not a State, for the State is destined to die) in which all mankind will join forces, entirely of its own free will, to launch the new struggle for the absolute mastery over nature, the final taming of its dark forces.

Nature which was discernible only through the screen of human relations so long as the class struggle pervading the whole of history was not concluded, will now manifest itself in its full immediacy to the collective will of mankind as the last barrier to its sway, the last remaining force that can be pitted against human freedom. The fight for ultimate freedom will thus be the final struggle for the absoluteness of the human race. In the end, then—if we may express the same idea in our own terms—humanity will itself become God.

Bolshevism thus turns out to be not a Russian Americanism but, on the contrary, a genuine emanation of the Russian spirit frozen into American tool steel.

5. The Basic Antinomy

We have so far made every endeavour to present the ideological world view of Bolshevism entirely free from prejudice and as objectively as possible. We sought—as will be readily understood—to suppress even the slightest hint of criticism and to allow the facts of the case to speak for themselves as well as against themselves. If in conclusion we propose to draw attention to the antinomy, to the basic cleavage which runs through the entire world view of Bolshevism, it is not because this is bound to reveal the whole system as ramshackle, but primarily because such an approach reveals a different cross-section and enables us to direct our searchlight from a new angle upon the inner structure.

Throughout our investigation—when we defined the initiating subject of the Bolshevik world view, again when we discussed the Bolshevik view of history and when we outlined its attitude to the problem of art—we have noted the emphatic stress laid by Bolshevism in manifold ways on supra-individual, impersonal forces, on blind elementary urges, on irrational volition. Yet, on the other hand Bolshevism was not only born as a system of rational thought, begotten by specific individuals, but in its entire practice it sets out with great thoroughness to rationalise the whole of life, including the Bolshevik Party's life, to make it intelligible, palpable, graspable, and above all it endeavoured to act wisely. Bolshevism thus strives to be unconsciously conscious or, more accurately, to be consciously unconscious: a tool in the hand of historic providence. Here the question must arise for Bolshevism as to how, in each individual case, it can be sure that any specific course of action adopted by it tallies with the great predestined line of unfolding world events. That judgment, after all, falls within the province of the personal, individual consciousness: but how, from this point of view, is a considered personal decision by an individual act of will at all possible?

That Bolshevism itself, perhaps unconsciously, is fully conscious of the acute difficulties raised by that problem is attested by a most curious phenomenon of its everyday life: it is the cult of the personalities of the leaders, carried to extreme lengths, its belief in authority as well as the belief in the revelatory power of the literature officially sanctioned by the Party. The antinomy which cannot be bridged by rational means is to be eliminated by establishing a firm relationship not susceptible to doubt between the supra-individual, impersonal power of the actual facts and the actual personalities of the power holders. In that way power itself, as an historic category transcending all individual human consciousness, picks its mediators and the heralds charged with proclaiming its designs which must be accepted as simply being there and whose sublime character as chosen instruments must not be questioned. We have already referred in passing to the transformation of Bolshevism into Leninism (Section 2). The full significance of that fact, which is crucial for the Bolshevik world view, is only now beginning to emerge.

If we had intended to confine ourselves to an account of Lenin's world view we should now have reached the point where we must pass from an account of his teachings to a characterisation of his personality. Lenin himself never doubted that the cause was being given tongue within him. Lenin always looked upon himself instinctively as a tool in the hand of an overwhelming supra-terrestrial power of which he was only the first servant. That he should have chosen to apostrophise his God by so earthly a name as "world proletariat" may be excused as a venial semantic aberration. But for Bolshevism as a world view this gives rise to a problem which in all its fateful import has only begun to dawn on Bolshevism since Lenin's death.

As a revealed world view not susceptible to testing either by interpersonal reason or by individual consciousness, Bolshevism is bound up for good or ill, for life or death with the miracle of the inspired personality. Who shall govern in Lenin's name? That question, on the face of it merely a Russian political issue of the moment, is in fact a question of ideology, of the Bolshevik world view. An attempt is being made to solve the problem by proclaiming a new principle of legitimate discipleship. Again the fact becomes clearly manifest that with the advent of Bolshevism West European socialism has entered a new stage: the stage of a religious movement, unique of its kind and still full of ferment.

Will a long life be granted to the "new Islam"? Let life itself give the answer.

6. Culture and Revolution

I.

In every corner of European culture, even the most inconspicuous, there is alarm and confusion. The moral ramparts of the old world have been shaken to their foundations, and all those in Europe whose thinking and feeling do not run upon well-worn lines are gripped by uneasiness and recklessly thrust themselves towards the unknown future. It becomes ever clearer that the old European culture, in all its strata and aspects has become hopelessly decrepit, that Europe is at a crossroads, that the danger of a final torpor and dissolution can be averted only by a heroic effort of will and mind.

It would seem natural that this consciousness of spiritual unease which possesses all the leading minds and hearts of Europe should be particularly obvious in the socialist section of society. For it is precisely this section of society which sees itself as called upon to serve as a transitional stage from the past to the future and in which therefore this clash of two irreconcilable principles should take on a particularly acute and critical character. But in fact this is not the case at all. Deep causes are at work here in a diametrically opposed direction. The predominance of Marxism with its decadently indifferent attitude to all the deeper enquiries of the human mind, an attitude inherited from the degenerating philosophy of the second half of the last century; its blind belief that the spiritual bases of the new socialist culture will form themselves of their own accord; its narrow prejudice against all attempts to anticipate and predict the future in its singular historical aspects, sharply distinguishing it from everything which human history has known to the present time—all this in contemporary Marxist socialism has fostered, however painful it may be to admit this, a spirit of cultural-philosophical moderation. This tendency, perhaps strong in criticism, but helpless in creative potency which in its opposition to the old cultural world is able to make use merely of the obsolete rust-eaten arms of its opponents. But this way the inner struggle in the world of contemporary culture threatens to turn into its spiritual suicide. The

This essay on Lukac's "History and Class Consciousness" was first published in Russian in *Znamya Borbi*, Berlin, March/July/August 1924. Nos. 1, 2, and 5. It was signed *M. A.*, Mark Avrelin—a pseudonym used by A. Steinberg since 1907.

experience of Marxist hegemony in the Russian revolution has made this abundantly clear. Clear to everybody except the Marxists them-selves—with very few exceptions.

When one looks at present-day Marxist literature of any persuasion, be it Leninist or minimalist, the first and general reaction must be depressing. It is as if nothing had happened, as if everything was quite in order! Both the main currents in contemporary Marxism are struggling furiously with each other only over the question of the practical and tactical application of the general theoretical and philosophical propositions; the principles themselves are taken for granted by both camps. And meanwhile events in Europe in general (let us recall no more than Germany and Austria) and above all the great lesson of Russia have subjected to devastating criticism all the original premises of Marxism: economism, centralism, the contempt for the free creative will, the scournful attitude to the particular historical fates of individual nations and states, to the idea of an organic entity itself. Faced with the great creative tasks which have fallen to the lot of Marxist socialism, Marxism has proved to be completely helpless both where its will has become law and where lack of will has become the law of its practice—i.e. in Russia and in the European West. The most insurmountable obstacle on the revolutionary road of Marxist socialism has turned out to be Marxism itself, its total lack of ability to build a new culture, its skill in destruction with its inability to construct. The revolution, drawn on by the energy of Marxist ideology, the Marxist "locomotive of history" was able to hurtle forward only upon rails laid earlier, laid moreover by engineers who were not socialists at all; but it overturned and fell down the embankment as soon as it came to the verge of the epoch, as soon as it came to an historical abyss. When it came to taking their reckless "leap into the kingdom of freedom", some, at the last moment, did not take the risk and stopped in their own tracks, on the very edge of the new kingdom, while others boldly rushed forward and plunged into the bottomless precipice. The "kingdom of freedom", the new socialist culture, is not gained freely, without spiritual effort: it is, as the Scriptures has it, exacted forcibly. But who among the Marxists has given thought to the inner essence of the future, who of them has even now seriously contemplated it? Any attempts in this sphere have been brushed aside and continue to be brushed aside as "vulgar utopianism", as "petty-bourgeois individualism", as symptoms of capitalist degeneration.

Yet the decline of capitalism is in its turn only a symptom of a deeper and persevering sickness. The entire universe of European values which, by the way, nursed and nurtured modern socialism too, threatens to collapse along with it. If all the values of European culture, all of them without exception, dissolve; if the whole of European morality is hurled into the abyss of the outworn, together with all of Europe's worship of progress in mechanization and technology; if the old aesthetics perishes and religion is eroded; if all the forms and ties of cultural creativity disintegrate; if the socialist revolution, in other words, is only the most obvious manifestation of the crisis of the whole of European culture,—then what is called upon to replace the great past? In a once holy place there is the abomination of desolation: can one really be content here with just a grimace of malicious laughter, of openly malignant joy? At whom are they laughing, these heralds of the European "scientific attitude", these apostles of decadent European positivism, these pupils, dazzled by electricity, of the epigones of materialism, these worshippers of the machine?—"Things will take shape" . . . "It will come out alright" . . . "One will get used to it". These are answers worthy of some gambler or company-promoter. Or is the entire reconstruction of the world on new socialist principles merely a grandiose capitalist enterprise, and is the kingdom of the proletariat a republic of small shareholders in some world-wide electrical engineering trust? Who will answer?

There is indeed no quieter and cosier nook in the whole of contemporary European culture than the world of Marxist meditations. This citadel of intellectual somnolence has as yet hardly been touched by the storm which is raging. All the alarming portents are waved aside with a stereotyped dogmatic "analysis". All the literature on the present crisis is invariably met by the Marxists with one and the same judgment: Spengler is a natural reflection of the pessimism common to the entire bourgeoisie, so is Keyserling; Tagore, though not entirely, is the same; anthroposophy is the same, all of contemporary Europe's fervent interest in the culture of the East is the same, the same, the same. . . .

The Russian populists should not share this attitude. All the literature on the present spiritual crisis is *their* literature. We have not yet forgotten that one of the first progenitors of the entire problem of the general European crisis was the forefather of populism—Herzen. For us socialism has never simply been super-capitalism. The problem of East and West is our original populist problem. We pay close attention to any interpretation of the meaning of the present age, to forecasts of the future, even when they emanate from circles which are alien and even hostile to us. From our point of view true thinkers, scholars, poets and artists speak for themselves, and not necessarily with the inscrutable assent of class interest. To all of this we have to pay attention. But we should listen with particular sensitivity to any stirrings in the socialist world—and such movement, outside the Marxist circle, undoubtedly exists. When the ice of Marxist thought breaks, then it will be Spring for us too.

We are still a long way from the Spring floods, but faint noises can already be detected and here and there cracks are showing in the solid cover of ice. New voices—as yet quite timid, it is true—can already be heard in the works of German, French, Italian Marxists. Appeals can be heard—now here, now there—for Marxist philosophy to be made more profound, for a re-evaluation of materialistic values, for a replacement of "materialism" by "realism", for a reunion of Marx with Proudhon, with Fichte, with a newly appraised Hegel, with the entire unbroken history of human thought. In this context we have to dwell first on the most remarkable of Marxist attempts of this kind: on George Lukacs's book "History and Class Consciousness", in which the extreme potentialities of Marxism and its natural limitations are most clearly to be seen. One of the most important events in the development of a new socialist culture will undoubtedly be Marxism's conquest of itself. Without this, contemporary socialism will never grasp the problem of culture, and without such a complete grasp, neither can the socialist revolution be successful.

II.

In George Lukacs's book "History and Class Consciousness", as already noted, the Marxist doctrine is indeed adequately presented. It is for this reason that this presentation deserves the most serious attention and the most thorough analysis. The problems of the socialist revolution are posed in this book in their full breadth, and they are indissolubly connected for the author with the fate of universal culture. This alone sharply distinguishes the book from the numerous Marxist works of recent times which treat the most vital subjects of contemporary history with misconceived profundity. George Lukacs has learnt nothing by heart and does not thrust his ideas on the reader. The most commonplace quotations from Marx sound on his lips like the articles of faith of a new heresy and the whole of his Marxism will perhaps sound in the ears of many Marxists, especially the erudites among them, like "idealistic gibberish". So much the better. If the Marxist movement is to haul itself out of that ideological bog into which it has been drawn during the last decades, if it is to merge in one stream with the loftiest aspirations of today, then Marxism will owe its salvation primarily to those few thinking people who are still to be found in the socialist upsurge and to whom our author undoubtedly belongs. But first of all a few words about the author himself.

In the world of Marxism George Lukacs is a new man: it is comparatively recently that he turned to it from a road leading in an entirely different direction. This, of course, shows in all his "Marxist" works of recent years. His earlier closeness to the Windelband-Rickert school, his former connection with Max Weber's Heidelberg circle have not passed without leaving their trace. Nor has there been a final obliteration of that fragrance of aestheticism which was noticeable in the author's earlier, pre-revolutionary works, devoted to problems of literary form and artistic style. The author, who joined the Soviet communist movement in Hungary and is now an émigré from that country, has taken up new themes but his methods of work remain the same. There is still the same broad horizon.

His learning has become even wider, his philosophical approach has become perhaps even deeper. The author read Kant and Hegel not after he had read Engels and Plekhanov but before he had read them, and he has attempted to understand Marx without the cribs of Kautsky or Kunow. All of this inevitably produced quite unique results and indeed in Lukacs's collection of articles we have a certain synthesis, which in richness of content undoubtedly surpasses anything that has been written by Marxists in any country during the last few years.

For Lukacs Marxism is not only a theory, not only an ideology, not only a world-view even, but an all-embracing philosophical system. As the only true philosophical system of our times, Marxism, in the view of Lukacs cannot be content with the mere superficial denial of the philosophical work of former generations but must raise this work to a higher level, must "uphold" it in the Hegelian sense, i.e. must inwardly transform it and make all its problems and, above all, the unsolved ones his own concern, must finally solve them anew. For him Marx not only continues Hegel's work but transforms it in the spirit of the Hegelian dialectic, against which—as we know—the greatest sin is the replacement of the synthesis by some shapeless antithesis. Such an antithesis, such a philosophical fragment devoid of any integrated sense is for the author the usual "vulgar", as he calls it, materialist Marxism. And he quotes with approbation Rickert's words to the effect that "materialism is the same as Platonism—only with a minus sign". The true hero of Marxism for Lukacs is the "young Marx", he in whom the strong brew of the truly Hegelian potion had not yet fermented. With unflagging energy the author collects drop after drop, seed after seed, all those elements of real Hegelianism in the literary heritage of Marx himself and of his associates and successors, because—how could it be otherwise? If the proletariat is indeed called upon to resurrect and liberate mankind, if Marxism indeed is the self-consciousness of our redeemer and saviour expressed in concepts, if—to put it briefly—proletarian socialism is in fact the last word of a dying culture and at the same time the first word of a nascent, new, universal culture, then socialist philosophy, Marxist and proletarian, not only cannot be poorer, in its range of problems, than the most grandiose of former philosophical systems, but must entirely embrace that system and even eclipse it in the sight of truth. Marxism is not simply Hegelianism, but super-Hegelianism, it is as it were the dialectic unity of Hegelianism and anti-Hegelianism. Such is the task, such is the programme.

It would of course be unforgivable to demand of the author that together with his programme he should at the same time present its final realisation. The grandiose design demands gradual fulfilment and one can only welcome the fact that at last amongst the Marxists,—among whom in the given instance one feels it is permissible—in spite of his subtle commentator—to include Karl Marx himself, there has resounded a voice which does not ring false when it utters the word "philosophy". However, what the author does offer so far allows us to anticipate the perspectives ahead, which should therefore be closely examined. After first giving a condensed exposition of the author's basic views, we shall then endeavour to evaluate them in detail.

The central place in Lukacs's book, taking up half of its extent, is occupied by the essay "Turning into things and the consciousness of the proletariat" (pp. 94 ff.). In relation to this essay all the others are as it were sketches. It is in this that we obtain the clearest impression of the new meaning which the author gives to "Marxism", the place which he allots to it in history of philosophy and the role which he ascribes to it in the contemporary historical struggles. It will be sufficient therefore to dwell in detail on this essay alone.

What is "turning into things"? The author borrows this term from earlier philosophical literature to characterise the whole of the contemporary capitalist bourgeois period of culture. For the author, Simmel's "Philosophy of Money" and Marx's "Capital" intersect in this term. According to Marx, capitalism turned human labour into a commodity and "commodity fetishism" became the philosophy of capitalism. The depersonalization of modern man, his conversion into a thing, his negative realization, as it were, this is the constant theme in recent decades of all contemporary philosophy of culture (Simmel, Weber and many others). Thus contemporary philosophy unconsciously continues Marx's work. The essence of this phenomenon lies in the fact that quantitative definitions completely overshadow the qualitative uniqueness of man, man is transformed into a digit and chunks of marketable time are cut out of his life. Capitalism evaluates a man by the weight of his working time and measures him with the yardstick of hours because the essence of capitalism is in calculation, in the mechanization of production and in the machine-like reproduction of life itself. Hence the whole of capitalist culture takes on the character of an enormous calculating office, and an accountant's ledger has become the Book of Genesis of bourgeois society. A universal accountant has become the master of life, and the whole of culture has bowed down before him.

Modern science has disintegrated into a number of specializations independent of each other. Law has degenerated into automatic legal procedure, the state into a bureaucratic apparatus, the family into a business transaction, literature—especially journalism—into a marketable conscience, a marketable emotion, a talent which can be bought and sold. The most inalienable in human existence, the uniqueness of man, his very spiritual image, his gifts—even these have been put up for sale, have been put on the "market", as the economists say. The logic of things has transformed man into a thing.

What has happened to the human world-view, to philosophy?

With great skill, Lukacs (all of whose predecessors in this Marxist matter are not fit even to be his apprentices) tries to show that the whole of modern philosophy, too, is merely the deepest expression in the sphere of ideas of the same order and tenor of things, and in this sense they are merely the product of capitalist economy and a further stimulus towards its development. From Spinoza and Leibnitz to Kant and Hegel we are dealing always with one and the same "bourgeois thinking".

Capitalist society has built its world according to its own image and likeness. The world is a world of mathematical science, i.e. a world which can be calculated, nature is a realm of measurable units, and all qualities are reduced to quantities; the universe, the spherical circulation is, as it were, a kind of international trade. In accordance with this turning of the world into a universe of things, the world of reason, too, acquires the character of a passively contemplated entity: reason is a knowledge of laws, and in the best case the ability to use to its advantage this or that intersection and conjunction of those laws (i.e. technology). On this point dogmatic rationalism passes immediately into critical rationalism, and the only essential distinction between this and its predecessor lies in the fact that it discovers an antinomy where for its predecessor there had been self-consistent integrity. But even this antinomy fits the essence of capitalism. Capitalism, aiming at rationalizing the whole of life, is in fact (let us recall no more than the capitalist division of labour, the theory of crises, etc.) a collection of partial rational systems which are not reduced to an ultimate unity and which leave room for competition, for the play of "chance", for the irrational. Thus bourgeois philosophy, too, is unable to cope with the problem of the irrational, with the problem of the immutably constant—with the problem of the all comprehensive unity. Kant's "thing in itself" is a perpetual reminder of this. Nor is bourgeois philosophy saved by its ethics—the ethics of Kant or Fichte. Reason, which creates the world, always turns out to be not of this world when it is a question of an actual social reality, and man is powerless to change that reality. Nor ought it to be changed—from the bourgeois point of view it is eternal, as the laws of nature are eternal, and one can merely set against it some moral postulate which, however, can never be realised; something to console the proletarian, perhaps?

But then in the depth of this world the proletariat is born, it grows and waxes strong, and the world begins gradually to change. The worker, as a single being, brings to the market his labour, his time, and his fate depends thereby on the fate of the entire structure of this world as a whole. It is not a question of the worker's psychology but of the role assigned to him in the world which has produced him and is in turn produced by him. In this world it is the destiny of the worker, finally depersonalised, to become the soul, the inner consciousness of the thing itself, its self-consciousness and thus the self-consciousness of the entire world of things. His natural attitude to things is the attitude at one and the same time of the producer of things and of the thing produced, or the product of production itself, i. e. of the thing itself. In this lies the essentially dialectic nature of his place in production. Hence the complete transformation of his view of the world, the complete transfiguration of the world of things as such. Things disappear for him and are reincarnated as processes. Instead of "reality" there are "tendencies", instead of a "nature" measured once and for all there is eternal becoming, change, continuous transition, "history". The class self-consciousness of the proletariat is the self-consciousness of the historical process as a whole, is the revelation of history in man, is man's true knowledge of himself. All the bourgeois antinomies (contradictions) are overcome. For the first time in history reason, developed and effective, is justified in ignoring the antinomy of freedom and necessity, of consciousness and being, of the rational and the irrational, of subject and object. The proletariat as a class is that "identical subject-object" which post-Kantian metaphysics sought in vain as the ultimate absolute. It is given to him to reconstruct the world of things into a world of pure history, in comparison with which all that has hitherto been will seem like a "prehistoric period", as Marx puts it. But for this very reason this reconstruction is not a fatal necessity but is the "free action of the proletariat itself". The socialist revolution is a free act!

Let the Marxists themselves determine to what extent such views are heretical, or to what extent they are orthodox. Our task is different. Lukacs's conception is undoubtedly in many respects independent and original and must be examined with care.

III.

In order to comprehend the new interpretation of Marxism proposed by G. Lukacs, it is necessary first of all to try and grasp what he understands by "social reality".

From the point of view of ordinary, "vulgar" Marxism, as the author himself puts it, the question is solved quite simply. The concept of reality is assumed *ab initio* and to be fully defined: reality is the totality of physical and biological processes occurring in space and time, it is the so-called world of experience within which social life—man and mankind—constitutes merely a small section completely subject to the laws of the whole of which it is part. In other words the only reality recognized by Marxism is the existence of nature, the laws of which are discoverable by the natural sciences: while social life is real only in so far as it can be demonstrated as an interplay and intersection of the multifarious laws of natural existence. The complex fabric of society consists entirely of sequences of causes and effect.—This is the essence of the scientific, "materialistic", understanding of society and, hence, also of history. The history of mankind is a chapter from the Book of Genesis which from beginning to end is one and the same codex of the laws of natural science.

But, as we have already noted, it is "materialism" which Lukacs considers to be an alien element in Marxism. In the language of philosophy this means that for Lukacs the fate of Marxism is not only not connected with the positivistic and naturalistic currents of contemporary thought, but on the contrary is deeply hostile to these currents. From his point of view the understanding of the world as a mechanism doomed to remain rigid in the iron fetters of "eternal laws" is the clearest expression of a purely bourgeois, "contemplative" attitude to reality, in terms of which the world is accessible only to an intellectual approach but cannot be the object of effective action and can never in its essence be changed. Meanwhile Marx, according to Lukacs, is distinguished from all previous thinkers by the fact that in his philosophy he aspired to change the world and not merely to understand it. Hence Marxism and naturalism are incompatible; society cannot be founded on nature as its prime basis: society must find its own basis within itself.

Thus, for Lukacs, the idea of a society independent of nature and sufficient unto itself turns the social world into a super-natural, a "meta"-"physical" essence. This follows from the definition. This in itself is no reproach, but one feels that if the author had taken his ideas to their logical conclusion, he would have had to attribute to this essence all those attributes which had always been attributed to the absolute spirit. Then we would have had, in all its novelty, not simply a "non-materialistic" Marxism, but a spiritualistic Marxism and Lukacs would have had to occupy vis-à-vis Marx approximately the position which, in his own opinion, Marx occupied vis-à-vis Hegel. But the author does not take his views to their logical conclusion and his failure to do so compels one in this case to assume that the spiritualistic deviation seemed dangerous to the author himself—and presumably not only for the likelihood of censorship? One would like to think that for an author with bold ideas there are no forbidden words in the philosophical dictionary and that it is only didactic considerations which impelled him to choose them with particular caution. All this however concerns not only the prognosis of the further development of his views but in part the diagnosis as well.

In contemporary social reality, in the author's opinion, the proletariat is that perfect "identity of subject and object" to whom alone true knowledge is given. Thereby Lukacs breaks not only with materialistic metaphysics, on which the "scientific" positivistic aspirations of Marxism are based, but also with the ordinary rationalistic theory of cognition which lies at its basis. The distance between subject and object, their eternal and inevitable opposition, is the general premise of all non-mystical and non-intuitive epistemological theories. Marxism always seems to have tacitly assumed this premise. In view of the entire structure of Marxist thought, any theory with a nuance of super-rationalism in it must inevitably seem deeply rectionary to Marxism—something which leads into the "low places" of religion, this *bête noir* from the historical abyss, in the Marxist understanding of the world. And here we have the neo-Marxist Lukacs taking this very decisive step: proletarian socialism turns out to be not only a doctrine of the super-natural essence of human society and of its historical development, but also a super-rational doctrine. An attempt is made to resurrect in Marxian Hegelianism not only the idea of freedom which lies dormant in it, but also the super-human, irrational sense of this idea. This very absoluteness of the idea of freedom undoubtedly gave Hegel the right to identify it with the central concept of religion: with God. Lukacs, who proclaims the proletariat to be the absolute bearer of historical freedom, thereby in the full sense of the word deifies the proletariat and is thus the first Marxist theologian.

This is not meant to be facetious—there is nothing humorous in it. A human organisation, invested with power, recognising itself as the custodian and bearer of absolute truth, ready with all the means at its disposal to suppress any attempt to raise any other concept in opposition to their concept of the meaning of historical life, such an organisation cannot be called, in the language of sociology, anything else but a church. State power as an instrument of the coercive incarnation of truth finds in Lukacs its philosophical apologist. But this is not an accidental phenomenon nor is it one merely associated with vital issues of our time—it is a genuine revelation of the innermost essence of Marxism as an actually operative historical force. To what extent this Marxism is derived from Marx is a question which is of no concern to us at all. Not all the pontiffs of Rome were good Christians. But outside the universal (Catholic) church there is no historical Christianity. Thus, that which in the chain of historical events had already become manifest as the true essence of the Marxist idea finds its verbal philosophical expression in Lukacs's reflections. It points to the absolute power of general abstract principles over actual historical reality and further, indissolubly connected with this idea, to the absolute subordination of these general principles to their actual personal carriers for whom their own consciousness is merely the depository of a higher, super-human, super-rational and super-natural wisdom. The tyranny of the absolute principle over the personal consciousness of its bearer cannot but transform the individual who has "seen the light" into a tyrant.

If Lenin had not existed, Marxism, as Lukacs understands it, would have had to invent him: the teacher "speaking as one empowered" is a foregone consequence of the teaching itself. The personality of Lenin is henceforth as inseparable from the fate of Marxism as Mohammedanism is from Mohammed. Future reflections on the essence of Marxism must of necessity try to grasp as a single phenomenon the teachings of Marx and the personality of Lenin. An absolute truth must be a concrete truth. The proletariat as the absolute subject-object must in actual reality be incarnated in a living person. Otherwise it would remain an empty abstraction for Lukacs, i.e. it would not be what it is for that man who deifies it, that proselyte, fervent to the last. "There is no absolute but the proletariat and

Lenin is its prophet"—the second part of the formula is a necessary consequence of the first.

Lukacs is consistent: his "tractatus" on Lenin confirms that his apostolic role is not the outcome of a chance mood. Issuing as he does from German classical idealism and medieval mysticism, the author inevitably makes Marxism one of the religious-mystical doctrines and Lenin—its beatified saint. The newly converted "Hellene" is better able to express the essence of the truth which has suddenly dawned upon him than the inarticulate barbarians who brought it forth. It is not the first time such things have happened.

IV.

True, Zinoviev, the supreme head of militant Marxism, declared at the last parade of the Comintern that for his new discoveries Lukacs should be counted a philosophical infidel, whom he, Zinoviev, "would not tolerate". Following him, a whole series of other critics, reviewers and censors of communist morals hastened to come to the defence of "truths known to every party member" (see *Pravda*, 25th July) against the dangers of Lukacs's concepts. All this however testifies to one thing only: the communist church cannot tolerate independence and free research even into its own dogmas. A truth which is not discredited from the lofty throne of the Central Committee cannot, by virtue of this very fact, be considered inaccurate. And the greater the originality, the greater its harm. Marxist freedom of thought is perhaps in fact more dangerous than any other: does it not threaten to undermine the foundations of the entire party hierarchy? The supreme ultimate truth is known only to the supreme hierarchs and, above all, it is only they who can know which of the truth is to be promulgated, and which is not to be disclosed. Lukacs's greatest sin, perhaps, lies in the fact that he has called some things by their real names and moreover has done so at an inopportune time. To declare aspirations to world authority in the realm of spiritual matters is least convenient of all in times of hesitations, doubts and great disillusionment. Lukacs has either been too late or—which is more likely—over-hasty. In either event he is equally wrong.

But in his argumentation with the Commintern he is *a limine* wrong.

Lukacs's theory of the absolute role of the proletariat as the bearer of freedom and truth suffers from the vital flaw that, while denying all previous criteria of the true and right, it not only does not offer others to replace them but eliminates, it would seem, all possibility of finding them. Let the aim of the socialist revolution be indeed the supreme law, but in each individual instance the question always is—does this or that actual collective action contribute to that end, and have the conditions and possible consequences of that action been properly evaluated? It is not the proletariat, cleverly constructed in the image and semblance of the

Hegelian absolute, which decides such questions—but individual people. And yet Lukacs has struck this part out of the list of "dramatis personae" altogether. The irrational, mystical theory of the cognition of historical reality opens, it is true, certain possibilities—but all of them are against Lukacs.

The first and, at first glance, simplest solution is that everything which the proletariat does is for the good. (Religious-mystical doctrines are always inclined to take an absolute view.) But the "proletariat" may err; or rather it may easily happen that behind the screen of the "proletariat" it is the petty bourgeois demon cavorting on the stage of history. There are many examples of this! On the other hand the converse case is possible: the "proletariat" itself, the primordial and original, may be suddenly transfigured into the image of some heavy-weight shopkeeper short of breath. Has not Lenin himself described in 1919 the partial restoration of private trade, as an exercise in breath relief.[1] How then can one tell when to hiss and when to applaud?

There is of course another way out: one can wait until the curtain comes down for the final results. The Marxists have always been wise after the event. But Lukacs is undoubtedly not a man who is wise after the event— his is a forward looking mind: otherwise there would be no need for all the fuss made. The very intent of his theory makes of it not a theory of eulogy, but a theory of action.

The last possibility is that the super-natural truth is revealed by supernatural means. As we have noted, it was in this direction that Lukacs turned when he pronounced Lenin a "theoretician of genius": "I and the Father are one"—Lenin and the proletariat are homogeneous. But will he believe in the reincarnation of Lenin, in the fact that his spirit has been resurrected in the form of a political trinity? Will he agree with Zinoviev that he, Lukacs, is a "revisionist", i.e. the most evil of heretics?

He has no option!—if he wants to remain a true son of the visible church. And thereby he will pronounce sentence on his own theory. He will either recant or he will cease to call it "orthodox Marxism", because within these limits there is not and indeed, according to Lukacs, there should not be room for any personal initiative which is not sanctioned from above— including initiative in the sphere of pure philosophical thought. Lukacs has contemplated the impossible: on his own responsibility and at his own risk he has attempted to deny in a new way the significance of the individual and has entered into unequal combat with his own personal fate.

Such personal failures are often the most fruitful and are always instructive.

---

1. Play on words in the original: *Peredyshka* means 'respite', 'breathing space' and was the term used by Lenin for the period after the signing of the armistice with Germany at Brest-Litovsk in March, 1918.

7. Education: The Shaping of the Soviet Citizen

I. The Inheritance of the Past

Reference books on the achievements of the Russian Revolution seldom fail to present in their diagrams, side by side with the tremendous increase in coal or machine-tool production, the exceedingly high standard of Soviet education as compared with that of pre-revolutionary Russia. The rise in the number of schools of all categories, of professors, teachers and pupils, and, above all, in the percentage of literate men and women is related in a manner which tends to suggest that education is concerned with measurable quantities rather than with qualities of mind and character. In the case of Soviet Russia, this may be partly due to the influence of Russian terminology. "It is time to realise," said Stalin in his speech of May 4th, 1935, "that of all the valuable capital the world possesses the most precious is man." There is certainly good reason for comparing human beings with some form of condensed capital. Still, a child's soul is something very different even from a precious stone, and the "output" of a school is only vaguely comparable with the yield of an oil-well. The difference is fundamental. Because man, even in the remotest part of the Soviet Union, is determined by his historical background. Thus he cannot be treated, especially in respect of his education, let alone of his re-education, as a raw material. Soviet education could not and did not start from scratch, and there is no way to assess its real achievements other than by an analysis of the "capital" inherited from the past, and by a description of the very peculiar "tools" at its disposal.

The most striking feature of the educational position in Imperial Russia, in the years preceding its downfall, was not so much the abnormal proportion of illiterate adults, when set against the standards attained in Western Europe, as the rapidly growing discrepancy between demand and supply of educational facilities. The Government and its supporters hated the general clamour for more and still more schools. "In Germany," said one of the leaders of the big landowners in 1906, "they praise the schoolmaster as the victor of Sedan. I warn you, the day is not far off, when our Reds will applaud him as the grave-digger of Old Russia." However, in

This essay was first published in English in *Our Soviet Ally*, London,, Fabian Society, 1943.

this, as in all other aspects of its policy, the Government was substantially on the defensive. After a prolonged struggle, compulsory schooling was accepted "in principle", and means were provided for the gradual extension of the elementary school network.

Bowing to political necessity, the Tsarist Government found its compensation in upholding the old school system with all its ties and bonds. Typical of the system was the subdivision of the very complicated structure, vertically as well as horizontally, into water-tight compartments. Those who went through the primary schools had no chance of admission to the secondary schools. Thereafter the highway to the universities became so narrow as only to admit the holders of a "classical" matriculation certificate. The chance of transfer from one type to another of secondary schools (of which there were no less than seven quite different types) was practically nil. "Divide and conquer" was the guiding principle, and this was applied as between the sexes by the formation of women's universities. (For a short time during the years of trouble 1905–7, the ordinary high school was thrown open to girls; but immediately afterwards the reactionaries in the most offensive terms ordered their expulsion.)

The main task prescribed for the educational institutions of all grades was the preservation of the traditional ways of life and the instilment of unswerving loyalty towards Throne, Altar and Empire. Aloofness from the troubles of the day and, generally, from all contemporary problems was law for pupil and teacher alike. The textbooks ignored the fact that Russia had lost a war against Japan, and the maps continued to mark Port Arthur as a Russian naval base. Russian literature was similarly treated. At a time when Tolstoy had long been recognised, both inside and outside Russia, as one of the classics of world-literature, pupils in Russian secondary schools were punished for reading *War and Peace*. That the abhorrence of the Present was bound to entail an ugly misrepresentation of the Past, is obvious.

A system of education lagging so far behind the times was doomed long before its actual destruction. Its breakdown was reflected in another phenomenon peculiar to pre-revolution Russia, the gradual growth of a second educational system, beside the official and in a way substituting for it. Free of the rigidity inherent in its rival, the new system automatically developed an elasticity which enabled it to respond to every aspect of the public demand.

Desire for knowledge was common in Russia to literate and illiterate alike. For the latter the only means of acquiring the longed-for knowledge was the spoken word, and, accordingly, the first task of the unofficial system of education was to spread oral tuition. It was supplied in abundance and supplemented by innumerable evening classes as well as by reading and study circles. The autobiographies of Gorki or Chaliapine testify how efficient this kind of education was even in the days of their boyhood. Thereafter it progressed by leaps and bounds. The educated Russian normally accepted it as his or her natural mission to share their spiritual bread with the hungry. Even Russian books were invisibly stamped with the mark "Common Property". As the influence of the unofficial education grew, all the distinctions of the old educational system became unimportant. What now really mattered, was whether one had acquired the essence of the "true" education.

The high reputation of the "second" system was derived from the fact that it had a curriculum of its own which, in direct opposition to the official one, bore a close relation to the actual problems of Russia's political and social life. The old system ignored the present out of fear of the future; the new revised even the past in the light of things to come. Pride of place in the new education was given to such subjects as Political Economy and Sociology, to the history of the French and other revolutions and, of course, to modern literature, Russian and foreign.

Of the two systems, the subversive had the particular advantage of being in tune with the craving for self-determination which swayed all the non-Russian peoples of the Tsar's Empire. Whilst the schools maintained by the State had scarcely any consideration for the most sacred traditions of the non-Russians, or, more exactly, of all non-Great Russians, the teachers and the teachings of the underground type were proclaiming emphatically that every ethnic group inside Russia was entitled to a life of its own. To these enthusiastic teachers, no matter whether they were "Great", "Little" or "White" Russians, Jews or Georgians, the Polish uprising of 1862, for instance, was an event no less glorious than the English or French Revolutions. In the past of Russia, in Russian literature and philosophy, they searched for and easily discovered those elements which agreed with their own ideal of universal brotherhood and justice. Thus they succeeded in winning the affection of conquered and oppressed peoples for a Russian commonwealth not yet born and only hoped for.

The main bearer of the new educational movement was Russia's Intelligentsia, a social group of a singular character, inseparably connected with the history of Russian culture. Every member of this group, held together only by common ideals, was supposed to be at least potentially a teacher in the people's service. For and with the people, was the Intelligentsia's motto. Teachers and educationists by the summons of the inner voice, they were continually conscious of a feeling of indebtedness towards the burdened and toiling. Was it not these, the producers of their daily bread, who had also created the Word, the Russian and all other languages, the main instrument of Thought and Knowledge? This was the semi-religious form in which the theories of Western socialism were assimilated by the Russian mind.

The fluctuating movement of All-Russia's Intelligentsia found its crystallisation points in an array of revolutionary parties, every one of which was constituted as an educational institution and represented, most literally, a school of thought. All of them considered themselves to be "parts" not of the existing "Russia", but of an ideal society which had yet to be called into being. Training of instructors and mass education with that purpose in view was, therefore, their main object. No one was qualified to lead who had not behind him years and years of such work. All the great Russian revolutionary leaders went through this militant school, starting as pupils in a reading circle and rising step by step to the position of revered "teachers". About 1905, the Russian political emigrés set up in Paris a full-fledged High School of Economics, and a few years later Maxim Gorki founded a special collect for Bolsheviks at his place of refuge, Capri.

At the time of the Revolution, the illegal schools inside the Tsarist educational system were ripe to emerge into the open and completely to replace their rivals.

II. The Educational Ideal of Marxist Russia

The establishment of the Soviet régime produced in Russia, alongside the political and social revolution, the overthrow of the inherited philosophy represented by the Orthodox Christian Church. Its place has been taken by Marxism, the official philosophy of the ruling Communist Party. Within the sphere of education this implies the adjustment of all educational aims to the social ideal of a classless society, which is the ultimate proclaimed goal of the Soviet Union.

The whole population of the Union is to be educated, taught and trained in such a way as to be able, everyone in his or her individual place, to perform the task allotted by the State. Thus the shaping of Soviet citizens worthy of the name is the general aim of Soviet education. A precise definition of the good Soviet citizen is now on Russia's Statute Book, the *Fundamental Law of the U.S.S.R.* In Chapter X of this Constitution is included a list of "Duties of Citizens", among them "to observe the laws, to maintain labour discipline, honestly to perform public duties and to respect the rules of socialist human intercourse" (Art. 130). For the understanding of the special characteristics of modern Russian education, the last few words are the most important. They presuppose a standard of human behaviour which can only be understood in the light of Marxist ethics.

What does the Soviet law mean by "socialist intercourse", and what are its "rules"?

The answer to these questions is to be found in the ideas the Marxists of Russia had always held about the moral and mental qualities of the working class. To the Russian disciples of Marx man in the factory represented even inside the capitalist world that higher type of human character which should be intentionally bred, so as to become universal in the coming classless society. In 1905, long before the Bolshevik Revolution, at the time of the mutiny aboard the battleship *Potemkin*,[1] Russian Marxists, in their attempt to explain why the Imperial Navy was more in step with the vanguard of the people than the army, pointed to the sociological likeness between a big naval vessel and a modern factory. Like the member of a battleship crew, the factory worker was found to become, sooner or later, aware of the fact that he is in the same boat with a great number of fellow-workers, that his individual fate is but a detail in the fortunes of a greater whole. His social position, the place held by him in the process of production, they said, predisposed him automatically to react to his environment in the right "socialist" way. It remained only to make explicit the different forms of this reaction, the "rules" governing it, in order to obtain the guiding principles of socialist education.

In the ideal image of the factory worker the feature most valued by the Soviet educationists is his presumed "Consciousness", i.e. his capacity to put the revolutionary mission of his class above his individual interests. To this level should be elevated all Soviet citizens, who should respect each other as befits members of a community engaged in a great work of liberation. Furthermore, in their intercourse they should pursue, to the total exclusion of every kind of national or racial discrimination, that class solidarity which is supposed to be ingrained in the workers all over the world. The tendency to discriminate against people of alien origin as well as against the "weaker sex" is continually exposed in the process of Soviet education as a "bourgeois prejudice". Particular stress is also laid on the sense of superiority which seems to be characteristic of the worker's attitude towards the machine. The industrial revolution, as it came in the West, involved the subservience of man to machinery; in the U.S.S.R. he is being taught to use it for his own social purposes. A similar sense of independence is being instilled into the child of the peasant towards *his* means of production, the soil. The underlying principle is that Man has to look upon himself as upon the Lord rather than the slave of Nature. There can be no doubt that by conferring upon the industrial worker the highest moral dignity Soviet education stimulates the shifting of country people to the cities and accelerates Russia's industrialisation.

With its economy based on rational planning, the Soviet Union needs the greatest possible number of citizens who respond easily to reason and are unlikely to be led astray by incalculable outbursts of emotion. In accordance with this need, Soviet education is set upon training the young generation in the virtues of self-control, of self-imposed discipline and of dutifulness towards both superiors and subordinates. Everyone should learn to lead and to be led. All these qualities are unmistakably martial

1. Subject of the most famous of the early Russian films.

virtues adapted to a rapidly progressing economy planned on the lines of a military campaign.

Together with will-power the Soviet education is trying to develop in all under its care the creative faculties of the intellect. Here again, the rapid expansion of the Union's economy demands a practically limitless number of inventors and explorers, of men and women capable of performing research work, in order to adjust difficulties and to improve the methods of work. The creative force of the human mind, it is thought, can most effectively be put into action by studying Marxist philosophy and science. The first, because it extols Man above all the heroes of past mythology (and to Marxism religion is nothing but mythology), thus imbuing the human mind with boundless self-confidence; the second, because it relects and reveals the immense power of the methodically working intellect.

All in all, Soviet education may be described as the mobilization to the full of Russia's moral and intellectual resources for the benefit of the great social experiment undertaken by the Soviet State.

III. Ways and Means

In drawing the picture of education under the Soviet regime we need to take several aspects into consideration.

First, the formal shape of the system of school and university, and the extent to which it is universally available.

Second, the content of the education provided, its purposefulness and the means by which it sets out to achieve its purpose.

Third, the network of extra-school organisations by which the efforts of the schools, etc.—again under control of the State purpose—are supplemented; and

Fourth, the role played in the education of the Soviet system by such bodies as Trade Unions, the Red Army, and above all the Communist Party.

Education, in the U.S.S.R., is not a separate part of life or an *adjunct* to the political system; it is a vital element in the system and continues from infancy to death. Unless this is clearly understood, we cannot grasp either what the Soviet educational system is trying to do or why education is a subject of such passionate interest to the rulers of the U.S.S.R.

Machinery

The machinery built up and used by the Soviet State for its educational purpose consists of two different sets of instruments, a regular school system and an extra network of training centres, supplementing each other and supplemented in their turn by a good many primarily non-educational institutions. A complete description of Soviet education has to take into account not merely the formal system, but *all* the main components and try to assess the part each of them is playing in the shaping of the Soviet citizen which is their common task.

In its outlines the Soviet school system resembles very much that of pre-revolutionary Russia. When the control of State education had been taken over by the exponents of Russia's unofficial educational system, they did not try to break it up, though they reformed it thoroughly in the democratic spirit of Russia's Intelligentsia. The inherited three-storey building, with its division into primary, secondary and high schools, has outlived the revolution. But inside the building there has been installed a lifting apparatus devised to carry the pupil, almost automatically, from the basement to the top. The instruction at every stage is preparatory to the requirements of the subsequent one, so as to make the intermediate examinations as easy as possible. Their passing depends entirely upon the abilities and the assiduity of the pupil. These facilities are implied in the "Right to education" guaranteed to the citizens of the U.S.S.R. by Article 121 of the Constitution.

Education in a State school, however, is in Soviet Russia as much a duty as a right. Whilst schooling is a State monopoly, elementary school training for boys and girls from 8 to 15 has, since 1930, been both universal and compulsory. The secondary school leads through an additional three years' course up to the highest stage, to institutions of university rank. In 1941 the Union's "school population" had already risen above the 37 million mark. The efforts to extend universal school education up to the age of 18, and thus to abolish the distinction between primary and secondary schools, were frustrated by the outbreak of war. At both stages the education was, however, till the autumn of 1940, free of charge. Wherever possible, it is being carried through in the appropriate vernacular. In such cases Russian is taught as a second language. Everywhere and at all stages, there is co-education.

Curriculum

Within the curriculum of the seven years' primary school the largest place, after Russian and Russian literature, is occupied by Natural Science, Mathematics, Geography and Social Science. The latter subject, the study of which begins at 13, plays in Soviet education the part assigned in the older form to moral instruction through religion; it bears some relation to the suggestions for "civics" as a compulsory subject in modern Britain. It comprises an introduction to Marxist philosophy, an exposition of the forces shaping modern society, an analysis of the internal structure and of the international position of the Soviet Union, of its ideals and, what is most important, of the duties incumbent on the individual citizen in respect of the whole Soviet community. Literature and history are taught in the same Marxist spirit, though in the last few years, with the growing of the war menace, much stress has been laid on the glorification of the Russian past. This blending of Marxist internationalism with old-fashioned traditional Russian patriotism in the Soviet text-books has been sponsored by Stalin himself. In geography also, special attention is given to the "greatness" and "uniqueness" of Soviet Russia. Even the teaching of foreign languages (usually English or German), which begins with the fourth school year, is being used to underline modern Russia's advancement in comparison with the outer world. Science is being taught in such a way as to open the mind of the pupil to the possibilities of its technical application, in industry as well as in agriculture. With that purpose in view, the whole primary school education in the early 'thirties was turned to "polytechnikisation", which means learning by producing in practice the various processes described and explained in the teacher's lessons. Thus boys and girls all over the country are being prepared for the vocational choice they are supposed to make with the completion of their elementary school education.

Hand in hand with the training of the intellect goes the developing of artistic inclinations (singing, dancing, acting, etc.), the steeling of the character and the hardening of the body through athletic exercises and games. After a period of extravagant experiments in self-government of and by the class members, following the tradition of Russia's unofficial education in the bygone pre-revolutionary days, discipline has been restored to a measure never achieved in Russia before. School administration is concentrated in the hands of a headmaster, who is, however, assisted by the whole body of teachers, instructors, a medical supervisor, representatives of the Parents' Soviet as well as by the most suitable among the pupils. For the children administrative activities within the school community provide the first opening to prove their capacity for leadership, to demonstrate strength of character and to put to test their common sense. Many similar opportunities are given to them during school excursions to places of work, in summer camps or on the occasion of a theatrical performance often produced entirely by the youngsters themselves.

Higher Education

On the conclusion of their primary training the pupils have to make up their mind whether they choose to go on studying or prefer to start productive work at once. In the first case, if they are in a ten years' school, they will stay where they are; otherwise they have the chance of being transferred to the higher type of school, and their choice of a definite vocation is then postponed for another three years. But even if they have decided to join up immediately in the army of the workers or the peasants, their education is by no means at an end. A dense network of technical training centers is spread all over the country, in which the young workers of both sexes receive, together with special vocational instruction, a considerable amount of additional general knowledge, for the purpose of making them "politically conscious". The enormous increase in the number of such institutions (as demonstrated by the figures given below) was dictated by the needs of industrialisation in conjunction with the mechanisation of agriculture. In order to direct the youth in ever-growing numbers to this type of "specialisation", the Government is deliberately discouraging their zeal for "scholarship". To that end and as an emergency measure, fees for the attendance at secondary and higher schools were re-introduced on October 2nd, 1940, in disregard of Article 121 of the Constitution.

The teaching personnel for both primary and secondary schools is being trained partly in special Training Institutions, of which there are several scores in the Soviet Union, partly in ordinary high schools, partly in the old universities, in which case the graduates have to acquire a supplementary pedagogical qualification. The total number of men and women who graduated in the last ten years as teachers, according to Prof. I. Trainin, is more than a quarter of a million. The teaching profession is held in high esteem throughout the Soviet Union.

Boys and girls of 18 who hold a secondary school certificate are entitled to compete for admission to one of the Union's 700-odd high schools which are training the most highly-qualified specialists for every branch of Soviet life, for industry and agriculture, for State and municipal administration, for educational and research work. A conspicuous feature of higher education in post-revolutionary Russia is its extreme specialisation. There are, for example, special high schools for statisticians and for teachers of geography. Needless to say, the great majority of the high schools are concerned to produce technicians. During the years 1928-32 the engineering colleges produced altogether 67,000 "industrial officers"; in the following five-year period the number of such graduates had risen to 211,000. (The corresponding figures for the lower technical schools were 98 and 318,000 respectively.) To counteract the educational disadvantages of specialisation, all students are obliged to study subjects of a "general interest", such as World History and, as a matter of course, the "dialectical materialism" of Marx, Lenin and Stalin.

Social Origins

However, the most striking feature of Soviet higher schools, particularly when compared with those of Imperial Russia, or with any other western country, is the social origin of the students. In 1914, figures drawn from eight universities, showed 57.1 per cent. of the students belonging to the upper and higher-middle class; the rest either derived from the lower-middle class or came of peasant stock. In 1931-5 about a half of all students came from the ranks of the urban workers. Taking into account that even in 1939 there were less than 30 per cent of wage and salary earners among the Union's adult population, we are entitled to say that in respect of higher education the working class in Russia has a privileged position. Whence are the sons and daughters of Russian workers getting the means for their five years' studies at a high school? The statistics tell us that in 1939 no less than 90 per cent of all students were maintained by State bursaries. And if bursaries are not available or insufficient, Soviet students manage to combine study with paid work.

> Every night from six until twelve [reports John Scott, an American observer who was himself working for many years in one of the newly created centres of Soviet industry] the street-cars and buses were crowded with adult students hurrying to and from schools with books and notebooks under their arms, discussing Leibnitz, Hegel, or Lenin, doing problems on their knees, and acting like high-school children during examination week in a New York subway. These students, however, were not adolescents, and it was not examination time. They were just the run of the population of the Soviet Union making up for several centuries of lost time.[2]

As in a flash, this vivid picture reveals the extent to which the Soviet population is making use of the equality of opportunity which is the corner-stone of the whole Soviet school system. But it reveals also that the application of this basic principle has still, even in Soviet Russia, its natural limits.

The State and Education

State control of school education is exercised for the greater part not by the Union but by the individual Union Republics. This enables the outline to be adjusted to the different conditions of life of the Union's various nationalities. The "determination of the basic principles in the sphere of education" is, of course, under Union jurisdiction (Constitution Art. 14). All matters concerning higher education are also under Union supervision. They are dealt with by a special Union Committee whose chairman is a member of the central government (Constitution Art. 70). The main instrument for implementing the Union's control is the federal budget. It is noteworthy that as late as 1937 almost 20 per cent of the whole expenditure was allocated to education (nearly as much as to defence); and even in the last pre-war budget the percentage was still over 12.

2. Scott, *Beyond the Urals*.

Semi-Official Education

Their own triumph over the old official educational system effectively convinced the builders of Soviet Russia that no system of State education could be considered secure, as long as there was room for a rival from outside. Hence their incessant efforts to control and absorb the whole educational potential of the country. Education begins at home. Therefore, under the Soviet régime, a second semi-official, semi-voluntary educational system has been built up which is designed to take hold of the child in its infancy, so as to detach it as early as possible from the uncontrolled and uncontrollable home atmosphere. Although respect for family life is now again in the ascendant in Russia, the educational influence of the family is being steadily eliminated. This is the chief aim of what is called "pre-school education".

Already the communal crèches in town and village achieve this purpose in part; and even more the network of kindergartens spread all over the country among all its peoples, including the most backward tribes of the farther North and the remotest East. The installation of a radio-station and the opening of a Kindergarten are usually the first civilising steps taken on some forlorn Arctic island. In the Murmansk region, to take one instance only, there were in 1937 forty-six Kindergartens with 2,430 children, and 8 special buildings at their disposal. Not less amazing are the corresponding figures for Kamchatka and the Chukotski peninsula. To the Kindergartens are often attached preparatory schools paving the way to the ordinary primary schools. All these institutions are in the care of specially trained personnel and are made as attractive as possible, so as to make them popular with the parents.

At the age of 7, when the youngsters are about to become liable to compulsory schooling, they become simultaneously eligible for full membership in the Communist organisation of the "Octyabryata", which means "the cubs of October", i.e. of the Revolution. There the little ones are educated under the guidance of older children, the "Young Pioneers", aged 12–16, who belong to the Communist organisation which prepares its members for joining the "Comsomol" (Communist League of Youth). The latter, with its membership of boys and girls between 16 and 23, is the last stage of the high road whch leads the young Soviet citizen to the very centre of the political life of the Union, the All-Union Communist Party.

Article 126 of the Constitution describes the Communist Party as the union of "the most active and politically conscious citizens." This gives the clue to the general aim of Party educational policy as pursued through all the stages of childhood and youth organisation. The official school system has the task of moulding in a general way the Soviet citizen; the semi-official co-partner that of finding and training recruits for the moral and intellectual élite which the Party aspires to be. As recruitment to the

Party itself is voluntary, so also is enrolment in the Pioneers and the other organisations. The various stages of pre-Party enrolment are, however, adjusted very nicely to the stages of the school system. Thus, elementary schoolchildren supply the candidates for entry to the organisations of Cubs and Pioneers, and students from secondary and higher schools join the Comsomol. The larger the membership of these preparatory groupings, the easier the selection of candidates for the Party itself, and the less likelihood that this will be dependent on accidental factors.

Herein lies the reason for the strenuous and successful efforts which have been made, ever since the early 'twenties, to extend the scope of these extra-school organisations. In 1926 Pioneers and Cubs between them mustered an army of some 2 million members; by 1935 this number had trebled. The membership of Comsomol grew even more rapidly, from a million and a half in 1926 to about 5½ millions in 1935. At the present time over one-half of all schoolchildren and students in the Union (nearly 19 out of 37 millions) are enrolled in one or other of the three organisations.

The Party devotes great care and attention to its juniors. Pioneers, for example, already possess their own super-club premises.[3] Richard Terrell in *Soviet Understanding* (1937), gives an eye-witness account of education in one or two of these institutions.

> In the Rostov Palace of Pioneers [he writes], I watched little boys studying models of ships, cranes and railway sidings such as were used on the Don river, at the port. They gave me a demonstration of the unloading of a ship. At Stalingrad, where tractors and other agricultural machines are made, the Palace contains models of internal-combustion machines in section. A lecturer explains the models and diagrams to a group of little boys and girls, who spend much of their time copying the models in crayon and mastering their intricacies perfectly.

Here, too, as in the ordinary course of Soviet education, much attention is paid to securing artistic efficiency.

The Work of Other Institutions

The State and the Party are assisted in their educational work by the efforts of a number of other institutions whose main objects are not primarily educational. Of these the most important are the Trade Unions, the Co-operative societies and above all the armed forces. All of them lent a hand in the liquidation of illiteracy.

The greatest service in this field was rendered by the Red Army, which for many years caused masses of illiterate recruits to undergo a course of elementary education. Since literacy became general among the younger

3. "Palaces" is the Russian word. Cf. "Palace of Labour."

generation, the young men in the armed forces are being provided with educational facilities of the widest scope. Even in time of war this work is unflinchingly carried on. "It is quite usual", reports the Soviet writer Y. Rykachev, "to meet a young Red Army man studying philosophy, history, some foreign language or psychology while the battle rages only a few miles ahead." Most of these front-line scholars are "corresponding" students of Soviet universities receiving special encouragement from the military command. Like the universities and the higher schools, the armed forces are one of the most fruitful recruiting grounds for the Comsomol.

No less attention is given by the Trade Unions to the improvement of the educational standard of grown-ups. In the first place, it is the workers' club which serves this purpose. The number of such clubs amounted to 6,000 in 1940; during the previous year they had to their credit the arrangement of over 1 million lectures and literary evenings, with audiences totalling more than 300 million. By 1940 the Trade Unions were responsible for nearly 15,000 special libraries. One of their duties is the selection of members suitable for higher technical education. A considerable part of the men and women who have passed their finals in the Soviet technical schools have been sent there by their respective Trade Unions. Not long before war broke out, the Unions were ordered to select half a million younger members for supplementary education in special factory schools. Now, in connection with evacuation measures, it is often the Trade Unions which have to take over the supervision of the whole school system.

However, in one way or another, every kind of Soviet activity has its particular educational aspect. Even service in the various branches of State and local administration is regarded as an opportunity for special education. The driving force behind all these feverish activities, the Communist Party, looks upon itself, true to its pre-revolutionary traditions, as an educational institution of the highest rank. The Party, also, moulds the entire cultural life of the Soviet Union (research work, artistic production, press, cinema, radio, etc.) to its own educational purpose, the formation of the Soviet citizen as the nearest present approach to the Communist ideal of man.

In fact, it would not be far from the truth to say that Soviet Russia is one great totalitarian school of socialist thought and action; and it is significant that its leader is addressed on the most solemn occasions as "our Teacher", and is proud to be described as the most faithful of the disciples of Lenin.

IV. The Results

The results brought about by the gigantic Soviet effort on the education front must be considered in regard both to quantity and quality.

In quantity the educational achievements are of such a size that they beat easily every record registered so far in human history. Only twenty-five years ago, to begin with the most vital point, 67 per cent or two-thirds of the population were illiterate; according to the census of 1939, the percentage of illiterates has sunk to 22.6, just a third of the pre-revolutionary level. Taken at their face value, these figures may, however, be misleading. An analysis of the details will show that even in pre-Soviet Russia in some parts of the country, particularly the big cities, the average of literacy was much nearer the present level. Still more revealing are the figures in relation to the sexes. At the beginning of 1939, 88.2 per cent of the males and 66.6 per cent of the females were literate; the corresponding figures for 1917 were 50 per cent and 15 per cent. This means that, in point of literacy the male half of the population had much less to gain than the female one, and that, on the other hand, the Soviet women have still far to go to catch up with the men, though the difference between the sexes has been considerably reduced. Soviet educationists are, none the less, fully entitled to claim that "illiteracy in the U.S.S.R. has been almost completely eliminated". Within the limits of the age group between 10 to 25, the proportion of illiterates is by now swiftly approaching zero. The residue of illiterates in this group belong almost exclusively to those backward nationalities which have only come into the the range of civilisation under Soviet rule. But in the advanced parts of the Union, not to speak of cities like Moscow or Leningrad, it is now a very rare occasion to find among the conscripted youth anyone who is not quite familiar with the art of reading and writing. On the whole, the Soviet Union is about to attain the standard of universal literacy.

The following table may convey a general idea how things are developing.

LITERATES AMONG PERSONS AGED OVER 9

	Urban Districts	Rural Districts
1926...................	76.3%	45.2%
1939...................	89.5%	76.8%

Like the males and females, the town and the country dweller are thus rapidly converging, which means that the peasantry is catching up on the townsfolk. As in many other respects, the Revolution has here, too, been particularly beneficial to the peasants and to the women; most of all to the womenfolk of the countryside.

A few more figures may illustrate the rapid extension of the school network since the Revolution. In 1917 there were in Russia about 94,000 elementary schools with 8 million pupils; the numbers are now over four times as great. Owing to the lack of suitable buildings, many schools, even in Moscow, work two and three shifts. Within the five immediately pre-war years alone, more than 20,000 new schools were built, most of them in the villages. At the time of the last Imperial census (1897), Russia had 1.3 million men and women with secondary or higher education, i.e. about 1 per cent of the whole population; by 1939 this number has increased to 14.2 million or to 8.41 per cent of the population. In the Ukraine the proportion was even higher (10.16 per cent), and the peak was reached in Stalin's native land, Georgia (12.46 per cent). These figures are among the highest ever reached by any community in the modern world. No less impressive are the figures relating to the high schools alone.

	High Schools	Students
1917...................	91	124,000
1940...................	700	600,000

This extraordinarily high standard is being upheld even in time of war. The number of places open to students during the term 1941-2 has increased by over 10 per cent against that of the previous year.

All these figures are concurrently indicative of the fact that the U.S.S.R. has at its disposal the largest number of men and women equipped with modern knowledge, and particularly, in accordance with the general trend of Soviet education, with technical knowledge. But are they equipped to make the appropriate use of their equipment? How deep is the scientific and literary knowledge they have acquired rooted in their mind? Has the intensive training, in conformity with the Communist pattern, not affected the independence of their judgment, their ability to live up to the requirements of genuine human dignity? Are these newly-shaped Soviet citizens normally developed personalities or a kind of mass-produced automatons in human disguise?

Statistics can give no answer to these questions which are, however, of vital importance for assessment of the quality of Soviet education. In order to discover its results in terms of quality, we have to turn our eyes to Soviet life as a whole; we must, mentally, plant ourselves in its very heart, and try to understand the cultural activities which are in progress there; we must get an adequate idea of Soviet literature, art, music; of the social climate which permeates, in the Soviet Union, the private life of every citizen.

This is a formidable task indeed. But there are other telling signs indicating, if only vaguely, the general direction in which Soviet humanity is travelling. The criticisms of Soviet education which are voiced time and again within the Union itself reveal not only its shortcomings from the official Communist point of view, but also the indestructibility of the Russian character which breaks through all the dams of educational planning. It is the Old Adam in the Russian, and in all the other human types of the Soviet Union, who revolts against the standardised type of a "cultured" Soviet citizen, into which he might have been pressed by sheer weight of political power. Owing to his powers of resistance, Marxist education in Soviet Russia is acquiring, with the progress of time, a specifically Russian tinge, and the result is a new blend of human character which is as much Russian as Marxist.

The present war, the acid test for Soviet education, proves beyond the shadow of a doubt that within the borders of the former Russian Empire, there has been brought up a new generation, in whom scientific knowledge, technical skill and efficiency, the results of the Communist educational effort, are organically combined with the perennial Russian characteristic, endurance, fortitude in reverse, and boundless love of the country. It is more than a symbol that the victors of Stalingrad are being decorated with orders named after the great warriors of the Imperial past, Suvorov and Kutuzov, and even after the military genius of the Orthodox church, Alexander Nevsky.

Culture

Before the Revolution "Kultura", the Russian equivalent of the English "Culture", meant to the mind of educated Russians first and foremost the quintessence of civilisation, its refinements and highest achievements in all spheres of creative spiritual life. As such, the word was quite foreign to common speech. At the present time, however, it is not only fully adopted by the Russian people in its entirety; not only did it find its way into all the non-Russian vernaculars of the Soviet Union, but it is appreciated in itself as a valuable acquisition of the masses. With its immense popularity, the word has also immensely gained in the scope of its meaning. "Kultura" still means all it had meant before, philosophical thought and scientific research, fine arts and a refined taste, chivalry and elegance; but it means also much more—conformity with the moral and intellectual standard of the average Soviet citizen, the required minimum of orderly behaviour and, of course, clean teeth and neat clothes. Significantly enough, all that is being done in the U.S.S.R. for the furthering of physical fitness goes under the heading "Phys-Kultura". And the famous "Park of Culture and Rest" along the Moscow river is a living monument to this linguistic innovation. The realisation of the big change the word has undergone provides us with a fitting measure for the appreciation of the cultural revolution through which Russia's population has passed in the last two and a half decades.

I. The Guiding Principles

The Revolution has brought culture to the people and has raised the people in a very short period to an extraordinarily high cultural level. What is true of Soviet education is equally true of the Union's cultural life. It is entirely determined by the principle of equality of opportunity.

Though the Constitution of the U.S.S.R. does not, as in the case of education or leisure, guarantee to the Soviet citizen a specific "right to culture", it emphasises that "the raising of the cultural level of the workers" is one of the main purposes which direct the whole planned economy of the country (Art. II). Whenever "culture" or "cultural life" are mentioned in the Constitution, they regularly occupy a place second only to that of "economy" and rank even higher than "defence" (Art. 68 [f]; Art. 131). This implies that every citizen of the Union is entitled to claim his part in the cultural life of the country in the same way as he is entitled to benefit from its prosperity and security. From this point of view the Soviet "right to education" is in itself, in the last resort, only a means to a cultural end, in so far as without education no one could possibly make a new contribution to the inherited culture nor even enjoy its fruits to the full.

In the articles of the Constitution just referred to, the Soviet State proclaims as its task to provide for the "development of economy, culture and defence". In regard to economic life it means first of all planned economy; the war has shown us what it meant in regard to defence. But what does it mean in regard to culture? Does the idea of planned culture make sense? Are the creative forces necessary for the development of culture able to be mobilised or regimented? Can the "cultural level" of a whole country be raised in a similar way as, say, the water-mark of Soviet lakes and rivers? That is exactly what the builders of Soviet Russia actually maintain. And we shall see that in the cultural sphere they have been, within certain limits, no less successful than in that of economy or defence.

Cultural development was conceived in Soviet Russia, since its inception, in accordance with a scheme drawn up on strictly Marxist lines. This scheme dictated, firstly, a rigorous selection of cultural values worthy of further cultivation; secondly, the segregation of those inherited values which had to be either sterilised or even rooted out. Selection resulted in the full vindication of Scientific Truth in all its refractions and of artistic beauty with all its radiations, but, at the same time, in a wholesale rejection of religious faith. It was this negative side of Soviet cultural planning which brought the whole enterprise into disrepute with the Western world. For many years it overshadowed entirely the other, the bright side of the picture. German anti-Russian propaganda would not have had the audacity to present Germany's Fuehrer to the world as the champion of European culture, were it not for the uncompromising attitude of the Soviet Government towards religion. Only a few among the believers all over the world realised that the fight of the "godless" Russian Communists against religion was not due to the uprising of some old barbarity, but, on the contrary, an attempt made by the partisans of modern European enlightenment to draw the practical conclusions from their scientific philosophy. This is borne out by the fact that in dealing with the other aspects of cultural life, apart from the religious, the rulers of

Soviet Russia have shown themselves as broadminded as was humanly possible.

Culture was to them the sum-total of all that Man has achieved in his struggle against Nature. It had, therefore, to be free of all limitations in space and time. It was conceived as a whole to which every people on earth and every epoch in history can make or has made its contribution. This cultural universalism is a quite logical extension of Marxist internationalism to human activities. Taking the broad view of the past and present alike, the Soviet Government created in the cultural sphere the theoretical basis for close collaboration of all the nationalities of the Union. There was no room left for cultural power-politics, say, of the Russians, on the one side; nor, on the other side, for cultural grievances on the part of the weaker nationalities. Soviet culture is intended to be neither Russian nor Georgian, nor tinged by any other national shade, but an interplay of many consonant colours, a rainbow, as it were, forestalling the coming cultural integration of mankind. Nothing seems to cause more delight to the eyes of the Soviet reader than lines like these: "The works of Shakespeare, Tolstoy, Goethe, Gorki, Swift, Chekhov, Balsac, Dostoevsky, Byron, Pushkin, Heine, Turgeniev, Maupassant and Sholokhov are now familiar friends of the remotest peoples of the U.S.S.R." (from an article by Y. Rykachev). All tongues and epochs are here deliberately intermingled, gathered together round one rallying-point, the Soviet Union itself.

It may or may not be a fact that Shakespeare, Swift and Byron are by now more at home in East-Siberian Yakutia than in their native land, and yet there is no doubt that this is, in general, what the Soviet cultural plan is aiming at. Within its framework a mass mobilisation of creative forces has been carried through; the educational system has been put into its service, and all available technical means are being used for its implementation. On November 7th, 1942, the last anniversary of the Revolution, *Pravda* wrote:

> The Soviet citizens emerged on the broad highway of cultural development. Before the young people opened up the wide vistas of art, science and literature. A new Soviet intelligentsia developed primarily from among the children of workers and peasants. They are the doctors, teachers, writers and artists. A new type of man has entered the history of mankind.

The balance-sheet of cultural planning during a period of twenty-five years is, in these few sentences, spread before us. It includes as its last asset even the highest prize of that planning, the "new type of man" or, in the phrase of S. and B. Webb, "Man Remade". Again we may be sceptical as to whether this ultimate goal of the planned cultural revolution has already been attained, or is, at best, only a justifiable anticipation. At any rate, it is worthwhile to survey the various items of this balance-sheet, not recoiling even before the difficult task of assessing the true value of the last one.

II. Planned Development of Culture

According to Marxist philosophy, human progress is basically progress in the development of the productive forces which serve humanity. The steady improvement of the technical means of production inspired and driven forward by science is, therefore, from the Marxist point of view, the most vital part in the "cultural superstructure" of human life. This means that science is the natural focal point where economic and cultural planning must meet, as soon as both are taken in hand. And that is what actually happened, in the early 'twenties, in Soviet Russia.

Simultaneously with the drafting of the first schemes for a unified economy, consideration was given to the organisation and systematic development of scientific research throughout the country. The most urgent task was the preservation of the scientists themselves and the winning of their sympathy for the socialist experiment. This was virtually achieved even in the years of the civil war. Then came the need for a rapid increase in the numbers of research workers, for providing them with the necessary equipment and for devising methods for their collaboration on an All-Union scale. These far more complicated problems were also one after another either solved or approaching solution when the German invasion came. However, the war has not merely wrought disruption on the scientific life of the country; in many ways it is stimulating research and inviting the Soviet scientists to new inventions and discoveries, particularly to those which are useful to the Union's defence.

A few details, supplemented by figures, may help to make the Soviet idea of planned science clearer.

The co-ordination of all the research work which is going on in the U.S.S.R. is entrusted to the Academy of Sciences, the opposite number of the British Royal Society. Founded in 1725, the Russian Academy was thoroughly reformed after the Revolution. In 1917 only one research institute was attached to it; in 1938 the figure was 58. In the same period the number of its Fellows rose from 45 to 130, and that of its Research Assistants from 109 to 3,420. In the early 'thirties, one Department of the old St. Petersburg Academy had been moved even as far as to Vladivostok on the shores of the Pacific. The grand total of the Union's research institutes exceeded 900 in 1939, and the number of men and women carrying on scientific work within their walls was in the neighbourhood of 30,000. The highly specialised research institutes are linked up with various People's Commissariats, for example, those of Heavy Industry, Public Health or Agriculture, and are being instructed by them, under the supervision of the All-Union's State Planning Committee, to deal, singly, or collectively, with the problems which Soviet life is continuously presenting. In one particular case—the preservation of agricultural produce—14 institutes have been brought together for a combined study of the problem. It was no accident that the man who was responsible for the first great Soviet plan of economic development, G. Krizhanovsky, became, in 1929, Vice-President of the Academy of Sciences.

The record of Soviet Technology, Physics, Biology, Agricultural and Medical Science bears witness that the hope expressed by Sir Peter Chalmers Mitchell, that the U.S.S.R. might easily become "a nursery of genius", is, to say the least of it, well founded. The equality of opportunity for higher education has resulted in a mass mobilisation of men and women blessed by nature with scientific abilities, so that the selection of the ablest from among the students of the Union's high schools for special training in scientific research is very unlikely to miscarry. It was the obvious success of the Soviet mass experiment as well as their own war-time experience that, in the opinion of Professor J. D. Bernal, brought home to the scientists of Great Britain that "planning of science is not only necessary but is also quite compatible with individual initiative and enterprise".

A special field of Soviet research is the well-organised exploration of the remote parts of the Union. Many valuable geographical discoveries have been made in the course of this exploration, many a territorial acquisition put for the first time on the map of the U.S.S.R. and, implicitly, on that of both hemispheres of our planet. Referring to the exciting successes of the Soviet flying explorers in the Arctic, a conservative London daily ventured, in 1937, the prophecy that for the future historian this "Conquest of an Empire"would perhaps be the only memorable event of our time. The title of H. P. Smolka's book *40,000 against the Arctic* (1937) intimates in a compressed formula how much planning and efficient organisation lies behind the triumphs of Soviet geography. Closely connected with the geographical exploration is the work of surveying and prospecting which is steadily going on in the peacefully conquered areas. In one of them only, the Murmansk region, 425 expeditions were working in the years 1920-34 (as many as 333 of these expeditions had been sent after the initiation of the first Five-Year Plan). If the number of all the scientifically qualified men and women who take part in this kind of work and the total of the personnel of all the factory and Kolkhoz laboratories is added to that of the professional scientists, the sum will by far exceed 100,000.

Geographical exploration involves ethnographical research, and the survey of the natural resources of the Union leads almost automatically to archaeological discoveries. In both these directions, in ethnographical width and in archaeological depth, the Soviet scientists have attained a high record, Many backward Soviet nationalites would never have come to historical life as active co-partners of Soviet culture, were it nor for the success of Soviet ethnography, in particular of its linguistic branch. As to archaeology, which according to the new Russian terminology is the basic part of the "History of Material Culture", it may suffice to note one fact only. Since the Revolution the Russian list of palaeolithic finds, so vital for the knowledge of prehistory, is ten times as long as before. The number of ethnographical museums and archaeological collections has increased immensely. There is scarcely an autonomous region in the U.S.S.R., not to speak of the Autonomous Republics, without at least one corresponding "national" museum. In a letter addressed last August to their British colleagues, Soviet archaeologists pointed out that even the war could not prevent them from continuing their collectively undertaken "investigations on the ancient history of the peoples of the U.S.S.R.".

Particular attention is given to historical research, in accordance with the traditions of the Russian intelligentsia, to the history of literature, not only of Russian literature or of other Soviet nationalities, but also to world literature as a whole. Alongside with new carefully prepared editions of Soviet Russia's classics (as for instance the edition of Tolstoy's works in 100 volumes) foreign classics (Shakespeare, Shelley and many, many others) have been and are being translated, even now, into Russian and a dozen other Soviet languages. The gigantic task which is being fulfilled by hundreds and hundreds of experts is, owing to the wider meaning associated in Russian with the word "Nauka" (Science), considered also as an integral part of scientific work. Actually it plays, within the framework of Soviet cultural planning, the part of a connecting link between Science and Art.

Difficult as the description of planned Soviet science may be, it is nothing in comparison with an attempt to present in a concise form the Soviet plans and what they have brought about in the fields of Literature, Theatrical art, Ballet, Music, Painting, Sculpture and Architecture. Each of these seven arts has to tell its own story of achievement and failure in Soviet Russia during the past twenty-five years. There is, however, one thing which unites them in a common progress. All of them have become tremendously popular with the broad masses of the Union's population; all have taken root in the most desolate expanses of the country; all are, though not with the same intensity, undergoing a process of rapid growth. The scale of this growth at any rate does not fall short of that which is characteristic of Soviet industry, of the armed forces and, of course, of Soviet education. The innate artistic abilities of the Russians and of many other Soviet peoples was an inherited "capital" which lent itself much more easily to full mobilisation than, say, the coal or iron resources of the Union.

Still, it was a job which had to be done. Simultaneously with the "liquidation of illiteracy", a flood of literary products, old and new, in prose and in verse, was let loose upon all peoples of the U.S.S.R. Here are some illustrative figures.

Year	Number of Books Printed
1913	86,000,000
1938	693,000,000
1939	701,000,000

Even the war, in its first year of heavy retreat, brought that last figure down only by one-half, to 350 million volumes. Since the Revolution, altogether 9,000 million copies of books and pamphlets have been issued. The annual output was, during this period, multiplied by eight. Soviet books are being printed in more than 100 languages. Tolstoy's and Chekhov's works have been published in sixty languages, Gorki's even in sixty-eight (with a total of nearly 40 million copies). In view of the tremendous increase in the number of libraries and in that of volumes in the old libraries, the effective circulation of books was in 1940 actually not eight- or ten-fold, but at least fifty times as much as in 1914. The 111,000 urban and rural clubs of the Union (before the Revolution their number was negligible), are doing their utmost in the services of literary education and of book distribution. The Government seizes every opportunity to put, for the sake of their popularity, the portraits of the Russian classics (Pushkin, Lermontov, Chekhov) on the postage stamps. Even cities and towns are being renamed after them. Tsarskoye Selo, the Windsor of Imperial Russia, bears now the name of the king of the Russian poets, Pushkin, and a whole province, as well as its capital, has been re-named after Gorki.

Coming back from the glorious dead to the living Soviet authors, we have to ask what the Soviet system has given them apart from an almost unlimited number of readers. "It is rather difficult to answer that question," says Vsevolod Ivanov, the well-known novelist, "because for us the Soviet system is like life itself. We are immersed in it like a disciple in the ideas of his teachers." It is probably this immersion which both helps and hampers the creative work of the protagonists of all the fine arts in Soviet Russia. Their number is legion, though it has risen in a proportion much smaller than the number of those whom they address. If they are sufficiently gifted and more or less in line with "the ideas of their teachers", they "receive invariably", in the words of the famous Soviet composer Dmitri Shostakovich, "tremendous support and assistance from the State and its leaders". But submerged as they are and as they by necessity must be in the irresistible flood of the dynamic Soviet life, they lack that serenity, that rest of mind, and self-control which seem to be the prerequisite of genuinely great art destined to tower high above its own age of creation. The texture and structure of Soviet poetry and prose, to stick to that form of creative art which had opened the world to Russian culture, is on the whole of a very high quality. So far, however, there has not yet appeared among the Soviet "Engineers of the soul", as the Soviet men and women of letters are being described since their first All-Union Congress in 1934, anyone who has the classical touch in his or her work, no one whose position in the cultural life of the country could be compared with the position of Pushkin under Tsar Nicholas I or even with that of Gorki when he was still a contemporary of Chekhov and Tolstoy.

No doubt that Shostakovich has, in his own words, "the largest audience of which any composer could dream". But has he ever been able to procure for himself, amidst the thunderstorms of his epoch, that undisturbed solitude which was so beneficial to his predecessors in the history of Russian music? And what is not so good for Soviet music, is perhaps worse still for the plastic arts in the Union. Dynamism and repose in one is a contradiction in terms. Trying to render the breathtaking speed of their surrounding life, Soviet artists are bound to sin against and derange their own aesthetic canons. Repeated attempts to find a new architectural style have not so far got beyond the stage of rough sketching.

The better were, from the start, the chances of artistic activities serving the day and bound to thrive in the air of publicity. The Soviet theatre, ballet and cinema are in full blossom. The latter, in particular, has broken new ground and acquired world fame, whilst the former still continue to profit from the traditions established before the Revolution. All of them have at their disposal, thanks to the gigantic scale on which the propagation of artistic activities has been deliberately undertaken, a practically limitless reserve of talent. So has music as far as performance is concerned. In many small Soviet cities concerts and recitals with programmes designated to satisfy the most refined taste are an everyday occurrence. In 1914 there were in Russia altogether 153 theatres and scarcely any cinemas; the respective figures at the end of 1938 were 790 and 30,000, not taking into account the 131 children's theatres and the amateur theatrical companies whose number goes into tens of thousands. Owing to the evacuation of theatre companies and orchestras, since the German invasion, the artistic life behind the front, in the eastern part of the Union, has received a new mighty impulse. On the other hand, the war was bound to bring to a standstill the promising development of that specific Soviet art, mass pageantry. The Unions of Soviet Writers, of Artists, of Composers and Musicians and of Actors, all used to collaborate with the All-Union Committee of Arts in evolving new schemes for popular mass entertainment with the active participation of the entertained themselves.

Those who are inclined to put chess into the category of fine arts, will be interested to learn at this juncture that chess tournaments are in Soviet Russia an occasion for mass enjoyment and that there are in the Soviet Union not less than 1½ million registered chess players.

III. The Survival of Pre-Revolutionary Russian Culture

Reference to the effect which the cultural traditions of pre-revolutionary Russia has had on the newly developed Soviet culture have already been made on previous pages. This older Russian culture, however, not only survives inside the Soviet Union as a recognisable thread interwoven into the tissue of the new cultural life, it still has a life of its own, embodied, first of all, in such an institution as the Russian Orthodox Church. A survey of Soviet culture, brief as it may be, is bound not to leave out of account these surviving elements of the past, if only for the purpose of finding out how the Soviet education and culture have succeeded in creating a really "new type of man".

One of the most influential factors in Soviet cultural life is the victory of the inherited Russian literary speech over its aggressive rivals of the first revolutionary years. For obvious reasons this linguistic struggle and the defeat of the aggressors passed, notwithstanding their vital importance for the development of Soviet culture, almost unnoticed by the outside world. As some other arts, the champions of the new Soviet culture were, in the late 'teens and early 'twenties, trying hard to "revolutionise" the literature, and not only the literary form, but also the Russian usage and even the Russian word itself. The signal fate of the poet Vladimir Mayakovsky, the driving force behind the Russian "Futurism", who had to capitulate before the necessities of Soviet cultural planning, stands out as a symbol of the Government's deliberate retreat on the "cultural front". The good old literary Russian has been rehabilitated and restored to its full rights in prose and in poetry, in the press and on the radio, in school and in the public meeting. Thus a strong bond has been established with the entire literary tradition of the past, a ring in a chain leading, link by link, to the very Slavonic origins of the Russian tongue. The distinctions between Eastern Slavonic languages, as, for example, between "Great" and "White" Russian, when confronted with their common roots, could not but lose their somewhat over-emphasised importance; and the close unity of all the Slavonic peoples of the Union, i.e. of three-quarters of its population, was thus reaffirmed anew. Not very different was the Soviet linguistic policy towards other Soviet peoples, and much the same was its effect on their cultural development.

The general line of Soviet cultural policy, to revise and to readjust the heritage taken over from the past rather than to suppress and to destroy it, was decisive even for the Government's utterly hostile attitude towards religion. The established Orthodox Church was separated from the State, even as the school, which in pre-Revolution days, particularly in the rural districts, was a domain of priestly control, was separated from the Church. With all that, the guiding principle of Russia's intelligentsia, that of "freedom of conscience", far from having been disowned, was time and again reaffirmed in the most solemn form. It is now embodied in Article 124 of the Constitution. Yet not without qualification. The second half of this article reads: "Freedom of religious worship and freedom of anti-religious propaganda is recognised for all citizens." The obvious implication is that the "believers" in the Soviet Union, be they Christians, Muslims or Jews, are denied the right, ensured to the atheists, agnostics, freethinkers and rationalists of all descriptions, to disseminate their faith and philosophy among their countrymen. The privileged position of the "godless" finds a noteworthy expression in yet another passage of the Constitution (Art. 129), in which the "right of asylum" of foreigners is extended to those "persecuted for their scientific activities". All Soviet commentators agree that the law provides hereby a refuge for all whose scientific convictions might bring them into collision with the anti-scientific, i.e. religious, philosophy predominant in their respective homelands. For, from the Marxist point of view, Science and Religion are incompatible. In so far as planned Soviet culture intended to be scientific in its very core, its promoters must regard every religious denomination as a school of thoughtlessness and prejudice. So do they regard every kind of philosophy, deviating from the Marxist dialectical materialism. Apart from the orthodox Marxism there is therefore no room left in Soviet Russia for Metaphysics, unless treated purely historically. Research into the history of human culture, however, comprises in the Soviet view the history of religious belief, and with all its opposition to philosophical idealism Soviet Russia has to its credit a new, most carefully revised, Russian edition of Plato's works.

The position of religious communities is, under the circumstances, exceptionally difficult. The more remarkable their survival. According to Soviet statistics, there were in the Union, on the eve of the war, 4,225 Orthodox churches and 37 monasteries, 1,312 mosques and nearly 1,000 synagogues. The number of religious communities with a membership of twenty or more amounted to 30,000. Compared with the pre-Revolution epoch, when Moscow alone was a city of "forty times forty churches", the effect of the "freedom of anti-religious propaganda" seems devastating. But to the religious mind the undaunted few make all the difference, and this small religious minority of the Soviet population, hardened by the trials of the last two and a half decades, is at any rate far from despair. That is why in the years preceding the war and in the critical time the U.S.S.R. is now going through we hear so frequently of new friendly contacts between the State and the Church. The support of the believers is by no means irrelevant to the Government; on the contrary, the Government realises that in relation to a considerable part of the population, in particular in the villages, this minority occupies the position of an influential élite. The more sincere is, therefore, the official appreciation of any expression of loyalty on the part of the churches, such as is contained, for instance, in the messages of congratulations sent by the Metropolitan Sergius of Moscow, the Primate of the Russian Orthodox Church, or by the head of the Orthodox Reformist Churches, Alexander Vedensky, to Stalin as the Commander in Chief of the Red Army on the occasion of its 25th anniversary. And not less sincere, too, for the same reason, are the declarations of tolerance repeatedly made, since 1936, by the Government. There is ample evidence that the day may not be far away when the religious outlook will be granted in the U.S.S.R. fairer conditions of competition with the official Marxist philosophy than at any time since the Revolution.

The scions of Soviet culture are often, in their moral and intellectual development, as good as the highest standards of older civilisations. The main point of difference is that they are atheists. If this negative criterion should be regarded as their distinctive mark, we may agree with the contention insistently proclaimed in Soviet Russia that a "new man" is set on foot. In his broadmindedness, in his longing for a quicker pace on the road of human progress, in his love of humanity not impeding in the least his enthusiastic self-abnegation in the service of his own country, he emerges as a most attractive cross-product of both the old Russian and the new Soviet culture. At the same time no specimen of the new type, contrary to the assumption sometimes made, has lost his own face, his unique individuality. If nothing else, the great number of heroic figures emerging on Russia's battlefields gives the lie to this malevolent assumption. Ilya Ehrenburg has every reason to emphasise:

> Only a blind man could declare that the Russians are a mass, that individuals do not exist in Russia. If they march to death without fear, it is because they desire a life worth defending. One can love life with such fervour and passion as to sacrifice one's own life for its triumph.

The Soviet novelist and war correspondent repeats here almost word by word the description of the Russian character given by that ardent Christian, Dostoevsky.

But what makes the Russian Christian ideal of a human being almost identical with the "new type of man" longed for in Soviet Russia is, first and foremost, the universalism common to both. It is unmistakably this universalist spirit which speaks out of the telegram sent from Kursk after the town's liberation to the Union of Soviet Writers in Moscow: "The Germans burnt down our libraries, and nearly all our Russian and world classics have been destroyed. Badly in need of works by Tolstoy, Pushkin, Lermontov, Shakespeare, and modern Soviet, English, American and French writers." "Moscow libraries", another news item tell us, "are collecting English, French, German, Italian and Spanish books, to form the basis of a foreign library in Stalingrad."

8. Socialist Religion or Religious Socialism?

There are certain problems which at first glance impress one as being no more than scholastic arguments. The attempt clearly to differentiate between religious socialism and socialist religion can, at the present state of the whole question regarding "socialism and religion", easily arouse the suspicion that one intends thereby no more than an acute exercise in logic. The very proposal of a marriage between religion and socialism, both to the great majority of socialists and the masses of religious believers, is for the present so Utopian an affair, so curiously strange, that the question about how the union is to be approached—whether it should result in the creation of a conscious socialist religion, or whether religion should gather socialism under its divine wings—must at the present juncture evoke the sarcastic response, "Who is interested in it?" Convince us first that socialism and religion can at least sit down together at the same table, then there will be some point in tackling the question as to who should predominate. Even then, however, the question will remain quite futile: if in a general sense there can be a union of socialism and religion, then it must automatically be socialist or religious, and the place of our exclusive "or" must then be taken by the closer linking "and". To put it briefly, the justification of our "or" is the first point which we must clarify.

Is it indeed true that socialist religion and religious socialism are mutually exclusive, that each is the opposite of the other, and in dismissing the argument, we place the whole problem of religion and socialism in grave danger of posing the question wrongly and thereby reaching a false solution. To demonstrate this point is the purpose of the following remarks which will again require a reference to certain chapters of logic, to the theory of concepts, and in particular to the principles on which new concepts are created.

Every idea of an empirical, especially a historical phenomenon is a kind of entity with an unlimited number of positive and negative attributes which tell us what it signifies and what it does not. At first glance one may think that it is not really important to know what the idea does not signify, as long as one is certain what it does signify. That would be correct,

This essay was first published in Yiddish in *Fraye Shriftn*, Warsaw, 1930, No. 10.

however, only if each idea were a world in itself, entirely isolated from all other ideas, that is to say an independent entity in the most precise sense of the word. Such absolutely isolated concepts are, however, beyond our grasp and will always remain so as long as our minds are ruled by logical thought. Thinking can be likened to the weaving of a net, in which the various ideas are but the knots in the thread of which the whole net is woven. This is the way in which every concept is bound up with all other concepts and its negative attributes are just those parts of the thread which lead to the concept centres of the fabric of thought. Just where the knot stops, that is where the endless cord begins to lead to the further creation of ideas; and that is how the thread of logic shows its validity, its inter-connection with the infinite. Without the negative attributes, the positive qualities of an idea are in a logical sense also negative, and what is left of all thinking, of logic, is a mere "No"—a negation.

The matter becomes particularly clear when one passes from the logical statics to the logical dynamics, where concepts are newly created, or at least renewed. Then it immediately becomes obvious that the logical *yes*, the positive features of an idea, and the logical *no*, its negative determi-nants, are indeed—without overdoing the simile—quite as firmly bound together as the knot and its connecting thread. Such a case of thought dynamics is, however, precisely our own case. Both socialism and religion are concepts not in a fossilized science but in living history that constantly renews itself. More than that. A spiritual approach between socialism and religion is, for the present, something that as yet has not been born, something that still has to be created, an idea, which has to point the way and not merely to gather up the strands of things already in being. The logical dynamics in our case, therefore, attains its highest intensity and provides us with an additional reason of passing from abstract theory to concrete application.

What is the object of trying to make religion socialistic and in giving socialism the mark of religion? The first answer that leaps to mind is that in this way we endow an old idea with new content, and enrich its positive core. This logical operation thus consists, to put it differently, in a kind of addition. But this also gives rise to the mistaken inference that it makes no difference whether socialism is linked to religion or religion to socialism. Nevertheless, the inference is a false one. Logical addition often implies at the same time the subtraction of something else, because in logic positive and negative are one and the tightening of one knot in the fabric of thought implies the loosening of several others. When I envisage the idea of religious socialism for my programme or ideal, I mean thereby not only that socialism can and should be also religious, but a good deal more: that this religious socialism be the only proper socialism and all the other non-religious forms be entirely excluded from the scope of socialism, so that they do not even bear its name. In other words, the positive conceptual "yes" implies a tendency to exclude all other similar forms of the given idea. So it is with a socialist religion which, in the sense that it is positively socialist, is also negative: non-Christian, non-Mohammedan, non-Judaic, and inherently aims at placing all other forms of religion under a ban, similarly to what its elder sister religions had done. To put it briefly, the biological struggle for survival is in a certain sense a mirror-image of the struggle in the purely spiritual realm. A firmly shaped idea, even if it is not conceived as a programme, carries within itself the desire for power, an energy for struggle. All the more so when it is a programme or an ideal.

Let it be clearly understood, that so far I have been dealing only with the spiritual sphere, the region of pure logical dynamics. Those who make the mistake of thinking that the things ideal are not real, may consider that the use of words such as struggle, power, energy etc. in the realm of thought is at best no more than a stylistic exercise. No sooner, however, does one pass from logic to psychology, from pure thought to the world of human thought, than it becomes clear to the most stubborn "realist" that ideas are forces, that they have a true reality, and even the *logos* itself (the Greek for *word*) often has an uncanny or magic influence. Even the man with no faith in pure logic must acknowledge that the system of ideas with which a man sets out to master the chaos in the world and in his own consciousness is of some consequence. One knot badly tied and the whole web can unravel, becoming no more than a spider's web, to use Nietzsche's word about Spinoza. One mistake in the world of thought and the whole of man is in danger of ceasing to be an intelligent being. One flaw in an ideological system and a whole state . . . . . "Stop!" . . . I can hear myself being interrupted. . . . "Does that mean that theory is important for practice and that without a firm theoretical basis any ideological edifice stands on quick-sands?" But is that anything new? Didn't we learn this in our schooldays, especially we socialists?—Certainly! How fine it would be, however, if in the hustle of daily life we bore in mind our schoolday wisdom.

It is life itself, that is the teacher, who has overtaken modern socialism that was once constructed on proper theoretical foundations and driven it into an acute, practical and ideological crisis. Life, and nothing else, has also ousted religion from its old exalted position and brought it to the point where it has to fight to-day for its bare existence. Times change quickly, but one's view of life develops slowly. Is it any wonder then that in philosophical syntheses which emerge in the course of daily strife, such as the synthesis of religion and socialism, not only the fine points of logic are forgotten, but also the underlying principles of logical thinking, and that from the whole of school wisdom one keeps in mind one principle only: not the interpretation, not the theory, but only the deed, the practice, is what really matters. Bold as it may be to say anything to the contrary, one is always obliged to recall anew that this thesis is itself an interpretation and not a statement of fact. Even the principle of the supremacy of practice is itself not a practical but a theoretical one. But if one is dealing with a fact still to be, with something which will be part of future practice, such as the union of socialism and religion, one must underline over and over again that out of all this religious socialism all that may emerge is an old wives' tale, if nothing worse, in view of the fact that at the outset there was no clarity of the final aim—true religious socialism or a brand-new socialist religion.

II

Such are the thoughts which at once rose to mind when I perused in the last issue of the "Fraie Shriften" the "Correspondence between Two Friends concerning Religion and Socialism". (Fr. Sh. No. 7-8, 129-144). In this discussion friend Reuben gets both the first and the last word, but it is by no means to be concluded that friend Simeon is at the end of his argument. Then why—inquires the reader, Levi,—has Reuben deserved the fifth and last letter in that correspondence? Possibly because he is keener in the pursuit of peace. "You seek a new way", he writes in the last paragraph of his final letter. "Show me that way. Then let us put together the fervour of our conceptions, because we are making for a common goal." In an earlier letter he observes, "We place in our conception of God the same longings which are so dear to us. And we both agree that socialism and religion to-day are interwoven ideas." But this is where Levi is moved to speak up instead of Simeon with a loud voice. "A total error! Your goals have nothing in common and your conceptions of God are not at all the same! Your fervours can never be combined, for they are to each other as fire and water. Simeon is a believer who longs for a religious socialism and Reuben is a socialist who is half-way to a socialist religion."

From our logical introduction we know now that a socialist religion must be different from any faith so far known to us. Reuben's letter in fact indicates a number of points which make this distinction absolutely clear. Firstly, he declares and repeats it several times that, in direct opposition to historical religions, man was not created by God, but on the contrary, man was the creator of God. "Without man," he writes, "there is no God and no religion. . . . God lives only in the human soul. . . . Abraham both recognised and created his Creator." (pp. 134, 141, 140). Naturally, a creator created out of the spirit of man is no more than a subjective human conception (p. 135). The content of such a conception is "the absolute eternal idea" which "I have created according to my human (that is divine) power. Man has the power to create the absolute and the eternal, and therefore his powers are themselves divine. It follows then that man must be potentially divine from the beginning of his life in the womb in order to be able to create the Almighty. This is intended in all seriousness. The god that is born in the human soul is certainly no abstract metaphysical idea, a transcendental sun which shines without giving heat, but a god whom one can "worship", from whom one can "seek comfort", with whom one can argue" (p. 141), because he is the "symbol of eternal goodness," "the absolute goodness itself." (p. 142) One might think that these last words make of Reuben's god a sort of shadow of the old God, the God we know from the Bible, the Koran or the Gospels. But that too would be a mistake! The idea of eternal Goodness is again not objective, but subjective: "Without constant re-creation by man, says Reuben, "the idea is no idea." (p. 134). Elsewhere he adds, "The eternity of a god is the eternity which men bestow on him according to their mind and mood" (p. 141). In accordance with his own intelligence and disposition, Reuben endows his god with something which becomes an "eternal foundation of socialist toil." This is the idea, says Reuben, which I serve and serve as I can." (p. 135)

To friend Simeon the whole approach appears bizarre. "When one considers the creator, i.e. man with all his faults," he writes to his objectivist opponent, "what is the product—an absolute idea or God? . . . There remains only an idea, no absolute, but an idol, not God" (p. 131). And therefore he wonders that anyone should be able to bow to the creation of his own thoughts. (p. 138). Friend Simeon, it seems to me wonders in vain. Men have shown that they can serve their own idea very well and even worship it. The theoretical bases of such worship is well known to the history of human thought. They are variously known as solipsism (which derives from Leibnitz's 'Monadology', absolute individualism (Stirner! an illegitimate son of Fichte the elder), anthropolatry (Dostoevsky's Kirilov and his other "supermen"), which have been subjects of research in psycho-pathology (autism, narcissism, etc). If Simeon had looked more closely he would have perceived that Friend Reuben makes no secret of his philosophical assumption. "The world", says he, "can lie outside man, God lives only in the human soul." The latter half of this sentence I have already cited above. Now I wish to underline the word *can* in the first half. Reuben, it seems, leaves the question open. Is not even the whole world "my imagination", "my property", as Stirner expressed it? The hypothetical form was chosen by him, as I see it, so that in the argument about God he would not stray into metaphysical digressions. Why, after all this progress can Reuben do no more than exchange God's world for a product of his own activity? What is the "absolute" if not the highest level of real being? Are but God, eternity and "absolute goodness, in which truth and beauty flow in one stream" (p. 143) my own offspring, then how can my creative powers reach their limits?—At the least, in the hollow ark of space and in the flowing continuity of time. Time and space, by the way, possess reality only by being woven into the web of logic, the objective, logical truth. When, however, truth has become "merged" with subjective good, then may the world cry in vain, but it will not escape from the "all-embracing element of human life", from the active-subjectivist "sense of holiness". (p. 130). All that remains real in Reuben's system is only one single Monad divine and creating God and everything which is good according to "divine motives": a Monad of will for which everything that is extraneous is at most a reflection of its own motives and aims. . . . Can anyone serve himself, asks Simeon. . . . Certainly, if the person concerned is a god. Can a human being be a god? Not just god's messenger, or a son of god, but actually *He* in all glory, God Himself, Father, Son and Holy Spirit in one person? . . . . Oh, subjectivity in the best way! All that is necessary is to register in the sect of "I-myself", the solipsists, those whose standpoint is that only my ego is actually real, or only I myself am real. But can such a fanatical representative of such a system be at the same time a representative of socialism? But this is indeed a thorny question!

From the three letters of Reuben it is quite clear that he is dedicated to socialism with heart and soul, incomparable to his own personal solipsism. Otherwise, how could it be that, suddenly, in the matter of solipsist consistency he failed so clumsily at the very outset of his journey? Saying then that "Man and God cling together", he at once makes the leap in his third letter from man-the-individual to the "people of Israel". Explicitly he adds that "God lives only through His people or through humanity" (p. 141). However, two pages later he inserts "incidentally" the following astonishing addendum: "Concrete man is not the only point of departure of religion. It is more correct to say that he is the transit-station, for he carries within him the legacy of the preceding culture of which he is also a product. But this is only incidentally." (p. 143). But why only "incidentally"? This is something of peculiar importance and hits the individualist standpoint of Reuben right in the middle! . . . I conclude therefore that his entire individualism is not very important to him. There is something else that he holds both dear and important—his need to place socialism on a firmer ideological foundation than that on which it totters to-day. As this need of his is a deeply seated personal feeling, he has attempted to construct an entire religious philosophical system on it. But almost at once he must have regretted it and abandoned his mistaken course. And so, his attitude of the "pursuit of peace" also becomes understandable. In fact, making God dependent on mankind, in the manner of Auguste Comte and Ludwig Feuerbach, does not deserve the name of genuine religion: the danger here arises not from individualist solipsism, but instead from collectivist solipsism. Reuben's innermost contradiction, which was revealed at the end of the argument, does nevertheless not entirely invalidate his line of thought. His main direction is open to us and demonstrates in a concrete manner how one can stray into an abyss when one sets out forcibly to inflate socialism into a religion, not only an abyss in the religious but also in the socialist sense. The matter is then quite simple: if God as the foundation of socialism is my private property, how much more so is socialism thus founded. To put it in Reuben's words: Socialism must consist "of the same dough as its eternal foundations" (p. 141), from the dough "which is kneaded in the warmth of the human heart." (p. 144). It is also clearly to be seen from Reuben's printed letters, that even the roses that grow in this warmth are not without thorns.

Arguing the case for subjectivism, Reuben exclaims, "Would that indeed Men were always a part of God, part of the One-on-High. All people would then be divine! But the plain fact is quite different. There are men who are saintly, those that are wicked and others in between." (p. 134). Here it becomes at once quite clear how wide the difference is between socialist religion and religious socialism. The same issue of "Fraie Shriften" contains a contribution by Roland-Holst, who relates that according to the beliefs which inspire the Swiss religious socialists, Leonard Ragatz and his friends, "something sacred is inherent even in the worst of men", for "man and the Kingdom of Heaven are not completely isolated from each other" and "God himself is at work in both man and the world" (pp. 120-121). That is religious! And that is also in the deepest sense socialist! As soon, however, as one divides people into categories, saints, sinners and those in between, and as soon as one also believes that he who is a revolutionary socialist is a saint and the one who is not, belongs at best to those in-between, so to speak ethically neither the one thing nor the other, then one finds oneself on the high road to socialist conceit . . . to Bolshevism. What does it matter that Friend Reuben loathes Bolshevism, that for him a Bolshevik is no better than an Inquisitor of old, the original man of evil (135), and that he is in particular an opponent of Marxism (p. 144). In this respect one may be able even to sleep more soundly with certain forms of Marxism than with Reuben's individualism. Marxism has at least objective categories for the purpose of distinguishing between friend and foe. Reuben's categories are, however, subjective. Reuben is prepared to give away the whole body of cool reasoning for a basinful of hot noodles. He has no option but to rely on his own skill of penetrating into someone else's heart. As subjectivist he will take another man's pulse and count according to an arithmetic in which two times two can sometimes make four and sometimes three-and-a-half. I'd be willing to say "So be it!" if Reuben were at least half a god. But since he is only simple flesh and blood and his religion, which he regards as the "eternity of each minute" (p. 144), is so consistently subjective that every moment in the minute is an absolute in itself, then the most logical form of this solipsist mania is the so-called momentalism. But how great can the danger become if all other socialist tribes were to make common cause with the tribe of Reuben and launch themselves on the conquest of the earth in order to subdue the whole world under this "religious" banner. Our only hope is that Reuben's "incidental" observation, his transition from isolated man to collective mankind, will become his highway, and the highway of his first letters . . . an incidental aberration.

This most probably will see the disappearance also of the last contradiction at which I must now pause a while. The contradiction touches no less on socialist faith itself than on the individual socialist believer. The deepest motive in Reuben's structure is, as we have seen, the need to establish socialist activity on a basis which would sanctify even the most ordinary work-a-day activity. And, therefore, he is so enthusiastic over Landauer's call to "immediate action." Nevertheless he is rather fearful that all those, "in the social order of the present, who demand suggestions for immediate action, do not carry within themselves the resolve to oppose the deeply rooted present ways of life." (pp. 136-7) How is this to be understood? It seems to me that, consciously or not, the contrast between the saintly and ordinary folk, not to speak of the wicked, once more plays a part here. The saintly, the conscious revolutionary socialists, have always to be wrapped in sanctity, their only profession being that of workers for the coming socialist upheaval. For this reason they need even to-day to build their economic way of life on a socialist basis. The great mass of morally average people, who to this day languish not only in physical but also spiritual slavery and who must be freed as quickly as possible by the saintly ones, can do no more than live "at God's mercy" (p. 141) until for them, too, redemption comes. This is more or less the way in which the idea of a socialist priesthood is formed from a revolutionary aristocracy in contrast to the great masses of ordinary people. Reluctantly I am reminded of Bolshevism again and Lenin's concept of "professional revolutionaries". In the context of our main theme this strikes me as more than merely a random thought induced by chance.

III

Our friend Reuben, having hardly started on the road of socialist religion, was obliged to turn away from it; Bolshevism proceeds with merciless logic. Reuben believes that "religion is possible only in a socialist guise" (p. 130), just as socialism is possible only within a profound religiosity (p. 130); Bolshevism proclaims, "Either communism or religion!" There is no place under the sun for both of them. Where Bolshevism holds sway, religion will be extirpated. And where faith is still unshaken, there is no prospect for a socialist revolution. When Russian Bolsheviks managed to publish the theoretical magazine, "Under the Banner of Marxism", Lenin in the congratulatory letter to his disciples pointed out that their most important task was the struggle against all kinds of clericalisms, from ecclesiastical beliefs to philosophical idealism. To-day we know that Lenin's fight against philosophers, priests and rabbis was not merely of theoretical intent, but thoroughly practical or, in fact, more practical than theoretical. Without any hesitation the most drastic and inhuman measures were used for the subjugation of the foe, and whatever else one might say, the fight was conducted with Marxist consistency. That is why in its essence Marxism is a religion, a philosophy with pretensions to unlimited autocracy and, in addition, with a morality which permits any sordid means to be used in the attainment of its sacred purpose.

As long as Marxism lacked power, its religious character was concealed by its supposedly scientific character. It therefore appeared to be "anti-religious", not because its own intention was to take the place of the Church, but only because the churches with their powerful organisations stood in the way of its work of spiritual liberation, and because with their "heavenly" nonsense they were deliberately confusing the minds of the proletariat and preventing it from recognising its closest "material" interest on this sinful earth.

Marxism indeed expressly proclaimed: "Religion is a private matter", thus indicating that it was prepared to reach a compromise with religion, saying in effect: "If you do not interfere in my natural economic-political sphere, I will continue to keep out of your supernatural metaphysical heavens. In this way we shall be able, each within his own limits, to conduct a spiritual struggle—you against scientific materialism, and I against your childish metaphysics and mythology." A symptom of this, in fact, very friendly attitude was the philosophical poverty in general of the whole of Marxist science. Apart from a few inferior writings like Kautsky's "Ethik", the West European Marxist school made not a single serious attempt to probe deeper in the basic premises of human thought, will and feeling. Even the more profound philosophical observations that are scattered in the writings of the young Marx remained unnoticed by the West European Marxists for more than half a century. This attitude first underwent a change at the moment when Russia made its appearance on the European horizon. Looking back we can see to-day that it was by no means fortuitous that it was the Russian émigré Plekhanov who, after Engels, was the first to build up Marxism into a philosophical system, uncovered its Spinozist-metaphysical roots, and published his book "The Monistic Concept of History" in Russian and in Russia. There, in the general moral revolutionary atmosphere it was perceived that Marxism had within itself a tendency towards a spiritual revolution and, if seriously believed in, Marxism could usurp of the old religions.

Shortly after the first Russian Revolution, Lunacharsky published the two volumes of his "Religion and Socialism", in which he tried to show that the relation of Marxist Socialism to religion was such as that of a subordinated concept. True, he had little success, because he omitted altogether to touch upon the most important point of the whole matter. The point is not, as the author believed, Marxist justice or its conception of beauty, but its notion of theoretical objectivity. It is superficial to put Marx's system on an equal basis with "the other four religions created by Jews" namely Judaism, Christianity, Islam and Spinoza's pantheism, as Lunacharsky did with exaggerated pathos, because all these four systems are based on an objective truth independent of man and mankind, while the Marxist idea of truth is through and through anthropological. For Marxism it is a rule that in the whole history of civilisation there is not a single manifestation which is not a function of the social-economic order of the period in question. This means, in other words, that even that which in the capitalist world is regarded as objective applies to that world alone, but for any other, and for the proletarian world, in particular, it is only a half-truth, if not a whole lie. According to Marxism the dominating truth, the allegedly "objective" truth is only the truth accepted by those who dominate. From which it follows that even proletarian Marxism itself becomes truly correct only when Marxism comes to power. Until then it is only a tendency towards truth. The world historical proletarian action, the socialist revolution alone, that can transform Marxist theory into objective truth. For Marxism, therefore, practice means more than confirmation of theory; it is itself a theorem, the centre-piece of the whole theoretical structure.*

All this was explicit in the well known statement by Marx, namely that philosophy should cease to try to understand the world and begin to change it instead. Naturally, people contented themselves with a banal interpretation of the passage, taking it to mean that practice was superior to theory. But Marxism had to become Russo-Bolshevist before its metaphysical-religious meaning could become visible. The passage was then treated seriously as really meaning that Marxism was chosen for a new Work of Creation, a new Genesis, because it had a living power enabling it to create a new world, a new sort of man and a new nature. The whole practice of Bolshevik dictatorship would have to be regarded as sheer lunacy unless we realised that it was impelled by a belief in the superhuman, divine power of a proletariat reared on Marxism. But while the proletariat is supposedly the only real creator of the world of the future, its "apostles" consider themselves entitled in the interests of their mission to decide on life and death, "who is and who is not to come to his end" and to deprive millions upon millions of people of their last shred of freedom, presuming to play the role before whole nations of a primordial force or of that of a judge on high. There is no Absolute but the proletariat and the Comintern is its prophet—that is the credo of the new Islam. Is Religion a "private matter"? Away with private matters! The proletarian master of the world knows nothing of private property. Body and soul, both are his.

*) See Georg Lukacs: "Geschichte und Klassenbewusstsein", Berlin, 1923 and my essay (Dr. A. Steinberg's) "Die Weltanschauung des Bolschewismus" in the German symposium "Staat, Recht und Wirtschaft des Bolschewismus", Berlin, 1925.

Such is the result when socialism becomes a religion and human aims, which may still be of the highest, are raised to the height of the Absolute. It is the old great experience that power corrupts. And what greater power can there be than the awareness that I or my creed embodies the Absolute? The prophet proved right a thousand times when he called upon man in God's name "to walk humbly with thy God" (Micah 6, 8). It is part of this humility that one should consider it again and yet again before proclaiming in one's own name anything about the absolute principle of our existence. Granted that logic is not the highest court of appeal, nevertheless it does afford some measure of validity. Ideas lead and can also mislead us. If you handle them crudely, they crumble in your hands, enveloping you in a cloud of dust that chokes and distorts your vision. Clarity, clarity and still more clarity, especially when dealing with public matters. Let us not be afraid of sharp arguments. Debate is better than decay. The crisis in present day socialism consists not only in the fact that its most active wing has gone aside and set itself up as a socialist religion. Should religious people who are activist and maximalist socialists, therefore, enter into competition with a false faith, the faith of people posing as gods? Heaven forbid! Their duty to-day is to say first of all: "No!" If, as religious people, as ethical socialists, they affirm that they had nothing of the sort in mind, but something entirely different, then the outcome will be, not a new kind of socialist religion, but a Jewish, a Christian and, (who knows?) even perhaps a Mohammedan . . . in short a religious socialism.

How can this be envisaged from a particular Jewish point of view. I should like to make this the subject of my next discussion.

9. Socialism and Messianism

I

In the problem of Jewish religious socialism, the main point is the question: Is there any particular relationship between the modern secular socialist movement and the basis of the Jewish faith—a belief in absolute redemption in a future of perfection? Are Socialism and Messianism two words for the same idea or, on the contrary, are they mutually exclusive? In other words, can Jewish religious maximalism be considered as a sort of sanction or approval of the socio-economic tendencies of present day non-religious society; or is it true that there is no bridge and there is no crossing from the new heaven and earth of the Jewish prophetic dream to the toil and strife that afflict simple flesh and blood in the everyday market of life? Two things will depend on the answer to this vital question: how far can a modern believing Jew admit into the deepest recesses of his heart the longings which are bred by the modern secularized spirit; and how far can a Jewish socialist be in harmony with the highest traditions of Judaism?

Even in this formulation the question appears sufficiently complicated. As in any of the more profound questions of cultural history, it is not possible to set down the first question mark without having first inwardly made a whole series of important assumptions. Before venturing any answer one has to make clear one's antecedents, to expound the meaning of the words used—in our case—of the term relationship.

When speaking of the relationship between religion and socialism, of their closer or more remote degree of kinship, one usually has first in mind, even though unconsciously, the historical dependence which connects the socialist ideal with the socio-ethical roots of the world religions. It will suffice here to recall one name, Jaurès, who with all the force of his fiery eloquence, in his book on the "new army", "L'armée nouvelle", tried to bar the way to the catastrophe of 1914. He roused the conscience of the French bourgeoisie by clearly demonstrating that the socialist pursuit of peace was no more than a direct legacy of true Christian morals. At the same time and in the same volcanic language he preached to the working men that without the gift they had received from the

This essay was first published in Yiddish in *Fraye Shriftn*, Warsaw, 1930, No. 10.

bourgeoisie in the vernacular translation of the Hebrew Bible, the enslaved proletariat would never have been able to sense the powerful urge towards a free and independent life. Not only the revolutionary spirit in the labour movement, but also its highest ideal of world peace and justice are derived, according to Jaurès from religion, that is from the Jewish element in Christianity which remains the yeast that always forces the human spirit to straighten its back and rise anew when the aim of freedom confronts a man. It is the most Christian element in Christianity. The same can be said also in this way: In modern revolutionary socialism, the revolutionary element is Judaistic; the socialist is Christian. Without the Judaeo-Christian world-view, socialism could not possibly have become the driving force of the new epoch. The religious legacy of the past is the historical basis of both the non-religious and anti-religious Labour movement in the culture of the so-called Christian world.

Let us assume that Jaurès, irrespective of his cultural make-up and historical background, is in the right, and that socialism is indeed the direct offspring of European Christendom. What then is the implication for our problem? Does it offer the Christian believer any approach to modern socialism? Does it enable the convinced socialist to find a new meaning in the ancient faith? How often does it happen that a father does not recognise his own flesh and blood, or his heir? And does not the Gospel urge a man to forsake father and mother and go where the new faith directs him? The union of two separate views or conceptions of the world in a single stream of thought requires more powerful resources than a sense of historical gratitude and the satisfaction of beholding one's direct descendents. In general, the recognition of de facto union tells us nothing—but really nothing at all about the possibility of an inner agreement. Of what use are the threads that extend from a historical manifestation into the past, when the past remains the past, and the present remains the present, as indeed it was for Jaurès? Union does not necessarily mean unity, and one cannot extract the essence of life through purely mental effort.

This becomes particularly obvious when we pass to the subject of socialism and Judaism. We Jews have inherited socialism not from our own forefathers or from our ancient Jewish religious culture, but from our non-Jewish environment. During the past century we have taken over a good deal from our surroundings, almost everything that the outside world held precious and holy. But as for the holiest thing in the European cultural heritage, Christianity itself, if we except its Jewish elements, we did not touch it even with the tips of our fingers, unless perhaps unwittingly. We have had nothing to do consciously with cultural apostasy, not even the most irreligious among us. We therefore treat as void also the union of socialism and religion which gives non-Jewish socialists and Christians the possibility, at least in philosophical theory, to conceive of each as part of a greater whole. We are thus left with no choice but either to deny any connection between Judaism and socialism, or to try to discover such a connection from the inside, from the innermost point of living Judaism, which is Messianism.

II

Why particularly from the point of Messianism is not difficult to see. Socialism is nurtured mainly by an ideal set in the future. In so far as it limits itself with the improvement of the working man's conditions here and now, it is at most only making preparation for socialist politics and is therefore not entitled to use the name it bears. It merely ranges itself with such social systems and tendencies as democratism, liberalism, conservatism and such like. These systems of thought and their programmes also keep an eye on the future, except that their tomorrow is the morrow of today. It is a tomorrow visible on the screen of today fused with today's past. In short, it is conceived as an outcome of the present. While true socialism wants just the opposite—to make the present a result of an ideal morrow—modern socialism has, from its very infancy, had its mind on Utopia, which is literally "a Land that Never Was", a land of nowhere (from the Greek *topos* meaning a place and *u* meaning not). Recognising the material realities of this world, socialism made sure from the start of the creation of an ethical ideal of a future world and an ideal future. The "Olam Haba", the World to Come, belongs to the Jewish concept and the Jewish idea of the Messianic Age. Secular socialism and Jewish Messianism are thus in one respect fully in agreement: both want to change the existing order of things. While for those who live only for the day it is the most obvious thing in the world that the present comes before the future, for those people who keep their eyes on an ideal future, it is this future that comes first with them, the present being something which will have to be changed by spiritual power in accordance with the shape of the future. Both in true socialism and in Jewish Messianism, this world is only the shadow cast on our day by the world-to-come. That is, by the way, the chief difference between Judaism and Christianity. Although the term *Christianity* means *Messianism* (for *Christos* is of course the Greek equivalent of the Hebrew *Messiah*, the Anointed One) and the Christian Messiah, Jesus, is immersed in the history of the past for believing Christians, whereas we Jews still await the time of Redemption with the Coming of the Messiah.

The area of agreement between Socialism and Messianism goes even further than that. Just as socialism holds fast on tomorrow for the sake of today, the ideal for the sake of present reality, similarly, Messianism is not, Heaven forbid, a means of sweetening away the bitterness of the present, but the norm by which every "today" must be regarded as a festival eve the eve of Redemption. Just as Maimonides' creed has it: "Even though he tarry, I will wait daily for the Messiah's coming." The Messianic ideal, like that of socialism, is non-romantic. Both have their faces turned not to a blissful childhood of the human race, not towards a lost Paradise which, like an image in a dream, is not to be re-created, but towards a ceaselessly materialising future. The future, however distant it may appear, is always closer and more real than even the immediate past. That which has been can never be recalled and can never be changed. But that which has to come is on its way and can come. The future-ness, if I may call it that, of socialism and Messianism makes them both essentially realistic. And since they are realistic, they must also approach closely in various details of their aim. In the Jewish view at least, there is only one Creator of the World and therefore there is only one world—and one sole reality.

But what can be more real for man than his own fate in an empirical world? "Not in Heaven . . ." it is written. The Torah did not remain in Heaven; it points the way for us here on earth. In the celestial spheres, man could possibly have been an entity on his own; but in this sinful world he must be a man among men. Even the loneliest, the most solitary of men cannot turn aside from the highways of life *("Derech Eretz")* from the relationship with fellow men. That is his fate—a tiny star among tiny stars, his so-called wholeness being only a grain of sand on the shore of an endless shore, a drop in the ocean. As Aristotle defined it once and for all, "Man is a political and social animal." Human fate is truly social political fate, which is elementary to any socialist. But does the Jewish socialist bear in mind that Messianism primarily aims at planting a heaven on earth and then raising earth to heaven? That the Jewish ideal of the future is throroughly socio-political? That the Kingdom of the Eternal, the universal rule of the Almighty which has to be established here on earth, means the dominion of harmony and social justice for all mankind?

Admittedly, Messianism has even higher aims than international brotherhood and social equality. Its maxima are higher than those of socialism. But as we shall see later, this is no defect but rather an advantage. For the moment let us consider to what extent the content of the Messianic ideal coincides with the ideal of socialism. As is well-known, justice and justice are not necessarily equal, and world peace is often a euphemism for world imperialism. In Christian polemics against the Jewish faith, the accusation figures conspicuously that Jews have for many generations dreamed of only one thing, Jewish dominion over entire mankind; the more they are humiliated, the more they long to rule over their masters; and one day be revenged for the persecution and affliction to which God himself has condemned them. Had there been even a scrap of truth in this accusation, the ways of socialism and Judaism could never possibly meet. Socialism would then have been the foe of Judaism, and Jewish socialism would have been a blatant heresy. The fact is, however, that the accusation about Jewish imperialist aims is, from first to last, false and defamatory, an the result of gross lack of understanding. One may think that it is not worth wasting two words on such stupidities when discussing Jewish Messianism in a Jewish context. Nevertheless, it is not so. Modern secular Judaism and especially Jewish Socialism will not entertain the thought that the Jewish people, with its belief in Messiah, has considered its own existence only as a means of leading the world to final Redemption, and that but for this awareness of mission, it would, like so many other people, have given up its right of independent existence. Has not just this pseudo-Messianism turned the world into hell for the Jewish people? It is the messianic principle or belief which has welded the people into a sort of group or association with a programme, a militant party, or an army camp which refuses to surrender as long as it flies its holy banner. So-called Jewish world dominion exists only in the hope and belief that the time will come when all the peoples of the earth will assemble beneath the same prophetic flag. The principal thing here is not the people itself, but its mission, not the party or the party rule, but the realization of its aims and ideal. As long as socialism is still formulated as a programme there must be a socialist party; as long as Messiah is delayed, the Messianic people must continue to live. The Jewish people therefore does not fight against the nations of the world, but always and everywhere against the rule of evil, all that is vicious in political and social practice, and against corruption in its own and the surrounding world.

I have used the word "fight", but "should fight" would be more correct. As in all big parties there is also in the party that calls itself the Jewish people much, far too much, corruption. It is therefore necessary to keep reminding oneself what being a Jew means. But is that any different from the world of socialism? There, too, is not the ideal turned into petty cash for the payment of small debts, when the fulfilment of socialism's greatest obligations which are at the same time its greatest privileges, is postponed not merely from day to day but actually from generation to generation? Although socialism does not cease to be socialism, and Judaism does not cease to be Messianic, peace and justice, which are the most important attributes of the Messianic era, should be the guiding principles of Jewish life, even at a time when God's glory is in the shadows. Similarly, in the capitalist epoch, the socialist movement should promote true international brotherhood and a morality that is above that which sets the standard for good and evil in the business world. Would that one could say at some time that there was no difference whatever between ideal and real life! Such a thought could occur, however, only to romantics, who tend to perceive the world of their fantasy as infallibly real. That is precisely where the anti-romantic realism, both of socialism and Messianism, is so pronounced, taking account as it does of the force of harsh reality, and not underrating it. Contained in the conception of Messianism is the idea of the "Messianic birth pangs" (or afflictions), the proposition that the new world cannot come to birth without pain. And yet another profound thought was bequeathed to us by our ancient philosophers of history: Messiah will come either in a generation made up entirely of saints or in a generation of evil-doers. It is a deep thought. Lest the idealist minority should fall into despair and become helpless amid the flood-waters of evil, the heart of believers was graced by a term of dialectic by the revelation that the overthrow of evil and the liberating revolution are imminent at the darkest moment of history, which may be close at hand and not remote. It is said, furthermore, that even in a generation made up of the wicked, one single saint, the Redeemer, can initiate a new epoch, the epoch of genuine justice.

We have thus reached the point where the kinship between socialism and Messianism becomes almost tangible. Justice and justice are not identical. Is the colloquial meaning of justice the same in the socialist idiom? At first glance there would seem to be no room for doubt. Is not socialism before all else a struggle for social justice? And on the other hand, is not the justice which will hold sway in the world after the advent of Messiah the justice of law and right? But justice as an aspect of Law is the frame of economy. The Redeemer, who is at the same time a righteous judge, can pass righteous judgment only when the law on which he bases his verdict is itself just. Every epoch, however, has its own conception of justice, that is to say, in so far as form is adjusted to content, and positive right to economic conditions of man's existence. That is the final theme offered by ancient Jewish thought, namely, that the Torah was created not for angels, but was given into the hands of men. It teaches righteousness not to creatures that have become static and frozen, but to living and evolving human beings. Jerusalem, as we know, was laid waste when its people held fast to the Law and refused to overstep its mark. The limit of right is, therefore, according to the Jewish conception, the lowest step of the supernormal, the moral force of right. This moral force, this longing for justice, is the initial spring which enables the ideas of justice to grow and flower, providing the possibility always to renew the conditions of the social order. The Jewish idea of justice and its scope for development, the need always to give it more content and more definition, makes it so spacious and viable, and so independent of time and age, that the entire socialist morality and the whole programme of the socialist economic order, can readily find an honorable place in the tabernacles of Messiah. The justice of the Prophets, the ancient Jewish social reformers, is not the maximal but the minimal programme of Jewish Messianism and in its nature belongs to the things that are without measure. So it should also be with the morality of the socialist idea of Justice.

I am aware that I am speaking here of socialist morality as though we knew precisely what the term meant. Far from it! Socialism is an abstraction, though no more pale abstraction than Messianism. I mean thereby that the tablets of socialist justice, like the principles of socialist concepts of good and evil in general, are nowadays even more worthless than blank tablets, to some extent void and to an even greater extent covered by deformed hierogliphs. This is no place for a critique of the morals of the Soviet Union. Even the morality of most of the anti-communist socialists offers a considerable field for critical examination. For the present, however, it will suffice to demonstrate that Jewish Messianism, which can easily accommodate the practical programme of socialism beneath its Utopian roof, can manage still more. It can serve as a criterion for an evaluation of the latest and the highest aims of socialism in action.

III

Until now, while drawing parallels between socialism and Messianism, I have deliberately touched upon only the formal idea of the future and its implications—the ideas of peace and justice which at one time appeared to be general principles. This, however, is characteristic of Messianism only in the smallest measure. Neither morality nor the idealistic conception of time are to be found at the real centre of Messianism. Its heart is truth, by which I mean divine Truth, in respect of which, everything that we today designate with that name is comparable to the shadow of a shadow. Messianism is a religious conception. Religion is not satisfied with relative dimensions. Its measure of measures is the absolute, God. And the Jewish God is before all else the God of Truth, and only after that the God of justice and peace. To put it differently, the highest standards for determining the relationship between man and his fellows must be founded on a deeper basis than that of human existence. We have seen that justice is really a pattern or mould which changes and, from epoch to epoch, must change its content. It is easy to prove that even international peace is in a certain sense a relative ideal, i.e. an idea with a changeable content. But it is not so with truth. Truth cannot by its very nature be a half-truth. A half-truth is a whole lie. And all we know so far is the knowledge that we do not know, that we want to know, and that the aim of one's endeavour to know truth, is independent of our fortuitous human nature. Only when the Messiah comes, "will the whole earth be full of knowledge as the sea is full of water." "Then," says the Prophet Jeremiah, "they shall teach no more every man his neighbour, and every man his brother saying, 'Know the Lord,' for they shall all know Me, from the least to the greatest." (Jer. 31:33). The fullness of understanding will be the most conspicuous sign of the "super-historical" Messianic era.

Super-historical? Is that not the same thing as super-empirical? Can Messianism, whose ideal knowledge steps across the threshold of historical reality, still be considered as one of the realistic, anti-romantic tendencies of the spirit? Or does that not turn the Messianic Utopia into a dream that can never be realised? A metaphysical fantasy, a castle in the air? But something that can never collapse because no one can dwell there? Where is the ladder which would enable us to ascend from the dust of the earth into the halls mirrored in heaven? Must we hope for miracles?

Yes indeed, for miracles! That is really the principal lesson to be learned from the whole discussion on socialism and religion, or socialism and Messianism. He who does not believe in miracles may with a clear conscience erase from his socialist credo the word *socialism*. He who does not discern today, after the Bolshevist experiment, that without the great miracle of a most radical revolution in the human spirit, socialism in practice can be no more than a diabolical caricature of its won ideal, remains, however secure or self-confident he may feel, the most naive of "Utopianas". Truth, the faith in its realisation, which is the heart of Messianism, compels us to understand justice and peace in a maximalist, super-historical sense: to raise justice to the level of love, and peace to the height of an all-embracing metaphysical harmony. From this potential it follows that people who long for absolute truth, justice and peace, must already now find the means of introducing a new quality into human relationships. If, on the contrary, one is satisfied with the present way of life *(derech-eretz)* which unites socialists and non-socialists, and holds that the nature of man can only develop naturally, that is, with the same cruel slowness as external nature, then the hope of any radical change in our social environment is childishly naive. Neither naive nor Utopian in the ordinary sense of the word, but on the contrary realistic and deliberate is the forecast that sees the world moving to a terrible catastrophe, the like of which the story of humankind has never seen, culminating in a war of all against all, a time of Gog and Magog when only a miracle can save us. Belief in a miracle, however, is itself no miracle. I refer only to its possibility as a belief that only with the help of faith, which Jews call the belief in Messianism, can the fiery volcano that bars us from the future be moved out of the way. Why fool ourselves? It is a supernatural problem which demands a belief in the power of truth, a belief in the superhuman strength of man, a belief in faith itself.

Messianism is the bridge of faith which shows us a road across the historical abyss, the way from exile to redemption. Not we alone are in exile. The Divine Presence is in exile; the whole world is in exile. We are not the only ones whom Messiah has to redeem; the whole world is in need of a Righteous Redeemer, indeed a Redeemer no less than Redemption. If it were otherwise we would not dare to talk of Messianism. The "ism" is in this instance of secondary importance; the real importance is in "Messiah". However brightly we may colour the idea of a perfect human society and perfect human relations, it will never cease to be an abstraction as long as we lack the power to realise the idea in the shape of a real and single person endowed with a heart of flesh and blood and compassion. Justice, however geometrically precise its outline remains nevertheless blind when it lacks the light of the human eye, and even deaf while it does not move the heart of the soul of man. Peace is never more than an adjustable idea in the absence of an individual living in higher harmony with the world, with the past, present and future, and with himself. Truth is a dream: it does not leave its imprint on concrete human thinking. Only faith in the Messiah makes this sinful earth the future home of a Higher Man, the ideal Superman. And just as each one of us has to regard himself as an eye-witness to the Revelation of the Law on Sinai, so each one has to think of himself as the First Man who partook of the Tree of Knowledge and thereby opened the way for the Last Man, for the Higher Man, the Messiah. There is no single person in the world—and this is the key to belief in the Messiah—whose heart is unable to set alight the Messianic Fires, the pains and suffering which are to herald the coming of the Redeemer. Each one is worthy of having the Redeemer within him— "*having*" in both senses—in the sense of possessing and in the sense of giving birth. So lofty is the conception which the Jewish faith has of human existence that it carries within itself the belief in the Messiah! Can then ancient Judaism be shamed by youthful socialism? Quite the contrary! There is much that socialism has still to learn both of Jewish religious ethics and of the concrete Messianic ideal in particular.

The socialist ideal is still far from being properly defined, and it lacks a clear image of the ideal individual. The problem of personality is the weakest point in modern socialism. The duty to form the spark of understanding in the world socialist movement, therefore falls upon Jewish socialism to put to the fore the individual's fate in the present-day world and of the individual in the world of the future.

Socialism opens our eyes to the present meaning of "justice". Jewish Messianism has to teach the world that there are deeper social targets than the endeavour of improving the economic standard of living. Truth will blossom forth from the earth, and with it perfection and holiness. The whole of socialism is no more than one point of Messianism. The ends of Messianism are higher, more real and more holy. The methods of the socialist movement have to be adapted to these aspirations. They have to become just as holy as the final human aspiration.

The Jewish voice should be the constant clearly distinguishable accompaniment of the universal socialist movement and should come from the prophetic depth with its demanding call: Pave the way . . .

10. Peoples and Ideals

I.

On reading my article in the third volume of *Fraie Shriften*, the eminent writer, Dr. Chaim Zhitlovsky, found it necessary, in a most friendly fashion, to present me with a challenge: "With us or against?" (Der Tog, New York, 22nd January 1928 and 5th February 1928). Assuredly, I should like to be counted among the friends rather then the enemies of Chaim Zhitlovsky; but I find it impossible to answer so provocative a demand with an equally short and direct answer, "Yes, I am with you!" The reason is that the insinuation underlying the challenge suggests many points which, as it seems to me, can be answered only with another query, a form of dialogue which, as the old joke has it, is truly Jewish. Long ago in Jericho, when Joshua put the question, "Are you for us or for our enemies", he got the answer—"No!" (Joshua 5, 13-15). In other words the question was badly worded, because there is a third possibility here.

"This way or that" affords, in general, no suitable means of combating that "psychology of discontent and longing" which Dr. Zhitlovsky discerns in the younger generation. Why is the younger generation dissatisfied if not precisely because it sees before it apparently only two roads: one leading to the cosmopolitan-assimilationist camp, the other into the camp of "secular progressive nationalism"? Neither road, however, offers any way out for the rising generation—particularly not the road of "assimilation" because it has never essentially been any more than an attempt to solve the Jewish problem on an individual basis. Only individuals can actively surrender to assimilation, not masses or a people as a whole. When the assimilation of West European Jews in the nineteenth century became a mass movement, instead of turning Jews into Germans, Frenchmen or Englishmen, it produced a rebirth of the old familiar Marrano-type and a new growth of clandestine penitents suffering even to the third and fourth generation from an inquisition of their own conscience. For the new generation, therefore, in so far as its thinking is influenced by Jewish-social considerations and is aware of the surrounding world, the way of assimilation is out of the question from the start. The "uncompromising battle"

This essay was first published in Yiddish in *Fraye Shriftn, Paris, 1928, No. 4*.

against outward assimilation waged by Chaim Zhitlovsky undoubtedly
rescued many Jewish individuals from a profound psychological peril.
Nevertheless, it remains important to draw a clear distinction between a
great number, even an unlimited number, of individuals and the living
organic entity which we call the Jewish people and for which assimilation, I
am convinced, is a danger not in the sense of an amputation, but of an
internal infection. Dr. Zhitlovsky, however will not acknowledge this. He
has for some years been speaking before the assembly of the Jewish
people, as it were, and thinks he has been addressing the atoms of which
the Jewish people is composed: the individual. In this regard I believe Dr.
Zhitlovsky to be a true son of the old European Haskalah or, or to put it
more precisely, a follower of an integrating individualism and not of the
newer differentiating collectivism. Many "hideous misunderstandings" to
use Zhitlovsky's own expression, might have been avoided, if the leaders of
the older generation had paid more attention to this modern and at the
same time truly Jewish collectivist trend of thought.

It might possibly have become clear then to the leaders of the older
generation why even "secular progressive nationalism" no longer possessed the power of releasing to-day's generation from "discontent and
yearning". The reason is practically the same; but to connect cause and
effect is in this case more complicated and must be proved at every step.

II.

In earlier essays of mine I described our "secular" nationalism as a
thoroughly "formalistic" standpoint, and I took the liberty of comparing it
with a velvet curtain before an empty Holy Ark. The comparison was not to
Dr. Zhitlovsky's liking. "Our nationalists", he writes, "always combine
their pure nationalism with some other ideal. . . . . Even the nationalism
which I serve heart and soul, became known as progressive nationalism
and proclaimed, more than once, that its only aim was—the realisation in
every corner of Jewish life of the four deeply rooted ideals of general
human progress: personal freedom and fulfilment, cultural attainment,
social justice and international brotherhood". Is such a "national ark of
holies—Chaim Zhitlovsky would say—"not very well stocked?" Is it not
"the best stocked of all?"

I do not deny that the ark is well filled. I would be so bold to say,
however, that it is filled with pure, clear, transparent air. Without air a man
suffocates; but air alone does not allay a man's hunger. Close analysis of the
kind of air for which we have to thank the blessed pen of Dr. Zhitlovsky,
reveals at once that personal freedom and fulfilment, cultural wealth,
social justice and international brotherhood are the elements without
which no man and no people can survive, or in these days even as much as
breathe. For that very reason, one would suppose, there would be no need

to confine them in some sort of "ark", particularly a "national" one. In other words, the nature of general human ethics is to breathe "where it will"; the way from a free ideal, abstractly formulated, leads at best to the isolated individual but never to the reality of an historic collective manifestation. No matter how many roots an abstract ideal may have, four or four times four, as long as it strikes no roots in the fertile soil of history, it remains suspended in the air and is like the air itself. How will it help to attach it to a national world-view or to dress it in a national skull-cap? An ideal remains an ideal, and a skull-cap but a skull-cap. Airy content cannot combine organically with velvet; one remains insubstantial, the other empty. And when the idealist content drops out, what remains but a threadbare formalist and negative nationalism? as B. A. Weinraub says ("Yiddishe Welt", Philadelphia, 17.2.1928).

Anyone who requires a living illustration of this should make a point of carefully perusing the article by Dr. Zhitlovsky already mentioned. Naturally, I do not doubt for a moment that the idealism and nationalism of Chaim Zhitlovsky are in his own mind closely interwoven. Therein lies the difference between the subjective and the objective, two worlds each governed by a different law of unity. On this subject Dr. Zhitlovsky himself once wrote a profound study "Relation of Historical Ideas" (*Historishe Ideen-Verbindungen*). Often deep down in a man's subjective mind two ideas dwell like a pair of doves. Once they break out into the wide world of objectivity, they inevitably have to part.

III.

The "twelve lines" which Dr. Zhitlovsky devotes to abstract idealism, and to the formalist general-national world-view, set out the first of the three theses which, according to the eminent author, must form the touchstone of any new line of thought in our national question—"Are you for us or our enemies?" (As though by design, the "Tog" printed this thesis in exactly twelve lines.) Thesis 'A' says: "The existence of the Jewish people and their free internal development are ends in themselves requiring no foundation in external ideas or ideals which have no relevance whatever to Jewish life and must be combatted as endangering its existence."

I have frequently perused these few lines, and every time I have wondered anew and ended up in the same state of indecision. If the existence of the Jewish people, which for Dr. Zhitlovsky is a people like all peoples, and an end in itself, if every nation can and must say, "I am also a human entity to be measured against you", what becomes of the fourth basic idea of "international brotherhood"? Everything I have ever learned from German philosophy, starting with Kant, about the idea of "end-in-itself" and "rule of objectives" cries in protest against the theory of Dr. Zhitlovsky. Wild associations intrude on the mind: "Sacra Egoisma" of the wicked Roman Emperor, the "national eros" of the Russian "German-eaters", the resurrection of the German Wotan cult, a whole Pantheon of old and new idols. But this cannot possibly be the intention of a Chaim Zhitlovsky! Thus there remains a question, and I must ask Dr. Zhitlovsky to clarify the initial argument of his challenge.

Dr. Zhitlovsky did indeed provide in advance a partial interpretation of his thesis. I must confess, however, that I underdstood the commentary no better than the text. "Ideals come", he observes, "and ideals go. But a nation wants to live for ever." Every word creates a new riddle! We know, firstly, that most human ideals are not older, roughly speaking, than the more significant of the surrounding peoples. The ideal of Christendom, for example, is older than all the Christian peoples without exception. Secondly, is the will to live for ever, itself everlasting? And thirdly, is "will" also an ideal, in so far as it deserves the name, not effective for ever? Fourthly, is not everlasting life, or immortality, an ideal in itself? And fifthly, does any compelling need arise for a people to wish just to live for ever in the world and not because of a higher purpose?

I could extend my list of questions even further, but enough! The fifth question is sufficiently pointed in itself, and it might be useful to pause for a while to consider it.

IV.

Whence comes the impulse, I ask, that makes peoples, and among them the Jewish people, to favour a straightforward nationalism, that is a national life as "end-in-itself"?

"Only to a lunatic," writes Dr. Zhitlovsky, "would it ever occur that a people would want to sacrifice itself for humanity down to a small remnant of itself". Let us, for a moment, substitute for the word "humanity" something more suitable, e.g. Truth, Faith, or God. Let us consider what the sentence would then convey. The first result would be that our Prophets would have to be included among Dr. Zhitlovsky's lunatics. Is then the faith of the "small remnant", the "remnant of the Yishuv", no more than a quotation from Isaiah? But among others to be included in the same lunatic circle would be all those who have harkened to the words of the Prophets as to Divine Truth, and that means the majority of the Jewish people of the last three and a half thousand years. Even to-day, at least half of the Jewish people is in its heart of hearts, I believe, true to the prophetic promise. With this lunatic promise the Jewish people survived Assyria and Egypt, the empires of Greece and Rome, Baghdad and Byzantium, the "Holy German Reich", and a long series of other social organisms both kosher and otherwise. For the prophetic promise the Jewish people sacrificed itself on the altars of the whole African-Asian-European world. One may ask, however: Has the iron faith of the people in its future, for which it has for thousands of years offered the perpetual sacrifice of its existence anything to do with "humanity"? I answer this question once again with one word: the Messiah. The opportunity will still occur to show that the Jewish ideal of Redemption comprises no more and no less than the absolute Deliverance-Ideal that underlies world history. It has as much relevance to the Messiah-Idea as any ideal which can be interpreted as a sort of mission. On this, too, there will be occasion to dwell again.

Our secular nationalism insists proudly on its clarity, on the fact that it has become emancipated from the thousand-year-old lunacy, and it does not doubt that thereby it serves the popular interest better than does the blind traditionalism. Happy are those who feel confident enough to rely on their own good sense! The riddle that still confronts me is: why do such leaders so often lack the courage to speak out and declare that they consider themselves the "masters" in active Jewish life, that they set their calculated programme above the blind instincts of the masses, and that their will must become a law of the people? Instead of openly dictating to the people they pretend that they are only their executive agents, their devoted followers. "In the life of a people" writes Dr. Zhitlovsky, "the people as a whole is the master," and in the course of speaking he declares "in the name of the people": "Long may they live! First of all live! and after that start thinking how to fill your life with ideals." When a disciple or envoy of the people, whose whole story contradicts the formalist doctrine or theory, begins to talk in this manner, the mind leaps at once to that excellent Talmudic rule: "Blame cannot be shifted to the employer", i.e. for such language the responsibility is not the people's, but only Dr. Zhitlovsky's. But why does he appeal to the people at all? A hint on solving this riddle was contained in my former essay: I fear that our secular end-in-itself nationalism stands in an odd relation to itself.

At this point we may pass to Dr. Zhitlovsky' a second thesis.

V.

The second thesis declares: "Jewish national existence and its free development must have a secular foundation in the widest possible sense of the term, in the sense of absolute spiritual freedom that recognises no limits, no prohibitions and no proscriptions in regard to what a Jew may believe and what he may not. Such absolute spiritual emancipation is possible only in the conditions of our own Jewish country or a cultural growth in our own Jewish language."

For the time being I avoid the question concerning the "conditions" of "absolute spiritual emancipation". I do so not because an "own Jewish country" and an "own Jewish language" are for me problematical words. On the contrary! But I am prompted to look into those terms and see what they embrace, which is a considerable matter in itself. For the purposes of our present theme it will be enough to analyse what our secular Jews really mean by the idea of "secularism".

If the term "secularism" signified truly and simply "absolute spiritual freedom", I would unhesitatingly subscribe to the thesis with both hands. What troubles me, however, is that according to modern secular usage the emphasis in the word "secularism" is not in unlimited freedom but precisely in its limitation. According to fashionable secular custom, a Jew may believe in whatever he wishes, even in the theosophy of Krishna-murti, but not in the basic hypotheses of our own "Credo", in the Jewish "I believe". As soon as a Jew remembers his Redeemer (Go-al-Tzedek), he is promptly warned that he is blundering into the bog and quick-sands of "World Mission", he is accused of being an assimilationist, and is suspected of heresy regarding "absolute freedom". I dislike the sophist in the cause of secularism quite as much as cursing in the name of Heaven. I demand that there should be no exclusion from the modern Jewish world even of those who want to be Jews "as God commanded". Yes, let our "progressive" world acknoweldge that even observing all the 613 commandments (mitzvot) is not a sin.

The true meaning of our secularism is not freedom of thought and conscience, but struggle: the fight against religious belief, tradition and the continuity of Jewish cultural development. If it were otherwise one would talk simply of freedom and not of secularisation. "Progressive" Jewish nationalism has in this respect been somewhat retrogressive. There was a time when the fight against tradition was a forward step, a mark of progress. The dialectic joke about historical development loses point, even for truly progressive thought, when the thinkers suddenly lose inclination midway for further progress. Our "free" secularism to-day is itself fettered by a tradition which is, however, in comparison with the actual and potential wealth of the old cultural heritage, as poor and barren as a "threadbare Hosanna". The progressive tradition lacks warmth and vitality because it is negative and its aim is always to castigate. At one time the formal principle of freedom of thought was itself of significance; to-day, when this aim has been achieved in the world at large, the world does not know what to do with it. In fact it makes use of it only to restrain the freedom of conscience of the beaten foe of old. At one time people hurled themselves against the bastions of the "Shulkhan Aruch"; but to-day they have provided themselves with a "Shulkhan Aruch" of their own, which however, stands on its head, turning every ancient commandment "Thou shalt not" into "Thou shalt", and vice versa. Until now the codifying ability of our worldliness has not had anything better to show.

So, who has to demand from whom freedom of thought and con-science—the old generation from the new, or the new generation from the old? Or it is right that the Day of Atonement should be a day of eating, and the Eve of Atonement a day of fast.

VI.

The third thesis of Dr. Zhitlovsky touches on assimilation. "The struggle against assimilation," he says, "is the prime and holiest duty of each one who feels any responsibility to Jewish historical destiny and seeks a full and complete Jewish emancipation".

At the very outset I observed that the anti-individualist younger generation would see "outward" assimilation as no less dreadful than assimilation in the innermost sense (or subjective sense), and that precisely because of this it would find as little satisfaction in "progressive nationalism" as in the road to the "Assimilationist cosmopolitan camp". After this long critical introduction it will, it seems to me, be a simple matter to explain briefly what I meant. Secular progressive nationalism, which denies that the Jewish people has always bowed to an ideal; which wants to persuade us, like a Dostoevsky (See Fr. Sh. No. 1), that the real intent of the Jewish will-to-live is merely to live; and that all Israel is, in other words, no more than the hero of the Christian legend of the Eternal Cain—such a nationalism is, to my mind, a form of crude assimilation even if it is unconscious. The "bitter uncompromising fight against assimilation" which I would very much have liked to lead under the banner of Chaim Zhitlovsky, must begin in one's own home, perhaps even in the heart. The individualism of the older generation is like a magnifying glass through which the danger outside appears far greater than it really is, the danger within much smaller. This arises from the fact that the ideal of individualism is a castle in the air, a product of subjective fantasy. Instead of clinging to the historical ideal of the people and teaching the people the meaning of "national existence", they find it possible to scold the nation as they would a naughty schoolboy and even offer it instruction. Wasted effort! The enquiry as to what is more worth-while, nation or ideal, is an academic question. The historical career of the Jewish people solved the problem long ago, and the road to nationhood can to-day lead only over the bridge of national ideal.

The proof of this lies in the "collectivism" of the new generation. According to anti-individualist theory, the national ideal of the individual has real roots only when it is the subjective expression of the objective ideal, i.e. of the power which binds the collective life of the people. It is possible to argue how the objective national idea should be interpreted subjectively, with what content the new age can and should compliment the inherited stock of national ideas, and in what direction the national spirit is able or unable further to develop. In the whole dispute, however, there must be acceptance beyond all doubt that national life and national religion are correlative ideas and that one has no meaning at all without the other. God and the world, the world and humanity, humanity and nation, nation and individual—these are the stages of Jewish national belief on which it is possible to descend into the furthest depths of the subjective spirit so as to mount anew to the greatest heights of objectivity. Yes, indeed! First mankind and then nation; and by the same token the nation takes precedence over the individual. Or does Chaim Zhitlovsky carry his individualism so far as to wish to deny it? Dr. Zhitlovsky is in error when he thinks that there is "a certain contradiction" between the Jewish belief "Thou hast chosen us" and the belief that any nation can bring salvation for mankind in general. The belief in the Jews as the Chosen People—an expression of the belief in a world Redeemer—does not imply a sort of monopolistic right, but the opposite—an obligation or responsibility for the fate or fortune of the whole world. This responsibility, according to Jewish thought, ought to be shared by all the people of the world. Missionaries of Judaism in the non-Jewish world might, before all else, have sought to interpret in all "seventy languages" the principle "Thou hast chosen us". I use the conditional "might have", but in truth the Jewish people, simply by the fact of its very existence, and through the power of its national literature, has always involuntarily fulfilled its missionary role. The Messianic ideas of the German Fichte, the French Michelet, the Polish Slowacki, the Russian Slavophiles, narodnik-populists, the brand-new Yevrazitzi, and even Marx who wanted to make a chosen people out of the proletariat, are nothing more than an attempt to interpret the true Jewish idea that one people must bear the responsibility for the whole world. Are we then, precisely we, to turn our backs on this inherited responsibility because we have become "secular" and "progressive"? If this is considered to be "progress" and "Freedom of thought", then it is far better to be a "blind retrograde."

"But", exclaims Dr. Zhitlovsky, "how can we as a nation take any active part in world history when we have no voice in it?" A question mark upon a question mark. We have no say in the affairs of the world? Then who has any say? Do those have it who sit in the seats of the scornful in Geneva? Those who argue with the mighty of London and Paris on the doling out of ginger-bread or punishment? Those who rely on the power of modern Assyria and Egypt? Those who trade in votes or the right to vote and call out "yea" or "nay" under orders? . . . . . . Heavens, what's happening to-day in our worldly world! What is this worldly world coming to! What a revolution has inner assimilation brought about even in the coolest of heads! How madly odd they picture our entire historic past, not to speak of the future! But no, I cannot believe that our Jewish people will sell back its birthright for another mess of pottage, even if it can get it in the earthenware dish of language and land.

The Jewish people still possesses immeasurable creative power in respect of which all the wealth of the world is not worth a penny. It also commands a potential of history-making activity. The question is, how can this hidden force be converted into effective action? This gives us all food for thought, and if you are not our enemies—, I will go further: If you are not at odds with yourselves, come to our aid.

11. Spinoza and Human Freedom (1632-1932)

"And seekest thou great things for thyself? Seek them not . . ."
(Jeremiah to Baruch, *Jeremiah*, 45, 5)

Three hundred years ago he was given the beautiful Jewish name Baruch, 'the blessed'. Twenty odd years later the blessed one became the accursed one—*Baruch* Spinoza had become *Arur* Spinoza ('cursed'). For reasons which to this day are not quite clear, the Jewish community of Amsterdam, the *kehilla,* excommunicated the young Talmudic scholar and mystic. Apparently, the path taken by the son of the pious communal leader, Miguel D'Espinoza, was from the outset (to speak *more geometrico*) "diametrically" opposed to that of the Law and its guardians. The 'cursed' one shrugged his shoulders and did not relinquish the blessing which his destiny had granted him at his birth. He translated his good Jewish name into Latin, the international language of contemporary learning and secure in its changed form of Benedictus (a name favoured by many Christian saints), he slowly continued on his way. He doubtless held, even then that "it is right to carry one's injuries with equanimity". This principle, which we find in Spinoza's most mature work, his *Ethic* (IV Appendix, heading XIV), is, incidentally, as deeply founded in Jewish as in Christian morality. The sources of both religions were, from his early life on, open to Spinoza's mind. Nevertheless, he did not convert to Christianity, not even after his exclusion from Jewish environment. His fundamental approach demanded that the Church be avoided no less than the Synagogue. Thus within several decades his auspicious Latin name also turned out to be a curse, from 'Benedictus' to 'Maledictus'.

Spinoza continued to be abused for over a hundred years. His principal work appeared several months after his death, in the year 1677, and yet in the second half of the XVIIIth century, the intellectual giant, Kant, who was by no means an obscurantist, would not touch the cursed book. The many sided genius, Leibniz, whose own system revolved about Spinoza's concept of substance, was not ashamed to be ashamed of having been personally acquainted with the Jewish heretic and remaining spiritually bound to him. When Lessing died (1781) and it became known that the famous writer had always regarded himself as Spinoza's disciple, it was of

This essay was first published in Yiddish in *Fraye Shriftn*, Warsaw, December 1932, No. 14.

all people the Father of the Jewish Enlightenment, Moses Mendelssohn, who sharply protested the attempt to dishonour his friend's memory with such a calumny. To the formula which Spinoza made the basis of his philosophical system, "God or Substance or Nature", the surrounding world replied with its formula: "Pantheism or Spinozism is Atheism". Branded with the mark of Cain of intellectual murder on his forehead, for a very long time Spinoza could only exert a secret influence. But at long last his hour to reveal himself did arrive. It was actually Mendelssohn's protest that brought this about. Immediately after the Jewish reformer came to Lessing's defence against the charge of Spinozism, German thinkers and poets, most of them good Christians, defended Spinoza against the accusation of atheism (1785). Jacobi, Herder and also Goethe became Spinoza's advocates. The philosophical dispute centred around the question whether pantheism, according to which God and Nature are identical, and consequently, all which exists is holy, still retains any relationship to religion. To this day the dispute has not been terminated. It is but forty years ago since the eminently Christian philosopher, Vladimir Soloviev, had to raise anew the issue of Spinoza's unjust treatment. Spinoza himself, who believed that at least a part of his soul was immortal, could have witnessed such debates today only with a scornful smile. Would it matter to him whether his system was religious or anti-religious? For him it was important to reveal in it the truth, that truth to which he had penetrated by his own efforts. And this he succeeded in doing only posthumously.

Both XVIIIth-century French materialism and early XIXth-century German idealism are based on Spinozism. "Matter is eternal and necessary," writes the Frenchman Holbach, in his "System of Nature", therein repeating two basic propositions of Spinoza's *Ethic* (Part I, propositions xi, xix). Spinoza's God-Nature has received another name: matter. Some time later the German Fichte recognized that only two philosophical systems are possible: Spinozism and its opposite (what he meant by this will become clearer later on). The young Schelling made much the same claim: "Spinoza's system will always be a model." If so, it implied that the newly appeared claimant may demand no less than "half of the philosophical domain". It was necessary to make peace with him. This task was carried out by the mighty Hegel. He took over Spinoza's world-plan, and built a world according to it. The drawing received colours, the skeleton became a living organism, but the world, the *universum*, was again God, though his utterable name was no longer "Nature" or even "Matter", but "Idea". As it is known, the intellectual empire which Hegel hammered together soon fell apart. Marxism inherited a large share: together with the dialectical method and evolutionary thought, also the belief in the "eternal and necessary" laws of nature and the conviction that absolutely nothing existed outside of nature. Thereby nature again acquired its 'French' honorary title—"Matter". The enthusiasm for "necessity" is doubtless the trait which, psychologically, makes Marx a close relation of Spinoza. Though neither were mathematicians, both derived the greatest pleasure from the iron discipline of mathematics. The spectacles for which the meek optician of Amsterdam polished lenses have not—to use Heine's saying—gone to waste: a substantial audience, ostensibly free of any interest in the fate of faith, gaze through them and cannot gaze long enough.

That is how it is in the wider world. And among us? Among us he has also fared well. Things are not what they once were. Not only have we given him back his good Jewish name, but we do not stop priding ourselves with it. We do not doubt in the least that he is one of us and we are proud of it. We translate his works; we assign him an ample niche in our history; at international congresses in his memory he is praised with particular zeal in Hebrew and in Yiddish; in Palestine, five years ago, at the 250th anniversary of his death, Joseph Klausner issued a manifesto invalidating the philosopher's excommunication, a gesture repeated this year (1932) by the Jewish Literary Society in Warsaw. There is surely no philosopher as popular among us as is 'Baruch' Spinoza. What has happened? How is one to understand this? The great respect shown for Spinoza in the surrounding world is altogether natural—for that world he is the bridge in the road leading from Descartes to Leibniz and even further, a link in a chain which binds together the entire history of philosophical thought in modern times. Everyone for whom the philosophical tradition is sacred must for that reason alone—regardless of his own philosophical views—hold Spinoza dear. But in our little secular world, philosophy with its pedigree is a stepchild, and Spinoza as a metaphysician has barely had any influence among us. Why then do we praise him to high heaven and boast about him? Why cannot we to this day pardon the wrong done to him in the year 1656? Simply because he is of our own blood? Because we wish to annex another bright star, even though he illumines foreign skies? In the present "encyclopaedic" period of our cultural development, during which our entire wealth is dissolving into separate atoms, into the letters of the alphabet, this question assumes the appearance of an answer. Yet something still remains obscure in this matter.

The key to the secret, I believe, is that we do not esteem Spinoza as a lover of philosophical truth, but as a great enemy of religious tradition. Not love for 'Baruch' but hatred for accursed "Theology" is the driving force in our Spinoza cult. Those who wish to make of Spinoza a Jewish national thinker often mention his having drawn from Jewish sources, which is true. Does it not suggest one should return directly to the original sources? Heaven forbid! For Spinoza's greatness consists precisely in his having, as it were, used up the Jewish sources to the last drop. Whoever is thirsty should go to him. From him one will learn how to ascend to the highest truth without the aid of sacred authorities and historical tradition, without commandments and good deeds—exclusively on the rungs of "geometrical" reason. Spinoza disburdens the Law of its yoke. He redeems the Jew from spiritual exile, leading him upon the broad path of human freedom.

He is a saint, for in the fire of his spirit—so it is believed—the Temple of Jerusalem is consumed for the third and last time.

II

In the wide world Spinoza is actually more thought of as a gravedigger than as a defender of human freedom. But the world could be wrong and we could be right. Which means we must take the book and examine it— the book being the *Ethic* with its five parts—a proper Pentateuch. From the very title-page we can discern whither we are being led. The fifth part, which marks the end of Spinoza's life work, is entitled: "Concerning the Power of the Intellect or Human Freedom". There we have it, don't we? Let us nonetheless not stand at the threshold but try to inspect the entire five-floor edifice.

Spinoza's main achievement is not that he expanded God into Nature, immuring Him, so to speak, in a prison, but the manner in which he turned that prison, Nature, into an absolute. The ancients, the early Greek stoics for example, already knew that God and Nature could be fused into one. That Nature was a "prison", that is, a network of immutable, iron laws, a mechanism wound up for eternity, was also no invention in Spinoza's day. The new idea was the insertion in the clock of eternity of a mirror, the looking-glass of a universal consciousness. Only thereby he made Nature absolute, something no predecessor had succeeded in doing, and if he was justified, no escape was left, and indeed, neither a chance for human action. To make this clear let us look at the chief points of Spinoza's system.

There exists only a single eternal infinity—the divine-natural substance. Substance is on the one hand extension, matter, the wholeness of all which is moved and moves. On the other hand it is consciousness, the wholeness of all ideas which are tied to one another in the same eternal order to which are tied the extended bodies. Can the picture in the mirror affect the object which it reflects? Obviously not. Similarly, thought cannot affect the material world. For all which transpires in the world is the eternal effect of the two-sided infinity which allows one idea to become fused with another and, in parallel fashion, allows one body to move another. "The natural laws according to which everything occurs and according to which everything changes from one form to another, are everywhere and always the same." (Ethic, III, Introduction). Whence it is deduced that "the body cannot determine the mind to think, nor the mind the body to remain in motion . . ." (III, 2), for one's soul is no more than the idea of one's body (II, 13).—Then how can one still talk about freedom as promised on the title-page? To this question the philosopher replies approximately as follows: To be free in the commonly understood sense of being able by oneself to initiate something new in the world is absolutely impossible and it is the greatest folly to hold otherwise. Even "God does not act from freedom of will" (I, 32, Corollary 1). Why are people so delighted with their imaginary freedom? ". . . true happiness and the pinnacle of freedom is to be a servant of God" (II, Note in fine, Argument 1). The young Spinoza began and ended his philosophical work with the ideal of leading the life of a "Servant of God", which in *Isaiah* is the name for Messiah (cf. *A Short Treatise on God, Man, and Human Welfare*, II, ch. 18). Being God's servant, serving Him in "intellectual love", meant to Spinoza the understanding that man is a particle of Divine Nature, a tiny wheel in the universal mechanism, and that man is himself an entity only insofar as the universe is reflected in his consciousness. And insofar as man understands it, he has clearly and sharply perceived his place in the world. Then he feels his power, refusing to let himself be driven by joy and grief, lusts and torments, confused thoughts and idle dreams, for then he is a "free man" in a free world (IV, 66-73; V, 36). In a "free" world? Yes! For to be free means to be at one with eternal law.

Already in his greater work, *Tractatus Theologico-Politicus* (1670), which appeared before the *Ethic*, Spinoza had declared that "the universal laws of nature, according to which all things exist and are determined, are only another name for the eternal decrees of God, which always involve eternal truth and necessity" (Chapter 3, beginning). On the basis of this statement I venture to assume that the five books of the *Ethic*, in which are recorded the most general laws of nature, so to speak its constitution, were for Spinoza a truly divine doctrine, a kind of Torah. The old Torah, which according to its innermost intent should be a second and higher nature, was given to ordinary humans of flesh and blood, not to the "angels around God's throne". And what of Spinoza's Torah, which is supposed to be neither above nor below nature, but an exact reflection of nature itself? Can this Torah be of use to those creatures compounded of a body and a soul? and further, is the constitution of nature capable of serving as a constitution for social life as well?

The philosopher, it would appear, has no doubts in the matter. He says plainly: "This doctrine confers advantages on social life, inasmuch as it teaches us not to despise, hate, or ridicule any one: not to be angry or envy anyone. For it teaches us that each one should be satisfied with what he has and ready to help his neighbour, not from effeminate pity or partiality or superstition, but guided by reason, depending on the needs of the time and the demands of the situation. Important is then its advantages also on state affairs, inasmuch as it teaches in what manner citizens should be governed, namely, that they should not be as slaves, but should do of their own free will what is best." (II, Note). Let us put aside the question whether being content with one's lot is compatible with a dynamic social

ideal. More difficult is the chief question of how Spinoza, led by his
geometrical reason, arrives at the conclusion of which completely contradicts one of his basic premises, the radical negation of "free will". An
explanation of how this contradiction may be resolved will also clarify for us
the social essence of Spinozism.

There is an old saying: "The Torah speaks in the language of men".
Spinoza's "Torah" is in this respect no exception. He himself knows very
well that in his nature there are no final causes, but only causes and effects,
premises and inferences. Therefore, the notion that there is yet something
incomplete in Nature is but childish nonsense. For has not Spinoza in his
'Genesis', Part One of the *Ethic*, "Concerning God", already spoken
clearly of this: "But to those who ask, 'Why did not God create all men in
such a manner that they might be governed by reason alone?' I make no
answer but this: Because material was not wanting to Him for the creating
of all things from the highest grade to the lowest; or speaking more
accurately, because the laws of His nature were so comprehensive as to
suffice for the creation of everything that infinite intellect can conceive . . ." (I, Appendix, final paragraph). In other words, greater perfection would have meant less perfection, and the desire to improve the world
means wishing to amend the Creation, to be mightier than the Infinite. In
the passage quoted above the discerning reader will catch a hint of another
important matter: The Divine Law—Spinoza calls it "immutable"—that
there must be in the world this variety:—great philosophers, sages, who
"are governed by reason alone" and sinister, stubborn fools, mathematicians and mad idlers, saints and villains. Whoever is wise is for that reason
righteous. But since the righteous man is wise, there must exist side by
side with him foolish villains, ordinary mortals, in speaking to whom one
must "weigh what the time requires"—in other words, according to their
foolish talk and their comprehension of will and reason, of good and evil, of
servitude and freedom. The philosopher needs not be angry with them,
nor deride them, but must accept them as the divine mother-nature has
made them. The cold and crystal-clear truth does not appease their thirst,
and thus it must be sweetened for their childish-womanish taste with
"usefulness". On that level on which one is worthy of drawing consequences from the idea of "substance", in any event one knows that
consequences are neither useful nor harmful, neither right nor wrong.
This is not to say that the doctrine concerning the divine substance cannot
be useful or harmful. At all events, in both cases it works haphazardly, in
agreement with the laws of nature. He who is fortunate enough to be wise
and therefore righteous, will conduct himself as described in the *Ethic*,
and he whose fate is otherwise ordained and who is doomed to be a fool and
a wrong-doer will be a fool and a wrongdoer as described in the *Ethic*.
Described! That should be remembered. Nowhere in Spinoza's *Ethic* is
there mention of commandments or good deeds; the term "thou shalt" and

"thou shalt not" are missing. He merely describes, merely relates how the free man and the slave live. Just as there is no wish to enslave, there is also none to liberate. Hermann Cohen has aptly said that in Spinoza's chief work, ethics has remained on the title-page. And now it is also understandable what Fichte meant when he said that only two philosophical systems are possible: Spinozism and its opposite. Philosophy is at the cross roads at the problem of freedom. One way leads to making necessity absolute, the other to making freedom absolute.

The result is that whoever is for freedom in the deepest sense of the word cannot take Spinoza's road. Spinozism cannot serve as the basis for a truly free social life. Even were we all suddenly to awake one morning as "free people" in Spinoza's own sense—something which is entirely impossible from his viewpoint—we would be separated from one another by an abyss. The fact that the Spinozian way to "freedom" is aristocratic, a goal for the select few, is not what matters. We, non-Spinozists, may hope that some day all individuals will become chosen ones. What is terrible is that every individual who takes that aristocratic path of salvation, must increasingly isolate himself from the surrounding world, increasingly become a model of the entire universe, Leibniz's "monad". This is not the place to prove this assertion in detail. For that, one would have to introduce the entire doctrine of "modes" of substance. So much, however, must be made clear: if "freedom", as Spinoza would have it, is living "in God", then it is a life in absolute, substantial, metaphysical isolation. For Spinoza's God is reflected in himself, and creating and created nature in him are one. A creature who acknowledges God is God's mirror, and the "intellectual love" for the creator of the universe is the infinite love with which he loves himself (V, 35).

When we examine Spinoza in the light of his own system, we see that he followed his aristocratic-individualistic path to the end. If this was his goal, he achieved it with his own reason. Indeed, was it not Nietzsche, also an exponent of individualistic aristocracy, who commented that it was not the world which excommunicated Spinoza, but the reverse. The dark, narrow, divided world that lulls itself with hope and trembles with fear is not his worry. It suffices him that he has found his way to the narrow crack through which the Infinite illuminates human existence. Almost 2,500 years ago there lived another Baruch, the first in our history, the disciple and friend of the prophet Jeremiah. In a grievous age, he sought "greatness" and above all "repose" for himself alone. What did the prophet, speaking in God's name, answer him? "And seekest thou great things for thyself? Seek them not; for, behold, I will bring evil upon all flesh . . ." (*Jeremiah*, 45, 5); nevertheless, he continues, "but thy life will I give unto thee for a prey in all places whither you go." Whether or not this passage is a mere coincidence must remain a deep secret.

III

Such is the situation. Both from the general philosophical and a religious point of view, it is not easy to dismiss Spinoza and his system. Of what avail is it that after Kant he is counted among the rationalist dogmatists? Of what use is it to us who oppose necessity and advocate freedom that to this day there is no system of freedom which can entirely cancel out Spinozism? What sort of comfort can we draw when the social philosophy which is based on Spinozism leads man to servitude, while no other philosophies have made man free? To battle against another's truth is much easier than living in peace with one's own. On the present occasion we can add that this is truly a memorial day for modern philosophy as a whole. Would it were a day of reckoning, a day to probing the ground-motives of our own thinking—for our freethinkers as well.

Why all the din and commotion? If the question of freedom in general is one of the most difficult and complicated in Spinoza's system, that of Spinoza's attitude towards freedom of the Jewish person and of the Jewish people is a riddle for schoolboys. To solve the riddle it suffices to leaf through the famous *Tractatus Theologico-Politicus*, a work which one can with a quiet conscience count among the masterpieces—of anti-Semitic literature. Here are the author's own words: "The love of the Hebrews for their country was not only patriotism, but also piety, and was cherished and nurtured by daily rites till, like their hatred of other nations, it became their second nature. Their daily worship was not only different from that of other peoples, it was actually directed against it, as it might well be, considering that they were a particular people and entirely apart from the rest. Such daily reprobation naturally gave rise to a lasting hatred, deeply implanted in the heart: for of all hatreds none is more deep and tenacious than that which springs from extreme devoutness or piety, and is itself cherished as pious. Nor was a general cause lacking for reflaming such hatred more and more, inasmuch as it was reciprocated; the surrounding nations regarding the Jews with a hatred even more intense." (Chapter 17, middle). Whoever imagines that Spinoza is speaking of the ancient past should read what he writes of his own day: "As to their continuance so long after dispersion and the loss of empire, there is nothing marvellous in it, for they so separated themselves from every other people as to draw down upon themselves universal hate . . ." (Chapter 3, near end). Who cannot but recognize in these words the chief argument of all anti-Semites in all lands and in all ages? And is it also known that since the time Spinoza became accepted in the world, his *Tractatus Theologico-Politicus*, especially in France and Germany, has been the principal literary source from which hatred towards Jews has drawn its sustenance?

But what sort of remedy does Rabbi Baruch—here we can permit ourselves to be familiar—propose for the world scourge known as the people of Israel? Spinoza's "national" programme with regard to the Jewish people is not less modern than his anti-Semitism. First, one must remember that nations are by no means natural things: "Nature does not create peoples, only individuals" (Chapter 17). Therefore a people without a state has no need to exist. If a people is as stubborn and stiff-necked as the Jews, one must see that they be assimilated. The author speaks to this point as follows: "When the king of Spain applying violence, left the choice to the Jews either to embrace the State religion or to be expelled, a large number of Jews accepted the 'faith of the Popes'. Those who adopted the state religion were admitted to all the native privileges of Spaniards, and became worthy of filling all honorable offices, with the result that they became so intermingled with the Spaniards as to leave of themselves no relic or remembrance. But exactly the opposite happened to those whom the king of Portugal compelled to adopt the religion of his country, for they always, though converted, lived apart, inasmuch as they were considered unworthy of any civic honours" (Chapter 3). This is incredible! The expulsion from Spain, the *autos-da-fé*, the martyrdom of the *conversos*—all belittled in favour of a natural solution of the Jewish problem by means of assimilation, with the proviso that there should be no half-measures, but that the *conversos* should be granted full rights. One may see from this, incidentally, that Spinoza stems from the Portuguese and not from the Spanish *conversos*. Otherwise he would be a living refutation of his own programme of assimilation through equal rights. A grandchild of Spanish or of Portuguese *conversos*, but what a grandchild! Yet our free-thinkers wish to enroll him in their national party. Is he worthy of being the saint of Jewish free-thought?

I have culled just a few excerpts from the *Tractatus Theologico-Politicus*. Had I examined this work systematically, chapter by chapter, I would have provided endless pleasure to our "liberals" who dance a national dance around "Baruch". They would have seen that their saint knowingly misquotes Jewish works from the Pentateuch to Maimonides; that he is an expert at grovelling when face to face with Christianity; that he defends the apostle Paul for having been "A Jew among Jews and a Greek among Greeks", i.e. a hypocrite; that Spinoza, the great, the refined, the master of all his feelings—is barbed, venomous, truculent, in brief that he has all the traits which the "free man" should not have. And perhaps the greatest shock for our new saint-enthusiasts would be to learn that circumcision is of the greatest importance to those who wish to ensure Jewish national existence in that it provides the Jews with a sign which is no less practical than the Chinaman's pigtail (all in chapter 3). Among Jews it is held in Spinoza's favour that he believed in the possibility of a future Jewish state.

Well, Spinoza wrote the *Tractatus* during the years of the tumultuous messianic movement when Sabbati Zevi's star shone brightly both in the East and in the West. It could easily have seemed at that time that Palestine would again become Eretz-Israel. What objection could Benedictus Spinoza have had to that? On the contrary! Let the stiff-necked Jews go wherever they wished, if only to be rid of them. This, too, in Spain is quite modern. No small number of *conversos'* grandchildren and a considerable number of XXth-century anti-Semites were equally friends of Zionism. Moreover, we know now that around the same time (1643), another *converso's* grandson, Isaac de la Peyrère, attempted to convince the Jews that were they all to submit to conversion they would, with the help of France, be able to settle in the "Holy Land". Assimilation-Zionism has a lengthy history . . .

To turn from *Ethic* to the *Tractatus* is like being hurled from bright daylight into a dark cave full of venomous snakes. Here too, of course, there are genuine sparks of genius, since the book has a great many other aims besides that of finishing off the Jewish people. One of Spinoza's principal efforts is to prove "That in a Free State every man may think what he likes, and say what he thinks" (Chapter 20), a view which we can accept without reservation and without ulterior motives. Indeed, let Spinoza think as he pleases regarding his origin. What emerges clearly from his works as a whole is that in describing the world, he also described the microcosm, Spinoza himself. He also contained all—"from the highest grade to the lowest". And the higher his estimate of man—the lower his estimate of the Jew. Nor is he justified by those who say that his development was not from the *Ethic* to the *Tractatus*, but the reverse. Spinoza, even when he came to feel himself wholly a "servant of God", a kind of messiah, never renounced the *Tractatus*. I respect him far too much to be so impudent as to do this for him. Nevertheless, he is, was, and will remain a false prophet, a pseudo-messiah.

One would not like to conclude on a derogatory note. A man who is destined to live and to affect others—in what direction is immaterial—for three hundred years must have some particular symbolical meanng for us. A symbol requires deciphering, though not necessarily be blessed. We have enough Baruchs, including quite a few significant ones. Indeed, we have a book—though hardly anyone knows of it—buried in the Apocrypha, the so-called *Baruch*. Let me cite a few lines from this unknown Baruch; let us hear what he believes and hopes for. "Then," he prophesies regarding the messianic age, "healing will descend in dew, and disease will withdraw, and anxiety and anguish and lamentation will pass from amongst men, and gladness will proceed through the whole earth . . . And judgments, and revilings, and contentions, and revenges, and blood, and passions, and envy, and hatred, and whatsoever things are like these shall be no more . . . And it will come to pass in those days that the reaper will not grow weary, nor those that build be toil-worn; for the works will of themselves speedily advance with those who do them in much tranquility. For that time is the consummation of that which is corruptible, and the beginning of that which is not corruptible." (*The Apocalypse of Baruch*, translated from Syriac, chapters 73-74.)

And here the matter stands: Baruch versus Benedictus, the true versus the false messiah.

12. Christianity in Crisis

Never since Christianity became a force in world civilisation has it been in such a critical condition as to-day.

The rupture that split Byzantium from Rome; the period of the Reformation which detached from the Roman Catholic Church the most vital religious forces of central and western Europe; even the time of the great French Revolution and its open war against the holiest Christian traditions (to mention but a few of the grave crises through which Christianity has passed during its two-thousand-year history), all these dangers seem no more than a warning by comparison with the crisis of to-day, no more than a threat which declares: "Beware! The anti-Christ, the 'Evil One', is prepared at any time to open a life-and-death struggle against your holy Christian faith!" Nevertheless, even during the last struggle in our own era, it never came to that. On the contrary, each of the crises I have mentioned, even the first apparent losses they inflicted, eventually brought the Church considerable advantage. If Byzantium had not broken away from the Roman Bishops, Christendom might never have been able so easily to capture Russia. But for the Reformation, Christendom might not have reached the honourable compromise with modern science and philosophy. And even the secularisation of political life, which resulted from the revolutionary upheaval towards the end of the eighteenth century, eventually enabled Christendom to find new ways of influencing social life and make use of those social forces which were ranged in opposition to official rule. To put it briefly, without the French Revolution a Christian labour movement would never have been possible. Considered together, it becomes clear, that all the great crises in the history of Christendom were pains of adaptation. The early mediaeval schism adapted the Church to its new geographic-ethnological environment; the Reformation, to the new scientific-technical culture which grew from the ferment in the Christian world; and the divorce which separated State and Church paved the way to the hearts of the European proletariat. This last fact calls for closer examination, if we wish to appreciate better where Christendom stands to-day and why its present-day crisis is more threatening than any that went before.

This essay was first published in Yiddish in *Fraye Shriftn*, Warsaw, 1934, No. 16.

Schism between western and eastern Christendoms, the emergence of independent non-Catholic churches in western Europe and the dilution of its practical dominion over people—all this could be treated by Christendom as a temporary affliction, since the Church, more than a thousand years old, was accustomed to thinking in terms of centuries and not days. Disregarding the acute dogmatic disputes which divide the various churches, each one of them nourished the hope that sooner or later they would all meet again at the same altar. Even the secularisation of political life, its "un-Christianization", while depriving the Church of its power did not rob it of its courage, because the more secular and indifferent politics became concerning faith, the freer became the conscience of man and the more amenable (or so said the Christian believer) to eternal truth. First, a man had to be a Christian perforce, and then he was allowed to be a Christian according to his own conscience. This was valid, of course, as long as the world in general remained essentially Christian, as long as it did not doubt that the highest human morality was Christian, and as long as it continued to allow "inner mission", or the freedom of Christian propaganda among the once formally Christian peoples. And so it came about that freedom of conscience, which once had to be wrung by force from the Catholic Church, became in the nineteenth century the prime demand of pious Catholics. In this matter they saw eye to eye with the democrats of the new age. But this was not enough. In order to retain leadership, the Church, in the Christian spirit, had to take up the cause of the new poor "freeman", the factory worker.

Pope Leo XIII pointed the way which had been foreseen by Dostoevsky as long ago as the 1870s. The time will come—Dostoevsky wrote in his *Diary of a Writer*—when the European workers will stretch forth their hands to take over the power of the state, but they will lack the necessary leadership. That is when the priests will meet them, bearing the cross, proclaiming: You are right, but you are poor, without education and experience in higher politics. Come to us! Trust in our thousand-year-old experience to rule over human passions, and we will take you where you wish to be. . . . The events after the war fulfilled that prophecy almost word by word. The fate of the European labour movement, so far at least as it was not dependent on Russia, was decided in Germany. And what happened there? The Social Democrats joined forces with the Catholics. "Rather with Rome than with Moscow" became for them a sort of religious dogma, until the "Romans" with Brüning at their head finally led them where "they" wished. And where was that? More of this later. For the time being let us stress the plain fact: in secularized Germany, religiously neutral, Catholicism was able to play a greater political role than it had been able in a Germany formally Christian; and this was actually a consequence of secularization. True enough, the whole German episode seemed more complicated. Catholicism was ranged here in opposition to the new secularism and at the same time to the old conservative Protestant "heresy". Nevertheless, Germany remains a classic example of the almost unlimited powers of adaptation with which Christendom made its way in the modern era. How was it that the greatest Marxist party in western Europe ever came to rely on Catholic loyalty? It was only for the reason that the ways of the old Church and the new Socialist movement had begun to run on parallel lines in secularized Europe. Both found themselves outside the ruling party; both belonged to the "commonalty". The free social life which kept developing in the nineteenth century outside the ruling establishment, or in obvious opposition to it, had become not just a shelter for revolutionary forces, but also a place of refuge for Christian tradition. This is where Socialism and Catholicism met. This is where they got to know each other, and from here they went forth arm in arm to found in partnership the Weimar Republic. A glance back at the years preceeding 1925 enables one to see that the great French Revolution had brought Catholicism not just harm but also great benefit. It restored to the Church of Rome that which it had lost in the period of the Reformation—temporal power in the greatest of all the reformed monarchies.

Now it is all over. Socialism which aimed at the abolition of classes and, in this way, to the opposition of state and people, led the way for the theory of absolutism, the "total state" which brushed aside all ideals of a "free society" except within narrow limits. Fascism, a side-effect of Socialism, disrupted the plans of Catholicism to rise once more to political greatness on the shoulders of the socialist atheists. "The system" which the National Socialist destroyed was really the Catholic-Socialist "accord", the "national" of the Nazis being directed both against socialist internationalism and against Christian-Catholic universalism. The loss of Germany left the Vatican a capital city without a land, and the Church a tower without a base. Italy was also as good as lost, Spain unsure, just like Poland and Austria—but that will be a chapter of its own (under II).

The totalitarian temporal state is the danger which Christendom has never before had to face. There is no running away from it, and there is no hiding, as after 1789, so as to wait for the right time to resume the march. The totalitarian secular state claims the young people, that is, the future. In particular, Nazism does in Germany just what Bolshevism does in Russia. In his book, *The Religious Crisis* (1934), Roger B. Lloyd quotes Lenin: "Either Bolshevism will triumph and destroy Christendom, or Christendom will triumph and destroy Bolshevism." The author comments, that even the Pope could have put his signature to those words. One point must be added to the remark of this British author: What Bolshevism is to Eastern Christendom, Fascism is to-day to Western Christendom. While the former offers comparison with mediaeval Islam, Fascism can be regarded as a sort of anti-Christian opponent to Islam. Christendom is at war on two fronts. Where will it find an ally? Both the

Catholic Church and the "Pravoslavny" (the Greek-Orthodox Church) are fighting without friends or any support from without. Since 1933 Protestantism has been overtaken by the same peril. After the French Revolution, Catholic Habsburgs, The Greek-Orthodox Romanoffs and the Protestant Hohenzollern concluded the "Holy Alliance" in order to rescue Christian tradition. Now there are no kings to don the garb of holiness and establish a united Christian front. Exactly nineteen hundred years after the "Redemption" according to Christian belief and Christian reckoning, Germany, like Russia, has become the land of the anti-Christ. Has Christendom still any future?

II

A philosophical theory which derives from the Danish thinker Kierkegaard has in recent times received much attention from the Germans, Jaspers and Heidegger. It suggests that the true nature of a person becomes apparent only when it is a matter of "to be or not to be". In Jewish terms it may be expressed in these words: Am I a Jew or not a Jew? Is my Jewishness indeed contained in my nature? I will know only when I stand face to face with "Him who kills and passes on", or when I have to answer the question whether I should commit a sin or be killed. German philosophers call such a situation a "border situation". That which happens to the individual can also be applied to great historical phenomena, even such as Christianity. During the past hundred years much study has been devoted to the question whether Christianity is still a living force. In Russia especially the question has been considered in depth. The fate of Christendom in the modern world was a grave problem not only for Dostoevsky or Vladimir Solovyev, but also for our contemporary Alexandr Alexandrovich Blok or Andrey Bely. Dostoevsky once exclaimed— "Christianity has not succeeded!" which was almost a cry of despair coming from a fervent Christian. Nevertheless there was no way of knowing what the truth was until Christianity slipped into its "border situation". To-day it can be said that as far as eastern Christendom is concerned it has resisted temptation. If it is destroyed, it will mean a destruction of a living faith of living Christians. But is it at all possible to destroy a living faith? "The Church is in need of a martyr"—these were the words in which the Metropolitan Benjamin of St. Petersburg refused in 1921 to sign a plea for his life when he had been sentenced to death. A faith for which people are ready to sacrifice their lives, lives on, and will live as long as the memory of its martyrs. Another question remains: Will Russian Christendom ever in our times, in the era of European history, emerge again from underground, from the catacombs into which it has been driven?

Even more serious is the state of Christendom in the heart of Europe. Shortly after World War I, Oswald Spengler in his two-volume "dirge" *The*

Decline of the West expressed his doubts on how far religion still had a future, and on whether its future lay no longer in Europe, but in the Orient, starting at the Russian border. Spengler was looking with the same pessimistic eyes as the west-European culture-pessimists. They all thought that Christianity, long enfeebled in Europe, would shortly die a natural death, because in the atmosphere of general indifference its forces would dissolve by themselves. They did not believe that it could possibly find itself in a border situation as in Russia. But in 1933 the impossible actually became a fact in Germany. At once the Christian problem became something which would reveal the entire future destiny of the principal two institutions of Christianity in Western Europe. If it was unable to face the challenge here, it would mean that it had become an empty vessel, form without content, a corpse whose burial had been overlooked at a proper time.

How does the Christian problem look in Germany to-day? Let us recall the most important stages through which it has passed since Nazism became a political factor, until now when both churches in the country are confronted with the dilemma "You should let yourself be slain, rather than commit a transgression".

The anti-Christian impulses of Nazism were recognised years ago. It is enough to glance through the most important Nazi books to get some idea of them. One can ignore Arthur Dinter's *"Die Sünde gegen Blut"* which gave rise to the jest in Germany, "A sinner has come out with ink against blood". Dinter soon became a spent force. But Alfred Rosenberg was destined to become the chief theoretician of Nazism. His *Der Mythus des XX.Jahrhunderts* (1930) is indeed no less anti-Christian than the heretical writings of Dinter. What Rosenberg preaches is a pure German, old Germanic "heroic" faith, which may not consider holy any translation from a foreign tongue, and this includes evangelism as it is to-day. "Neopaganism", "new idolatry"—such are the labels which pious Christians attach to Rosenberg's system that rejects the principle of "Christian love". The book has been excommunicated by the Vatican, which could with no less justification have excommunicated Hitler's *Mein Kampf,* the real evangelism of Nazi Germany. Apart from being imbued with an anti-Christian spirit, it displays attitudes which can be regarded only as hymns of praise for the ancient Graeco-Roman paganism, or as unembellished contempt for Christianity. Hitler declares, rather like the old Frankish atheists, that but for Christianity there would have been no violence and no terror. Pious Christians and just ordinary educated people could shake their heads at these words a thousand times, but the words remained and the book is now approaching a sale of three million copies. The widely travelled American churchman, Charles McFarland, went in the autumn of 1933 on a special visit to Germany in order to learn from Hitler's own mouth what might happen to the German Church. In his book *The New*

Church and the New Germany—a study of Church and State, he gives the Christian world the joyless news that there is nothing good to be expected from Hitler, if only because in religious matters Hitler is an ignoramus. Of Rosenberg, with whom he also conversed, McFarland writes that he is "the high priest of a theory which has become a sort of religion and shakes the very foundations of the teaching of Jesus", both religious and moral.

Nazism was first seen to be aiming at the creation of "a sort of religion" when its actions gave clear interpretation to its words. Its anti-Christian course, however, has been clear enough right from the start. But what did the German Churches do to warn their people of the new idolatry? There are two answers to this question, for Catholicism and Protestantism each sought its own solution.

Protestantism took the simplest view of the matter. Politically close to the German monarchist attitude, the leaders of over twenty Protestant Churches in Germany regarded the National Socialists as hired workers employed in building the "King's Highway", in this case the way to the restoration of the Prussian Protestant Hohenzollern Monarchy. As soon as they were ready, however, to exploit the Nazi drive, they were also ready to make ideological sacrifices so that it should appear that they were hand in hand with the gangsters on the theoretical front. They took with extraordinary zeal to anti-Semitism (see e.g. the hypocritical study by the Berlin professor of theology, Ernst Selin, *Abolish the Bible?* which appeared in 1932). Protestant theology began at once to debate such questions as "Church and People" (which became the title of a book published precisely in January 1933 by the former Magdeburg General Superintendent, Johannes Eger), and "Religion and Race" (the work by the Frankfurt professor, Julius Richter)—questions which from the Christian stand-point had long since been disposed. Protestant theology sank to the level of short-sighted German nationalist politics and, just like the German National Party, woke up to the fact that it had taken a wrong and crooked turn only after it had already happened.

It was otherwise with Catholicism. Of all Christian churches, it is best at sniffing up the scent of an approaching upheaval in the world. The post-war nationalism, which made the nation into an absolute, had aroused the suspicion of the Vatican at a comparatively early stage. Well remembered are the thunderbolts which it hurled against both the French chauvinists who are now grouped under the banner of Action Francaise, and against the German Nazis. But how did it happen that the pious "Roman" Brüning became—doubtless with the Papal blessing—the victim of German democracy? Georg Bernhard, the well-known liberal publicist, in his book *Der Selbstmord der Deutschen Republik* (1933) tries to provide an answer, but it is an unsatisfactory one because he treats the problem separate from Catholic world history. For Catholicism in Germany there was more at stake than merely the future of German Catholics. One may suppose that

Rome looked forward to becoming finally "the third who rejoices", the one who laughs last. Bolshevism was a mortal foe; Nazism the mortal enemy of Bolshevism; was it possible, therefore, that the enemy of our enemy would be our friend? No! That would have been short-sighted opportunist politics, blind to the possibility that the enemy of our enemy might turn to be our enemy too. Unlike Protestantism, Catholicism was aware that a wave of nationalism was rising in the world, anti-Christian, idolatrous and bowing only to physical might. And yet Catholicism was willing to speculate on the chance that its enemies would devour each other. A terrible gamble, a gamble with poison gas! And who knows, but that the argument was really a counsel of despair? Despair, according to Catholic doctrine, is one of the seven Deadly Sins.

The real aim of modern Catholic policy can be no more than a matter of conjecture; yet events of the last eighteen months provide singular confirmation. In the summer of 1933 the Pope quickly concluded a concordat with Nazi Germany. For their part the Catholic priests in the German Churches began to prepare the public for martyrdom, and a great many Catholic zealots earned the distinction of consignment to the concentration camps. At the same time, Protestant churchmen had just about dropped to their knees before anti-Christian power. That was just what Catholicism was waiting for. If Protestantism had entirely submitted and allied itself for life and death with Nazism, Catholicism would itself have been able to monopolise central Europe and eventually the whole of the western world. The history of the Reformation would thus have ended sooner than anyone would have expected. On one side would have been ranged Bolshevism, or more generally Marxism, on the other side Nazism, so to speak from afar, pretending to be neutral and pacifist, patient and passive, but prepared for the greatest sacrifices. Sooner or later the Catholic Church, the other two opponents having snapped off each other's head, would again assume the entire guardianship over the fortunes of humanity—so more or less the mills of the future were grinding in the heads of the Catholic pundits trying in the first third of the XXth Century to feel the pulse of the ultimate third.

Protestantism knows, at least instinctively, the Catholic way of reasoning, and there is no doubt that its opposition to Catholic pressure in church life draws its sustenance largely from the fear of losing any influence it ever had in world Christendom. Consequently, there has developed a sort of competition in self-sacrifice, while even the Protestants are now at one in seeing that the whole fate of European Christian culture has become twisted in Germany into one tangled knot. The struggle of the old German Protestantism carried on officially against the so-called new Protestant sect, which is in truth pure Nazism, and therefore anti-Christian, or "German Christian", wins the attention of the world press principally from the purely political point of view. The world was amazed when it heard the echo of a protest from the enslaved land. Moreover, it seemed to come from a dark and remote corner and from Luther's and Calvin's grandchildren. The world saw in this a beginning of an opposition movement against the Nazi dictator. It interpreted the demand for religious freedom as a political demand, and it expected to see Prussian generals and German nationalist Junkers behind the religious preachers. Naturally, religious and cultural politics are closely bound up with politics in general. If, however, the German Church had been the true advance guard of a movement, or force, fighting even for a minimum of civil freedom, then the significance of the fight would have exceeded its immediate results. Christianity might have become capable again of reformation under entirely different conditions, capable of a cultural revolution with results no less important than at the beginning of the "new history". Religion and Socialism might then have been able to enter into a new alliance, not like the one they made in "the Land of Egypt", and not like the alliance of the Social Democrats and Catholics in the bogus republican Germany of Weimar.

While Protestantism has once again to learn to believe in its world mission and because of its experience in Germany needs to go to school again, Catholicism treats Germany as a chessman, though a most important one on a board which extends over the earth. The catastrophe of Marxism in Austria is incomprehensible unless it is studied in the light of Catholic world policy. It is part of basic Catholic principle that at any point in the world the Church should be able to rely on the "secular arm". The greater the Nazi danger became in central Europe, the more urgent it became for Catholicism to rescue and hold Austria at the very least, regarding it as the bridge to the Catholic provinces of Nazi Germany, Bavaria, the Rhineland and the Saar region. The leaders of the Austrian Social Democrats believed, for the same reason, that the Catholics would not wish to quarrel with them. What shortsightedness! They did not understand that the watchman on the church tower had his eyes on distant days. At a time which, in the Catholic way of thinking, was certain to bring the final battle between two atheisms, the nationalist and internationalist, when Europe might become the victim of another world war in which the victor might well be the non-Christian Far East, Japan and its vassals—at such a time Catholicism had to free itself of all "provisional" obligations. This was a more important consideration than a signature to this or that parliamentary agreement. But were Marxists ever in a position to understand Catholic world policy? They took it for granted that Christianity was dead and that its only certain dominion was in the church-yard.

III

The Christian church-yard has suddenly sprung to life. Christians in Russia are showing a heroism comparable to that of their ancient forerunners in the times of the Roman tyrants. The Catholic Church is waging war against Marxist workers in Austria. In Germany it has taken up a hostile attitude to Nazism in a spirit of bravery and defiance. It vies thereby with the Protestants, who have brought to life Luther's proud declarations, "Here I stand. I can do no other!" Who would have believed all this a mere twenty years ago?

Twenty years ago saw the outbreak of World War I which brought to the fore the crisis involving all modern civilisation. European civilisation was and remained Christian, a fact which had been forgotten. Bolshevism gave a jolt to the memory; but Russia is Europe and not-Europe. European Christians, however, turned over and tried to sleep again. Then they were overtaken by the year 1933, and after this shock it was really impossible to dream again.

The anti-Christian character of Nazism is generally well-known. Most of its anti-Christian tendencies, however, have become confused with its anti-Semitism. People imagine that because Christianity sprang from Jewish roots, those who wish to uproot Judaism must also reduce Christianity to ruins. That is logical, but Nazism's own logic lies fathoms deeper. Anti-Semitism itself is in Nazism not the point of departure, but the result of a series of other assumptions: The blood, claim the Nazi theoreticians, is the soul. As the blood is, so is the "Race"—this determines the kind of spirit and the kind of culture. *Adam*, man, originates from the *adamah*, the earth, the land. *Dam*, (blood), *adam* (man) and *adamah* (earth)—race, culture and land are therefore three which become one. A people which is not pure of race and does not occupy its own land, is not a people, culturally speaking, and therefore has no place in the world. So how is it to-day with the German people? Almost half of it is scattered abroad; the race is not pure and even its culture is mixed. And so it follows that the Germans should begin an "ingathering of exiles" (imperialism), purify the blood (anti-Semitism), and resurrect the old-German "culture" (anti-Christianity). The inference is that even if there had been no Jews at all in Germany, Nazism would still have been anti-Semitic, because pure blood is necessary before all else for pure culture, and German culture was contaminated not only as a result of Jewish assimilation but long before as a result of un-Germanic, Asian-Semitic Christianity. In other words, the deeper motive of Nazi anti-Semitism is its anti-Christian, politico-cultural Pan-Germanism.

As long as the German Protestants believed that the anti-Christian temper of Nazism was an offspring of its anti-Semitism, they themselves tried to make a scape-goat of the Jews. When it became clear, however, that this was the sort of he-goat that would carry off into the desert the Christian faith itself and no other, then for the first time both Churches in Germany felt the earth shaking beneath their feet. For the first time they took a stand for "God's word" in the Hebrew Bible against the "aryan paragraph", and for the management of their own communal affairs.

Monday, November 13, 1933, was in this respect a historic day. It was the day after the plebiscite which had brought the Nazis an almost hundred per cent victory. The Nazi sect in the hastily united Protestant and "Evangelical Church" ("German Christians") felt so powerful that it tore the Christian mask from its face and at a great German gathering declared open war against the Bible, against the "Jewish rebel", Paul, and even against "the poor man riding on an ass", as Jesus is depicted in Christian tradition. Twenty thousand "Christians", among them a few thousand recently created dignitaries, acclaimed "Bravo!", jostled and shouted "Heil!". It was the sort of scene that is described in the "Story of the Apostle": "Some therefore cried one thing, and some another, for the assembly was confused, and the more part knew not wherefore they were come together" (*Acts*, 19, 32). They had been assembled so that with their blessing the Nazis could uproot Jewish Christianity from German soil. Anti-Semitic demagogues had the role of helping to popularise the idea in those circles which had done particularly well out of the persecution of the Jews—the academics and the middle classes.

The storm, however, brought forth a counter-storm. The collection of sermons *Your Word is the Shield of Your Church* (1934) (i.e. God's Word) in which the most important old-Protestant preachers ranged in battle against Nazi idolatry, from Friedrich Bodelschwingh to Martin Niemöller, express their view, is testimony of the deep agitation and a feeling that, whether one wishes it or not, at least the historical importance of the Jewish people as the creator of the Christian religion must be defended. "In vain", preaches Niemöller, "do we seek another people which has in morals, custom and law held so firmly to its faith as the Jews . . . The history of the Jewish religion is no more than the history of the reforms, often serious and far-reaching or profound, and of reformation right up to the time of Jesus and even later" (p. 121). One must try and understand how sacred the principle of reformation is for a Protestant pastor, if one wishes to appreciate the full import of this historically based compliment. Whenever the Bible is called in question, there is no other way of defending it than by taking sides with the people which expressed "God's word" in its Hebrew language, in its Holy Tongue. To the Catholics who always have their "Holy father" in Rome, the "Holy Script" is not as important as for the Evangelical Chruch. The dangerous state of Christendom, however, as shown principally and particularly in the rivalry between Catholics and Protestants (already mentioned) compels the German Catholics to profess the utmost enthusiasm for the glory of the Old Testament and thus also for the glory of old Judaism.

What alarm was created, as we all know, at the end of 1933 by the five sermons of Cardinal Michael von Faulhaber of Munich on *"Judaism, Christendom and Germanism"*! There was a rush for the book when it appeared in print, and shots were fired at the Cardinal's windows. A few quotations from his sermons will serve to explain why the book must have the effect on Hitler's and Rosenberg's devotees as a red rag on a bull. "It is a fact in the history of civilisation", declares this Catholic prelate in his first sermon, "that nowhere in pre-Christian times can we find so great a number of noble spirits as among the people of the Old Bible. Among no other people can we find a literature like the Books of Moses with their childishly beautiful tales; the Books of Samuel and Kings with their classic art, to relate (as our Germanists may prove for themselves) the chronicles with its liturgical laws; the Book of Job with its great problem of suffering; the Psalms and their prayers deep as the soul; the Wisdom Books and their understanding of everyday life; the Books of the Four Major and Sixteen Minor Prophets and their popular orations; the Books of the Maccabees in which the old heroism and faith glow once again. To-day when so much has been learned of the history and literature of other pre-Christian peoples . . . science must bear witness on behalf of the people at the Jordan: You have surpassed all others in loftiness; of all ancient people you have given us the highest religious values." (p. 12). Speaking of "the social values of the Bible" the Cardinal reaches this conclusion at the end of his third sermon: "He who does not believe in the Holy Spirit and does not regard these books as God's word . . . must consider the people of Israel as the supermen of world history. There is no alternative. Either we believe in the Holy Spirit of the Holy Books, or we must say to the Jewish people: You are the most gifted race in all history." Race" indeed, if you atheists are so keen on "blood".

If you try to sum up the dispute between Nazism and Christendom, which is still at full heat, then you find a purely political result which for the time being amounts almost to nothing. That does not mean, however, that the struggle may not finally lead to very important political changes. At the moment one cannot doubt that by their pressure or challenge the Nazis have awakened western European Christendom to a new vitality, and caused them to remember the deep foundations of European culture and its Jewish-Christian origins. Both sides in fact realised that between Christianity and the deification of "blood and earth" no compromise was possible, unless Naxism renounced its most arrogant dreams or Christianity ceased to exist on German soil. There are to-day not a few signs which indicate that at the worst Christianity in Germany will vanish underground as in Russia, because there are still among the Germans enough living Christians with a living faith. The situation is set for a tragic climax. Prophecy in this case is not a matter of logic, but of faith. To comprehend it rationally, one must attempt a prognosis for the entire condition of the modern world. Not only the confirmed pessimists foresee a second world war; the fear pursues even tender-hearted optimists in their nightmares. Such a war could result in an entirely new situation. Whose prospects are the best? The Nazis, who have created the anti-Christian religious movement in Germany? The Catholics, who reckon that their hour will come after the war between Gog and Magog? Bolshevism which interprets this expression to suit itself as a sort of civil war in the lap of capitalist imperialism? Japan, that is flexing its muscles to conquer the world? Or is there possibly some still hidden ethical force of which we know not to-day, but which lives among us as a great silent faith? Who can tell? This is not a rational problem. It is a matter of faith.

IV

A world built on the foundations of "Jewish" Christianity is shaken. The Bible is the centre of conflict. Catholic and Protestant dignitaries once again give testimony for the two-thousand-year old book. Other "dignitaries" would consign it to flames as soon as possible. And what have the People of the Book themselves to say about this? The people whom others are ready to cast into the fire together with their Scrolls of the Law? The People of the Book, the People of Wisdom and Understanding pretend not to be aware of a matter that so closely affects them, or even to know of a dispute among the gentiles on whether the Bible is kosher or carrion! The question is far from clear even within the "four ells" of Jewish life. Our attitude is: Christianity, Catholicism, Greek Orthodoxy, Protestantism . . . . Priests, pastors, Pope . . . not our concern! and then suddenly you hear a remark: If Hitler has been sent to destroy the Church, then perhaps, after all, he will earn our thanks.

Beyond belief, even in the telling. And yet so it is. So widespread is ignorance on all matters touching faith in our little secularised Jewish world, that our Jews do not even begin to understand how closely the future of the Jewish people is bound with the future of Christendom. They have all got into their heads that since the secular world has granted citizen rights to the Jews, it must be a better and more moral world, and therefore closer to the Jews than a system that requires faith in a Kingdom which is "not of this world". Now the time has come to realize that this irreligious world, "world of ours", is just as capable of doing with the Jews what the ancient pious Christian world did, and even more. The connection between an irreligious world and Jewish civil rights is not a logical necessity . . . and even less so in a world that is not merely irreligious but anti-Christian like the world of the Nazis, with whom there is no language in which the Jews can hold discussion. And with the Christians? Should we answer "no concern of ours"? Our great-grandfathers and forefathers before them were very deeply concerned indeed.

It is a great mistake to believe that the relationship between Jewry and Christendom consisted only in the fact that the Christians always persecuted the Jews and the Jews always answered with lamentations and curses. Their relations were much more complex than that. Quite apart from the first early Christian centuries, when the separation of the two sections (Christians and Jews) was no easy divorce, they maintained mutual interests that were both lively and cordial throughout the Middle Ages. It is necessary only to read the accounts of the Judeo-Christian debates of the XIII-th to the XV-th centuries (the dispute in Barcelona, e.g. in 1263, or that in Tortosa in 1412), to see clearly how well, irrespective of acute antagonisms, they understood each other, Christian and Jew, Jew and Christian; how many beliefs they held in common; and how familiar the opposing claims and counter-claims sounded in both Christian and Jewish ears. Both parties took their stand on the Bible and they disputed only as to the right interpretation of prophetic passages. Can one imagine such a debate taking place to-day between Alfred Rosenberg and one of our modern Jewish scholars? It would be impossible! The abyss between them is unbridgeable.

People using a common language are under its spiritual influence, and therefore Christians and Jews have not ceased for more than a thousand years to influence each other. This is a great theme which cannot be exhausted or disposed of in passing. Two or three instances will perhaps give some indication of its importance and scope. Monogamy among the Jews is without doubt a result of Christian influence. Is there any need to stress the far-reaching effects that this form of family life has had on the entire spiritual development of the Jewish people during the past few hundred years? The vitality of the belief in the Messiah—who will want to deny that one of the sources of its nourishment was the Christian belief in the "Second Coming" of their own Messiah? Or consider, for example, such a phenomenon as "Tsadikism"—would it have been possible without the awe of the Catholics for their priest or the Greek-Orthodox belief in their Elder or the monk? On the other hand, the whole Reformation has for long been seen as "re-judaising", as a "yiddishing" of Christianity. Jews and Christians may assess the reciprocal influences as positive or negative; their existence is a plain fact which is not possible to erase from our Book of Chronicles.

Let us for a moment imagine that Christianity has vanished around us; that the bridges to a world which has reverted to idolatry have been burned; that the Jewish belief in one God, one World and therefore One Human Race, is once again the belief only of some scattered people; that this people is separated from its natural historical environment by a wall of hate, blood-libels and bloodstained persecution; and that in the Christian church a picture of some sort of Hitler hangs over the altar instead of a picture of Jesus (as actually happened according to the Protestant Berlin pastor, Dr. Jacobi, in May 1934!). Let us imagine all this and then ask ourselves: if it depends on us, even in a small way, whether such a possibility can be prevented, should we do something about it, or is it all one to us, what becomes of Christianity? It seems to me that there is only one possible answer to this question. Give help and more help! Let us help as far as it is in our power to help.

Have we any power? This is a great and difficult question, once again a sort of question which can better be answered on the basis of faith and confidence than on the uncertain scales of reason. The world around us takes on a new aspect. We relied on secularism and we have been repaid for our naive enthusiasm with a resounding slap in the face. We relied on European Socialism, itself now in a predicament from which it can only be rescued by holy faith. We did not want to know that in the European world there still existed moral forces outside the political and social fields. We must therefore turn again and seek them and go on seeking. We must not be ashamed if we find them in quiet corners which we had thought were dark and remote.

The Jewish people is faced to-day with a choice between two alternatives—either to flee into a spiritual ghetto into which it is being driven from outside and into which it is being drawn by its own frightened senses—or to step out with head held high across the world whither its ancient destiny directs it. "Lo, it is a people that shall dwell alone and shall not be reckoned among the nations." In the mouth of Balaam it was rather a curse than a blessing. In any case, it was true only for the generation of the desert. Should we return to the desert? Even if we are compelled to do so, we will shout from the desert with all our might: "Prepare a way!" We shall have to call upon all who still possess some spark of faith, truth, righteousness and spirit, even though the whole world around is, this entire temporal world, turned into a desert. If Christianity is indeed an enemy of the world, then it is our friend. Would that Jewry might live to achieve its own "re-Judaising"; then it might also achieve the "re-Judaising" of Christendom and with it the world. Then the Prophets would still have the last word—not Balaam, but the Prophet Isaiah—"And all the nations will flow unto Him."

13. Our Controversy with Christianity

The dispute that Jews and Christians have been conducting against each other for nearly two millennia has lately entered a totally new phase.

Christianity, which until quite recently was the accuser that either demanded the truth of its Jewish opponent or testified and rendered judgment against him, is now itself in the position of such an accused and stands before judges no less severe than the members of the "holy authorities" of the past. The persecuted Christians can draw but little consolation from the knowledge that those who had become their bitterest enemies had nevertheless never ceased to hate the Jews. For one of the principal accusations voiced in the newly launched anti-Christian trial is actually the argument that the Christians themselves are "Jews" in spirit. Thus, today both sides find themselves in the same situation, not one against the other as in the past, but side by side, face to face with a common foe. From the Jewish point of view, is such a partnership of genuine value? Does it constitute a foundation on which one can build? On this basis, can one at the very least offer a prognosis with regard to the further development of Christian-Jewish as well as Jewish-Christian relations?

In attempting to answer this question, historical parallels will be of little help. True, history already provides instances in which Jews and Christians found themselves together on the side of the oppressed, facing a common enemy, such for instance as Islam after its victories in Spain. Everywhere and invariably, however, this third power was an outside factor and consequently less dangerous in the realm of the innermost spiritual culture. In this respect the situation today is vastly different. The enemy who now seeks utterly to destroy Christian culture is in fact the child it has itself borne and therefore represents a greatly increased threat to its existence. It is no longer a question of a schism of sorts within the Church itself which occurred during the division into Roman and Greek Christianity, or during the rise of the Protestant "heresy". It is in effect an anti-Christian revolution among Christian nations, the Germans and Italians, as among the Russians at an earlier time. It is a mass movement, with "nationalist" and "socialist" ideas which in their deepest spiritual origins are themselves Christian. Never in its entire history has Christen-

This essay was first published in Yiddish in *Oifn Sheidweg*, Paris 1939, Volume I.

dom encountered dangers of such an extent. Those charged with the responsibility for its future are well aware of this fact. Just as the world around them changes, so they themselves begin to change and so does their view of past friends and foes, including the Jews.

In this new situation of world history it behooves the Jewish people also to revise its position in its controversy with Christianity. With utmost care the Jews must look into the future of their own relations with Christianity and discover for themselves whether there is anything or anyone to be relied on. To be able to do this, we must first of all attempt to examine how far we have got in our controversy and, furthermore, where Christianity stands today as seen from our vantage point. Only then will it be possible for us to indicate with more or less clarity the main lines of a consistent Jewish policy with regard to the world of Christian believers.

I

From the first Christian centuries onward, since the establishment of the fundamentals of Christian philosophy, to the threshold of most recent times, the dispute between us and the Christians was in essence theological and dogmatic. The Church and the Synagogue both stood on the same foundation, namely—the Bible, for its books were "Holy Scriptures" both for us and for them. We held that to build further on the same foundation, for the sake of Heaven, it was necessary to erect a fence around this foundation, and then another and yet another, with the result that we embarked on the road of the Talmud. Whereas the Christians erected on the Bible a second storey, a "New Testament", possessing allegedly an even greater sanctity. They began to claim that only stubborn Talmud-Jews were capable of transforming a bare foundation into a completed building, and a half-truth into a whole faith. They regarded the Jews as half-baked Christians, whereas they on the other hand became for us "red hot" heretics who had "breached the wall", broken through all the fences and fallen into "bad ways", devoid of the protection of the strict Jewish Law.

From earliest times there were linked with this a series of theological theses which both sides continuously brought against each other. The dogmatically important among them were the arguments for-and-against the Trinity, for-and-against the Christian dogma that the Creator of the universe is one Being in the form of three images, including that of Jesus the "Messiah", who became flesh-and-blood, "born of woman", in order to bring salvation, through his life and his death and redeem all mankind. The Jewish people rejected this interpretation of "God", not only because of its being the people of "Hear O Israel the Lord our God the Lord is One", but also because it never ceased waiting for the true redemption and the true Redeemer, prior, during and after the rise of Christianity alike.

It is essential to recall all this here and keep it well in mind, as otherwise it would be difficult to grasp what constituted the compromise reached by the Judaic and the Christian world in the era of emancipation, nor what it may mean today in the counter-emancipation era, should such a compromise be discussed in earnest at all. For there can be no doubt that Jewish emancipation was based on a religious compromise on both the Jewish and the Christian sides. We attached more emphasis to the fact that Jews were accorded equal rights with Christians, on condition that they abandoned their "national" character. Only subsequently this led to Jewish reform, that is to say to a compromise on the part of the Jewish faith with regard to the surrounding non-Jewish environment. (This, first of all, was explained in Simon Dubnow's teaching.) In fact, however, the very concept of "nation" as viewed by Jews prior to the emancipation was a religious one; it may even be described as fundamental to the Jewish faith. Consequently, on the Jewish side the so-called "national" concession (during the period of the French revolution and of Napoleon I, and later in Germany) was actually a form of treason. It was thus in fact that the Jewish religious reform began. But it is even more important to remember that it was precisely this that enabled the Christian world to emancipate the Jews, since to begin with it was a world of a reformed, liberalized, open-to-compromise Christianity. In the Middle Ages, when a Jew wished to attain equal rights with Christians, he was forced to convert to Christianity, that is to say to accept the Christian messiah, Jesus of Nazareth, and all that this implied; whereas towards the close of the eighteenth century the only thing demanded of us was to abandon the belief in our own Messiah and all that went with it. Concessions, and explicitly religious ones, were, therefore made on both sides.

It is worth while to examine the special reasons we usually tend to forget about the perspectives of the Christian-Jewish controversy while considering this subject.

The anti-Jewish elements in Christendom, particularly the cruel persecutions of Jews in the name of the Christian faith, led us gradually to develop an anti-Christian complex. "Can any good come out of the 'shtetl' of Nazareth?"—this question dating back to the Evangelical period became for us a means of judging good and bad in the world surrounding us. If it was good, then it must perforce be non-Christian; if it was Christian, then it could not be good; the emancipation was favourable for Jews, therefore the proof is that it was not the fruit of Christianity. The Middle Ages in Europe were thoroughly saturated with Christianity; hence it was a period that was all bad. Confirmation of this can be found in abundance in the recent non-Jewish philosophy of history. Although, if we would look into the matter more closely, we would immediately perceive that most of the Britons or Germans who condemned the Middle Ages did so not because this period was Christian, but because it was Roman

Catholic, i.e. not sufficiently Christian in their view, not purely Evangelical or Reformed Protestant. We assumed that following the secularization of the surrounding Christian world, it itself pronounced us right in our dispute with Christianity. Nevertheless it was an error. Even the most extreme agnostics in the Christian camp still hold Christian morality to be on a higher spiritual level than the Jewish and that Christianity in general, notwithstanding the dogma of the Trinity, is a step forward on the previous general human development. In our secret hearts many among us thought that this might perhaps be true. In any event, we no longer conducted disputations on whether God could in fact become a man of flesh and blood, as was done in the past, e.g. in the days of Nachmanides and of Joseph Albo. Why conduct disputations when the whole controversy, praised be the Almighty, had been abandoned along with the old laws and the even more ancient Torah? And the verdict? It is quite clear: neither one thing nor another, since both sides were in the wrong; since both relied on false authorities, on miracles and fairy tales; since even their common ground, the Bible, was suspended in the air. The ground which today links the Jew with the Christian is incomparably firmer—man with his fellow-man, the ground of common sense, the truth not of some nebulous belief but of transparently clear science!

Who, then, of our modern saints who once lived with the faith (. . . . "the just shall live by his faith"—Habakkuk 2:4), believing in an a-religious scientific truth, could have foreseen that in the second third of the thoroughly scientific twentieth century a new world trial would be started against the Jews, and this especially on the basis of some new racial science? And that the attorney for the defense of the Jewish people would be none other than a Christian priest! The very same priest who still believes today, just as in the darkest Middle Ages, that where God is concerned, three principles are relevant: that God's word became flesh and that flesh was turned back into spirit; that it must even today be demanded of us, as it had been a thousand and fifteen hundred years ago, that we confess our sins, repent, and finally admit who is the true messiah. How did it happen that this priest took upon himself our defense when his foes were also our enemies? Can anything good come of this? Or—the very opposite?

Even in normal times it is prudent to know one's friends, no less than one's foes, especially at present when mortal danger threatens the whole of Jewry.

II

What is the position of the Christian side at present? In order to simplify the question that has already grown quite complex, let us for the time being set aside the vast Eastern Church and the various Protestant denominations. The future of the Eastern Church is almost entirely bound up with the future fate of Russia, and thus constitutes a subject in its own right, whereas Protestantism is in a large measure divided by countries and states, so that, for example, it is difficult to refer under a single heading to its German, English and American branches. It is different with the Roman Catholic Church which, as its very name indicates, is not merely international, but supra-national, universal, or in other words—a world church. Statistics show, that the Catholic faith is the most widespread of all religions on earth, encompassing more than 300 million souls. For us here it is especially significant because the dispute with Judaism was conducted in the name of Christendom chiefly by the Roman Church. If it is true in fact that now it is in the process of revising its arguments against the Jewish "unbelievers", this must of necessity exert a tremendous effect primarily on all other Christian denominations. But is it actually embarked on such a course?

The uncommonly strong impression that the death of the last Pope made on Jews everywhere is a sign that it is well understood in our ranks how important it is at present to have the Roman Curia aligned on the side of general human justice and, particularly, of tolerance towards the Jews. Rabbis of different tendencies eulogized Pope Pius XI no less warmly than, for instance, the representatives of the World Jewish Congress. Judging by his essential humanity, it is just possible that he was one of the "righteous among the nations". Nevertheless it would be fundamentally false to consider the whole complex of Judeo-Christian relations solely in connection with the character of the personage in St. Peter's seat, even if we consider it only within the framework of secular international politics. The policies of the Vatican, both in general and in regard to the Jews, have their ancient deep roots which exert their influence under every Pope, whatever the situation of the particular time.

From the point of view of constitutional law, the Catholic Church is an absolute monarchy, hence it matters greatly who wears the papal crown. But precisely because the Church may at any time acquire "a new king", we must be on our guard not to confuse the personal factors with the "eternal" ones in the policies of the Catholic Church. We do not as yet know who will reign tomorrow in the Vatican, whether it will be the erstwhile papal right hand, the Secretary of State Pacelli, or another cardinal closer in spirit to the Italo-German militarism. The guiding rule should be, on the one hand, "Put not your trust in man", not to rely too much on the kind hearts of human beings, and on the other hand—not to be too fearful of their ill will. If Catholic world politics should demand it, then even Pacelli can ally himself with the worst Jew-haters, and conversely—Mussolini's candidates, della Costa or Massimi, may execute a very sharp turn about against fascism and nazism. The proof may be seen in the Catholic politics which prevailed in the seventeen years of the Papacy of Achilles Ratti, that is Pius XI.

Nearly two-thirds of the initial period of his reign were devoted largely to fighting "godless" communism, even though by nature the last Pope was not a fighter at all, but a man "dwelling in tents", a quiet, dreamy "easy-chair scholar" (see the fine French biography, "Vie de Pie Onze, Life of Pius XI, by Alfred Perrier, 27th Edition, 1937). The anti-nationalist leanings of the Vatican's policy were more boldly expressed only during the final third of his term. This, too, was done after a period of protracted hesitations and then only gradually. Even after Nazism had already bared its fangs, Pius XI first declared his trust by means of the Corcordat published in the summer of 1933. In other words, in view of the anti-communist spirit of Nazism, its anti-clerical spirit was of little importance in the eyes of the Pope. In 1934 the Vatican gave its blessing to the annihilation of the Socialist-Labour Movement in Austria, as well as to the local, albeit not complete anti-Semitism. Since 1935, Italian Fascism, again with the Pope's blessing, carried out the subjugation of Abyssinia. Since 1936, his blessing was bestowed on the Spanish Fascists, although anti-Catholic elements were also present amongst them. It may be said that were it not for the last few years, neither we nor the world in general would have known what a friend we lost in Pius XI, and what a forceful opponent he was of German and Italian racism. How, then, can the transformation he underwent in his very last years be explained?

This radical evolution, whether of the Pope personally, or of the Vatican's Secretary of State in general, faithfully mirrors the development in the world outside the Catholic Church. Only of late has it become clear, even for those who for a long time pretended that they could not see, that the upheaval in Germany was not only a political, not only a social, but also a spiritual revolution of as great a depth as the Bolshevist revolution in Russia. The virulent anti-Catholic expressions in Hitler's "Mein Kampf", in Alfred Rosenberg's "The Myth of the Twentieth Century", and in many other books by less prominent Nazis, which were at first interpreted as mere talk, were gradually being put into practice. As S. K. Padover justly described it in the last issue of New York's "Forum and Century" (February 1938), the Catholic Church in Germany became, after the Jews, scapegoat number two. "Nuns were being kept in prison and priests in concentration camps, Catholic leaders were being shot, the houses of cardinals destroyed . . . such is the news coming almost daily from the German Reich," It was war, and a religious war at that, the strife of a new faith against the old Christian faith and tradition.

The Vatican was quick to grasp that Bolshevism was more than anti-Christian, that it arrived like a new Islam of sorts in order to replace all the old world religions, including Christianity. That totalitarian nationalism was also capable of taking up this challenge, was absorbed with deliberate slowness. For years after years there was still hope in the Vatican that it would be possible to avoid a war on two fronts, against communist internationalism and anti-communist hypernationalism. But step by step the Catholic world perceived that the new racist nationalism was also capable of overflowing the borders of a state and cause a spiritual flood. In the wake of the spiritual annexation of Italy by German racism in 1938, the waves of that flood rolled up to the foot of the Catholic Ararat, the Vatican Palace and the "Eternal City" of Rome. "With aching hearts we were forced to witness how the holy city was inundated with crosses which are not the crosses of our Lord the King, Jesus Christ", stated Pius XI after Hitler's journey to Rome in May 1938. It was therefore clear that the German swastika together with the Fascist sign, just like the five pointed Bolshevist star, were pagan, anti-Christian and the emblem of Satan.

Henceforth a change occurred in the fundamentals of the Catholic Church's stand towards Judaism. The current international, materialistic, "scientific" anti-Semitism stands revealed in Nazism not as an anti-Bolshevist element, as had been understood even a few years ago, but as anti-Christian. The "religious" anti-Christian character of the new German anti-Semitism was sharply delineated in Edmond Vermeil's last book, "The Theoreticians of the German Revolution" as well as in the volume entitled: "The Religious Question in Germany" by another Parisian scholar, the Catholic professor, Count R. D'Arcourt (both appeared in 1938). We hear the same from the American James M. Jillis who writes in his own monthly journal "The Catholic World" (Vol. 148. p. 515 ff) concerning the anti-Jewish persecutions in Germany as follows: "The deepest foundation, the very root of this is the truth which up to the present is cherished by all Jews insofar as they have not forgotten their biblical heritage, that God is the supreme Lord, to whom all the kings with all their power are subservient, existing only as long as they remain faithful to God." This truth, however, is upheld no less by pious Christians than by the Jew, with his "long memory", who still remembers the Bible. The "war of Amalek", i.e. of Nazi Germany, against the Jews had to expand into a war against Christians, at least against the Catholic Church, which, similarly to the Jewish people, is also an international force continuing the spiritual tradition—again like the Jewish people—dating not from today and not from yesterday but continuing unbroken, without intervals, millennium after millennium.

Since olden times it has been part of the Catholic tradition to keep the Jewish people in existence. Today this tradition assumes a new form, that of maintaining its own existence together with that of the Jewish people. This is an enormous difference compared with anything that existed previously. The dispute regarding the Trinity is postponed to await a more favourable time; who knows for how long. It is no longer the problem of the "second storey" but of the first as well, and the foundation itself. Satan's symbols and signs multiply like locusts. Miracles and wonders were not lacking. Germany and Italy allied themselves with Japan, the most powerful state of the old deeply-rooted pre-Christian pagan world. In such circumstances, French Masons, Anglo-Saxon heretics, and even Jews are welcome as friends. Are we then to remain no more than a passive object of this friendship?

III

And where do we stand now? The signs of the friendly mood we can at present perceive in Christendom bear, almost without exception, a purely opportunistic character. It seems to be the need of the hour. Ordinarily our orientation is based not on spiritual forces, but rather on political ones and, therefore, mainly on the so-called democratic countries. Is it not a fact that the storm of protest following the November 1938 pogrom in Germany was strongest in the democratic monarchy of Great Britain and the democratic republic of the United States of America? Since there was no such reaction in the democratic republic of France we, the opportunistic believers in "Realpolitik" that we are, hasten to explain this in the terms of "Realpolitik". For this reason, the Catholic Church rather pleased us since it itself was drawing closer to the "democracies". If the Freemason Herriot, chairman of the French Chamber of Deputies, may pay tribute to the Pope in Parliament in a speech delivered on January 12th, 1939, then why should we not do so? As a result we are inclined to look at the Vatican and its pro-Jewish policies solely from a political point of view, thereby increasing the danger that we may once again harm ourselves, not only in a spiritual, but especially, in a political sense.

We should begin to free ourselves from the abstract concept of "democracy". The spiritual essence of any country is far more significant than the external form of its political life. At present the United States of America still draws spiritual sustenance from puritan Biblical Christianity. As William Bullitt, the American Ambassador to France said recently (22nd February 1938), "Our faith is old. We are a young nation, always close to the soil and to the Bible. We believe in the commandment: Thou shalt not bear false witness. . . . We believe in the commandment: Thou shall not covet a stranger's property. We believe in the commandment: Thou shalt not kill!" The English keep to the Bible and the Ten Commandments with equal firmness; the prestige maintained by the Jewish people in the eyes of the Anglo-Saxons is a reflection of the prestige they attach to the Jewish Scriptures. In France, where the Bible is not cherished with quite so much zeal, the historical fate of the Jewish people is of little concern to anyone. Only when we take into earnest consideration these definitely "non-political" facts, can we find a correct approach to the newest policies of the Vatican.

To understand the spirit of their policies, one must first of all bear in mind that it is a policy of the spirit, that spiritual factors in human history play the main role in their calculations. True the Catholic Church strives for power, but for power over the human soul. It is prepared to enter into compromise with every factor of political power as long as it is not a competitor for the soul or the spirit of man. As soon as racism embarked on such a competition, the Catholic Church at once became its opponent. If, at present, it supports the abstract idea of democracy, because it believes that the latter's spiritual-revolutionary role has come to an end and now needs the protection of the Church. The 2000-year old Church is in the habit of making long-term prognoses, frequently for a whole generation in advance. It is now taking into account what may occur after another world war or even after a much longer period of general European decay without a war. It is already preparing itself to assume the leadership of a new European regeneration movement, be it even in the form of political democracy. In all this, it will not surrender even an iota of Christian dogma. It recognizes in the Jews a factor as eternal as it is itself. In this particular, Judaism seems to the Church to be preferable to Nazism and all manner of other transitory secular "isms". This is not the time for it to conduct a dispute with us. It is not a matter of the immediate moment, but for future generations and centuries to deal with.

If we grasp all this, we will be saved from entertaining dangerous political illusions and avoid equally dangerous spiritual threats. It is a political illusion to think that the Catholic Church values Jewish emancipation. Should events prove that the decisive political forces in the world are indifferent to this matter, the Church will not quarrel with them. If in Germany, for example, Nazism will be replaced by a monarchy or a military dictatorship, thus putting an end to the anti-Christian war and to racism, but leaving the Jews in their present condition, this would not deter the Vatican for a single moment from making peace with Germany. Nevertheless, our own policy as regards the Catholic Church should not depend exclusively on its attitude to emancipation. To attain equal rights, we must first of all exist. And today we realize, as we look ahead into the future, that for the majority of the Jewish people it is actually a matter of life and death. This problem concerns *us*, not me or you or him, but us Jews, the Jewish people as a whole. This point brings us face to face with a new spiritual danger relating to the Jewish Christian controversy. Christianity, or at any rate, the Catholic Church has a special interest in keeping the Jewish people alive, for it is a living witness of the historical side of the Christian tradition. But is it especially interested in preserving the Jewish faith? One may retort with another question: is it possible that a Jewish people should exist without Judaism? To this one may reply that this is precisely the approach used by our secularised circles. Why then should the Roman Church not go a step further and introduce the idea of a separate Jewish national church within the general Catholic framework? This is already being discussed by various Catholic groups. There is no doubt that for the sake of a mess of pottage, i.e. "more rights" and, particularly, if they could go on bearing the name "Jew", some of our disoriented elements would agree even to conversion. Thus the question of conversion within our ranks is now relevant, especially in Catholic countries. Is our controversy with Christianity then to end with Jacob's selling his birthright back to Esau?

The birthright—that is the main point. Anyone who reads Chapters 25 and 27 of Genesis attentively senses immediately that the case of Jacob and Esau contains a profound secret. It brings to mind the story of the three rings in Lessing's "Nathan der Weise". Who actually inherited the genuine ring, who is really the eldest son, can be ascertained only by their behaviour. Are we ourselves to-day as firmly convinced as our fathers and grandfathers had been that our Jewish genealogy in fact reaches back to the first born among the world's religions, to their true source? As long as we lack this firm conviction, then Christian protection that may be our fate, constitutes the major spiritual threat to which we have ever been exposed throughout our entire history. The fathers of the Reform Movement aspired that we become a sort of church and, actually, it might be fulfilled for a part of our people, but in the form of a Jewish-Christian Church. Conversely, however, if we accept the support of Christianity while we are spiritually strong and armed, then we can accept it freely and without fear. What more, we can then accept it as equals, for in a deeper sense Christianity today needs our good will no less than we need its concern.

But for such an understanding to develop, not only between Jews and Christians, but between Judaism and Christianity—until the great present threat to all mankind shall have passed—it is necessary for ourselves to be really Jews, such Jews as the Almighty commanded us to be.

SECTION D

Towards the Future

1. Moscow, New York, Jerusalem

Over a century ago, the French Jewish thinker, Joseph Salvador (1796–1873), the spiritual forerunner of Moses Hess and James Darmesteter, offered the Jewish people a brief formula relating to their political situation in the world: Paris, Rome, Jerusalem. Three words, three names, three principles. Paris—the birthplace of the great French Revolution and of the free secular man and citizen of the world; Rome—the capital of the Catholic Church and the chief buttress of religious tradition and of supra-individual spiritual power; Jerusalem—the origin of the most free and humane of religions, the place where eternal peace would one day be made between Paris and Rome, between revolution and tradition, sealing the evolutionary urge of the individual and society built on firm historical foundations. The road which leads Jewry through the whole world from Jerusalem to Jerusalem would bring all the people of the earth to the only possible world religion, to the sublime secular religion— to liberty, equality, fraternity. Such were the hopes and beliefs of the son of a French Jew, offspring of a Spanish *converso* and of a Catholic mother who through her love of a Jew acquired a love of Jews in general.

In our own era of world politics, Salvador would have been among our most widely acknowledged thinkers and leaders. He was one of the first who, in the new West European environment, searched anew to find for the Jewish people their own way out of the bewitched labyrinth of world politics. Thus with magnificent instinct, consciously or otherwise, he performed what has always been the most important task of Jewish creative thought.

Is it perhaps wrong to say that world politics is the backbone of the entire Jewish history? Or that the true Jewish creative spirit, from the Prophets onwards, has always held to its aim of determining the world-political situation of the Jewish people, in order to formulate on this basis a concrete world-political, world-historical programme? Is not the whole Bible a continuous affirmation of the primacy of external politics in Jewish life? Did not later Jewry sometimes forget that medieval Rome was only a reincarnation of old Edom, and Byzantium and Kiev the heir of Greece?

This essay was first published in Yiddish in *Fraye Shriftn*, Warsaw, 1930, No. 7/8.

409

Why then are our most important figures in world politics so little appreciated among our new-style nationalists?

Why should a name like Joseph Salvador be known to us only because of the polemics which Hess launched against him, and Hess again only insofar as he can be utilized for deriving all sorts of "minimalisms"? The reason for this, it seems to me, is that our new-style nationalism has lost, with its predilection for ideas, the desire to make fine distinctions. People appear to prefer a discourse that appeals to the heart to a critical inquiry into the deepest prerequisites of national existence. The demands of the hour outweigh, they consider, the world of eternity. Anybody referring to world-historical missions, declare the so-called enemies of sophistry, is a true brother to the preacher of "the world mission", the false prophets of assimilation. If Salvador's Jerusalem is the world capital of the future, our Jewish towns and townlets have to reject him. Is he really a "prophet"? Then no doubt he is a prevaricator. What benefit to us is East and West in the same town, since we are minimalists, ready to be satisfied with little, and demanding no more than some permanent place along the East Wall of our local synagogue.

The suggestion that the idea of "world-mission" and national consciousness are mutually exclusive is, as I once observed elsewhere in passing, a result of muddled logic. If we dislike a man's hat, we believe that the head that wears it is empty. The phrase, "Light from the East", we translate as "Darkness from the West". The world "mission" is in fact only a literal Latin translation, originating in Western Europe, derived in Yiddish from the Hebrew word *sh'likhut*. A *sheliakh* is a person who has undertaken to do something, and in this sense the task he has before him is called *sh'likhut*. If the task is strictly defined, affirmed in effect in a document, then it is designated with the Greek word "programme". Has it ever occurred to anyone to oppose a party just because it has a programme? Even to entertain such a notion is senseless. A voluntary association of people who wish to work together can be created only on the basis of a more or less clearly formulated programme. Even when considering an individual, we esteem him not when he lives aimlessly, but when he displays a certain will and plan, and when he is aware that his life must serve some purpose. Marxism has accustomed us to the thought that among individuals there are also classes comparable to organized spiritual units, spiritual organisms. One can go further and say that with Marx himself the idea of class is no more than the result of his recognition that the proletariat has its own world-historical mission. It is therefore no exaggeration to say that never in world history has there been a time when humanity stood so clearly in the balance as in the present historic hour, under the constellation of Libra, measuring, weighing, and drawing up an account of itself for the moment ahead. In just such an epoch of prognosis and programme may not the Jewish people, who for thousands of years have never ceased to strain their eyes looking into the remote future, now consider the purpose of their existence? Is it for them alone to live without awareness of their national mission, to live without plan or programme, just at random?

The question is not whether the Jewish people have a mission; the question is what is their mission? For the Jewish socialist this gives rise to a further important question: What has the Jewish national mission to do with that of the general working man? Do the socialist and Jewish programmes lend themselves to amalgamation in a harmonious whole? In any event, one thing is clear: a socialism which avoids the raising of such questions is perhaps a socialism of Jews, with a literature in Yiddish, but not a Jewish socialism. It would be a parallel to a Jewish nationalism formulated according to a code of non-Jewish analphabets but not to that of the spiritual history of Judaism, of the code of our own historical experience.

Ever since its existence as an historical entity, the Jewish people assumed the part of the speaker of the nations, as their *Advocatus Dei* (cf. Isaiah, 2). That is the real meaning of the selection of the Jews or any nation as a chosen people. He who denies the Jewish mission in the world, denies his descent even when he swears three times a day by the Latin word "nation".

If, however, anyone asks me: Well now, those Western European theoreticians of the world-mission, were not they the first who hit upon the discovery that the Jew is only a Jew so far as he is not a Jew? I would answer: Quite right! The ideology of the Jewish world-mission, in that particular case, coincides partly with the ideology of assimilation. But can the particular prove anything against the general? A convert will also prove from Scripture that a Jew may accept conversion, and a traitor that the prophet Isaiah was an assimilationist. Should we, therefore, on that account, relegate the Torah, as the saying goes, to a corner and excommunicate the prophets? On the contrary! We have to make every effort to redeem the Torah from incompetent hands and to liberate its right interpretation from those who badly misread it.

The main error of the ideologists of world-mission lay in their to one-sided and too abstract formulation of the real content of the Jewish mission-idea. The Talmud sharply distinguishes between a messenger for delivery and one for reception. The meaning of the Jewish mission is two-fold, not only to bestow upon the world the sacred gift, but also to receive something from the world itself. It is just this duality of the Jewish conception of mission that remained unrevealed to the Western Europen Jewish thinkers of the nineteenth century. It seemed to them that European culture, which the Jewish people had accepted from its

European surroundings, had little to do with the mission-idea, and that the modern way of life was only a means to an end, only an instrument for breaking down the wall that separated the Jewish tradition from its worldly environment. Judaism, they considered, had a task in relation to the world, and not the world in relation to Judaism. The mission of non-Jewish humanity lay beyond their horizon, because these thinkers were in fact not too weak but too strong in their national approach which was a nationalism of a peculiar character. It sounds like a paradox and yet those who denied the Jewish "nation" were too one-sidedly Jewish in spirit. Even in the work of such a philosopher as Hermann Cohen one can perceive it at every turn. His Judaism was to him an imitation of German ideology, a message for "delivery", and not for "reception". He considered the Jewish religion to be a closed world-view which needed neither expansion nor development. The world, it seemed to him, was too poor to make any gifts to Judaism, and Judaism was too rich and too satisfied with its possessions to wish to accept anything from outside. The consciously assimilated Jews, unknowingly but essentially Jewish in their preaching of the world religion, were really defenders of the faith of the medieval ghetto.

The one-sidedness of the mission-idea is connected with its abstract character. The world in which Judaism pursues its mission, and needs further to pursue it, was regarded by most of the adherents of the mission-theory as a mirror-like plane, without peak or declivity, grey and cold as ice. According to them the peoples of the world whom Judaism addresses are dumb, and all dumb people have one language, an abbreviated, abstract sign-language. Jewish exposition had to be boiling hot in order to melt the thousand-year-old ice, but the words had to be adapted to the average human intelligence, to suit, like algebraic symbols, every time and every place. One God, truth, righteousness and peace—this is the frame within which the essence of Judaism could be placed and transmitted. They considered that in order to spread the Jewish faith in the world they had to popularize it, to lower it to the level of the common people, and strip it of all its historical garments. The link between the theory of world-mission and the internal Jewish reformation in Germany, even with the anti-historical *Haskalah* of the eighteenth century, is almost tangible. But, like the one-sidedness of the theory, its abstract character is ultimately no more than a ghetto legacy. When one learns a foreign language, one begins with speaking it, and only much later does one understand what the speakers of the language are trying to convey. The assimilated Jewish apologists of the world-mission idea thought that the world was dumb, because they themselves were deaf. That was the reason why the translation of *sh'likhut* into germanized Latin (mission) turned out to be so inept. The way Salvador used the term showed us how much better it could have been rendered.

Joseph Salvador was assuredly a representative of the world-mission ideology, and yet there was a great distance between him and his friends in

Germany. The chief difference consisted in that, firstly, Salvador understood the Jewish task in the world as the logical corollary to the European
world concerning Judaism; secondly, he defined the Jewish world-
historical task not in an ethico-abstract sense but in a concrete way in the
light of philosophy of history. To Salvador, Paris and Rome were not just
ethico-religious categories, but also names of two defined world-historical,
world-political epochs: the period from 1789, the year of the birth of the
French Revolution, till 1815, the year in which the upheaval spent itself,
and the period from 1815 to 1848 as the pause between the old and the
newer revolutionary epochs. Therefore, his Jerusalem was not just a name
for an idea transcending history, but a plastic expression of a concrete
universal historical task: the early rebuilding of Zion with Western
European help, preferably French. Had worldly nationalists not been so
detached from the world, the fate of Salvador's "Utopia" might have
proved to them that a maximum programme of a believer is often
incomparably more real than the mixture of scattered programme points.
The great approach to world politics adapted to the times is the call that
sounds from Salvador's triangular formula.

II

It is obvious that in the formula: Paris, Rome, Jerusalem, only the last
term at most can remain unchanged today. More will be said about this
later. Meanwhile let us consider why, in the present situation, Paris and
Rome must give place to Russia and America, to Moscow and New York.
    Seventy years ago, when Salvador surveyed the political globe in order
to determine the two poles and hence to ascertain where Judaism stood in
the world, Paris and Rome were two diametrically opposite points through
which passed the axis of the Western European scene and therefore of the
universe. Europe then still reigned over all the other continents, and in
Europe itself France was the volcanic centre where at almost any moment
a new pillar of fire could erupt. Ten years later the Paris commune
demonstrated that the Utopian Salvador was not only a French patriot but
also a politician of acute perception, more precisely, that the French
patriotism of Salvador had a general humanitarian basis—that is to say, also
a Jewish basis if one accepts that "Jewish" is in its essence tied to the
world's progressive tendencies. At that time even medieval Rome was far
from having ended its role. It is enough here to mention only the policies of
Pope Leo XIII and the Catholic workers' movement nurtured by him.
Since then, however, much water has flowed down the Seine and the
Tiber. Europe is no longer Europe, and the most significant West
European capitals are receding ever more rapidly into provincialism. Our
old planet is once again changing its political poles, and this is most
conspicuously manifest in relation to Paris.
    Not so long ago the Russian poet Valery Bryusov wrote in his poem

"Paris": "And every day may here acquire historic greatness." That was at the beginning of this century. After 1905, after 1917, Paris had to yield its historic revolutionary role to the Paris of the East—to Moscow. The city that once stood at the head of the social movement and taught the world how to build a just political order was now obliged to follow the lead of other countries that had surged ahead. As a rule, ideas are seldom realized in the place where they have originated. In order to blossom and bear fruit they need, apparently, to be transplanted to an unfamiliar climate. Liberty, Equality, and Fraternity were three shoots that took root in French soil. When the hothead Babeuf, however, demanded that the plantlet should become a flower, he became a sacrifice to a distant future in a strange and unknown country. French socialism, the direct offspring of French republican democratism, was destined to flower in Germany and bear weighty fruit in Russia.

Who would now dispute that if revolution has any meaning for our times it is only when it signifies the spiritual renewal of man on a new economic basis. Western European man, may, however, still possess the force to battle against a crumbling national order, against national oppression, and other objective evils, but not against himself. The development of the productive potential has revealed a dialectic of which dialectic materialism had never even dreamed. Between man and man, and also between man and his own historical mission, there has arisen in the West a mount of things of material needs that narrows his historical horizon, obscures his view of the future, and shackles him more severely than the chains of which Marx and Engels wrote in the Communist Manifesto. The proletarian of the West has also nowadays something to lose and, dazzled by the false glitter of capitalist civilisation, stands helpless, in the truest sense of the word unconscious, relying blindly on leaders who have been openly or secretly bought. His liberation can no longer come from himself or through himself alone. For this he needs a jolt from outside, the impulse of a new people in world history, from a land uncluttered with things and not inhabited by automatons, but with living, sensitive people. Such a land is Russia.

The mention of Moscow evokes immediately the image of Bolshevism. And yet Bolshevism is no more than a link in the chain of Russian history, one of the stages in the East European historical process, part and not the whole. The Russian revolution has proceeded for over a century, from the Decembrists onwards. The Decembrists, as is well known, were the pupils of Paris, like later Russian revolutionary generations enlightened in the West. Gradually, however, the pupils became independent, and Russia became unnoticeably the teacher of Western Europe, where acute minds had early foreseen precisely what would happen. Back in the 1870s Disraeli had based his anti-Russian policy in the Balkans on the belief that Russian penetration of Western Europe would create the greatest danger for the whole economic and social order. At that time Marxism in Russia was scarcely known, but both in Russia and abroad, it was felt that the Russian people had something new to tell the world and that it possessed a gigantic force which could overturn the world.

One after the other, champions arose on Russian soil proclaiming to all mankind, with unlimited faith in their power, a life and death struggle: death to the mean petty-bourgeoisie of Western Europe; death to the pettiness of so-called politics; an end once and for all to the oppression of people by people! Long live Liberty, Equality, Fraternity! These sound like old, familiar, outworn French expressions, and yet how fresh was their ring in Russian! Fresh and new, for "the Russian was not yet accustomed to talking of freedom and to carry at the same time"—as Herzen expressed it—"a gendarme in his heart"; to talk of equality and at the same time to hold that the difference between high and low was God-ordained; to preach fraternity while behaving like Cain and Abel. The Russian said what he thought, and was ready to do what he said. To translate the fine Western European words into acts was the mission which Russia undertook, and that has been the mightiest power in Russian culture of the past hundred years. Moscow was not Bolshevik, but Bolshevism was Muscovite.

Bolshevism is Muscovite, trully Russian, in its terrific impulse, in its historical scope, in the zeal with which it applied itself to the realization of the West European socialist programme, and in some ways not Russian in its practical methods, in its cunning diplomacy, and above all in the cruelty with which it tramples on the life of the individual. Not Russian, for the distinguishing mark of Russian culture is the singular depth of its interpersonal relationships, which Bolshevism combats with relentless hostility.

To explain what I mean by Russian "depth", I want to point to its opposite, to the behaviour of people toward each other in Western countries. Among Europeans a man is primarily the sum of a limited number of abstract, biological and sociological determinants: age, sex, race, occupation, property, education. In the Western world measure is taken of every one as of a recruit to the army with its established standards and, behold, he is dressed from head to foot in uniform clothes which hide his personality and make his individual image indiscernible. There a man is valued not as an independently existing substance, but as a bundle of attributes. He is assessed according to the place he holds in his environment, in other words, his place is valued higher than he himself. It follows that the products, both material and spiritual, have a higher rating than the producers themselves, the human souls. People have become, so to speak, things among things, and even in relation to himself a man is turned into a material thing alien to himself. People are to one another like shadows out of a price-list. That is why, basically, there is no hope that the renewal of

humanity will begin in the West and that "Paris" will ever again illumine
the world. For this to happen Western man would have to approach as
closely again to his fellow and himself as only the Russian is capable of
doing today.

Among the Russians a person is first a person, and only afterwards old or
young, man or woman, one "of our own" or a stranger, a worker or a
peasant, high or low, shoemaker or professor. A Russian does not inquire
of a man what he does, where he comes from, or what his training has been,
but only what he is. Instinctively he is interested in the man himself, his
substance, and not in his outward appearance which could be defined in
abstract terms. I once expressed it in this way: in the West a "person"
derives from the Latin "persona", that is to say, "a mask"; but its Russian
equivalent is a "litchnost", from "lik, litso" (face). He does not wear a mask.
He has his own face and looks the other man straight in the eye and into his
very soul. If he is good, his goodness is endless. If he is cruel, he is
frightful, like a wild animal. Good or bad, he is naturally broad-minded,
over lifesize in his feelings and his strivings, as lavish as God-given nature
itself. It is therefore no wonder that the young Russian society, storming
on its way, has in scarcely a hundred years overtaken the old Western
civilisation, and in many respects has even surpassed it. Other people,
other tempos.

The spiritual role which Russia, with its literature, music and theatre,
plays in the world of Western Europe is well and widely recognized. Less
attention has been paid to the significance of Russia regarding future world
history. Such recognition is largely prevented by the "episode" of Bolshevism. Russia's influence in the world is today manifested under a
pseudonym, under the name "Comintern". When, however, the great
admiration which Westerners of today, whether workers or intellectuals,
show for Moscow, is subjected to close examination, it is quickly seen to
have been evoked by Russia rather than by Bolshevism. Communist youth
abroad is accustomed to a freer, a more humane and heroic way of life and
believes naively that it follows the Bolshevik programme, whereas in truth
Bolshevism is by comparison a secondary ingredient mainly nourished by
the Russian national spirit. Was it not known in Russia before Bolshevism
that to abide by formalities was narrow-minded, that to pursue honours
was despicable, to boast of success was shameful, and that money was dirt?
It is interesting to note that even Russian communists often do not notice
how they confuse the Russian idea with the Communist or revolutionary
idea. In his recently published autobiography, Leon Trotzky criticizes a
number of German and other foreign socialist leaders for their petty-
bourgeois attitude to women, to children, to distinction, to making a living
and so on. He believes that inherently in their whole mental make-up,
they have never been revolutionaries, that from the beginning, from their
"six days of Genesis", they remained Germans, Frenchmen, Poles, but

never Russians. Seen at a distance, the meaning of "Russian" is "revolutionary", because in contact with the congealed West European way of life, the Russian conception of morals works like dynamite.

The great cultural and moral influence of Russia in the world is at the same time the means by which Russian political influence spreads in other countries. Moral attraction and repulsion are the same as mechanical forces in nature. On this depends, in every historical epoch, the universal political constellation, the individual destiny of nations and their correlation with each other. If we add to this that Russia has one face turned towards Europe and the other towards Asia, and that her influence extends in this way into the Islamic-Indian-Chinese-Japanese world, then we begin to grasp why Russia was destined to grow into a paramount problem of world history, and why no people in the world today can, on its way into the future, avoid Moscow.

III

Just as Moscow is today the Paris of old, so New York has replaced Rome.

Rome, the Eternal City, was for almost two thousand years on end the focus of the Western world, first as the Rome of the sons of Jupiter, and then of the Christian Caesars, the Popes. Old imperial Rome established the Pax Romana in the world, an armed state of international peace; whilst the Christian Rome watched over the inner peace in people's souls. In both cases the method was the same—dictatorship. The Catholic priests, the legions of the cross, took over with the old Roman law the classical idea of world dominion. The Catholic faith became a religious imperialism. Relying on its secular arm, the Catholic Church created a world-system which was wider and more real for the Christian of the West than the natural world, which it hoped entirely to absorb. To a wide extent this aim succeeded. The Christian believer felt himself to be as if in a fortress in the world, enclosing within its walls earth and heaven, time and eternity, hell as well as paradise. Relying on the guides appointed in the highest quarter, the bearers of the "Holy Ghost", he felt that he could never become lost in this all-embracing world structure; all his doubts were easily allayed, and peace in his heart was assured for ever. The greatest monument to the Catholic world-view, so regarded even by non-Catholics, is Dante's *Divine Comedy* : for every kind of human feeling, for every shade of good and evil thought, there is here room which transcends time and space.

The need for comfort, his striving for inner security and harmony, is no less deeply rooted in man than his urge for instability and movement, his longing to release himself. The Catholic dictatorship made clever use of this conservative force in the human spirit, but was never able entirely to annul the equally strong impulse to change whatever was once achieved, to create some disorder, and to protest. However admirable a system of thought may be, if it is set within limits, the human spirit will sooner or later come up against the frontiers, will conceive the desire to see what is happening on the other side, and find its inheritance narrow and restricted. The inherited values of religious life, peace and security, suddenly fall in price, the sweet joy of Sabbath becomes an affliction, and life loses colour. West European history for the past three hundred years is the history of the ordinary man and his wanderings in a world without end, and almost without aim. It is a time of religious crisis. Without a firm centre, however, without organized idea or purpose, no culture can continue to exist. In the absence of an absolute, the holy idea, relative or commonplace aims are made to serve instead. People begin to make distinctions between various types of the ordinary, one kind of workday and another, and to the first chapter of the Book of Genesis are added new verses and a new Sabbath. So it came about that the secularized peoples of Western Europe have, one after the other, transferred sanctity to matters which have no religious significance, such as the state, law, and economy—in brief—the nation and its household affairs. It has been no different in the Jewish fold.

Rome, Christendom were supra-international. Secular, revolutionary Paris laid the stress on "national". All the great states which arose in Western Europe during the anti-religious epoch bear the stamp of "nation" and are "national states". Nevertheless, the old Roman and Christian internationalism did manage to survive in the new times. Expelled from politics it escaped into economies. The busiest day in the new week became its holiday. Economy and its twin sister technology became, in times of greatest national divisions, the bridges between the nations. The internationalism of modern capitalism on the one hand, and that of proletarian socialism on the other, display old Christian, religious, the "Roman" tendency therein. If Moscow is indeed destined to become the capital of spiritual, revolutionary socialism, it will be not only the second Paris but also, as the Slavophiles have always aspired "the Third Rome". For the moment we are far from that. For the time being, materialist, Marxist socialism, and also therefore Bolshevism, and the ethico-religious Russian-Roman trend are overlaid by unlimited economic-technological ambitions, by the idolatry of productive capacities, and the worship of the factory chimney. In this way socialist internationalism drops to the level of capitalist internationalism and becomes a sort of underwriter on the world market. In the market, however, it is the one with the purse who calls the tune. At the base of exclusively technico-economic progress, the heir to the power of Rome is not the beggarly Moscow shopkeeper but New York's opulent Wall Street.

Indeed, if there were no Russia in the modern era with its revolutionary, maximalist spirit, one could safely predict that the whole world would within a short time become Americanized. America, which Goethe with prophetic vision once described as "the land of illimited possibilities", was from the start the ready soil for the highest development of the progressive tendencies of a secularized Christian culture. Like a ripe fruit from the English mother-tree, the American republic, great and free as she was, could never be otherwise than tolerant to other people, regardless of language or race. In a land which had by revolutionary action broken away from its own national roots, the national principle had eventually to give way to the state principle, and the supra-national state principle had again to link up with the economic principle, which by its nature even among the West European nations became the main pillar of internationalism. In this way the apparatus of state, which in Europe to this day acts in great measure as the protector of national culture and independence, became in America the armour of the economy and of capitalist accumulation. The republic of traders and farmers, not having either a state nationality or a state religion, seemed expressly created to promote capitalist internationalism itself as a state of religion. It has not been done formally, but the younger American generations absorbed the ideology with their mother's milk. In his well known study on the Puritans, Max Weber has shown that the so-called "Father of the American Constitution" had no other purpose than to make capitalism a sort of religious system. However that may be, the particular American spirit, "Americanism", is a fact, and its historical significance becomes daily more obvious. The First World War drew in fact in this respect too a concluding line. It is a mistake to think that the success of Americanism in the world is only an effect of the top prize which Uncle Sam drew in the lottery of the Great War. Present-day American wealth makes such a deep impression because it plainly demonstrates that the American system, if one accepts its basic hypotheses, is the most logical of all moral systems: it promises only what it can deliver and is as good as its word. Who desires a more honest marriage with morality?

More honourable and consistent than materialistic socialism, Americanism proclaims quite clearly that all talk of the mission of peoples, classes or individuals is an empty dream, an old wives' tale. The earth on which we live is just like time in which we exist; it is not a vestibule but rather the main hall where we are to witness here and now the finest of all possible spectacles entitled: grasp whatever you can! Push your way through! Let no one take your place! You are a person, a human being, and that means you have a ticket as good as anyone's. But a ticket without a number. If your elbows are strong enough, you will push your way through to the front, where you will be delighted with the world-show, and the weaker and the more gentle people will envy you. But woe to you if you are short-winded and soft-natured! You will be trodden under foot, and you will have only yourself to blame. For competition is the highest law, the battle of all against all, and the world is not for idlers. To toil and enjoy, each according to his power and taste, these are two pillars on which American morality reposes. Should a heretic raise any doubts whether human society can survive on such pillars, the American answer is: "See for yourself!— There's sure something to see in America.

In America and wherever Americanism holds sway, it is possible to observe how free competition enables the most forceful drivers to grasp the reins of the ruling class and of economic life, and hold them fast while driving the free and equal citizens like horses in harness. The masters themselves, the task masters, possess a whole collection of whips: the media, pictorial persuasion, sport, all kinds of amenities for every taste. But all is overruled by the whip-morality! It is due to American morals that the weary drudge of a horse draws on its last strength and runs still faster in the drive to overtake the other creatures harnessed like itself. Without this American morality the merciless pace of the economic and technical development of the new world would not have been possible; with it that development was the most natural thing in the world. Therefore it is clearly understandable how Americanism and its propaganda so easily succeed among all enjoying violence, whether they are Capitalists or Bolsheviks: once a man becomes convinced that to establish a record is the highest aim in life, he will believe that to become out of breath is a healthy exercise, and even dropping to the ground he will bless his masters. That is the spirit which enables millions of people in New York, living tens of storeys high, to go scrambling over each other's heads.

The dominant spirit in New York is the spirit of numbers uncounted, of measures without matter, of weight without counterweight. Economics is all for the sake of economics; technology for that of technology; and to hurry along in order not to miss speed. That is the highest attainment of secularised West European culture, of Americanism. Just as Russia has one face turned to Europe and another to Asia, so America flashes its electric eyes over the entire old world in order to hypnotise and subdue it. The magic of ancient Rome now spreads from New York. Rome cast a spell upon peoples with its angelic music of the spheres; New York tries to deafen them with the din of its satanic mills. And so Russia, land of the living soul wherever men live, must clash with America. Moscow and New York are nowadays the two poles of the world's globe.

IV

The development of all peoples takes place today just between these two polar points, and how much more so that of the Jewish people. And why much more so? Let us consult the historical atlas. A glance at the pre-war ethnographic map reveals that for more than a century, half of the Jewish people lived in Russia and thus came directly under Russian influence. With the mass emigration of Russian Jews to America, Russian influence on Jews was carried across the Atlantic, and to other countries on the way from Moscow to New York: Germany, France, England. Russian Jews thus became the carriers and cement of national Jewish unity and wrote, for all time, one of the finest pages in our history. If the Jewish people is to-day placed so firmly on the globe, not the least important reason for this is that it had since the nineteenth century one foot still in Russia and the other in America. This is the secret of our present national equilibrium. Granted, there is another factor which must not be overlooked: the *kibbutz-galuiot*, the ingathering of the dispersed communities which is a consequence of technical progress. Old commentaries expound that *Eretz Yisrael* may also be called *Eretz Tzvi*, Land of the Deer, because when Messiah comes it will stretch like the hide of a deer. The ancients did not foresee that the union of the scattered people could come about even before Messianic times through the mutual contraction of all the lands of the Exile. Not even an earthquake was needed as a prerequisite. It was sufficient to that end to release the genius of technology. It may be noted that the journey today from Moscow to New York takes little longer than the journey from Paris to Rome a hundred years ago, in Salvador's time. Spiritually united by the Russian Jews and geographically linked by technological knowledge which becomes ever more Americanised, the dispersed and scattered people are, in fact, more than any people living within territorial boundaries depen-dent on the general political trends at the two magnetic poles, Moscow and New York.

Is then the influence of Russia on the Russian Jews, and through them on Jewry in general, really so powerful? Our worldly nationalists who, as I have frequently noted, are essentially shamefaced assimiliationists, have no liking for talk of alien influence on modern Jewish culture, just as they dislike any talk of a national mission. When I speak of Jewish world problems, and at the same time of actual outside influence on the present-day Jewish spirit, I run the risk of being torn apart as a "double-dyed" assimilationist. Nevertheless I hold that to err in the service of truth is preferable to remaining in agreement with a generally accepted untruth.

The story of Russia's influence upon Jewry has not yet been written. This is a theme that will certainly one day find its master. The matter is more than important. Incidental observations on the theme made in passing and to be found here and there in our standard literary histories will not suffice, as for example that Jehudah Leib Gordon in his creative work relied a good deal on Nekrasov, or that Abraham Reisin was a disciple of Chekhov. The essay of Baal Machshoves on the significance of the Ukraine for Yiddish literature is probably the only attempt to generalize in this field. But, in fact, the theme is wider than a question of only literary history. The problem touches upon the whole recent history of the Jewish people and therefore also on its situation in the modern world. Does anyone really believe that socialism would in any event have become a force in Jewish national life even if Russia had remained outside our historical horizon? Does anyone think that the socialist movement arose only from material poverty and not simultaneously also from spiritual superabundance? Or that even the Zionist movement would ever have become that which it is, an unconscious Messianism, if its centre had not been situated in the classic land of maximalist world policies, Russia? The part played by Russian Jews in the Jewish national and socialist movement is usually explained by their numbers and by their deprivations. It is not realized that mass without force is immobile and that grief without hope may strangle. Hope and joy of life are certainly Jewish national assets, and yet all this might have remained dead or immobilized for who can tell how long, but for the thrust from without. The leaders of the so-called Bilu, the pioneers of the Jewish intellectuals in Russia, were not only disappointed assimilationists; they were to a still greater degree Jewish "narodniki" (populists). Having the same zeal as that with which the Russians went to the people, these Russified populists went to the land of the people. The importance attached among us today to agriculture, to land and labour, is in general derived from the colossal peasant folk, the Russians, whom we encountered in the course of our history. One should not forget that the heroic father of the Halutzim (avant garde) movement, Aaron David Gordon, like Mahatma Gandhi, was a Tolstoyan. His teaching of the renewal of man, his physical and spiritual sustenance, is a remarkable and at the moment the most successful synthesis of Russianism and Judaism. It is the Russo-Jewish, Asian-European protest against the over-estimation of West European-American civilisation among us Jews.

The protest has come betimes. Surely our people, placed between the two poles of the modern world, are no less influenced by America and Americanism than by Russia and Russianism. As in the whole world, the two waves clash in Jewish life and the effect of the former is particularly noticeable. The majority of Zionists are inclined, in respect of foreign policy, to rely entirely on the brand-new "Pax Romana", on Anglo-American pacifism. They disregard the hypocrisy which cries to heaven, and the fact that the Washington and London pursuit of peace is no more than the creation of a world arena for "free competition", for the highly publicised conflict of all against all (bellum omnium contra omnes) in which victory from the start will be assured for the strongest and richest. This is the Jewish Americanism which gave birth to the Agency. Not the daughter, however, is to blame but the father. Those are to blame who wish to annex the Jewish Orient to the West and want to make Jerusalem a suburb of New York. Even Herzl in his *Alt-Neuland* sinned deeply in this particular. The danger is today incomparably greater and for a score of reasons, in the first place, because Americanism has pierced our hearts.

The most terrible of the terrible events which have come to pass this summer (1930) in Eretz Israel is the echo they have awakened within the Jewish confines. Hate, vengeance, pride and all manner of evils mentioned and unmentioned in the *Al-Het* (confession of sins) have suddenly been unleashed abroad. And throughout the turmoil ran the battle cry: Hands off our Home! Here the say is ours! Ours? Is the awareness of collective property the deepest basis of Jewish national sentiment? Have we then no right on which to appeal other than the rights of returning absentee landlords? Is Eretz Israel no more than our national bulwark, a courtyard secured with guns?

Fifteen years ago the war made world socialism bankrupt and it is not yet back on its feet. The war in Palestine must on no account lead to the same result in our own foreign policy. It would be a sin against the Jewish spirit and the land in which it was cradled to bring home the vices of the Canaanites abroad. It is a sin to learn Torah from Ishmaelites. Not so long ago Martin Buber told a gathering that one of the most esteemed Zionist leaders in Palestine, to whom he put the question, "What do you think of the Arabs?" answered, "Yes, a considerable people, but a lowly race." Buber went on to say, "In my youth, I heard precisely the same words spoken almost in the same tone of voice by the Poles against our Jews." What have we to boast about? The white collar? The colour of our skin which has gone pale in exile? Are we in truth no better than Jewish Poles? Englishmen? Yankees? Was it only unsatisfied lordly pride which made us cry out down the centuries with the failing strength of our souls, "Next year in Jerusalem!"?

If I forget thee, O Jerusalem, let my right hand forget her cunning! That was the oath we took on all the rivers and seas of the old and new world. Everywhere, among all the seventy-seven nations, we clung to the thought that our city is not like other cities, that the earth on which it stands is holy, and its towers are fire from heaven. Jerusalem of old was for us only an attempt to build the true, ideal, world-Jerusalem, the Jerusalem on High. And now it has come to this, that in Jerusalem itself we forget Jerusalem. This is the most dreadful catastrophe that can befall us. Do we care no longer about our right hand? Does our left hand know what the right is doing? Do we imagine that the world can manage well enough without us? Without our prophecy, and without our feeling or even our view of world history? Do we really believe that in the conflict between New York and Moscow, Jerusalem will be able to remain disinterested?

That is the most important question facing our future world-policy. Each one of us, the Jewish "I" has to stand up and declare.

2. Faith (Bitochn)

Faith? Yes, faith—trust in God. Indeed! Bitter and frightful as Jewish conditions are today, we must not accept the thought that some sort of 'Jewish problem' exists, that the very existence of the Jewish people is subject to question. Can the Jewish people, God forbid, cease to exist? Only together with the whole world. Yes, with this world and the world beyond bestowed on us and kept by us and the surrounding world for fully three thousand years. Anyone who is prepared even to consider the destruction of the world no longer belongs among us, thus having forfeited his place. We do not understand his language, nor can he comprehend what we say. May the True Judge be blessed! In the Jewish world of today it is only possible to communicate with one another for those who still have faith or at least long for their fainting hearts to become alive and strong again. In my opinion most Jewish sceptics could be classified under the latter heading. Their twisted, sceptical smile and ironic glances are all too frequently a mere disguise to cover up their searing heartache, their yearning for faith, for consolation, for trust. How can they, and we along with them, be helped?

It may be that those of us who have faith and those who are allegedly non-believers, are in fact not two distinctly separate types of souls. If it is true that just as in the Jewish sceptic there nearly always glows a ray of hope, so the worm of scepticism, of doubt, must gnaw today even in the most faithful believer. If this is true, then there remains but one way to overcome our inner foe, our Jewish weak-heartedness, one way for the pious and for the freethinkers. That is the way of wisdom.

Opening the "Gate of Faith" in Rabbi Bahya b. Joseph ibn Pakuda's *Hovot Ha'levavot* (Duties of the Heart), I rediscovered at once on "the threshold of the Gate" the fundamental concept underlying this entire work, namely that as our other most sublime duties, so the duty of faith "has its roots in reason". Needless to say, the pious author is referring not to ordinary faith and not to confidence in the future of our people, but to Jewish faith in the original sense, to reliance on God in every particular and in every individual situation. Who can say, however, whether we will

This essay was first published in Yiddish in *Oifn Sheidweg*, Paris, 1939.

ultimately arrive at the point to which our ancient sages always led us, if only we embark on the old road of wisdom and reason?

Faith based on the foundations of reason—that ought to be our common path, no matter what differences of opinion divide us on other particulars. Thus only those will be excluded who cut the roots of reason and sow and reap the poisonous harvest of despair. They are excluded because they place themselves outside. Let us not give them any more thought regardless of our sense of compassion, and let us attempt to apply the quality of intelligent faith quite concretely to the concrete Jewish situation.

I

We see with open eyes that our situation is frightful and bitter. Year in, year out entire Jewish communities are destroyed one after another, millions of Jewish individuals are forced to endure the harshest, most cruel torture, thousands upon thousands curse the day they were born and do away with themselves. We are experiencing the multiple destruction of nearly all our national, social and spiritual values. Those who counted on the abstract national principle now see how the guaranteed rights of the Jewish minorities have been turned into a mockery; those who placed all their national hopes on having their own country now stand in the land of Israel once again face-to-face with the Exile and the Ghetto; while in the lands abroad signs multiply of an even greater dispersion, not of a new ingathering of exiles. Those who hoped that the Jewish nation would benefit by the proletarian class-struggle must now admit that a totally proletarianized people does not tolerate any classes and, as a corollary, any type of socialist struggle. Those dedicated to our Jewish culture, both Yiddish and Hebrew, are well aware that we must mobilize our last reserves to prevent the collapse of that which required so much effort and toil to build. Ordinary Jews bewail the destruction of the old way of life. But at the same time we are undergoing the destruction of emancipation, assimilation and, the increasing number of converts to Christianity notwithstanding, of conversion itself. We are no longer certain even of our 'race', of the Jewish type of individual, because the enemy forces into our borders a mass of persons who are neither objectively nor subjectively Jews. What then is to befall us? Utter ruin? But we have agreed that not the slightest hint of such a question mark must appear in our script.

As long as we consider our position from the inside and only thus, it is impossible for us to assess it accurately. A survey demands by its very essence that we stand 'above' that on which our look is concentrated. In general, one can assess a thing only when one has in mind a definite set value with which one may compare it. Today, however in formulating our diagnoses of the Jewish situation, we tend not to venture beyond our borders. If we do make comparisons with other circumstances, it is always by means of examples taken from our own history. This would be of some value if our historical memories themselves were not circumscribed within the sphere of the Jewish "little world". Our world historiography has not yet succeeded in opening a window from the Jewish microcosm into the great world beyond. On the contrary, one may state that it has in fact overcast our vision of God's world in its wholeness and unity, that vision which was at the origin of classical Jewish thinking. Of what avail is it to ask, for instance: Is the present situation just as bad as that which prevailed during the Crusades, or during the expulsion from Spain, or during the bloody years of 1648 and 1649? What use is it, if what we have in mind are situations long since past, again observed only from the inside? We go back centuries into the past and remain treading water in the same small spot. It appears to me that nine-tenths of our present extremely pessimistic prognoses are the result of our being unwilling to look with an open mind either on our past or our present.

To look at the Jewish situation with an open mind means to be willing to see it as it is in the light of world history. The historical past trodden by the Jewish people has always been a universal historical path, and had this fact not been transmitted to us by our forebears, we should have come up against it now, in the second third of the twentieth Christian century. Lately pious Jews have taken to quoting frequently from Rabbi Yohanan's words as cited in *Midrash Rabba* on Deuteronomy: "Every misfortune which the Jewish people and the other peoples of the world have in common is a misfortune, but one which descended on the Jewish people alone is not a misfortune." In other words, essentially it is not a great calamity even for the Jews themselves. With what a clear and open mind our sages of the past looked at the world about them and at their own people!

The current calamity of the House of Israel is indeed a calamity, an enormous one, for the catastrophe of the world as a whole is enormous and its fortunes look black. We are, first of all, the victims of a world war which has been going on for several years. This is no mere rhetorical statement. In a work by the French historian Jacques Bardot I came across the following description of the present situation in Europe: "today, as a quarter of a century ago, Great Britain finds itself side by side with France in a war against Germany. Secret agents are meanwhile making attacks on electrical installations, or ships, and yet the whole atmosphere is that of war. It is a war in disguise, a financial and economic war, a war which aims to undermine the spiritual forces, a war of nerves, a war cut on Hitler's pattern, but a war none the less" (*Revue de Deux Mondes*, Vo. 51. pp. 561 and 567). The theme then is no longer the Japanese war against China, nor is it Abyssinia, or even Spain, or Austria and Czecho-Slovakia, but quite literally a second world war which is a direct successor of the first war. In this present war we became one of the first victims, but not the very first and not the only one. The Amalekites and the Philistines are ranged against us. But they are not yet in the saddle, and it seems reasonable to hope that it will never come to pass. These hopes are shared today by many of the great peoples the world over. Our misfortune is their misfortune. "If it should be preordained that the democracies lose this war", writes the well-known English publicist, Wickham Steed, "then a murky cloud may quite possibly settle over human souls for a period of decades, if not centuries" (article "What Says British Politics" in Contemporary Review, Vol. 155, p. 650). Thus the common calamity, theirs and ours, becomes an enormous and terrifying one. But we do not stand alone in the world, we are not isolated and our bond with the future is doubly strengthened. The sole question is where are we to obtain again a pair of hands that will remain extended heavenward and not be lowered until the earth swallows Amalek and his entire community!

In recent years we have lost some important ground: our numbers have shrunk, we have grown poorer, thousands have been cast to far away countries whose names our ancestors never even heard of; masses of Jews walk about sick at heart and yet, despite all, the existence of the Jewish people is not shattered. Let us draw a comparison with what is happening around us. How many pause to reflect for a moment on the bitter fate of the Abyssinian population (which, too, has a history of a couple of thousand years), on the frightful chastisement being inflicted on the Chinese people, on the destruction of the thousand-year old state of Austria, on the Spanish victims, on the suffering that the Czech nation is undergoing. We would do well to review this list over and over again. We have not, God be praised, been sold into slavery as has the Czech people. Our intelligentsia has not been completely exterminated as it was in wretched Ethiopia. Nor have we reached the abyss into which the Chinese, with the oldest culture on earth, have been forced. Our independence is not being threatened from without, as is the case today for many highly esteemed old and new European national states, and our people does not suffer in its *total* entirety from any dictatorship of one or another type. Can we really think that it is so fortunate nowadays to be a German or an Italian? I have seen Italians whose faces flushed with shame at the mention of the current situation in their beloved land. Let us not be envious! Let us not envy the foolish "Aryan" nations, seemingly so fortunate, which are in fact slaves to slaves who do not even sense how "the earth doth quake", as is written in Proverbs 30:21-22, "for a servant when he reigneth; and a churl when he is filled with food".

In brief, as things stand today in the world, our situation as viewed from the outside and our condition from the material point of view of our existence are *approximately* such that even those who do not follow in the old ways may nevertheless pronounce the benediction on this evil, as one "blesses the good". This approximation should, of course, be underlined twice and thrice.

II

Is this half a consolation? In a pessimistic work on the Jewish problem ("Sh'eylat Yisrael" in Ha'olam, 1939, Vol. 18, p. 336) the Hebrew writer S. Rawidowicz polemicizes against Rabbi Yohanan's above mentioned philosophical view of Jewish misfortunes in the following words: "It may be that a calamity which is shared by many offers half a consolation. But after half the calamity has thus been removed, the remainder is still more than we can bear, even today, not to speak of days to come." In the context of what has been stated above, this argument seems to be twice as valid. First of all, how can we actually profit from the fact that things are just as bad for others, and perhaps even worse. Secondly, should we really discover some solace in the current troubles of the world's nations? The fact still remains that this applies to but one aspect—to our material circumstances (to put it in its broader sense); where then is the second half, the spiritual side? Is there another historic people in the world whose spiritual essence is in the same danger as that hovering over the living Jewish spirit? This second question must be answered first, because the very meaning of consolation is the innermost link between consolation and faith and constitutes an eternal problem which must always be posed anew only after one has grasped and analyzed the concrete spiritual condition prevailing in the world. (About 12 years ago I wrote a series of articles on this theme in the *Freie Shriften*.)

Again then, where do we stand and where stands the world in the spiritual sense? This is not the place to disentangle this question even as to its principal points. Suffice it to list them here.

First of all let us consider the subject of belief. Truly, today Judaism still stands not a whit more firmly on its age-old foundations than, say Christianity. Does anyone yet remember how assured was the Russian philosophy of history in the preceding century (with its Aksakov, Khomiakov and Dostoevsky), that the main attribute of the Russian spirit was the genuine Christian faith of the Russian man? Did not German Protestants advance the very same argument with regard to the German, "the Lutheran man"? And what is the position of the Christian faith in both Russia and Germany? Even in England, the most Christian country in present day Europe, it was possible recently for A. P. Herbert, the representative of Oxford University in Parliament and a very popular writer, to utter the witticism that the Christians are "a forgotten sect". Herbert is a wit and his remark is an exaggeration. As for us Jews, I refer to those who practice Judaism, this type of exaggeration would nevertheless not in any way be a jest, for whatever the conditions may be, the Jewish "sect" is less forgotten than ever. Whether we wish it or not, the "Divine Name" shines on all our foreheads and the entire world situation forces each and every one of us to detect once again a glint of the sacred spark in the other's eyes. Not only the Jewish people is alive, but the Jewish faith lives as well. In comparison it is probably the most vital of all the old world religions. And, the Lord be praised, it was spared the temptation of signing any agreements with those who are evil.

However, was not Jewish morale and Jewish culture undermined meanwhile, not more and possibly less than the morale and culture of the world as a whole? It is not we alone who are slapped and pretend that nothing happened. There are scattered throughout the world powerful nations who are pulled by the tail, stabbed in their sides, while they pretend to be napping and feeling nothing. There is no doubt that internal enemies, traitors and deceivers of the most destructive sort, who wreck and pull down our own house, exist in our midst in large numbers. But have we not witnessed with our own eyes how Chinese are destroying China, Spaniards—Spain, and Czechs—Czechoslovakia? There are enough creatures who betray their country, their people, their language and of all the spiritual possessions still left to them for a few worthless coins; there are enough people of this type also among the world nations. As far as culture is concerned, whoever thinks that human beings are capable of surviving on this earth while the Book and the People of the Book are totally wiped out from human memory, simply does not comprehend the meaning of the terms 'human being' or 'culture' or, above all, 'cultured human being'. As long as the Jewish 'Holy Scriptures' continue in existence, Jewish culture will be a source, a fountainhead of the creative spirit for both Jews and non-Jews, since a Jewish body devoid of a living Jewish soul is altogether inconceivable. In what other people is its culture so deeply embedded as in ours?

Do we lack unity? Are our ideologies of yesterday or the day before yesterday disintegrating? Well, and what is their condition elsewhere? And has more than a shred survived of yesterday's and the day before yesterday's ideologies in Russia, in Germany, or in Italy? The ideologues, the theorists, (even of Russian Communism) are refugees, émigrés, and their systems have long since been shaken off by the Almighty. Their Divine inspiration, too, is in exile. A frightful crisis has enveloped the world and all the varieties of socio-political philosophies are melting in the smelting-furnace of world history: socialism as well as liberalism, (even the British kind!) and conservatism too. The so-called democracy has fallen by the wayside altogether. Wherever some spiritual freedom still remains, there is practically no remnant of spiritual unity and where there is unity, it is evil in spirit. Against this background it is quite miraculous how well the Jewish ideologies stand up. Even in this, the Jews are still the age-old stiff-necked people they have always been.

III

It would therefore follow that our portion of the calamities which have inundated the world is at least not greater, either materially or spiritually, than that which has befallen other nations. What then is the consolation we can draw from this? How does this improve the Jewish condition in general or even that of the individual Jew? Even should it prove true that suffering shared by others is easier to bear, can this kindle the flame of faith in tortured Jewish hearts? Every man of faith bears within himself, no matter what befalls him, the comfort of consolation. But surely not everyone who has found consolation in such measure that he is prepared to reach a compromise with his bitter fate, is likely as a result of this alone to become a man of faith.

Thus formulated, the question leads one directly to the answer. That "sorrow shared is sorrow halved", and that, as the Russian proverb has it, "Company in distress makes trouble less". These sayings are known not only to the Germans and Russians, but to all the nations. But the innermost root or source of the entire matter was apparently discovered by our ancient sages when they instituted the custom of expressing condolences immediately after a burial with the words: "May God console the Mourners of Zion and Jerusalem!" It cannot console me that apart from myself many others are also bowed by their misfortunes. I have lived through the horror of the destruction of my own home; I can barely stand on my feet; yet all around I hear voices saying: You should know that no matter how dreadful your present ruin and how profound your sorrow, there exists within yourself an even deeper sorrow; you face today an even greater ruin, the destruction of the Temple, and in this calamity of yours you are bound fast to your entire people, with its past, its present and its future. Yes, with its future too! And if the name of Jerusalem is capable of awakening in the sorrowing heart an echo of an eternal Jewish emotion; and if in the consciousness of the mourner there still is room for the "memory of Temple's destruction", then his own immediate, personal ruin and the blessed memory of the loved one he has lost will blend and intermingle with the emotions, memories and hopes which have characterized the history of the Jewish people on the chart of world history. It is thus that we may find consolation; thus can a more intense pain displace a lesser one, and a sorrow that has no outlet can thus be swept away on the waves of solace to the very shores of faith. For the true meaning of Jewish mourning, of the "mourner of Zion", is not sadness for sadness' sake, but quite the reverse: the uplifting memory of what existed before the destruction, the spiritual exaltation directed upward, to the radiant age of the prophet's "and it shall be in the end of days". One of the Habad hassidim expressed it aptly when he said: "To sorrow is to rot. However, there are two ways. One kernel rots in a sack and putrifies, but another kernel, rotting in the soil, grows a healthy tree." This is the dialectic of Jewish sadness hence, frequently it is for us more than "half a consolation", when we are enabled to mingle our personal trials and tribulations with those of the whole community. It is a time of trouble to Jacob and through it he will be saved: since it is the calamity of the whole Jewish people, it *must* and will ultimately grow into something good.

What applies to the Jewish individual with regard to the Jewish community as a whole applies exactly in the same way to the relationship between the Jewish community and the world as a whole. If the catastrophes that befall us begin to threaten our will to live and to fight; if there is a likelihood of our drifting into that despair and sadness described as "rotting in a sack", then we must immerse ourselves in the enormous misfortune of the *entire world* , we must extend our melancholy prognosis to a world-historical absurdity, we must arrive at the conclusion that humanity will at any moment begin once again to run about on all fours, devour one another's flesh and drink one another's blood. And this, not metaphorically but literally, and across the full extent of our planet. Only when we experience the most extreme depths of agony destined for all humanity, when we listen to the heart of the world, will we, the Jewish community as a whole, hear the voices answering us: "Let the mourners of earth and heaven be consoled!" And through this the gates of faith will open before us.

We—and the world! The covenant of Abraham and the covenant of Noah. Had there not been a covenant in the wake of the flood, there could not have been a covenant "among the pieces" nor a link between evil fates. The Jewish people has always lived with the consciousness of this fact; without this consciousness it is prevented today not only from assuming its old faith anew, but even from finding solace in its sufferings. Those among us, however, who have faith, hope and belief and are convinced that the Jewish people is even today capable and worthy and therefore also likely— as it was two and three thousand years ago—of showing the world the way out of the most profound depths. With signs and wonders! The signs are the letters and words that whole millennia cannot erase, and of the wonders, the first and most important will be—our own faith.

We can rely on the latter. As Jeremiah said: "Blessed be the man who has faith", blessed be the true, the honest, the strong man of faith. Today he is our prophet, our sage, our hero.

3. The Tribes of Israel

I

How different is the attitude of the non-Jews to that of the Jews in regard to the unity of the people of Israel, a unity that continues to exist despite its recurring dispersions!

Among the non-Jews, in particular those with outspoken sympathies for the Jews, they are mostly confined to fellow countrymen who have lived since time immemorial alongside them. Yet, this also constitutes the limit of their philo-Semitic inclinations, whereas their dislike of Jews comprehends the entire nation, that is to say, all the communities of the Diaspora without distinction. Furthermore, the symptoms of this hostility are directed indiscriminately not against the one generation only, but against all earlier generations and even against those still unborn. The reverse obtains among Jews. There is not a Jew with the good of his people at heart, whose love would not embrace the whole House of Israel, in space and time, in the Diaspora and Eretz Israel, in the past and in the future. Those in our midst who separate the Jewish community in the country in which they live from the rest of Israel, who raise partitions between one component and another in the House of Israel, exclude themselves, according to the accepted view, from the totality of the Jewish people, and are inevitably numbered among the assimilationists, among the deliberate destroyers of the unity of our people. Generally speaking, our transgressors and traitors follow, apparently, in the footsteps of the non-Jewish 'lovers of Israel', while the external enemies of Israel adopt an attitude of hostility and envy characteristic of the fanatical wing among our own orthodoxy. But those who, in their folly, go so far as to call themselves "Aryans", widen the gulf that separates them from the spirit of our people and put themselves beyond the pale of those who seek the welfare and integrity from within. Is this not an amazing phenomenon that deserves investigation?

Is it possible that a saint should err, that the wicked should be right? On the other hand, that the righteous and the unrighteous should join forces,

This essay was first published in Hebrew in *Metsudah*, Essays and Studies edited by Simon Rawidowicz, Ararat Publishing Society, London, 1943. We are grateful for the permission to reprint this essay to Mr. William Margulies and Mr. Alex Margulies.

432

that the wise and foolish should become bedfellows? There must be a reason for this. If the accepted approach of Jewish nationalism requires re-examination, if it is still an obscure doctrine that has not been exhaustively elucidated, let us investigate our position as far as possible in the light of history.

Undoubtedly Israel is one people, just as its name is one. As we know by tradition the roots of this unity lie in the uniqueness of one distinguished and distinctive individual whose personal name was Jacob-Israel, who was the father and head of the House of Israel and consequently of all the Children of Israel. Hence the name 'Israel' serves equally as a plural and as a singular. The Jewish masses, with their native linguistic genius, still jestingly contrapose, to this day, *Kelal Yisrael* ('the totality of Israel') to Reb Yisrael ('the individual Jew'), Patriarch Israel—to his millions of descend-ants, the people as a whole—to the individual. It may well be that our whole doctrine of modern nationalism, which recognizes only, on the one hand, the total nation, and on the other, individuals, and completely ignores separate groups that occupy an intermediate position between the individual and the entire community of Israel, is not founded on a popular conception that is lacking in depth. This view, like that of the modern nationalists, accords with the comparison of the Children of Israel to the sand of the sea, but is entirely unsuited to the second simile, which complements the first and seeks to raise the seed of Abraham to the plane of the host of heavens. For there reigns not the anarchy of dust, but the absolute order of the constellation of the Zodiac, whose number corre-sponds to that of the tribes of Israel.

The category and concept of 'Tribe' is a principle that has almost disappeared from the ambit of the new Jewish thought, and possibly this loss accounts for the decline of the inspiration of our thinking, and confusion prevails in respect of the word 'Israel', which is full of the clean and unclean, so that no one knows who is pure and who is impure. It is not impossible that the restoration of this loss may also help to solve the question that was presented anew in the preamble of this essay as a kind of riddle: 'Is it possible that a saint should err?'

II

For the sake of accuracy let us proceed to study the question in the light of our history. What was the nature of the tribe in Israel in ancient times? How and when did it disappear? And is it true that after it had passed into oblivion, the Jewish people proceeded on its way as though its different tribes had never existed? Needless to say, each question must be answered here with the utmost brevity.

According to tradition, the merit of the father, called Israel, brought it about that each of his sons was himself raised to the status of a father, that is to say, not to become the head of a mighty nation with a great future destined to play a leading role in the world, but to be the ancestor and chief of one of the sections within the framework of the people that unites them all, namely, the tribe. Hence the first definition of 'Israelite' denotes, like 'Israel' itself, not only the names of an *individual*, but also that of a *particular group*. It is certain (both according to scientific research and according to tradition) that in the period of the past known to us, the *people of Israel* was in the Land of Israel an assembly of clans, a community of different groups, each one with its specific complexion and its personal features; a type of its own, as though it had a special soul, living, articulate being created in the image and likeness of its particular regional heritage. Judah—the lion among them—dwelt in mountain fastnesses, was a mighty hunter, and heroic warrior; indeed he is in nature not unlike his uncle and neighbour 'Edom'. Zebulon 'dwelt by the shore of the sea'. Issachar 'couched down between hillocks. Dan was 'a serpant by the way'. As for Asher, 'his bread was rich', and he also 'dipped his foot in oil'. And Joseph—'his land was blessed', etc. (the blessing of Jacob and Moses, *Genesis* , XLIX and *Deuteronomy* XXXIII). Such are the tribes, the tribes and clans of Israel—not endless piles of sand whose forms are transient, but hosts upon hosts, each one with his own banner and mode of life, everything being in accord with his natural environment and individual history. In the light of this, individual Providence watching over each tribe, we can understand the history of our people in those days, the abundance of blessings and blights that simultaneously overwhelmed their life in their own land, until the time arrived when 'the ten tribes' were exiled and only Judah remained, and the people of Israel were transformed into a single tribe. From this it follows, according to the conventional view, that even the category of tribe itself should be absorbed in the concept of the people.

However, the accepted view fell into the ditch of error. This is evidenced by the blessed remembrance of the fact preserved among the people and the number of the tribes. Not only do we not find in all our literature any indication of a negative attitude to the fact that Israel in its youth was divided into separate tribes, but, on the contrary, until the time of Menasseh ben Israel, and in the countries of Eastern Europe until and including the time of Benjamin III, one of the most cherished dreams of our people was ever the restoration of his lost tribes, since it was accepted that all ten of them were in actual existence and were living in a given place till such time as it was the Divine will that their whereabouts should be revealed.

Additional proof of the correctness of this conception is to be seen in the duality that marks the remnant of Israel, separating precisely between a descendent of Judah, who is termed simply an Israelite, and a Levite, who, if genealogically worthy, may even be numbered among the community of the House of Aaron. We know how meticulously careful about this distinction between the sacred and the profane each one of our holy congregations is to this day. Whosoever should venture to assert that there is no difference between the lineage of one Israelite and another—i.e., that a Kohen is like a Levi and a Levi like an Israelite—is, by his own testimony, seen to have no portion among the Chosen People.

All this serves to prove that the concept of the tribe and the recollection of the tribes as they existed in ancient times is still very much alive, at least within the precincts of the Synagogue. However, not a few among our people ask today: What have we to do with the Synagogue, and what connection is there between the assimilationists with their erroneous doctrines and the regulations of the *Shulchan Aruch*? But there is an answer to this query, which is based not on religious customs but on the experiences to which the Jewish people was actually subjected repeatedly in 'mundane affairs', that is to say, in the world as the unbelievers themselves know it. It will suffice to mention in this connection the dichotomy between the Sephardim and Ashkenazim after the former had been banished from their homeland. French Jews, in particular, then took the view that the Sephardim were descended from the most important tribe in Israel, namely Judah; hence they are related to the House of David and many of them belonged to the royal family, whereas the other Israelites were of lower rank and were rightly subordinated to them. This unwarrantable belief, which a number of Sephardic writers proceeded to disseminate among the Gentiles, was responsible for the fact that at the time of the French Revolution, at the close of the eighteenth century, the Sephardim were the first to receive the rights of citizenship. However, not the notion itself is of primary importance here, nor the underlying deception (possibly the Sephardim themselves believed in the truth of the assertion), but the actual conditions of life that provided a generally accepted notion bearing the name of one of the ancient tribes of Israel. This false notion illuminates for us events of a secular character, events that occurred continuously during the existence of the world-wide Golah. It is an unchangeable law of nature that the Jewish people, so dispersed and fragmented, should assume the form of many tribes, when one section is as far removed from the other as West from East and South from North. What occurred of old in the Land of Israel, whose total length is mainly 'from Dan to Beer-sheba', is bound *a fortiori* to recur on an even greater scale in the Dispersion which stretches from Mesopotamia to the Pacific, all depending on the place and time of the closest surroundings. In all its history Israel changes the appearance of its various tribes and there is no epoch in which there is an absence of a plurality of communes and their mutual strife.

Our historian Simon Dubnow, who followed in the footsteps of Graetz, taught us to give consideration in every age to the question: Which Jewish settlement or 'centre' stood at the head of the whole people as 'leader' and exercised spiritual hegemony? In my humble opinion the term 'centre', which is used by both Ahad Ha'am and his colleague, Simon Dubnow, is not large enough to accommodate our subject in all its aspects and nuances. We are not concerned with the relationship of one part of the Jewish people with its other parts, but—as a preliminary consideration thereto—with the specific character of each community *per se* in relation to the special conditions of its life. Who, for example, will fail to recognize that the life of the Jews in Spain not only led at the time to the spiritual hegemony of the Sephardic community, but also left its imprint on every individual Jew of that land, and that this type, both physically and spiritually, is stamped with the quality of soul and the attributes of their own environment, of the non-Jewish Spaniards? And who will deny—if we proceed from the general to the particular—that it would have been impossible anywhere but in Spain for the man R. Yehudah Halevi, with all his many and powerful inner contradictions—his human desires and sublime yearnings, his pride and humility, his courage and his resolution, to go 'like a sheep to the slaughter'? To draw a lesson from another example, if we are to return from the particular to the general—would it have been feasible that the type of 'Hassidim', with their absolute faith in their *Tsadikim* , should have appeared anywhere outside of the Catholic-Polish environment? But in truth these are no more than headings of the tribal history of the thousands upon thousands of Jews.

III

Now this realization, even in its initial stage, has much to teach us, and the exposition here has an entirely practical purpose.

Today, just after the calamity, destruction and holocaust of war, we all lament that the Jewish people, which is one, lacks unity. The devotees of unity are of the opinion that we are riddled with the disease of sectarianism than which there is not greater misfortune. However, there is no healthy human society that would forgo public discussion in all matters relating to its most vital interests. The nations who thought that less divergence of opinion means greater strength were like Sodom and ended like Gomorrah. Such a view is to be rejected outright. The malady of our people does not consist in the proliferation of parties, great and small, and certainly not in the conflicts between the economic classes, which are wholly unconnected with our internal life, but solely to the multiplicity of tribes that our people breeds. Regarding this particular aspect of our history, Scripture does not say *va-yishretsu* ('and they swarmed') but *va-yitrotsetsu* ('and they struggled together'), as it is stated 'Two *(shenei)* nations are in thy womb'—read not *shenei* but *shonim* ('different'). We are inclined to overlook the travail of growing tribes. We ignore the natural difficulty inherent in the gathering of our exiles. A cosmopolitan people, which is dispersed over the whole world, must of necessity be, in view of the great number of its parts, like a spherical mirror—a monade—which reflects all the physical and spiritual contrasts in the entire world, or like an individual that contains all that is comprised in the totality of the human species. On the other hand, the affairs of each individual Jewish tribe are not generally so complicated; indeed, relatively they are quite simple. Who can say whether the whole complex of problems with which the new Eretz Israel bristles is not to be explained, most simply, as due to her conceiving a new tribe, which is still an unborn embryo.

Diagnosis of the disease is half its cure. We could in future be saved much surgery, if only we were prepared to examine our position in the world, and in particular the plurality of Jewry's tribes despite the unity of its soul, with a vigilant and penetrating eye. This blessing has also a practical meaning. Consider what many of our people, who speak in its name as though they were authorized by it, demand what we should do to that great tribe of Israel that is bound by the shackles of the Soviet territories. Some ban it because the majority of the Jews in Russia are presumed to be irreligious; others are agreeable to sever this limb from the living body of Israel only out of fear that the Jews there will oppose the Zionist idea. Both groups demonstrate that their love of Israel and faith fall short at least of those of Rabbi Israel Baal Hashem, who even grieved over the loss of the deliberate apostates that became, in their day, adherents of the false doctrines of Jacob Frank. Whoever gives up a single tribe of Israel sins not only against his own soul but also against the spirit and history of Israel. The story of Gibeah is proof: so long as there is a judge and justice in Israel it is impossible for even the smallest tribe to be severed from our people (Judges XXI: 4, 6, 15). This is shown most emphatically by the son of man, Ezekiel. Who are 'the dry bones' seen by the prophet through the holy spirit? Are they the individuals of 'the whole house of Israel'? The *Qra* ('the text to be read') and the *Ketiv* ('the text as it is written') provide the answer: Far be it! The dry bones from which the spirit of life had departed are the tribes of Israel after they had become separated from one another: 'Judah and the house of Israel his companions' on the one hand, and on the other, 'Ephraim and the tribes of Israel his companions' (Ezekiel XXXVII 11, 16, 19). There is no national revival save a new covenant between all the tribes of Israel in their entirety. That which was shall also be; that which happened in the days of Ezekiel after the first Destruction will also come to pass after our last Destruction.

IV

There are public affairs pertaining to the whole Jewish people that are the joint concern of all its tribes without distinction, as we have learnt:

'Jerusalem was not apportioned among the tribes' (Sotah 45 b). There are other matters that, despite their general character, are nevertheless the sole concern of one tribe or of a league of united tribes; for example, the first shock-troops that conquered the Land in the days of Joshua son of Nun. In the period of the exile, the dispersion of the people among various kingdoms and the separation of the tribes from one another gave rise to the Talmudic principle: 'The law of the kingdom is valid'. Hence one of the important matters that should be placed on our agenda is the drawing of a clear and definite line between the Jewish public tasks that are to be divided among the tribes and those that are not. This is not a utopian goal. Strange as it may seem, during the Flood of our times 'the *Hassid* (as well as the *Mitnagged*) have perished out of the earth' (cf. Micah VII:2) and their children have joined forces. It is not inconceivable too, that the differences between the Jewish labourer and employer are inconsequential. Therefore, it cannot be doubted that for the rebuilding of Jerusalem and its daughter cities we are duty-bound and able to work together in unison. Nevertheless, the various tribes with their individual domains still exist and there is no likelihood of their disappearing in the near future.

From this we may learn that there is a solution to the riddle to which we alluded above. The entire truth is not with the devotees of unity in our midst, and the nature of their love is different from that of the hatred of the nefarious anti-Semites. Whereas the intent of the hate evinced by the evil men is concrete and consolidated and embraces the House of Israel as a whole together with its individuals, including all its separate communities, down to the last person, be it a son and daughter of Jewish descent, the love of our Jewish patriots that are informed by the contemporary spirit is extremely abstract and seeks a short-cut by ignoring the reality of our tribes. Let us not be extreme in our love as are our enemies in their enmity, which does not distinguish between individual Jews, whether they are pious or impious, whether one is a grandson of an apostate mother or a Jew proper, nor differentiates between one tribe and another. We dare not deny that those of our coreligionists, whose favour primarily is bestowed upon the Jewish tribe that accepts their platform and speaks their language, are but partly right.

If good men have erred, it is worthwhile searching for the grain of truth in their error; and if the truth is published by the wanton liars there is reason to suspect that the truth is not to be taken at its face value. We must 'divide the statement'; we must accept the principle of the doctrine of Israel's unity without vitiating the manifest historic fact of the existence of our tribes. Whoever prays for our redemption, must pray not only for the ingathering of individual exiles, and not only for the salvation of the Golah as a whole, but for the ingathering of 'the dispersed', in the plural—the redemption of the tribes of Israel.

4. The Future of Continental Jewry

This very problematical subject, The Future of Continental Jewry, is included in a series of lectures concerning this huge complex "Religion after the War." Within this framework, the title of my address contains by itself a twofold implication: (a) That the prospects of the Jewish Faith after the War are dependent on the survival of the Jews of the European mainland; (b) assuming that Continental Jewry is not without a future, the continuation of its existence is likely to involve a change in its spiritual outlook. Even after the unique catastrophe which has in the last decade overtaken European Jewry, it still will persist and, more than that, it still might be called upon to play a notable part in upholding and re-vitalising the Jewish creed.

Reasoning about the future is, of course, a venturesome undertaking. All we can do, when trying to foresee future developments is to draw conditional conclusions. Even so, it is a game of chess played against Providence. One of the most decisive factors in all mundane affairs is the human will. Much will certainly depend on the free will of the remnants of the European Jews themselves, whether they will make the necessary effort to rebuild their life on European soil and to reassert themselves as an entity formed by their own history and tradition.

"European Jewry"?

But is it permissible at all to speak of European Jewry as a whole? *Is* there, *was* there such an entity, such a sociologically definable group with an identity of its own?

Though the European Continent is a geographical term, geography alone cannot help us in finding the solution. History, particularly the history of the inter-war period, must be studied. West of the frontiers of the Soviet Union it was broadly true that the majority of our community shared in a substantial measure of spiritual and intellectual freedom. That was not the case within the borders of the U.S.S.R. where 3,000,000 Jews,

This text which is a summary of an address delivered in London to the Society for the Study of Religions on 13 December 1944 was first published in English in *Religions*, London, January 1945, No. 50.

or nearly 1/3 of the Jewish population of Europe were separated by this demarcation line from the rest. This separation produced among the Jewries of Europe outside Russia (in conjunction with a number of other causes) a specific consciousness of belonging to the same world. Before the last war and the Russian Revolution we used to differentiate between East European and West European Jews. The distinction was derived mainly from the fact that in the West the Jews were emancipated and enjoyed recognised rights of citizenship, whilst in the East legally they lived still under mediaeval conditions. After the last war this distinction assumed a new meaning. Apart from the fact that the line dividing West and East has shifted further to the East, and notwithstanding the full emancipation of the Russian Jews, there still remained a difference in relation to the real measure of personal freedom between the West and East to the detriment of the East, a fact which gave a new emphasis to the Europe-mindedness, of all the Jewries, from Riga and Warsaw to Paris and London.

The general spiritual background common to all the European Jewries found its manifold expression in movements, currents of opinion and schools of thought in which the Jewish population of the different countries participated without any regard to State frontiers. They knitted the different Jewries together and transformed them into one great community of six or seven million souls, or, to be more exact, into one great family of communities, every one of them with its own characteristics.

These communities had to face the problem of preserving and rejuvenating the old religious tradition of Israel. It certainly presented a less formidable task on the banks of the Vistula or the Niemen than in Paris or London. Zionism, in its essence a secularised or modernised form of Jewish Messianism, linked up all European Jewries with the constructive work in Palestine. Philosophers, artists or musicians of special Jewish interest usually became the common property of all European Jewries. Hebrew, the sacred language of worship, was, as a medium of modern literary production, rather gaining than losing ground, and even Yiddish, the popular idiom of the East European Jewish masses thanks to its achievements in literature and the theatre, as to its prestige among the Westernised Jews, was markedly on the upgrade. In the last resort all these phenomena were the effect of a steadily increasing interchange of blood in the last few generations.

Disintegration

To complete the picture, it should also be remembered that, parallel with this consolidation of Continental Jewry, a process of disintegration was in progress, due partly to intermarriage between Jews and Gentiles, partly to formal conversions of Jews to Christianity or other causes of severance between the individual Jew and his people. (Among the latter the most conspicuous were those caused by the profession of Rationalism, Agnosticism and last but not least, the Marxian variety of Atheism.) It appears, however, arguable that the loss in numbers thus incurred was, on the whole, beneficial to the Jewish body, insofar as it reflected the working of a selective factor destined to absorb the less steadfast elements of old Israel. All in all, it can be said, were it not for the catastrophe now afflicting us, Continental Jewry could have entered a Europe united in peace and justice as one body predestined, perhaps more than any other component of European life, to serve the great cause of Western Unity.

Yet Continental Jewry as it was has ceased to exist. Numerically it is only a small fraction of what it used to be (hardly more than one-fifth to one-fourth of its previous strength, *i.e.*, about one and a half out of the previous six-seven millions); economically it is ruined, and spiritually, mentally—well, he is a bold man who finds the words to describe the mental condition of a million Lazaruses coming back from hell. Facing the facts, and the hardest of the facts, the figures, one feels almost compelled to shut one's eyes and ears and keep silent, remembering Isaiah: "Come, my people, enter thou into thy chambers, and shut thy doors about thee . . . . until the wrath be overpast. For, behold, the Lord comes out of his place to punish the inhabitants of the earth for their iniquity." (Is. 26: 20-21).

The present is inscrutable. But we have a notion of the past, and out of the depths of this past we may pierce the mists of to-day and get a glimpse of the probable future. This change seems to be all the greater in the case of the Jewish people, just because its past experience is so long and so rich in lessons applicable to the coming years.

To the plain question, Are we entitled to expect a resurrection of Continental Jewry? It is history itself which dictates the answer. How many Jewries have, in the course of the last twenty centuries, been destroyed and again resuscitated? Does this succession of miracles not imply some general principle, akin to a law governing the destinies of Israel?

"Horror Vacui"

Studying the past, we find that it is natural to the Jewish people to abhor empty space, to wit, a space empty of Jews—as natural as, according to what was once thought, to Nature herself. In mediaeval science they used to call it "Horror vacui," by this term of art they were trying to account for the capacity of expansion characteristic of certain forms of matter. According to Hegel this capacity is an essential feature, not of matter, but of the spiritual as such. Be that as it may, there is no doubt that among the dwellers of the earth this capacity is not equally distributed. Some peoples tend more to "replenish the earth" (Gen. 1: 28), whereas others are not so heedful of God's first blessing to man, or act accordingly only in certain periods of their history. Well, the Jews are, in this respect, I should say, at least as mobile as the British. And they remained so, true to form, during 25 centuries. With their Mother-Country always in spiritual sight, they never felt lost or lonely in their tiny colonies in the remotest corners of the world. There is, therefore, no reason to assume that the Jews will take leave of Europe for good.

No doubt, there were periods when this or that part of Europe was a "vacuum," in the sense that it was devoid of Jewish inhabitants. The best example is Spain after the expulsion of 1492. But this and similar exceptions, when adequately analysed, rather confirm than overthrow the rule. Spain got rid of her Jews devoted to Judaism, but the faithful Spanish Jews never got rid of Spain, of the Spanish tongue, and of so many other features typical up till now of a considerable part of the so called "Sephardim" which is the Hebrew equivalent of Spaniards. And that was tantamount to an indication that a return, in due course, of the Sephardim to Sepharad, *i.e.*, to Spain, was somehow always in their minds. If this subdued dreamy hope has not come true, the reason was that both parties, Jews as well as the Spaniards, still hesitated to make peace.

In recent times, Jewish history has most conspicuously repeated itself in the case of Russia's Jews. The bulk of the Jews who used to emigrate in big numbers from the Empire of the Tsars to the Transatlantic Republic retained through generations their identity and their ardent interest in things Russian and their sentimental attitude to the "old home." Even to-day much of the anti-Soviet feeling apparent in the U.S.A. is due to the disappointment felt by American Jews of Russian extraction in view of the course the Revolution of 1917 has since taken. It may be possible to detach Jews from the soil of the native land, but not from their own attachment to the best in the spirit of that land. This sentiment alone might suffice to make the resettlement of Jews in Europe a practicable proposition.

Happily, the course of the present struggle has proved that Europe was essentially mightier than her internal enemies, that she was always worth praying for, in the Synagogue not less than in the Church. This is, I think, the instinctive reaction of every genuinely Jewish heart to the great tragedy unrolling before our eyes. Europe as a whole has not betrayed her Jews who are among her oldest inhabitants, nor are they likely to betray Europe. "There will always be"—a Continental Jewry.

Palestine and Europe

I am fully aware that my humble opinion clashes with very pronounced views advanced recently by a number of Jewish leaders, particularly as far as the return of Continental Jews to the Continent from their different countries of refuge is concerned. There is a strong tendency to advocate an "evacuation" of the Jews remaining on the Continent, first of all the children, into Palestine. This is certainly desirable and advisable, at any rate as an emergency measure, so long as the red flood has not subsided. However, wholesale evacuation which does not take into account the ingrained Jewish "horror vacui" will be undertaken in vain. We may still live to see a movement in reverse, of Jews temporarily settled in Palestine going back to Europe.

All this pre-supposes the fulfilment of certain conditions. Europe should not banish the Jews, and the Jewish people, on its part, should not proclaim Europe out of bounds. That is exactly what happened in the case of Spain, four and a half centuries ago. The Jewish urge to 'replenish.' empty spaces is by no means boundless. The Children of Israel, (and therein they are so different from the British), persistently recoiled from advancing into a world that was spiritually not congenial to their own. It is a fallacy to assume that the Jews are scattered all over the world. This is true only of those parts of the world, where Christian or Islamic civilisation is predominant. The dispersion of Israel was never universal. It has been said, Trade follows the flag, and Jews follow Trade. To agree with the facts, this formula needs amplification. The Jews always followed only the flag and trade of kindred civilisations. With a Germany putting her clock back behind the time of her conversion to Christianity, and relapsing into a pre-Roman paganism, the bonds might have become severed for the entire period of the spiritual 'black-out.' With the badly affected heart of Europe forcibly restored to its normal functioning, the traditional Jewish feelings toward Europe as a whole must, in their turn, become normal again.

The resurrection of Continental Jewry will lastly be dependent on the restoration of Europe's true spirit, of that Western civilisation whose deeper foundations are common to Jew and Gentile. Will there be, within the boundaries of this restored European civilisation, a special place for the Jewish religion? Will Europe be willing to listen to a special message the Jews may have to deliver, and if so, have we the right to expect that a resuscitated Continental Jewry will live up to its religious task?

A Europe united in peace and justice and flanked on both sides, to the East as well as to the West, by two mighty Unions, the Soviet and the American, each with its own civilisation, by no means alien to the European civilisation and yet more or less different from the latter, can persist as a separate component of the New World Order under the sole condition that all peoples of Europe should become conscious of their common spiritual heritage, and that this common spiritual origin should actually determine everyday life. Europe will need an idea of her own, rooted unshakably in her common history. I think, RAJ is a fitting abbreviation of what all of us have in mind when we are on the lookout for such a ruling, all-comprehending European idea. R stands for Rome, for

Roman order and equity, *A* for Athens, for Athenian Wisdom and Science and *J*, of course, for Jerusalem, for Religion and Ethics. (No European, I hope, will mind the Sanscrit sound of the three-pronged word.)

Jewry and the European Tradition

Now, the question arises whether Continental Jewry may be called upon to represent some specific shade of that European tradition insofar as it goes back to ancient Jerusalem. From the purely Jewish point of view there is no doubt about it. Jews devoted to their creed never ceased to believe that they are the trustees charged with the preservation of the tradition of the Holy Land in all its purity and integrity. This is, certainly, not the Christian view. And yet, on the whole, Christians, too, valued the tangible presence of Old Israel, in flesh as much as in spirit, as one of the precious assets of Christendom. To the Christians the Jews were the living witnesses of the living Christ. How much more will be this the case in the Europe to come when, drawing closer to each other, the various Christian communions will have to look for a common denominator. I venture to say that under these conditions the Bible will regain the position of the first source of religious inspiration and of the last resource in the defence of the faith. The greater part of the Book of Books, however, is written in a language which is a living language only among Jews. If we are really moving towards a new revival of European Humanism, more than one Erasmus will have to go to school to the people of the Book. Weak in numbers and impoverished, Continental Jewry is bound to re-occupy its proper place in a re-Christianised Europe if only its core will remain true to the spirit. In a world, on one side over-emphasising the technical aspect of Western Civilisation, on the other, replacing Deity by the human race, Continental Jewry may be instrumental in imparting new life to old Adam, to that Biblical conception of Man which sees in him what he truly is—the link between the created Nature and the Creator. Thanks to the close ties interconnecting the Children of Israel in all parts of the world, the European Jews may become the most successful missionaries of the European spirit outside Europe as well.

Let me now deal in brief with the last of my points.

What reason have we for the hope that the European Jews, weighed upon the scales of their present fate, will not be found wanting? Is it not a fact that, on the eve of the catastrophe, the signs of decline in Jewish religious life were only too obvious? Why should we now expect a change of mind and of heart?

I am entitled to presume that, if Europe as a whole will pursue the way traced for her by the most farsighted among her men of action, the European Jews, or at least that part of them who never lost sight of the vision of Israel's prophets, are not likely to go astray or to lag behind. True, in the last 50 years or so a growing number of Jewish men and women with an irresistible longing for a guiding ideal used to make up the loss of their trust in the coming of Messiah and of the Promised Time by some inferior substitute. Strong attraction had for them especially the Marxian variety of pseudo-Messianism. Others were more inclined to put their entire confidence in the ambiguous blessings of scientific progress. But rather than see in these facts an indication of religious sterility, I would say that the driving force behind all such aberrations was a legitimate dissatisfaction with the general trend of European life. Now we know that their uneasiness was a form of veiled foreknowledge, in face of a real evil, of a lingering disease which was to reveal itself later as a devouring plague. With the passing of the crisis it is not unsafe to assume that its symptoms, as reflected in Jewish life, will disappear in their turn. And whatever else the Jewish "horror vacui" may signify, it is first and foremost the expression of a genuine abhorrence of the void in the spiritual sphere.

Those Who Fall Away

It is not unlikely that owing to the devastation of these critical years many Jews lacking Jewish substance will seek spiritual food not in the Synagogue but somewhere else. To my mind, this would be another occasion for applying the maxim of Deuteronomy (20:8); "What man is there that is fearful and fainthearted?—let him go." Numbers alone are not decisive. As it is written in another chapter of the same book (7:7); "The Lord did not set his love upon you because ye were more in numbers than any people; for ye were the fewest of all people." How true is this in Europe to-day, and at the same time how inspiring.

To this I should like to add only one "if" more. If Continental Jewry will again take to heart what is taught since time immemorial by the Law and the Prophets, its future is built on a rock.

> *God hath no shape, nor can the artist's hands*
> *His figure frame in shining gold or wood;*
> *God's holy image—God sent—only stands*
> *Within the bosom of the wise and good.*
>
> STATIUS

5. Between the Pieces of Abraham's Covenant (Ben Habtarim)

"The sun went down and it was dark" and a great fearful blackness descended upon the earth. The principle of Mercy departed from it; it was subdued and passed away, while the principle of Justice grew ever stronger. On such a day all of us are called to be judged, all the creatures in the world, whether sons of the Covenant or as the slaves of slaves; not a people, nor a tribe, not a single one is excepted. The entire globe, the whole inhabited earth is split, with slits and breaches puncturing it. Even the current of time, that symbol of regular constancy, is also cleft, cut across, rent into pieces. The present does not link the past with the future as before, but separates them completely instead. The past is a chaos, the future a void, and between the two halves, those familiar pieces "each half over against the other", there yawns an abyss. With our own eyes we see the bird of prey swoop down upon the carcasses, but where is the Spirit which hovers over the face of the deep? Behold a smoking furnace and a flaming torch are passing between the pieces, but alas, there is no visionary, no vision, no one paying heed.

True, there is no end to the verbiage, the lectures and the inventions relating to "the new order" of the future world that will emerge out of the present abyss. And simultaneously, the past too is frequently being subjected to critical scrutiny. On the face of it, nearly all of us became as the judges and like unto those who prophesy. In fact, however, in vain is our judgment and to no purpose our anticipation of the things to come, if we fail to abandon our ways of glorifying and exalting our myopia as though it were the most superior virtue, if we fail to note that gathering single ears or harvesting the corners of the fields of historical memory, is no more than a form of forgetting. How can a mere scrap satisfy the lion? How can the pit be filled with its own dug-up earth?

Let us look and see where we stand, how the standards in matters of history have declined, particularly in their philosophical study which is obligatory, since theory is   necessity for practice, how these have

This essay was first published in Hebrew in *Yalkut*, London, 1942, No. II. We are grateful for the permission to reprint this essay to Mr. William Margulies and Mr. Alex Margulies.

deteriorated since the days of the First World War to the present time. Then in the third year of hostilities, it was plain to see that the end had come for a great, universal era in the annals of mankind, and that in this final period a completely new chapter was ceaselessly and without pause taking shape which, although it still had no name is likely to serve in the main as the crowning result of the whole preceding historical development. Whatever we recall regarding the climate of man's life about one generation ago, will immediately show how lofty was the apex of human thinking in those days as compared to its low state today. This comparison is the initial step in the reasoning that will lead us outwards from the history of our days which to all appearances does not at all depend on us, as we do on an inner consciousness which always contains something of the power of the acts of Creation, of that colossal creative power that utilizes even chaos as building material. For we have nowhere else to look for relief and deliverance!

Approximately 25 years ago all the sages of western and eastern Europe, in anticipation of the coming event, declared unanimously that the time had come to put an end to the age of division and confusion of tongues in international life. And if the war which was raging in the world was indeed a holy war, it is only because it was the very last in the chain of the troubles never ceasing from the days of primitive man; because, to begin with, it was launched for the sake of peace; because its end, along with the abundant blessings in its wake, will attest to its healthy roots. Even in Germany many of its thinkers did not consider this matter in any other light. And what is the last blessing that in the view of succeeding generations of the enlightened people the world over needed to fight for? To put it briefly: an ingathering of the exiles of the Tower of Babel; the gathering together of all the sons of Noah into one league under the rainbow of the world covenant valid until the end of time. We all know that it was the fortune of this aspiration to lead to the first experiment in achieving mankind's unity. Even though it is today clear and obvious to all that the League of Nations in Geneva was stillborn at the very start, there is no birth without conception, and no conception without knowledge, devoid of idea and spirit.

Even more serious was the idea of transition in the internal life of each and every nation, particularly with regard to relations between social strata. Those who justified the old ways fell into confusion and retreated, while those who yearned for the future prepared themselves for entirely new acts of creation in the fullest sense of the word: "a new earth and a new sky"—it was from this perspective that they looked at the future. Whether Marxists or opponents of Marx, socialists all over the world were united in the belief that the dawn of fulfillment had arrived for their ideal. The latter too caused conception and the pregnancy ran its whole course. A covenant of peace between the nations, a pact of justice and equity within every people—these were the principal headings in the scroll heralding the future that hovered over the last war's valley of death. And just as the new experiment was about to enter the sphere of international laws, so there was no want of endeavour to carry out the new commandments in the socio-economic sphere. In the very midst of the war came the great revolution in Russia, proving that not everything was futile and that there was hope for all who thirsted for justice. Again it should be emphasized that the quintessence of the matter lay neither in the fruit nor in the seed, but rather in the tree itself and in its trunk, or to put it more accurately, the inclination and the will which leads to planting and fruit-bearing. If all the vintners who hoped to produce grapes were instead to bring forth wild grapes, yet would their original good intention not be wasted, and the fate of the thing they created would indicate the secret of creation in general, that is, the secret of "the broken vessels" and "the dispersal of the divine sparks." Who knew in advance that within socialism two parties were struggling, the one wedded to the concept of liberty and popular government, and the other paying homage to tyranny and violence, and that as time passed the elder would serve the younger? Who can fathom that which is hidden? Consequently, it behooves us to admit even today that at the time to which we are referring, the socialist movement had rightly enjoyed the presumption of propriety and honesty.

Such an evaluation fits all the more the desires of the so-called "small" nations for an emancipated policy, independent of the will of others who take inordinate pride in their size. Their transgressions after they succeeded in establishing their first and second edifice, like Poland for example, do not prove the iniquity of their original point of departure, when they were following their own pillars of fire and cloud. As in other spheres, their subsequent development cannot be a proof as to what their beginning had been. Here we have to plead the cause of our own people. The Jews could not dissociate themselves in spirit from all the other nations at a time when the latter appeared to be "becoming Jewish". For, since olden times, all our prayers have always concluded with the peace blessing; our world-to-come was bedded into foundations of justice and equity; and the love of liberty has been ingrained in our hearts from the most ancient days. The approach to historical events which typified that period, namely—profound examination and breadth of opinion appealed to the spirit of our people even more. We are Hebrews, the sons of Eber, but we should be described rather as the people of the past (*avar* in Hebrew); when we look back our eyes gaze towards the days of the Beginning, of Creation, and when we direct our attention to what lies ahead, our never ending yearning embraces the Messianic age, thus moving from one extreme of historical time to the opposite extreme. This also means that we are extremists, who press the coming of the Messianic end of days. In our people, breadth of vision and impatience are mated and joined into one. Therefore we grasped too much and held nothing; hence we wandered and lost our way, as it was predestined from the day of our emergence as a nation, and as was invariably our wont, and as all nations proceeded at that time. Even though our longing was in vain, we did save our soul. Until the numberless trials and tribulations befell us during the past decade.

In the meantime, little by little, the earth assumed a new look which was old. Its spiritual elation was interrupted midway and with progressively increasing speed it descended into the lowest Hell. And we knew it not and with our minds distracted, we too sank lower and lower. The black bitterness with regard to the present world became superimposed on the pure white of faith related to the end of days, which is our life and the length of our days; we told ourselves that what was done could not be reversed and that henceforth and forever more our way will be as their way. They cried peace to the wicked and we too fell into the trap. They chose not to be concerned with the interests of the community, disregarded their own flesh and blood, did their worst to the League of Nations, ostracized the moderates, and associated themselves with the leaders of a perverted generation;—and we too lived in near isolation, turned our eyes away from the acts of deception directed at others, were guilty of unfounded hatred and by way of compromise lent a helping hand to our foes. Now the day of vengeance and requital has come, for us and for them. License has been granted to the sword, the plague and the beasts of prey. And still we wait to hear what the gentile nations will say, and still we call round at the doors of their ruined palaces and castles. Have we then no ruins within our own borders? Can we not make our moral stock-taking for our own selves?

It will suffice to compare the pattern for the future which is before the outside world today, with the main outline of the pattern mentioned above, to realize that this is not a propitious time to rely on the leaders of the host nations and their ways. In the entire Anglo-Saxon world the faith in natural progress has contracted and faded; it has indeed all but vanished. Restraint, such as was unknown in the olden days, is spreading among the experts on matters of state, as well as the exaggerated care to keep their statement vague. Who among those listening to their words will decide where the emphasis is to be placed and whether their hearts are turning to the left or to the right? In any event there is no doubt that parsimony is increasing in the world and that only a lean future awaits man's progeny. What we did not learn from their declarations, we sensed in their silence. There is no hint of the words of our prophets, which until recently everyone knew by heart, namely that it was mandatory for the art of war and its strategies to disappear, the heavens having decreed that all instruments of destruction would vanish entirely. Also it is not even mentioned that the League of Nations was to make the whole world into one single unit. They assure us only that we will live securely under the shadow of well-armed skies, but provide no answer to the question "armed against whom?" Since Bolshevist Russia is also reckoned among the victims of the catastrophe, who then is envisaged as the enemy of the future? From which direction is the trouble to come? Or can it be that the danger will not originate from any unforseen direction at all, but from among ourselves?

The same applies to internal matters in the realm of social and economic structure. Even the more modest programmes and demands of socialism appear to have been erased from the agenda and declared taboo. The international labour movement has disintegrated and makes no demands, while the rulers of Russia are forced to look to their opponents for assistance. Instead, the wealthy and mercenary boast of being the benefactors of the weak and the future unemployed. Neither the meat of the legendary bull, nor the reserved old wine awaits them at the time of grace and the Feast, but only bread to eat and a garment to wear, and even this without promise. Similarly, the "small" nations, the humble and poor people have likewise not attained a better portion in this hereafter. The name of the Jewish people is not mentioned or listed in any way, as though it did not actually exist, but was only an allegory—an allegory and mockery in the mouths of those seeking to destroy us. The new order that the righteous of our time are demanding and proclaiming in the English tongue is not really a major world order as formulated during the last war, but only a minor world order in which the Jewish people and the Jews have not been granted a place at all.

Not out of despair and for the sake of denigration have these words been said; on the contrary, they were uttered in order to strengthen weak hands and were promoted by indomitable faith that our world was not created, Heaven forbid, for chaos but for its inhabitants "to live together as brothers", with the Jews included among them. If that is so, then the Seed of Abraham is indeed fortunate having been born to recall from the depth of the abyss, things primeval and ancient, the past which does not pass away, but generates even in the darkest hour, for those who remember it, a lasting asset for the world to come. They are irritated and apprehensive, afraid to look into the abyss, to grasp why and where they have been flung—so it is our great and grave mandate to eradicate the lie from the face of the earth and make the truth to grow instead, precisely as it is. They spread illusions in order to deceive people; they deliberately build castles in the air as ephemeral delusions. It is our unqualified right to bring them to judgment before the whole of the past and the whole of the future, and to create a bond to join the two for ever and ever. Their cures are as false as idols, their eyes are shut fast as though they had never seen a single ray of light; let us open wide our own eyes.

Our heritage serves to show that "between the pieces" is the propitious hour for entering a covenant and renewing one that had been concluded. From our prophets we know that the beginning of all beginnings in exalted matters such as these is "proclaim liberty, every man to his brother, and every man to his neighbour" (Jeremiah 34-17). Redemption cannot come except to a generation that is either all righteous or all wicked, and since we are as far from belonging to the category of "all righteous" as earth is from heaven, no alternative remains for us but to accept with good grace the responsibility that we all were guilty: to admit and confess that all of us—in all our tribes, families, political parties and sects—are indeed guilt-laden and faithless. This will stand in the breach among the pieces and as a result we shall live and inherit.

At a time which is by way of being an interlude and a precarious one at that, one should not hand down judgments on life and death, on the life of our people and the life of the entire world, except in things above and beyond time, and may Providence deliver us.

6. Timidity and Audacity in Modern Jewish Thought

Since our general theme is *"Timidity and Audacity in Jewish Thought"*, I propose to begin with some observations on the title itself. I believe that we are dealing with an important problem, for it is, in my opinion, this very timidity which hinders the progress of Jewish thought today; it is therefore necessary to ask oneself: whence comes this timidity?

Anyone who has studied the history of Jewish thought knows that the application of moral categories to this system of thought has its origin in the separation of the Europeanized and the traditional schools of thought. Merely to mention the name Mendelssohn in this context is probably enough: it is since his time, the dawning of emancipation, that the "enlightened" on the one hand and the "traditionalists" on the other have begun to level accusations at each other.

The enlightened proclaimed that, after the resounding clarion-call of the new epoch, after the walls which divided the Jewish world from the world outside had tumbled in ruins, it was only because of timidity of thought that the boldness needed to face the world outside, and to adjust Jewish life to the new conditions, was still lacking. The traditionalists, for their part, accused the other side of a lack of boldness, maintaining that, even if one had not the strength to continue in the traditional Jewish way of life, one ought to have the audacity to hold fast to the continuity of Jewish thought.

Furthermore, when we speak of the timidity or the audacity of Jewish thought, we need to have some idea of what is meant by Jewish thought as such. I feel that it must first be admitted as an essential fact that there really exists a continuous Jewish manner of thinking which possesses an identity of its own, that there actually exists something resembling collective thought and that, in consequence, one may speak of Jewish thought and not merely of the thought of Jewish thinkers, which is something entirely different.

For example, I would venture to say that Spinoza, although Jewish in his intellectual and spiritual origins, does not have a place in Jewish thought as we nowadays understand it. There exists another example of a great Jewish

The text of this address delivered on 28 September 1959 to the Second Colloquium of Jewish Intellectuals of French Language, held in Paris, was first published in French in *La Conscience Juive*, Données et Débats, by Presses Universitaires de France, Paris, 1963.

thinker, nearer to our own times, Henri Bergson, but I likewise doubt whether it is possible to find a place for him within the framework of Jewish thought. Conversely, if he will allow me to say so, I consider that the philosophy of M. Vladimir Jankélevitch, little though I know of his work, is evolving in a direction which would allow him to take a place in the history of Jewish thought.

I am citing these examples merely in order to make the point that it is very difficult to categorise any particular thought as being a Jewish thought, but what is not here in question is that there exists a continuous stream which has persisted unbroken into our times and which can be described as being the stream of Jewish thought.

It is since the end of the eighteenth century that Jewish thought has become Europeanized. Although it derives from the original trend of our thought, it has developed, in a particular sense, in opposition to this traditional trend. Now it is for this very reason that the two opposing trends have remained on common ground, however restricted and limited this ground may be. Like the Orthodox thinkers, the Jewish freethinkers were inspired by the goal of maintaining the continuity of Jewish thought albeit by means of criticism and purification of the tradition which they believed they could thus save for the new age of enlightenment (the *Haskala* in Hebrew). Following on from this argument, the idea spread that there exist certain very simple values known to all, concerning everyday morality, values which had been preserved even in separation. This everyday morality was not even considered as being only a Jewish morality but as a human morality, having a general character, well-defined values and a system of virtues and vices. It is in this sense that it was held that audacity was a virtue, something to be accepted, and timidity a vice. For some, it was timidity obstinately to refuse to examine, even from a distance, any reforms in Jewish tradition, whereas the Orthodox, for their part, regarded those Jews who had been led astray by Europeanized thought as victims of a dishonourable surrender caused by timidity, by lack of courage, even by cowardice.

The traditionalists considered that, faced with this new world, it was a matter of the greatest possible audacity to remain behind our traditional rampart, to continue in the way of that which has a value in itself, independently of the history of the outside world. But what is history of the outside world?

"Outside history" is, indeed, a problematic notion. And what is history itself? One might think that evolution constitutes a quality, a symptom of the historical process as such, whereas in fact it is only an idea formed under the influence of certain stages in human experience. This idea of evolution may be found even in the Biblical account of creation. Man is always at the centre of creation according to our religious tradition. Thus evolution is a special aspect of an individual historical process. Accordingly, it is possible to conceive a whole succession of evolutionary developments.

The idea that evolution implies consecutive stages is one which proceeds solely from modern thinking; in turn, it is no more than a system of a certain state in the evolution of thought. Seen in this context, one may affirm that Jewish thought is basically an indivisible entity and that it is present in its entirety in each of the stages which develop against the background of historical time.

Jewish thought if present in its entirety in the primordial tradition which is basic to Judaism. Such a conception is not identical with Franz Rosenzweig's idea of eternity outside time. It is a conception of something, however, which cannot be described in a precise way. Even the glass of water in front of me is a unity in itself, a whole, despite the fact that each exposition of this unity is evolving in time. How much more, then, does Jewish thought constitute a unity in itself independent of the consecutive stages which in their projection have evolved the image of a movement forward. Yet, in reality, the image as a whole, as already indicated, is fully anticipated in the initial stage of the process.

But, if such be the case, the question arises where is the place for Jewish virtues generally and, in particular, for audacity? Would it not be more correct to confront the problem of virtues with the evolution of our Europeanized thought which, in its movement forward continually boasts of being audacious? To reply to this, we must take a glance backwards.

When one considers the separation of these two trends during the first historical period at the end of the eighteenth and the beginning of the nineteenth centuries, one may note that this period is characterised by the fierce struggle between the 'enlightened' and the 'obscurantists', those who remained in the shadows. At this period, Hasidism was, for the *Maskilim*, the enlightened ones, the quintessence of obscurantism. Then, towards the end of the nineteenth century, what happened? It was precisely thanks to the enlightened that Hasidism experienced its renaissance. And it was, indeed, a true renaissance. It was discovered that it was Hasidism and not our secularized, Europeanized thinking which contained something very valuable for the new time.

From the very fact that we are present here, it is clear that our problems are eternal ones. With regard to eternity, I do not think it necessary to make a distinction between that which, being within the process of time, lasts from infinity to infinity and that which is outside time. What matters is that there are problems which remain important for human thought and human beings, Jews and non-Jews, alike.

In moving from the beginnings of Hasidism to more recent times, we may note that one of the effects of our secularized thinking is the nineteenth century idea of a Jewish nation and it is because of this that the notion of audacity has taken on a new meaning. A little impatience is creeping in, there is a desire to see some actual result from the thinking. At the same time, the accusation of timidity is also receiving a new meaning: the argument is advanced that, if we remain locked up in traditional Jewish thought, in a state of siege so to speak, there is no possibility of moving from thought to action; we are condemned to inaction. However, it is necessary to make a distinction beween audacity in action, which takes its origins from thought, and audacity in thought itself. It is perhaps no exaggeration to say that our idea of a nation had its origins rather in the timidity of Jewish thought.

All those who have reflected upon the evolution of European thought during the nineteenth century are well aware that our secularized nationalism was no more than an application of certain external ideas to Jewish reality. I do not wish to deny that it was perhaps audacious even to attempt to draw practical conclusions from certain ideological concepts and more audacious yet to attempt to bring them to realization. I am thinking of the State of Israel. Naturally, in order to conceive of the possibility of recreating a Jewish State in Israel, much audacity was required. In order to impose this idea on the outside world, how much more audacity was needed!

But our Europeanized thought had, at the same time, another effect. Modern Jewish philosophy was making its appearance. It is very interesting to note that this philosophical movement had to suffer from the partisans of our idea of a nation, just as the old tradition had, in its day, to suffer from similar attacks. It was said, in the camps of the Jewish nationalists, that it was still timidity which was pushing Jewish thought in the direction of European philosophy, that to make spiritual concessions to the outside world was timidity. I do not think, however, that there is any lack of heroic vigour in the thinking of Hermann Cohen or of Rosenzweig: for them to proclaim, in the face of the outside world, that no system of philosophy is possible unless Jewish tradition forms a part of it required much real courage, much audacity of thought. What did Cohen do? He constructed a system of general philosophy which, according to him, could not have been constructed without its system of ethics and this latter was based on prophetic monotheism, that is to say, on ancient Jewish tradition. Thus general philosophy, philosophy as such, finds itself annexed, so to speak, to our sacred tradition which becomes a *sine qua non* for the progress of philosophical thought.

It was therefore very important for modern philosophy to penetrate the real meaning of traditional Jewish philosophy and especially of what is called prophetic Messianism.

With this idea was associated the conception that the Jews and Jewish thought have a special duty towards the world, a mission to fulfil, a message to make known and it is therein that the justification resided for the continued existence of the ethnic group, known as the Jewish people.

Now this very idea of a mission was regarded by our secular thinkers as a manifestation of timidity, of assimilation, adaptation to the outside world, resulting from a certain weakness of the spirit. It would be interesting on this point to make a close examination of the relevant literature; one would continually find repetitions of the same accusations: timidity, submissiveness, lack of courage, etc. And why? For Jewish nationalism the idea of a mission is the expression of a feeling of insecurity. The philosophers, say their adversaries, were unable to make peace with this very simple idea that we are a people like any other and that we have the right to exist like any other among them.

In my modest view, it was rather audacity and courage that were required by thinkers rooted in Jewish tradition, such as Cohen or Rosenzweig, in order to confront the outside world within the framework of Jewish thought. Moreover it is very important nowadays that we should understand one another with regard to such attitudes as are described as courageous on the one hand and timorous on the other.

When we look at the outside world as it is today, we must acknowledge that it has undergone great changes during the 150 years that have elapsed since Mendelssohn and his disciples. Now the question is no longer one of a confrontation of Judaism with Christianity, since Christianity in turn is entering into a period of siege. Even in the West we are no longer encircled by a Christian world; we must take into account the whole planet and the majority of humanity is far from being a monotheistic majority any longer. Christianity now finds itself confronted by dangerous enemies such as Buddhism and, atheism. It is often said that the world is divided between atheism and Christianity. It is certainly true that the world is divided. But, though it may be true that the Eastern world is an atheist world, it is not true that the West is Christian. For example, in England, the poor attendance at churches is deplored; statistics have established that scarcely ten per cent of the population goes to church—a fact which is all the more striking in so far as England has the reputation of being the most Christian country in Europe.

Now, it is not only Christianity but all the ancient traditions of our world which are being threatened. We must face up to this new situation. The world of today is evolving towards a uniform civilization; a great unity is in the process of being established on this small planet which we inhabit. In spite of all political divisions, it must be realized that it is the same civilisation which, to give a very precise example, unites the USA and the USSR; it is the same ideal of a civilisation based on exact sciences, on technology; it is the same goal of material well-being which is pursued on the one side as it is on the other, a goal which it is intended should be attained by technical means. And the result is that all the ancient traditions of human culture are in danger of disappearing. When I visited India three years ago, I was in a position to see to what extent Indian intellectuals are concerned about the future of Indian culture and thought, because the majority of their intellectuals are becoming Europeanized as was the case with our Jewish intellectuals a century ago.

This is, then, a very grave danger for others as well as for ourselves. I am not referring to assimilation of the Jewish people but to its integration into the rest of humanity. I would prefer to concentrate on our tradition which has, to my mind, a value in itself appertaining to the individuality of the person. Along with the danger to all spiritual traditions throughout the world, there arises a threat to Man as an individual. When we think about the world of the future, we above all envisage mankind as being united. Certainly that will come. I sincerely hope that future generations will not be so torn by political conflict, that a common prosperity will prevail, and that the same values might even be shared by the entire world. But what values? What will be the place of Man as an individual in that world? I find it hard to imagine. The individual survives through his refusal to conform to the outside world. But, when the entire environment in which he lives is based on a desire for uniformity, there exists a danger, not only for the cultural and spiritual traditions of the past, but also for the individual as such, and this wherever it may be, among Jews or Christians, Europeans or Asians.

In such a situation, I believe that audacity is required to bring Jewish thought into action against this imperious movement which predominates in our world. Audacity is necessary, certainly, but the continuity of Jewish thought itself bears witness to the fact that, in times past, we have possessed this courage and that there has grown up in us a reserve of courage and of audacity which will enable us to effect this mobilisation.

Of course, this could not be achieved without faith. On this point I should like to say that our whole spiritual tradition bears witness to the presence of faith in Jewish thought, one might say ever since Abraham. It is written: "Abraham believed in the Lord and he counted it to him for righteousness" (*Genesis*, 15,6). Of course, this revelation of 'belief' (*Emunah* in Hebrew) may be translated in various ways without the use of the word 'faith'. Whatever may be the case, this Biblical 'belief' implies acceptance of an eternal justice, of unshakeable principles of human behaviour. It is true that one cannot have intellectual courage without faith but, at the same time, thought is also concerned with realities. I believe that a certain intuitive knowledge has been transformed in the Jewish heart into faith; this belief was such that it surpassed even the highest degree of knowledge. What then is this primordial intuitive belief of Judaism? That the world was created, which is to say that it is essentially fragile and our entire tradition never ceases to stress this fact. We hold the doctrine that the Eternal built and destroyed the world time and again. The existence of the world thus appears to be dominated by a rhythm of construction and destruction. Thanks to this intuitive knowledge, being fully aware of the fact tht the world is fragile, we are predestined to face up to the world of today, this world which is becoming more and more uniform, predestined to make a stand against it by our refusal to conform, by our resolution and by our belief in Jewish thought.

Fragility . . . Here it would be proper to refer to the *"Laws of Repentance"* in the *Code of Maimonides*. According to him, the world must be seen as being suspended between destruction and construction, between continuity of existence and the end of existence, so that everything depends on the sum total of human actions, whether good or ill, on the balance between good and evil. A single act by one man may upset the balance, and thus the continued existence of the world or its annihilation depends on the free will of each one of us. When one considers the present-day situation in international politics, when one considers that a madman might come to power and, simply by pressing a button, unleash a catastrophe for the human race, one comes to realize that Maimonides was, in some measure, a prophet and not merely a thinker inspired by Jewish tradition. Thank God, we have not yet come to this pass. Nonetheless, given the primordial intuitive knowledge of Judaism which is written down in the first chapter of *Genesis*, we should not be surprised that we have reached the present state of affairs, since we know that the world, from its beginnings, is fragile and that, in consequence, the existence of humanity, as also the life of the individual, are all the more fragile.

To appreciate the great importance for us all of our tradition, of the necessity for maintaining and for reinterpreting Jewish thought in its continuity, it is necessary, in my opinion, to have an idea of God. This is the point which logically outweighs the fragility of the world, just as it is a means of reassurance for the individual man. The psychiatrists among us could, I believe, bear witness to the fact that there exists a means of healing by faith and it is this faith that must be resurrected in order to forestall the collective insanity of the human race. Does this mean belief in a miracle? By no means! This 'miracle' derives from the collective experience of the Jewish people and constitutes an element in Jewish tradition. This latter is founded on the intuitive knowledge that Man has the power to oppose destruction and to contribute to the continuity of existence.

The great idea which is preserved in our tradition is that Man is somehow within the same category as Deity. He is made in the likeness of God. This great idea is, of course, one that Christianity has also adopted, but in what sense? By making a Man-God, whereas, for us, each man is, in a sense, 'God' and by the very fact that the Eternal is unique, each human visage is unique. This idea is precisely formulated in the *Mishna (Sanhedrin,* chap. 4, 5). It is there written that God created all living beings according to their kinds whereas Man was created alone, in order to show that he is equivalent to the Universe, unique like the Universe and, it must be added, like the Creator of the Universe. One also finds therein a splendid piece of imagery which brings out the difference between an earthly king and God. When an earthly king has his likeness stamped on the coinage, all the coins are alike in this portrait, whereas God—the *Mishna* goes on to say—has stamped his image in the faces of all men and yet not one resembles another. Each is therefore of himself and in himself a unique being and, consequently, well-qualified to act, as it were, as an associate of the Creator.

In the book of *Genesis*, we find also the story of the Flood. The human race was in danger of being wiped out. The Creator of the world, however, in His mercy, decided to make peace with humanity and to accord it a sign of the divine love for the whole of creation. This sign was the rainbow. How wise! What is the rainbow? It is light divided into its multiplicity of colours, a symbol of diversity in the world. Diversity, the negation of uniformity, guarantees the future of the human race; only diversity warrants the possibility of a perpetual maintenance of existence for the human race. If we do not wish to see the human race degraded to the level of a flock of sheep—a contingency foreseen by the prophets of the nineteenth century such as Nietzsche—we must have diversity in historical existence. We must lift our eyes to the sky and to the multi-coloured arch in the clouds. We must remember that it is the symbol of a treaty made by the Creator for the continued existence of the human race.

A further word about Messianism. When Cohen or Rosenzweig spoke of Messianism were they inspired by faith in a personal Messiah? Whatever may be the case, it would not be just to maintain, with regard to Jewish tradition in its continuity, that it has ever been lacking in boldness and faith in awaiting a Messiah in a human individual, a real incarnation of the Messianic idea in a corporeal individual. As far as our traditional thought is concerned, it was not a question of a general ideal, but of a man possessed of moral and intellectual perfection. This great principle, this perfect man who must every day be awaited, is a safeguard against the false grandeur of Man. We live in an age where false grandeur impresses the whole human race. The name Messiah has even been applied to dictators of recent periods of history.

But let us return to our central theme, that of making a stand against the fragility of the world. Should an atheist go on asking: "What is the point in the existence of the world? Let it go to pieces!" At that point there ceases to be any common ground between the atheist and those who have chosen existence. Of course, in order for the world to exist, love is required, not merely the love of one man for another, but love of the world. One must love the world, one must love existence as such. One must accept that being is of greater value than not being. One must be opposed to Satan who, to quote *Dosfoevsky*, is the essence of non-existence.

When we now ask ourselves: where is the timidity of Jewish thought today and where the audacity, it seems that, in order to put oneself on the side of audacity, one must also put oneself on the side of traditional Jewish thought. This is not too difficult. May I once more quote the *Pentateuch,* where it is written: "I have set before you life and death . . . therefore choose life" (Deuteronomy, 30, 19). This is the first commandment of Judaism implying commitment. If one lives, one has already made a choice, one has chosen life rather than death. And this concerns each individual life. If we live, we have aligned ourselves with life against death.

Of course, a bold upsurge of audacity is necessary to reaffirm today these very simple truths which have been rooted in Jewish intuitive knowledge for millennia. It is necessary because, in our times, people prefer to live on the surface. Now, in the profundity of life and above all in Jewish thought, there remains ever present this intuitive knowledge of the fragility of the world and it is therefore up to us to make the choice; in favour of the human race, of ourselves both as Jews and as individuals, or—against.

7. Why Remain Jewish?

A *Traditional Approach*

Anyone dedicated to the Jewish religious tradition must be on the alert to face the challenge to the essence of the Jewish faith.

It is one of the most prominent sages of Israel of the 1st Century of the Christian era, Rabbi Eleazar ben Arakh, who enjoins us "to study the Torah with application and to know what answer to give to the Epicuros". The "Epicuros", i.e. the Epicurean, is a name used in the Talmudic literature as a generic term defining the impious, the unbeliever, or more precisely, the heretic. Any dialogue between a believing Jew and Jewish non-believers is thus qualified by the ancient precept, which can incidentally be found in the Prayer Book, as an encounter not only permitted but even encouraged by the Jewish tradition. The exhortation closely to study the Torah apparently implies that such a study would enable the diligent student to discover in the sacred text an intrinsic refutation of any line of thought inconsistent with the traditional faith. But forearmed with the required knowledge, the man of learning should always be ready to deal properly with the exponents of a false philosophy.

To the great majority of our freethinkers all this may appear naive, antiquated and, at any rate, beside the point under consideration. However, to those amongst us who continue in the Jewish traditional way of life and try to think and to act accordingly, the very question "Why remain Jewish?" is bound to appear as a stumbling block designed to lure them off their road and to lead them into temptation. To them it sounds like one of the questions invented by the sophisticated ancient Greeks to expose logic itself as a self-contradictory absurdity. What answer should I give to a man who would ask me whether I was prepared to be a party to the destruction of the universe? For in his self-awareness the Jewish believer knows himself as a citizen of an historical universe whose existence depends as much on his own resolve to foster his Jewishness as this

The text of this address delivered to the Second Conference of Jewish Intellectuals held in London in June 1965 was first published in English in abbreviated form in the *Jewish Spectator*, New York, November 1965.

Jewishness is an end-product of the whole preceding process of universal history. To put before himself the question whether it is worth while to sustain his Jewish life in its integrity or to renounce it, would for the mind of the faithful Jew imply the admission that he was facing the tragic dilemma to be or not to be, and above all, that he was already placing himself, though only tentatively, outside the boundaries of the inherited Kingdom of God. In short, the question under consideration is clearly a heretical one which no faithful Jew could ever address to himself. Has he, then, to close his eyes to the fact that so many of his fellow Jews are fighting a hard uphill fight in search of the right solution to the problem of their Jewish existence?—Certainly not! It is obviously a case in which the ancient maxim concerning heretics becomes operative.

Provided with the credentials for negotiating with heretics, we have to consider first what is the true meaning of the crucial WHY in our query and to whom precisely it is addressed. A preliminary analysis in such an awkward situation can do no harm and may forestall misunderstanding.

The heretical challenge could be based on the presumption that it does not matter whether those called to account for their will to carry on as Jews, or at least for their reluctance to shed their Jewishness, whatever this may signify, are traditionalists or emancipated from the yoke of the Torah. Yet, such an assumption is in itself anathema to the Jewish believer. It is obviously based on the widely accepted view that with the steadily expanding secularisation of Jewish life that classical definition of a Jew by the token of his Jewish faith had lost its validity; that, in other words, the hard realities of our historical existence were giving the lie to any attempt at a logically correct generalisation applicable to all human beings regarding themselves, or who are being regarded by others, as Jews. Consequently, there was no other alternative but to approach every individual case in accordance with its own merits, and, as far as our particular question is concerned, to resign oneself to collating a great variety of answers, all equally worthy of recording.

This seemingly unbiased, objective and, on the face of it, scientific approach is entirely unacceptable to those steeped in the "Faith of Abraham". They unflinchingly cling to the classical definition of a Jew. Whoever indulges in the riddle, Who is a Jew?, reveals in their view a fault in the balance of his Jewish mind. To the well balanced Jewish mind it remains true to-day as it was unquestionable a hundred and a thousand years ago that there are no Jews in the world showing in their eyes some gleam of Jewishness who could be what they are if the living force of our perennial faith had not been preserved in its effectiveness throughout the ages. Not a single Jewish man or woman, let alone the Jewish people as a whole, or the Jewish culture, could have survived without this historical *Vis vitalis*. One may be disinterested in all which concerns the Jewish body politic, or social; but who could make bold to deny in a general way that individual existence was invariably rooted in the historical past? There are, of course, the uprooted who are sometimes afraid and ashamed even to glance at their genealogy propagating, as it were, a specific cult of intellectual parricide. However, there are extreme border cases. Besides, how can the uprooted, insofar as they are unaware of the historical continuity informing the individual existence, be qualified to pronounce judgment on what is and what is not the essence of Jewish history. A byproduct of a process of dissolution and atomisation of the primordial radioactive substratum of Jewish existence running parallel to the process of its constant wholesome radiation these mostly innocent victims of total assimilation have been metaphorically characterised as "human dust". The Talmud has a harsh word for them: "Though alive, they may be called dead" (Berakhoth, 18b). Does that mean that they should remorselessly be written off?—At this critical point which for many seems to be one of no return, the traditional definition of the Jew acquires the character of the magic formula.

Instead of excluding anyone, the formula "A Jew is a human being of the Jewish creed" reveals itself as all-inclusive, for its corollary is the Law: "A Jew is a Jew even if he is a sinner". The rejection of the Jewish creed through secularisation certainly is a sin from the traditional point of view and even more so is the severing of all links with the Jewish people by way of total assimilation. Nonetheless, both categories of Jews, immersed as they are in error and sin, do not cease to belong to the all-embracing community of Israel. If there are "dead souls" in the House of Israel, they should be revived and resurrected; if the aberration of secular nationalism is gaining ground, it should be exposed as a flagrant deviation from the genuinely Jewish persuasion; if even amongst the Jewish believers themselves there is strife and an abundance of conflicting philosophies, no one should give up the hope that eternal truth will in the end prevail. In no circumstances can the Jewish traditionalist be discouraged by the fact that he belongs to-day to an outmoded minority. Is not the minority status as such, since Deuteronomy, through the age of the Maccabees, and up to our own days vindicated by the Jewish tradition? Yet, just because Jewishness is to its devotees a living reality, they can well understand that to those who are alienated from its primary sources it may become in the changing world of ours one of the most problematic historical phenomena and that they might prefer to turn a blind eye to it altogether.

The preliminary analysis is intended to show that the WHY? in our question acquires at least three different meanings each dependent on the specific categories of Jews confronted by it. In the case of the totally assimilated the WHY? sounds rather like a HOW?—How can one best efface the last traces of his or her Jewish origin in a world moving rapidly towards the emancipation of the individual from all rudiments of group history? How make it clear to the world outside, to which even the converted half-Jew remains a Jew, that there is nothing real in the empty shell of this irritating name?—Quite different is the meaning of the WHY? in correlation to the various adherents of Jewish secularism. To them it sounds rather as an interrogative What? What should they substitute for the discarded Jewish creed in order to rationalise their Jewish self-awareness, to make it understandable to themselves and to others, in the first place to their own children?—Finally to the traditionalist, as indicated, the WHY? is overshadowed by a Who? and a Which? Who, precisely, is the challenger and which specific kind of heresy is represented by him.

Whoever he may be, the plain duty of the traditionalist is to avoid the pitfall of unwarranted polemics and, before counterattacking the individual assailant, to find the common overtones in all the voices raised against the validity of the Jewish creed in our time.

It is being stressed over and over again that, since we live in an age of rapid change, the very spirit of traditionalism has become obliterated and was condemned to wither away. The Jewish traditionalist, therefore, implicitly represented a lost cause. His obstinacy was of no avail and inadvertently strengthened the argument of the assimilationist. At the same time traditionalism was slowing down the process of adaptation of the Jewish people to the requirement of national life in its secularised environment. Tradition, it is being said, leads to fossilisation, to stagnation, and who can be so blindfolded as not to see that in our time to lag behind was tantamount to foregoing any chance of survival?

Against this the Jewish traditionalist has to recall some hard facts of our people's history. Far from being a factor of deadly intellectual stagnation, the Jewish tradition constantly stimulated its own evolution and transformation. Our whole sacred literature from the Pentateuch onwards proves it, testifying to the immense variety of ways and means by which our inherited faith, nowadays called "Judaism", came to terms with the requirements of a new age without impairing the integrity of its substance. Was the epoch of Hellenism, for instance, not an age of rapid change? Did not a hurricane of change blow during the centuries of the decline and fall of the Roman Empire and of the advance of Christianity? Shall we, further, remind ourselves of the emergence and the triumphs of Islam? Or of the Crusades, or the horrors of the Inquisition? In all these cases the Jewish tradition responded to the challenge of the respective age and adapted itself in one way or another to its requirements. As a rule the adaptation signified not a selling out of articles of the Jewish *credo* but, on the contrary, the propping up of its protective walls and a deepening of its intellectual resources. The story is told in detail in the unique history of Jewish religious thought. Is the present situation, one may ask, basically different from anything that happened to our tradition in the past?

This, indeed, is what the children of the modern age often presume. Let us then consider to what an extent their supposition is justified.

Admittedly, universal history does not know of another age which was entirely determined by the predominance of science and scientific thinking. It is not for nothing that we call our time the technological age. As a consequence of the conquests of applied science, all peoples on the face of our planet are coming ever nearer one to another and all their particular cultural traditions tend to dissolve and to flow into one gigantic melting pot. The ascendency of the scientific mentality, coupled with an utter disdain for any claim to possess super-empirical knowledge, brought religion the world over into disrepute as though it were identical with superstition and, as an after effect, undermined the authority of the erstwhile sacred moral principles. The order of the day is atheism, either forthrightly professed or disguised as agnosticism. It appears, thus, that in this rapidly expanding kingdom of No-God (lo-el in the Biblical phrase), there is no refuge for the Jewish religious tradition, and that, consequently, if one is anxious to safeguard the survival of the Jewish people, which is the duty of the faithful Jew he has no choice but to accept secular nationalism as the best means to this end.

Yet, the conclusion is by no means cogent. The Jewish tradition teaches us to look beyond the horizon of current history. Any historical stage reached is but a stop on the way of the final goal of universal history, towards the Messianic age, or post-history, so to speak. No one could insist that modern science has contributed to the improvement of human nature and was paving the way to universal redemption. One is rather justified in asserting that the improvement of the external material conditions of human life entails moral degeneration, a lowering of moral standards and a marked deterioration in all relations between individual human beings, including even those within the family. The balance sheet of our age is not drawn up yet and will in all probability reveal, side by side with its impressive assets, very heavy, perhaps altogether unbearable liabilities. One is almost tempted to exclaim: God help us! But to that we come a little later.

Quite apart from all that, philosophically speaking, the uncritical assumption that religion and science essentially contradict one another and are mutually incompatible, has no foundation in fact; it has long since been exposed by the history of human thought, including our own as a fallacy. A certain tension between the two certainly exists and friction is from time to time unavoidable. However, be that as it may, our own tradition has proved great flexibility and the ability to adjust itself in a reasonable way to the real achievements of science. The crucial point is not whether this or that scientific discovery was or was not anticipated by our prophets and sages, but whether science has a rightful claim to be the sole judge of what is true and what is not. Incidentally, science qua science has never arrogated to itself this right to unrivalled dominion over the human mind and heart. It is the blind worshippers of science who propagate such a misconception, whilst the true scientist carries on his work unperturbed

by the clash of opinions about things in which he is agnostically not
interested. We may remember: When Laplace was asked by Napoleon
what he thought of the existence of God, the eminent scientist replied,
"Majesty, in my daily work I don't make any use of this hypothesis." In
contrast to Laplace, the co-author of the Kant-Laplace cosmogenic theory,
the philosopher Immanuel Kant, when engaged on the construction of a
theory of ethics, could not help to fall back on the God-idea.

Can our scientific age, an age of turmoil and moral confusion, can we as
Jews carry on our daily lives and work without this idea? Here at last is the
point where one has to speak up.

"Why remain Jewish?"—a heretical question, as we know, to the Jewish
believer, is all the same one which he has to take up when it is voiced by
secularised or assimilated fellow Jews. Try as he may to place himself for
the sake of argument on their common ground which seems to be identical
with that of common sense, a moment must come for the disciple of the
sages to interrupt the worldly conversation with the admonition: "Higia
zman Kriath Shema! . . . ."—It is time to cite the verse: "Listen (and
understand!) Oh Israel . . . . . ."

The hour has indeed struck for the Jewish traditionalist to make a special
effort in explaining to all exponents of the so-called common sense not only
why his steadfastness gives sense and direction to his own individual
existence, but also why he is firmly convinced that faithfulness to the God
of Israel represents in our age of radical change one of the few guiding
threads predestined to lead human kind out of the maze in which it is
trapped. Modern decapitated theology, a theology without the Theos, a
striking parallel to the "Psychology without the psyche" of the last century,
is hardly able to fulfill this task. What we need is personal courage to
formulate anew one's traditional *credo* in the plain "language of the sons of
Adam", to use the phrase of our ancient sages. And how gratifying it is to
know that the Jewish tradition leaves its followers the widest freedom of
movement in the field of thought expression.

To begin literally with the "Beginning", or more precisely with "In the
Beginning" (Bereshith!), it is most important to note that the central idea
animating the Jewish tradition is that of creation. The universe is a created
universe and all its living inhabitants are therefore creatures. Aristotle
could not prove the eternity of the world's existence in time and space;
neither does modern science testify one way or another, either in favour of
the Greek conception of a no-beginning or of the Jewish belief in creation
ex nihilo. Yet, the Jewish belief in perpetual creation and re-creation of the
world, the affirmation of nature as a *natura naturata*, as a created one,
correlated with the world's Creator, *the natura naturans*, in Spinoza's
phrase, is the very core of the Jewish tradition. Not less important is to
realize, in this context, that we are here confronted not with an abstract
philosophical thought, but with a deeply laid intuition concerning the

human condition and all it implies. Anything created, including man, could not have been created, which is *a fortiori* true of the products of man's handiwork. Nothing created can be said to be self-supporting in the ontological sense, to carry the ground of its existence in itself. The intrinsic attribute of every created substance is its fragility. Fragile is every individual creature and so are all human institutions, as it is, incidentally, borne out by the whole history of the human race. Trust can be put only in an Entity which is not created, which is not encompassed in the limits of space and time, in a word, in the transmundane Creator Himself. Who can say whether this trust based on the primordial Jewish intuition of the fragility of nations, empires and the world itself, is not the real clue to the mystery of Jewish survival?

However, the first word of the Torah is not its last word. Dependent on the Creator of the universe, as man is, he is from his own beginnings distinguished by godlikeness, having been created as it is written, "in the image of God". Like his Progenitor, man is creative. "Everything created", teaches the Midrash, "wants to be worked upon . . . . even man is in need of being improved". That is the interpretation of the words in Genesis: ". . . . that he is created to be done *(la'asoth)*". The meaning is clear. The work of creation goes on forever and in this endless creative process man is chosen to co-operate, as it were, with the Almighty, both in the outside world and by working for his own perfection.

Furthermore, the godlikeness of man finds its expression in the miraculous uniqueness of every single human being, of every single face. This most remarkable moral discovery is incorporated in the Mishnah which draws the practical conclusion therefrom that the destruction of a human being is tantamount to an attempt to destroy the universe, whilst the saving of a living human creature is comparable to the re-affirmation of the whole work or creation. *(Sanhedrin, IV, 5)* In short, according to the Jewish tradition, the main attributes of the human being are his creativeness, uniqueness, and the microcosmic form of his existence as though he were the world's sparkling mirror.

Entirely in line with traditional Jewish awareness of man's election and his metaphysical dignity, Maimonides taught, in his own age of change, that even a single act for good or ill of a single human being may determine the world's fate. This fate is, according to his *Code*, always in a precarious equilibrium; the existence of the world depends perpetually on whether the sum total of the good deeds outweighs that of the wrong-doing; in consequence, one additional misdeed, might, God forbid, bring down the scale with the good deeds in it and with it the entire habitat of the human race. Not so long ago the whole idea of Maimonides together with its picturesque elaboration could have appeared as a fantastic exaggeration of a moralist out of touch with reality. But things are moving in the technological age of ours very quickly, and lo!, Maimonides' vision reveals prophetic farsightedness. We have in fact reached the stage when one man's hand by pressing on a certain button may smash the world, as we know it, to smithereens

We live in a time of growing depreciation of all spiritual and moral values, whereas the virtues and vices of the individual, and first of all his sense of moral responsibility, become all important. Technological progress tends to transform the earth from pole to pole in one integrated, though overcrowded, power-house. But where from will be supplied the wisdom and the rectitude and the inspiration for using unprecedented material force in the service of the higher and highest aspiration of humanity, if not from the treasures accumulated by the generations gone by? The custodians of the Jewish tradition looking as is their duty, beyond the horizon of current history, believe in all humility that they are holding on trust for the future one of the most important legacies of the historical past. Against the threatening degradation of the human personality through universal uniformity of thought and behaviour, they are safeguarding the ages-old valiant Jewish con-conformism. Above all, they pray that the united human race should be assembled in accordance with the hope and vision of Israel's prophets, at the foot of the Lord's mountain and around a restored Tower of Babel.

Yes, they are given to prayer. One of the most frightening signs of the times seems to be modern Man's fateful loneliness. The communication lines between him and his fellow men are disrupted. He is losing his ability to penetrate the heart of others and his fellow men, in turn, are about to discard any interest in his individual destiny. In his isolation his conscience becomes dumb, and so even the outlet of speaking to oneself is barred to him. Where should he turn to find relief? In such a state of mind bordering on despair men used to invoke the absolute principle of existence by ardent prayer. Alas, modern man does not and cannot pray, for his lips are sealed by the seven seals of an apocalyptic agnosticism.

If there were no other reasons for cultivating the Jewish tradition in the modern world, this alone, the fact that faithful Jews are thoroughly educated in the ancient "House of Prayer", would suffice to make them missionaries in the midst of their own people. But the reasons, as we have seen, are many. Still, it should not be overlooked that no tradition can claim to be Jewish if it does not care for the Jewish way of life.

Is this the complete answer to the heretical question, Why remain Jewish?—It is certainly not more than an outline, but it indicates the frame within which the dialogue can go on. The ball, if I am allowed to say so, is now in the court of the other side, of the *sitra achra*, in the cabbalistic usage. Let the other side give its reply to the questions implicitly set out here. For the precept of Rabbi Eleazar ben Arakh, our actual starting point, demanding from us to know how to respond to the heretic's challenge, includes, in my humble opinion, also the instructions to elaborate beforehand the questions to be put to the Epicuros in return.

8. The Jewish Idea of Education in Our Age

Jewish education has a long history. Throughout this history it never betrayed its main purpose—to carry forward, from generation to generation, the inherited knowledge of "What is good" (*Ma tov*—Micah, 6, 8) and thus to safeguard the continuity of Israel's meaningful existence. As the Psalmist has it—"The Lord established a testimony in Jacob, and appointed a law in Israel, which he commanded our fathers, that they should make them known to their children: that the generation to come might know them, even the children which should be born, who should arise and tell them to their children" . . . (Ps. 78, 5-6). In a word—education in the House of Israel is a sacred duty. However, irrevocable as this duty remained, in its scope and content Jewish education followed the general line of the people's destinies and faithfully reflected the successive phases of its evolution. From age to age, the emphasis in the interpretation of the central idea of Jewish education changed, and so did the dividing line between the substance of the matter and the accidental by-ways to be used in the practical educational effort. Is it, then, not justified to assume that in our own age which is so different from all preceding epochs of human history, we have to face up once again to the vital problem, how the Jewish idea of education might be brought into correlation with the exigencies of the present time?

Our time: We live in an age which carries us at an ever-quickening pace towards the consummation of world history. Our dwelling place lies open from pole to pole, and continents and oceans are but islands and lakes on its surface. From outer space, Man is about to get sight of the whole globe as of one visible object. In spite of all international divisions and tensions, East is West and West is East, since our essentially technological civilization is common to both. The entire human race is engaged in a frantic competition for the attainment of identical scientific goals. Who will deny that the next generations are chosen to live, to work and to co-operate in one world, under the same roof, as it were?

Simultaneously with the geographical shrinking of the Earth, the

The text of this address delivered at the Symposium on International Cooperation for Jewish Education at the World Jewish Congress Fourth Plenary Assembly in Stockholm was first published in English in *World Jewish Congress Fourth Plenary Assembly, Stockholm, 2nd-12th August, 1959*, Booklet No. IV: *Symposium on International Cooperation in Jewish Education, 6th August 1959*.

physical basis of Man's historical evolution, History itself assumes that image of unity which was preconceived at its very beginning, in its *Bereshith*. For this is fundamental to the traditional Jewish conception of the historical process: similarly as mankind first appeared on the earthly scene as a single family, so the human race will in the end, *beacharith ha'yomim*, re-create and restore itself once again as one family with the nations of the world as its members. True, we are in the wake of terrible decades of cruelty and bloodshed, but ever more clearly it is realized from one end of the world to the other that what had happened was fratricide, a crime against humanity. Neither wars, nor revolutions, nor volcanic eruptions of hatred have the power any more to obstruct the great converging movement of our age which brings into interplay the most disparate historical traditions of the past. We are confronted with a mighty confluence of formerly isolated streams of cultural energy. Originally a mere idea, World History is about to become real.

The internationalism, characteristic of our age, the democratization of modern society, the rapidly growing weight of the masses—of mass production, mass communication, and mass reproduction—in every sphere of human activity, they all represent various aspects of one and the same process of universal coalescence. Humanity is in search of some common level of civilized existence and is groping towards the best possible average. The word of the Prophet: "Every valley shall be exalted, and every mountain and hill shall be made low" (Isaiah, 40, 4), seems to come true, and whether one rejoices at the prospect of its fulfilment or deplores it, the fact remains that it is fraught with far-reaching consequences both for the human race as a whole and for our own people in particular.

The common standard of civilization looming ahead implies the levelling down of earlier outstanding standards of collective cultural achievements not less than the levelling up of the ways of life of the so-called "backward" peoples. Universal equalization and assimilation must needs work both ways. In all circumstances the single human being will be exposed to the danger of losing his individuality and, in the last resort, of becoming a mass product. Even in our day the effacement of personality is a striking drawback within the general advancement of scientific knowledge and rational organization of social life. The sense of individual responsibility is on the decline. The highly complicated machinery of modern civilized life serves as an excuse for passing the burden of decision to the expert, whilst the experts themselves are confined each to his special compartment. Recent experience demonstrates to what disastrous consequences this human condition may lead when a whole people entrusts its destiny to a single expert in making history—to the dictator. And yet, the more the technological civilization of our age expands, the heavier becomes its pressure on personal conscience, on personal feeling and on personal taste.

It is obvious that the Jewish population of the world cannot escape the impact of the new age. The process of Jewish assimilation released and stimulated by the emancipation of the Jews, first in the West and since 1917 also in the East, is now overtaken by an even mightier process of universal cultural equalization and is being superimposed by it. To resist this redoubled pressure in order to secure our meaningful existence as a separate entity we have at our disposal outside Israel's borders nothing more, but also nothing less, than the idea of Jewish education. In Israel the position is, of course, basically different: there, Jewish life is a natural produce of the land; there, in the words of the old adage, "the air itself" educates. But what about the people in dispersion? Are we still able to ward off the concentric onslaught of the forces threatening to efface the differences between human groups moulded by past history, and incessantly working for their mutual adjustment and integration into a worldwide homogeneous society?—No doubt, thanks to its technological achievements, the new age has brought closer the various parts of the Diaspora and provided all of them with an easy access to Israel, their natural centre. None the less, the chances of the Diaspora's survival would be slender indeed, were it not for that hope which is the soul of the Jewish idea of education.

When we turn our attention to the present state of Jewish education in the Diaspora, we are inclined to take its idea for granted. It very often seems to us that, having defined Jewish education as the principal means for our collective survival, we have disposed of all the problems related to the deeper meaning of our educational endeavours. In assessing the educational position in this or that country we look in the first place for figures; we count the Jewish schools in operation, we try to ascertain the total number of children attending them and the number of hours dedicated to Jewish subjects. This is certainly very important and entirely in line with the statistical obsession of our age. But statistics is even in our time not enough. We may, for instance, discover that what Jewish education in the U.S.A. is gaining in extension, it is losing in depth, and that with its "shallowness" the self-identification as Jews is of vanishing consequence for the new generation. Is this the effect of the irresistible attraction of the specifically American way of life or of the universal tendency towards uniformity, or the result of both intertwined? Be it as it may, the phenomenon is not restricted to the U.S.A. alone. We can also observe it in Latin America and in Western Europe, not to speak of the East where facilities for Jewish education hardly exist and conformity is the order of the day.

Apart from the external factors impeding Jewish education in our time, we have to take into account the fact that we are, amongst ourselves, deeply divided as to the exact meaning of the very term "survival", though it is meant to indicate the ultimate aim of Jewish education. What should "survive" and how? To the truly faithful the answer to this question presents no difficulty: the Lord's chosen people is in duty bound to persevere in its progress along the traditional way as the custodian of Eternal Truth. But the great majority of those who nowadays identify themselves as Jews by the token of the Jewish faith do not hesitate to pour water into the old wine of our religious traditions and to mould their various educational systems in a modernized style. Opposed to all of them is that worldly conception according to which the Jewish people is not a religious community but, even in dispersion, a nation among nations engaged, as any other, in a struggle for collective existence; hence the network of secular Jewish schools. Yet another bone of contention is the language of tuition, and although Hebrew has driven Yiddish into the background, the Yiddish trend is still far from unconditional surrender. Can there be any doubt that this fight of all against all in the fields and gardens of Jewish education is one of the main obstacles on the way to its consolidation? Surely, the growing confusion weakens the interest in Jewish education amongst the uncommitted and thus imperils from within its avowed end, the survival of the Diaspora, whatever this may mean to our various spiritual and temporal schools of thought.

Is there a way out of this confusion? Can we devise a rational plan by which a turn towards a reversal in our deteriorating educational position could be stimulated?—This indeed is what I dare to believe and what I shall try to explain first on the theoretical and then on the practical level.

Our first and foremost task in the present circumstances is to reanimate the Jewish idea of education in an open-minded and frank confrontation with the tendencies and propensities of our age. In the introductory remark to this exposition the Psalmist's voice reminded us that it was the "Testimony established in Jacob" and the "Law appointed in Israel" which were at the basis of our original educational system. Is this Testimony and this Law still valid in our age? We all agree, I presume, that the survival of our people as a self-centred cultural entity, since the year 70 of the Christian era, is mainly due to the unrelenting educational effort inspired by Faith. But this source of inspiration, we are advised on all sides, has now dried up; under the intense radiation of the Sun of Science and Reason the old fountainhead of our creative energy was condemned to evaporation. We had, therefore, either to look for other sources of inspiration or to try and do without it. Is it really so? Is such an approach realistic at all? I beg to doubt and to differ.

Jewish education stands and falls with the conviction that practical commonsense is by no means the only criterion of rational human endeavour. From the purely practical point of view, the Jewish school in the Diaspora has but little to offer either to the pupils in training or to their parents, if their common interest is concentrated on the things of this world, i.e. the greatest possible chance of achieving success within the surrounding non-Jewish community. It is often stressed that a timely training in the skill of Jewish self-identification helps to keep the balance of one's mind and emotions, particularly in situations of social conflict in a world not altogether friendly to individuals of Jewish origin. In other words, Jewish schooling appears to be the safest antidote against the effects of anti-Semitic poison. However, one may despair of the future of Jewish education in the Diaspora, if it is to live by this poison only. We are looking to a better future for the whole of mankind and not to the perpetuation of the evils of our day. Making our younger generation immune against the psychological dangers of the anti-Semitic disease has practical importance, but it does not appear very likely that the great mass of Jewish parents would be persuaded to give their children a Jewish education out of fear— not fear of God, but of the Satanic nature of man.

Certainly, we have educational institutions which, in the practical sense, offer much more than the usual type of Sunday or Supplementary School. Leaving aside the higher schools devoted to the professional training of Rabbis and teachers, we have to take into consideration, in the first place, the existing Day-Schools. Their number is increasing as if in response to the challenge of our age. Their overall purpose is to train our young in their formative years to live a full life within the confines of the Jewish community. It may be anticipated that from amongst the graduates of these schools will emerge the bulk of our social workers and creative personalities in the generation to come: they will not only live as Jews, but also make a living as Jews. But will they stay on in the Diaspora? Is Israel not created for them and they for Israel? Why should they wish to be exposed to all the inevitable inner conflicts and temptations of Diaspora life, when before them the gates to Israel stand wide open? We have to face the fact that, with the exception of a part of our orthodox Day-Schools, the rest are preparatory schools for *Aliyah,* and the training received in them—a thorough-going *Hachsharah* for the absorption in Israel. And so we have to ask again: but what about the Diaspora? How can we provide here for a change of guard?

Let us then take recourse to the Jewish idea of education and let us see what may be its specific message in our age.

The emphasis in our age is on conformity and its universalization. Against this there is the fact that the Jewish people has, through the ages, strongly adhered to the principle of nonconformity and has contrived a system of education by virtue of which it maintained itself in historical existence as one indivisible entity. In a general way traditional Jewish education could, therefore, be described as training for an existence not conforming to the predominant historical forces. The school was only one of the many classrooms in that all-embracing educational establishment called Jewish life. Education had precedence even before the natural order of things: "He who teaches his friend's son Torah"—says the Talmud—"is, as it were, his begetter" (Sanhedrin, 19b) because one's son is but a vehicle for carrying on Israel's nonconformist Law and the Testimony of nonconformism "established in Jacob".

The principle of nonconformism which animates the idea of Jewish education assumes tremendous significance in our age. At a time which is dominated by the tendency to flatten out differences between cultural traditions of the past, it becomes vitally important to counter-balance the drift towards dull equalization by a forceful re-assertion of the human value of nonconformity. In continuity with our educational tradition we may be preordained to cultivate in our home and school the type of human being soon most urgently to be needed by humanity, if its degeneration into a state of amorphous homogeneity is to be avoided. The idea of a united humanity deriving from our idea of education is modelled not on the image of a heap of sand, but on that of the symphonic harmony of the celestial spheres, each within its own orbit contributing to the miraculous consonance of the cosmic whole. If for no other reason, let us in our age, for its own sake, reassert the value of nonconformity.

However, the principle of nonconformity deriving from the Jewish idea of education has a double meaning. No less than to Israel and Jacob as a collective entity, it applies to every one of Israel's children. It demands from everyone within the House of Israel not conformity with the general rule of the law, as is often presumed, but its free acceptance by way of a constantly renewed and reaffirmed covenant. No one can remove from one's shoulders the burden of responsibility which one imposes on one's self. The children of Abraham, Isaac and Jacob are meant to be "like the stars in the sky" each one radiating its own light, the light of personal conscience. It is most important to put this specific aspect of our educational idea into the right perspective. Jewish self-identification should above all include the identification of the Jew as a self, as a free human being fully responsible for all his or her doings. In an age when human personality is in jeopardy, Jewish education is charged with the task of mobilizing the younger generation in the struggle for the independence and the uniqueness of every human being. For this, too, is inherent in the Jewish idea of education. In the light of this idea the discovery was made that human individuality is comparable with the universe and, that it thus presents within the framework of the macrocosm a microcosm, as unique as the universe and its Creator. A direct way leads from the Proverbial advice to "train the child according to his ways" (Proverbs 22, 6) to the Mishna in *Sanhedrin* where the uniqueness of every human being is explicitly emphasized (Chapter IV, 5). If Jewish education in the Diaspora has a future—and it is up to us that it should have a future—Jewish personalism will have a say not only within our own house, but also far beyond.

All this is closely related to the vision of "the time to come", *Le'atid lavo*, inherent in our idea of education. Without this vision of the Messianic age, in which human history should attain its glorious consummation, our strenuous efforts to keep our people in being by a steady current of educational effort would be meaningless. We need our "generation to come" for the promised "time to come", the *dor acharon* for the *acharit ha'yomim*. In a general way, the Messianic idea is incorporated in all our educational systems, not excluding the worldly ones in which the Messianic hope is represented by the socialist ideal. However, in most of the modern conceptions of Messianism its very core, the Messiah himself is missing, that concrete image of the "Higher Man" who might at any moment appear in our own midst and, remaining a plain human being, reveal himself as the perfect embodiment of virtue and wisdom. There is nothing in modern science which contradicts such a hopeful expectation. And yet, just in this technological age of ours, the vision of the beautiful image of spiritual perfection invoked for the eye of the young is likely to produce an ineffaceable impression. In fact, all of us, old and young, have constantly to train ourselves in the Jewish art of looking for human perfection. This, incidentally, is the educational significance of the fundamental Jewish conception of the God-likeness of Man which is, therefore, inseparable from the Jewish idea of education. In the quest for perfection incarnate, our young will not easily succumb to the temptation of the time, to the idolization of the favourites of the fleeting hour. In substance, this is implied in the Jewish principle of non-conformism which teaches us in anticipation of "the time to come" to keep a distance in regard to all things of this world, the *olam ha'zeh*.

The confrontation of the Jewish idea of education with the tendencies of our age thus suggests more concentration of our educational effort on training of character, on hardening of the will, on cultivation of genuinely Jewish virtues, than on the purely intellectual aspect of instruction and tuition. The emphasis today should be on morals, rather than on study. Vital as the conveying and acquisition of Jewish knowledge remains, our time demands that the strengthening of the character of our children and grandchildren should become the main object of a truly modern Jewish education.

The concrete practical conclusions to be drawn from the foregoing theoretical assessment of our crucial problem are manifold.

First of all, in view of the general character of the problem, which in substance is identical throughout the Diaspora, it would appear that any approach to its solution should be undertaken on an international scale. Although the specific conditions of Jewish life outside Israel vary from country to country, all our communities in dispersion are subject, more or less directly, to the impact of the spirit of the age. This, as I have tried to show, is heading in the direction of equalization and assimilation. To inaugurate a vigorous resistance against the universally felt pressure, we have to undertake an effective concentration of all the forces active in the sphere of Jewish education wherever they may be found in order to safeguard our inherited human values. Within the structure of the House of Israel no stone should be left unturned. The response to the universal challenge must equally be universal.

The visualized concentration might find its first expression in a Conference on Jewish Education at which all our communities, not to forget the smaller and smallest, should be adequately represented. World Jewry is not without experience as to the international aspect of co-operation in the field of education. The Department of Education and Culture of the Jewish Agency, together with its Department for Religious Education, have accumulated a great deal of such experience; it relates mainly to the adjustment of Jewish education in the Diaspora, through the medium of Hebrew, to the educational and cultural achievements in Israel. In a practical way, the problem of international co-operation in the sphere of Jewish education has been actively faced by the Claims Conference. The cultural policy pursued by the World Jewish Congress in the last ten years or so is a further instance of the consideration given to the international character of Jewish culture in general. Other pertinent illustrations could easily be added. In short, it is being realized far and wide that our educational position cannot be properly evaluated and dealt with other than in a world-wide perspective. The awareness of this fact is the common ground of all our educational trends, from the extreme orthodox to the extreme worldly. In consequence, Jewish opinion seems to be well prepared for the idea of a World Conference on Education now envisaged.

Plausible as the idea of such a Conference may appear, it should be borne in mind that it might defeat its own main purpose, i.e. the concentration of our educational efforts on a world-wide scale, if its composition were not to reflect the diversity of our educational trends. The goal before the Conference should be of a two-fold character; on the one hand, the integration of our geographically separated communities in a common effort and, on the other, the proclamation of a truce—a "Truce of God" in the medieval phrase—amongst our educational parties. Odd as it may sound, I venture to state that our age demands from us all a new *cheshbon ha'nefesh,* the redressing of the balance of our souls, as it were. Far be it from me to suggest that we should strike a bargain or make concessions in things spiritual. But why not follow the precept of our sages and judge the endeavours of all our educational trends *le'kaf z'chut,* according to their intrinsic value? Should we agree that in our age it is imperative to accentuate the ethical aspect in Jewish education, we may discover that the common ground of our various educational trends is wider than we are usually inclined to presume. It would be an event of greatest moment were it possible, prior to the Conference, to delineate the extent of our concensus on educational matters.

In all circumstances, the World Conference on Jewish Education should not disperse without leaving behind some tangible results. In the first place, it must lead to the establishment of a permanent central agency for Jewish education, and devise methods of financing the new institution. This should function: *(a)* as a world centre for the collection and distribution of every kind of information relevant to Jewish education; *(b)* as a clearing-house for Jewish schools in need of teaching personnel and for candidates aspiring to join the teaching profession; *(c)* as an institute stimulating research into specific educational problems. One of the most urgent problems is the improvement of the status of the Jewish teacher in the community. Provision should be made for a gradual expansion of the new central institution to enable it to extend its special care to the educational needs of the smaller communities which, owing to lack of support from outside, are in danger of disintegration. Furthermore, the central educational agency will have to take the initiative, perhaps in collaboration with the Jewish Agency, in putting the training of teachers for the Diaspora on solid foundations, and in stimulating the production of textbooks and other teaching materials. Obviously, the tasks of the envisaged educational agency would be immense and could be accomplished only over a long period. This being so, the first step in the right direction should be made by the Conference itself.

The creation of the central institution may at first have merely symbolical significance. But symbols sometimes possess a reality of their own. As the outward expression of the determination of the Diaspora to transform itself into a world-wide union for mutual educational assistance, the new agency is likely to ignite sparks of active educational energy where it is now dormant. This applies particularly to those among our adults who have unwittingly deprived their children of Jewish education. It is unavoidable that in the years to come the problem of adult education will gain in importance and occupy its deserved place within the working plan of the central educational agency. Simultaneously, the intimate correlation between Jewish education and cultural creativeness in the Diaspora will be thrown into relief, with the consequence that, along with Jewish education, the new agency will also include Jewish culture within its purview.

If the proposed World Conference will prove a successful experiment in our international co-operation and bring forth results on the envisaged lines, the hour may be auspicious for looking ever further ahead. What we actually need is a total mobilization of Diaspora Jewry for a fundamental reversal in our educational position. A mobilization plan of such scope cannot be improvized. Much careful thought must be given to it before it will become mature and suitable for translation into a blueprint. However, it is perhaps not unlikely that a central agency for Diaspora education with a research institute attached to it may decide to treat the mobilization plan as a matter of urgency and give it high priority on the list of its research projects.

All the practical propositions here touched upon are conceived in the light of the Jewish idea of education. It is my firm conviction that only in this light, in the perspective of our traditional nonconformism, can we—as the biblical phrase goes—"see light" in the maze of our present educational position. Looking back to our historical past, we find that in spite of all its singular characteristics the present position is not without analogy in relation to epochs gone by. The closest similarity to our time presents the great age of Hellenism. Then, too, the Jewish idea was in danger to be overwhelmed and absorbed by the Greek *Paideia*, the Hellenistic ideal of human education. And yet, the Jewish resistance movement conquered. Let us, then, in our opposition against the dangers of the modern diluted "Hellenism" draw inspiration also from the days of old. The last word should be ours.

A most welcome coincidence enables me to conclude by citing one of Sweden's foremost writers, August Strindberg. In his *Historical Miniatures*, a volume that begins with antiquity and leads through history up to modern times, there appears everywhere and at any period the lonely figure of a Jew who utters his stalwart "No" in the face of the splendours of contemporary civilization, be it in Athens of the time of Socrates or in the reign of the Queen of Sweden, Christine. In many guises he refuses to conform to the spirit of any of the successive ages, all for the sake of the *Le'atid La'vo*, of that Messianic age which is still to come. Thus, the Jewish tradition of nonconformity is revealed by the Swedish genius as the leaven of world history. I believe, this conception is valid even today.

9. A Parliament of World Education

Non-Governmental Organisations and Unesco

May I introduce my remarks on the place the International Non-Governmental Organisations—NGOs for short—occupy in Unesco with reference to the fact that my own Organisation, the World Jewish Congress, was already represented at Unesco's Constituent Assembly convened in London in 1945. My observations are thus based on an experience covering the whole period since then and until this last 8th Session of the General Conference of Unesco.

The legal basis for the co-operation between the NGOs and Unesco is a clause of Unesco's Constitution which is, however, rather vague and, moreover, envisages consultative arrangements only with single NGOs. A wise Frenchman has observed that it is a mistake to study a functioning machine only by examination of the inventor's blueprints.

In this clause the emphasis appears to be placed on the particle *non*. It appears that the common denominator of the NGOs in question is the fact that they are *Non*-Governmental, divorced from state power. However, there is an old Talmudic saying that the undertone of every "No" is a "Yes", of every negation an affirmation. This applies fully to our case. With progress of time, the emphasis in the description of the NGOs has evermore shifted to the term "international".

The internationalism of a state is derived from its particular sovereignty; an NGO is essentially loyal to a principle transgressing state borders. It is always a free Republic of the Mind devoted to an ideal above the territorial basis of human existence—be it an educational ideal, the endeavour to further scientific research, to cultivate a certain aspect of human existence (such as childhood or womanhood) or to develop a specific cultural tradition maintained through the ages in all parts of the world, as is the case with the World Jewish Congress.

Is there an interest relating to Unesco common to all the NGOs? In the

The text of this address which was broadcast in English on 15 December 1954 by the Radio Department of Unesco at the close of the Fourth General Conference of Unesco in Montevideo was first published in *World Jewish Affairs*, London, 15 December 1954.

479

first place, this interest consists in their common aim to improve their status within the House of Unesco. Indeed, this gave originally the impulse for their getting together and organising themselves as a body, a process which proved to be advantageous for both Unesco and the NGOs, saving time and effort on both sides.

Integration of Human Ideals

But something more was bound to result from the transformation of the amorphous mass of the NGOs into a well-organised body. They were rapidly growing in numbers and have by now reached a figure which is approximately twice as high as the number of Unesco's Member States. Taken together, they represent a movement towards the integration of all human ideals through co-existence within Unesco. Thus, the NGOs contribute their full share in paving the way for the materialisation of the supreme universalistic ideal of Unesco.

It can safely be said that there is today no other inter-governmental organisation wherein the body of the NGOs is likely to become such a vital factor in the life of the whole as within Unesco. Looking back over a period of nine years and surveying the progress made, one is tempted to state that Unesco is on the way to growing into a Two-House Parliament of the World's Education, Science and Culture, with the Lower House, the body of the NGOs, increasingly becoming the legitimate representation of all the Republics of the Mind now in existence.

In this respect the 8th Plenary Session of Unesco's General Conference is a marked step forward. The collective comments of the NGOs on the Draft Programme for the next two years played a notable part in the deliberations of the Conference, and may provide the future historian of Unesco with a documentary proof that consultative provisions of Unesco's Constitution have already become a full-blooded reality, growing in importance far beyond the limits visualised by the Constituent Assembly of Unesco.

Does this not clearly indicate that the climate of our age is singularly propitious for the growth of a universalistic internationalism in both its aspects—one determined by governmental guidance and the other blossoming forth out of spontaneous voluntary effort?

About the Author

Aaron Zacharovich Steinberg whose pen name was M. Avrelin, was born in Dvinsk, Russia on 12 June 1891. He was a descendant of Rashi. His father, Zorach Steinberg, was a well-established merchant and his mother, Chiena (Elyachev), was a sister of the Yiddish literary critic Baal-Makhshovas. Jewish tradition and Haskalah co-existed in his house where he and his brother Nachman received a traditional Jewish education.

Dr. Steinberg studied philosophy and law at the universities of St. Petersburg and Heidelberg. He obtained a Doctorate at Heidelberg in 1913. He was Professor of Philosophy and Secretary of the Philosophical Association at St. Petersburg from 1918 to 1923 where he was a co-founder and member of the Board of the Institute of Higher Jewish Studies. In 1923 he went to Berlin and in 1934 moved to England where he married Sophie Rosenblatt in 1935. During his Berlin years, he was among the founders of YIVO (1924). A personal friend and collaborator of Simon Dubnov, Dr. Steinberg translated Dubnov's ten-volume *World History of the Jewish People* from Russian into German (1925-29), his two-volume *History of Chasidism* (1931) from Hebrew into German, edited with Dubnov the three-volume abbreviated *World History* and edited *Simon Dubnov, the Man and His Work*, a centenary volume (1963).

In 1941 he joined the leadership of the World Jewish Congress and became head of its Cultural Department on its establishment in 1948. He retired from this position in 1968. During World War II Dr. Steinberg was a member of the WJC Research Committee in London, working in close cooperation with the Institute of Jewish Affairs in New York. As jurist, historian and philosopher, he made original contributions to post-war planning for the reconstruction of Jewish life in Europe and the moral and material restitution of Jewish losses.

Dr. Steinberg represented the WJC at UNESCO from its inception in 1946 until 1967. In this capacity he participated in UNESCO's Textbook Revision Programme and achieved the acceptance of Jewish history as part of universal history in the monumental UNESCO *History of the Scientific and Cultural Development of Mankind* and took part in UNESCO's

General Conferences. During Dr. Steinberg's Directorship of the Cultural Department, the WJC sent prayerbooks and other Judaica to the liberated areas in Europe, published such important series as *The Popular Jewish Library, Bibliothèque Juive, Biblioteca Popular Judia, Jewish History Pamphlets,* etc.; sponsored the publication *i.a.* of the Yiddish philosophical journal *Davke* (Buenos Aires) and the Yiddish literary journal *Di Goldene Keyt* (Tel-Aviv), and in 1964 established the *Jewish Journal of Sociology.* Dr. Steinberg was a member of the Institute of Jewish Affairs Board of Management from 1967 until his death. On his retirement in 1968, he was elected an Honorary Member of the WJC Governing Board. He wrote in Russian, Hebrew, Yiddish, English, French, German and Spanish.

Apart from hundreds of articles in all these languages, he wrote: *The Two-Chamber System in Russia* (1913); *Dostoevsky's Philosophy of Freedom* (1924); *Dostoevsky in London* (1923); *Dostoevsky* (1966).

He was active in formulating the guidelines governing the policy of the Memorial Foundation for Jewish Culture and in establishing better relations between Christian Churches and the Jews.

Dr. Steinberg died in London on 10 August 1975.

Index